W9-ASJ-307

Reconsidering Israel and Judah

Sources for Biblical and Theological Study

General Editor:
David W. Baker
Ashland Theological Seminary

1. *The Flowering of Old Testament Theology: A Reader in Twentieth-Century Old Testament Theology, 1930–1990*
   edited by Ben C. Ollenburger, Elmer A. Martens, and Gerhard F. Hasel
2. *Beyond Form Criticism: Essays in Old Testament Literary Criticism*
   edited by Paul R. House
3. *A Song of Power and the Power of Song: Essays on the Book of Deuteronomy*
   edited by Duane L. Christensen
4. *"I Studied Inscriptions from before the Flood": Ancient Near Eastern, Literary, and Linguistic Approaches to Genesis 1–11*
   edited by Richard S. Hess and David Toshio Tsumura
5. *"The Place Is Too Small for Us": The Israelite Prophets in Recent Scholarship*
   edited by Robert P. Gordon
6. *Community, Identity, and Ideology: Social Science Approaches to the Hebrew Bible*
   edited by Charles E. Carter and Carol L. Meyers
7. *Israel's Past in Present Research: Essays on Ancient Israelite Historiography*
   edited by V. Philips Long
8. *Reconsidering Israel and Judah: Recent Studies on the Deuteronomistic History*
   edited by Gary N. Knoppers and J. Gordon McConville

Reconsidering Israel and Judah

Recent Studies on the Deuteronomistic History

edited by

Gary N. Knoppers
and
J. Gordon McConville

WITHDRAWN
Regis College Library
15 ST. MARY STREET
TORONTO, ONTARIO, CANADA
M4Y 2R5

BS
1286.5
.R43
2000

Eisenbrauns
Winona Lake, Indiana
2000

© 2000 by Eisenbrauns.
All rights reserved.
Printed in the United States of America.

Library of Congress Cataloging-in-Publication Data

Reconsidering Israel and Judah : recent studies on the Deuteronomistic history / edited by Gary N. Knoppers and J. Gordon McConville
p. cm. — (Sources for biblical and theological study)
Includes bibliographical references (p.) and index.
ISBN 1-57506-037-X (cloth : alk. paper)
1. Bible. O.T. Former Prophets—Criticism, interpretation, etc.
2. Deuteronomistic history (Biblical criticism) 3. Jews—History—To 586 B.C.—Historiography. I. Knoppers, Gary N., 1956–
II. McConville, J. G. (J. Gordon) III. Series.

BS1286.5 .R43 2000
222′.06–dc21
Regis College Library
15 ST. MARY STREET
TORONTO, ONTARIO, CANADA
M4Y 2R5
00-035326
CIP

The paper used in this publication meets the minimum requirements of the American National Standard for Information Sciences—Permanence of Paper for Printed Library Materials, ANSI Z39.48-1984.♾

Dedicated to our children,

*Theresa Maria and David Joel
Knoppers*

and

*Alistair Gordon, Carys Elizabeth,
Andrew Samuel Walter, and Claire Alexandra
McConville*

CONTENTS

Part 2
Deuteronomy, Joshua, Judges

Part 3
Samuel, Kings

Part 4
New Directions

Indexes

Series Preface

Old Testament scholarship is well served by several recent works which detail, to a greater or lesser extent, the progress made in the study of the Old Testament. Some survey the range of interpretation over long stretches of time, while others concern themselves with a smaller chronological or geographical segment of the field. There are also brief *entrées* into the various subdisciplines of Old Testament study included in the standard introductions as well as in several useful series. All of these provide secondary syntheses of various aspects of Old Testament research. All refer to, and base their discussions upon, various seminal works by Old Testament scholars which have proven pivotal in the development and flourishing of the various aspects of the discipline.

The main avenue into the various areas of Old Testament inquiry, especially for the beginner, has been until now mainly through the filter of these interpreters. Even on a pedagogical level, however, it is beneficial for a student to be able to interact with foundational works firsthand. This contact will not only provide insight into the content of an area, but hopefully will also lead to the sharpening of critical abilities through interaction with various viewpoints. This series seeks to address this need by including not only key, ground-breaking works, but also significant responses to these. This allows the student to appreciate the process of scholarly development through interaction.

The series is also directed toward scholars. In a period of burgeoning knowledge and significant publication in many places and languages around the world, this series will endeavor to make easily accessible significant, but at times hard to find, contributions. Each volume will contain essays, articles, extracts, and the like, presenting in a manageable scope the growth and development of one of a number of different aspects of Old Testament studies. Most volumes will contain previously published material, with synthetic essays by the editor(s) of the individual volume.

Some volumes, however, are expected to contain significant, previously unpublished works. To facilitate access to students and scholars, all entries will appear in English and will be newly typeset. If students are excited by the study of Scripture and scholars are encouraged in amicable dialogue, this series would have fulfilled its purpose.

DAVID W. BAKER, *series editor*
Ashland Theological Seminary

Publisher's Note

Articles republished here are reprinted without alteration, except for minor matters of style not affecting meaning. Page numbers of the original publication are marked with double brackets ([[267]], for example). Other editorial notes or supplementations are also marked with double brackets, including editorially-supplied translations of foreign words. Footnotes are numbered consecutively throughout each article, even when the original publication used another system. No attempt has been made to bring transliteration systems into conformity with a single style.

In the introductions to each part below, reference to works included in the respective "additional reading" sections is made by in-text citation; bibliographic information for all other works is provided in footnotes.

EDITORS' PREFACE

Gary Knoppers has shouldered the burden of providing the introduction to the present volume and allowed me, in the kind of *quid pro quo* that joint editorships are made of, the lighter task of writing a preface on behalf of us both. This gives me the chance, first of all, to say that it has been a great privilege to work with him on this volume. While we (plainly) share a long-standing interest in the Historical Books of the Old Testament, we had not met before the SBL Meeting of 1995, at which David Baker instigated the idea that we work together on the project. We then had the opportunity to meet for our preliminary discussions about the shape of the volume during a sabbatical that Gary spent with his family at the Oxford Centre for Hebrew Studies in 1995–1996. For me, one of the most rewarding things about the project has been this cooperation itself. Gary is certainly one of the leading contemporary scholars on the subject of the Deuteronomistic History, so it has not only been an honor to be associated with him in a volume of essays on the subject but also a stimulating experience.

The study of the Historical Books (to use a rather general term for Joshua, Judges, Samuel, and Kings) is inescapable in the study of the Old Testament. My own academic interest in them is a kind of spin-off of my primary research focus on Deuteronomy. But Deuteronomy studies quickly pose the question about the relation of that book to those that follow it in the canonical order (whether Hebrew or Christian), hence the sobriquet *Deuteronomistic History* for the subject matter in question, a term, of course, that usually includes Deuteronomy itself. But other interfaces are equally important, not least the Prophetic Books, with their tantalizing overlaps at certain points (e.g., 2 Kings 18–20; Isaiah 36–38), and the union forged between the two blocks by the traditional Jewish nomenclature of Former Prophets and Latter Prophets. Modern study of the history of Israel is intertwined with them too, for obvious reasons. So it is not surprising that these books have often been at the heart of developments in critical theories about the Old Testament itself (witness the place of 2 Kings 22–23 in the reconstructions of Israel's history since Wellhausen and the modern disputes about the historicity of King David).

It follows that scholarly work on the Historical Books is bound to be extremely diverse, reflecting a range of interests on the part of authors and of orientations toward the ramified issues of Old Testament study. The reader has spotted in the last sentence the usual prefatorial apologia concerning the choice of essays included in the present volume. The choice arose, of course, from our discussions of the current trends in the study of the subject. In retrospect, it is hard to trace the story more precisely than that. A number of the essays here could hardly have been omitted and therefore selected themselves. Others have been chosen because of the particular interests of one or the other of us. In the process of editing, however, we have, to an extent, lost sight of who originally proposed what, as we liaised with authors and publishers, shared editing tasks (also with our colleagues at Eisenbrauns), and wrote short introductions to each essay.

No doubt the volume would look different had it been edited by only one of us. Yet the volume as it stands is not a "compromise." I say this because of our slightly different published views of the composition of the DH, which are somewhat reflected in the contributions from each of us included here. (The official "spin" on this is that I selected Gary's and he selected mine! However, the inclusion of both may perhaps also be justified as a kind of commentary on our cooperation). In any case, the compilation is based on our perception of the aspects of scholarly study of the Historical Books that ought to be present in a volume intended to offer a learning resource to those who are developing an interest in the subject.

The concept of the structure of the volume will be clear to the reader. Part 1 gathers essays that have become significant reference points in the subject area in general. These highlight essentially methodological issues, which recur implicitly or explicitly in many of the essays that follow. We have then grouped essays according to the books of the DH, rather than pursuing a rigorously methodological demarcation of the material, an approach that would probably have foundered on the sheer diversity of the available literature. It follows that essays of quite different kinds (historical, literary, etc.) are set alongside each other. This means that the reader is invited to survey and comprehend the interpretive landscape, though we hope that we have not left him or her without some help. We have concluded, however, with a section that offers pointers to the diversity of methods (principally recent ones) that now operate in the scholarly study of these books.

Acknowledgments

We owe a debt of gratitude to a number of people. Our thanks go first to David Baker, the series editor, who is indefatigable in his perception of needs in the world of scholarship and the classroom and in his ability to mobilize resources to meet them. We are also immensely grateful to our friends at Eisenbrauns, especially Beverly Fields and Jim Eisenbraun himself, who have spent long hours on the developing manuscript. (There have undoubtedly been others too, whose labors I have not seen.) A mass of detail is involved in resetting hundreds of pages of essays of quite disparate origins and styles. We have been delighted to be able to reproduce a number of important essays in English for the first time, which we know is an expensive and labor-intensive task. Our sincere thanks go to Peter Daniels, for his extensive work on nine of the translated articles, and to Sam Heldenbrand, for translating the Lemaire article; we hope we have not interfered unduly with the end product!

There are wider debts, of course, not least to all our colleagues who have had an inestimable part in the development of our thinking about Old Testament scholarship. Our thanks go last and above all to our wives and families, who have shouldered many of the burdens of our academic vocations. In recognition of their support, we are glad to dedicate this volume to our children.

Abbreviations

On Deuteronomy and the Deuteronomistic History

D	Deuteronomy or the old deuteronomic law code
DH	Deuteronomistic History
Dtr	deuteronomistic, or the Deuteronomist
Dtr^1	the Josianic Deuteronomist
Dtr^2	the exilic Deuteronomist
DtrG	the exilic, deuteronomistic historian (= DtrH)
DtrH	the exilic, deuteronomistic historian
DtrP	the exilic, prophetic redactor of the Deuteronomistic History
DtrN	the exilic or early postexilic, nomistic redactor(s) of the Deuteronomistic History

General

diss.	dissertation
DN	divine name
E	the Elohist
ET	English translation
Fest. (or Fs.)	Festschrift
H	the Holiness Code
J	the Yahwist
Jer C	a series of speeches in the book of Jeremiah with affinities to Deuteronomy
K	*Kethiv*, the (Hebrew) text as written
KJV	King James Version
JPSV	Jewish Publication Society Version
Luc	Lucifer of Cagliari
LXX	Septuagint version
LXX^A	Codex Alexandrinus to the Septuagint
LXX^B	Codex Vaticanus to the Septuagint
LXX^L	the Lucianic recension or the majority of the Lucianic manuscripts of the Septuagint

LXX^N	Codex Basiliano-Vaticanus to the Septuagint
ms(s)	manuscript(s)
MT	the Masoretic (Hebrew) Text of the Scriptures
NEB	New English Bible
NIV	New International Version
NJPS(V)	New Jewish Publication Society Version (1985)
NRSV	New Revised Standard Version
OG	the Old Greek text
OL	the Old Latin version of the Bible
OT	Old Testament
P	the Priestly writer(s)
pl.	plural
PN	personal name
Q	*Qere*, the (Hebrew) text as it should be read
rell	*reliqui*, the rest of the selected Greek cursives
Rgns	ΒΑΣΙΛΕΙΩΝ, the Septuagintal books of Reigns or Kingdoms
RSV	Revised Standard Version
sg.	singular
Syr	the Syriac Peshiṭta
SyrH	the Syro-Hexapla
Tg	Targum
Vg.	the Vulgate
VL	Old Latin
*	an asterisk on some scripture passages designates an earlier or older form of a passage as reconstructed by modern scholars

Reference Works

AASF.B	Annales Academiae Scientiarum Fennicae, Series B
AASOR	Annual of the American Schools of Oriental Research
ABD	D. N. Freedman (ed.). *Anchor Bible Dictionary.* 6 Vols. New York: Doubleday, 1992
AcOr	*Acta orientalia*
ADAW.PH	Abhandlungen der Deutschen Akademie der Wissenchaften zu Berlin: Philosophisch-historische Klasse
AfO	*Archiv für Orientforschung*
AHW	W. von Soden. *Akkadisches Handwörterbuch.* 3 Vols. Wiesbaden: Harrassowitz, 1965–81
AJSL	*American Journal of Semitic Languages and Literature*
AmSc	*American Scholar*
AnBib	Analecta Biblica
A(nc)B	Anchor Bible
ANEH	W. W. Hallo and W. K. Simpson. *The Ancient Near East: A History.* New York: Harcourt Brace Jovanovich, 1971

ANESTP J. B. Pritchard (ed.). *Ancient Near East Supplementary Texts and Pictures*. Princeton: Princeton University Press, 1969
ANET J. B. Prichard (ed.). *Ancient Near Eastern Texts Relating to the Old Testament*. Princeton: Princeton University Press, 1950; 3d ed., 1978
AnOr Analecta Orientalia
AnSc *Annals of Science*
AOAT Alter Orient und Altes Testament
AOr *Archiv Orientální*
AR(AB) D. D. Luckenbill (ed.). *Ancient Records of Assyria and Babylonia*. 2 Vols. London: Histories and Mysteries of Man, 1989
ARE J. H. Breasted (ed.). *Ancient Records of Egypt*. 5 Vols. Chicago, 1905–7. Reprinted, New York, 1962
ARM Archives royales de Mari
ArOr *Archiv Orientální*
ASA Association of Social Anthropologists
ASOR American Schools of Oriental Research
ATANT Abhandlungen zur Theologie des Alten und Neuen Testaments
ATD Das Alte Testament Deutsch
ATS(AT) Arbeiten zu Text und Sprache im Alten Testament
BA *Biblical Archaeologist*
BAL Berichte über die Verhandlungen der Sächsischen Akademie der Wissenschaften zu Leipzig
BAR(eader) *Biblical Archaeologist Reader*
BAR(ev) *Biblical Archaeology Review*
BASOR *Bulletin of the American Schools of Oriental Research*
BBB Bonner biblische Beiträge
BDB F. Brown, S. R. Driver, and C. A. Briggs. *Hebrew and English Lexicon of the Old Testament*. Oxford: Clarendon, 1953
BETL Bibliotheca ephemeridum theologicarum lovaniensium
BEvT(h) Beiträge zur evangelischen Theologie
BGBH Beiträge zur Geschichte der biblischen Hermeneutik
BHK[3] R. Kittle. *Biblia hebraica*. 3d ed.
BHS *Biblia hebraica stuttgartensia*
Bib *Biblica*
B(ib)I(nt) *Biblical Interpretation*
BibOr Biblica et orientalia
BIES *Bulletin of the Israel Exploration Society* (= *Yediot*)
BIOSCS *Bulletin of the International Organization for Septuagint and Cognate Studies*
BJRL *Bulletin of the John Rylands University Library of Manchester*
BKAT Biblischer Kommentar: Altes Testament
BN *Biblische Notizen*
BOT Boeken van het Oude Testament
BRev *Bible Review*
BTB *Biblical Theology Bulletin*

BWANT Beiträge zur Wissenschaft vom Alten und Neuen Testament
BZ *Biblische Zeitschrift*
BZAW Beihefte zur *Zeitschrift für die Alttestamentliche Wissenschaft*
CAD A. L. Oppenheim et al. (eds.). *The Assyrian Dictionary of the Oriental Institute of the University of Chicago*. Chicago: Oriental Institute of the University of Chicago, 1956–
CBC Cambridge Bible Commentary
CBQ *Catholic Biblical Quarterly*
CBQMS Catholic Biblical Quarterly Monograph Series
CentB Century Bible
CEPOA Cahiers de Centre d'Études du Proche Orient Ancien
CHM *Cahiers d'histoire mondiale*
C(on)BOT Coniectanea biblica, Old Testament
CRAIBL *Comptes rendus de l'Académie des inscriptions et belles-lettres*
DOTT D. W. Thomas (ed.). *Documents from Old Testament Times*. London/New York: Harper, 1958
EAEHL M. Avi-Yonah (ed.). *Encyclopedia of Archaeological Excavations in the Holy Land*. 4 Vols. Jerusalem: Israel Exploration Society, 1993
Ebib Études bibliques
EF Erträge der Forschung
EnBr *Encyclopaedia Britannica*
EncJud *Encyclopaedia Judaica*
E(r)I(sr) *Eretz Israel*
EstBib *Estudios Bíblicos*
ETL *Ephemerides theologicae lovanienses*
ETR *Études théologiques et religieuses*
EvT(h) *Evangelische Theologie*
ExpTim *Expository Times*
FGLP Forschungen zur Geschichte und Lehre des Protestantismus
FOTL Forms of the Old Testament Literature
FRLANT Forschungen zur Religion und Literatur des Alten und Neuen Testaments
FSTRP Forschungen zur systematischen Theologie und Religionsphilosophie
GS *Gesammelte Studien*
GTA Göttinger theologische Arbeiten
HAR *Hebrew Annual Review*
HAT Handbuch zum Alten Testament
Hen *Henoch*
HK Hand-Kommentar zum Alten Testament
HSAT Die heilige Schrift des Alten Testaments
HSM Harvard Semitic Monographs
HSS Harvard Semitic Studies
HTR *Harvard Theological Review*
HUCA *Hebrew Union College Annual*
ICC International Critical Commentary

IDB	G. A. Buttrick (ed.). *Interpreter's Dictionary of the Bible.* 4 Vols. Nashville: Abingdon, 1962–76
IDBSup	K. Crim (ed.). *Interpreter's Dictionary of the Bible Supplementary Volume.* Nashville: Abingdon, 1976
IEJ	*Israel Exploration Journal*
Int	*Interpretation*
IOSOT	International Organization for the Study of the Old Testament
ISLL	Illinois Studies in Language and Literature
JAAR	*Journal of the American Academy of Religion*
JANES(CU)	*Journal of the Ancient Near Eastern Society of Columbia University*
JAOS	*Journal of the American Oriental Society*
JAOS.S	Journal of the American Oriental Society Supplement
JBL	*Journal of Biblical Literature*
JCS	*Journal of Cuneiform Studies*
JDT	*Jahrbücher für deutsche Theologie*
JHI	*Journal of the History of Ideas*
JJS	*Journal of Jewish Studies*
JNES	*Journal of Near Eastern Studies*
JR	*Journal of Religion*
JSOT	*Journal for the Study of the Old Testament*
JSOTS(up)S	Journal for the Study of the Old Testament Supplement Series
JSS	*Journal of Semitic Studies*
JTC	*Journal for Theology and the Church*
JTS	*Journal of Theological Studies*
JTSA	*Journal of Theology for Southern Africa*
JWCI	*Journal of the Warburg and Courtauld Institutes*
KAI	H. Donner and W. Röllig. *Kanaanäische und aramäische Inschriften.* 3 Vols. 3d ed. Wiesbaden: Harrassowitz, 1971–76
KAT	Kommentar zum Alten Testament. Leipzig: Scholl
KEHAT	Kurzgefasstes exegetisches Handbuch zum Alten Testament
KHC	Kurzer Hand-Commentar zum Alten Testament
KK	*queried*
KTU	M. Dietrich, O. Loretz, and J. Sanmartín (eds.). *Die keilalphabetischen Texte aus Ugarit.* Alter Orient und Altes Testament 24. Kevelaer: Butzon & Bercker / Neukirchen-Vluyn: Neukirchener Verlag, 1976
LÄS	Leipziger Ägyptologische Studien
LCL	Loeb Classical Library
Leš	*Lešonénu*
MVAG	Mitteilungen der vorderasiatisch-ägyptischen Gesellschaft
NCB	New Century Bible
NedTT	*Nederlands theologisch tijdschrift*
OBO	Orbis biblicus et orientalis
OBT	Overtures to Biblical Theology
Or	*Orientalia*
OTL	Old Testament Library

OTS	*Oudtestamentische Studiën*
PEQ	*Palestine Exploration Quarterly*
PJ	*Palästina-Jahrbuch*
PMLA	*Proceedings of the Modern Language Association of America*
PW	Pauly-Wissowa, *Real-Encyclopädie der classischen Altertumswissenschaft*
RA	*Revue d'assyriologie et d'archéologie orientale*
RB	*Revue biblique*
RGG	*Die Religion in Geschichte und Gegenwart*
RHP(h)R	*Revue d'histoire et de philosophie religieuses*
RR	*Radical Religion*
RT	*Recueil de Travaux Rélatifs à la Philologie et à l'Archéologie Égyptiennes et Assyriennes*
SB	Sources bibliques
SBA	Studies in Biblical Archaeology
SBB	Stuttgarter biblische Beiträge
SBLDS	Society of Biblical Literature Dissertation Series
SBLSCS	Society of Biblical Literature Septuagint and Cognate Studies
SBS	Stuttgarter Bibelstudien
SBT(h)	Studies in Biblical Theology
SBTS	Sources for Biblical and Theological Study
ScrHier	*Scripta Hierosolymitana*
SJOT	*Scandinavian Journal of the Old Testament*
SKGG	Schriften der Königsberger Gelehrten Gesellschaft
SOTSMS	Society for Old Testament Study Monograph Series
SPAW	Sitzungsberichte der preussischen Akademie der Wissenschaften
SR	*Studies in the Renaissance*
SSEA	Schriften der Studiengemeinschaft der Evangelischen Akademien
STh	*Studia theologica*
STT	O. R. Gurney, J. J. Finkelstein, and P. Hulin (eds.). *The Sultantepe Tablets.* 2 Vols. Occasional Publications of the British School of Archaeology at Ankara 3/7. London, 1957–64
SVT	Supplements to Vetus Testament (= VTSup)
SWBA	The Social World of Biblical Antiquity
TAVO	*Tübinger Atlas des Vorderen Orients*
TB(ü)	Theologische Bücherei
TC	Torch Commentary
TDOT	G. J. Botterweck, H. Ringgren, and H.-J. Fabry (eds.). *Theological Dictionary of the Old Testament.* Grand Rapids, Michigan: Eerdmans, 1977–
THAT	E. Jenni and C. Westermann (eds.). *Theologisches Handwörterbuch zum Alten Testament.* 2 Vols. Munich: Chr. Kaiser / Zurich: Theologischer Verlag, 1971–76
T(h)LZ	*Theologische Literaturzeitung*
ThR(u)	*Theologische Rundschau*
ThStud	*Theologische Studiën*

T(h)WAT G. J. Botterweck, H. Ringgren, and H. J. Fabry (eds.). *Theologisches Wörterbuch zum Alten Testament*. Stuttgart: Kohlhammer, 1933–69
T(h)Z *Theologische Zeitschrift*
TLZ *Theologische Literaturzeitung*
TUMSR Trinity University Monograph Series in Religion
TWAT G. J. Botterweck, H. Ringgren, and H. J. Fabry (eds.). *Theologisches Wörterbuch zum Alten Testament*. Stuttgart: Kohlhammer, 1933–69
TynBul *Tyndale Bulletin*
UF *Ugarit-Forschungen*
UGAÄ Untersuchungen zur Geschichte und Altertumskunde Ägyptens
Urk. IV K. Sethe. *Urkunden der 18. Dynastie*. Vol. 4. Urkunden des Ägyptischen Altertums. Leipzig: Hinrichs, 1906–9
USQR *Union Seminary Quarterly Review*
VF *Verkündigung und Forschung*
VT *Vetus Testamentum*
VTSup Vetus Testamentum Supplements
WMANT Wissenschaftliche Monographien zum Alten und Neuen Testament
WO *Die Welt des Orients*
WuD *Wort und Dienst*
YOS Yale Oriental Series
ZA *Zeitschrift für Assyriologie*
ZÄS *Zeitschrift für Ägyptische Sprache und Altertumskunde*
ZAW *Zeitschrift für die alttestamentliche Wissenschaft*
ZDMG *Zeitschrift der deutschen morgenländischenGesellschaft*
ZDPV *Zeitschrift des deutschen Palästina-Vereins*
ZKT *Zeitschrift für katholische Theologie*
ZT(h)K *Zeitschrift für Theologie und Kirche*

Introduction

GARY N. KNOPPERS

The Deuteronomic or, more properly, Deuteronomistic History is a modern theoretical construct which holds that the books of Deuteronomy, Joshua, Judges, Samuel, and Kings constitute a single work, unified by a basic homogeneity in language, style, and content. The work covers much of Israel's history—from the time just before Israel entered the land (Deuteronomy) to the exiles of the Northern (2 Kings 17; 722 B.C.E.) and Southern Kingdoms (2 Kings 25; 586 B.C.E.). That most scholars in the second half of the twentieth century have viewed the books of Deuteronomy through 2 Kings as essentially one corpus owes much to the influence of Martin Noth's classic study of the Deuteronomistic History, contained in his larger *Überlieferungsgeschichtliche Studien.*[1] According to Noth, the Deuteronomist incorporated the deuteronomic law into the beginning of his work, framing it with speeches by Moses.[2] The Deuteronomist then added other sources, such as tales of conquest and settlement, prophetic narratives and speeches, official annals and records. The Deuteronomist organized these disparate materials, shaped them, and inserted his own retrospective and anticipatory comments (often in the mouths of major characters) at critical junctures in his history. As the chapter of Noth's work included here ("The Central Theological Ideas," pp. 20–30) indicates, Noth considered these speeches, prayers, and summarizing reflections as demarcating the major sections within the Deuteronomistic History.[3] The Deuteronomist employed the old deuteronomic

1. M. Noth, *Überlieferungsgeschichtliche Studien: Die sammelnden und bearbeitenden Geschichtswerke im Alten Testament* (Schriften der Königsberger Gelehrten Gesellschaft Geisteswissenschaftliche Klasse 18. Jh. H. 2 Bd. 1; Tübingen: Max Niemeyer, 1943). The first part of this work has been translated as *The Deuteronomistic History* (2d ed.; JSOTSup 15; Sheffield: JSOT Press, 1991).

2. *The Deuteronomistic History,* 27–60

3. Originally published as "Die theologischen Leitgedanken," in his *Überlieferungsgeschichtliche Studien,* 100–110, and later translated in *The Deuteronomistic History,* 134–45.

law code, or at least select portions within it, as a standard by which to judge the actions of major figures within his history.[4] The unity the Deuteronomist imposed upon the resulting work was literary, thematic, and chronological. Covering almost a millennium of Israel's existence, from the time of Moses to the end of the monarchy, the movement of the Deuteronomistic History found its chronological high point in Solomon's construction of the Temple (1 Kgs 6:1).[5]

Because the Deuteronomist's compositional technique included selection, edition, and composition, the resulting work was not merely a collection of sources, but a coherent work manifesting a deliberate design and a uniformity of purpose.[6] In advancing this point of view, Noth was reacting to both those scholars who focused their attention solely upon isolated historical books without recognizing their relationship to others and those who attempted to identify strands within the Former Prophets (Joshua through Kings) continuous with or analogous to the sources (JEDP) of the Pentateuch. In Noth's view, the partition of the Deuteronomistic History into discrete books was a later development which in some cases did justice to the natural transitions within the work (e.g., Deuteronomy to Joshua) but in other cases did not (e.g., Judges to Samuel). Noth's presentation of the Deuteronomist as both author and redactor was ingenious. Noth could acknowledge discrepancies between passages by appealing to the Deuteronomist as the redactor of disparate sources. Yet he could also speak of the overarching unity of Deuteronomy through 2 Kings by appealing to the Deuteronomist as an author who carefully composed his history according to an elaborate design.

The scholarly reaction to Noth's work has been generally quite favorable.[7] Noth's theory was, in fact, so persuasive that until a few years ago

4. Noth, *The Deuteronomistic History*, 134–38.

5. Ibid., 34–44. Most scholars have disputed, however, Noth's reckoning of deuteronomistic chronology. Noth thought that the 480 (LXX: 440)-year figure of 1 Kgs 6:1 marked the halfway point in the Deuteronomist's version of Israelite history—480 years (or 12 generations of 40 years each) after the exodus and 480 years until the Babylonian exile. But this calculation is difficult to reconcile with the various chronological markers contained within the work. See, for example, the comments of Rofé (p. 464 n. 8) in this volume.

6. Noth, *The Deuteronomistic History*, 26.

7. It is beyond the scope of this work to furnish a complete history of criticism. Overviews may be found in J. Gordon McConville, "The Old Testament Historical Books in Modern Scholarship," *Themelios* 22/3 (1997) 3–13; and in Gary N. Knoppers, *Two Nations under God: The Deuteronomistic History of Solomon and the Dual Monarchies*, vol. 1: *The Reign of Solomon and the Rise of Jeroboam* (HSM 52; Atlanta: Scholars Press, 1993) 17–56. The most recent and extensive treatment is that of T. Römer and A. de Pury, "L'historiographie deutéronomiste (HD): Histoire de la recherche et enjeux du débat," in *Israël construit son histoire: L'historiographie deutéronomiste à la lumière des recherches récentes* (ed. A. de Pury, T. Römer, and J.-D. Macchi; Le Monde de la Bible 34; Geneva: Labor et Fides, 1996) 9–120.

most, albeit not all, scholars accepted it.[8] All of the essays in this book are indebted to Noth's work, and many build on it. This is not to say that commentators universally agree with particular aspects of Noth's literary analysis and argumentation. Far from it, many have found particular facets of Noth's work wanting. As the present collection of essays amply attests, there is a bewildering diversity of opinion on the questions of sources, authorship, date, provenance, and redaction. But most of these same scholars, while disagreeing with Noth and with one another about a variety of issues, continue to affirm the existence of a Deuteronomistic History. Hence, for these commentators, the larger argument has stood, even as they have taken issue with the particular means employed to sustain it. The debate continues, however, to be lively. Within the past decade an increasing number of scholars have called into question a number of central tenets and assumptions of the Deuteronomistic History hypothesis. For these scholars, the hypothesis itself, and not just particular aspects of it, needs to be completely revised or rejected altogether.

The present collection of works, which contains previously published essays and one new essay, attempts to provide readers with an understanding of the important developments, methodologies, and points of view in this ongoing debate. One of the advantages of the Sources for Biblical and Theological Studies series is its concern to translate important works originally written in French, German, Italian, or Spanish for a broader English-speaking audience. The publisher is to be highly commended for presenting no fewer than ten such essays (Dietrich and Naumann, Herrmann, Lemaire, Kraus, Lohfink, Plöger, Römer, Smend, Veijola, and Weippert) in the present volume. Another benefit of the Sources for Biblical and Theological Studies series is the concern to communicate not only a sense of the current debate at the end of the twentieth century but also the context of this debate, that is, how this discussion took shape over the course of the past half century. This book contains both current essays—works published for the first time or within the past few decades—and older essays—works written during the last thirty to fifty years that employ a certain methodology or pursue a certain argument—that have had a sizable influence on other scholars. Detailed forewords written by the editors immediately precede each of the essays. What follows is a broader introduction to the context in which these essays were originally published.

8. Two notable exceptions were O. Eissfeldt, *The Old Testament: An Introduction* (New York: Harper & Row, 1965) 241–48; and G. Fohrer, *Introduction to the Old Testament* (Nashville: Abingdon, 1968), who writes, "we have a series of books Deuteronomy–Kings, each composed or edited in a different way" (p. 195).

Refinements or Redactions?

Already within Noth's own time there were scholars who developed his insights and pushed his hypothesis in new directions. Some scholars believed that Noth did not do full justice to the ways in which the Deuteronomist structured his presentation. Others sought to temper Noth's judgments on certain issues. The essay by Otto Plöger, "Speeches and Prayers in the Deuteronomistic and Chronistic Histories" (pp. 31–46), explores one of the major means by which the Deuteronomist and the Chronicler unify their histories.[9] To be sure, Noth also recognized that deuteronomistically-worded speeches, prayers, and summarizing reflections orchestrate the transitions between major epochs.[10] But, as Plöger demonstrates, close examination of these compositions, as well as the links between them, provides key insights into deuteronomistic theology. Contrary to Noth's assertion that the use of this literary device was unique to the Deuteronomistic History,[11] Plöger shows that the same technique is also well represented in the Chronicler's work.

In her contribution to this volume, "Histories and History: Promise and Fulfillment in the Deuteronomistic History" (pp. 47–61), Helga Weippert draws attention to a promise-fulfillment schema in the deuteronomistic writing as foundational to deuteronomistic perceptions of divine action in history.[12] The existence of this prophecy-fulfillment pattern was not probed by Noth, but it was noticed and developed by von Rad.[13] In any case, this schema is one indication of unity within the disparate sections that make up the Deuteronomistic History. Weippert demonstrates that the pattern operates on both short-range and long-range levels.

9. Plöger's essay was originally published as "Reden und Gebete im deuteronomistischen und chronistischen Geschichtswerk," in *Festschrift für Günther Dehn zum 75. Geburtstag* (ed. W. Schneemelcher; Neukirchen-Vluyn: Neukirchener Verlag, 1967) 35–49. The essay was reproduced in his *Aus der Spätzeit des Alten Testaments* (Göttingen: Vandenhoeck & Ruprecht, 1975) 50–66.

10. Noth, *The Deuteronomistic History*, 18–20. But, as many scholars have recognized, these compositions are more numerous than Noth acknowledged: Knoppers, *Two Nations under God*, 1.26–27.

11. Noth recognized, of course, that the Chronicler composed speeches and prayers, but he contended that the Chronicler did not situate these compositions at critical points in his narrative (*The Deuteronomistic History*, 18–20). Noth reiterates this view in the second part of his *Überlieferungsgeschichtliche Studien*, 156, 160–61, translated as *The Chronicler's History* (JSOTSup 50; Sheffield: JSOT Press, 1987) 76, 80–81.

12. Originally published as H. Weippert, "Geschichten und Geschichte: Verheißung und Erfüllung im deuteronomistischen Geschichtswerk," in *Congress Volume: Leuven, 1989* (ed. J. A. Emerton; VTSup 43; Leiden: Brill, 1991) 116–31.

13. Gerhard von Rad, "The Deuteronomic Theology of History in I and II Kings," *The Problem of the Hexateuch and Other Essays* (New York: McGraw-Hill, 1966) 205–21.

One of the major ways in which scholars have sought to modify Noth's hypothesis is to contest his pessimistic conception of the Deuteronomist's purpose. In Noth's understanding of the Deuteronomist's project, the history of Israel was a disaster, a record of "ever-intensifying decline."[14] The record of the monarchy was a dismal failure. The Deuteronomist viewed the collapse of Israel as a nation as "final and definitive" and "expressed no hope for the future."[15] But is such a grim assessment the best way of grasping the author's purpose? Both Gerhard von Rad and Hans Walter Wolff challenge these negative conclusions. Von Rad points to an alternation between themes of "gospel" and "law" in Samuel–Kings. The Davidic promises delay the exile (e.g., 1 Kgs 11:11–13, 31–35), while King Jehoiachin's release from prison (2 Kgs 25:27–30) adumbrates the ultimate revival of David's line, signaling that the Deuteronomistic History ends with a messianic promise and not with a final judgment.[16] Disagreeing with the treatments of both Noth and von Rad, Wolff's essay, "The Kerygma of the Deuteronomic Historical Work" (pp. 62–78), cites the importance of turning (*šûb*) to Yhwh in Deuteronomy, Judges, and Kings to argue that the Deuteronomistic History advances a clear element of hope to its readers.[17] Divine judgment does not entail Israel's doom but calls the exiles to repentance, because the people's return (*šûb*) to God can elicit God's compassionate return (*šûb*) to them (1 Kgs 8:46–53).

The different criticisms of Noth's treatment by von Rad and Wolff raise the larger question of whether Noth's notion of a single author is adequate to account for the diversity of material and perspectives evident within the Deuteronomistic History. If von Rad and Wolff disagree with Noth on the issues of theme and purpose, Frank Cross and Rudolf Smend challenge Noth's notion that the deuteronomistic writing was the product of one exilic author. Cross and Smend, and the schools of thought they have come to represent, do not believe that one can attribute all of the diversity within the Deuteronomistic History to heterogeneous sources that the Deuteronomist incorporated, but did not rewrite, within his work. In their view, the thematic diversity extends to deuteronomistic commentary itself. In other words, Cross and Smend acknowledge the main features of the theological arguments raised by Noth, von Rad, and Wolff, but they dispute whether all of these distinct themes stem from the work of a

14. Noth, *The Deuteronomistic History,* 122.

15. Ibid., 143.

16. Von Rad, "The Deuteronomic Theology," 218–21.

17. Originally published as H. W. Wolff, "Das Kerygma des deuteronomistischen Geschichtswerk," *ZAW* 73 (1961) 171–86. The essay was translated as "The Kerygma of the Deuteronomic Historical Work," in *The Vitality of Old Testament Traditions* (ed. W. Brueggemann and H. W. Wolff; Atlanta: John Knox, 1975) 83–100.

single author. Instead, they posit a series of editions to account for this heterogeneity.

In his essay, "The Themes of the Book of Kings and the Structure of the Deuteronomistic History" (pp. 79–94), Cross revives and significantly modifies an older hypothesis of a two-stage redaction of the Deuteronomistic History.[18] Whereas some critics of the late nineteenth and early twentieth centuries believed that an older form of the Deuteronomistic History was substantially supplemented and edited in the period of the exile, Cross argues that the main edition of the Deuteronomistic History (Dtr^1) dates to the time of King Josiah (r. 640–609 B.C.E.). The author created a contrast between two main themes in the divided monarchy–the sin of Jeroboam and the promises to David–to support Josiah's revival of the Davidic state. This primary Josianic edition of the Deuteronomistic History was later retouched and revised in a much less extensive edition in the exile (Dtr^2). The exilic writer (Dtr^2) lightly edited the earlier work, laconically recorded the destruction of Jerusalem, and introduced the subtheme of Manasseh's apostasy, attributing the destruction of Judah to his perfidy. The views of Cross have had a major impact on many scholars. The essays by Halpern, Knoppers, Lemaire, Lohfink, McCarter, McKenzie, Nelson, Römer, and Weippert in this collection have all been influenced, to some degree, by Cross's redactional analysis.

Smend agrees with Noth in rejecting the extension of Pentateuchal source criticism into Kings and in acknowledging the necessity of speaking of a Deuteronomistic History. But like Cross, Smend revives and significantly modifies an older theory of composition, in this case, the multi-edition reconstruction of Alfred Jepsen.[19] In his essay "The Law and the Nations: A Contribution to Deuteronomistic Tradition History" (pp. 95–110), Smend argues that the work of a nomistic deuteronomistic editor is present in Joshua (1:7–9; 13:1b–6; chap. 23) and Judges (1:1–2:5, 17, 20–21, 23).[20] Smend surmises that, in addition to Noth's Deuteronomist (Dtr*G*[*eschichte*] or Dtr*H*[*istorie*]), there must have been a second (Dtr*N*[*omist*]).[21] Smend's views have been developed and refined by a number of scholars, the most influential being Walter Dietrich and Timo

18. Published in Frank Moore Cross, *Canaanite Myth and Hebrew Epic* (Cambridge: Harvard University Press, 1973) 274–89. An older form of this essay appeared five years earlier, "The Structure of the Deuteronomic History," in *Perspectives in Jewish Learning* (Annual of the College of Jewish Studies 3; Chicago: College of Jewish Studies, 1968) 9–24.

19. A. Jepsen, *Die Quellen des Königsbuches* (2d ed.; Halle: Max Niemeyer, 1956).

20. Originally published as R. Smend, "Das Gesetz und die Völker: Ein Beitrag zur deuteronomistischen Redaktionsgeschichte," in *Probleme biblischer Theologie: Festschrift Gerhard von Rad* (ed. H. W. Wolff; Munich: Kaiser, 1971) 494–509.

21. Smend and Dietrich originally called the first edition DtrG but later termed it DtrH.

Veijola. Dietrich revises Smend's redactional analysis in his examination of prophetic narratives and speeches in Kings, arguing for a major prophetically-oriented redaction of the Deuteronomistic History in addition to the DtrH and DtrN editions posited by Smend.[22] Dietrich believes that these prophetic materials were added to an older literary layer (DtrH) but prior to a later nomistic redaction (DtrN). DtrP assails the political and cultic apostasy of Northern royalty, while DtrN adds material of a nomistic nature, containing assorted legal sayings and the law code itself. Veijola accepts the nomenclature proposed by Dietrich (DtrH, DtrP, DtrN) but advocates a different reconstruction of DtrH and DtrN (see below). Dietrich believes that all three redactions date to the Babylonian exile and were completed by 560 B.C.E., but Smend is inclined to think that there was a longer chronological gap between redactions. Smend situates DtrN, which he conceives as representing the work of more than one writer, in the early postexilic period.[23]

Deuteronomy, Joshua, and Judges

While Cross and Smend are interested in the larger purpose(s) and redaction of the Deuteronomistic History, other scholars have explored important issues within particular books or portions thereof. The essay by Thomas Römer, "Deuteronomy and the Question of Origins" (pp. 112–38), addresses an issue to which Noth gave insufficient attention–the relationship between Deuteronomy and the rest of the Deuteronomistic History and, more specifically, the deuteronomistic editing of the old deuteronomic law code.[24] In Noth's view, the work of the Deuteronomist was largely confined to framing this code with (deuteronomistically authored) speeches of Moses.[25] But many scholars have come to believe that the deuteronomistic editing of Deuteronomy was more pervasive than Noth allowed and that this editing extended to the code itself. Moreover, even allowing for certain later additions,[26] the internal testimony of Deuteronomy is complex.[27] In the view of Römer, both Deuteronomy and the

22. Walter Dietrich, *Prophetie und Geschichte* (FRLANT 108; Göttingen: Vandenhoeck & Ruprecht, 1972).

23. R. Smend, *Die Enstehung des Alten Testaments* (4th ed.; Stuttgart: Kohlhammer, 1989) 124–25.

24. Originally published as T. Römer, "Le Deutéronome à la quête des origines," *Le Pentateuque: Débats et recherches* (Lectio Divina 151; Paris: du Cerf, 1992) 65–98.

25. Noth, *The Deuteronomistic History,* 28–34.

26. Of which Noth thought there were many (ibid., 32–33).

27. See the earlier volume in this series edited by Duane Christensen, *A Song of Power and the Power of Song: Essays on the Book of Deuteronomy* (SBTS 3; Winona Lake, Ind.: Eisenbrauns, 1993).

Deuteronomistic History speak with more than one voice on the question of Israel's national origins. The essay by Roy Porter, "The Succession of Joshua" (pp. 139–62), examines the formal elements in the deuteronomistic version of the Moses-Joshua succession.[28] Porter thinks that the practice and ideology of royal succession in Israel and the ancient Near East play an essential role in shaping how the Deuteronomist depicted the transfer of national authority from Moses to Joshua in Deuteronomy and Joshua.

The essay "Gilgal: A Contribution to the Cultic History of Israel" (pp. 163–78) by Hans-Joachim Kraus shows one standard way in which the Deuteronomistic History has been used by scholars over the past century.[29] Individual texts are drawn from various parts of the deuteronomistic work to reconstruct the history of a particular site or sanctuary. Gilgal is featured prominently in the conquest and early monarchy. Aside from being commemorated as the first site the Israelites encounter upon crossing the Jordan (Josh 4:19–20) and the place at which the Israelites hold the Passover sacrifice (Josh 5:9–10), Gilgal also functions as a base of Israelite operations well into the period of the Judges (Josh 9:6, 10:6–43, 14:6; Judg 21:5). The goal of Richard Nelson's essay, "The Role of the Priesthood in the Deuteronomistic History" (pp. 179–93), is different in nature from Kraus's goal.[30] Rather than using the Deuteronomistic History to reconstruct history, Nelson employs the work to get at the historiographical and theological concerns of the Deuteronomist. Many scholars have contended that the Deuteronomist did not have an active interest in sacrifice and cultic affairs, even though he insisted on centralization.[31] Nelson qualifies this judgment by pursuing an issue neglected by Noth. Nelson argues that the Deuteronomist was interested in the history of the priesthood insofar as this history was related to other topics of interest to him. In this respect, the evidence provided by the Deuteronomistic History, however incidental this testimony may be, can contribute to a much larger project–reconstructing the history of religion(s) in ancient Israel and Judah.

One of the reasons that scholars before the time of Noth spoke of the Pentateuchal sources (JEDP) continuing into at least some of the historical books is the presence of Priestly language and themes at the end of

28. First published in *Proclamation and Presence: Old Testament Essays in Honor of Gwynne Henton Davies* (ed. J. I. Durham and J. R. Porter; London: SCM / Richmond: John Knox, 1970) 102–32. A new and corrected edition of this volume was published by Mercer University Press (Macon, Ga., 1983).

29. Originally published as H.-J. Kraus, "Gilgal: Ein Beitrag zur Kultusgeschichte Israels," *VT* 1 (1951) 181–99.

30. Nelson's article was originally published in *Congress Volume: Leuven, 1989* (ed. J. A. Emerton; VTSup 43; Leiden: Brill, 1991) 132–47.

31. See, for instance, Noth, *The Deuteronomistic History*, 137–39.

Deuteronomy and in the book of Joshua (especially within Joshua 13–22). Noth handled the issue by contending that these chapters in Joshua composed a later addition to the Deuteronomistic History.[32] The essays by Wenham and Van Seters revisit this issue in interesting, but different, ways. In a close comparison of prominent concerns in Deuteronomy and Joshua, Gordon Wenham ("The Deuteronomic Theology of the Book of Joshua," pp. 194–203) demonstrates that these books (including Joshua 13–22) share a number of important themes.[33] John Van Seters takes a different approach from that employed by Wenham. In "The Deuteronomist from Joshua to Samuel" (pp. 204–39), Van Seters argues for a whole series of interpolations to the text, mostly of a Priestly character but also deuteronomistic and Yahwistic.[34] In this manner, Van Seters is able to maintain a high degree of unity within the (original) deuteronomistic narrative.

Another problem that the text of Joshua posed for Noth's theory is the existence of two apparent conclusions to this section of the deuteronomistic record–Joshua's farewell speech (Josh 23:2–16) and the speeches spoken by Joshua in the following covenant ceremony (Josh 24:1–28). The detailed study by David Sperling, "Joshua 24 Re-examined" (pp. 240–58), addresses the authorship and provenance of the latter passage.[35] Whereas Noth viewed Josh 24:1–28 as a later interpolation, influenced by deuteronomistic themes, and Van Seters sees this account as the conclusion to the Yahwistic History (J), Sperling's study of language, style, and content argues that this material was authored by a writer living sometime in the eighth century B.C.E. If this is the case, the piece cannot be identified with either the work of the Deuteronomist or with any of the four Pentateuchal sources (JEDP).

Samuel and Kings

In treating the book of Samuel, many scholars operating with a historical-critical methodology have argued that the Deuteronomist had access to extensive source materials. These older sources are thought to have been incorporated with some light deuteronomistic editing into the larger

32. Ibid., 66–68. Noth's comments on the other so-called Priestly portions of Deuteronomy and Joshua are also relevant. They appear in a latter portion of his *Überlieferungsgeschichtliche Studien*, translated as *The Chronicler's History*, 111–34. On the issue of Priestly editing in Deuteronomy and Joshua, see also the essays by Porter, Römer, Sperling, and Van Seters in this volume.

33. Originally published as G. Wenham, "The Deuteronomic Theology of the Book of Joshua," *JBL* 90 (1971) 40–48.

34. Originally published in J. Van Seters, *In Search of History* (New Haven: Yale University Press, 1983) 322–53. This work has recently been reprinted by Eisenbrauns (1997).

35. Sperling's essay was originally published in *HUCA* 58 (1987) 119–36.

record of the development of the united monarchy. The contribution of Kyle McCarter, "The Apology of David" (pp. 260–75), stands out as an exemplar of this approach.[36] He argues that one of these putative sources, the history of David's rise, defined by McCarter as 1 Sam 16:14–2 Sam 5:10*, originally functioned as a literary legitimation of David's ascendancy to kingship over all Israel. Because the author presents this detailed, bloody, and much-contested sequence of events as conforming to God's will, McCarter favors both an early date and a Southern provenance for the narrative.

If McCarter sees the Deuteronomist(s) as lightly editing the sources bequeathed to him, a more complex picture emerges in the treatment of the same material by Walter Dietrich and Thomas Naumann ("The David-Saul Narrative," pp. 276–313).[37] In his earlier work, Dietrich argued that an exilic editor (DtrP) redacted an earlier historical account of the kingdoms dating to between 587 and 580 B.C.E. (DtrH) by inserting prophetic speeches and stories in Kings, substantially revising and expanding the earlier history. In this essay, Dietrich and Naumann take a broader approach, addressing both diachronic and synchronic methods of interpretation. They contend that a blend of traditional forms of scholarly criticism and recent literary approaches can best deal with the complexities of the Samuel narrative. In his contribution, entitled "David's Rise and Saul's Demise: Narrative Analogy in 1 Samuel 24–26" (pp. 319–39), Robert Gordon focuses his attention on the internal literary dynamics of one unit within the larger Samuel narrative.[38] If Dietrich and Naumann call for a union of older historically centered approaches–such as source criticism (the isolation of sources underlying the Masoretic Text) and redaction criticism (the history of the editing of the Samuel narratives); and newer literary approaches, such as narratological criticism, which concentrate on the text as it is–Gordon attempts to create exactly such a fusion. His essay, which was written in advance of much of the new literary work on Samuel, argues that the story of Nabal (1 Samuel 25) should be read in conjunction with and set over against the narratives depicting David's rise and Saul's demise. Hence, whereas 1 Samuel 24 and 26 were regarded as variant forms of a single tradition, Gordon shows how the latter represents a development from the former. The intervening chapter (1 Samuel 25) contributes to this development by casting Nabal as a "type" of Saul.

36. Originally published as P. Kyle McCarter, "The Apology of David," *JBL* 99 (1980) 489–504.

37. Originally published in W. Dietrich and T. Naumann, *Die Samuelbücher* (Erträge der Forschung 287; Darmstadt: Wissenschaftliche Buchgesellschaft, 1995) 47–86.

38. Originally published as R. P. Gordon, "David's Rise and Saul's Demise: Narrative Analogy in 1 Samuel 24–26," *TynBul* 31 (1980) 37–64.

As might be expected, the analysis of Solomon's rise by Timo Veijola ("Solomon: The Firstborn of Bathsheba," pp. 340–57), shares more in common with the analysis of Dietrich and Naumann than it does with the analysis of Gordon.[39] Veijola's methodology involves detecting sources underlying the text, tracing a sequence of deuteronomistic editions of the text, and isolating later additions to that text. In his judgment, the earliest (reconstructed) version of the David and Bathsheba narrative presented Solomon as the firstborn son of this couple. Embarrassed by the implications of this story, a later redactor added a narrative detailing the death of the firstborn. In this manner, the redactor legitimated Solomon's birth. The contrast between the essay authored by Dietrich and Naumann and the one authored by Veijola demonstrates a larger point about biblical scholarship: even scholars working with the same redactional model can come to different conclusions about the history and import of given narratives.

In the view of Noth and many other scholars, the divisions between the primary units within the larger deuteronomistic narrative are provided by speeches, prayers, and summarizing reflections. Two essays in this volume deal with one of the major deuteronomistic compositions: the prayer of Solomon at the dedication of the Temple (1 Kings 8). Gordon McConville's contribution, "1 Kgs 8:46–53 and the Deuteronomic Hope" (pp. 358–69), engages Solomon's petitions for those Israelites who find themselves in exile and compares these petitions with the statements about the possibility of the people's return from exile found in Deut 30:1–10.[40] The fact that the two passages share similar terminology yet offer different hopes for the future suggests differences in perspective and authorship. In contrast to the redactional models proposed by Cross and Smend, McConville favors an interpretive model that underscores the distinctive nature and individual integrity of each of the books that make up the Deuteronomistic History.[41]

My essay, "Prayer and Propaganda: The Dedication of Solomon's Temple and the Deuteronomist's Program" (pp. 370–96), deals with a number of literary, historical, and theological questions.[42] In contrast to critics who contend for many redactions of 1 Kings 8, I argue for its

39. Originally published as T. Veijola, "Salomo: Der Erstgeborene Bathsebas," in *Studies in the Historical Books of the Old Testament* (ed. J. A. Emerton; VTSup 30; Leiden: Brill, 1979) 230–50.

40. Originally published as J. G. McConville, "1 Kings VIII 46–53 and the Deuteronomic Hope," *VT* 42 (1992) 67–79.

41. See further his essay, idem, "Narrative and Meaning in the Books of Kings," *Bib* 70 (1989) 31–49.

42. Originally published as G. Knoppers, "Prayer and Propaganda: The Dedication of Solomon's Temple and the Deuteronomist's Program," *CBQ* 57 (1995) 229–54.

essential unity, pointing out that a series of complementary literary frames within the chapter cumulatively highlight the role of the Temple as a place of prayer. Rather than seeing the *topos* of prayer as an exilic devaluation of the Temple's importance (Noth), I argue that a preexilic Deuteronomist, writing in the context of Josiah's campaign for centralization, shaped the Solomonic petitions to underscore the Temple's pivotal role in addressing all sorts of predicaments in which the people might find themselves. If the authors of Deuteronomy centralize sacrifice, the Deuteronomist ventures a step further by centralizing prayer.

The royal speech of Solomon is an important marker in the deuteronomistic history of the united kingdom, but the prophetic speeches against the Northern kings are important markers in the deuteronomistic account of the Israelite kingdom. In his study of these prophetic addresses, entitled "Dog Food and Bird Food: The Oracles against the Dynasties in the Book of Kings" (pp. 397–420), Steven McKenzie explores whether a major prophetic source or history may be recovered from these texts. He finds that the speeches are much more heavily edited by the Deuteronomist than some have supposed. Although he thinks that the Deuteronomist may have had access to some individual prophetic stories, McKenzie very much doubts that an earlier prophetic history underlies any of these oracles.

If the prophetic oracles against the Northern dynasties are considered to be one key indication of the deuteronomistic stance toward the Northern Kingdom, Nathan's dynastic oracle (2 Sam 7:5–16) is considered to be a pivotal text for understanding the deuteronomistic portrayal of the united monarchy and the later kingdom of Judah. As the earlier essay by Herrmann indicates, the Davidic promises have been much discussed in recent literature. This is not only because many scholars consider Nathan's oracle to be a deuteronomistic composition but also because the Deuteronomist uses these promises as a cipher to structure his account of the Judahite monarchy. Norbert Lohfink engages in a detailed text-critical and exegetical study of one particular text in Kings that bears on this larger issue ("Which Oracle Granted Perdurability to the Davidides? A Textual Problem in 2 Kgs 8:19 and the Function of the Dynastic Oracle in the Deuteronomistic History," pp. 421–43).[43] In Lohfink's judgment, not 2 Samuel 7, but the conditional dynastic oracles of 1 Kgs 2:4a, 8:25a, and 9:5b provide the best insight into the perspective of the Deuteronomist (Dtr[1]) on the issue of the dynastic promises. The failure of Solomon to

43. Originally published as N. Lohfink, "Welches Orakel gab den Davididen Dauer? Ein Textproblem in 2 Kön 8,19 und das Funktionieren der dynastischen Orakel im deuteronomistischen Geschichtswerk," in *Lingering over Words: Studies in Ancient Near Eastern Literature in Honor of William L. Moran* (ed. T. Abusch, J. Huehnergard, and P. Steinkeller; HSS 37; Atlanta: Scholars Press, 1990) 349–70.

abide by these conditions does not mean, however, that all hope is lost for the descendants of David. On the contrary, the pledge of Yhwh to grant the sons of David continuing 'rule' (*nîr*) in Jerusalem supports their right to govern in Jerusalem and Judah.[44]

Many New Directions

Over the past half century, research on Deuteronomy through Kings has been dominated by one model—Noth's Deuteronomistic History hypothesis. The success of this theory has inspired many important studies of the Former Prophets and opened new possibilities for research. But there is also a negative side to the strong influence exercised by this one model. As is the case with any dominant hypothesis, new and competing hypotheses may be crowded out or neglected altogether. Research can become ossified, never venturing outside the limits of the theory first traced by the master. A number of contributions contained in this volume overtly challenge the assumptions and tenets of the Deuteronomistic History hypothesis.[45] Others pursue new directions not imagined even a few decades ago.

If Cross and Smend emend Noth's redactional analysis by positing two and three editions, respectively, André Lemaire contends that these emendations do not go far enough. Citing variations in the regnal formulae of Northern and Southern kings, Lemaire's essay, "Concerning the Redactional History of the Books of Kings" (pp. 446–61), posits multiple preexilic editions in addition to the Josianic and exilic editions advocated by Cross.[46] In advancing this general point of view, Lemaire is not alone. A variety of other recent scholars have argued for a sequence of preexilic editions. The history and conception of the deuteronomistic work evident in Lemaire's proposal are quite different from those implicit in the models proposed by Noth, Cross, and Smend. Rather than thinking of a work that underwent one, two, or even three major editions, Lemaire envisions a basic work being constantly updated and expanded over the course of a few hundred years.[47]

44. In this respect, Lohfink's position resembles that of Baruch Halpern, *The First Historians: The Hebrew Bible and History* (San Francisco: Harper & Row, 1988; repr. University Park: The Pennsylvania State University Press, 1996).

45. On the import of these recent challenges, scholars come to different conclusions. See further J. Gordon McConville, "Old Testament Historical Books," and my "Is There a Future for the Deuteronomistic History?" in *The Future of the Deuteronomistic History* (ed. Thomas Römer; BETL147; Leuven: Peeters, forthcoming).

46. Lemaire's essay was originally published as "Vers l'histoire de la rédaction des Livres des Rois," in *ZAW* 98 (1986) 221–36.

47. For a more detailed discussion of this general approach, see Gary N. Knoppers, *Two Nations under God,* 1.42–45, and the references cited there.

The compositional model proposed by Alexander Rofé in his essay "Ephraimite versus Deuteronomistic History" (pp. 462–74) departs from both the theory proposed by Noth and the revisions of that theory proposed by various other scholars.[48] Rofé contends that Noth either overlooked or ignored decisive older arguments for a major block in the narrative–Joshua 24 through 1 Samuel 12–being fundamentally nondeuteronomistic in character. Instead, Rofé speaks of Joshua 24 through 1 Samuel 12* as constituting a coherent, (North) Israel-oriented, predeuteronomistic history. Only at a later point was this unit incorporated into the larger Deuteronomistic History.

As Julio Trebolle Barrera observes in the introduction to his essay "Redaction, Recension, and Midrash in the Books of Kings" (pp. 475–92), the work of Noth coincided with a back-to-the-Masoretic-Text movement in biblical studies on the continent.[49] As a result, the insights afforded by a century of manuscript discoveries, clarifying the relationship between the Greek and Hebrew texts of Samuel and Kings, were largely passed over. With the discovery of a variety of Hebrew texts at Qumran, some of which resemble the Greek witnesses to certain biblical books, scholars have gained unprecedented insight into the development of the biblical text in the last centuries B.C.E. and the first centuries C.E. As Trebolle Barrera shows, many of the variants between Hebrew, Greek, and Old Latin texts of Kings do not constitute tendentious alterations of a standard and fixed text but form genuine witnesses in their own right to different text-types extant in the history of the biblical writings. Such readings can reflect earlier stages in the process of editing and redacting the biblical text than are reflected in the received rabbinic text. Hence, Trebolle Barrera's essay moves beyond the traditional boundary between "lower criticism" (textual criticism, form criticism) and "higher criticism" (historical criticism, source criticism, redaction criticism).

Another boundary observed in much criticism of the Deuteronomistic History is the demarcation between literary criticism and comparative Semitics. Happily, a number of scholars have broken down this boundary by offering studies that relate the findings of ancient Near Eastern epigraphy, history, and archaeology to the Deuteronomistic History. The works of Porter, Van Seters, and McCarter (mentioned above) contribute to this discussion.[50] Two other essays included in this volume make comparison with ancient Mediterranean texts their primary focus. Narratives pertain-

48. Rofé's essay was first published in *Storia e Tradizioni di Israele: Scritti in Onore di J. Alberto Soggin* (ed. D. Garrone and F. Israel; Brescia: Paideia, 1991) 221–35.

49. Originally published as J. Trebolle Barrera, "Redaction, Recension, and Midrash in the Books of Kings," *BIOSCS* 15 (1982) 12–35.

50. In fact, the work of Van Seters contains an extensive discussion of ancient Greek, Mesopotamian, and Egyptian historiography (*In Search of History*, 8–187).

ing to the reigns of both David (2 Samuel 7) and Solomon (1 Kgs 3:5–14) comprise the topic of Siegfried Herrmann's essay, entitled "The Royal Novella in Egypt and Israel: A Contribution to the History of Forms in the Historical Books of the Old Testament" (pp. 493–515).[51] Herrmann argues that these pivotal passages may be best understood by comparing them with ancient Egyptian royal novellas, which date from the Egyptian Middle Kingdom onward. In his essay "The Counsel of the 'Elders' to Rehoboam and Its Implications" (pp. 516–39), Moshe Weinfeld offers detailed comparisons between the advice Rehoboam receives at the Assembly at Shechem (1 Kgs 12:6–7) and the advice provided to rulers in ancient Near Eastern diplomatic texts.[52] He discovers a number of parallels in phraseology, literary genres, and conceptual ideals. Weinfeld thinks that the Chronicler's later rewriting and softening of this advice (2 Chr 10:7) misses some of the diplomatic nuances of his source text.

One of the assumptions underlying Weinfeld's piece, as well as most others reprinted in this volume, is that the Deuteronomist(s) wrote a work of history. The product of the Deuteronomist's labors belongs to the larger genre of ancient historiography. This is not to say that Noth and others who followed him believed that this work lacked legendary elements or was free of bias and ideology. Quite the contrary, as we have seen, Noth thought that the Deuteronomist employed sundry traditions, of varying quality, and left his own unmistakable stamp on the material he included within his work. Like other ancient historians, the Deuteronomist exercised considerable latitude in composing his work. Nevertheless, Noth thought that the Deuteronomist employed his sources in a conscientious manner and intended his writing to be "a compilation and explanation of the extant traditions concerning the history of his people."[53] In the past decade, however, a number of scholars have avidly disputed applying the label *history* to most, if not all, of the Former Prophets. According to these scholars, the deuteronomistic authors produced a work of literary fiction or national etiology but not a work of historiography.[54] Few, if any, correspondences are said to exist between the events mentioned in this work and external history. In his previously unpublished essay, entitled

51. Originally published as S. Herrmann, "Die Königsnovelle in Ägypten und in Israel: Ein Beitrag zur Gattungsgeschichte in den Geschichtsbüchern des Alten Testaments," *Wissenschaftliche Zeitschrift der Universität Leipzig* 3 (1953–54) 51–62 and republished in his *Gesammelte Studien zur Geschichte und Theologie des Alten Testaments* (Munich: Chr. Kaiser, 1986) 120–44.

52. Weinfeld's article was originally published in *MAARAV* 3 (1982) 27–53.

53. Noth, *The Deuteronomistic History*, 133. His comments on the Chronicler's work are also relevant (*The Chronicler's History*, 75–95).

54. The assessment is tied to differing notions of what constitutes history and to differing notions about what one may reconstruct, if anything, about the united and early divided

"The State of Israelite History" (pp. 540–65), Baruch Halpern surveys this new development and assesses what he considers to be the merits and demerits of this trend in biblical studies. On the basis of comparisons with Northwest Semitic epigraphy, history, and archaeology, Halpern concludes that there is still much to be said for viewing the Deuteronomist's work as an example of ancient history writing.

At the time in which Noth wrote, biblical studies were dominated by a certain range of critical methodologies–source criticism, form criticism, redaction criticism, historical criticism, and the like. To be sure, some studies paid keen attention to literary motifs but with a clear view toward the larger task of historical reconstruction. The past two decades have witnessed the emergence of new approaches in literary criticism, sociological criticism, and feminist studies, which have provided clear alternatives, if not also challenges, to these older forms of scholarly work. Some commentators have seen the contrast between historical-critical and literary studies as essentially a difference between diachronic and synchronic concerns. Whereas historical-critical investigation purportedly involves excavating a sequence of layers within a text and commenting on the original contexts of these reconstructed narratives, newer forms of literary criticism comment on the structure and content of the (Hebrew) text as it has come down to us. But this statement of contrast is, as David Gunn shows ("New Directions in the Study of Hebrew Narrative," pp. 566–77), too simplistic.[55] In his insightful overview of new interpretive strategies, he points out that many recent literary studies have rejected the possibility of achieving a normative reading of the text. Some have opted instead for a variety of reader-oriented theories. Such approaches neither presume nor seek a reliable narrator. In Gunn's view, reader-oriented theories do not require, much less prefer, the delimitation of a Deuteronomistic History. Hence, the newer forms of literary criticism have succeeded in bringing a host of new considerations to bear on old issues and in raising a variety of new considerations to bear on our readings of biblical texts.

The essay by Cheryl Exum, "The Centre Cannot Hold: Thematic and Textual Instabilities in Judges" (pp. 578–600), stands out as an example of one type of new literary criticism.[56] Many traditional readings of Judges posit an apostasy, punishment, repentance, and deliverance cycle, but Exum contends that "increasing corruption and an atmosphere of hopelessness characterize the book."[57] Moreover, traditional readings largely

monarchies (Gary N. Knoppers, "The Vanishing Solomon: The Disappearance of the United Monarchy from Recent Histories of Ancient Israel," *JBL* 116 [1997] 19–44).

55. Gunn's essay was originally published in *JSOT* 39 (1987) 65–75.

56. Exum's article was originally published in *CBQ* 52 (1990) 410–31.

57. J. C. Exum, "The Centre Cannot Hold," 411 (p. 580 in this volume).

ignore God's role in Israel's political and moral instability. Exum's study focuses on the increasingly problematic character of the book's human protagonists and on the increasingly ambiguous role of the deity. Inasmuch as Judges ultimately deconstructs itself, the book reveals a crisis of both human and divine leadership.

In his contribution ("What, if Anything, Is 1 Samuel?" pp. 601–14), David Jobling registers both appreciation for and criticism of some new literary studies on 1 Samuel.[58] He points out how the results of literary studies are inherently dependent on the limits provided by one's choice of a text. The issue is very much related to the larger topic of the Deuteronomistic History, because many literary scholars have accepted the notion of a Deuteronomistic History even while they have chosen to focus on only one limited section, usually a book, within it. Despite the insights of historical criticism and redaction criticism, scholars have often continued to follow uncritically the ancient divisions made by the text's canonizers. The idea of "1 Samuel" is already an interpretation, and the reading of this material is very much affected by whether one regards 1 Samuel as a beginning or as a continuation. Jobling's study shows that historical criticism and literary criticism cannot be entirely separate and discrete enterprises but are inevitably linked together.

One may get the impression from the essays included in this volume that the study of the Deuteronomistic History is a much more complex enterprise at the end of the twentieth century than it was at its beginning. This impression may accurately characterize the field of biblical studies as a whole. In the context of such change, it would be tempting to explain this diversification as resulting from the different assumptions and methods at work in contemporary scholarship. Such a conclusion, however, would be too simplistic. To be sure, various presuppositions, traditions, commitments, models, and methods inevitably lead to different conclusions. But the differences of opinion about the Deuteronomistic History may also say something about the work itself. As the various contributions to this volume attest, there are profound textual, literary, theological, and historical issues involved in the interpretation of Deuteronomy and the Former Prophets. Cheryl Exum comments in the introduction to her essay on Judges that this biblical book is a multilayered, dense narrative construct. What is true of Judges is also true, perhaps even more so, of the Deuteronomistic History itself. But one of the remarkable features of the deuteronomistic historical work is that it continues to offer fascinating answers to the wide variety of questions brought to it by modern interpreters. In this respect, the unity and diversity of the Deuteronomistic History may be regarded as two poles exercising some constraint upon

58. Jobling's essay was originally published in *SJOT* 7 (1993) 17–31.

each other. What remains to be seen is whether the diversity of recent scholarly study will increase in the years ahead or whether the concept of unity, as commonly adopted in the nomenclature of the Deuteronomistic History, will continue to exert major influence.

Appendix 1
Summary of M. Noth's Major Work on the Deuteronomistic History

Martin Noth, *Überlieferungsgeschichtliche Studien: Die sammelnden und bearbeitenden Geschichtswerke im Alten Testament* (Schriften der königsberger Gelehrten Gesellschaft, Geisteswissenschaftliche Klasse 18. Jh. H. 2 Bd. 1; Tübingen: Max Niemeyer, 1943). Second and third (unaltered) editions of the same work were published in 1957 and 1967.

The first part of this work was first translated as *The Deuteronomistic History* (JSOTSup 15; Sheffield: JSOT Press, 1981). To complicate matters, this translation was reworked, corrected, and repaginated as *The Deuteronomistic History* (2d ed.; JSOTSup 15; Sheffield: JSOT Press, 1991).

The second part of Noth's *Überlieferungsgeschichtliche Studien: Die sammelnden und bearbeitenden Geschichtswerke im Alten Testament* has been translated as *The Chronicler's History* (JSOTSup 50; Sheffield: JSOT Press, 1987).

Noth's comments on the other so-called Priestly portions of Deuteronomy and Joshua also appear in a latter portion (the second half) of his *Überlieferungsgeschichtliche Studien*, translated as *The Chronicler's History*, 111–34.

Appendix 2
Abbreviations Related to the Deuteronomistic History

There has been little consistency in the use of abbreviations relating to the Deuteronomistic History. Some inconsistencies have been caused by differences of opinion about the number of redactors and their dates, and some have been caused by different uses of the same abbreviations by scholars who *do* agree with each other about deuteronomistic theory.

In this volume, the DH (or, spelled out, the Deuteronomistic History) refers to the *work* of the Deuteronomist, which usually is considered to be the history encompassing Deuteronomy through 2 Kings. Dtr refers to the Deuteronomist, *the person*, who edited or redacted the Deuteronomistic History. In the view of some scholars, there was one definitive, exilic edition of the Deuteronomistic History. As opposed to this hypothesis, some scholars believe that there were two redactors. They use Dtr^1 to refer to a person who worked during the reign of the reformer-king, Josiah. Dtr^2 refers to a later, exilic Deuteronomist. To complicate matters further, there were, according to another group of scholars, three different exilic (and postexilic) editions of the deuteronomistic work: DtrH (or DtrG), DtrP, and DtrN. The reader is advised to refer to the list of abbreviations and to this introduction for these distinctions while reading this book.

Part 1

The Theory of a Deuteronomistic History and Its Refinements

The Central Theological Ideas

MARTIN NOTH

The main thesis of Noth's seminal work is well known, namely, that the DH is a unified product of an exilic historian who uses available sources and supplements them with his own compositions in order to support his interpretation of Israel's history. Every part of Noth's book is so germane to the debates that followed that it is difficult to make a selection from it. The many questions it raises include the following: is the DH a unified composition? How do the "books" relate to the redaction as a whole? What is the attitude to the temple and monarchy? Is there hope for the future of the covenant people? These questions surface frequently in the pages of the present volume. The passage reproduced here is the final chapter of the monograph. It is chosen because it focuses on the historian's fundamental theological attitudes and his motive for writing. The important contentions are Dtr's equation of "law" and "covenant," his negative attitude to cultic matters and consequent view of the temple as hardly more than a place of prayer, his insistence, conversely, on the requirement of a single place of worship, and his low expectation of future restoration for Israel. The last point prompted the response of Wolff (included here, pp. 62–78), among others. And the question of the temple and monarchy has much to do with the understanding of the basic character of the work. E. W. Nicholson's judgment, in the preface to the edition from which the present pages are excerpted, is still valid: "This is a 'classic' work in the sense that it still remains the fundamental study of the corpus of literature with which it is concerned."

[[89]] Dtr did not write his history to provide entertainment in hours of leisure or to satisfy a curiosity about national history, but intended it to

Reprinted with permission from Martin Noth, *The Deuteronomistic History* (JSOTSup 15; Sheffield: JSOT Press, 1981 [Eng. trans. of the 1957 German edition]). The excerpt selected is chapter thirteen, "The Central Theological Ideas," 89–99, 141–42.

teach the true meaning of the history of Israel from the occupation to the destruction of the old order. The meaning which he discovered was that God was recognisably at work in this history, continuously meeting the accelerating moral decline with warnings and punishments and, finally, when these proved fruitless, with total annihilation. Dtr, then, perceives a just divine retribution in the history of the people, though not so much (as yet) in the fate of the individual. He sees this as the great unifying factor in the course of events, and speaks of it not in general terms but in relation to the countless specific details reported in the extant traditions. Thus Dtr approached his work with a definite theological conviction. He certainly does not think that the history of the Israelite people is a mere random example of the fate of peoples whose end is at hand but rather regards it as a unique case, quite apart from the fact that the people concerned are his own people. Dtr gives various hints that God honoured the Israelite people with a special role and thus placed them under a special obligation, which was formulated in the Deuteronomic law which Dtr places at the beginning of his history; this law was essentially intended to keep them from forsaking God in any way, that is, to demand an exclusive bond with the one God and thereby to assure the worship of one particular God–an exclusiveness unique in the history of ancient religion. The very fact that Dtr repeatedly mentions apostasy, although he uses no specific technical term for it, shows that he seeks not to describe just any collective fate, but to portray the development of a nation living under particular conditions.

In this task, Dtr focuses his attention upon specific theological presuppositions to which he alludes only occasionally in his narrative and which he does not articulate or expound as a whole; clearly, he expects the reader to be familiar with them. His interest centres on the special bond between God and people to which he refers when, with the old [[90]] traditions (1 Sam 9:16; 2 Sam 7:7f., etc.) in mind, he speaks of Israel as "God's people" (1 Sam 12:22; 1 Kgs 8:16, 16:2, etc.; cf. also 1 Kgs 8:53). He did find the extremely unusual concept of a "chosen people" in the Deuteronomic law (Deut 14:2) and its framework (Deut 7:6), but does not himself use it to characterise the position of the people of Israel. However it seems that, following tradition, he liked to describe the relationship between God and people as a "covenant"; here he did not have in mind the act of making a covenant in its original sense but rather the permanent regulation, as defined in the law, of the relationship between God and people. This is shown by his independent use of the term "ark of the covenant of Yahweh" to describe the ark and his habit of incorporating this term into his source material instead of using the older expression "ark of Yahweh." Moreover, in Deut 9:9ff. he equates the concepts of "covenant" and "law" (cf. Deut 4:13), and in Deut 10:1ff. regards the stone tablets which contain the basic law, the decalogue, as the contents of the ark (cf. 1 Kgs 8:9, 21). Thus in his view the special relationship between God and people is confirmed through the promulgation of the law, of which the Deuteronomic law is, according to Deut 5:28ff., the authentic divine exposition. This relationship is therefore–here he merely follows the old tradition–confirmed once in history by the theophany on the mountain of God to which he gives the name Horeb (Deut 4:10ff.) and it is associated with miraculous manifestations of divine powers to which Dtr alludes as a matter of general knowledge in his frequent references to "being brought up out of Egypt." Among these manifestations–and here Dtr follows the content of the old "occupation tradition" (von Rad)–is the conquest of the "good" land of Palestine (Deut 1:35, etc.) which was already promised to the ancestors, and described by Dtr on the basis of detailed accounts in the sources; this conquest succeeded because God "was with Moses and Joshua" (Deut 31:8; Josh 1:5, 17; 3:7) and shaped the course of events. Further examples so ordered of how Dtr saw divine intervention in history are seen, for example, where the kings whose territory has been promised to the Israelite tribes stubbornly resist their passage (cf. Deut 2:26ff.) and so bring about their own elimination.

Of the events from the sphere of the "Sinai tradition" which are of fundamental importance for the relationship between God and people, Dtr has, then, mentioned only–and that briefly–the theophany on Horeb and the promulgation of the [[91]] decalogue, going into detail only when he gives the whole Deuteronomic law with connecting passages by way of exposition of the decalogue. From the sphere of the "occupation tradition"[1] he occasionally refers in passing to the promise of the land to the Israelites' ancestors and the bringing up from Egypt and then, following a summary of the period of the wanderings in the wilderness, he describes the conquest of Palestine in detail because he had a specific source at hand. All these things prepared the way for the real theme of his history, the conduct and fate of the people once they had settled in Palestine. Dtr constructed his history as he did in order to show that the early events committed the people to unbroken loyalty to God as manifested in observance of the law, the more so because (as Dtr says in 1 Kgs 8:23, in connection with Deut 7:9, 12) this God "keeps covenant and steadfast love" and is, moreover, a just judge who passes the right sentence not only on individuals (1 Kgs 8:31f.) but also on the people as a whole, even if he

1. On this traditional material, cf. G. von Rad [[ET: "The Form-Critical Problem of the Hexateuch," *The Problem of the Hexateuch and Other Essays* (Edinburgh: Oliver and Boyd, 1966) 1–78]].

waits patiently and in the "judges" period gives the people one "saviour" after another despite their unfaithfulness and, what is more, meets the people's demand for a king, recognises the king as his "anointed" (1 Sam 12:3, 5) and gives the monarchy a chance to prove itself beneficial to the people (1 Sam 12:20ff.) in their subsequent history. For Dtr then the demand for observance of the divine law has as its background the fact that God has manifested himself and acted at the beginning of Israelite history and has repeatedly intervened to help.

Although in this traditional history of the Israelite people Dtr has little chance to mention that God's actions were intended to have an effect on the whole world, he does so once, in 1 Kgs 8:41–43, where he makes "foreigners," that is, members of other races, pray to the God of Israel who "causes his name to dwell" in the temple of Jerusalem and then goes so far as to make it an ideal to be realised in the future that one day "all the peoples of the earth" will "learn to know and fear" this God (cf. 8:60). In similar fashion the prophet Ezekiel, roughly contemporary with Dtr, speaks of the purpose of God's action. Similarly Dtr presents the history of Israel as a preparation for greater things. However, this idea does not take on any significance for Dtr; in his casual statement of it he is merely imitating a manner of speaking popular in his time. In general he saw the history of Israel as a self-contained process which began with specific manifestations of power and came to a [[92]] definitive end with the destruction of Jerusalem.

In keeping with all his presuppositions Dtr has centred his history on the theme of worship of God as required by the law, or defined in a strict, rather narrow sense; for he is interested not so much in the development of possible forms of worship of God as in the various possible forms of deviation from this worship which could be construed as apostasy and how these were realised in history. Hence, the law is needed not in a positive role to prescribe the forms of worship, which were indicated by current religious practice throughout the ancient Near East, but rather to prohibit the forms of worship which were wrong; this was in fact one of Dtr's main concerns. According to Dtr, the law itself was stated in its essentials in the decalogue; since, according to Deut 10:1ff., the stone tablets on which the original text of the decalogue had been inscribed were deposited in the "ark of the covenant of Yahweh," the ark took on a central importance for Dtr. On one hand, then, he saw the decalogue on the stone tablets as the original form of God's law, withheld from the gaze of the profane, concealed and guarded by cultic officials. On the other hand, the document of practical significance was the Deuteronomic law, the authentic exposition of the decalogue; and he means the Deuteronomic law, when he speaks of "the law (of Moses)," when he requires it to be read out regularly (Deut 31:10ff.) and reports that Joshua obeyed this requirement (Josh 8:34), or when he refers to the law in the course of general admonitions (Josh 23:6; 1 Kgs 2:3; 2 Kgs 10:31; 17:13), or when he speaks of the observance of some particular clause of the law (Josh 8:31; 2 Kgs 14:6; 23:21). In each of these instances we can prove that Dtr is alluding to the Deuteronomic law. Thinking of the application of the Deuteronomic law under Josiah, he pays particular and disproportionate attention to the religious prescriptions contained in the law (cf. above, pp. 81f. [[not reprinted here]]) and these prescriptions have considerable influence on his view of cult and of the general nature of men's worship of God.

Because Dtr takes so much notice of the cultic prescriptions in the Deuteronomic law, he adopts a strongly negative attitude toward particular aspects of cult; and since, out of all the regulations on worship contained in the law, he gives special, one-sided attention to matters of cult, he forms a generally pessimistic view of the possibilities of men's worship. In taking this view he has correctly understood the attitude of the Deuteronomic law to cultic activities; for, apart from the fact [[93]] that the commandment to have a single place of worship implies that the practice of cult must be drastically reduced, the law shows a distinct lack of interest in the observance of cult and is interested instead in preventing all manner of cults and cult practices which it thinks illegitimate. Similarly there is no sign that Dtr was actively interested in the performance of cult activities and he likes to confer upon cult objects and institutions a significance not strictly speaking cultic, as well as indicating their original and actual function. He does not ignore an activity of cult sanctioned by the Deuteronomic law or deny that it was authorised but he attaches no special importance to it. For example, he sees the ark in its role as the "ark of the covenant of Yahweh" principally as the repository of the autograph of the fundamentally important decalogue. Naturally he was well aware of its original cultic significance and recognises this by introducing the (levitical) priests as bearers of the ark (Joshua 3–4, 6; 1 Kgs 8:1–13), thereby entrusting this sacred object to certain persons who had the exclusive right to perform cult activities. However, he never relates the ark directly to cultic practices, not even in Josh 8:*30–35, which he added himself; here he explicitly mentions the presence of the ark among the Israelite tribes, which seems appropriate, given Joshua 3–4 and 6, but he mentions it, not as part of the preliminaries of sacrifice, but only just before the subsequent reading of the law.

It is even more remarkable that Dtr is not interested in cult proper as part of his conception of the significance of the temple in Jerusalem as described in Solomon's prayer of dedication (1 Kgs 8:14–53). In 1 Kgs 8:5 Dtr does follow his source in saying that the bringing of the ark to the temple was accompanied with great sacrifices, and in his own addition

(1 Kgs 8:62ff.) he tells of abundant sacrifices following the prayer of dedication.[2] This he thought self-evident and legitimate. He accepts, then, that sacrifice was inevitably a customary form of worship, provided that it took a form authorised by the Deuteronomic law, but he gives it such a peripheral importance that Solomon's prayer of dedication says nothing whatsoever on the role of the temple as a place of sacrifice, even though Dtr must surely have known that this was originally its main practical function. Dtr took over the formula in the Deuteronomic law which describes the temple as the "dwelling" "chosen" by God for his "name." However, whereas the Deuteronomic law had used this formula to justify [[94]] the recognition of the temple as a legitimate place of sacrifice (cf. Deut 12:13f. and passim), Dtr surpassed the Deuteronomic law in devaluing cultic sacrifice and completely disregarding sacrifice altogether, and so formulated his own conception of the significance of the temple. For him the temple is little more than a place towards which one turns in prayer, the location of the invisible divine presence–this is more or less what is meant by "the dwelling place of God's name" in this place–which determines the direction in which one should pray, the Kibla.[3] The only other function attributed to the temple is in vv. 31f., that of the place of divine judgements, which are responsible for determining the verdict related to the administration of justice in particular, prescribed cases. In this passage, allusions to sacrifice are conspicuous by their absence, the more so because the formal religious occasions mentioned in Solomon's prayer of dedication were normally accompanied by supplicatory sacrifices. One can be sure that Dtr has in mind the situation in his own time, when the temple had been destroyed and a sacrificial cult on the usual scale was therefore no longer practicable in Jerusalem, but the prayers of those who remained in the land and of those who had been deported probably were directed towards the site of the old temple, in memory of the past, although they could no longer be supported by supplicatory sacrifice.[4] This is certainly what happened; but it is still curious that Dtr knew perfectly well that the temple used to be a centre of regular sacrifices, and, although he did not regard other aspects of his own time as normal, but saw in his own time the end of the history of his people, he even so did not see the end of regulated cult as any great loss. Thus he lets Solomon describe

2. Following his source (cf. *ʾz* [['then']] in 1 Kgs 8:12, and on this see chap. 8, n. 45 [[not reprinted here]]). Dtr has regarded the moving of the ark and the dedication of the temple as two separate actions performed at different times, both related to sacrificial practices.

3. Subsequently the temple retained its significance as the place towards which prayers were directed, cf. Dan 6:11 and the fact that the synagogues of which we know in the period after Christ faced Jerusalem.

4. Of course the story in Daniel 6 (cf. n. 3 above) has been transposed into the exilic period when the temple had been destroyed and sacrificial worship temporarily suspended.

the significance of the temple which he has just built without so much as mentioning sacrifice. In this Dtr is in direct succession to the Deuteronomic law. His concern with the temple as the place of sacrifice is purely negative; he expresses this not in the prayer of dedication but in comments which recur throughout his account of the subsequent history of the monarchy. Here he follows the assertion in the Deuteronomic law that the temple is the one legitimate centre for cult at such times as it may be appropriate to perform sacrifices. Dtr found such sacrifices acceptable, provided that they took a legitimate form, but did not lay any stress upon them. On the positive side, however, in the long prayer of dedication Dtr characterises the erection of the temple as an historical milestone and goes on to extract from the "Books of [[95]] the Chronicles of the Kings of Judah" any material relevant to the temple. The value which the temple of Jerusalem had for him is entirely based on its actual historical role, which he explained–drawing upon the Deuteronomic law–as the "dwelling place for Yahweh's name" in Jerusalem, the city "chosen" by Yahweh for this purpose (cf. 1 Kgs 11:13, 32, 34, 36; 14:21; 2 Kgs 21:7, 23:27); further, he adduces the fact that it was the repository of the holy ark with the tablets of the law (cf. 1 Kgs 8:9, 21), and finally, the fact that it was, in accordance with the Deuteronomic law, the one and only legitimate centre of the cult, so long as cultic sacrifice was carried out.

We cannot tell how Dtr thought that the Deuteronomic requirement that there be only one place of worship had been met in the time before Solomon built the temple; for he assumes that the law was familiar from the time of Moses onward, and must therefore have taken for granted that even in earlier times some temporary provision was made to meet what he considers the most important requirement of the law. However, he has said nothing definite about the matter. In fact, he has simply reported all manner of sacrifices found in his old sources without censuring them on the ground of this stipulation of a single place of worship. He probably allowed the law to be interpreted fairly loosely in this temporary situation. Josh 8:*30–35, which he inserted himself, reports the sacrifice authorised by the command of Moses in Deut 27:2ff. and then mentions the presence of the ark. Even though this is not supported by Deuteronomy 27 and the ark is not connected explicitly with the sacrifice, it suggests that Dtr might consider sacrifice with the ark at hand to be justified; this would make the sacrifice in Shiloh legitimate (1 Sam 1:3ff.; 2:12ff.). Gideon's sacrifice (Judg 6:11–24) was, of course, explained adequately by the appearance of God's messenger or God himself;[5] the same is true of Solomon's sacrifice

5. Naturally this also applies to Manoah's sacrifice in Judg 13:19f. but, like the rest of the story of Samson, this story was probably not added to Dtr's account until later.

in Gibeon. Elsewhere Dtr tacitly uses the presence of a "man of God" or the like as a justification for sacrifices performed outside Jerusalem before the completion of the Jerusalem temple; this would apply to the sacrifice at the "high place" of an unknown city in the presence of Samuel (1 Sam 9:12ff.) and even to Elijah's sacrifice on Mount Carmel (1 Kgs 18:30ff.).[6] Dtr probably based this view upon 1 Sam 10:8 and 13:7b–14—the secondary part of the old Saul tradition which, however, had formed a part of Dtr's source. Here it was a sin for Saul to perform a sacrifice without [[96]] waiting for Samuel. Dtr also dealt with Samuel's sacrifices in parts of the history composed by himself—for example the account of the great assembly in Mizpah (1 Sam 7:9f.), and the report that Samuel built an altar in Ramah (1 Sam 7:17). On the other hand, Dtr probably did not regard the activity in 1 Sam 14:33–35 as a sacrifice, since sacrifice is not explicitly mentioned here, but probably saw it as a "profane slaughter" in the sense of Deut 12:20ff., even though the incident was originally understood to be a sacrifice, as is shown by the reference to the altar in v. 35. In general, however, Dtr seems to have kept as close as possible to his sources, even in a matter of such importance to him, without altering or even adding comments to them. This is in keeping with his basically favourable opinion regarding the traditions to which he had access. In accordance with this he was apparently relatively lenient about the sacrifices made in the different cult centres in Israel before the time of Solomon, finding some way to justify such practices and not interpreting the stipulation of a single place of worship as strictly as the Deuteronomic law sets it out, until the Jerusalem temple was built. This is a further proof that Dtr did not intend to write his history to fit a pre-determined theory but took the tradition into account and somewhat modified any strictness of theory. Tradition gave a favourable picture of Samuel; therefore, because of his division of history into periods, Dtr saw reason to include Samuel in the series of "judges" to whom he is consistently favourably disposed. This means that he does not criticise, on the basis of the Deuteronomic law, the sacrifices which the traditions report that Samuel offered, in the way that he later criticises sacrifices offered by the kings of Israel and Judah, whom he tends to view negatively. Instead, in his discussion of Samuel's action, he interprets the

6. Elijah's sacrifice took place when the Jerusalem temple was standing—Dtr considered this the sole lawful centre of cult and his view covered the Israelite kingdom as well, as is shown by his running commentary on the Israelite kings. Here then Dtr makes extraordinarily large concessions to the tradition, even if this is an exceptional case. Furthermore, the appearance of this particular instance in the Books of Kings, which are agreed to be the work of a "deuteronomistic editor," i.e., compiled by a deuteronomistic writer, shows that the occurrence of similar sacrificial scenes in 1 and 2 Samuel does not prove that they do not belong to Dtr's work.

stipulation in the Deuteronomic law that there should be only one place of worship as if it were not strictly binding before the time of Solomon. He judges other instances in the same manner. It appears to be the tradition about Samuel, however, which matters to him whenever he inquires into the application of the regulation about the single place of worship prior to Solomon. Thus in his account of the period before the Jerusalem temple was built, Dtr uses only the highly generalised Deuteronomic warning against worshipping other gods as a criterion by which to judge historical events and characters. We see this in the way he adapts the history of the "judges." It is only with Solomon that he begins to [[97]] make sacrifices on "high places" outside Jerusalem the main transgression against the law, in his critical examination of the history which he is describing.

Finally we must raise the question of what historical developments Dtr anticipated for the future. Admittedly his theme is the past history of his people, as written down and, as far as he was concerned, at an end. However, the pre-exilic prophets saw the catastrophe which they predicted not as a final end but as the beginning of a new era. Similarly, Dtr could have seen the end of the period of history which he depicts as the end of a self-contained historical process, without thinking that his people could go no further; and he could have used the interpretative summaries, which he adds, to answer the question that readily suggests itself: would not the history which he wrote attain its full meaning in the future, in conditions which had yet to develop out of the ruins of the old order, the more so because in Dtr's time people were intensely hopeful that a new order of things would emerge from all these catastrophes? It is very telling that Dtr does not take up this question and does not use the opportunity to discuss the future goal of history. Clearly he saw the divine judgement which was acted out in his account of the external collapse of Israel as a nation as something final and definitive and he expressed no hope for the future, not even in the very modest and simple form of an expectation that the deported and dispersed people would be gathered together. On one hand, it was appropriate to threaten deportation as the final divine punishment for disobedience, as Dtr emphasises in the introductory speech by Moses in Deut 4:25–28 and then more briefly and at times only allusively in Joshua's speech in Josh 23:15b–16 and in Samuel's speech in 1 Sam 12:25. On the other hand, there was every reason to speak of the more distant future in connection with reflection on the past destruction of the northern kingdom and on the future destruction of the state of Judah in 2 Kgs 17:7ff. and 21:12ff. or in a final remark at the end of the whole work. The most unambiguous information on this point is to be had in the last part of Solomon's prayer of dedication (1 Kgs 8:44–53). At this early stage Dtr makes Solomon look at the possibility of future dispersion but he is thinking only that the prayers of the dispersed people would then be directed towards the site of the Jerusalem temple; he makes Solomon wish that these prayers be heard but he makes the prayers contain nothing but a petition for forgiveness of past guilt without even [[98]] suggesting that the nation might later be reassembled and reconstructed. Under these circumstances Dtr cannot mean the improvement in the deported Jehoiachin's personal fortunes (2 Kgs 25:27–30) to herald a new age. Apart from the fact that the subject matter of this event does not lend itself to such a comprehensive interpretation, in view of what we have said above, Dtr would have no reason to take such a view. On the contrary, he shows his usual scrupulous respect for historical fact in reporting the last information that he has about the history of the Judaean monarchy as a simple fact.

On this matter, then, Dtr's theological outlook corresponds to that of the Deuteronomic law most closely. In the light of conditions in its own time, the Deuteronomic law sees nothing but the order of things given and willed by God in the time of Moses, without ever considering an historical purpose outside this present situation.[7] Similarly, the possibility of the destruction of the people, already envisaged by the Deuteronomic law as punishment for disobedience, was now for Dtr an accomplished historical reality. Thus he thought that the order of things as put forward in the Deuteronomic law had reached a final end, an end which his whole history is intent upon explaining as a divine judgement. The close relationship of the Deuteronomic law to the contemporary situation because of intervening historical events, was the cause of Dtr's concentration upon the past. Dtr clearly knew nothing about the additions to the Deuteronomic law which postulate a new future.[8] In any case, his interpretation of the facts and, probably, the time in which he wrote, are far closer to those of the original Deuteronomic law than to those of the author of the secondary passages.[9]

Not even the occasional reference to God's intention to deal with all peoples by his activity causes Dtr to look at the future; here too he does

7. Cf. von Rad [[*Das Gottesvolk im Deuteronomium* (BWANT 47; Stuttgart: Kohlhammer, 1929)]] 60ff.

8. Cf. ibid., 70f.

9. It is striking that such additions are found only in Deuteronomy and not in Joshua–Kings, where there was every opportunity to supplement the text in a similar way. We must conclude that this revision was not carried out until Deuteronomy had been detached from the body of Dtr's work and included in the Pentateuch (cf. on this, Chapter 25 [of *Überlieferungsgeschichtliche Studien* = *The Chronicler's History*, 143–47]). Given its role as a canonical document for the post-exilic community, the Pentateuch could not tolerate the idea that the destruction of Jerusalem in 587 was the final end. Meanwhile this revision did not affect the rest of Dtr.

not go beyond the situation of his own time. This is strange, as the prophets who are closest to him chronologically, Deutero-Isaiah (Isa 52:10) and Ezekiel (Ezek 36:36 and passim), endow God's future actions with the goal that "all peoples" should see them and should come to recognise God. Dtr did use this last statement but did not relate the nations' knowledge of God to great events of the future but to present and visible circumstances, even if this knowledge of God would take some time to arise and grow in them; here he has in mind the existence of the holy place in Jerusalem with which "the great name of God" and the contemplation of God's great deeds [[99]] in the past are associated (1 Kgs 8:41–43), the answering of Israel's prayers which God receives in this holy place (1 Kgs 8:60) and finally the divine judgement pronounced on people and sanctuary which will make "all peoples" attend to the judging God (1 Kgs 9:7–9). Here again Dtr is interested exclusively in the past and present.

All this at least tells us what Dtr's spiritual world is not. His work is not of an official nature, nor did it come from the priestly sphere—we have demonstrated his significant lack of interest in cult—nor is it rooted in the attitude of the governing class, for his censure of the monarchy as an institution and his description of it as a secondary phenomenon in the history of the nation are crucial to his approach to history. The view that the great final catastrophes were a divine judgement towards which the Israelite people were precipitated in the course of their history is in the spirit of the "writing" prophets, but this spirit is not a determining factor in Dtr's work, as we see from the complete absence of projection into the future. This fact also rules out the possibility that Dtr followed the ideology of the so-called national prophets. The negative characteristics of Dtr are exactly the same as those in the Deuteronomic law. Furthermore, there is no evidence that Dtr was commissioned by an individual or by a particular group. Hence the history was probably the independent project of a man whom the historical catastrophes he witnessed had inspired with curiosity about the meaning of what had happened, and who tried to answer this question in a comprehensive and self-contained historical account, using those traditions concerning the history of his people to which he had access.[10]

10. The fact that Dtr had access to such a variety of literary sources might suggest that he had stayed behind in the homeland rather than being deported. The preservation of these sources must at the very least indicate that they survived the great catastrophes; they would be most readily available in the homeland. Besides, the best explanation of Dtr's familiarity with local traditions attached to the region of Bethel and Mizpah (cf. above, p. 85 [[not reprinted here]]) would be that he lived in Palestine and, better still, this particular region. Finally, it would seem more likely that one of those who stayed in the land would omit to express any expectation for the future.

Speech and Prayer in the Deuteronomistic and the Chronicler's Histories

OTTO PLÖGER

This study by Plöger argues that speeches, prayers, and summarizing reflections orchestrate the transitions between periods in both the Deuteronomistic and Chronistic Histories. He demonstrates that a number of links exist between the speeches and theological summaries in the Deuteronomist's work and that the form and placement of these compositions provide interesting insights into deuteronomistic ideology. In his treatment of summarizing orations in the Chronicler's work, Plöger takes aim at Noth's claim that this literary device is used in a very different way in Chronicles, Ezra, and Nehemiah from the way it is used in the Deuteronomistic History (DH). Plöger shows that the Chronicler employs speeches and prayers by major figures to delimit a certain period, such as the united monarchy of David and Solomon; to honor a certain event, such as the construction of the Temple; and to introduce new eras, such as the divided monarchy. Also of interest is the manner in which the Chronicler develops a series of echoes between prayers, such as the prayers spoken by David at two different points in his reign (1 Chr 17:16–27 // 2 Sam 7:18–29; 1 Chr 29:10–19). Plöger employs comparisons between the use of prayers in the Deuteronomistic History (DH), on the one hand, and the use of prayers in the Chronicler's History (understood as Chronicles, Ezra, and Nehemiah) and Daniel, on the other hand, to shed some light on the different attitudes toward the future that one finds in the exilic and postexilic periods.

Translated and reprinted with permission, from "Reden und Gebete im deuteronomistischen und chronistischen Geschichtswerk," in *Festschrift für Günther Dehn zum 75. Geburtstag* (ed. W. Schneemelcher; Neukirchen-Vluyn: Neukirchener Verlag, 1957) 35–49; reprinted in O. Plöger, *Aus der Spätzeit des Alten Testaments* (Göttingen: Vandenhoeck & Ruprecht, 1975) 50–66. Translation by Peter T. Daniels. All English scripture quotations in this article have been taken from the RSV translation of the Bible.

I

[[35]] Authorial reflections presented in the form of speeches or summaries introduced at specific climaxes or turning points of the presentation spanning the so-called Former Prophets (Joshua through 2 Kings) have often been taken as a special feature of a unified and self-contained conception of the Deuteronomistic History (DH). As it happens, this opinion, which was clearly set forth particularly by Noth,[1] is far from being generally accepted. But even if we consider it more correct to take Joshua through 2 Kings as a continuation of the old Pentateuchal sources and as a result regard the activity of the Deuteronomist(s) more in terms of redactional editing, we still will not be able to escape the observation that, at specific, important transitions in Old Testament history, backward- or forward-looking programmatic overviews are supplied that do not primarily report events or more generally tell stories. For the moment let us pass over Moses' speech in the introductory chapters of Deuteronomy, which is certainly strongly deuteronomistically colored, in order not to strain unnecessarily the bounds of the limited space available to us. First, let us acquaint ourselves with Noth's remarks, in order to gain a bit of insight into the situation.

> For example, at the very beginning of Joshua 1, . . . Joshua briefly addresses the Transjordanian tribes in front of all the tribes of Israel; he briefly outlines the task of occupation of the land that lies before them west of the Jordan. Most important, after the Israelites have occupied the land, Dtr. [the Deuteronomist] has Joshua, in Joshua 23, make a long, solemn speech to the gathered tribes. In this he formulates the most important instructions for behaviour in the land they have now come to possess. By means of this speech, the course of the narrative moves into the period of the "judges". And as with the transition from this "judges" period to the Kings period, Dtr. marks it with a quite lengthy speech by Samuel in 1 Samuel 12. In it are presented to the gathering of the people the lessons to be learnt from the vicissitudes of history hitherto and, once again, it is concluded by an admonition to the people concerning their future. Finally, after the completion of the temple in Jerusalem—an event that was of fundamental importance to Dtr.'s theological interpretation of history—King Solomon makes a detailed speech in the form of a prayer to God, which thoroughly expounds the significance of the new sanctuary for the

1. M. Noth, *Überlieferungsgeschichtliche Studien: Die sammelnden und bearbeitenden Geschichtswerke im Alten Testament* (Schriften der Königsberger Gelehrten Gesellschaft Geisteswissenschaftliche Klasse 18. Jh. H. 2 Bd. 1; Tübingen: Max Niemeyer, 1943) 1–110. [[The first part of this work has been translated as *The Deuteronomistic History* (2d ed.; JSOTSup 15; Sheffield: JSOT Press, 1991).]]

present, and especially for the future (1 Kings 8:14ff.). Elsewhere the summarising reflections upon history which sum up the action are presented by Dtr. himself as part of the narrative, whether because they did not lend themselves to reproduction in speeches or because there were not suitable historical figures to make the speeches. Such is the case in Joshua 12 concerning the results of the occupation of the land, and in the programmatic statement for the book of Judges in Judg. 2:11ff.; this presents an anticipatory survey of the cyclical nature of the course of history in the "judges" period in a manner which is quite understandable within the limits of Dtr's point of view. Similarly the writer appends to the story of the end of the Israelite state a retrospective reflection upon the grim outcome of the monarchic period in Israel and Judah (2 Kings 17:7ff.).[2]

⟦36⟧ There is thus no doubt that, by presenting his summary remarks in the form of sermon-like speeches, the Deuteronomist himself expressed a preference for the speech form and, in fact, seems to have chosen it over other forms of self-expression the majority of the time. Given, then, the fact that a prayer was chosen for the sort of summary reflection that appears at the center, the climax of the entire work (in connection with the dedication of the Temple), one wonders why the prayer form was more highly valued and was considered more suitable than the sermon-like speech form that had previously been used. Other considerations must have come into play. The older, certainly predeuteronomistic, consecration speech in 1 Kgs 8:12–13 must have provided an opportunity to have Solomon give further utterance in the form of a prayer. This is also reminiscent of David's prayer in 2 Sam 7:18–29, which, likewise predeuteronomic, has been placed in connection with the planning of the Temple construction, albeit secondarily. Moreover, the hymnic-narrative framework of Solomon's prayer in 1 Kgs 8:14–21 and 54–61 has likewise been inserted in order to preserve the more usual speech form to some extent.

In addition to the speeches identified by Noth (Joshua 1, 23; 1 Samuel 12) and Solomon's Temple dedication prayer, which is unique but provided motive and narrative structure, there are also the summaries or reviews in Joshua 12, Judg 2:11ff., and 2 Kgs 17:7ff. These (setting aside 2 Kgs 17:7ff. for the moment) are not nearly as significant as the great speeches, for (1) the sober enumeration in Joshua 12 is completely overshadowed by Joshua's speech in chap. 23 (which must be considered to connect to it directly); (2) the long survey in Judg 2:11ff., which likewise is also connected with Joshua 23, is clearly recognizable as the personal opinion of the Deuteronomist regarding the events of the period of the judges. As a continuation to the Joshua 23 speech, it includes only what

2. Ibid., 5–6 ⟦*Deuteronomistic History,* 18–19⟧.

had already been indicated summarily in the last sentences of Joshua's speech. [[37]] In this way it introduces us to the institution of the "judges." These three chapters–Joshua 12, 23, and Judg 2:11ff.–then, can be seen as a relatively self-contained unit that concludes the land-taking process and leads into the period of judges, with Joshua's great speech at the midpoint, and the conclusion and introduction also being included.

Returning to 2 Kgs 17:7–things are quite different with this great peroration, which deals with the period of kings up to the fall of the Northern Kingdom. One could hardly say that the collapse of the kingdom of Ephraim was not a suitable occasion for a programmatic speech or that the Isaiah narratives introduced into 2 Kings 18ff. did not present the Deuteronomist with a fitting speaker in the person of this prophet. But in this case the Deuteronomist refrained from putting a speech in the mouth of a historical personality and clearly introduced a separate reflection for special reasons. It so happens that, in the presentation of the time extending from the dedication of the Temple to the Ephraimite catastrophe, no further summary homily from the pen of the Deuteronomist is to be found, although an event such as the so-called division of the kingdom under Solomon's successor, Rehoboam, would have been serious enough to warrant it. The Deuteronomist was probably satisfied with the prophetic proclamations, such as the ones put in the mouths of the prophet Ahijah of Shiloh in 1 Kgs 11:29ff. and the man of God Shemaiah in 1 Kgs 12:22ff. (if the second passage is not to be regarded as a postdeuteronomic insertion). This probably explains the absence of these introspective pieces during the period cited: the prophets' words interlarded here and there, the entire Elijah-Elisha complex, the appearance of nameless men of God and prophets were felt to be sufficient and made a programmatic reflection superfluous. Since the prophets' endeavors and message of admonition are also referred to in two passages (v. 13, within a divine speech, and v. 23) within the great peroration of 2 Kgs 17:7ff., we will not go far astray by seeing 2 Kgs 17:7ff. as a summary of the prophetic message in general, insofar as it appeared suitable to the Deuteronomist (setting aside, for example, any eschatological expectation). Consequently, we may consider this passage to be an indirect speech by the Deuteronomist on the entire preexilic period of the prophets. In a similarly generalizing way, Zechariah (chap. 1) attempts to link up with the message of the earlier prophets.

Note that certain prophetic speeches, such as the speeches of Ahijah of Shiloh in 1 Kgs 11:29ff. and 1 Kings 14, seem thoroughly deuteronomistic. Prophetic writings also contain sermon-like chapters–one thinks of perhaps Jeremiah 7 or 11–that approach deuteronomistic speech, just as certain individual features of these speeches are obviously prophetic in origin.[3] [[38]] Let us simply say in conclusion that the contemplative homilies of the deuteronomistic historian are set forth in the form of speeches and also that where another form of rendition has been chosen, as in the Temple dedication prayer of Solomon or in the great peroration in 2 Kgs 17:7ff., at least a speech-like form can be recognized throughout. Furthermore, a particular form of prophetic proclamation provided the necessary lineaments for this deuteronomistic speech in a simplified way,[4] whenever it suited the historian's purposes.

It has rightly been pointed out that at the end of the Deuteronomistic History any hopeful outlook for a better future is absent.[5] I return to this subject here because it will become relevant later on. This lack of hope weighs even more heavily, because the observed dependency on a prophetic form of speech and the affinity for the prophetic message that goes with it must have exposed the historian to some prospects for the future. The proclamations of the preexilic prophets do occasionally evidence clear signs of hope. But any indication of a better future has obviously been intentionally avoided in the Deuteronomistic History. Neither the broadening of the field of view to the foreigners (reminiscent of Ezekiel) in the Temple dedication prayer of Solomon (1 Kgs 8:43, 60) nor the notice forming the conclusion of the History about the "elevation" of the captured King Jehoiachin (2 Kgs 25:27ff.) can be considered positive indications in this context. They would yield a gleam of hope too weak in comparison with the concrete expectations that are also expressed in "nonsuspicious" passages in the preexilic prophets (see, for example, Isa 1:21–26). Nevertheless this line of inquiry is not fully satisfactory. It is indeed striking that the concluding reflection on the period of the kings is not placed at the end of the entire work, but occurs in conjunction with the fall of the Northern Kingdom. Indeed Judah is also drawn into this homily (2 Kgs 17:19–20), albeit in a somewhat subsidiary fashion, and it would not have been difficult to add a similar comment after the collapse of Judah, if it had been important to the Deuteronomist. But this too he did not do. Did he assign a much greater significance to the events that he

3. Cf. specific usages in the Temple dedication prayer, 1 Kgs 8:43, and especially in v. 60, which recall Ezekiel; Noth, *Überlieferungsgeschichtliche Studien*, 102–3 [[*Deuteronomistic History*, 136–37]].

4. Nevertheless the consideration offered by L. Köhler ("Die hebräische Rechtsgemeinde," *Jahresbericht der Universität Zürich* [1930–31] 17–18), looking at the deuteronomistic pareneses, that neither the prophet nor the popular speaker, but the preacher, speaks in this parenetic-didactic way should not be overlooked. We need only add, as Köhler appears to accept, that without previous prophetic proclamation, the development of this sort of sermon-like speech is not really imaginable.

5. Cf. Noth, *Überlieferungsgeschichtliche Studien*, 107ff. [[*Deuteronomistic History*, 142–45]].

had to report for the remaining history of Judah, especially the Josianic reform that lay close to his heart (2 Kings 22–23), so that it did not appear advisable to him [[39]] to conclude the entire work with a negative evaluation similar to the evaluation he had delivered in 2 Kgs 17:7ff.? But he was no prophet. The answer that came to Ezekiel as he was led over the valley of bones of his people (Ezekiel 37) was not available to the Deuteronomist in his review of the history of his people. So he left open what in his time he could not close. "His time" must have in fact been the situation around 560 B.C. when, after the death of Nebuchadnezzar, the fragmentation of the Neo-Babylonian kingdom began to become apparent. But there was still insufficient knowledge available to establish concrete expectations.

II

If in a similar way we consider the other great historical work of the Old Testament, the Chronicler's work, which spans the two books of Chronicles plus Ezra and Nehemiah, we can consult quite a few investigations recently dedicated to understanding this historical work. Gerhard von Rad[6] has devoted special attention to the meaning of the name *Israel* and to the pronounced elevation of David and the Levites. He has rightly taken notice of the Chronicler's limited relationship to the deuteronomistic school. Noth in his above-mentioned *Überlieferungsgeschichtliche Studien*[7] insightfully investigated the peculiarity and independence of this historian, who intended to present the history of the origin of his postexilic community. In this process we can disregard Kurt Galling's[8] division of the work into an earlier and later Chronicler, though in certain contexts this division is enlightening. However, it is certainly not inconsequential that Galling assigns the overwhelming part of the speeches to be discussed here to the second Chronicler.

First of all, I agree with von Rad's well-founded opinion that the Chronicler's work should be considered in the deuteronomistic tradition rather than in the Priestly. It would then certainly need to be added that such a dependence on the Deuteronomist is not in the end conditioned by the material handled by the Chronicler, because he does not begin his narrative presentation until David. For the preceding period of Israelite history, the main focus of the Priestly writing, he was satisfied with meager

6. G. von Rad, *Das Geschichtsbild des chronistischen Werkes* (BWANT 4/3; Stuttgart: Kohlhammer, 1930).

7. Noth, *Überlieferungsgeschichtliche Studien*, 110–80 [[English translation: *The Chronicler's History* (JSOTSup 50; Sheffield: JSOT Press, 1987)]].

8. K. Galling, *Die Bücher der Chronik: Esra und Nehemia* (ATD 12; Göttingen: Vandenhoeck & Ruprecht, 1954).

genealogical data, whose sketchiness is even more evident if we take into account the considerable secondary expansions of the list.[9] The Chronicler's stylistic trick of bridging longer ⟦40⟧ time-spans with genealogies is also more reminiscent of the Priestly writing. The deuteronomistic method, especially the distinctive form of marking historical breaks with detailed speeches (which also occurs in Priestly writings; recall the conclusions of covenants analyzing the course of history and the divine speeches [Genesis 9, 17] connected with them), appears not to have been used by the Chronicler. He has richly favored us with long and short speeches and prayers, but they are inserted wherever they seem to fit, without indicating important turning points in history in the deuteronomistic sense. There is a question, however, whether Noth's opinion[10] requires supplementation.

A large proportion of the deuteronomistic speeches belongs to the pre-Davidic period (Joshua 1, 23; 1 Samuel 12), which the Chronicler has excluded from the narrative portion of his presentation. The Temple dedication prayer of Solomon, however, he has incorporated with modifications and also with a view toward the significance that he has attached to David, associating with him the events relating to the Temple construction via additional speeches and prayers placed on David's lips. Obviously he has understood the preparations for Temple construction under David and the erection of the Temple under Solomon as a coherent act, just as he interpreted the return of the Temple furnishings under the Cyrus edict and the restoration of the Temple under Zerubbabel on the one hand and the appearance of Ezra and Nehemiah on the other as one great event. In regard to the pre-Davidic period, after the genealogical prelude, the ascent of the Ark and the consequent erection of a Temple along with the preparations undertaken by David are the real beginning of his presentation. He will underline its importance by means of several speeches by David. All in all, the Chronicler has followed his deuteronomistic forerunner in this matter; after the transportation of the Ark he too reports Nathan's prediction with the subsequent prayer of David (1 Chr 17:4–14, 16–27 // 2 Samuel 7), though not without making a few simple but significant alterations.[11] This also holds for God's speeches to Solomon (2 Chr 1:8–10, 11–12 // 1 Kgs 3:4–14; and 2 Chr 7:12–22 // 1 Kgs 9:3–9), which indeed have been taken over, again with a few alterations. Obviously, however, the Chronicler does not have the same purpose that the Deuteronomist had, namely, to divide Solomon's reign into positively and negatively

9. Noth, *Überlieferungsgeschichtliche Studien*, 117ff. ⟦*Chronicler's History*, 36ff.⟧.

10. Ibid., 156, 160–61 ⟦Eng., 76, 80–88⟧.

11. Cf. von Rad, *Geschichtsbild des chronistischen Werkes*, 123ff.; Galling, *Bücher der Chronik*, 53ff.

evaluated portions and to signal the beginning of each portion with a speech from God. Likewise, the Chronicler's Temple dedication prayer of Solomon (2 Chr 6:1–2, 4–10, 14–42 // 1 Kings 8), especially in the second half and at the end, diverges from the deuteronomistic account. But overall, the dependence on the deuteronomistic *Vorlage* is unmistakable, [[41]] and in my opinion this is also clear in that the Chronicler is definitely aware of the secondary Song of Thanks by David in 2 Samuel 22. The song must have been known to him in a completely different form and was inserted, certainly not accidentally, between the Ark narrative and the Nathan pericope in 1 Chr 16:8–36, as a prelude to the theme of Temple construction that was especially close to the Chronicler's heart. The material unique to the Chronicler comes next, closely packed, and continues until the end of 1 Chronicles. The end of 1 Chronicles contains David's frequent speeches of encouragement, some to Solomon (1 Chr 22:7–16, 28:9–10 and 20–21) and some to the people (1 Chr 22:18–19, 28:2–8, 29:1–5). They retrospectively allow David to take part in the planning of the Temple construction and are rounded off with a special prayer of David (1 Chr 29:10–19). This clearly concludes in prayer form the section that had begun in prayer form (1 Chr 17:16–27). The prayer form may have been chosen because it was suggested by 1 Chr 17:16–27. In view of his frequent speeches, prayer forms a worthy closing point for David's participation in the Temple construction.

For the period after Solomon, as mentioned before, the Deuteronomist introduced no larger overviews in speech form. Evidently, the prophets and men of God, who appeared in his sources and whose words he interpolated into his own account, were enough to satisfy him. In this respect, the Chronicler again follows the deuteronomistic model, though in considerably modified form. He does not allow traditional sources to speak, but now and then, in part going beyond the Deuteronomist, he has prophets or prophet-like figures appear or has, say, Elijah intervene in Judahite relations in the form of a letter (2 Chr 21:12–15). The Deuteronomist brings the period of the kings to a conclusion with a sermon that may be interpreted as a speech summarizing the entire institution of prophcy (2 Kgs 17:7ff.), inserted like an appendix to the fall of the Northern Kingdom and, consequently, foreshadowing the Judahite catastrophe to some extent. The Chronicler then attempted to reuse this marker but in a way that corresponded to his interpretation of the period of the monarchy. His primary interest was not in an evaluation of the monarchy and the period identified with this institution; rather, it was to see in the Jewish community of his time the legitimate successor of the powerful united Israel that came into existence under David. Therefore, the sundering of the united kingdom under Solomon's successor, Rehoboam, must have carried an entirely different weight for him than for the Deuteronomist. For the Chronicler, after devoting so much space and and so many details to the Temple as the cultic-national heart of all Israel, the split was less a political event than a schismatic action. He expresses this by having the Judahite king, Abijah, extend a great call of repentance to the Israelites of the North (2 Chr 13:4–12) immediately after the division of the kingdom. Likewise, just before the end of the Northern Kingdom, again he has a Judahite king, Hezekiah, call the North [[42]] to repentance (2 Chr 30:6–9). Thus the division of the kingdom is the deep cut that divides the Davidic-Solomonic period (the period of planning and building the Temple) from the period of the Judahite kings. The two calls to repentance by Abijah and Hezekiah interpret the period of the Judahite kings as more akin to a period of two separate "churches" than as a period of two separate kingdoms. Admittedly, this characteristic is less conspicuous because, between Abijah and Hezekiah, the Chronicler has quite a few prophets or charismatics give sermon-like addresses. The great prayer of Jehoshaphat (2 Chr 20:5–12) especially stands out during this period, and it will lay further claim to our attention below.

It is interesting to see how the Chronicler proceeds as soon as his deuteronomistic model has run its course. It is readily apparent that he has no special interest in the period after Hezekiah. Until the fall of Jerusalem, he follows his deuteronomistic source, though with a few variations (Manasseh's conversion, 2 Chr 33:11ff.; Josiah's death, 2 Chr 35:20ff.), and he also gives due consideration to Josiah's reform. Nonetheless, one receives the impression that Hezekiah's reform, which is not particularly distinctive historically, lay much closer to his heart. There is clearly a special reason for this, for at the very moment of the collapse of the schismatic Northern Kingdom, a fundamental, virtually new, construction of Judah should have been undertaken (2 Chronicles 29–31). It is not by chance that the Chronicler attempts to gloss over the reign of Manasseh, so negatively evaluated in 2 Kings, by employing the Deuteronomist's division of Solomon's reign into good and bad halves and applying it to the reign of Manasseh. But in this case the good and bad halves are reversed, and the first (worse) half includes a quotation attributed to the Davidic-Solomonic era (2 Chr 33:7–8) but formulated by the Deuteronomist. The period after Josiah is considerably abbreviated, and the destruction of the Temple is conspicuously brief. In goal-oriented fashion, the Chronicler directs the Cyrus edict forward (2 Chr 36:22–23; in more detail in Ezra 1:2–4). Within the period beginning with the Cyrus edict—that is, in the presentation found in the books of Ezra and Nehemiah—we observe a conspicuous diminution in detailed speeches. This is not to say that the Chronicler has completely renounced them! We find a short message of encouragement given to a man called Shechaniah in Ezra 10:2ff., and appended to it are a few proverbial instructions from Ezra. In Neh 5:8–11 Nehemiah gives a short speech to prevent the enslavement of fellow Jews (compare Neh 13:25–27). These are not programmatic speeches of fundamental significance, however, but instructions relating to particular conflicts. In any case, they are partly incorporated from a source (Neh 5:8ff., 13:25ff.) and thus are not to be ascribed to the Chronicler. The absence of detailed speeches [[43]] can certainly be explained adequately by the fact that the relatively short period (about one hundred years) from the Cyrus edict to the end of Nehemiah's activity was sufficiently subdivided by particular acts. Therefore, marking specific time-spans with homilies was superfluous. Above and beyond this, in Ezra–Nehemiah the Chronicler employs deuteronomistic methods to a much greater extent by introducing into his presentation unedited or only slightly altered documents. For example, there are numerous lists[12] or document-like information in Aramaic[13] and, above all, the detailed Nehemiah Memoirs in Nehemiah 1ff.[14] We need not go into the authenticity of the documents and lists here, since the Chronicler has clearly attached importance to their documentary character. Certain markers had already been transmitted to the Chronicler, such as Cyrus's decree, which he formulated as an opening to the first subsection, comprising Ezra 1 through Ezra 6, the Temple rededication; the next subpart is introduced by Ezra's "certificate of appointment" (Ezra 7) and concludes, at least in the opinion of the Chronicler, with the climax, the penitential prayer of Ezra (Ezra 9) regarding the awkward question of mixed marriages;[15] he begins the last part with the Nehemiah

12. Ezra 2:1ff., 8:1ff.; Neh 7:6ff., 10:1ff.; also the lists in Nehemiah 11–12; the extent to which this is a matter of supplementary expansions does not need to be dealt with here. In any case, it would be difficult to maintain this for all of the lists.

13. Ezra 4:11ff., 5:7ff., 6:3ff., 7:12ff.

14. For want of space we pass over the opinion of H. H. Schaeder (*Esra, der Schreiber* [Tübingen: Mohr, 1930]) and others that the book of Ezra is an "Ezra memoir," analogous to one of the memoirs in the book of Nehemiah. This opinion is in fact very controversial.

15. Ezra's reading of the law was not reported right away in connection with the mixed marriages question but was bound up with Nehemiah's task at a later time. Thus the report about the reading of the law in Nehemiah 8 was inserted into the Nehemiah presentation only secondarily (so the majority of recent interpretations). This sequence of events was fashioned by the Chronicler so that the activities of the two men culminated at the climactic closing point of his entire presentation in a common work, as at the beginning he had similarly placed retrospective emphasis on the unanimity of David and Solomon with regard to the Temple construction. Obviously, the Chronicler had a specific view of the course of events. First he pursued Ezra's effectiveness up to a certain conclusion (the solution of the mixed marriages question) and then Nehemiah's activity likewise to an approximate conclusion (the building of the wall, *synoikismos* [['peopling of the area']]), in order to conclude the activity of the two men with the reading of the law and the solemnities loosely connected with it (on the

Memoirs, though for the moment we will leave open the question of whether the prayer at the beginning of these memoirs (Neh 1:5–11) is original or formulated by the Chronicler. As with the prayer of Ezra in the second subpart, he has inserted into the third subsection a theologically important climax in the form of the great prayer in Nehemiah 9.

Thus, compared to the deuteronomistic presentation, [[44]] the Chronicler appears to use detailed speeches more freely. He uses them to emphasize what is in his opinion an important period of time (David, Solomon, and the Temple construction) or to present a further stretch of time as relatively unified, by bracketing it with similar speeches (the period of the divided kingdom). But he also narrates shorter periods whose depicted events are concluded with a special climax, a detailed prayer. The Chronicler certainly distinguishes himself from the Deuteronomist by choosing the prayer form considerably more often. I would suggest that prayer was used by the Chronicler as a medium of presentation more than speeches.

III

In considering the Chronicler's speeches, it may be best first to summarize von Rad's rich study[16] of these speeches as Levitical addresses and then briefly consider what the custom was at the time of the Chronicler. Von Rad discovered a particular feature that lends this speech its sermon-like character. The Chronicler's speech borrowed certain words (not always easily identified) from other, principally prophetic, books of the Bible. These words, though not always literally quoted, are appealed to as "biblical texts," especially in the climaxes of the speeches.[17] The Chronicler's occasional practice (2 Chr 30:6ff.) of sending couriers to instruct the population of the land could support von Rad's opinion that the Chronicler adopted a speech form in use during his time.[18] These speeches largely consisted of exhortation or encouragement in circumstances of war–in other words, the Chronicler's speeches have the form of war addresses.

occasion of the wall-building). This was then rounded off by some supplement-like reports. Whether one comes closer to historical reality if one reverses the temporal ordering of the Chronicler and places Nehemiah before Ezra is a much-discussed question that, despite certain indications, is to be considered skeptically. However, we cannot go into this here.

16. G. von Rad, "Die levitische Predigt in den Büchern der Chronik," *Festschrift für O. Procksch* (1934) 113–24. [[Translated as "The Levitical Sermon in I and II Chronicles," in Gerhard von Rad, *The Problem of the Hexateuch and Other Essays* (New York: McGraw-Hill, 1966) 267–80.]]

17. Ibid., 115ff. [[= "Levitical Sermon," 269ff.]]; cf. also his "Geschichtsbild," 15 n. 48.

18. Ibid., 125 [[= "Levitical Sermon," 278]].

This does not necessarily prove that they were used during wars, since the selection of situations was done by the Chronicler. Nevertheless, the question can be asked whether in the postexilic period the sending out of messages occurred in connection with preparations for war—just as in earlier times messages were necessary for assembling a levy. This could be why the Chronicler not only had the charismatics give a speech, but also on one occasion he even had the king give one. The style of warlike address was also retained when nonmilitary plans commenced.[19]

⟦45⟧ In the Chronicler's History, there are some correspondences between the speeches and the prayers. It is not hard to imagine that a short sermon of encouragement in particular cases was motivated by a preceding prayer, as the example in 2 Chronicles 20 shows (vv. 5–12: Jehoshaphat's prayer; vv. 15–17: the address of a charismatic). Consequently, we must consider whether the Chronicler, with his relatively common use of prayers, was not following a custom in his community, a custom that arose historically during the Exile, when prayer played a special role of replacing sacrifices. It would then be all the more understandable that the Chronicler placed so much value on prayer and perhaps explains why he elevated prayer over speeches.

Setting aside the question of the content of the prayers for the moment, we observe first an increase in the number of of detailed prayers in the Chronicler's History compared to the Deuteronomist's History. The Deuteronomist would have taken the prayer of David after Nathan's promise (2 Samuel 7) from his source and, in a similar way, prompted by the ancient passage about the ark, formulated Solomon's Temple dedication prayer, which despite its hymnic setting still exhibits narrative elements throughout. The Chronicler adopted both. Then, also prompted by the prayer of David after Nathan's prediction, he once again added a prayer by David in 1 Chr 29:10–19. In light of David's numerous preceding speeches, he was then able to use two prayers to frame David's participation in Temple-building with dignity and effect. Indeed, it was so important to him that he appears to have framed the narrative portion of his entire work with two long prayers. David's Song of Thanks in 2 Sam 22:2–51, a postdeuteronomistic addition parallel to Psalm 18, appears to have been already known to him; he took it over, fully reworked it, using phrases extracted from three other psalms (105:1–15; 96:1b–13a; 106:1, 47–48), and inserted it at the point where the conveyance of the Ark begins the royal ritual (1 Chr 16:8–36). Correspondingly, at one of the climaxes of the history of the postexilic community, he rounds off the por-

19. Cf. David's encouragement of Solomon before beginning Temple construction (1 Chr 22:13, 28:20–21); also the addresses in connection with Asa's cult reform (2 Chr 15:1ff.) and Jehoshaphat's legal innovations (2 Chr 19:9ff.).

trait of the newly constructed community with a great prayer (Neh 9:5–37). As a penitential prayer it is not fully appropriate to the situation under Nehemiah, but with its effective conclusion it will clearly prepare the way for the unanimous, binding oath taken by the community and reported in Neh 10:1ff.[20] This prayer may also be considered in terms of its relationship with Psalm 78, but it shows affinities to some extent with the prayer of Ezra formulated by the Chronicler (Ezra 9:15), in its stress on the righteousness of God (vv. 8 and 33). Its formal significance, because it is associated with the covenant (Nehemiah 10) and [[46]] the wall dedication (Neh 12:27ff.), obviously consists in serving as the conclusion to the Chronicler's work, which had begun with the ritual activities of David.

Two additional, extensive prayers are found in Ezra–Nehemiah: the prayer of Ezra (Ezra 9:6–15) and the prayer of Nehemiah (Neh 1:5–11). However, the formal significance of these prayers clearly must be sought elsewhere. Despite the thoughts expressed by Hölscher, Noth, Galling, and others, it seems to me that Nehemiah's prayer must have originally been a component of his Memoirs[21] and must have also given the Chronicler the idea of putting a prayer on Ezra's lips, in view of the significance that he ascribed to him. This is especially true since, in this way, in the concluding part of the Chronicler's History, the common deeds and behavior of the two men could be placed in splendid parallelism to the unanimity of David and Solomon, which was also expressed in prayers in the first main section of the presentation.

A prominent place is also certainly given to the great prayer of Jehoshaphat in 2 Chr 20:5–12. Here it is a good idea to recall that the significance of this king in the Chronicler's narrative has been considerably expanded in comparison to the deuteronomistic presentation. Legal reforms are ascribed to Jehoshaphat (2 Chr 19:5ff.); he strives for a proper cult, through which he somewhat makes up for the ugly transgression of a military operation in collusion with the schismatic king of the North [[2 Chr 18:1–19:3]]. This recognition, that he had directed his heart to seek God (2 Chr 19:3), appears to be virtually the key word for the following prayer, in which Jehoshaphat is presented as a humble king trusting in God alone. In this way his piety continues along the course taken by David and Solomon, as the allusion to the Temple dedication prayer in 2 Chr 20:9 shows.

Thus the Chronicler followed no strict principle in his employment of prayers but used a free hand, similar to what we already observed in his speeches and addresses. If a particular event already marked by detailed speeches or a historical personality close to the Chronicler's heart needed

20. Galling, *Bücher der Chronik*, 240.

21. Cf. W. Rudolph, *Esra und Nehemia* (HAT 20; Tübingen: Mohr, 1949) 105–6.

to be emphasized with dignity, then he typically chose the technique of prayer to present the story. This reflected his intentions impressively, as did the speeches. There is thus no way that content influenced the special choice of the prayer form. The prayers formulated by the Chronicler do not particularly signify any more than what could also have been said in speeches. The reason that the Chronicler occasionally awards the favored spot to prayer must, rather, be sought in the nature of prayer itself. In a sermon-like address one can certainly confess what one believes, but it is more vivid to say it in prayer if one [[47]] requests the actualization of what one believes and confesses. Along these lines, just a few more considerations may be added in closing.

In the monograph mentioned above, von Rad[22] refers to the significance given to David in the Chronicler's work and seeks to do justice to it with the help of a messianic idea but without excessively stressing the eschatological element, which customarily appears instantly in connection with messianic thought. The Chronicler's view of the significance of the Davidic monarchy for Israel as messianic, however, can in my opinion only be understood and considered valid in light of the contruction of the Jewish community in the postexilic period, beginning with the reconstruction of the Temple and closing with the activity of Ezra and Nehemiah. This is how the Chronicler has composed the sections of his presentation. What since David, in the Chronicler's view, appears as "Israel"–has maintained obedience to God's instruction and God's prophetic word and has won a new form in the postexilic period in the activity of God-filled men–is the true Israel. This true Israel has remained what it was from the beginning, a special creation of God. No break with the past can shatter this continuity, but neither can any marked eschatological expectation give this ritual- and law-based community more than what it already possesses. In the framework of history, there is no room for eschatological expectation; what can be done, and what may be necessary, is to remedy any abuses that may appear. And in fact it is not by chance that, after portraying the ideal Israel (Neh 12:44ff.), the Chronicler reports the scandals (Neh 13:4ff.) taken from the Nehemiah Memoirs as "partial aberrations"[23] and Nehemiah's resolution of the problems simply as an aside.

This is the context in which we must seek to understand the individuality of some of the prayers formulated by the Chronicler,[24] variations

22. Von Rad, *Geschichtsbild des chronistischen Werkes*, 119ff., together with pp. 18ff.

23. Galling, *Bücher der Chronik*, 250.

24. I have limited myself to the three great prayers (David's, 1 Chr 29:10ff.; Jehoshaphat's, 2 Chr 20:6ff.; Ezra's, Ezra 9:6ff.) that without question derived from the Chronicler. But the prayers that he inherited may also have undergone significant alteration in his hands (e.g., David's prayer in 1 Chr 17:6ff. and Solomon's Temple dedication prayer). In Neh 9:5ff., the selection of particular Psalms passages is also not without importance.

bound to a particular situation: the context was the piety of the late Old Testament period. It was not the only contributing factor, but it was of special significance. In the prayer of David concluding the preparations for the building of the Temple (1 Chr 29:10–19), v. 15 states: "For we are strangers before thee, and sojourners, as all our fathers were; our days on earth are like a shadow, and there is no abiding." Following this, v. 18 requests God to preserve forever what is now to be done in preparation for building [[48]] the Temple. These expressions, resignedly skeptical yet trusting in God, correspond to the prayer of Jehoshaphat in the standard acknowledgement of personal powerlessness. "We do not know what to do, but our eyes are upon you," says 2 Chr 20:12. Understandably, Ezra's entire penitential prayer (Ezra 9:6–15) exhibits a similar mood, finding its climax in the last verse: "O LORD, the God of Israel, thou art just, for we are left a remnant that has survived, as is now the case. Behold, we are before thee in our guilt, for none can stand before thee because of this." Certainly in this last passage there is a clear reference to the mixed marriage question, which could damage the integrity of the saved remnant, the true Israel. But this thread of human guilt and human powerlessness runs through the Chronicler's prayers (and also appears occasionally in the speeches). It is also emphasized in the great final act of reading the law and taking a binding oath, which is to say, in the final construction of the true Israel. Nonetheless, one particular understanding of the Chronicler is revealed by the mood of guilt—namely that, by means of sincere prayers and the confession of transgressions, the resulting troubles will not jeopardize the existence of the new community. Here indeed lies the special significance of prayer for the life of the community to which the Chronicler belonged. This is also why he has made prayer so significant in his presentation: God causes the sincere to succeed, and honorable confession and sincere prayer are effective aids to bringing the community through the inevitable times of trouble. This appears to be the same attitude adopted a little later by the Maccabean movement. They regarded the religious conflict that began with the persecution and oppression of Antiochus IV Epiphanes as a period of hardship and affliction such as there had not been in Israel since the prophets ceased (1 Macc 9:27). Nevertheless, they also considered it a time of travail within history that courage in faith and devotion to faith could overcome and during which, if need be, comfort could be taken from the hope of a personal resurrection, which, however, possessed no apocalyptic character at all. A noneschatological view of the life and history of the community continued from the Chronicler to the Maccabean movement and certainly contributed a considerable impulse to the later Maccabean restoration. This is not to say that what had remained alive of anticipation and hope in prophetic eschatology had become unknown or overlooked. But it was adopted by a community to which monarchy, Temple ritual, prophecy (everything meaningful in Israel's previous history) had made a valuable contribution.

Here an elaboration is needed, but only a brief sketch can be drawn. The affinity between Ezra's penitential prayer (Ezra 9:6ff.) and the great penitential prayer in Dan 9:4–19 is frequently [[49]] mentioned. However likely it may seem that the author of Daniel introduced a strange prayer into his presentation that he did not write, we must consider the context in which Daniel's prayer now stands in contrast to the historical situation of the Ezra prayer. The apocalypticist writing at the beginning of the Maccabean Revolt has the seer in the time of the Exile strive to understand correctly the seventy years that were foreseen as the duration of the Exile, according to Jer 25:11 and other passages. The Chronicler's History also mentions these seventy years in passing (2 Chr 36:21) and has them end with the arrival of Cyrus. That is, he has them end at the point in time in which, in the Chronicler's opinion, the first steps toward the construction of the new community, the true Israel, were undertaken. So it sounds virtually like a protest when a different understanding of the seventy years has been put in the mouth of the exilic seer Daniel (Daniel 9). An extension of this time period is now to reach into the future of the apocalypticist, and indeed, as we can judge from an overall understanding of the book of Daniel, the things now commencing under Antiochus Epiphanes are apocalyptic in character and proclaim the great eschatological turning point. One need only compare the date—which remains in the framework of history—given in 1 Macc 9:27 ("Thus there was great distress in Israel, such as had not been since the time that prophets ceased to appear among them") and the interpretation of the exciting events given there with the eschatologically interpreted date in Dan 12:1 ("a time of travail such as there has never been since people existed on earth") to clearly recognize the contradictory understanding of the same circumstances. It is the clear protest of an eschatological perspective on history in Daniel to the de-eschatologized approach to history found in the Chronicler's History that comes newly to life in the Maccabean movement. This sheds light on what had certainly been a long-latent rift *within the antihellenistic opposition*—a rift that continued in the Temple-restoration activities of the Maccabees on the one hand and in the consistently eschatological approach of the Hasideans, the "pious" ones of 1 Maccabees, and the factions of the Pharisees and Essenes that developed from them. This was a far-reaching and serious rift, because none of these factions would give up its claim to the honorable ascription of the "true Israel." But prayer proceeding from a common root in faith and piety, as counterpointed for us in Ezra 9 and Daniel 9, can be served equally by either point of view.

"Histories" and "History"

Promise and Fulfillment in the Deuteronomistic Historical Work

HELGA WEIPPERT

Weippert finds in von Rad's category of promise–fulfillment a key to understanding the DH. The arc of promise–fulfillment is present at all levels in the DH, crossing genres, spanning greater and lesser stretches of text, and deriving from different periods. This is demonstrated by close attention to a number of passages from Judges, Samuel, and Kings, respectively. Weippert concludes that promise–fulfillment is found by redactors in their *Vorlagen* and that they prove worthy successors in their ability to develop the concept.

The present esssay does not offer a general theory of the composition of the DH. However, as Weippert's examples show, she works within the theory of the DH and the limits normally given to it, while assuming a number of redactions.* The essay is interesting, however, as an attempt to characterize the DH in terms of its underlying theological tendencies.

* Elsewhere she proposes a combination of redactions and preexisting "blocks" of material: "Das deuteronomistische Geschichtswerk: Sein Ziel und Ende in der neueren Forschung," *TRu* 50 (1985) 213–49.

Translated and reprinted with permission from "Geschichten und Geschichte: Verheissung und Erfüllung im deuteronomistischen Geschichtswerk," in *Congress Volume: Leuven, 1989* (ed. J. A. Emerton; VTSup 43; Leiden: Brill, 1991) 116–31. Translation by Peter T. Daniels. The RSV has been used for all English scripture citations in this translation.

Author's note: This is part of a more comprehensive investigation that I am preparing for publication. It will include references to sources and secondary literature in more detail than is possible here.

As with many traditional critical treatments, there is an implicit hermeneutic here—namely, the belief that it is possible to identify the intentions of the various authors of the text. For Weippert, the concept of promise–fulfillment helps identify the text's natural boundaries, and the parts are precisely parts of a greater whole, this last being a "canonical" postulate. All of these elements are disputed (Gunn, Jobling). However, Weippert's proposal of a theological concept as unifying category (like Wolff's rather different one) offers an alternative to approaches that emphasize the reader's part in interpretation much more strongly.

[[116]] In the Deuteronomistic History[1] (but not only there and not everywhere in it) the storytellers and history-writers are not content with describing events, connections between events, and the course of history in spare, journalistic style. Rather, they often precede their presentation of events with authoritative proclamation of them and afterward record the fulfillment of the promise. There thus arise narratives, compositions, and histories that follow the scheme of promise–fulfillment. The authors derived the certainty that the promises actually determined the schedule of future events from their belief in the history-effecting authority of the divine word.[2] Now this does not mean that they put every promise into the mouth of God or one of his representatives. Alongside the authority of the speaker who guaranteed the fulfillment of the prediction comes with equal legitimacy the authoritative form of the utterance that calls on God as the guarantor of an announcement of the future (see, for example, Judg 11:35, 1 Sam 1:23). It follows from this that promises were not tied to any particular genre. A word of God, a prophetic saying, a curse, a blessing, a judgment, or indeed a vow all had the same character as a promise.

The property of promises to establish the future, whether for good or ill, and [[117]] the possibility of making various forms of speech into a vehicle of promises, make it difficult to distinguish them from other future-related speech-genres such as wishes, requests, or commands, and in fact the distinctions are fluid. The Old Testament texts indicate in two ways that we should not yield to the modern desire for a narrower delimitation of what might properly be called a promise: first, they use only nonspecific *verba dicendi* [['speech words']] to preface a promise (*ʾmr, brk, dbr, nšbʿ* [['say, bless, tell, take an oath']], etc.); second, the signs of fulfillment (that is, the notices that, by portraying the event, expressly refer back to

1. By this I mean the history presented in Deuteronomy 1 through 2 Kings 25.

2. In this area, G. von Rad's 1947 work was ground-breaking: "Die deuteronomistische Geschichtstheologie in den Königsbüchern," *Gesammelte Studien zum Alten Testament* (Munich, 1958) 189–204.

the previous prophecy) indicate that the Old Testament authors regarded any number of genres as promises.[3]

What the promises announce verbally as inevitable future events the fulfillment reports tell retrospectively as past events. Thus, the promise–fulfillment schema proves to be a generally symmetric pattern of presentation that portrays the event as that which was already named in advance, as a once-and-for-all authoritatively established future. Narrated promises refer to a past future, which with the fulfillment of the promise became present; yet this present is only ever spoken of in the texts as something past. The promise–fulfillment schema thus belongs to the narrative genres that retain in words smaller or larger portions of a past time.

In this retrospective recounting of past event, the narrator selects from the occurrences what to tell and what to be silent about; he decides which periods he will report and which he will pass over. In order to be able to represent whole sequences despite leaving out events and skipping over times, he brings the promise–fulfillment schema into play, since it makes a bridge between a narrated promise and its narrated fulfillment that spans the events and times that have not been narrated. The link can be shorter or longer. Promise and fulfillment can abut each other directly in time and content, or lie far from each other. This is echoed on the literary level, where the two can stand more closely together or more widely apart. If [[118]] a promise is fulfilled within a single narrative, then this is a narrative use of the promise–fulfillment schema; if the arc between the two spans a wider distance but is limited to a portion of the Deuteronomistic History, then one may speak of a compositional use of the schema. Last, where the schema encompasses major sections and brackets them together, then in all probability this is a redactional usage.[4]

The Schema within a Narrative

Within the Deuteronomistic History, the promise–fulfillment schema occurs more than sixty times as a narrative stylistic device—that is, a promise appears together with the report of its fulfillment in the context of a single narrative. In these instances the schema does not have a text-spanning function; it has a text-structuring function.

3. Against the narrowing of the concept by E. Würthwein, "Prophetisches Wort und Geschichte in den Königsbüchern: Zu einer These Gerhard von Rads," in *Altes Testament und christliche Verkündigung: Festschrift für A. H. J. Gunneweg zum 65. Geburtstag* (ed. M. Oeming and A. Graupner; Stuttgart, 1987) 399–411, at 410.

4. I. L. Seeligmann already observed the use of the schema on the various literary levels ("Die Auffassung der Prophetie in der deuteronomistischen und chronistischen Geschichtsschreibung," *Congress Volume: Göttingen, 1977* [VTSup 29; Leiden, 1978] 254–84, at 258–64).

Conquest and war narratives are constructed on this narrative pattern, such as: Israel's passage over the Jordan (Joshua 3), the conquest of Jericho (Joshua 6) and Ai (Joshua 8), the victories over Adoni-zedek (Joshua 10) and Jabin of Hazor (Joshua 11), Judah's campaign against the Canaanites (Judg 1:1–4), and Deborah and Barak's triumph over Sisera (Judges 4). The schema is repeated in the description of David's battles against the Philistines (1 Sam 23:1–13, 2 Sam 5:17–25) and the Amalekites (1 Sam 30:1–20), as well as in Israel's wars with the Syrians (1 Kgs 20:13–30) and the Moabites (2 Kgs 3:13–27). Under the sign of promise are Saul's anointment to kingship (1 Sam 9:15–17, 10:1), David's entry into Hebron (2 Sam 2:1–7), and Hazael's usurpation of the Syrian throne (2 Kgs 8:13–15); this sign also appears negatively in the prediction of inflation in besieged Samaria (2 Kgs 7:1, 16, 18). Jotham's curse of Abimelech and the Shechemites, once pronounced, ran its ineluctable destructive course (Judg 9:16–57).

Promises are not limited to preceding the sort of events that we too would traditionally ascribe to the realm of history.[5] They also interfere with the course of nature: at the [[119]] Jordan crossing they staunch the flow of water (Josh 3:8, 14–17); they cause the sun and moon to stand still at the battle of Gibeon (Josh 10:12–14); or they bring about drought (1 Kgs 17:1, 7; 18:2) or rain (1 Kgs 18:1, 41–45). The fact that Samson (Judg 13:3–5, 24), Samuel (1 Sam 1:11, 17, 19–20) and his brothers and sisters (1 Sam 2:20–21), and even the son of the Shunammite (2 Kgs 4:16–17) saw the light of day is narrated, not as fascinating family history, but as the fulfillment of promises. Correspondingly, the narrators also present death, not simply as the limit of life due to sickness or bad luck but as a previously announced event: as with Jephthah's daughter (Judg 11:30–31, 34–39), David's first son by Bathsheba (2 Sam 12:14–18), one of Jeroboam I's sons (1 Kgs 14:1–6, 12–13, 17–18), an unnamed prophet (1 Kgs 20:36), an officer in Samaria (2 Kgs 7:2, 17–20), and kings Ahaziah (2 Kgs 1:4, 16–17), Ben-hadad (2 Kgs 8:10, 14–15), and Sennacherib (2 Kgs 19:7, 37). Similarly, Naaman's recovery (2 Kgs 5:10, 14) and Gehazi's illness (2 Kgs 5:27) are presented as the results of promises. To round off the list of examples, we must also recall tales of miracles, such as the jar of meal that was not spent (1 Kgs 17:14–16), the miraculous multiplication of loaves (2 Kgs 4:43–44), and the altar in Bethel that burst asunder as a result of the command of the man of God (1 Kgs 13:3, 5).

5. On the notion that "the systematic introduction of nonhuman factors (what was earlier called 'Nature') into history" is again required, see H. Lutz, "Braudels *La Méditerranée*: Zur Problematik eines Modellanspruchs," in *Formen der Geschichtsschreibung* (ed. R. Koselleck, H. Lutz, and J. Rüsen; Munich: Deutsche Taschenbuch, 1982) 320–52, at 348.

These stories, which I have only briefly recalled by referring to key features, are classified into quite different narrative genres, including the genre of Yahweh war, legends, historical narratives, birth narratives, and prophetic miracle tales. They come from a variety of storytellers, with their individual circles of tradents; they pursue special purposes and address different listeners. Some texts may not have been passed down as tales but instead owe their existence to creative writing. This material, so variable with respect to genre and origin, takes on unity in that it all employs the schema of promise–fulfillment as the basic structure of the narrative. A widespread fondness for this narrative principle may thus be assumed.

If a promise and its fulfillment follow closely [[120]] together within a narrative, then the symmetry between the two elements can be boring, since the promise tells the ending of the narrative in advance. A more precise reflection on the texts, however, shows that, though the narrative pattern was symmetric in principle, it was applied asymmetrically in practice. This is indicated by the differences in extent between the passages promising and reporting the fulfillment. Only rarely is the balance between the two approximately preserved, as with the episode of the two prophets during one of the Israelite–Syrian wars (1 Kgs 20:35–36). Symbolically, the episode is meant to illustrate the guilt of the Israelite king who after his victory at Aphek did not kill the Syrian king but, flouting the decree of the ban, concluded a treaty with him. In the episode, a prophet orders his companion to strike him, but he refuses.

> Then he said to him, "Because you have not obeyed the voice of the LORD, behold, as soon as you have gone from me, a lion will kill you." And as soon as he had departed from him, a lion met him and killed him. (1 Kgs 20:36)

An expansive promise followed by a concise report of fulfillment is found in 2 Kgs 1:16–17, in the text in which Elijah prophesies the death of Ahaziah.

> Thus says Yahweh, "Because you have sent messengers to inquire of Baal-zebub, the god of Ekron,–is it because there is no god in Israel to inquire of his word?–therefore, you shall not come down from the bed to which you have gone, but you shall surely die." (2 Kgs 1:16)

The fulfillment report notes the death of Ahaziah with one [[Hebrew]] word, "he died," adding for completeness, "according to the word of the LORD, which Elijah had spoken" (2 Kgs 1:17). Representing the converse case is the narrative of the fulfillment of Jotham's curse (Judg 9:16–57). The curse occupies just four lines.

> [L]et fire come out from Abimelech,
> and devour the citizens of Shechem, and Beth-millo;
> and let fire come out from the citizens of Shechem, and from Beth-millo,
> and devour Abimelech. (Judg 9:20)

⟦121⟧ The ensuing fulfullment report tells in 35 verses of the complicated events that finally led to Abimelech's preparing a bloodbath for the Shechemites, to the death of a thousand men and women in the smoke and flames of the burning of the temple of El-berith, and to Abimelech's finding an ignominious end in the siege of Thebez (Judg 9:22–57).

The formal imbalance between promise and fulfillment made it possible for the narrators to include detailed information about the action in the promise and then offer the fulfillment simply as an outcome (2 Kgs 1:16–17). Conversely, what is depicted with close attention to detail in the fulfillment report can be reduced in the anticipatory promise to its bare essentials (Judg 9:16–57). But above all, promises are where the narrators can make visible what in their opinion lies invisibly behind the things about which they can speak, but about which on the narrative plane they must keep silent.[6]

Let us consider the two prophets of 1 Kgs 20:35–36, one of whom refuses the order of the other to strike him. The promise states that by his refusal he has not heeded Yahweh's word and therefore must die. Thus the promise evaluates the preceding conflict morally and teaches on the basis of this interpretation, not on the basis of the event in itself, that the pronouncement of death is justified. If we reduce the episode to its outward components–a prophet refuses his colleague's request for him to strike him, departs, and is killed by a lion–then the things that happen do not fit together into a coherent event. They are only made to constitute a unified event by means of the promise that, like an interpretive commentary, holds together what on the narrative plane falls apart.[7]

The same holds for the narrative of the dying king, Ahaziah (2 Kgs 1:16–17). The fulfillment report notes only with lapidary brevity that the king died. The far more detailed pronouncement of death by Elijah does nothing at all to specify the outward circumstances that led to his death. Of Ahaziah's fall from the roof as the causal trigger of his injury and death (2 Kgs 1:2), nothing is said. Instead, the narrator ⟦122⟧ detects a transgression by the king in the attempted inquiry of Baal-zebub. The death

6. See in this sense G. Hentschel, *Die Elijaerzählungen: Zum Verhältnis von historischem Geschehen und geschichtlicher Erfahrung* (Leipzig, 1977) 340, on 2 Kgs 1:1–17: "They [that is, the tradents] did not look just at the outward, verifiable events but sought hard to find the deeper connections."

7. On this I agree with Würthwein, "Prophetisches Wort und Geschichte in den Königsbüchern," 401–10.

certificate, as it were, that had already been issued by the narrator in the promise of Elijah therefore gives a transgression against God as the reason for death. By this means he produces a unified event consisting of the attempted inquiry of Baal-zebub and the death of Ahaziah, a unity that does not exist on the narrative plane.

Jotham's curse differs only slightly. It concludes a long speech (Judg 9:16–20) in which Jotham blames Abimelech and the Shechemites for the eradication of the house of Jerubbaal (Judg 9:1–6). If Abimelech and the Shechemites have acted properly with their bloody deed, then they will live happily and peacefully together; but if they have done wrong, then Jotham's curse will fall upon them (Judg 9:19–20). Only after placing this prognosis before the following catastrophe report (Judg 9:22–57) can the report be read as proof of Abimelech's and the Shechemites' guilt. The fact that Gaal stirred up the Shechemites against Abimelech, that Abimelech in turn had the Shechemites cut down and immolated in their temple, and that he himself at last, struck by a millstone during the siege of Thebez, had his servant kill him has no causal connection whatsoever with the eradication of the family of Jerubbaal.

As in the episode of the two prophets and the case of the death of King Ahaziah, lines of connection are missing on the narrative plane that could gather the individual happenings together into a unified event. The connection comes in each case only by means of the promise, and here it is moral categories that make possible the conjunction of isolated phenomena that, only then, produces the unified event. What is narrated retrospectively obtains its character as an event only as a result of the promise, which organizes isolated phenomena into a value system, lifting them out of contingency and thereby making them worthy of telling. The narrators base their decisions about what to tell, what to omit, and how the connections between individual events arise on that value system, since it provides them with the moral categories according to which the course of events in the world may be evaluated and portrayed.

The fact that the narrators could distinguish between the telling of events and the interpretive function of promises that, on the one hand, they narrated as it were "objectively," "as it really was"[8] and, on the other hand, left [[123]] the interpretation to a (for the most part) expressly identified person, calls to mind the practice of our daily newspapers, in which the comment columns are formally distinguished from the news pages and are provided with the signature of the columnist.

8. On this quotation, see R. Vierhaus, "Rankes Begriff der historischen Objektivität," in *Objektivität und Parteilichkeit in der Geschichtswissenschaft* (ed. R. Koselleck, W. J. Mommsen, and J. Rüsen; Munich: Deutsche Taschenbuch, 1977) 63–76.

The Schema as a Means of Composition Extending beyond Individual Narratives

When it came to connecting narratives and the individual events portrayed in them into a course of events that cohered in time and content, this could be managed in a variety of ways. But when a narrator also wanted to show that there was an inner coherence that corresponded to the external matter of the narrative, then the promise–fulfillment schema was available for the purpose, since it could extend backward and forward across long narrative distances within the history.

The literary traces left behind in the Deuteronomistic History by the compositions—rather than compositions, we might just as well speak of partial redactions—show that narrative materials from different periods were often gathered according to the promise–fulfillment schema, although various principles of doing so came into play. In what follows, just three of these procedures are discussed, one each from Judges, Samuel, and Kings.

The function of promises to link individual texts emerges most clearly in Judges in the narrative clusters that have gathered around the figures of Gideon (Judg 6:11–8:28), Jephthah (Judg 10:17–12:7), and Samson (Judg 13:2–16:31). At the beginning of each is a promise that programmatically anticipates what is told in the following narratives. In the case of Gideon it is first Yahweh's messenger, then God himself, who assure Gideon that God is with him and promise him victory over the Midianites (Judg 6:12, 16); two signs requested by Gideon confirm this promise (Judg 6:36–40). The narratives about Jephthah begin with a conditional promise pronounced by the leaders of Gilead: "Who is the man that will begin to fight against the Ammonites? He shall be head [[124]] over all the inhabitants of Gilead" (Judg 10:18). The leaders repeat their promise to Jephthah; he acquiesces to their blandishments and is installed in his office (Judg 11:8–11) in order to undertake the battle with the Ammonites. The motto character of the introductory promise can be most easily recognized in the Samson stories. It is again placed in the mouth of Yahweh's messenger. He prophesies the birth of a son to the hitherto-childless wife of Manoah the Danite: the child will be dedicated to God, and it will be his task to begin to free the Israelites from the power of the Philistines (Judg 13:3–5). As the woman tells her husband of the encounter, and Yahweh's messenger returns at Manoah's request and repeats his promise, however, the talk this time is only of the child's future as a Nazirite; there is no more word of his role as savior from Philistine oppression (Judg 13:6–14). In this difference is expressed the programmatic character of the introductory promise, which stands like a superscription over what follows. The promise is carried forward by the recognition that the farcically told individual actions of Samson against the Philistines enact a motto, and thus the promise subordinates them to an overall concept and raises Samson's private disputes to the level of folktale. It creates the unity and thereby also the meaning of the whole.

The compositional structure of the books of Samuel rests on a large number of promises. From them proceeds a network of narrative threads that tend toward the fulfillment of the promises. As these narrative threads are closely interwoven, run alongside each other, supplement one another, compete with and supersede one another and contradict, so arise tensions and their resolutions, the course of events is distributed onto several planes, and in this way the simultaneity of the nonsimultaneous can be accomplished, as well as the intertwining of progression and regression, in which "every future contains a past and everything past contains a future."[9]

On the one hand, there is Samuel, born (1 Sam 1:19–20) following a divine promise confirmed by the priest Eli in Shiloh (1 Sam 1:17), as a result of his mother's vow (1 Sam 1:11) dedicated to priestly duties (1 Sam 1:21–28), and willingly taking these duties upon himself (1 Sam 2:18, 26). But there too are the two sons of Eli, Hophni and Phineas, who should follow their father in the priestly office but do not honorably carry out the [[125]] obligations associated with it (1 Sam 2:11–17, 22–25). In this initial narrative constellation, the sequence of the fall of the Elides and the rise of Samuel is anticipated and made simultaneous. The fact that the Elides will be able to exercise the priestly office in the future only in extremely difficult circumstances and that it is therefore indirectly open to Samuel is summarized in a prophecy spoken by a man of God (1 Sam 2:27–36; cf. 1 Sam 3:10–14); the death of Eli's two sons confirms it (1 Sam 4:11).

Samuel's rise can no longer be stopped. The stories equip him with priestly, prophetic, and judgelike characteristics and thus ascribe all power to him; nonetheless, the people crave a king (1 Samuel 8), and Samuel is styled "kingmaker."[10]

> Tomorrow about this time I will send you a man from the land of Benjamin, and you shall anoint him to be prince over my people Israel. He shall save my people from the hand of the Philistines; for I have seen the affliction of my people, because their cry has come to me. (1 Sam 9:16)

9. R. Koselleck, "Wozu noch Historie?" in *Seminar: Geschichte und Theorie: Umrisse einer Historik* (ed. H. M. Baumgartner and J. Rüsen; Frankfurt, 1976) 17–35 (= *Historische Zeitschrift* 212 [1971] 1–18); quotation from p. 20.

10. For this concept, see S. Herrmann, *Ursprung und Funktion der Prophetie im Alten Israel* (Rheinisch-Westfälische Akademie der Wissenschaften, Vorträge, Geisteswissenschaften 208; Opladen: Westdeutscher, 1976) 21–24.

With this divine promise to Samuel a momentum is reintroduced into the story in that the replacement of the one by the other is contained in it. Of course, the promise is fulfilled (1 Sam 9:14, 17; 10:1). *Praedicationes sunt servandae* ⟦'pronouncements must be obeyed/attended to'⟧, and the predicted success in war also begins to become apparent (1 Sam 14:47–48).[11] But the Philistines cannot be permanently overcome (1 Sam 14:52). Another change in regime is due, and typically it is again prophetic promises that relate the fall of Saul and the rise of David to each other. Samuel prophesies to Saul as follows:

> But now your kingdom shall not continue; the LORD has sought out a man after his own heart; and the LORD has appointed him to be prince over his people, because you have not kept what the LORD commanded you. (1 Sam 13:14)

⟦126⟧ And:

> The LORD has torn the kingdom of Israel from you this day, and has given it to a neighbor of yours, who is better than you. (1 Sam 15:28)

Samuel's ghost, conjured from the underworld, repeats the prophecy he pronounced while alive and now also names the rival of Saul:

> The LORD has done to you as he spoke by me; for the LORD has torn the kingdom out of your hand and given it to your neighbor, David. (1 Sam 28:17)

When Saul himself (1 Sam 24:20b, 21) and his son Jonathan (1 Sam 20:13, 23:17) must recognize David as the future king with solemn oaths—that is, in a genre of speech involving a promise—then the past and what is to come are most closely intertwined. When at David's elevation to king of Israel reference is made several times to divine promises relating to it (2 Sam 3:9–10, 18; 5:2; cf. 6:21), the event itself is framed by promises reaching both back and forward. In this way it appears as though the long effect of the promises has been put in the scales to balance the ephemerality of events[12] in order to show that what now happens was not unfore-

11. Of course, a monument to Saul has been erected here on David's model, but it cannot be a deuteronomistic memorial according to either its form or its content; so H. J. Stoebe, *Das erste Buch Samuelis* (KAT 8; Gütersloh: Mohn, 1973) 277.

12. "Les événements sont poussière: Ils traversent l'histoire comme des lueurs brèves; à peine naissent-ils qu'ils retournent déjà à la nuit et souvent à l'oublie" ⟦'Events are the ephemera of history; they pass across its stage like fireflies, hardly glimpsed before they settle back into darkness and as often as not into oblivion'⟧; so F. Braudel, *La Mediterranée et le monde mediterranéen à l'époque du Philippe II* (8th ed.; Paris, 1987) 2.223; but see also p. 519. ⟦ET: *The Mediterranean and the Mediterranean World in the Age of Philip II* (New York: Harper & Row, 1972–73); quotation is from vol. 2, p. 901 of the English edition.⟧

seen but was predicted. The experience that events develop and are bound up in complex scenarios that diverge from other sequences, yet that behind both stands the same effective power, has here been expressed by means of promises.

The subplots, too, on that stage of the past follow a similar pattern. Promises elevated David to the throne, but promises also impose duty on him. Solemn vows charge him with the care of Saul's survivors (1 Sam 20:14–16, 24:22; cf. 2 Sam 9:1, 3, 7). Solemn commitments promise him the destruction of his enemies, even those very Saulides (1 Sam 20:15, 24:5, 25:29, 26:8). While the narratives drive forward along the paths previously laid down by the promises, they make the impossible possible: they show David as victor in the struggle for power [[127]] yet without fighting—that is, one who does *not* have the blood of the Saulides on his hands.

David's kingship is established; now the narrative turns to the continuance of the new royal house.[13] This theme also is treated in the form of a promise in Nathan's oracle, which assures David of the permanence of his dynasty (2 Sam 7:1–15). The fulfillment is reported in 1 Kings 1–2 with the accesion of Solomon. The arc of promise between 2 Sam 7:1–15 and 1 Kings 1–2 admittedly does not run single-mindedly toward this point. Instead, a new word of God proclaimed by Samuel in 2 Samuel 12 provides a counterpoint that, while it does not abolish the dynastic promise, nevertheless stands in its way as a hindrance. Yahweh will "take" from David, not the kingdom, but the harem "and give it to the one close to him" (2 Sam 12:11). Absalom's rebellion is heralded. As David has already reached the peak of royal power, the counterpromise reduces him contrapuntally to his human measure.[14]

With promise and counterpromise, both often bound up in a single divine utterance, the presentation stretching from 1 Samuel 1 to 1 Kings 2 succeeds in breaking up the rigid succession of Eli, Samuel, Saul, David, and Solomon and explaining the changes in rulership as a course of events dovetailed into each other in time and substance. Thus, each time, the future grows out of the past and within itself carries the past on. Where past and future interpenetrate in this way, nothing is reversible. The promises bind the old and the new together. They can do this because, according to the conviction expressed in them, the same God brings about rise and fall, progress and regress.

13. Cf. L. Rost, "Die Überlieferung von der Thronnachfolge Davids," *Das kleine Credo und andere Studien zum Alten Testament* (Heidelberg, 1965) 119–253 (= BWANT 3/6; Stuttgart: Kohlhammer, 1926] 60): "Yahweh will no longer be enlarging the realm but will be its guardian, the guarantor of the greatness that has been achieved."

14. On the background, see H. J. Stoebe, "David und Uria: Überlegungen zur Überlieferung von 2 Sam 11," *Bib* 67 (1986) 388–96.

The portrayal of the history of the divided kingdoms in the books of Kings is essentially determined by prophecies of disaster. There are three post-narrative but predeuteronomistic judgments of rejection on the descendants of Jeroboam I, Baasha, and Ahab (in 1 Kgs 14:7, 10–11; 16:2–4; 21:21–22, 24) that in their basic elements and the sequencing of these are quite [[128]] stereotypical but nonetheless are placed in the mouths of the three prophets–Ahijah, Jehu, and Elijah. Models for the three antidynastic sayings are found in the narrative of Jehu's revolt (2 Kgs 9:7–10, 26, 36–37) and perhaps also in 1 Kgs 21:19b, 23.[15] What relates in that place to unique events, however, the composition takes up in a generalizing way for repeated interpretations of events. While it thus explains history by means of the principle of repeatability, it does not postulate repeating situations at the level of events; rather, it infers from narrative contents that are quite differently composed in terms of both time and characters that these are analogous in their inner relations of cause and effect.

If the recognition and description of "historical patterns" comprise the actual historical task of the historian,[16] and therefore if Augustine's equating of *historia ipsa* [['history itself']] with the *ordo temporum* [['ordering of the times']] is right,[17] then this task can only be managed by means of three basic insights about time: the principles of the irreversibility of events, of repeatability, and of the simultaneity of the unsimultaneous. When the compositions that underlie the Deuteronomistic History used the schema of promise–fulfillment as described above, they applied these three principles using the possibilities of expression of their time,[18] even if only for the re-presentation of brief periods of time: in Judges in relation to individual figures, in Samuel perhaps first to delineate family histories, in Kings for presenting periods of fifty years or so. Even if these compositional works thus do not really deserve the label "history," with their schema of [[129]] promise–fulfillment so variously applied, they nevertheless transmitted to the redactors a model for historiographic interpretation.

15. For a fuller treatment of this group of texts: A. F. Campbell, *Of Prophets and Kings: A Late Ninth-Century Document (1 Samuel 1–2 Kings 10)* (Washington, D.C.: Catholic Biblical Association, 1986) 32–41. Differing from Campbell, I understand 1 Kgs 16:1–4 to be compositional, not redactional.

16. So with R. Koselleck, "Geschichte, Geschichten und formalen Zeitstrukturen," in *Wozu noch Geschichte?* (ed. W. Oelmüller; Munich, 1977) 253–66, esp. 255–56.

17. L. Honnefelder, "Die Einmaligkeit des Geschichtlichen: Die philosophischen Voraussetzungen der Geschichtsdeutung Augustins," *Zeitschrift für philosophische Forschung* 40 (1986) 33–51.

18. Koselleck, "Geschichte, Geschichten und formalen Zeitstrukturen," 260: "In it [that is, the Judeo-Christian tradition] theological definitions of time are found that run crosswise to 'empirical' data. Without thematizing 'history,' the Judeo-Christian interpretations imported standards that at the same time indirectly showed historical structures, as they had never been formulated before, or anywhere else."

The Schema as a Means of Redaction Extending beyond Individual Narratives and Compositions

The redactors proved to be worthy trustees. If the schema of promise–fulfillment was present in narrative or composition at points in the past that were in their view significant, they extended the arcs of promise, whether in short narratives or in medium-length compositions by means of far-reaching new arcs. Typical of this ever-further reach into the future is the narrative of the death of Jeroboam's son Abijah in 1 Kgs 14:1–6, 13a, 17–18.[19] On the narrative plane, Ahijah announces the death of the child, and what the prophet announces comes to pass. The composition broadens the announcement of death to all the male descendants of Jeroboam (vv. 7, 10–11).[20] The promise arc that now stretches beyond the individual narrative ends in the narrative of Baasha's revolution in 1 Kgs 15:27, 29. The redaction goes even further and has the prophet Ahijah in vv. 15–16 (v. 13b is also redactionary) take much more into his scope; now he also prophesies the exile of Israel. Thus, the long gap extending as far as 2 Kgs 17:7–23, 18:11–12, and nearly two hundred years, is bridged. Nathan's reprimand of David in 2 Sam 12:7–12, 13b, 14 grew in a similar manner.[21] In its narrative kernel (vv. 7a, 13b, 14), it identifies only David as guilty, but shifts his death sentence to the first son that Bathsheba bore him, and yet his fate is still fulfilled within the narrative (2 Sam 12:18). The composition extends the pronouncement of judgment on David to future interfamilial quarrels, with Absalom's revolt specifically in mind (vv. 11–12). And 2 Sam 16:22 does in fact relate that Absalom took over David's harem. Only with the redaction is David's guilt pictured as particularly serious, given the background of God's earlier favorable deeds toward him, and therefore extending the punishment *ʿad-ʿôlâm* [['to eternity']] as well: nevermore shall the sword depart from the House of David (vv. 7b–10).

[[130]] The royal oracle that forms the core of the divine promise of the everlasting Davidic dynasty was fit into its present context compositionally (2 Sam 7:8b, 9, 11b, 12, 14a, 15a, 16)[22] without pointing any further than Solomon's enthronement in 1 Kings 1–2. The theme of building

19. On the delimitation of the narrative entity, there is general consensus; cf. E. Würthwein, *Die Bücher der Könige: 1 Könige 1–16* (Göttingen, 1977; 2d ed., 1985) 172–79.

20. See n. 15.

21. For the text division, I follow Rost, "Die Überlieferung von der Thronnachfolge Davids," 201–7 (= BWANT 3/6, pp. 92–99).

22. So with M. Weippert, "Assyrische Prophetien der Zeit Asarhaddons und Assurbanipals," in *Assyrian Royal Inscriptions: New Horizons in Literary, Ideological, and Historical Analysis* (ed. F. M. Fales; Rome, 1981) 71–115, at 105; H. Weippert, "Die Ätiologie des Nordreiches und seines Königshauses (I Reg 11, 29–40)," *ZAW* 95 (1983) 344–75, at 352–53.

the temple (vv. 5b–7, 13), which anticipates 1 Kings 6; 7:13–8:66, belongs to the redaction.[23] Also, in the pronouncement of the man of God against the priest Eli in Shiloh in 1 Sam 2:27–36, vv. 35–36 constitute a redactional supplement that, far beyond the immediate events, has the replacement of the Elides by the Zadokites under Solomon in mind (1 Kgs 2:35b) and the subordination of the "priests of the high places" to the Jerusalem priesthood on the occasion of the Josianic reform (2 Kgs 23:9).[24] Possibly belonging in this set is the narrative of the altar at Bethel, which in 1 Kgs 13:3, 5 is destroyed according to the prediction, but in the redactional context is henceforth intended to be read only as a sign confirming the promise of the birth of King Josiah and his activity against this altar (v. 2b), a prophecy that is meant to cast a long arc across text and time, reaching as far as 2 Kgs 23:15–18, 20.[25]

Even if the way was not paved for the redactors through promises previously given either in narrative or in composition, they nevertheless turned again and again to the proven instrument of promise–fulfillment. With the change in leadership from Moses to Joshua or, in literary terms, with the joining of the Deuteronomic frame-portions with the book of Joshua, the divine assurance that God will be with Joshua as he had been with Moses is inserted as a connecting link that creates a material and literary continuity (Deut 31:8, 23; Josh 1:5, 17; 3:7; 6:27).[26] The network of promises and fulfillments, [[131]] connected with the theme of rest from enemies and spread throughout the text from Deut 3:20 to 1 Kgs 8:56, means to unify distinct compositions under an overarching point of view.[27] Only redactional and probably also postredactional narratives sketch the picture of "Solomon in all his glory" (Matt 6:29),[28] and only to this Solomon does God promise wisdom, honor, and riches in his nocturnal appearance in Gibeon (1 Kgs 3:4–15). This promise was to be more

23. So most recently E.-J. Waschke, "Das Verhältnis alttestamentlicher Überlieferungen im Schnittpunkt der Dynastiezusage und die Dynastiezusage im Spiegel alttestamentlicher Überlieferungen," *ZAW* 99 (1987) 157–79, at 165 with n. 40.

24. So with Stoebe, *Das erste Buch Samuelis*, 120.

25. Things are similar with the thrice-dying king in 1 Kgs 22:35, 37, 40. H. Weippert, "Ahab el campeador? Redaktionsgeschichtliche Untersuchungen zu 1 Kön 22," *Bib* 69 (1988) 457–79.

26. Summary in N. Lohfink, "Die deuteronomistische Darstellung des Übergangs der Führung Israels von Moses auf Josue: Ein Beitrag zur alttestamentlichen Theologie des Amtes," *Scholastik* 37 (1962) 32–44.

27. G. Braulik, "Zur deuteronomistischen Konzeption von Freiheit und Frieden," *Studien zur Theologie des Deuteronomiums* (Stuttgart, 1988) 219–30 (first pub.: VTSup 36; Leiden, 1985] 29–39).

28. So with Würthwein, *1 Könige 1–16*, 146–47.

than fulfilled in the eyes of his own people and all the world through the course of the Solomon story.[29]

This free use of the promise–fulfillment schema by the redactors also indicates that they had learned from their predecessors. Though narrative, compositional, and redactional promise-arcs grew out of each other in stages, reaching ever further into the future, there can be no doubt that "history" arose from the "histories."[30]

29. 1 Kgs 3:28; 5:9–14, 15–32; 7:13–51; 10:1–13, 23–29; 11:41–43.

30. Cf. also Weippert, "Ahab el campeador?" 478–79 n. 36.

The Kerygma of the Deuteronomistic Historical Work

Hans Walter Wolff

In Wolff's famous essay, he accepts at the outset the main premises of Noth. First, the DH was written in the exile, essentially by a single author. (Wolff's second Dtr is only tentatively postulated and plays a small role; his concept of two deuteronomistic writers is quite different from that of Cross [pp. 79–94], whose first writer is Josianic.) Second, history is the fulfillment of words of God proclaimed by Moses. His essay, then, attempts little new at the level of composition, but rather addresses a question of interpretation arising from Noth's work: why would the historian expend his energy simply to proclaim that the ancient threat of final judgment had now been fulfilled?

For answer he looks first, not to the end of the story, which sends ambiguous messages, but to key moments within it. There he finds an ever-changing history based on a reciprocal movement between God's word and Israel's actions. Each new phase of this history is different, because events have irreversible consequences (a motif also in Weippert's essay [pp. 47–61]); even so, God continues with his people. This is his first answer to the idea that Israel's history had been brought to an irrevocable end. Only after establishing this does he go on to develop the point for which the essay is best known, namely that the history is characterized throughout by the theme of repentance, which he then sees as the content of Dtr's exhortation to the people of the exilic time.

In his study of the key passages Deut 4:29–31, 30:1–10; 1 Kgs 8:46–53, Wolff highlights the important question of the relationship between Deuteronomy, Kings, and Jeremiah, thus bringing studies of the DH into the wider arena of exilic theology.

Reprinted with permission from Walter Brueggemann and Hans Walter Wolff (eds.), *The Vitality of Old Testament Traditions* (Atlanta: John Knox Press, 1975) 83–100, 141–43 (Eng. Trans. by Frederick C. Prussner of "Das Kerygma des deuteronomistischen Geschichtswerk," *ZAW* [1961] 171–86). "DtrH" has been changed to "the DH" where appropriate in this essay, for reasons of inner-volume consistency.

⟦83⟧ With an unprecedented force, Israel's prophets in the eighth and seventh centuries B.C. disclosed the present human reality as simply a part of God's ongoing history. Men such as Hosea, Isaiah, and Jeremiah, in their anticipation of new, cataclysmic, divinely initiated happenings, exposed the guilt of their own time and moved it into the clear light of divine actions which had occurred earlier. The result was almost necessarily a quick attention to the ongoing movement of things and to the interconnection of all events, particularly because the prophetic word encompassed the whole of current world history.[1]

And, as one of the fruits of prophecy, there came into being in the sixth century B.C. a gigantic historical work, unparalleled in the surrounding world. It stands before us today as the Old Testament books of Deuteronomy, Joshua, Judges, Samuel, and Kings. It follows the course of approximately seven centuries of Israelite history from the time of Moses to the Babylonian exile. With scrupulous care, it assimilates both literary traditions and facts which were experienced directly, and, in the process, achieves an astonishingly unified design.

After a variety of preliminary inquiries, Martin Noth in 1943, demonstrated this convincingly and in detail with his studies on the history of the traditions used in the work.[2] His results in essence were confirmed by Alfred Jepsen's investigations which—surprisingly enough, because independently—also took the sources of the books of Kings as their starting point.[3] For this reason we can accept ⟦84⟧ Noth's results in wide measure. In the deuteronomistic historical work (DH)[4] traditional materials have been put in systematic order, and then have been highlighted by certain new passages; and these usually come in the form of speeches delivered by the most important historical figures. The work probably originated around 550 in the territory of Judah–Benjamin.

Author's note: ⟦This article first appeared in German in⟧ *Zeitschrift für die Alttestamentliche Wissenschaft* 73 (1961) 171–86. Reprinted in Hans Walter Wolff, *Gesammelte Studien zum Alten Testament* (Munich: Chr. Kaiser Verlag, 1964). ⟦It⟧ was first presented as a guest lecture to the theological faculty of the University of Göttingen on July 15, 1960. It is translated and included here by permission of *Zeitschrift für die Alttestamentliche Wissenschaft* and Chr. Kaiser Verlag.

1. Cf. H. W. Wolff, "Das Geschichtsverständnis der alttestamentlichen Prophetie," *EvTh* 20 (1960) 218–35.

2. Martin Noth, *Überlieferungsgeschichtliche Studien I, Die sammelnden und bearbeitenden Geschichtswerke im Alten Testament* (Tübingen: Max Niemeyer Verlag, 1943, 2d ed., 1957).

3. Alfred Jepsen, *Die Quellen des Königsbuches* (Halle: Max Niemeyer Verlag, 1953, 2d ed., 1956). The manuscript of the book was already completed in 1939, i.e., before the appearance of Noth's studies (p. 116).

4. Translator's note: Wolff's abbreviation is DtrG (for "deuteronomistisches Geschichtswerk").

The theological assumptions of the work are set forward in a generally clear and persuasive fashion. History is understood as the accomplishment of the word of God which prophets had proclaimed, and more especially, as the fulfillment of the words of Moses that stand at the beginning of the whole work in Deuteronomy. And always in the foreground looms the question of whether Israel is still the people of God—since having put herself in jeopardy by apostasy.

But what Dtr intended to proclaim with this kind of format has, in my opinion, not been satisfactorily explained. What sermon, by means of his extensive work, does he want to give to his sixth-century contemporaries? They were, remember, the mere remnants of Israel, without king, without the Jerusalem temple, without sovereignty over their land, therefore without their own state and without organized public worship. It is generally agreed that to find the DH's kerygma is important—the work is after all a child of prophecy and it has the usual prophetic urgency to issue a command. But what is that command?

I

Martin Noth holds that "the punishment for disobedience, . . . considered by Deuteronomy as a [mere] possibility [but one] which would lead to the destruction of the nation, had now, for Dtr become an accomplished fact," so that "for him the order of things which Deuteronomy had presupposed had come to its final end," and therefore "the actual purpose of his entire historical presentation" was to show that this final end must "be understood as divine judgment."[5] In this view, of course, there is no room for a hopeful future. Quite the reverse: the judgment is to be "viewed as something definitive and final."[6] This perspective is well sustained by the various speeches and reflections whereby Dtr presents his view of history. [[85]] What they say is something like this: "If you transgress the covenant order which Yahweh your God has appointed for you and you go and serve other gods and worship them, then Yahweh's anger will be kindled against you, and you shall be quickly blotted out from the good land which he has given to you."[7]

To begin with, one can only ask why an Israelite of the sixth century B.C. would even reach for his pen if he only wanted to explain the final end of Israel's history as the righteous judgment of God. Gerhard von Rad has answered this question by pointing out that this historical work repre-

5. Op. cit., 109.

6. Op. cit., 108.

7. Thus Josh 23:16; similarly Deut 4:25–28; 1 Sam 12:14–15, 25; 1 Kgs 9:8–9; 2 Kgs 17:23, 21:14–15.

sents "a great judgment doxology which has been transposed from the cultic to the literary realm," and which confesses before God "in order that thou mightest be justified in thy sentence" (Ps 51:6 [51:4]).[8]

On the other hand, von Rad views the DH as really more concerned with the "problem of the operation of Yahweh's word in history." Alongside Deuteronomy's word of malediction and the words of threat by the prophets there stands the other word of the promise of salvation which is contained in the Nathan oracle, but which appears to be as yet unfulfilled. In the mention at the very end (2 Kgs 25:27ff.) of Jehoiachin's pardon, the DH may be said to be pointing "to an opportunity with which Yahweh can start over again."[9] Indeed, von Rad considers "the true thematic content of this work . . . [to be] a messianic one."[10] In this view, Dtr did not at all intend only to teach that the exile was a righteous judgment and fulfillment of the threat which Moses and the prophets had proclaimed. Rather, he wanted his readers to expect that beyond that, sometime, the promise made to David of salvation would also be fulfilled.

The final scene does indeed raise serious questions about Noth's thesis that the DH presents only the end of Israel's history. One cannot be satisfied with Noth's interpretation that Dtr, "because of his own peculiar conscientiousness and reverence for the actual course of events, . . . simply reported as such this last fact known to him on the subject of the history of the Judean kings."[11] That interpretation simply does not comport with the idea that Dtr–as Noth himself insists–used the greatest of care in selecting and organizing his materials.[12]

[[86]] On the other side, it is even less clear to me why one should recognize in this final passage "the beginning of the hoped for deliverance,"[13] as though, in addition to declaring the righteous judgment of God. Dtr wanted also to stimulate hope in the fulfillment of the Nathan oracle. This is already contradicted by the fact that the information from the year 561 in 2 Kgs 25:27–30 contains no reference at all to the Nathan oracle whereas the Jerusalem catastrophe of the year 587 is specifically seen by the DH in 2 Kgs 24:2 as coming "according to the word which Yahweh had spoken by his servants, the prophets." And apart from everything else, the notion of a windfall hope is flatly inconsistent with the Nathan oracle,

8. Gerhard von Rad, *Theologie des Alten Testaments* (Munich: Chr. Kaiser Verlag, 2d ed., 1958) 1.340. English Translation by D. M. G. Stalker, *Old Testament Theology* (New York: Harper & Row Publishers, 1962) 1.343.

9. Op. cit., 341.

10. Op. cit., 342.

11. Op. cit., 108.

12. Op. cit., 11.

13. Thus Enno Janssen, *Juda in der Exilszeit* (Göttingen: Vandenhoeck and Ruprecht, 1956) 76.

whose fulfillment, the DH invariably maintains, is contingent on obedience to the word of Moses in Deuteronomy.[14] Even kings are subject to the covenant word which Moses had proclaimed.[15] By that covenant are measured not only the kings of the Northern Kingdom but in the end even the Davidic rulers.[16] When the covenant word is abandoned, the Nathan oracle, too, is no longer in force. It would therefore be very hard to maintain that the DH is giving rein to hope based on the Nathan oracle–and doing so by this lone brittle piece about Jehoiachin's elevation.

This note about an actual event is precisely, however, what makes it impossible to hold that the deuteronomistic historian intended nothing more than to point to the Jerusalem catastrophe of 587 as a justified and final divine judgment and, therefore, as the deserved ending of Israel's history.

What then *does* the Deuteronomist want to say to his contemporaries?

II

The very size of the work requires us to ask whether the Deuteronomist did not have a rather complex intention in mind. Had he wanted to arouse hope by means of the Nathan oracle, he should have selected a much narrower and shorter sector from history. What was the purpose of his detailed treatment of the time of Moses, Joshua, the judges, and Samuel? If, on the other hand, it had been his aim to show that Yahweh had accomplished his ancient threat issued at the making of the covenant with Moses and that the history of Israel had now rightly come to its end, then one must ask, in view [[87]] of the sheer volume of his presentation, why it did not terminate at a much earlier point. Why does he keep his readers occupied with the ups and downs of events, concatenated through the centuries?

His treatment of the period of the judges already points out to us an answer. He obviously sets great store in showing that apostasy begins immediately following the time of Joshua. "The people served Yahweh as long as Joshua lived" (Judg 2:7). But immediately after the occupation of the land apostasy sets in. Therewith he invokes Hosea's view of history. He does not envision just a few instances of disloyalty, but states unabashedly that *all* of Israel "did what was evil in the sight of Yahweh and served the baalim" (2:11).

> They departed from Yahweh, the God of their fathers, who had led them out of Egypt, and followed other gods from among the nations

14. 1 Kgs 2:3–4; 9:5–7.
15. Deut 17:18f.
16. 2 Kgs 18:6; 21:8f.; 23:25.

> who were round about and worshiped them; but Yahweh they offended. . . . [Whereupon] the anger of Yahweh was kindled against Israel . . . and he sold them into the hands of their enemies round about and they were no longer able to withstand their enemies. (vv. 12 and 14)

That very cycle, according to the DH—the whole nation's apostasy and Yahweh's burning anger—had led to the end of the Northern Kingdom, and in Manasseh's days had sealed the fate of Judah and Jerusalem.[17] Why then did Israel's history not come to its end at that time?

> When they cried to Yahweh,[18] then Yahweh raised up judges who delivered them from the hand of those plunderers. . . . For Yahweh was moved to pity by their wailing because of those who afflicted and oppressed them. (vv. 16, 18)

To cry to Yahweh—this caused the reversal which followed upon both accomplished apostasy and the burning anger of Yahweh—who had, before, carried out his judgment by handing the people over to their enemies. Upon every deliverance there follows in the time of the judges a new apostasy, generation after generation. Why did Israel's history nonetheless continue? Because Israel implored Yahweh anew and because Yahweh was moved to pity.

[[88]] This pattern of apostasy and turning to Yahweh, of catastrophes and deliverances, does not, however, remain without consequences for the history of God's people. Yahweh ordains a new twist to history. According to the original promise Israel was to take over the whole land, but now it is said,

> I will not drive out before them any of the peoples which Joshua had left at his death, in order to test Israel by them whether they will walk in the ways of Yahweh. (2:21–22)

The symbiosis with Canaan appears to the deuteronomistic historian to be a new enactment by Yahweh in history, coming at the end of a long phase of disobedience (cf. Judg 3:4). But as an added new enactment there appears also the martial protection which Yahweh provides Israel, in the saviors he raises up.

The period of the judges is thereby clearly set apart from the time of Moses and Joshua. But just as clearly, the time of the kings is later set apart from the period of the judges. The great farewell speech of Samuel in 1 Samuel 12 emphasizes this latter difference forcefully. The judges were deliverers whom Yahweh sent because of Israel's prayers. Their king,

17. 2 Kgs 17:15–18; 21:2–25; 23:26.

18. With regard to this text see 3d ed. of Rudolf Kittel's *Biblia Hebraica* (Stuttgart: Bibelanstalt, 1949); restored with reference to 3:9, 15 and elsewhere.

however, they have demanded in defiant protest against the will of Yahweh. This desire by the people opposes Yahweh's very sovereignty, which Dtr sees as the capstone of the period of the Judges.[19] As a result of this rebellion against Yahweh the old covenantal order of the sacred tribal league breaks and falls apart—with disastrous consequences.[20] Israel was to become a state like all the states round about.

Nevertheless, even following this rebellion against the covenant God—a rebellion which makes even the apostasy under the judges seem piffling—Israel's history does not come to an end. Yahweh condescends to heed his people and he himself establishes a king for it (1 Sam 12:13b). Indeed, in David he chooses the king as his king and at the same time chooses Jerusalem as the place where the name of Yahweh will find a dwelling (1 Kgs 8:16). Both of these enactments are completely new elements in history. They follow upon Israel's rebellious protest against Yahweh's kingship.

But this new ordering of history does not occur without further ado any more than it did in the time of the judges. The continuation [[89]] of Samuel's farewell speech in 1 Sam 12:14–15 demonstrates this. Israel is admonished to remain, along with her king, under subjection to Yahweh and to listen to his voice. In a thunderstorm at the time of the wheat harvest Israel comes to know the judgment upon her rebellion (vv. 17–18). Then Israel entreats Samuel to intercede with Yahweh:

> Pray for your servants to Yahweh, your God, that we may not die. For we added to all our sins this wrong, to desire a king for ourselves. (v. 19)

Israel knows that her end has been deserved. Thereupon Samuel's assurance of salvation occurs:

> Do not be afraid! To be sure, you have done this wrong. . . . But Yahweh will not cast away his people for his great name's sake, but it has pleased Yahweh to make you his people. (vv. 20, 22)

The time of the judges does not return any more than the time of Joshua had returned earlier. History, in its reciprocal movement between Yahweh's word and Israel's conduct, is irreversible. And the salvation history never breaks off, even amid the catastrophe brought down by apostasy and by Yahweh's judgments—though that history does seem to stand still for a moment. The reversal of judgment is again initiated by Israel's cry to Yahweh. That is shown by this second deep incision into the course of Israel's history, which, *mutatis mutandis*, corresponds perfectly to the first one. The cry represents an appeal for Yahweh's watchful compassion

19. 1 Sam 12:10–13; cf. Judg 8:23; 1 Sam 8:7.
20. 1 Sam 8:10ff.

on his people; and this compassion brings Israel under new enactments and into an entirely new phase of her salvation history.

In the Deuteronomist's own time the third and last phase of Israel's history, namely that of her national existence, came to its end. Ever since King Manasseh's apostasy it was irrevocable that Judah also, as was true of Israel, would be rejected, including Jerusalem, the chosen city, and the house where Yahweh's name dwelled.[21] But that judgment, now carried out, and conclusive as it seems, is merely one more in the chain of historical reversals, and there is no reason to think that it, too, will not be reversed, if the people repent. Therefore, to maintain that Yahweh, in the Deuteronomist's eyes, wanted [[90]] to pass final judgment on Israel's history, and irredeemably end it, is really to overstate the case. To be sure, this judgment does appear especially harsh. The state of Israel, the state of Judah, and even the chosen city are rejected. But who can say whether a completely new phase could not come about, again with wholly new enactments for Yahweh's own people, as had been true after the earlier rejections? Why otherwise would Dtr have reached back so far and presented such a steady chain of reversals?

However, amid this hour of deepest catastrophe, there is not much brief for teaching hope. Noth has pointed out with complete justification that such an intention, if it exists, would have to be recognizable in the great speeches.[22] But still, if Judges 2 and 1 Samuel 12 are to be believed, there is yet room for hope: the cry to Yahweh, with a confession of guilt, a prayer for deliverance, and a willingness to give renewed obedience, may be efficacious again.

III

If a summons to such is the true and actual kerygma of the DH, then it should appear clearly not only at the main junctures of history but should also be in full view elsewhere in the great speeches. Is this the case?

Judg 2:11ff. and 1 Samuel 12 have just shown us how decisive a role for the continuation of salvation history was played by Israel's turning to Yahweh. In 1 Samuel 12 the return occurs as the result of a pointed admonition speech by Samuel (vv. 14–15). Indeed, we find the theme "return" in almost all of the important passages which enable us to recognize Dtr's intention. On the other hand, nowhere do we encounter an encouragement to hope.

21. 2 Kgs 21:12–13; 23:27. "Israel," "Judah," "Jerusalem" here signify national entities and the monarchy. Otherwise it would be incomprehensible why a king like Manasseh is not mentioned explicitly.

22. Op. cit., 108.

The catchword *shûb* for 'return' is found as early as 1 Sam 7:3 in Samuel's address:

> If you want to return [*shābîm*] to Yahweh with all your heart then remove the foreign gods and the Ashtarts from your midst and direct your heart to Yahweh and serve him alone, so that he will rescue you out of the hand of the Philistines.

⟦91⟧ Israel obeys and experiences deliverance in the trouble with the Philistines.

In a decisive passage, 2 Kings 17, where the Deuteronomist pauses to meditate on the end of the state of Israel, he summarizes (v. 13) the message of Yahweh spoken "by all prophets and seers of Israel and Judah" as the single word *shûbû*!

> Turn back [*shûbû*] from your evil ways and observe my commandments and statutes strictly according to the instruction which I gave to your fathers and which I sent to you by my servants the prophets.

Because the call to return and thereby also the covenant made with the fathers (v. 15) were ignored, the final judgment upon Israel took place. It is not so much the total apostasy which makes the judgment final as the contemptuous disregard of the call to return.

A return will reverse the judgment, though it might already have been decreed. This is shown by the DH in the case of one who is for him the brightest figure in all of Israel's history, Josiah (2 Kgs 23:25):

> There had never been a king like him, who turned [*shāb*] to Yahweh with all his heart and with all his soul and with all his strength, completely in accordance with the instruction of Moses; and after him there arose no one like him.

He is not depicted as the faithful one who never yielded to apostasy. Neither is he shown as one trusting in a word of promise. Rather, he is presented precisely, and only, as the one who returned.

Thus the theme "return" appears at important highpoints of the deuteronomistic presentation of history, and it thereby demonstrates through different examples what Israel should hear and do under judgment in the exile.

But could it be that this idea of return is still subordinate to the Deuteronomist's emphasis on judgment for the time of the apostasy?

IV

In order to answer this question I must ask another: does Dtr state specifically what Israel should do in the hour of judgment? ⟦92⟧ Yes, he does, and a passage of particular prominence–Solomon's prayer at the dedication of the temple.

The catchword *shûb* occurs in the prayer no less than four times. First of all, in 1 Kgs 8:33 and 35 where the thought is found that Israel might be defeated by an enemy or might be the victim of a drought "because they have sinned against thee." In both instances it is said:

> If they turn back to thee and confess thy name, and pray and make supplication to thee in this house, then hear thou in heaven and forgive the sin of thy people.

These two instances confirm first of all only that to return is the imperative of the hour for the DH whenever judgment takes place because of apostasy, as we have already seen in Judg 2:1; 1 Samuel 7 and 12; and indirectly in 2 Kings 17 and 23:25.

But does this imperative also obtain for the hour in which Israel now finds herself, far from her destroyed sanctuary? The prayer at the dedication of the temple gives (in 1 Kgs 8:46–53) a precise answer to this and does so with marked detail:

> If they sin against thee . . . and thou art angry with them, and dost give them to an enemy, so that their conquerors carry them away to the land of the enemy, far or near, and they take it [punishment] to heart in the land where they are held captive, and repent [*w^e^shābû*] and make supplication to thee in the land of their captivity and say, "We have sinned and have acted perversely, we have been ungodly," and if they turn to thee [*weshābû ʾēlêkā*] with all their heart and soul in the land of their enemy, and pray to thee, in the direction of their land which thou didst give to their fathers, and towards the city which thou hast chosen, and towards the house which I have built for thy name, then hear thou in heaven their prayer and their supplication.

This passage has for two reasons extraordinary importance for our question about the actual kerygma of the DH. In the first place, it stands at a turning point–at the introduction to the third major phase of Israel's history. And second, in this passage explicitly Dtr shows his concern for the judgment now overtaking Israel, and he thereupon expressly takes up the question, what should Israel do in this hour? Martin Noth has properly pointed out [[93]] that, if the Deuteronomist had wanted to give rein to hope for any "dawning new future," it is precisely in this passage that he would have done it.[23] But on the other hand the DH does *not* say that this judgment, collapse and exile, cataclysmic as it is, is final, or that Israel can do nothing more than submit to it as just and hopeless. No, he says a third

23. Op. cit., 108.

thing, and leaves open the possibility of hope: the cry to Yahweh is once more necessary. The confession of guilt, and so, the acknowledgement of Yahweh's justice, belong to a returning with all one's heart and with all one's soul (v. 48). But the prayer does not only point backward to a history, the final ending of which is recognized as just. It is true that the emphasis is not on what follows, but it is nevertheless expected, without being expressed in definite hopes, that Israel will once more be heard, and find pity among the nations as "Yahweh's people and possession" (v. 51). The imperative at the moment is to turn back to Yahweh with all one's heart and all one's soul. This turning back, however, is regarded even here as a change to a new phase in the history of salvation.

V

There are yet two other passages within the DH where the question of what to do in the exile is raised. Both passages provide the same answer–return to Yahweh, your God!–and both appear within the Moses speeches in Deuteronomy. This may mean that the Deuteronomist wanted Israel to read his whole work from its beginning as a summons to return in the midst of judgment. But here we are faced with the difficult literary-critical question whether the two passages present us with Dtr's own formulations.

The first and more detailed passage, Deut 30:1–10, is considered by Martin Noth to belong to the older components of Deuteronomy. These he sees represented in 4:44–30:20. In his opinion, they should not be related too closely to the DH but were, rather, taken over by Dtr as a whole.[24]

Now Deut 30:1–10 presupposes at first sight the same situation in the exile as 1 Kgs 8:46ff. Here too, it is asked, what should be done now that the sentence of judgment has been carried out? And here too, it is answered with the catchword *shûb* 'return', which is repeated three times (vv. 2, 8, 10):

> [[94]] When someday all these words come upon you, the blessing and the curse which I have set before you, and you take it to heart among all the nations where Yahweh your God has expelled you, and you turn back [*w^eshabtā*] to Yahweh your God, and you listen to his voice according to all that I command you this day, [v. 3] then Yahweh, your God, will turn your fortunes around and have compassion upon you . . . [v. 7] and Yahweh will lay all the curses upon your persecutors. . . . [v. 8] But you shall turn back [*tāshûb*] and listen to the voice of Yahweh, and keep all his commandments which I am today giving you. . . . [v. 9] Yahweh will again

24. Op. cit., 16.

> take delight in you for your best, as he took delight in your fathers, if you listen to the word of Yahweh, your God, so that you keep his commandments and his statutes which are written in this book of instruction–if you [this is said once more as a summary at the conclusion under the main catch word] turn back [*tāshûb*] to Yahweh your God with all your heart and with all your soul.

Even a preliminary analysis shows that 30:1–10 with its formulations in the singular is to be attached to chap. 28 with its theme of blessing and curse (I omit chap. 29 because of its use of the plural). The introduction–"when all these words come upon thee"[25]–reaches back recognizably to the introductory words of blessing and curse in 28:2 ("When thou hearest . . . all these blessings shall come upon thee") and 28:15 ("when thou dost not hear . . . all of these curses will come upon thee"). Cf. also v. 45. More specifically, the promise of Yahweh's abundant gifts in 30:9a takes up the exact wording of 28:11a, and the statement about Yahweh's delight in Israel in 30:9b consciously refers back to 28:63. Neither of these statements is found in this formulation anywhere else in the DH, but the latter one is still to be seen in Jer 32:41. Deut 30:1–10, therefore, unquestionably presupposes chap. 28–all of it, even the exilic additions in 28:45ff.

In this connection, a comparison of the formulation, "listen to the voice of Yahweh, thy God, to keep his commandments and statutes" (30:10a) shows that 30:1–10 stands closer to the addition 28:45ff. (cf. 45b) than to the older text (cf. 28:1, 15). In addition, both 28:45ff. and 30:1–10 themselves presuppose the written ⟦95⟧ "book of this instruction" (compare 30:10 with 28:58, 61). For this reason the only question can be whether 30:1–10 was formulated at the same time as 28:45ff. or later.

Now 30:1–10 reveals some peculiar linguistic elements which occur neither in chap. 28 nor anywhere else in the DH but which, rather, are thoroughly characteristic of the Jeremiah traditions. Notice only the following: *ndḥ, hiphil* for 'dispersing' in v. 1 appears often in Jeremiah (16:15, 32:37, and 46:28 in the same connection as here); *shûb sh^{e}bût* (v. 3) in Jer 29:14; 30:3, 18 and elsewhere; *qbṣ, piel* in vv. 3–4 for the gathering of the dispersed in Jer 23:3, 29:14, 32:37; the circumcision of the heart in v. 6 in Jer 4:4b and 9:25–26; the "delight of Yahweh" in Jer 32:41 as well as Deut 28:63 and 30:9. Together with this last very typical expression there are still others which in the appendage to the curses (28:45ff.) recall the Jeremiah traditions. I mention as the most striking in 28:49 "the nation from afar whose language thou dost not understand" (= Jer 5:15), and in 28:53

25. Translator's note: I have used *thou, thee,* and *thy* in the explications whenever the Hebrew (and Wolff's German) indicates second person *singular*; the distinction from the plural is often significant.

the description of extreme distress when people consume the flesh of their sons and daughters (=Jer 19:9). Thus words of threat in 28:45ff. are taken over from the Jeremiah tradition, while 30:1–10 makes use of salvation words of the Jeremiah tradition. This indicates that 28:45ff. and 30:1–10 go back to the same author, who in these sections closely followed the Jeremiah traditions.

There are also in our Deuteronomy passage several close connections with the DH. The most impressive connection is with 1 Kgs 8:46ff., through the use of the rare expression 'to take something to heart' (*hēshîb ʾel-lēb* in Deut 30:1b and in 1 Kgs 8:47a; compare also *hākînû lᵉbabᵉkem ʾel yhwh* ⟦'direct your hearts to Yahweh'⟧ in 1 Sam 7:3). The expression which speaks of the "love for Yahweh for the sake of your life" (30:6b) is found in similar form in Josh 23:11, and the phrase about the "coming of the words" (30:1) in Josh 23:14. It is also especially instructive at this point to recall the frequent appearance of *shûb* at the climaxes of the DH. In this connection needs to compare the peculiar correspondence between man's return and Yahweh's return in 30:2f., 9f. and 2 Kgs 23:25f. Finally, mention should be made of the frequent references ⟦96⟧ to "this book of instruction" in 30:10 as well as in Josh 1:8, 23:6; 1 Kgs 2:3; 2 Kgs 17:37; 23:3, 24f., the last example being the most notable.

All in all, the language of Deut 30:1–10 (and 28:45ff.) shows clearer harmony with the Jeremiah traditions than with the later deuteronomistic elements, with the possible exception of 1 Kgs 8:46ff. We may maintain as our tentative results: (1) Deut 30:1–10 belongs in content and language with 28:45ff. (2) Both of the sections have been influenced by the Jeremiah traditions. (3) Both nevertheless have affinities with the language of the DH. (4) And both emphasize the theme "return" as the summons of the DH for his day.

Manifestly, the two passages did not belong to any earlier body of material; they are contemporary with the DH. The question is only, were these sections composed by the deuteronomistic historian? If so—and Martin Noth would have us believe so[26]—then we must assume that the historian enriched his picture of Moses by including Jeremiah traditions, and these inclusions account for the changes in language from the other

26. At this point one needs to take account of Jepsen's observations ⟦n. 3⟧ establishing a clear relationship between the Jeremiah traditions and his R II (equated with the DH op. cit., 100f.) for the books of Kings as well. Jepsen must count, for the books of Kings, too, on at least two deuteronomistic hands. His assignment of 1 Kgs 8:27–39 (except for 29αβ, 30, 36αβ) to a "priestly" redaction and of 1 Kgs 8:44–53 to a "nebiistic" redaction is noteworthy for our question. It is clear that both know the theme of a "return"; cf. pp. 15ff. and 80ff., also the summarizing sections in Jepsen, pp. 76 and 94. From this starting point the coalescence of Deuteronomy and the DH in Deuteronomy 28–30 should be examined anew!

speeches in the DH. Or should we, on the contrary, assume a *second* writer from the deuteronomistic circle, who carried the theme of the history work specifically back into Moses' time in order to insure that the entire work would be read and taken to heart in his own day?[27]

I am inclined toward the latter view. A parallel instance also suggests it. The two parts of Deut 4:25–31 are clearly by two different authors: vv. 25–28 employ the plural while vv. 29–31 use the singular. And, further, the second part (vv. 29–31) is clearly by the same author as 30:1–10 and 28:45ff. So if, as Noth suggests,[28] the first part is by the Deuteronomist, then the second part (as well as 30:1–10 and 28:45ff.) cannot be by him, but must be by someone else, who was trying to graft not only deuteronomistic kerygma but also Jeremiah traditions onto the older material of Deuteronomy. Let us consider this second part (4:29–31) and its authorship more closely:

> Then from there thou shalt seek Yahweh thy God and shalt find him, if thou askest for him with all thy heart and all thy soul. When thou art in trouble and all these words are [[97]] come upon thee in the last days, then thou wilt turn back [*wᵉshabtā*] to Yahweh thy God and listen to his voice. For Yahweh thy God is a merciful God. He will not abandon or destroy thee and will not forget the covenant which he promised by oath to thy fathers.

Thematically, of course, this passage flows directly from the one before it (vv. 25–28); but the use of the singular sets it clearly apart. On the other hand, in both matter and style it is absolutely uniform with 30:1–10. Verse 29 takes over words of the Jeremiah tradition (Jer 29:13); v. 30 recalls Hosea (3:5; 5:15); *shûb* is constructed only here (v. 30) and in 30:2 with *ʿad* (*yahweh*) [['to Yahweh']], otherwise never in the DH (30:10, as usual, has *ʾel* [['to']]. Here, too, the text speaks of the "fulfillment of all those words" (4:30; cf. 30:1). If 4:39 belongs to the same addition, then the reappearance there of the expression *hēshîb ʾel lēbab* ('take it to heart') is a significant recollection of 30:1 and 1 Kgs 8:47.

The close thematic and linguistic relationship between 4:29–31 and 30:1–10 suggests they are both part of one author's effort to mesh Deuteronomy with the DH. I concede, however, that this deutero-Deuteronomist, this second author, is still just a hypothesis. Final clarity can only be obtained by a new and urgently needed examination, on the basis of Deuteronomy 28–30 and Deuteronomy 4, of the literary interconnection of Deuteronomy and the DH.

27. Hans Wilhelm Hertzberg, *Die Bücher Josua, Richter, Ruth* (Göttingen: Vandenhoeck and Ruprecht, 1954) 8, like Jepsen, presupposes a "group of theologians."

28. Op. cit., 38f.

If the deutero-Deuteronomist hypothesis is correct, however, it means that more than just one writer in the deuteronomic circle found the call for a return to be the one of utmost moment for his own day. Indeed, the second writer found it so momentous that he proclaimed it twice over–before and after the incorporation of Deuteronomy–as the decisive and final word of Moses for the generation of the exiles. Thereby the reader was directed from the start to a proper understanding of the entire work. Much later that work would present King Solomon, in the prayer at the temple's dedication, as the great advocate of the return, and Josiah, the last model king, as the shining example of proper return.

VI

The question, how the return as proclaimed by the DH was to take place, can be discussed here only briefly. [[98]]

(1) It should occur as an unqualified turning to Yahweh in prayer. Judg 2:16, 3:9, 1 Sam 12:19; and 1 Kgs 8:47 reveal this most clearly. Included are a confession of guilt, a plea for deliverance, and a willingness to renew obedience.

(2) Such a return includes a "listening to the voice of Yahweh, your God, according to the instruction of Moses" and listening to the continued reminders of the prophets. The example of Josiah in 2 Kgs 23:25 and the summary of prophetic preaching in 2 Kgs 17:13 point to this. This means first of all the removal of foreign gods, as is shown especially in 1 Sam 7:3 and also in 2 Kgs 23:24. In Deut 4:30 and 30:2, 8, 10 "turning back" and "listening to the voice of Yahweh" have become an indissoluble combination.

(3) The non-cultic character of the return is noteworthy. The passionate concern for warding off the foreign cults shows no corresponding positive interest in carrying out certain Yahweh rituals. This is especially true of the Jerusalem temple. In all essentials it is only a place of prayer, and nearness to it is never required–in the exile it is enough to turn in its direction.[29] The DH has in mind essentially a service of prayer, wherein everything depends on a turning to Yahweh's voice itself as it became known through Moses and the prophets.

(4) It is especially the second writer from the deuteronomistic circle, recognizable in Deut 4:29–31 and 30:1–10, who clearly demonstrates that the DH considers the return to be less a human deed and more a psychological event, promised by Yahweh, that will follow after his judgment upon them. The return is thus promised in 4:29f. for the time of affliction,

29. Compare M. Noth, op. cit., 104f.

in close parallel with Hosea's and Jeremiah's words of promise.[30] In 30:8 too, the return is plainly part of the promise. The presupposition in 4:30f. as in 30:2f. is Yahweh's watchful compassion—he, for his part, will never forget the covenant affirmed by oath with the fathers (4:31). To be sure, since the time is close when Yahweh's compassion will break through, 30:1f. and 10 put more emphasis on the conditional character of the return; but it is nevertheless maintained that "Yahweh *will* circumcise the heart" (v. 6). Thus the return in 4:30, as well as in the corresponding redaction in Hos 3:5, constitutes [[99]] in fact the eschatological salvation "at the end of the days."[31]

Because of this stress on Yahweh's agency, the deuteronomistic preaching lacks the character of legalistic urging. The deuteronomistic historians educate their contemporaries towards the expected return by their tremendous and most patiently developed picture of salvation history—an ongoing history, of which the present generation is the living part. To return, to turn back to the covenant with the fathers which Yahweh still has not forgotten is all that remains for Israel to do. In the time of affliction it offers the only possibility for salvation.

Thus the work serves as an urgent invitation to a return to the God of salvation history. This third kerygma in the Old Testament writings grows out of the "emotion of praise and of remorse" in terms of which Israel otherwise spoke of her history.[32]

VII

In all of this one cannot say that Dtr combined his idea of return with any *specific* hope. Considering his open-ended view of history, concretes and predictables would be absurd. As in the days of the judges and the kings one should, rather, count on completely new arrangements by Yahweh. Only Deut 30:4 [30:5] speaks of a return to the land; 1 Kgs 8:49f. confines itself to a prayer for justice and mercy for the people of God among the foreign nations. The humility associated with the return stands in the way of any specific hopes. 1 Kings 8 speaks just as little of a new king as it does of a return home. The king has come under judgment along with Israel and her national state. When Jehoiachin is allowed to take off his prison garments this means little more than that God is still acting for his people. Thus the DH has recorded this event out of respect for the facts. He does

30. Compare Hos 2:9, 3:5, 5:15; Jer 3:1, 22–4:2; on this see H. W. Wolff, *Hosea* (Neukirchen: Verlag der Buchhandlung des Erziehungsvereins, 1961) 43, 79f., and H. W. Wolff, "Das Thema 'Umkehr' in der alttestamentlichen Prophetie," *ZTK* 48 (1951) 138ff.

31. Cf. Wolff, *Hosea*, 79.

32. G. von Rad, op. cit., 114; Engl. translation, 108.

not, however, attach any messianic hopes to it. Messianic hopes are perhaps what Jeremiah's opponents, such as Hananiah saw in the event: they had been waiting so long for the king's return that their hopes had become delirious.[33] As a disciple of Jeremiah the deuteronomistic historian is much more reserved.

Perhaps one of the wholly new arrangements is to be the office of witness which the people of God will occupy in the midst of the nations, just as Jehoiachin remains in a distant land, eating at the [[100]] royal table as long as he lives, enjoying a strange preeminence above the other kings (2 Kgs 25:28–29). The ruined temple will in any case become a witness for the God of Israel among the nations (1 Kgs 9:8–9). Whoever prays there will, according to Solomon's intercession, be heard, even if he is a foreigner from a far country, "in order that all the nations may know thy name" (1 Kgs 8:41–43). These new arrangements, however, are hidden and cannot be fitted at all into a program of hope.

By contrast, Israel must expect, even when she turns back, to remain in affliction for "many days." The Deuteronomist points to such a possibility at the very beginning of his work in his picture of the generation of Moses (Deut 1:45–46). The return cannot be thought of as a ticket to restoration or betterment.

Deut 29:28 [29:29] expresses this with great clarity:[34]

> That which is still hidden [i.e., in the future] belongs to Yahweh; but that which has been revealed [i.e., the past] concerns us and our children forever, that we may carry out all the words of his instruction.

This revealed word now contains the summons to return (in the text of Deuteronomy that summons follows immediately). To return means that Israel will listen with her whole heart to the voice of her God alone and expect every good from him alone in order that she may become God's agent in the midst of all nations. This is, if I understand it correctly, the peculiar interest of this first comprehensive history not only of the Old Testament but of world literature.

33. Jer 28:4. Cf. M. Noth, "Die Katastrophe von Jerusalem im Jahre 587 v. Chr. und ihre Bedeutung für Israel," *RHPhR* (1953) 82–102 = *Gesammelte Studien zum Alten Testament*, 2.346–71; English translation by D. R. Ap-Thomas, "The Jerusalem Catastrophe of 587 B.C. and Its Significance for Israel," in *The Laws in the Pentateuch and Other Studies* (Philadelphia: Fortress Press, 1967) 267.

34. E. Janssen, op. cit., 74, has characterized the word *return* as a hermeneutic rule of the deuteronomic school. Janssen shows on the basis of the passage in Judg 10:6–16 that the DH holds out hope for Israel only by way of a return.

The Themes of the Book of Kings and the Structure of the Deuteronomistic History

Frank Moore Cross

In this essay, Cross bases his argument for separating preexilic and exilic layers of the Deuteronomistic History on a thematic analysis of Kings. He traces two major themes running through Kings: "the sin of Jeroboam," which reverberates throughout the narration of the Northern Kingdom, and the promises to David, which restrain divine wrath in the history of Judah. Successive Northern kings perpetuate Jeroboam's sin to the great detriment of Israel. Forming a stark contrast with the first theme are the promises to David first articulated in 2 Sam 7:1–16 and repeated often in Kings. Whereas Jeroboam stands out as the symbol of infidelity, David stands out as the symbol of faithfulness to the deity. The second theme finds its climax in Josiah, the successor to David (2 Kgs 22:2). Josiah tries to restore the kingdom of David to its former glory, centralizes the cultus in accordance with deuteronomic law, and ensures that a national Passover is celebrated. The juxtaposition of these two themes—the sin of Jeroboam and the promises to David—forms the basis of the Josianic reform. In this reconstruction, the first edition of the Deuteronomistic History was produced during Josiah's reign as a programmatic document acclaiming his revival of the Davidic state.

Cross posits a second much less extensive edition of the Deuteronomistic History stemming from the period of the exile, Dtr^2. This exilic editor retouched the earlier work, laconically recorded the destruction of Jerusalem, and brought the history up to date. Dtr^2 blamed the destruction of Judah on King Manasseh's apostasy. 2 Kgs 23:25b–25:30 are the work of this much more pessimistic exilic editor.

Reprinted with permission from Frank Moore Cross, *Canaanite Myth and Hebrew Epic: Essays in the History of the Religion of Israel* (Cambridge: Harvard University Press, 1973) 274–89.

The Contemporary Discussion of the Structure of the Deuteronomistic History

[[274]] The contemporary discussion of the structure of the Deuteronomistic[1] History was initiated by the brilliant essay of Martin Noth, *Überlieferungsgeschichtliche Studien.*[2] Noth radically revised literary-critical views which asserted that the books of the Former Prophets, namely Joshua, Judges, Samuel, and Kings, grew into their present shape out of sources combined in a series of redactions. He viewed the whole, Joshua through Kings, as a single historical work, created by a highly original author during the Exile, about 550 B.C. Diverse sources, sometimes rewritten in the peculiar deuteronomistic rhetoric, sometimes not, were selected and informed by a framework into a unity expressing the theological and historical slant of the editor. An older form of Deuteronomy, supplied with a new deuteronomistic introduction and conclusion,[3] was prefixed to the historical work paper, together forming a great deuteronomistic block of tradition. This work stands over against the Tetrateuch, Genesis through Numbers, or what is more appropriately called the Priestly work.[4]

The framework of the Deuteronomistic History is marked in particular by speeches in pure deuteronomistic style patterned after Deuteronomy, the whole of which is cast as the last speech of Moses to Israel. These passages include the speeches of Joshua (Josh 1:11–15; and 23), the address of Samuel (1 Sam 12:1–24), and the prayer of Solomon (1 Kgs 8:12–51). [[275]] Oddly, Noth ignores the oracle of Nathan and the Prayer of David (2 Sam 7:1–16 and 7:18–29) which surely belong to this series.[5]

1. In M. Noth's usage "deuteronomistic" (Dtr) identifies the hand of the exilic author of the great work Joshua–Kings and the framework of Deuteronomy. Deuteronomic (Dt) is reserved for the old core of the book of Deuteronomy (Dtn), that is, the legal code and its immediate, framing passages. In our discussion, the above sigla are modified only by the use of Dtr^1 to designate the seventh-century author of the Deuteronomistic History, Dtr^2 to apply to the exilic editor of the work. This involves a change in the terminology used in my lecture underlying the present essay published under the title, "The Structure of the Deuteronomic [*sic!*] History," *Perspectives in Jewish Learning,* Annual of the College of Jewish Studies 3 (Chicago, 1968) 9–24.

2. The essay, hereafter designated *ÜGS* was first published in 1943; the second (unchanged) edition in Tübingen, 1957.

3. Deut 1:1–4:43 and 31:1–32:44 (excepting secondary material). Deut 33:1–34:12 was later added to Dtn, taken from the end of the Priestly Work (Genesis–Numbers).

4. See F. M. Cross, "The Priestly Tabernacle," *BAR* 1, 216–17: and chap. 11 in *Canaanite Myth.*

5. See chap. 9 [[in *Canaanite Myth*]] and D. J. McCarthy, "II Samuel 7 and the Structure of the Deuteronomic History," *JBL* 84 (1965) 131–38.

Other major deuteronomistic summaries include Judg 2:11–22, and especially 2 Kgs 17:7–18, 20–23, the deuteronomistic peroration on the fall of Samaria.

The theme running through the framework of the deuteronomistic history, according to Noth, is a proclamation of unrelieved and irreversible doom. The story of Israel is a story of apostasy and idolatry. The inevitable result has been the visitation of God's judgment and the curses of the covenant: death, disease, captivity, destruction. In the era of the kings, the violation of the law of the central sanctuary comes to the fore. In the sin of Jeroboam (northern) Israel earned God's rejection, and in Manasseh's grave apostasy Judah was damned to irrevocable destruction. The deuteronomistic author, according to Noth, thus addressed his work to the exiles. His theology of history, revealed in the framework of his great work, justified God's wrath and explained the exiles' plight.

Older literary critics, as well as their more recent followers, argued for two editions of the deuteronomistic complex of traditions, one preexilic, the basic promulgation of the Deuteronomistic History, and one exilic, retouching the earlier edition to bring it up to date. We need not review here the variety of views nor their specific arguments.[6] Some of their arguments are very strong, for example, the use of the expression "to this day," not merely in the sources but also in portions by the deuteronomistic author, which presumes the existence of the Judaean state, notably 2 Kgs 8:22 and 16:6.[7] The increase in epigraphic material of the late seventh and early sixth century, including the extraordinary series from Tel ʿArad, has made clear that the complex syntactical style of the Deuteronomist (if not his peculiar archaizing forms) [[276]] characterized late preexilic prose.[8] It has been argued also that the availability of sources to the deuteronomistic editor requires a preexilic date.[9] Nevertheless, from our point of view, the strongest arguments for the preexilic date of the basic promulgation of the Deuteronomistic History have not yet entered

6. The "orthodox" literary-critical viewpoint was framed by Kuenen and Wellhausen, in particular, and survives in such recent works as R. H. Pfeiffer, *Introduction to the Old Testament* (New York: Harper and Brothers, 1941) 277ff.; and John Gray, *I & II Kings. A Commentary* (London: SCM Press, 1963) 13ff. Cf. O. Eissfeldt, *Einleitung in das Alte Testament*, 3rd ed. (Tübingen: Mohr, 1964) 321–30; 376–404. A Jepsen, *Die Quellen des Königsbuches*, 2nd ed. (Halle: Niemayer, 1956), while assuming two primary redactors in his complex analysis, is in basic agreement with M. Noth (though independent). He holds that the exilic "prophetic" redactor gave to an earlier "priestly" history of the two kingdoms its essential framework and deuteronomistic stamp.

7. Cf. 1 Kgs 8:8; 9:21; 10:12; 12:19; 2 Kgs 10:27; 14:7; 17:23.

8. It goes without saying that it persisted into the early exilic age, or at least was imitated accurately in the later period.

9. See W. F. Albright, *The Biblical Period* (Pittsburgh, 1950) 45–46 and n. 108.

into the discussion (see below). Yet the view of M. Noth has increasingly gained sway, especially in German circles, and much recent writing presumes his basic position as the foundation for further research.

Two important recent studies have attempted to bring modification to Noth's view of the essential purpose and teaching of the Deuteronomist. Gerhard von Rad in his *Studies in Deuteronomy* took up again the question of the deuteronomistic theology of history in the Book of Kings.[10] Von Rad was anxious to emphasize not only the motifs of lawsuit and judgment which follow upon the breach of covenant law (as stressed almost exclusively by Noth), but also to develop a counter-theme in the deuteronomistic presentation of the history of the kingdom, that is, the theme of grace, God's promise to David which was eternal and hence the ground of hope. In the oracle of Nathan to David, and its persistent reiteration in later Judaean reigns, von Rad found a major deuteronomistic theme. Moreover, it appears that the Deuteronomist never really repudiated this promise.[11] In 2 Sam 7:13–16, Yahweh addressed David concerning his seed, "and I will establish the throne of his kingship forever. I will become his father and he my son; whenever he commits iniquity I will discipline him with the rod of men and the stripes of the children of men, but my faithfulness I will not turn aside from him . . . your dynasty shall be firm and your kingship forever before ⟨me⟩: your throne shall be established forever." Von Rad speaks of this repeated theme as proving that in the day of the Deuteronomist[12] there remained a cycle of "messianic conceptions," a hope that the [[277]] Davidic house would be reestablished after the Exile. The final notice in 2 Kgs 25:27–30, recording the release of Jehoiachin, was taken by von Rad as having a special theological significance, alluding to the hope of salvation in the Davidic dynasty.

We must confess that Noth has the better of the argument when it comes to the interpretation of 2 Kgs 25:27–30.[13] That Jehoiachin was released from prison and lived off the bounty of the Babylonian crown—still in exile for the remainder of his days—is a thin thread upon which to hang the expectation of the fulfillment of the promises to David. Yet von Rad has singled out a theme, the promise to the house of David, which must

10. Gerhard von Rad, *Studies in Deuteronomy. SBT* 9 (London, 1953) 74–79. Cf. his *Old Testament Theology* (New York: Harper, 1962) 1.334–47.

11. In certain passages, 1 Kgs 9:6–9, for example, the eternal decree of kingship is followed by a specific reference to the Exile and the destruction of the temple. With Kuenen and most earlier commentators we should regard the passage as secondary, in direct conflict with 2 Sam 7:18–29 and the deuteronomistic theme to be discussed below. Cf. 2 Kgs 20:17–18, an obvious addition.

12. That is, in the Exile, of course, von Rad follows Noth fully in his dating of the Deuteronomist.

13. Noth, *ÜGS*, 108.

be dealt with systematically; the neglect of this theme is a serious failure in Noth's study.

H. W. Wolff recently has taken up again the Deuteronomist's future hope or, as he puts it, the Deuteronomist's *kērygma.*[14] He finds Noth's analysis of the Deuteronomist's doctrine of history defective in its portrayal of the end of Israel as a monochromatic picture of unmitigated judgment. He cannot conceive of the Deuteronomist taking up the tedious task of composing a great theology of history as a labor devised and designed to teach only the message that the disaster of Israel is final. At the same time Wolff rejects von Rad's position, noting the qualification of the eternal decree of Davidic kingship in 1 Kgs 9:6–9, 2 Kgs 24:2, and so on.[15] Wolff seeks a note of grace, a modest future hope in certain deuteronomistic passages which call for repentance and which promise that when Israel cries out to God and repudiates her apostate ways he will repent of his evil and listen to their prayers.[16] Nothing is said of the restoration of the house of David. The only clear hope is that the Lord will restore a repentant people to his covenant.

⟦278⟧ Wolff correctly discerns a theme of hope which comes from the hand of a deuteronomistic editor in the Exile (our Dtr^{2}), especially in Deut 4:25–31 and 30:1–20 (framing the old Deuteronomic work), and in the addition to Solomon's prayer in 1 Kgs 8:46–53. One may question, however, whether the alternating pattern of grace and judgment in the deuteronomistic notices of the era of the Judges had as its original setting the exilic situation. It is easier to understand it as exhortation to reform with the hope of national salvation.[17] Here one listens with sympathy to von Rad's plaintive comment that "it is difficult to think that the editing of the Book of Judges and that of the Book of Kings could have taken place as a single piece of work."[18] At all events, Wolff has not given an adequate

14. H. W. Wolff, "Das Kerygma das deuteronomistischen Geschichtswerkes," *ZAW* 73 (1961) 171–86. Incidentally, the importation of the term *kērygma* into the form criticism of the Hebrew Bible is to be deplored as an inelegant and presumptuous anachronism.

15. On the former passage, see above, n. 11. The cycle of passages attributing the fall of the Davidic house to the sin of Manasseh belong to a special exilic group and will be dealt with below.

16. The chief passages are Judg 2:18; 1 Sam 12:1–24; and (dealing with repentance) 1 Sam 7:3; 1 Kgs 8:33, 35; 2 Kgs 17:13; 23:25. A series more explicitly related to exile or captivity is 1 Kgs 8:46–53; Deut 4:25–31; 30:1–10 (the latter two form a later hand than the Deuteronomist proper in Wolff's view: i.e., they are secondary to the Exilic */sic!/* work). See Wolff, "Das Kerygma," 180ff.; Noth, *ÜGS*, 17, 109. Only Deut 30:4 speaks explicitly of a return from Exile.

17. See further below. Note that 1 Sam 12:25 is to be taken as a secondary addition (Dtr^{2}).

18. G. von Rad, *Old Testament Theology*, 1.347.

explanation of the persistent, and in many ways major, theme of the book of Kings: the promises to David. If von Rad's handling of this theme is unconvincing, we are not thereby justified in ignoring it. The persistence of the deuteronomistic stress upon the eternal decree of Davidic kingship cannot be explained as a survival of royal ideology taken over mechanically from monarchist sources. It *must* be pertinent to the deuteronomistic theology of history.

We are left unsatisfied by each of these attempts to analyze the themes of the Deuteronomistic History, especially in their treatment of Kings. Each seems too simple, incapable of handling the complexity of the theological lore in the great collection. In short, it appears that these fresh attempts to examine the history of the deuteronomistic tradition, while casting much light on the deuteronomistic corpus, leave many embarrassing contradictions and unsolved problems.

The Two Themes of the First Edition of the Deuteronomistic History (Dtr¹)

We desire first to analyze the latter part of the Deuteronomistic History, especially the Book of Kings. Here we should find the climactic section of the history. As the historian draws closer to his own times, we expect him to express his intent most clearly both in specifically theological or parenetic sections which would constitute his framework and the shaping of special themes which unify his work.[19]

There are indeed two grand themes or bundles of themes running [[279]] through the Book of Kings. In combination these themes must stem from a very specific setting having a specific social function. We shall argue that they belong properly to a Josianic edition of the Deuteronomistic History.

(1) One theme is summed up in the following saying:

> This thing became the sin of the house of Jeroboam to crush (it) and to destroy (it) from the face of the earth.[20]

The crucial event in the history of the Northern Kingdom was the sin of Jeroboam.

Earlier, Ahijah of the prophetic circle of Shiloh had prophesied that, if Jeroboam acted faithfully as did David, he would be given a sure house. This promise was not an eternal decree after the pattern of the oracle of Nathan to David. Ahijah added the qualification that while the seed of

19. Cf. G. von Rad, *Studies in Deuteronomy*, 75 and n. 2.

20. 1 Kgs 13:34 (reading *hdbr* with LXX, Syr, et al.).

David would be chastised for a season, God would not afflict Judah forever.[21] In this statement we must understand that the oracle presumes an ultimate reunion of the two kingdoms under a Davidid. In 1 Kgs 12:26–33, we read a strongly deuteronomistic description of Jeroboam's arch-crime, namely the establishment of a countercultus in Bethel and Dan. The account assumes that Jeroboam's motivation is fear that traditions of the central sanctuary which David brought together and focused upon Zion would ultimately lure his people back to the Davidic house even as the national shrine of Jerusalem attracted them in the time of the pilgrimage feasts. Hence, he established new shrines at ancient holy places of the north, introducing an idolatrous iconography and a syncretistic cult.[22] An account of the prophecy of "a man of God and of Judah," otherwise unidentified, follows. The prophet is made to give utterance to one of the most astonishing as well as rare instances of a *vaticinium post eventum* ⟦'prophecy after the event'⟧ found in the Bible, obviously shaped by an overenthusiastic editor's hand: "He cried against the altar [of Bethel] . . . 'Altar, Altar, thus saith Yahweh: behold a son will be born to the house of David, Josiah by name, and he will sacrifice upon you the priests of the high places who burn incense on you, and human bones ⟦280⟧ ⟨he⟩ will burn upon you' " (1 Kgs 13:2–5). The reform of Josiah is here anticipated, preparing the reader's mind for the coming climax.

Ahijah of Shiloh also proclaimed an oracle which would be repeated almost verbatim, like a refrain, pointing forward to the crescendo of this theme in Kings, the fall of the North.

> Thus saith Yahweh, God of Israel: "Because I exalted you from the midst of the people and made you commander (*nāgîd*) over my people Israel, tearing the kingdom from the house of David to give it to you, yet you have not been like my servant David . . . but have done evil . . . casting me behind your back, therefore I will bring evil on the house of Jeroboam and will cut off from Jeroboam every male, whatever his status, and I shall consume the house of Jeroboam, as one burns up dung and it is gone. He of (the house of) Jeroboam who dies in the city the dogs shall devour, and he who dies in the field the birds of the heaven shall eat." (1 Kgs 14:7–11)

The grisly fulfillment of Ahijah's prophecy is carefully noted in 1 Kgs 15:29.[23] "Jehu the son of Hanani proclaimed against Baasha, '. . . behold I

21. 1 Kgs 11:29–39, esp. v. 39.

22. We are not concerned here with reconstructing the actual, historical character of the cultus of Jeroboam. We have argued (chap. 3 ⟦in *Canaanite Myth*⟧) that, in choosing Bethel and in reverting to a bull iconography (in place of the cherubim of Jerusalem and earlier of Shiloh), he actually was attempting to "out-archaize" Jerusalem.

23. Cf. 2 Kgs 17:7–23.

will consume Baasha and his house and I will make his house to be like the house of Jeroboam son of Nebat. He (of the house) of Baasha who dies in the city the dogs shall devour, and his dead in the field the birds of the heaven shall eat'" (1 Kgs 16:1–4).

Against each king of Israel in turn the judgment comes, "[he] did evil in the eyes of Yahweh, doing evil above all who were before him, and he walked in the way of Jeroboam."

Elijah the Tishbite prophesied against Ahab:

> Thus saith Yahweh, "Have you murdered and also taken possession? . . . in the place where the dogs lapped the blood of Naboth, the dogs will lap your blood, even you . . . Behold I will bring on you evil and I will consume you and cut off from Ahab every male, whatever his status, in Israel, and I will make your house like the house of Jeroboam the son of Nebat and like the house of Baasha . . . and also concerning Jezebel Yahweh has spoken, saying, the dogs shall eat Jezebel in the plo⟨t⟩ of Jezreel. He (of the house) of Ahab who dies in the city the dogs shall devour, and he who dies in the field the birds of the heaven shall eat."[24]

⟦281⟧ The word of Yahweh was in part delayed (1 Kgs 21:29), in part fulfilled in Ahab's death (1 Kgs 22:37f.) and in Ahaziah's death. The prophecy was roundly fulfilled in the revolution of Jehu in which the king (Ahab's son Joram) together with the "seventy sons of Ahab" and Jezebel the queen mother were slaughtered in Jezreel and in Samaria (2 Kgs 9:1–10:11).

Elijah's prophecy against the house of Ahab no doubt goes back to an old poetic oracle. The earlier oracles, in wording at least, were shaped to it by the Deuteronomist so that a refrain-like rhythm is given to the theme of prophetic decree and fulfillment.

The string of oracles and judgments which make up this theme in Kings is completed in the great peroration in the fall of Samaria in 2 Kgs 17:1–23. Here the Deuteronomist reached the first great climax of the last section of his work and rang the changes on his theme of Jeroboam's sin and Israel's judgment.

> And Yahweh rejected the entire seed of Israel and afflicted them and gave them into the hands of spoilers until he had cast them out from his presence. For he tore Israel from the house of David and they made Jeroboam, the son of Nebat, king, and Jeroboam enticed Israel away from Yahweh and caused them to sin a great sin. The children of Israel walked in all the sins of Jeroboam which he did; they did not turn aside from it

24. 1 Kgs 21:17–29. Cf. also the prophecies of 1 Kgs 20:42f.: Micaiah in 1 Kgs 22:8–28; and of Elijah in 2 Kgs 1:2–17.

> until Yahweh turned Israel aside from his presence, as he had spoken through all his servants the prophets, and Israel was taken captive from off their land to Assyria until this day. (2 Kgs 17:20–23)

The lawsuit of Yahweh is complete. The verdict is rendered. The curses of the covenant are effected. In Jeroboam's monstrous sin, Israel's doom was sealed.

(2) The second theme we wish to analyze begins in 2 Samuel 7 and runs through the book of Kings. It may be tersely put in the refrain-like phrase:

> for the sake of David my servant and for the sake of Jerusalem which I have chosen.[25]

An alloform is the expression "so that David my servant will have a fief always before me in Jerusalem, the city I have chosen for myself to [[282]] put my name there."[26] The crucial event in Judah, comparable to the sin of Jeroboam was the faithfulness of David. Through much of Kings this theme of grace and hope parallels the dark theme of judgment. David established Yahweh's sanctuary in Jerusalem, an eternal shrine on chosen Zion; Jeroboam established the rival shrine of Bethel, a cultus abhorrent to Yahweh, bringing eternal condemnation. David in Kings is the symbol of fidelity, Jeroboam the symbol of infidelity. In view of the antimonarchical elements surviving in Deuteronomic (Dt) tradition, notably in the law of the king (Deut 17:14–20), and in certain sources in the books of Judges and Samuel, it is remarkable to discover that the Deuteronomist in 2 Samuel 7 and in Kings shares in unqualified form the ideology of the Judaean monarchy.[27]

We have discussed at some length in the last chapter the deuteronomistic character of both the so-called oracle of Nathan in 2 Sam 7:11b–16 and the prayer of David in 2 Sam 7:18–29. In promising an eternal throne to the Davidic dynasty the Deuteronomist appears to take up specific elements of the royal liturgy also found reflected in Ps 89:20–38.[28] The prayer of David, framed in wholly deuteronomistic language, echoes similar hopes and expectations for the permanence of the Davidic house.[29]

In 1 Kings 11 the Deuteronomist condemned Solomon for his apostasy and idolatry. The ten tribes were "torn away" from the Judaean king

25. 1 Kgs 11:12, 13, 32, 34, 36; 15:4; 2 Kgs 8:19; 19:34 (quoting Isa 37:35); 20:6.

26. 1 Kgs 11:36; 15:4; 2 Kgs 8:19; 2 Chr 21:7.

27. See chap. 9 [[of *Canaanite Myth*]]. Cf. G. von Rad, *Studies in Deuteronomy*, 89; *Old Testament Theology*, 1.344ff.

28. See chap. 9 [[of *Canaanite Myth*]] for a translation of this text.

29. See chap. 9 [[of *Canaanite Myth*]].

and given to Jeroboam. Solomon thus "did evil in the sight of Yahweh" and went not fully after Yahweh as did David his father. Yet even in the context of Solomon's sin we find the following formula: "Yet in your days I shall not do it [that is, rend away the northern tribes], for the sake of David your father" (1 Kgs 11:12–13). Again, it is said of Solomon by Ahijah:

> But I shall not take the whole kingdom from his hand for I will make him a prince (*nāśîʾ*) all the days of his life for the sake of David my servant whom I have chosen, who has kept my commandments and statutes . . . to his son I will give one tribe in order that there may be a fief for David my servant always before me in Jerusalem the city which I have chosen for myself, to place my name [[283]] there. (1 Kgs 11:34–36)

Even in the context of Ahijah's prophecy of the division of the kingdom, however, we find the striking promise, "And I will afflict the seed of David on this account yet not always."[30]

The refrain persists. Of Abijah we read: "but his heart was not perfect with Yahweh his god as the heart of David his father. Yet for the sake of David Yahweh his god gave him a fief in Jerusalem in setting up his son after him and in establishing Jerusalem because David did that which was right in the eyes of Yahweh" (1 Kgs 15:3–5a).

Jehoram of Judah "walked in the ways of the kings of Israel . . . and did that which was evil in the eyes of Yahweh. But Yahweh was unwilling to destroy Judah for the sake of David his servant as he promised him to give him a fief for his sons always" (2 Kgs 8:18–19).

Interwoven with these repeated formulae is another element belonging to this theme. While the kings of Israel were always condemned, each having done "that which was evil in the eyes of Yahweh," judgment does not come automatically upon the kings of Judah. Certain kings, Asa, Jehoshaphat, Joash, Hezekiah, and above all Josiah "did that which was right in the eyes of Yahweh, as did David his father." Even King David and Hezekiah had peccadilloes. Josiah alone escaped all criticism. Josiah "did that which was right in the eyes of Yahweh and walked in all the ways of David his father and did not turn aside to the right or to the left" (2 Kgs 22:2). "And like him there was no king before him turning to Yahweh with his whole mind and soul and strength according to all the law of Moses" (2 Kgs 23:25a).

The second theme reaches its climax in the reform of Josiah, 2 Kgs 22:1–23:25. We have been prepared for this climax. Josiah, as already predicted, becomes the protagonist of the drama, extirpating the counter-

30. See above, n. 21.

cultus of Jeroboam at Bethel. He attempted to restore the kingdom or empire of David in all detail. The cultus was centralized according to the ancient law of the sanctuary, and Passover was celebrated as it had not been "since the days of the Judges." The story of the renewal of the covenant and the resurrection of the Davidic empire by the reincorporation of the North is told at a length not given to the labors of other approved kings after David.

[[284]] The deuteronomistic historian thus contrasted two themes, the sin of Jeroboam and the faithfulness of David and Josiah. Jeroboam led Israel into idolatry and ultimate destruction as all the prophets had warned. In Josiah who cleansed the sanctuary founded by David and brought a final end to the shrine founded by Jeroboam, in Josiah who sought Yahweh with all his heart, the promises to David were to be fulfilled. Punishment and salvation had indeed alternated in the history of Judah . . . as in the era of the Judges. Yahweh has afflicted Judah, but will not forever.

The two themes in the deuteronomistic book of Kings appear to reflect two theological stances, one stemming from the old Deuteronomic covenant theology which regarded destruction of dynasty and people as tied necessarily to apostasy, and a second, drawn from the royal ideology in Judah: the eternal promises to David. In the second instance, while chastisement has regularly come upon Judah in her seasons of apostasy, hope remains in the Davidic house to which Yahweh has sworn fidelity for David's sake, and for Jerusalem, the city of God. A righteous scion of David has sprung from Judah.

In fact, the juxtaposition of the two themes, of threat and promise, provide the platform of the Josianic reform. The Deuteronomistic History, insofar as these themes reflect its central concerns, may be described as a propaganda work of the Josianic reformation and imperial program. In particular, the document speaks to the North, calling Israel to return to Judah and to Yahweh's sole legitimate shrine in Jerusalem, asserting the claims of the ancient Davidic monarchy upon all Israel. Even the destruction of Bethel and the cults of the high places was predicted by the prophets, pointing to the centrality of Josiah's role for northern Israel. It speaks equally or more emphatically to Judah. Its restoration to ancient grandeur depends on the return of the nation to the covenant of Yahweh and on the wholehearted return of her king to the ways of David, the servant of Yahweh. In Josiah is centered the hope of a new Israel and the renewing of the "sure mercies" shown to David.[31] Judah's idolatry has been its undoing again and again in the past. The days of the Judges, of Samuel and

31. Cf. Isa 55:3; 2 Chr 6:42.

Saul reveal a pattern of alternating judgment and deliverance. But in David and in his son Josiah is salvation.

Before the pericope on Manasseh there is no hint in the Deuteronomistic History that hope in the Davidic house and in ultimate national [[285]] salvation is futile. The very persistence of this theme of hope in the promises to David and his house is proof that it was relevant to the original audience or readership of the deuteronomistic historian. It is not enough that the faithfulness of God and Jerusalem merely delay the end, postpone disaster. The historian has combined his motifs of the old covenant forms of the league and of the north, with those taken from the royal theology of the Davidids to create a complex and eloquent program, or rather, one may say, he has written a great sermon to rally Israel to the new possibility of salvation, through obedience to the ancient covenant of Yahweh, and hope in the new David, King Josiah.

The Theme of the Exilic Edition of the History (Dtr[2])

There is to be found in the Deuteronomistic History a subtheme which we have suppressed until now in the interest of clarifying the major motifs of the Josianic edition of Kings. We should attribute this subtheme to the exilic editor (Dtr[2]) who retouched or overwrote the deuteronomistic work to bring it up to date in the Exile, to record the fall of Jerusalem, and to reshape the history, with a minimum of reworking, into a document relevant to exiles for whom the bright expectations of the Josianic era were hopelessly past.

This subtheme is found articulated most clearly in the pericope dealing with Manasseh and the significance of his sins of syncretism and idolatry, in 2 Kgs 21:2–15. The section is modeled almost exactly on the section treating the fall of Samaria.

> He [Manasseh] set up the image of Asherah which he had made in the house of which Yahweh had said to David and to his son Solomon, "In this house and in Jerusalem which I chose of all the tribes of Israel, I will set my name forever, nor will I again cause Israel's foot to wander from the land which I have given to their fathers, only if they be careful to do according to all which I commanded them and to all the law which my servant Moses commanded them." But they did not listen, and Manasseh led them astray so that they did more evil than the nations which Yahweh destroyed before the children of Israel. And Yahweh spoke by his servants the prophets saying, because Manasseh the king of Judah has done these abominations . . . and caused Israel to sin with his idols, therefore, thus saith Yahweh, god of Israel, "Behold I shall bring such evil on Jerusalem and on Judah that the two ears of whoever hears of it shall tingle.

> And I will extend over Jerusalem the cord of Samaria and the plummet [[286]] of Ahab's house, and I will wipe out Jerusalem as one wipes out a dish, wiping it and turning it upside down. I shall cast off the remnant of my possession and I will give them into the hand of their enemies, and they shall become spoil and prey for looting to all their enemies." (2 Kgs 21:7–14)

One is struck by the weakness of the phrase, "Yahweh spoke by his servants the prophets, saying. . . ." No specific prophet is named by name. Moreover, no prophecies concerning Manasseh's great sin, and the inevitable rejection it entailed, are to be found in the earlier parts of the Deuteronomistic History. Not one.[32] On the contrary, the hopes of the reader have been steadily titillated by the promises. Everything has pointed to a future salvation in virtue of the fidelity of Yahweh to the Davidic house and to Josiah, who called for a wholehearted return to the god of Israel's covenant. Moreover, we are driven to ask, why is the culprit not Solomon or even Rehoboam? In short, there are a number of reasons to suppose that the attribution of Judah's demise to the unforgivable sins of Manasseh is tacked on and not integral to the original structure of the history.

The same must be said for the content of the prophecy of Hulda which speaks of the delay of disaster owing to Josiah's piety and penitence.[33]

Attached to the end of the account of Josiah's reforms we find the following significant addition:

> and after [Josiah] none like him arose. Yet Yahweh did not turn back from the heat of his great wrath which was kindled against Judah on account of all the vexations with which Manasseh vexed him. And Yahweh said, "Also Judah I will turn aside from my presence even as I turned aside Israel, and I will reject this city which I have chosen, Jerusalem, and the house of which I said, my name shall be there." (2 Kgs 23:25b–27)

This is evidently from the hand of an exilic editor.

[[287]] There are a sprinkling of passages in the deuteronomistic work which threaten defeat and captivity. These need not necessarily stem from

32. We speak here of the Deuteronomist's work. Whether the exilic editor had in mind prophecies of Micah, Zephaniah, and especially Jeremiah, we cannot tell. The absence of explicit allusion to Jeremiah's prophecies in the Deuteronomistic History is most extraordinary if we suppose the latter to be an exilic work. The silence is far easier to explain if we suppose that the great history had its principal edition in the time of Josiah. The close ties between Jeremiah and the deuteronomistic school, early and late, are well known, of course, as is the traditional attribution of the Book of Kings to Jeremiah himself (Babylonian Talmud, Baba Batra 15a).

33. 2 Kgs 22:15–20. No doubt there is an old nucleus in Hulda's prophecy which predates Josiah's *unpeaceful* end.

an exilic editor. Captivity and exile were all too familiar fates in the Neo-Assyrian age. More important, the threat of exile or captivity was common in the curses of Ancient Near Eastern treaties and came naturally over into the curses attached to Israel's covenant.[34] Nevertheless, there are a limited number of passages which appear to be addressed to exiles and to call for their repentance, or in one case even promise restoration of the captives to their land. These latter are most naturally regarded as coming from the hand of an exilic editor.

Such passages include Deut 4:27–31 which is addressed to captives "scattered among the nations whither Yahweh will lead you away," and gives to them the assurance that Yahweh will not "forget the covenant of your fathers." Deut 30:1–10, promising return from captivity, must be coupled with Deut 4:27–31 as an exilic addition in a style distinct from the hand of the primary deuteronomistic author (Dtr^1). Other passages which include short glosses can be listed: Deut 28:36f., 63–68; 29:27; Josh 23:11–13, 15f.; 1 Sam 12:25; 1 Kgs 2:4; 6:11–13; 8:25b, 46–53; 9:4–9; 2 Kgs 17:19; 20:17f.[35]

The Two Editions of the Deuteronomistic History

We are pressed to the conclusion by these data that there were two editions of the Deuteronomistic History, one written in the era of Josiah as a programmatic document of his reform and of his revival of the Davidic state. In this edition the themes of judgment and hope interact to provide a powerful motivation both for the return to the austere and jealous god of old Israel, and for the reunion of the alienated half-kingdoms of Israel and Judah under the aegis of Josiah. The second edition, completed about 550 B.C., not only updated the history by adding a chronicle of events subsequent to Josiah's reign, it also attempted to transform the work into a sermon on history addressed to Judaean exiles. In this revision the account of Manasseh's reign in [[288]] particular was retouched, conforming Judah's fate to that of Samaria and Manasseh's role to that of Jeroboam. This new element does not exhauast the work of the exilic Deuteronomist, but in general the retouching by his pen was light, not wholly obscuring the earlier framework.

When we examine the exilic editor's account of the fall of Jerusalem and the captivity of Judah, we find that the story is told laconically. There

34. See D. R. Hillers, *Treaty-Curses and the Old Testament Prophets* (Rome: Pontifical Biblical Institute, 1964) 34 and passim. Cf. J. Harvey, "Le 'Rib-pattern,' réquisitoire prophétique sur la rupture de l'alliance," *Bib* 43 (1962), esp. 180, 189, 196.

35. Obviously the end of the history, 2 Kgs 23:26–25:30, belongs to the exilic sections. Certainly other passages may be described as suspect: e.g., Deut 30:11–20; and 1 Kgs 3:14.

is no peroration in the fall of Jerusalem, much less an elaborate one like that upon the destruction of Samaria. The events are recorded without comment, without theological reflection. This is remarkable, given the Deuteronomist's penchant for composing final addresses, edifying prayers, and theological exhortations on significant events. One might argue that the Deuteronomist has said his say, has said earlier all that is necessary to prepare the reader for an understanding of the fall of Jerusalem. However, it must be said that the deuteronomistic historian never tires of repetition of his themes and clichés and is fond of bracketing events and periods with an explicit theological framework. The omission of a final, edifying discourse on the fall of chosen Zion and the Davidic crown is better explained by attributing these final terse paragraphs of the history to a less articulate exilic editor.

In the light of our understanding of the two editions of the work and their different tendencies, the primary edition (Dtr^1) from the author of the era of Josiah, the second (Dtr^2) from a late Deuteronomist of the Exile, a number of puzzles and apparent contradictions in the Deuteronomistic History are dissolved or explained. Little or no hint of inevitable disaster is found in the deuteronomistic historian's framework and transitional passages in Joshua, Judges, and Samuel. Yet the Book of Kings and the Deuteronomistic History in its final form offer little hope to Judah, as Noth has correctly maintained. In the retouching of the original work by an exilic hand, the original theme of hope is overwritten and contradicted, namely the expectation of the restoration of the state under a righteous Davidid to the remembered greatness of the golden age of David. Von Rad's instincts were correct in searching here for an element of grace and hope. The strange shape of the exilic edition with its muted hope of repentance (as Wolff has described it) and possible return (Deut 30:1–10) is best explained, we believe, by the relatively modest extent of the exilic editor's work and his fidelity in preserving intact the work of the Josianic Deuteronomist. This explains the lack of a peroration on Jerusalem's fall. This explains the [[289]] anti-climax of Josiah's reign, falling as it does, in the present form of the history, after Judah's fate has been sealed by Manasseh. This explains the contrast between the Deuteronomistic History and the great works of the Exile with their lively hope of restoration; of the eternal covenant and return (the Priestly work), of a new Exodus and Conquest (Second Isaiah), and of a new allotment of the land, a new Temple, and a new Davidid (Ezekiel).[36] The failure of such a dominant

36. I hope to discuss elsewhere the date of the Priestly work and of Ezekiel 40–48: see F. M. Cross, "The Priestly Tabernacle [[in Light of Recent Research," in *Temple and High Places in Biblical Times* (ed. A. Biran; Jerusalem: The Nelson Glueck School of Biblical Archaeology, 1981) 169–80]]. See also chap. 11 of *Canaanite Myth.*

theme of God's coming restoration can be explained best by removing the primary Deuteronomistic History from the setting of the Exile.

Our analysis of the themes of the Deuteronomistic History has led us to views which superficially resemble positions taken in the nineteenth century. At least we have opted for dating the fundamental composition of the Deuteronomistic History in the era of Josiah. At the same time, we must assert broad agreement with Noth's description of the primary deuteronomistic historian (Noth's Dtr, our Dtr[1]) as a creative author and historian and our full agreement with the sharp distinction made by Noth and the late Ivan Engnell between the Tetrateuch (or Priestly work) and the Deuteronomistic History. In our view, however, the Priestly work is the work par excellence of the mid-sixth century B.C.: essentially, the Deuteronomistic History is a work of the late Kingdom, suffering only minor modification by a member of the deuteronomistic school in the Exile.

The Law and the Nations

A Contribution to Deuteronomistic Tradition History

RUDOLF SMEND

Smend's influential thesis is that the basic narrative layer of the Deuteronomistic History (DH) has undergone at least one major redaction at the hands of a "nomistic" editor–that is, one whose dominant concern is obedience to the Torah of Moses. This redaction, which he calls DtrN, is characterized not only by its interest in law but also by the perspective that remnants of enemy nations remain in the land even after Joshua's military operations.

Smend's analysis, with its admittedly narrow basis, culminates in a call for further similar work, and when this call was taken up, his name became attached to a "school." In his own study, the number of redactions is left open, but it (or they) is (are) essentially "nomistic." The now familiar tripartite redactional pattern–DtrG (DtrH), DtrP, DtrN, with the interposed "prophetic" redaction–is not initiated here but owes more to W. Dietrich, *Prophetie und Geschichte*, which was already known to Smend in dissertation form (see n. 58).

The differences between Smend and F. M. Cross, therefore, need to be carefully understood. They differ methodologically, Smend's analysis beginning at the sentence level, whereas Cross's was based on large-scale trends in the whole work. This may explain why later work, such as that of M. O'Brien, *The Deuteronomistic Hypothesis Reassessed* (OBO 92; Göttingen: Vandenhoeck & Ruprecht, 1989), could attempt to combine the two approaches.

Translated and reprinted with permission from "Das Gesetz und die Völker: Ein Beitrag zur deuteronomistischen Redaktionsgeschichte," in *Probleme biblischer Theologie: Festschrift Gerhard von Rad* (ed. H. W. Wolff; Munich: Chr. Kaiser, 1971) 494–509. Translation by Peter T. Daniels. All English scripture quotations have been taken from the RSV.

Joshua 1:7–9

[[494]] The Bible's description of the Israelites' taking of Palestine west of the Jordan begins in Josh 1:1–9 with God's address to Joshua, the successor of the recently deceased Moses. The passage continues the narrative of the beginning and end of Deuteronomy; the basic material is unquestionably by the author of those passages—the author of the Deuteronomistic History (DtrH). The statement "be strong and of good courage; for you shall cause this people to inherit the land which I swore to their fathers to give to them" (v. 6) most likely belongs to the same material.[1] However, the following sentence is curious. The double imperative at the beginning of v. 6 is repeated and is now introduced by רק 'only' and intensified by מאד 'very'. Then, instead of the reason given in v. 6, a further specification is added and developed thus: "Only be strong and very courageous, being careful to do according to all the law which Moses my servant commanded you; turn not from it to the right hand or to the left, that you may have good success wherever you go" (the original text of v. 7).[2] Not satisfied with this, v. 8 varies the instruction in v. 7 and continues in a particular direction: "This book of the law shall not depart out of your mouth, but you shall meditate on it day and night, that you may be careful to do according to all that is written in it; for then you shall make your way prosperous, and then you shall have good success." Verse 9, finally, steers back to v. 6. The phrase "Be strong and of good courage" is picked up once again, [[495]] this time qualified and explained by the words "be not frightened, neither be dismayed" and the reference to the divine help, wherever Joshua may go. Now, however, it is specified and grounded in a different, more direct way than is implied in vv. 7–8.

How do the components of this sequence of verses relate to each other, and how is this relationship to be explained? Between vv. 6 and 7 is a clear break. Verse 6 succinctly demands courage of Joshua in the imminent battle for the Promised Land; the reason given is also a firm commitment made by God: the plan will succeed. By contrast, v. 7 gives the general order to behave in accordance with the commands issued by Moses and not to stray from them either to the left or to the right. The image, though partly obscured, is one of a journey. In return, Joshua is promised success on all his journeys. In contrast to v. 6, the generalization

1. The correspondence with Deut 31:6–8 has been offered as evidence for the contrary view (for vv. 5bβ–6); see M. Noth in the first edition of his commentary. But see N. Lohfink, *Scholastik* 37 (1962) 32ff. The relation between v. 6 and vv. 7–8 is not directly affected by the minor uncertainty.

2. The phrase כל־התורה is a later insertion. It can generally be recognized as an addition by its absence from the LXX and by the following ממנו.

in v. 7, signaled by the opening word "only,"[3] is also a limitation: success is linked to Joshua's holding strictly to Moses' commands. The modified repetition of the double imperative "be strong and very courageous," which connects v. 7 to v. 6, is very interesting. The words lose something of their color in the process; indeed, they are "twisted into an entirely different meaning."[4] If in v. 6 they have their usual meaning of courage and intrepidity in war, then in v. 7 they can only mean "make every effort; do your utmost."[5] The difference shows even more clearly in that the words are *repeated*. The repetition is made for the purpose of the interpretation. But this assumption presupposes a temporal and material gap between the drafting of vv. 6 and 7. The author of v. 7 is thus probably not the same as the author of the Deuteronomistic History.[6] Verse 6 already lay before him as text; he provided its earliest exegesis, basing his interpretation on its opening words, taking it in the sense of obedience to the law, in a way that both generalized and restricted it.

Verse 8 belongs with v. 7. The motif of obedience to the law is even stronger in v. 8 than in v. 7. While in that place obedience to the commands of Moses appeared only in a restrained way, so that the word "law" was later felt to be lacking and inserted into the Hebrew text after the Greek translation, v. 8, in contrast, could not be clearer. It is not just the law (or its individual commands) that is of concern here; it is the *book* of the law and what is written in it. The tension with the situation to which the text purports to belong [[496]] is even more evident in v. 8 than in v. 7: "Joshua had his hands full during the conquest of Canaan and no time to devote himself day and night to the lawbook."[7] Furthermore, v. 8 runs surprisingly parallel to v. 7. Verse 8b is only a slight variation of v. 7b, and v. 8a sounds like an instruction about how to understand the words "be careful to do according to . . ." of v. 7a: that is, by the reading of the law. Does this mean that v. 8 relates to v. 7 as v. 7 relates to v. 6? (Parallels to the vocabulary of v. 8 are generally found in later, extradeuteronomistic literature.[8]) We must leave the question open for the moment. If the

3. Noth's translation *jedenfalls* 'in any case' obscures this; C. Steuernagel's *jedoch* 'however' is better.

4. R. Smend, *Die Erzählung des Hexateuch auf Ihre Quellen untersucht* (Berlin: G. Reimer, 1912) 280.

5. A. B. Ehrlich, *Randglossen zur Hebräischen Bibel: textkritisches, sprachliches, und sachliches* (Leipzig: J. C. Hinrichs, 1908–14), ad loc.

6. The secondary character is also indicated by the absence of any correspondences to v. 7(–8) in the Deuteronomic parallels to v. 6 (Deut 3:21–22, 31:7–8, 23) (Steuernagel, ad loc.).

7. Ehrlich, ad loc.

8. Isa 59:21, Ps 1:2–3. There must be a direct connection between our passage and the Psalms passage. According to the usual interpretation, the priority goes to Josh 1:8; but see Steuernagel, ad loc.

answer is positive, then we have two distinct stages of interpretation of the original deuteronomistic text before us, of which the second rested on the first and then carried it further.[9]

A recognition of the difference between the inserts and and the original text did not inhibit the later writer from repeating the words that had constituted the starting-point for the additions once again at the end (v. 9). This time he did not add his own interpretation, thus demonstrating that it was not his intent to annul the preexisting text.[10]

Thus, the deuteronomistic redactorial activity in our example was not a single event.[11] Rather, here as elsewhere in the Old Testament, we see at work the process that H. W. Hertzberg called *Nachgeschichte* 'post-history'.[12] Texts like ours "ask to be read vertically,"[13] which means that the tradition-historical, historical, and theological interpretation of the strata, individually and [[497]] as an ensemble, goes far beyond their literary-critical separation.[14] The above investigation of Josh 1:7–9, admittedly, has revealed rather little about the entirety of the Deuteronomistic History. Parallel observations on other texts must be adduced if we are to make good our claim that this passage the original deuteronomistic text has been subject not just to glossing but to a fairly deliberate editing; that, alongside the author of the Deuteronomistic History (DtrH) there was thus another author (or several); for whose work, because of the legal or nomistic scope of his (their) labor on the work of his (their) predecessor, we use the siglum DtrN. For this reason we now turn to other texts.

9. Something similar may possibly be seen in Josh 8:30–35.

10. Within our chapter, v. 9 refers not only to v. 6a (9aα) but also to vv. 5bα (9bα) and 7bβ (9bβ). The separation of vv. 7 and 8 would initially suggest that the author of v. 8 was the author of v. 9; the misunderstanding of vv. 7aβ–9a as a speech by Moses (which leads Noth to separate v. 9b from the preceding because God is named there in the third person) could have already been known to the author of v. 8 but not to the author of v. 7. For the translation of the first two words of v. 9, see Ehrlich, ad loc.

11. Noth, too, had originally, in the first edition of his commentary and in the *Überlieferungsgeschichtlichen Studien* (Halle: M. Niemyer [1943] 41 n. 4), taken vv. 7–9 as a later addition; in the second edition of the commentary, however, he changed his mind.

12. H. W. Hertzberg, BZAW 66 (Berlin: de Gruyter, 1936) 110ff. = *Beiträge zur Traditionsgeschichte und Theologie des Alten Testaments* (Göttingen: Vandenhoeck & Ruprecht, 1962) 69ff.

13. See Hertzberg on Josh 1:8.

14. This corrects some literary-critical judgments, on the basis of which Steuernagel places Josh 1:9, not with vv. 7–8, but with vv. 5–6. This wrong conclusion is understandable in light of the fact that later Deuteronomists characteristically worked with the vocabulary of their predecessors. The relationship of v. 7–8 to v. 6 is overlooked by G. Fohrer (*Einleitung in das Alte Testament* [Heidelberg: Quelle & Meyer, 1965] 219–20) when he assigns priority to vv. 7–8 over vv. 3–6, 9, 12–18. The relation of those verses to Deuteronomy is a question in itself.

Joshua 13:1bβ–6

The next substantial section of the Deuteronomistic History, the division of the land west of the Jordan after its conquest, again begins with an address to Joshua by God: "Now Joshua was old and advanced in years; and the LORD said to him, 'You are now old and advanced in years . . .' " (Josh 13:1abα).

Martin Noth contested the assignment of Josh 13:1–21:42 as a whole to the original Deuteronomistic History and ascribed it to a later deuteronomistic editor(s). I cannot agree. Noth's main argument is the repetition of the sentence from Josh 13:1a, "Now Joshua was old and advanced in years," in Josh 23:1b in the introduction of Joshua's farewell address to the Israelites. Noth argues correctly that this "sentence in a literarily unified whole . . . is not likely to have originated in such widely separated passages."[15] Which of the two passages has priority? Noth opts for 23:1. His observation that the sentence about Joshua's age "must actually have introduced Joshua's final words"[16] at first sounds reasonable. A secondary [[498]] transfer from 23:1 to an earlier point in time, however, with the purpose of "interpolating the section on tribal geography as a literary afterthought" (Noth) is even less plausible (after all, looking back from the later point in time, the sentence seems wildly premature) than a secondary repetition of the sentence at the point where it makes sense–at the beginning of the farewell address,[17] assuming in this case that it had originally stood at the beginning of the division of the land. Naturally, this sort of vague conjecture based on limited evidence cannot prove decisive, and neither does it do so for Noth. His judgment is based on his presupposition, secure in his mind, that Joshua 23 belongs to the original Deuteronomistic History. Further along in our investigation, this presupposition will prove untenable; the identity of Josh 13:1a and Josh 23:1b will no longer constitute an obstacle but instead will support the suggestion that the initial words of Joshua 13 go back to the author of the Deuteronomistic History (DtrH). If we consider the passage without reference to Joshua 23, we find a striking formal relationship with Josh 1:1–2a that points in the same direction. In both cases the explicit precondition for what follows is presented first: "after the death of Moses, the servant of the LORD"; "and Joshua was old and well advanced in years." The divine speech follows, in both cases beginning with the repetition of the explicit precondition: "Moses my servant is dead," and "you are old and advanced in years." Then

15. Noth, *Das Buch Josua*, 2d ed. (Tübingen: J. C. B. Mohr, 1953) 10.

16. Ibid.

17. The repetition would certainly not be "unmotivated" (Noth, *Josua*, 1st ed., xiv).

in 1:2b the divine command to Joshua comes directly, introduced by ועתה 'and now'. The parallel in chap. 13 does not appear until v. 7. In between, in vv. 1bβ–6, comes a long piece that lists a whole series of geographical details about the land and thereby deals more precisely with the fact that the conquest has not yet been completed. It has been said that in a divine speech "a geographical discussion, especially at such great length, simply does not" fit.[18] A comparison of chap. 13 with the structure of Josh 1:1–2 thoroughly confirms this essentially esthetic impression, and both these factors suggest that the geographical piece has been secondarily inserted into its present context.

Analysis of the text sustains this assumption. We begin at the end. Directly following the command for Israel to draw lots for the land as an inheritance (13:6b) comes the new command: "Now therefore divide this land for an inheritance . . ." (v. 7). This sequence is inconceivable in an original context. In addition to being incompatible in form, it is incompatable in content. First of all ⟦499⟧, there is a question about the identity of the recipient of the land to be divided. Verse 6b simply talks about Israel, but v. 7 talks about the nine and a half tribes, which is in accord with the presentation of DtrH, according to which two and a half tribes are already settled in Transjordan (Deut 3:12–13, 18–22; Josh 1:12–15, 22:1–6). Furthermore, and above all, there is a noticeable difference regarding what land is to be divided. The nine and a half tribes, according to DtrH's conception, receive the now-conquered Cisjordan. However, according to v. 6b, what is to be distributed to "Israel" is the areas enumerated (clearly in several literary strata) in vv. 2–6a, territories located on the periphery of the land, facing the coast.[19] It is called the "the land that still remains" (2a), whose inhabitants Yahweh has yet to drive out before the Israelites (6aβγ).[20] The half-verse 6b, introduced by רק, which we have already encountered in 1:7 (though in a somewhat different sense), connects this proclamation[21] to the older context that reappears in v. 7.[22] It achieves this goal only in part, succeeding somewhat less than the sentence in 1:9 that has a corresponding function, namely, to resolve the material tension between the different literary strata.

18. Ehrlich, ad loc.

19. For the geography, see Noth, ad loc.

20. Strictly taken, this statement refers only to the peoples named in 6aα; the sentence, which is presumably later than the preceding one, however, naturally also includes the inhabitants of the areas listed in 2b–5.

21. The excision of 6a, so that 6b abuts 5 (Steuernagel), does not seem to me a major relief. Verse 6b requires something like 6aβγ before it. The suffix in הפלה is possibly oriented toward the הארץ in v. 7. Verse 6b would have to belong to the same literary stage as v. 6aβγ.

22. Josh 13:7 would originally have been followed by 18:2ff. Others have seen this before, though some of the details of their arguments are not convincing.

It would not be incorrect to view the interpolation as beginning with the words "this is the land that still remains . . ." in v. 2. But something more must be said about the connection between the insertion and the older text. The directly preceding sentence, 1bβ, probably already belonged to the older text, that is, to the DH.[23] But in that context, it undoubtedly meant something other than the interpretation found in vv. 2ff.: the land, though conquered, [[500]] still largely needs to be *possessed.*[24] In fact, for the interpretation to fit, the wording probably had to be altered.[25] Given its present interpretation, it must be attributed to the later stratum, just as, by the same token, given its earlier interpretation, it must be attributed to the older. The two strata overlap in it. This is similar to what happens in Josh 1:6–9 with "be strong and of good courage," to which the later layer lays claim, giving it a new interpretation.

In the context of the later stratum (that is, according to the way it is explicated in vv. 2–6), v. 1bβ unquestionably means: the land in large measure has not yet been conquered. This statement decidedly contrasts with DtrH's presentation. The summary passages Josh 10:40–43 and 11:16–20, 23 explicitily claim the total conquest of the land and the nearly total expulsion of its inhabitants. Gaps that might be found in the individual listings[26] do not resolve the contradiction any more than the (correct) insight that the areas and peoples enumerated in 13:2–6 lay on Israel's periphery.[27] The statement of 13:1bβ is just too significant and sweeping.

In conclusion, Josh 13:1bβ–6, just like 1:7–9, is a later person's interpretive addition to the narrative of DtrH. Certain formal similarities have

23. The explanatory recommencement in v. 2 is evidence of this. Another proof is the still-visible direct connection between 13:1bβ and the probable one-time continuation in *18:2ff. Against belonging to the older layer one could certainly adduce the analogy of Josh 1:1–2; the phrase את־הארץ הזאת in v. 7 does not necessarily require the presence of הארץ in 1bβ preceding it. Above all, let it be said that 1bβ, at least in its present wording, is much more easily understood along with 2ff. than in the context of the DtrH. On the separation of v. 1abα (whoever its author may be considered to be), see Smend, *Erzählung*, 321–22; O. Eissfeldt, *Hexateuch-Synopse* (1922) 227*; H. Holzinger in Kautzsch and Bertholet, ad loc.; Steuernagel (ad loc.) in part, suggesting that vv. 2ff. are in turn later elaborations of 1bβ.

24. Cf. Holzinger (KHC) and especially Noth, ad loc.; Hertzberg (ad loc.) holds a different view: "Originally it might generally have been said that much land still remained to be conquered."

25. See W. Rudolph, *Der "Elohist" von Exodus bis Josua* (Berlin: Töpelmann, 1938) 211–12.

26. The coastal plain is not mentioned in the second list; however, Gaza appears as the boundary point in the first list (10:41).

27. Cf. Rudolph, ibid., 240–41. In Joshua 23 these people, who live "from the Jordan to the Great Sea in the West" (v. 4), are considered to be close to the Israelites—"cheek by jowl" with them. The enumeration in 13:2–6 is conventional. Its geographic data are scarcely either clear or important to our author any longer. He uses them to indicate the totality of the peoples remaining in the land.

also been shown, and the language in v. 6aβγb reads like that of a Deuteronomist. The content, however, has not yet been considered. So far, therefore, our result from chap. 1 remains unconnected to that of chap. 13: chap. 13 has been supplemented by someone whose closest interest is in the law; chap. 1 by someone whose deepest concern is the incomplete possession of the land and the continued existence of foreign peoples in it. The relation between the two, however, will soon appear.

Joshua 23

⟦501⟧ The narrative of conquering and possessing the land is brought to an end by the DtrH in Josh 21:43–45. We learn once more that Yahweh has given the Israelites the entire land and that none of the enemies have withstood them; the outcome is solemnly described with the word "peace." The promise, it is expressly stated, has been fulfilled without reservation. An epilogue (22:1–6) relates the discharge of the two and a half Transjordanian tribes.[28]

The next deuteronomistic text is Joshua 23, the speech of warning and admonition to the Israelites by the aged Joshua. Noth ascribes the chapter to the deuteronomistic historian. Can this be maintained?

Just a brief glance shows us how similar Joshua 23 is to the other texts whose secondary character within the Deuteronomistic History we have already observed. Again an important role is played by "these left-over peoples" (הגוים [האלה] הנשארים האלה; vv. 4, 7, 12). Joshua apportioned their land to the Israelites as their hereditary possession (v. 4); Yahweh will drive them out before the Israelites, who will take possession of their land (v. 5). This is all formulated in correspondence to 13:1bβ, 6aβb and is stated in reference to those verses. Verse 6 is also strongly reminiscent of the "nomistic" insert in Josh 1:7–8: "Only be strong and very courageous, being careful to do according to all the law which Moses my servant commanded you; turn not from it to the right hand or to the left." The clause "be strong and of good courage" in 1:6 is rather strongly redirected toward obedience to the commands of Moses in 1:7; the combination of the two originally-quite-different components remained in place, not least through the maintenance of 1:6, the boldness and force of which was forever visible. In 23:6, the second component of the introductory double imperative is omitted and replaced by the intensification מאד 'very', taken over from 1:7. This combination has its original meaning behind it; it has become "language of edification" (E. Käsemann). Enough leveling has taken place

28. Verse 5 is to be recognized without further ado as an addition corresponding to 1:7–8.

that the juxtaposition of doing the commands of Moses (1:7) and doing what is written in the lawbook (1:8) dissolves, and the statements are combined into a single sentence.

The cited components of Joshua 23 cannot be wrenched from their context.[29] Consequently, the chapter belongs not to DtrH but to a later redaction. This presupposes 1:7–9 and 13:1bβ–6; [[502]] if we distinguish two stages of redaction in 1:7–8, then the second stage was already in existence in chap. 23. One could hypothesize that in chap. 23 a still later hand was writing. In this case, we would be facing no less than four deuteronomistic stages of redaction in this small section alone. Fortunately, this is probably not the case, however. In chap. 23 an idea becomes clearly apparent; it is in this idea that the preceding passages find their place and only through this conception do they realize their fullest character. It appears that behind sections that individually could be considered more or less accidental glosses there stands a redaction that is wide-ranging in its scope and standing. The siglum DtrN, mentioned in passing above on Josh 1:7–9, is indeed justified.

The starting-point for chap. 23 is the conditions described in Josh 21:43–45: Israel was at peace from its enemies all around (23:1a in accordance with 21:44a); none was able to withstand the Israelites (23:9b in accordance with 21:44b); the promise was completely fulfilled (23:14b in accordance with 21:45).[30] On closer inspection, however, differences begin to appear. While 21:44b reads "not one of all their enemies had withstood them, for the LORD had given all their enemies into their hands," 23:9b says more succinctly: "No man has been able to withstand you to this day." This statement expresses a limitation precisely to the past, and the notice regarding all of the enemies of Israel is passed over in silence. This was not accidental, as shown by the positive presentation. Two categories of peoples are distinguished (גוים, not as in 21:44 and 23:1: איבים = enemies). Yahweh had dealt victoriously in the past with the one, in the sight of Israel; they disappeared (v. 3). Additionally, however, there were "those who remained,"[31] the "remnant" (v. 12), whose territory had already been apportioned among the Israelites, and whom Yahweh will drive out (v. 5), according to his word. At present they are still there, and

29. Noth (ad loc.) attempts this with some of the components (esp. vv. 5, 13a) but in the process cannot eliminate the "somewhat suprising presupposition of still-present remnants of the expelled peoples" and as a result achieves only a partial understanding of the text.

30. Noth for a while even regarded Josh 21:43–45 as secondary with respect to DtrH, because clauses from Joshua 23 were inappropriately anticipated there (*Überlieferungsgeschichtliche Studien*, 45); the relationship is the other way around.

31. The words הנשארים האלה [['these left-overs']] in vv. 7, 12 can (with Noth) be considered an addition, but one that suitably clarifies (in accordance with v. 4).

perhaps Yahweh (contrary to his word) will not proceed with the expulsion (v. 13a), especially if the Israelites mingle too closely with them and begin to honor their gods (vv. 12, 7). The law against doing so is found in the law of Moses (v. 6). "Until this very day" the Israelites have behaved properly—that is, they have depended on Yahweh (v. 8)—and so Yahweh has "until this very day" expelled the peoples (vv. 9–10). Corresponding to the appeal to continue such behavior (namely, to depend on Yahweh and to love him, v. 11; cf. v. 8), there already comes from the lips of the dying Joshua (v. 14a) a description of the role that the peoples remaining [[503]] in the land will play for the Israelites, and indeed an ominous limitation on this role of the peoples: it will cease when the Israelites are exterminated from this land (v. 13b; cf. 15bβγ, 16b). The "good words" of Yahweh (cf. 21:45) are placed alongside his "evil words," which will be fulfilled if Israel violates God's instructions (ברית [['covenant']]), just as the good words have already been fulfilled (vv. 14b–16).

The author speaks through Joshua's mouth to people of his own time, but naturally not without trappings, which he added as a matter of course through historicizing back-projection. However, these are such that it does not take much guesswork to imagine roughly the (exilic at the earliest) situation from which and to which it was written. Naturally the goal here was not only the interpretation and cause of the present state of affairs but, even more, an appeal to behave in a way that might still avert the full effects of the catastrophe.[32]

Joshua 23, like the texts discussed above, was inserted into the preexisting literary context of DtrH. The new statements should not be understood as replacing the old ones but as validating and supporting them. They accomplish this in the only way possible, by modifying them. The overwhelming mighty deed of Yahweh for his people now no longer stands in the foreground, as it did for DtrH, although it is in no way denied. Whereas that concept allowed for nothing less than a complete conquest in a single blow, with the almost complete eradication of the previous inhabitants,[33] we now see the more ambiguous, rather confused, arduous, dangerous reality of the cohabitation between Israel and the peoples in the land. It so happens (and, as we shall see, it is not just by accident) that an image thus emerges that corresponds better to the actual course of events than DtrH's image. The two images stand more in a relationship of rivalry with each other than in supplementation, much as the portrayals of Israel's occupation of Palestine by modern scholars. The nomistic redactor inserted his image into the picture drawn by his predeces-

32. Cf. H. W. Wolff, *Gesammelte Studien zum Alten Testament* (Munich: Kaiser, 1964) 308ff.

33. Cf. my *Elemente alttestamentlichen Geschichtsdenkens* (1969) 27–28.

sor as well as he could but not so well that he avoided being inconsistent or forcings things–to the benefit of literary critics.

In a treatment of chap. 23, chap. 24 must not be overlooked. The points of contact are obvious. In both chapters Joshua convenes the Israelites; both times he gives a speech in [[504]] which he presents the previous acts of Yahweh, on the basis which he appeals to them to decide for him. It has long been accepted that chap. 24 served as the model for the composition of chap. 23. Noth first made this suggestion, then renounced it, and then came back to it again.[34] The sequence of the two chapters has always presented greater difficulties. Noth, proceeding from what was for him an unquestioned assumption that chap. 23 belonged to DtrH, argued as follows: "The Deuteronomist . . . can hardly have incorporated into his work the narrative he used for a model. Instead, in the deuteronomistic editing it was included secondarily as an appendix in the deuteronomistic book of Joshua."[35] But Joshua 23 does *not* come from DtrH, and what we have previously said about the author's attitude to chap. 23 in relation to the texts that lay before him can also hold for its relation to Joshua 24. His purpose here was not to replace the older text any more than it was in chaps. 1 and 13.[36] Rather, he left it in, at least as an "appendix,"[37] after he had revised its basic message for his own time. The double summons to the assembly (23:2a, 24:1) must have been less of a problem for him than for us. The repetition of 13:1a in 23:1b shows that he was not finicky about such things. We have already seen that "repetition" was one of his literary devices; we will soon find him using it again.

Judges 2:17, 20–21, 23

In the programmatic presentation of the period of the judges (Judg 2:10ff.), the first clear voice is that of DtrH. The opponents, whose gods the Israelites follow and into whose hand Yahweh gives the Israelites, are "the peoples (עמים) all around" or "the enemies (איבים) all around" (vv. 12, 14), following the terms of Josh 21:44. There is no mention[38] of the

34. *Josua*, 1st ed., 101; *Überlieferungsgeschichtliche Studien*, 9 n. 1; *Josua*, 2d ed., 133.

35. *Josua*, 2d ed., 10.

36. The motivation proposed in Smend, *Erzählung des Hexateuch*, 315, and elsewhere (annoyance about the role of Shechem) does not contradict this. Compare the role of Shechem in DtrN in Josh 8:30–35.

37. Noth, *Josua*, 1st ed., xiii.

38. M. Weinfeld ("Period of the Conquest and Judges as Seen by the Earlier and Later Sources," *VT* 17 [1967] 104–5) attempts to bring Joshua 23 into line with our text, in the process assigning too much weight to the fact that the "peoples who remain" lie on the periphery of the land according to Josh 13:2–6.

"peoples (גוים) who remain" in Josh 23:4, 7, 12, 13.[39] Incidentally, albeit with variations, a passage like this shows how much DtrN learned [[505]] from DtrH. He took from here (though no doubt not only from here) the thought that Yahweh avenged the Israelites' honoring of the gods of the other peoples by the hand of those very peoples and modified it in accordance with his different understanding of the manner and outcome of the occupation.

And of course he did this with his distinctively nomistic vocabulary. Evidence for this is found in the present text, namely, in Judg 2:17. No quarrel about the secondary character of this verse is possible. Its insertion into the context is, and not for the first time in DtrN, achieved by resumption: the beginning of v. 18 repeats the declaration of v. 16a in the form of a subordinate clause. In terms of content, v. 17 breaks through DtrH's generational schema in blatant contradiction of v. 19. Moreover, the "judges" here have a function different from their role in DtrH: here they are something like law-preachers.[40]

The cycle of the judges schema comes to a close in v. 19 with the death of the judge and the Israelites' renewed idolatry, now stronger than ever. Apparently without transition, there follows in v. 20 the continuation known from v. 14: "So the anger of the LORD was kindled against Israel"—but only apparently, for what follows breaks with the previous schema. The words about Yahweh's wrath are followed by words about his action, not directly as in v. 14, but only three verses later (v. 23). In between is a divine speech—or, better, soliloquy (Israel is mentioned in the third person)—that motivates the action. In this speech, v. 22 is secondary (Yahweh is now in the third person, and from this point on).[41] The elements of vv. 20b, 21, on the other hand, are already known to us: because "this people" (גוי) has transgressed Yahweh's command, he will drive out no more of the peoples (גוים) whom Joshua allowed to remain. The evil that was envisioned as a possibility in Joshua 23 has now taken place. The conditions (v. 12) for Yahweh's halting the expulsion of the inhabitants of the land (v. 13a) have become reality because of the Israelites' apostasy (Judg 2:11–13);[42] the divine proclamation then changes in tone from one that was conditional to one that now has just cause, and the act follows hard on its heels. The connection of thought also appears in the wording; we need only mention v. 20 עבר ברית [['transgress covenant']], which is like

39. The fact that DtrN also names the first category (גוים) in Josh 23:3, 4b(?), 9 means nothing.

40. Cf. W. Richter, *Die Bearbeitungen des "Retterbuches" in der deuteronomischen Epoche* (Bonner Biblische Beiträge; Bonn: Hanstein, 1964) 33–34.

41. Cf. ibid., 37.

42. There is no need to assign any one of these verses to DtrN; DtrN is a supplementer, not an independent narrator for whom one has to prove a continuous composition.

Josh 23:16; v. 21 הוריש [['dispossess']], like Josh 23:5 (versus Judg 2:3 גרש [['drive out']]), or even more precisely הוסיף להוריש [['continue to dispossess']] like Josh 23:13. In these verses the continuation from that place is before us; it comes from DtrN.

The content of 3:1–6, which follows the concise description of God's intention henceforth in 2:23, is confused and, as all previous efforts show, very difficult for the literary critic to untangle. Possibly it goes like this: 3:5–6 belongs to 2:20–21, 23, and the rest was added successively.[43] We cannot discover any components of the verse before DtrN; it appears from this that, on the contrary, the work of the deuteronomistic School was not complete even with DtrN.

Judges 1:1–2:9

We now go back a little in the biblical sequence and consider a text in a somewhat more theoretical way.

The narrative of the "covenant renewal at Shechem" ends with the dismissal of the people (Josh 24:28). Notices of the death and burial of Joshua (vv. 29–30) follow this. DtrH continues with the observation that Israel had served Yahweh "all the days of Joshua and all the days of the elders who outlived Joshua and had known[44] all the work which the LORD did for Israel" (v. 31). The evident continuation is Judg 2:10: "And all that generation also were gathered to their fathers; and there arose another generation after them who did not know the LORD or the work which he had done for Israel." Thus commences the period of the judges, whose course is set in motion by the new generation's evil (v. 11).[45]

What stands between Josh 24:31 and Judg 2:10 is a later insertion. At the end of the insertion, the editor employed the method of resumption in an especially striking way, in order to restore the lost connection.[46] Josh 24:28–31 is repeated in Judg 2:6–9, with extensive rearrangement and a

43. So Richter, ibid., 38ff.

44. Here perhaps orginally "had seen"; cf. Judg 2:7; and ibid., 47.

45. The original connection between vv. 10 and 11 is disputed by W. Beyerlin in *Tradition und Situation: Studien zur alttestamentlichen Prophetie Artur Weiser zum 70. Geburtstag* (ed. E. Würthwein and O. Kaiser; Göttingen: Vandenhoeck & Ruprecht, 1963) 7–8. But his arguments do not hold water. The change of subject between vv. 10 and 11 is explained by the formulaic nature of v. 11. The cause of the unfaithfulness of Israel in vv. 11–19, does not contradict the cause given in v. 10, especially when the secondary character of v. 17 and the element of escalation in v. 19 are taken into account. In v. 19 it is hard to see (with Rudolph, ibid., 243) a reference to the depravity of Joshua's generation.

46. Cf. I. L. Seeligmann, "Hebräische Erzählung und biblische Geschichtsschreibung," *ThZ* 18 (1962) 322ff. and especially the individual proofs in Richter, ibid., 46ff. Somewhat differently, T. C. Vriezen, *VT* 17 (1967) 336ff.

few small alterations. The number of alterations is an indication of the secondary character of Judg 2:6–9.

⟦507⟧ Judg 1:1–2:5,[47] while it was inserted by a later redactor into DtrH's work, nevertheless cannot have come from the pen of that redactor, at least not for the most part. This is not the place to discuss in detail the multifarious historical and tradition-historical problems of Judges 1; what interests us is the redaction-historical question of the role and possibly the origin of this admittedly old text in its present context. The key must lie in the later appendix, 2:1–5, and, to be precise, in the angel's speech that constitutes its main section (vv. 1b–3).[48] Here the Israelites are reproached for their behavior in relation to the prior occupants of the land: they have not heeded God's command not to mingle with them but rather to tear down their altars. Yahweh will no longer drive out the occupants of the land; they together with their gods will oppress the Israelites and become a snare to them. Though it seems to do violence to Judges 1 to want to understand it in the sense of this speech, this seems to be what has happened. The "non-possession catalogue" of Judg 1:19, 21, 27–35, originally a collection of the gaps in Israelite possession as they simply were forced by the balance of military power, now obviously justifies the accusation of wrong behavior in relation to the previous inhabitants of the land and thus of disobedience to Yahweh.[49]

Who inserted Judg 1:1–2:5 here? Without question, it must be someone later than DtrH, since clearly his work was interrupted. It makes sense to consider DtrN, already known to us as an interpolator in DtrH. The most important piece of evidence is the correspondence between the content of the insertion and DtrN in the fundamental fact that the land has not been fully conquered and the complete eradication of the previous inhabitants is still to come, if it is even to be achieved at all. A difference has been found in that the noneradication in our text is regarded as a sin, whereas in Joshua 23 and Judg 2:20–21, 23 (that is, in DtrN), it is regarded as a divine punishment for sin.[50] This opposition is questionable: the noneradication is also proclaimed a divine punishment in Judg 2:3. A line can be drawn from Joshua 23 not just to Judg 2:20–21, 23 but also to Judg 2:1b–3, with the proviso that in the latter the disobedience of the Israel-

47. Josh 24:32–33 is of no importance to the present argument.

48. Cf. especially Rudolph, ibid., 263–64.

49. Cf. K. Budde on 1:19; Rudolph, ibid.; Weinfeld, ibid., 94–95. Admittedly, we could see a more precise reference to Judges 1 in Judg 2:2; this difficulty would be lessened if Judg 2:1–5 were an originally independent narrative; cf. H. Gressmann, ad loc. (in that case, the assumption is probably required that v. 2 has replaced an original, certainly more concrete argument).

50. Weinfeld, ibid., 100ff.

ites, which changes the divine proclamation from conditional to [[508]] unconditional, is obviously considered to be given concrete form in the data of the "non-possession catalogue." It is difficult to support the theory that DtrN, following Joshua 23, as it were, on the same level, wrote both Judg 2:1b–3 and Judg 2:20–21, 23, which are in substance doublet, as if this were, so to speak, a single argument. Since Judg 2:20–21, 23 unquestionably comes from his pen, his relation to 2:1b–3 would have to be different. Did he have 2:1b–3 already in its present form before him, so that the striking correspondence between Josh 23:13b and Judg 2:3b[51] can be attributed to literary dependence on the part of the Joshua text, and thus, did DtrN create Judg 2:20b, 21 on the model of 2:1b–3? Judg 2:1b–3 has relationships with Exod 23:20–33, 34:11–16; Num 33:50–55; and Deut 7:1–5,[52] the clarification of which may be significant not only for our question in the narrow sense but also for the question of DtrN's tradition-historical orientation.

In any case the insight that Judg 1:1–2:5 was probably introduced into DtrH's work by DtrN is of great value. It reveals that DtrN not only relied on his own reasoning but also had old material available. Unfortunately, we do not have the means to decide whether Judg 1:1–2:5 lay before him as a fragment or as a component of a more comprehensive literary work. The second possibility should not be rejected out of hand prematurely, especially if we remember that, in general, the chance of longer documents surviving into the exilic and postexilic period must have exceeded that of shorter works. In the context of further observations on deuteronomistic editorial activity, even within the Tetrateuch, new perspectives may emerge on the old dispute about whether Judges 1 comprises the conclusion of the Yahwistic source of the Pentateuch.[53]

For DtrN, the existence of foreign peoples in the land was certainly a vexing contemporary problem. But he did not simply project it back from his time into the past to the period of the occupation of the land. Instead, there was available to him an old document on that period that was of the utmost importance and authenticity precisely on the subject that interested him. Thus he had the best evidence in the tradition as a resource for his project; conversely, this tradition had him for its best interpreter, even if he did not always take the old statements in every point as they were originally meant. For now we can only speculate on the exact relationship

51. Judg 2:20 together with its ancillaries (or continuations) in Judg 3:1–6 may be considered dependant on the motif there.

52. Cf., for instance, N. Lohfink, *Das Hauptgebot: eine Untersuchung literarischer Einleitungsfragen zu Dtn 5–11* (Anbib 20; Rome: Pontifical Biblical Institute, 1963) 172ff.

53. Most recently O. Kaiser, *Einleitung in das Alte Testament: Eine Einführung in ihre Ergebnisse und Probleme* (2d ed.; Gütersloh: Mohn, 1969) 73–74.

between them. Did Judges 1 open his eyes to the problem in the [[509]] present and thus in this respect already have a priority in the tradition? If Judges 1 already lay before DtrN along with its interpretation in Judg 2:1b–3, then his work consisted of accepting and incorporating this interpretation into DtrH's larger presentation of the taking of the land, which also was available to him. Lest DtrN's tradition-historical lineage be presented too simply, let it be remembered that the tradition of the incomplete conquest of the land was not only available in the form of Judges 1. In Josh 13:2–6 DtrH also uses a preexisting inventory of nonconquered areas. It differs significantly from the account in Judges 1,[54] though it seems that these divergences would not have particularly troubled DtrN.[55] Narrative consistency was obviously not a major concern of his anywhere else, either; but rather, saturating the material with his theological conceptions was.

Our investigation has pursued the goal of proving the existence of a systematic reworking of the Deuteronomistic History, the principal motif of which was the law. In this essay, only the deuteronomistic presentation of the occupation of the land was examined.[56] The study could be expanded, however, to cover what preceded and followed; within the Deuteronomistic History, DtrN first speaks in Deut 1:5 and does not fall silent until the end of 2 Kings.[57] I cannot attempt even a rough sketch of the profile of the nomistic redactor on the basis of the small amount of material covered here.[58] Even in respect of what has been proposed here, a series of questions—tradition-historical, historical, and theological—could be asked; perhaps some preliminary answers would even be possible. But it seems to me it would be better to wait until the exegetical foundation is broader.

54. In Judges 1, the situation during the period of the judges is described; in Josh 13:2–6, however, the setting is the period of the monarchy.

55. See above, n. 27.

56. This article originated in a seminar on the redaction of the book of Joshua that I taught in the winter semester of 1967–68. I am happy to find myself in agreement in many places with a book by G. Schmitt, *Du sollst keinen Frieden schließen mit den Bewohnern des Landes* (BWANT 5/11; Stuttgart: Kohlhammer, 1970), which at the time this article was submitted was not yet available.

57. For Kings, some of the analytical work has already been completed in W. Dietrich, *Prophetie und Geschichte: Eine redaktionsgeschichtliche Untersuchung zum deuteronomistischen Geschichtswerk* (Diss. ev. theol., Münster, 1970; published as FRLANT 108; Göttingen: Vandenhoeck & Ruprecht, 1972).

58. This essay does not cover all of the material in the book of Joshua, of course.

Part 2

Deuteronomy, Joshua, Judges

Deuteronomy in Search of Origins

THOMAS RÖMER

Römer explores a number of questions about the relationship between Deuteronomy and the Deuteronomistic History. Römer is one of many scholars who think that the deuteronomistic editing of the old Deuteronomic law code was more pervasive than previous scholars allowed. This raises at least two questions. First, what was the function and purpose of this exilic edition of Deuteronomy? Second, how does the view of Israel's national origins in the older form of Deuteronomy compare with the view evinced by the deuteronomistic edition of Deuteronomy? In response to the first question, Römer believes that the exilic edition of Deuteronomy was shaped to provide the community with a new sense of coherent identity by presenting an ideal, formative period in the past. Römer addresses the second question by examining allusions to "the fathers" in Deuteronomy. He argues that in older sections of Deuteronomy citations of "the fathers" refer to the exodus generation. Israel's national history was thought to begin with God's actions on behalf of these fathers. Only in the final stages of the editing of Deuteronomy, when the work goes from being simply the introduction to the Deuteronomistic History to becoming the conclusion to the Pentateuch, does one find references to "the fathers" as alluding to Israelite ancestors, most prominently Abraham, Isaac, and Jacob.

Translated and reprinted with permission, from "Le Deutéronome à la quête des origines," in *Le Pentateuque: Débats et recherches* (ed. P. Haudebert; Lectio Divina 151; Paris: Éditions du Cerf, 1992) 65–98. Translation by Peter T. Daniels. The RSV has been used for the citation of most of the biblical passages in English. To distinguish between second-person singular and plural pronouns used in both Hebrew and French, "thee" and "thou" have been used for singular and "you" for plural in some English scripture quotations.

Deuteronomy's Pivotal Position

[[65]] The book of Deuteronomy occupies a unique position in the Hebrew Bible. First, it concludes the first portion of the Bible, the Torah or Pentateuch. But at the same time it serves as a prologue to the books that are called the "historical" books (Joshua to 2 Kings) and thus constitutes the opening of what since Martin Noth has been called the "Deuteronomistic History."[1] Because of this pivotal position, it is not in the least surprising that there have been proposals to see Deuteronomy as the very "center" of the entire Old Testament. For Siegfried Herrmann, Deuteronomy functions as a "prism," filtering the old traditions of the Tetrateuch (Genesis to Numbers) to give them the Deuteronomic aspect under which they appear in the succeeding books.[2] In the current state of exegetical research on the Pentateuch,[3] this appealing [[66]] description of Deuteronomy has not found unanimous acceptance, notably because it implies knowledge and use of the non-Priestly traditions of the Tetrateuch by the authors of Deuteronomy. And it is precisely the relationship between the block of Genesis to Numbers and Deuteronomy that is currently under discussion.[4] For some exegetes (Martin Rose, John Van Seters, and others), Deuteronomy, traditionally considered an interim conclusion, has become instead a "cornerstone" on which was built first the edifice of the Deuteronomistic History and second, as an expansion of this original corpus, the texts of the Pentateuch labeled "Yahwist."[5]

Nonetheless, all this questioning of received ideas merely confirms the central place that must be assigned to Deuteronomy in order to understand both the Pentateuch and the Deuteronomistic History. Deuter-

1. Martin Noth, *Überlieferungsgeschichtliche Studien: Die sammelnden und bearbeitenden Geschichtswerke im Alten Testament* (3d ed.; Darmstadt: Wissenschaftliche Buchgesellschaft, 1967; 1st ed., 1943). English translation: *The Deuteronomistic History* (JSOTSup 15; Sheffield: JSOT Press, 1981).

2. Siegfried Herrmann, "Die konstruktive Restauration: Das Deuteronomium als Mitte biblischer Theologie," in *Probleme biblischer Theologie* (G. von Rad Festschrift; ed. Hans Walter Wolff; Munich: Kaiser, 1971) 155–70.

3. On this subject, see Albert de Pury and Thomas Römer, "Le Pentateuque en question: Position du problème et brève histoire de la recherche," in *La Pentateuque en question* (2d ed.; ed. A. de Pury; Le Monde de la Bible; Geneva: Labor et Fides, 1991) 9–80; Jacques Briend, "La 'Crise' du Pentateuque," *Revue de l'Institut catholique de Paris* 29 (1989) 49–62.

4. See Norbert Lohfink, "Deutéronome et Pentateuque: État de la recherche," in *Le Pentateuque: Débats et recherches* [[(Lectio Divina 151; Paris: du Cerf, 1992) 35ff.]].

5. See notably Martin Rose, *Deuteronomist und Jahwist: Untersuchungen zu den Berührungspunkten beider Literaturwerke* (ATANT 67; Zurich: Theologischer Verlag, 1981); idem, "La Croissance du corpus historiographique de la Bible: Une proposition," *Revue de théologie et de philosophie* 118 (1986) 217–36; John Van Seters, *In Search of History: Historiography in the Ancient World and the Origins of Biblical History* (New Haven: Yale University Press, 1983 [[repr. Winona Lake, Ind.: Eisenbrauns, 1997]]).

onomy remains the touchstone of every theory of the formation of the Torah and of the deuteronomistic movement.

This importance of the last book of the Pentateuch does not fit very well with our "Salvation History" framework of reading, since such a reading implies a "chronology," a progression in the story of YHWH with his people. In fact, from the beginning of the book to the end, not much new happens apart from the installation of Joshua as the successor of Moses (Deut 31:7ff.) and the [[67]] death of the latter (Deut 34:1ff.). The narrative progression that takes place between the arrival in Transjordan, related in the book of Numbers, and the conquest of Cisjordan, treated in the book of Joshua, could thus be accommodated in a single short chapter. Of course, there is plenty of "history" in Deuteronomy, but it appears in retrospective or prospective texts that are not organized according to a chronological principle. In the great historical canvas stretching from the creation of the world (Genesis) through the end of the kingdom of Judah (2 Kings), Deuteronomy marks a pause. This phenomenon deserves our attention. If Deuteronomy was not intended to cohere with a linear history, then what is its purpose?

The "Purpose" of Deuteronomy

To speak of the "purpose" of Deuteronomy might prove to be a trap. It is always chancy and perhaps a bit arbitrary to wish to reduce a document to one specific intention. Furthermore, as regards Deuteronomy, the diachronic question cannot be neglected. The "primitive Deuteronomy" certainly looked different from the book in its present form. The initial version of Deuteronomy, which probably consisted primarily of a legislative code (perhaps principally Deuteronomy 12–18*)[6] provided with an introduction (Deut 6:4ff.*?)[7] and a conclusion [[68]] (Deuteronomy 26ff.*),[8] provoked, perhaps even legitimated, the "reform" of Josiah described in

6. Georg Braulik, *Die deuteronomischen Gesetze und der Dekalog: Studien zum Aufbau von Deuteronomium 12–26* (SBS 145; Stuttgart: Katholisches Bibelwerk, 1991) 116. Braulik defends the thesis that the Ten Commandments constituted for the exilic redaction of Deuteronomy the organizing principle of the legislative material. Since this principle is less clearly perceptible in Deuteronomy 12–18*, it follows that these were the chapters that formed the preexilic core with which the deuteronomistic redaction had to come to terms.

7. For Albrecht Alt ("Die Heimat des Deuteronomiums," *Kleine Schriften zur Geschichte des Volkes Israels* [Munich: Beck, 1953] 2.250–75 at p. 253), there was no doubt about the validity of this thesis; see recently Andrew David Hastings Mayes, *Deuteronomy* (NCB; Grand Rapids: Eerdmans, 1979) 48; Felix García López, *Le Deutéronome* (CE 63; Paris, 1988) 19. For other hypotheses, see Horst Dietrich Preuss, *Deuteronomium* (EF 164; Darmstadt: Wissenschaftliche Buchgesellschaft, 1982) 26ff.

8. For the end of the original Deuteronomy, see the differing theories of Mayes, *Deuteronomy*, 48; and García López, *Le Deutéronome*, 47ff.

2 Kings 22–23.[9] This Josianic Deuteronomy, whose delimitation remains extremely difficult, was probably not yet conceived as a Mosaic discourse[10] but was written in a triumphalistic context (the fruit of a certain independence of the kingdom of Judah from the Assyrians). Several decades later, Deuteronomy emerged totally transformed, after being considerably enlarged, and was inserted into the Deuteronomistic History. The work of the deuteronomistic redaction gave Deuteronomy, *grosso modo* [['broadly speaking']], its current form and structure. This *deuteronomistic* edition of Deuteronomy, then, is what I take as the starting-point of my inquiry: it is, in fact, a much less hypothetical corpus than the "original Deuteronomy," and the idea of a deuteronomistic redaction of Deuteronomy rests on the unanimous consensus of exegetes.

Even so, this last statement has to be modified [[69]] immediately in regard to current theories of the Deuteronomistic History and, of course, the understanding of Deuteronomy. Martin Noth's theory of a single deuteronomistic author/writer compiling his work, after the fall of Jerusalem but before 539 B.C., has for quite a while been considerably modified. Noth himself already made the statement, without giving it much attention,[11] that numerous deuteronomistic texts reveal the contribution of many hands. To this may be added the impression that a variety of positions on the attitude toward the monarchy or even on the possibility of a future after the catastrophe may be found in the deuteronomistic work. The systematization of these facts has given rise to two different models.[12]

9. See the works of N. Lohfink, especially "Zur neueren Diskussion über 2 Kön 22–23," in *Das Deuteronomium: Entstehung, Gestalt und Botschaft* (ed. N. Lohfink; BETL 68; Louvain: Peeters, 1985) 24–48; idem, "The Cult Reform of Josiah of Judah: 2 Kings 22–23 as a Source for the History of Israelite Religion," in *Ancient Israelite Religion: Essays in Honor of F. M. Cross* (ed. Patrick D. Miller et al.; Philadelphia: Fortress, 1987) 459–76. We cannot enter into the debate about the composition of the "original Deuteronomy." While Lohfink and others (see N. Lohfink, "Culture Shock and Theology: A Discussion of Theology as a Cultural and Sociological Phenomenon Based on the Example of Deuteronomic Law," *BTB* 7 [1977] 12–22; Moshe Weinfeld, "The Emergence of the Deuteronomic Movement: The Historical Antecedents," in *Das Deuteronomium:* [[*Entstehung, Gestalt und Botschaft*]] [ed. N. Lohfink]; [[Louvain: Louvain University Press/Peeters, 1985]] 76–98) defend an original publication in the time of Hezekiah, R. E. Clements, in his recent introduction to Deuteronomy, maintains the classic thesis of dating to the Josianic period (*Deuteronomy* [Old Testament Guides; Sheffield: JSOT Press, 1989] 71). The opinion that 2 Kings 22–23 contains no historical details has also been defended. It is supposed to be a purely fictitious tale exploiting the stratagem of "recovered ancient documents"; see Bernd Jørg Diebner and Claudia Nauerth, "Die Inventio des *spr htwrh* in 2 Kön 22: Struktur, Intention und Funktion von Auffindungslegenden," *Dielheimer Blätter zum Alten Testament* 18 (1984) 95–118.

10. M. Rose, Bemerkungen zum historischen Fundament des Josia-Bildes in II Reg 22f.," *ZAW* 89 (1977) 50–63 at 56 n. 26; García López, *Le Deutéronome*, 16.

11. E.g., Noth, *Überlieferungsgeschichtliche Studien*, 33ff.

12. See Rainer Albertz, "Die Intentionen der Träger des Deuteronomistischen Geschichtswerks," in *Schöpfung und Befreiung* (C. Westermann Festschrift; ed. R. Albertz et al.;

The first model is that of *two editions* of the historical work; a first, preexilic edition is postulated during the reign of Josiah (ending somewhere in 2 Kings 22ff.), and a second after the catastrophe of the exile (adding 2 Kings 24–25 and other supplements). This theory, developed by Frank Moore Cross[13] and widely adopted especially in the English-speaking world,[14] nonetheless [[70]] poses two problems: it is difficult to locate a convincing end to the preexilic edition, and the allusions to the exile within deuteronomistic texts are so numerous that their elimination from the first edition looks rather like begging the question.

The second model is that of *successive redactional layers*, elaborated by Rudolf Smend and his students.[15] After the first exilic edition, ascribed to a deuteronomistic historian (DtrH), they postulate numerous additions and insertions by a prophetic Deuteronomist (DtrP) and several nomistic Deuteronomists (DtrN). This model is currently adopted by a considerable number of European scholars. Thus Norbert Lohfink proposes to complete it with a "DtrL" (the preexilic layer of Josiah's time, containing a history of the conquest) and a "DtrÜ" (in some sense the final redactor of the Deuteronomistic History in the postexilic period).[16] This approach risks inflating the number of redactional layers (and sigla), whose precise extent no one has yet defined in the deuteronomistic work; and the descriptions of certain "layers" often appear quite arbitrary.[17]

Stuttgart: Calwer, 1989) 37–53 esp. 39ff.; Enzo Cortese, "Theories concerning Dtr: A Possible Rapprochement," in *Pentateuchal and Deuteronomistic Studies: Papers Read at the XIIIth IOSOT Congress, Leuven 1989* (Louvain: Louvain University Press/Peeters, 1990) 179–90.

13. Frank Moore Cross, "The Themes of the Book of Kings and the Structure of the Deuteronomistic History," *Canaanite Myth and Hebrew Epic: Essays in the History of the Religion of Israel* (Cambridge: Harvard University Press, 1973) 274–89 [[pp. 79–94 in this volume]]; see the favorable presentation of this thesis in Rolf Rendtorff, *Introduction à l'Ancien Testament* (Paris: du Cerf, 1989) 314ff.

14. See, among the recent publications offering modifications of Cross's theory, Iain William Provan, *Hezekiah and the Books of Kings* (BZAW 172; Berlin: de Gruyter, 1988) (Provan postulates a Josianic edition ending at 2 Kgs 19:37; the rest is to be attributed to an exilic redaction); Mark O'Brien, *The Deuteronomistic History Hypothesis: A Reassessment* (OBO 92; Fribourg: Éditions Universitaires, 1989) (O'Brien places the end of the Josianic edition at 2 Kgs 23:23 and suggests three exilic redactional layers). These studies, together with many others that could be added, clearly show the hesitation as to the ending of the preexilic deuteronomistic work.

15. A summary of this model is found in Rudolf Smend, *Die Entstehung des Alten Testaments* (Theologische Wissenschaft 1; Stuttgart: Kohlhammer, 1978) 111ff.

16. N. Lohfink, "Kerygmata des Deuteronomistischen Geschichtswerks," in *Die Botschaft und die Boten* (H. W. Wolff Festschrift; ed. Jörg Jeremias and Lothar Perlitt; Neukirchen-Vluyn: Neukirchener Verlag, 1981) 87–100.

17. For example, is it judicious to name a layer "nomistic" when the entire deuteronomistic work revolves around the Law? See also the critical remarks of Albertz, "Intentionen," 40.

Faced with this situation, it seems to me more prudent to once again take seriously the *coherence* (despite the great complexity) of the deuteronomistic ideology and style[18] and to return, in a way, to Noth's position. Thus I shall work with the model of a Deuteronomistic History [[71]] edited by a "school," or better a "coalition," of scribes, former court functionaries, and "liberal" priests during the exile.[19] This edition underwent a considerable number of successive additions coming from the same milieu. Since, in my opinion, we do not have sufficient criteria for distinguishing these secondary additions, I will lump them all together under the siglum "Dtr^2."[20]

Deuteronomy's autonomy is only relative. Serving as the prologue to the Deuteronomistic History, which attempts to "make sense" of the catastrophe of the exile, its purpose must be understood within this context. The ideological crisis for the small kingdom of Judah signified by the exile of 597–587 can scarcely be overestimated. The pillars on which the identity of the people rested–king, Temple, land–had been knocked down. It was thus necessary to reinvent a new identity; and actually, a search for identity is always a search for "origins" as well.

So deuteronomistic Deuteronomy, conceived as far as chapter 30 as a great Mosaic discourse (with a few minor interruptions), transports the exiled community, for whom in my opinion it was intended,[21] into a situation of origins. By directly addressing their audience, the [[72]] Deuteronomists in a way made them into contemporaries of Moses, and this

18. If the deuteronomistic work appears to take ambiguous positions on certain points, we might see them either as the reflection of disputes within the deuteronomistic movement (what party does not have "factions"?) or else as a desire to exhibit to the addressees the complexity of an institution like the monarchy (see my "Mouvement deutéronomiste face à la royauté: Monarchistes ou anarchistes?" *Lumière et Vie* 178 [1986] 13–27).

19. The idea of a "coalition" much more easily explains the complexity of the Deuteronomistic History than the identification of its authors as a specific sociological group; see Albertz, "Intentionen," 48ff.; Clements, *Deuteronomy,* 78ff.; Erhard Blum, *Studien zur Komposition des Pentateuch* (BZAW 189; Berlin: de Gruyter, 1990) 341ff.

20. For a comparable approach, see Rose ("La croissance du corpus," 224ff.), who distinguishes between an "old Deuteronomistic layer" and a "new Deuteronomistic layer."

21. The location of the deuteronomistic enterprise in Palestine, contemplated by Noth, remains a widespread opinion among exegetes (see recently Albertz, "Intentionen," 49, 52 n. 64). However, a careful analysis of the texts very clearly reveals a Babylonian perspective. During the past few decades, an increasing number of investigators have placed the Deuteronomists among the exiles in Babylon, see esp. Ernest Wilson Nicholson, *Preaching to the Exiles: A Study of the Prose Traditions in the Book of Jeremiah* (Oxford: Blackwell, 1970) 117ff.; Jan Alberto Soggin, *Introduzione all'Antico Testamento* (Biblioteca di cultura religiosa 14; Brescia: Paideia, 1987) 215; Christopher R. Seitz, *Theology in Conflict: Reactions to the Exile in the Book of Jeremiah* (BZAW 176; Berlin: de Gruyter, 1989) 294ff.; Blum, *Studien zur Komposition,* 339ff. The rest of my article will also provide arguments in favor of an exilic location of the deuteronomistic enterprise.

transparent fiction corresponds well with the actual situation of the exiled community: as at the time of Moses, they are again/anew outside the land, and they await (re)entry. They find themselves in a desert, in "a land of want," in a place where "the need for divine aid makes itself felt most urgently."[22] We have the impression that by situating their addressees at the "origins" of Yahwistic faith, the Deuteronomists wished to temporarily wipe out entire centuries of history to signify that a new beginning was possible.

The purpose of Deuteronomy is visible (in addition to numerous parenetic passages) in what can be called "rhetorical techniques." This refers especially to the following phenomena:

(1) *Numeruswechsel* [['change of number']] is the name given to the continual variation between second-person singular [[here "thou"]] and plural [[here "you"]], sometimes within a single clause. A randomly chosen example is Deut 6:14–15: "You shall not go after other gods, of the gods of the peoples who are round about you; for YHWH thy God in the midst of thee is a jealous God." This distinctive characteristic of Deuteronomy[23] has been discussed in many dissertations,[24] without achieving a consensus. The *Numeruswechsel* has been used to distinguish the different literary layers, the "thou" sections being attributed to the original Deuteronomy, the "you" sections [[73]] to the deuteronomistic redaction.[25] Taken as an absolute, this approach quickly leads to an impasse. It is thus necessary above all to interpret the *Numeruswechsel* as a stylistic phenomenon.[26] The frequent interchange between "thou" and "you" serves first of all to hold the attention of the addressee, but it also expresses the fact that the community can be spoken to as an individual and that, consequently, each

22. For the symbolism of the desert, see A. de Pury, "L'image de désert dans l'Ancien Testament," in *Le Désert: Image et réalité (Actes du Colloque de Cartigny 1983)* (Cahiers du Centre d'Étude du Proch-Orient Ancien 3; Louvain: Peeters, 1989) 11–126, at 126.

23. It is not limited to Deuteronomy alone; see Exodus 21ff., Leviticus 19, etc.

24. See among recent works: Christopher Begg, *Contributions to the Elucidation of the Composition of Deuteronomy with Special Attention to the Significance of the Numeruswechsel* (Ph.D. diss., Louvain University, 1978); see also idem, "The Significance of the Numeruswechsel in Deuteronomy: The 'Pre-History' of the Question," *ETL* 55 (1979) 116–24; Yoshihide Suzuki, *The "Numeruswechsel" Sections of Deuteronomy* (Ph.D. Dissertation, Claremont Graduate School, 1982); William Robert Higgs, *A Stylistic Analysis of the Numeruswechsel Sections of Deuteronomy* (Ph.D Dissertation, Southern Baptist Theological Seminary, 1982).

25. G. Minette de Tillesse, "Sections 'tu' et sections 'vous' dans le Deutéronome," *VT* 12 (1962) 29–87.

26. N. Lohfink, *Das Hauptgebot: Eine Untersuchung literarischer Einleitungsfragen zu Dtn 5–11* (AnBib 20; Rome: Pontifical Biblical Institute, 1963) 239ff.; G. Braulik, *Die Mittel deuteronomischer Rhetorik erhoben aus Dtn 4, 1–40* (AnBib 68; Rome: Pontifical Biblical Institute, 1978) 146ff.

individual ("thou") represents the community ("you").[27] In this way, the responsibility of each individual to the instructions given by an intermediary of Moses with respect to the land-taking is stressed. This responsibility is linked to a *decision*. This aspect of decision is stressed by a second rhetorical technique.

(2) As we have already noticed, the Deuteronomists turned the addressees of Deuteronomy into contemporaries of Moses. In the process they distinguished, especially in the historical introduction of Deuteronomy 1–3, two Mosaic generations, the first generation, who died in the desert, and the following generation, who were promised possession of the land. Curiously, the addressees of Deuteronomy are identified sometimes with the first, sometimes with the second desert generation. And to push still further: Moses can tell his addressees that they are already dead. Thus Deut 1:34–35: "YHWH heard *your* words, and was angered, and he swore, 'Not one of these men of this evil generation shall see the good land which I swore to give to *your* fathers' "[28] (see also the "you" in 1:41ff.); and 2:14 states [[74]] that "the entire generation, that is, the men of war, had perished from the camp, as YHWH had sworn to *them*." Corresponding to this double identification (in 3:18ff. the "you" designates the generation of the conquest) is the end of the Mosaic discourse in 30:15ff., where the issue is one of choice: "See, I have set before thee this day life and good, death and evil. . . . Therefore choose life, that thou and thy descendants may live" (Deut 30:15, 19b). That is, the addressees must make a decision, and on their own decision will depend in the final analysis their identification with one or the other of the generations presented in Deuteronomy 1–3: the generation of death or the generation of life. It is certainly not an accident that this dual identification and the call to decide between life and death are found in emphasized fashion in the chapters that *frame* the testament of Moses (Deuteronomy 1–3, 30). This "ambiguity" in the identification of the addressees shows that the Deuteronomist is not attempting at all to conceal its fictive character. Perlitt is right to note that the deuteronomistic desire to make past history present, with a parenetic goal, pays no heed to chronology. The Deuteronomists knew that their audience was capable of understanding this elimination of

27. Pierre Buis and Jacques Leclercq, *Le Deutéronome* (SB; Paris: Gabalda, 1963) 9. These few remarks are not intended in the slightest to "close the book" on the *Numeruswechsel*. The diachronic investigations of F. García López (notably "Analyse littéraire de Deutéronome V–XI," *RB* 84 [1977] 481–522; 85 [1978] 5–41) especially deserve attention. For our purposes it seems legitimate to me to concentrate on the *effect* on the addressees provoked by the interchange between "thou" and "you."

28. L. Perlitt (*Deuteronomium* [BKAT 5/2; Neukirchen-Vluyn: Neukirchener Verlag, 1991] 115) thinks that v. 35 "provides a religious lesson to the head-shakers."

periodization and of applying to themselves the history presented.[29] This "pact" between author and reader includes "play" with the tradition, as well as "play" with the generations.

A very good example of this play is found in Deuteronomy 30, in the proclamation of the possibility of a happy future.

> Yhwh thy God will bring thee into the land which thy fathers possessed [*yrš*], that thou mayest possess it; and he will make thee more prosperous [*yṭb, Hiphil*] and numerous [*rbh, Hiphil*] than thy fathers. . . . For Yhwh will again take delight [*śwś*] in prospering thee, as he took delight in thy *fathers*. (Deut 30:5, 9b)

If one is wondering who the "fathers" alluded to are, the concordance provides a ready answer. The "fathers" of 30:5, 9 are the addressees of 28:63: "As YHWH took delight [*śwś*] in doing you good [*yṭb, Hiphil*] and multiplying you [*rbh, Hiphil*], so will YHWH take delight in bringing ruin upon you and destroying you; and you shall be plucked off the land which you are entering to take possession of it [*yrš*]." ⟦75⟧ In fact, these are the only two texts in all of Deuteronomy that combine *yṭb–rbh, Hiphil*; likewise the root *śwś* appears in Deuteronomy only in 28:63 and 30:9.[30] This means that the addressees to whom future curses are announced in the fiction of 28:45–46—and who experienced them in the reality of their life—are presented as *fathers* in 30:5, 9. Thus the addressees are transformed into *sons* for whom happiness again becomes possible.

Elsewhere, this play with the generations can express an insistence on *continuity*, despite the fracture of the exile. Gerhard von Rad observed that Deuteronomy is preoccupied with a "generational problem."[31] The crisis of the exile signified a crisis in faith in YHWH, especially regarding the new generations, who were at risk of being born outside the traditional framework of Israelite religion. This crisis explains the insistence in Deuteronomy on the teaching of the history of YHWH with Israel as well as the central role that the writer assigns to the *pater familias* ⟦'head of household'⟧ in this transmission of knowledge.[32] Deut 6:20ff. is a parade example.

> When thy son asks thee in time to come, "What is the meaning of the testimonies and the statutes and the ordinances which YHWH your God commanded you?" then thou shalt say to thy son, "We were Pharaoh's

29. Ibid., 134.

30. Note also the root *yrš* in both texts.

31. Gerhard von Rad ⟦*Old Testament Theology* (New York: Harper & Row, 1962) 1.225⟧.

32. On this subject, see José Loza, "Les Catéchèses étiologiques dans l'Ancien Testament," *RB* 78 (1971) 481–500; A. de Pury and T. Römer, "Mémoire et catéchisme dans l'Ancien Testament," in *Histoire et conscience historique dans les civilisations du Proche-Orient ancien* (ed. A. de Pury; Cahiers du CEPOA 5; Louvain: Peeters, 1989) 81–92.

> slaves in Egypt; and YHWH brought us out of Egypt with a mighty hand; and YHWH showed signs and wonders, great and grievous, against Egypt and against Pharaoh and all his household, before our eyes; and he brought us out from there, that he might bring us in and give us the land which he swore to our fathers." (Deut 6:20–23)

This catechism brings into play three generations. The "thou" designates the present generation, the "son" anticipates the generation [[76]] to come, and the "fathers" evoke the past generation. Past, present, and future are linked by these means, and the *ʾābôt* [['fathers']] recall the origins on which rests the history of YHWH with Israel. But what origins are they talking about? This question leads us to inquire into the "identity" of the fathers in Deuteronomy.

Reference to "Fathers" in Deuteronomy

The *ʾābôt,* the fathers or ancestors, play an extremely important role for deuteronomistic Deuteronomy. They appear about fifty times in theologically important contexts,[33] often within stereotyped expressions. There are the following formulas:

1. The most important group relates fathers to an oath of YHWH (expressed by the root *šbʿ*, *Niphal*). It concerns primarily the ground (*ʾădāmâ*) or the land (*ʾereṣ*) sworn to the fathers,[34] but there is also the covenant (*bĕrît*) sworn to the fathers;[35] three other texts do not immediately specify the content of the oath.[36]
2. The fathers appear further in the definition of YHWH as *ʾĕlohê ʾābôt* the 'God of the fathers'.[37]
3. Another series speaks of the addressees' and the fathers' "not knowing," epecially "other gods, which neither thou nor thy fathers have known."[38] [[77]]

33. I leave aside the following instances: Deut 5:16; 21:13, 18ff.; 22:15–16, 19, 21, 29; 23:1 (father [sg.] in legislative texts); see also 27:16, 20, 22; Deut 18:8; 24:16 (fathers [pl.] in legislative texts); Deut 32:6 (Yhwh as father); 32:7 (he who transmits knowledge like a father); 33:9 (Levi's father).

34. Deut 1:8, 35; 6:1, 18, 23; 7:13; 8:1; 10:11; 11:9; 11:21; 19:8; 26:3; 26:15; 28:11; 30:20; 31:7, 20, 21 (? the Masoretic Text has no object; see the apparatus of BHS and my *Israels Väter* [OBO 99; Fribourg: Éditions Universitaires, 1990] 184ff.); 34:4 (Abraham, Isaac, Jacob without the appellative "fathers").

35. Deut 4:31, 7:12, 8:18, 29:11ff.

36. Deut 7:8, 9:15, 13:18.

37. Deut 1:11, 21; 4:1; 6:3; 12:1; 26:7; 27:3; 29:24.

38. Other gods: 13:7[6], 28:64; 32:18; manna: 8:3, 16; people: 28:36.

4. Finally, there are a few other references to fathers that cannot be classified among the stereotyped expressions.[39]

These frequent references to fathers in Deuteronomy have scarcely been mined by exegetes. The reason is probably that they have never been problematic. In reading Deuteronomy first of all as the *end* of the Pentateuch, is it not obvious that the fathers in Deuteronomy recall the patriarchal traditions of Genesis? Furthermore, certain texts in Deuteronomy explicitly identify the fathers with the patriarchs. Thus, directly after the first mention of the *ʾābôt* in Deuteronomy (1:8), it is made clear by apposition that these fathers must be understood to be Abraham, Isaac, and Jacob, and these names are found in the last chapter of the book as well (Deut 34:4).[40] In this way, the names of the patriarchs form a quasi inclusio, reinforcing the identification fathers = patriarchs, currently accepted.

Still, the question must be asked: who in the redactional process is responsible for this identification? We have already seen that the fathers in Deut 30:5, 9, interpreted within the context of Deuteronomy, do not make any sort of allusion to the patriarchs. If we analyze the occurrences of the *ʾābôt* in terms of the context of deuteronomistic Deuteronomy, paying attention to the semantic fields within which they appear and considering Deuteronomy first of all as the prelude to the Deuteronomistic History, we arrive, in my opinion, at the following conclusion: for the deuteronomistic school, the fathers mentioned in the book of Deuteronomy are not Abraham, Isaac, and Jacob but are often a generation in Egypt, namely, the generation of the Exodus; in other [[78]] texts they designate the ancestors in general, without reference to a specific generation.[41] This pays attention to the fact that Deuteronomy's search for origins ends in Egypt. For the deuteronomistic redactors of Deuteronomy, the history of Israel begins in Egypt; the mention of the fathers serves to evoke these beginnings or to provide a condensed summary of YHWH's continual interven-

39. Deut 4:37; 5:3; 10:15, 22; 26:5; 30:5, 9; Deut 5:9 ("sin of the fathers"); and 31:16 ("lie down with his fathers") have a different status: unique within Deuteronomy, these expressions recur as stereotypical phrases in other books of the Old Testament.

40. The other texts identifying the fathers with the patriarchs are: Deut 6:10, 9:5, 29:12, 30:20. In 9:27 the names Abraham, Isaac, and Jacob appear without the appellative "fathers."

41. I have presented this theory in detail in *Israels Väter*, esp. pp. 9–271. It is inspired principally by an idea of J. Van Seters, "Confessional Reformulation in the Exilic Period," *VT* 22 (1972) 448–59. The conclusions of *Israels Väter* have been severely criticized by N. Lohfink, *Die Väter Israels im Deuteronomium: Zu einem Buch von Thomas Römer* (OBO 111; Fribourg: Éditions Universitaires, 1991). As I said in the rejoinder appended to Lohfink's work (pp. 111ff.), his criticism is based principally on an interpretation of Deuteronomy as the conclusion of the pre-Priestly "Pentateuch." In regard to the deuteronomistic context, I do not find sufficient arguments in Lohfink's treatment to persuade me to modify my theory.

tion on behalf of his people as well as his "present reality" in relation to past generations.

Within the bounds of this article, it is impossible to support this theory with a detailed analysis of every text mentioning the fathers.[42] We must be satisfied with more general remarks, illustrated with sample texts.

The "Non-knowing" of the Fathers

This formula first of all places the addressees in continuity with the fathers[43] but at the same time marks a "rupture" that occurs on the plane of the present generation. In regard to manna, "[which thou didst not know nor] did thy fathers know" (Deut 8:3, 16), it was a positive new thing in the activity of YHWH for his people. In the other cases, the expression "not knowing" evokes a crisis situation. Thus, in chapter 28, the exile is decribed as the fact of being led by YHWH toward "a nation that neither thou nor thy fathers have known" (v. 36) or as a situation in which they serve "other gods, which neither thou [[79]] nor thy fathers have known" (v. 64). This "novelty" of the deportation, which constitutes a threat to the relationship with YHWH, underlines the responsibility of the present generation, placed between the "preexilic" fathers and the future generations mentioned in the same context.

The *ʾĕlōhîm ʾăḥērîm* [['other gods']] against whom the Deuteronomists are constantly on guard[44] are characterized by this expression of not knowing in 13:7[6] and 32:17 to stress the rupture that their worship constitutes with respect to the history of YHWH with Israel.

In all of these texts, the fathers do not designate a specific generation. They symbolize Israel's past after Egypt or in the land (Deuteronomy 28); allusions to a patriarchal tradition are not found.

The "God of the Fathers"

In Deuteronomy, YHWH is presented eight times as the "God of the fathers." Most of the texts using this epithet belong to the secondary deuteronomistic layers (Dtr^2).[45] This explains, on the one hand, the less frequent use of this epithet in the rest of the Deuteronomistic History (and its

42. For a detailed treatment of the question, see my *Israels Väter*.

43. The fathers are never mentioned alone (for Deut 8:16 see v. 3); on the other hand *ʾăšer lōʾ yādaʿ* [['which thou didst not know']] is found without "fathers": Deut 11:28; 13:3, 14; 28:33; 29:25.

44. See the table of occurrences in García López, "Analyse littéraire," 43 n. 248; and my *Israels Väter*, 85–88.

45. They are, in my opinion, 4:1, 6:3, 12:1, 27:3, 29:24. The attribution of 1:11, 21 is difficult.

absence from the book of Jeremiah) and, on the other hand, its great popularity in the books of Chronicles.[46]

The "God of the fathers" appears primarily in introductions to the different sections of Deuteronomy.[47] This is a deliberate usage expressing the deuteronomistic [[80]] concern for the *continuity* of the generations. In fact, the mention of the "God of thy fathers" or "God of your fathers" is as a general rule preceded or followed by a "thy God" or a "your God" (see 1:10, 11; 1:21; 4:1, 2; 6:2, 3; and so on). In this way, the Deuteronomists insist on the fact that YHWH is the God of the present generation, perhaps against all evidence, just as he had been the God of the preceding generations. This rhetorical technique placed in the service of the kerygma is again reinforced by the fact that YHWH as the "God of the fathers" fairly frequently (four times out of eight) accompanies reminders of divine promises (*dbr*) to the addressees, as in Deut 1:11: "May YHWH, the God of *your fathers*, make you a thousand times more numerous than you are, and bless you, as he has promised *you*!"[48] The God who addresses the present generation is the same one who addressed the fathers. In most cases the fathers are the *ancestors in general* of the exiled community. In fact, these texts do not follow the Mosaic fiction to the letter. Thus Deut 12:1 ("These are the statutes and ordinances which you shall be careful to do in the land which YHWH, the God of thy fathers, has given thee to possess . . .") is formulated in such a way as to speak directly to the present and future addressees. In this verse, the relative clause "which I command thee [today]" is missing, a specification that in the Mosaic fiction frequently accompanies the legislative details, and the gift of the land is presupposed as having already been completed [[81]] (the perfect *ntn* is used, rather than the habitual participle).[49] Other references to the God of the fathers suggest a

46. The "God of the fathers" is attested 26 times in 1–2 Chronicles and 3 times in Ezra; see my *Israels Väter*, 344ff.

47. Deut 4:1, the new introduction (Dtr^2) after the historical summary in Deut 1–3; 6:3, the introduction to the *Shemaʿ* (the beginning of the original Deuteronomy?); 12:1, the prologue to the legislative code (the God of the fathers in 26:7, together with 12:1, forms a frame around the law collection); 27:3, beginning of the last section of the Mosaic discourse.

48. I will make two incidental remarks on this verse in passing. (1) In contrast to the land, the idea of multiplication (Deut 1:10ff.; 6:3; 7:13; 8:1; 10:22; 28:62; 30:5, 16) in Deuteronomy is not based on a *declaration* to the fathers. Only 13:18 makes the link with an oath addressed to the fathers, but it is a Dtr^2 text (see M. Rose, *Der Ausschließlichkeitsanspruch Jahwes: Deuteronomische Schultheologie und die Volksfrömmigkeit der späten Königszeit* [BWANT 106; Stuttgart: Kohlhammer, 1975] 99ff.). (2) The *kaʾăšer dbr* [['as he has promised']] in 1:11 (and other places) does not refer to a specific text (see the hesitations of Dieter Eduard Skweres, *Die Rückverweise im Buch Deuteronomium* [AnBib 79; Rome: Pontifical Biblical Institute, 1979] 174ff.). This phenomenon of "fictitious citations" will be found again in the analysis of the formula *(ka)ʾăšer.*

49. Because of this *ntn*, N. Lohfink ("Dtn 12, 1 und Gen 15, 18: Das dem Samen geschenkte Land als Geltungsbereich des deuteronomischen Gesetzes," in *Die Väter Israels:*

more specific identification with the ancestors in Egypt. If we compare the historical summary in Deut 26:5ff. (v. 7: "We cried to YHWH, the God of our fathers") with its "cousin" text in Num 20:15ff., without committing ourselves on the literary interdependence of these two texts,[50] it follows that these fathers do not refer to the patriarchs but to the generations going down to or living in Egypt. The same Egyptian perspective is visible in 29:24[25], where the catastrophe of the exile is explained as follows: "because they forsook the covenant of YHWH, the God of their fathers, which he made with them when he brought them out of the land of Egypt."[51] Let us now pause a few moments to consider the relationship between the fathers and the *bĕrît* ⟦'covenant'⟧ in Deuteronomy.

The Covenant Sworn to the Fathers

⟦82⟧ In Deuteronomy, this *bĕrît* sworn to the fathers is clearly rooted in the tradition of the giving of the law at Horeb. Let us begin with Deut 7:12: "the covenant and the steadfast love [*ḥsd*] which YHWH swore to thy fathers" is defined in v. 9 as "covenant and steadfast love [*ḥsd*][52] with those who love him and keep his commandments, to a thousand generations." The *bĕrît* is placed, in an obvious way, in the context of the Decalogue (see Deut 5:9ff.) and the revelation of the law.[53] The same context stands out

---

Beiträge zur Theologie der Patriarchenüberlieferungen im Alten Testament [F. J. Scharbert Festschrift; ed. M. Görg; Stuttgart: Katholisches Bibelwerk, 1989] 183–210) thinks that Deut 12:1 refers to Gen 15:18. Independent of the problem of the date of Genesis 15, the parallels between these two texts seem rather indistinct to me (see Lohfink's concessions, pp. 179ff.).

50. Most exegetes consider Num 20:15ff. to be the older text; see, e.g., N. Lohfink, "Un exemple de théologie de l'histoire dans l'ancien Israël: Dt 26, 5–9," *Archivio di filosofia* 39 (1971) 189–99; Siegfried Kreuzer, *Die Frühgeschichte Israels in Bekenntnis und Verkündigung des Alten Testaments* (BZAW 178; Berlin: de Gruyter, 1989); J. Briend, "Rite et parole en Dt 26, 1–11," in *Rituels: Mélanges offerts à Pierre-Marie Gy o.p.* (ed. Paul de Clerck and Erich Palazzo; Paris: Éditions du Cerf, 1990) 85–98. Nonetheless, to me it seems instead that Num 20:15ff. is a Dtr^2 text (see my *Israels Väter*, 551ff.) that corrects certain unusual features of Deut 26:5ff. (the Wandering Aramean) and introduces the *mlʾk*, often found in late texts (according to Blum [*Studien zur Komposition*, 119], in this postexilic text the word probably designates Moses). For a late dating of Num 20:15ff., see also J. Van Seters, "The Conquest of Sihon's Kingdom: A Literary Examination," *JBL* 91 (1972) 182–97; Siegfried Mittmann, "Num 20, 14–21: Eine redaktionelle Kompilation," in *Wort und Geschichte* (Kurt Elliger Festschrift; AOAT 18; Kevelaer: Butzon & Bercker / Neukirchen-Vluyn: Neukirchener Verlag, 1973) 143–49.

51. It is not entirely clear with whom the covenant is made: with "them" or with the "fathers," the LXX opting for the latter solution (*ha dietheto tois patrasin autôn* ⟦'which he made with their fathers'⟧), as in the parallel text, 1 Kgs 9:9. Even so, Deuteronomy nowhere else speaks of *making* a covenant with the fathers. In any case, the fathers designate a generation in Egypt, namely the generation of the Exodus, since Deut 29:23ff.[24ff.] is spoken by a generation that survived the catastrophe (for further details, see my *Israels Väter*, 128–33).

52. For this combination, see esp. 1 Kgs 8:23.

53. The vow specified in Deut 7:8 probably refers to this same covenant, or generally to an action by YHWH in Egypt (see Ezek 20:5ff.).

in 4:31: "He will not forget [*škḥ*] the covenant of thy *fathers* which he *swore* to them." This verse forms an inclusio with 4:23,[54] where the addressees are warned not to forget [*škḥ*] "the covenant of YHWH *your* God, which he *made* with you." In what follows (vv. 23ff.: the proscription of images, the jealous God), this covenant is once again identified as the covenant at Horeb.[55] We can moreover note that Deuteronomy makes an important difference between the verbs *šbʿ* in the *Niphal* [['swore']] and *krt* [['cut or make' (a covenant)]] in regard to the covenant. Throughout the book the *bĕrît* is exclusively *sworn* to the fathers, it is only *made* with the addressees.[56] In a way it is the theologoumenon of "promise and fulfilment." In this context the statement of Deut 5:3 can also be understood: "Not with our fathers did YHWH [[83]] make this covenant, but with us, who are all of us here alive this day." How much more could the present reality of this covenant be emphasized for the exiled community, which had become "contemporary" with Moses? To be sure, the covenant had been promised by oath to the fathers in *Egypt*,[57] but its (new) realization depends on the *hic et nunc* [['here and now']]. Thus the Deuteronomists of the second generation (since Deut 4:31, 5:2, 7:7ff., 8:18[?], 29:12 probably belong to the Dtr^2 stage) remind the exiles of the Exodus origin of the covenant by means of the fathers, and this covenant remains or, better, must become again the foundation of the relationship with YHWH.

The Land Sworn to the Fathers

This proclamation occupies the central position among the expressions concerning the *ʾābôt* [['fathers']]. Formally speaking, this formula can be divided into three groups.[58]

54. See Braulik, *Die Mittel deuteronomischer Rhetorik*, 77ff.; A. D. H. Mayes, "Deuteronomy 4 and the Literary Criticism of Deuteronomy," *JBL* 100 (1981) 23–51, at p. 25.

55. See C. Begg, "The Literary Criticism of Deut 4:1–10: Contributions to a Continuing Discussion," *Études théologiques de Louvain* 56 (1980) 10–55, at p. 52.

56. Covenant–addressees–*krt*: 4:23; 5:2; 9:9; 28:69; 29:11, 13; 31:16 (for 29:24, see n. 51). Covenant–fathers–*nšbʿ*: 4:31; 7:12; 8:18; 29:12.

57. The fathers of Deut 5:3 are not necessarily limited to the generations in Egypt. They might more generally symbolize for the exiled community the "past" that need not be taken into account. From this perspective, Deut 5:3 is not terribly far from the proclamation of the new covenant in Jer 31:31ff. Aside from the (late) insertion of the names Abraham, Isaac, and Jacob in 29:12, Deuteronomy has no interest whatsoever in a covenant with the patriarchs. Furthermore, in the Pentateuch this idea is attested only in Priestly texts (Exod 2:24, 6:2ff.; Lev 26:42; see also 2 Kgs 13:23; 1 Chr 16:15–18 = Ps 105:8–11); the stories in Genesis (Genesis 15, 17) mention only a covenant with Abraham.

58. Following a method used by R. Rendtorff, *Das überlieferungsgeschichtliche Problem des Pentateuch* (BZAW 174; Berlin: de Gruyter, 1977) 47–50; English translation: *The Problem of the Process of Transmission in the Pentateuch* (JSOTSup 89; Sheffield: JSOT Press, 1990).

- A first group (I) simply speaks of the land/ground that YHWH has sworn to the fathers.[59]
- A second group (II) specifies *lātēt lāhem* 'to give to "them"'[60]—that is, the recipients of the oath and of the land appear at first sight to be identical.
- A third group (III) specifies *lātēt lānû* 'to give to us' [[84]] or *lātēt lāk* 'to give to thee'[61]—that is, the recipients of the oath are distinguished from those of the land.

The temptation to see in these three groups an evolution "from shorter to longer" or to attribute them to three different redactional layers must nonetheless be resisted.

Actually, all of the texts with the short version of the oath are among the Dtr^2 texts, while the group II and III formulas are found in both Dtr and Dtr^2 texts.[62] The double specification of the oath with *lātēt lāhem* and *lātēt lāk* probably goes back to the deuteronomistic concept of two desert generations;[63] certainly, it stresses the openness of this oath as regards its definitive recipient. This expression about the land, sworn to the fathers, runs through every part of Deuteronomy except the legislative code in Deuteronomy 12ff.,[64] confirming once again the theory that the pre-deuteronomistic level of the book is found principally in these chapters. The constant refrain of the oath regarding the land also has very interesting compositional functions that we cannot go into here.[65]

59. Deut 6:18; 8:1; (19:8a;) 31:20, 21.

60. Deut 1:8, 35; (19:8b;) 10:11; 11:9, 21; 30:20; 31:7.

61. *Lānû* [['to us']] 6:23; 26:3, 25; *lāk* [['to thee']] 6:10; 7:13; 28:11; (34:4).

62. Group II: Dtr: 1:8, 35; (10:11?;) 31:7; Dtr^2: 11:9, 21; 30:20. Group III: Dtr: 6:10*, 28:11; Dtr^2: 6:23; 7:13; 26:3, 15. For arguments concerning this classification, see my *Israels Väter*, 137ff. Deut 19:8, which differs greatly from the other texts, is postdeuteronomistic, probably presupposing the Priestly texts; see Alexander Rofé, "The History of the Cities of Refuge in Biblical Law," *ScrHier* 21 (*Studies in the Bible*, ed. S. Japhet; Jerusalem: Magnes, 1986) 205–39.

63. The constructions with *lātēt lānû* [['to give to us']] are presupposed to be spoken by a (already/again) living speaker in the land. The *lāhem* [['to them']] in 10:11 and 31:7 could refer to the fathers and/or their descendants. In 1:8 and 11:9, after *lāhem* the 'descendants' (*zrʿ*) are found as second recipient.

64. Aside from Deut 19:8 (a postdeuteronomistic text, see n. 62) and 26:3 (the deuteronomistic conclusion of the legislative code).

65. Group II is especially used for "structuring" (see my *Israels Väter*, 226ff.). Some indications: 1:8 and 30:20 mark the beginning and end of the Mosaic discourse; 1:8 and 10:11 frame all of the "historical recapitulations" (chaps. 1–3; 5; 9:7–10, 11) of Deuteronomy (moreover the construction *bwʾ wyrš* 'go and take possession' linked to an oath made to the fathers is found in Deuteronomy first in 1:8 and last in 10:11); 1:35, 11:9, and 31:7 are linked by the evocation of Joshua and thus prepare for what follows (see Josh 1:6).

[[85]] For a reader coming from the book of Genesis, the discourse about the land sworn to the fathers easily evokes the promises of the land in the patriarchal narratives. And in the final form of Deuteronomy, the names Abraham, Isaac, and Jacob are found in some texts that deal with the land oath (1:8, 6:10, 30:20, 34:4). Futhermore, does not the constant use of *(ka)ʾăšer nišbaʿ* [['as he swore']] correspond to our "cf.," quoting something like the text of Genesis, as has often been thought?[66] However, if we look more closely, we realize that the verb *šbʿ Niphal* [['swore']] is very rarely attested in Genesis 12ff. and then only in texts that have long been considered late and dependent on the Deuteronomistic History (Gen 22:16, 24:7, 26:3, 50:24).[67] It is also far from certain that the expression *(ka)ʾăšer nišbaʿ* refers to a specific text on every occasion.[68]

Let us first attempt to interpret the land oath on the basis of the *deuteronomistic* context of Deuteronomy. We can state at this point that all the references to the land sworn to the fathers are found in semantic fields evoking Egypt, the Exodus, or the annihilation of enemies (linked to the tradition of the "war of YHWH").

Thus Deut 26:15 contains a prayer (Dtr²) forming the conclusion of the legislative collection, which is to be recited by every generation *in* the land: "Look down from thy holy habitation, from heaven, and bless thy people Israel and the ground which thou hast given us, as thou didst swear to our fathers, a land flowing with milk and honey." This description of the land is frequent in Deuteronomy, and moreover every occurrence of *zābat ḥālāb ûdĕbāš* [['flowing with milk and honey']] is connected to the *fathers* (the oath regarding the land: 11:9, 26:15, 31:20; the God of the fathers: 6:3, 26:9, 27:3). [[86]] Of course, this expression never appears in the patriarchal traditions; it is typical rather of the Exodus tradition,[69] as shown (among other things) by its first occurrence in the Pentateuch in Exod 3:8, 17, on the occasion of the call of Moses. Thus the great Jewish commentator Nachmanides (1194–1270), who has unfortunately found few followers, was right to remark that the fathers in this context apparently do not designate the patriarchs but the (first?) generation of the Exodus.[70]

66. See Skweres, *Die Rückverweise*; for *kaʾăšer*, see also Jacob Milgrom, "Profane Slaughter and a Formulaic Key to the Composition of Deuteronomy," *HUCA* 47 (1976) 1–17.

67. According to Rudolf Kilian (*Die vorpriesterlichen Abrahamsüberlieferungen literarkritisch und traditionsgeschichtlich untersucht* [BBB 24; Bonn: P. Hanstein, 1966] 204ff.), these texts are to be attributed to a redactor close to the Chronicler's History. See also A. de Pury, *Promesse divine et légende cultuelle dans le cycle de Jacob: Genèse 28 et les traditions patriarcales* (2 vols.; Paris: Gabalda, 1975) 332ff.

68. See Blum's critique of Skweres's position, in *Studien zur Komposition*, 172ff.

69. Siegfried Herrmann, *Die prophetischen Heilserwartungen im Alten Testament: Ursprung und Gestaltwandel* (BWANT 85; Stuttgart: Kohlhammer, 1965) 66 n. 3, 76.

70. Ramban (Nachmanides), *Commentary on the Torah: Deuteronomy* (trans. Charles B. Chavel; New York: Shilo, 1976) 315.

Let us take yet another example: Deut 6:18ff. serves as motivation for the exhortation not to test YHWH and to keep his commandments (v. 16ff.). Thus, "that it may go well with thee and that thou mayest go in and take possession of the good land which YHWH swore to give to thy fathers by thrusting out all thine enemies from before thee, as YHWH has promised." First we note a "military" context[71] typical of the books of Exodus (see, e.g., Exod 23:27ff.) and Deuteronomy but totally contradicting the "pacifist" attitude of the patriarchal narratives concerning other peoples.[72] Furthermore, the use of the adjective *ṭôbâ* ⟦'good'⟧ to describe the Promised Land is not found in Genesis either. The parallels (Exod 3:8, Num 14:7) again go back to the exodus tradition. This is the context in which the fathers must be located, the recipients of the oath of YHWH. For the Deuteronomists, therefore, the land was promised to fathers in Egypt. Moreover, the Old Testament in Ezekiel 20 clearly ⟦87⟧ attests the tradition of an oath of God in Egypt.[73] In this historical summary, YHWH reminds the addressees of their origins in Egypt. "I made myself known unto them in the land of Egypt, when I lifted up mine hand unto them,[74] to bring them forth out of the land of Egypt into a land that I had espied for them, flowing with milk and honey, which is the glory of all lands" (Ezek 20:5b, 6, KJV). Several verses later, this generation in Egypt is rightly called "fathers" (20:18, 24, and so on) and the end of this text proclaims for the exiled Israel entrance into "the country for the which I lifted up mine hand to give it to your *fathers*" (Ezek 20:42, KJV).

The use of this word in Ezekiel 20 is quite close to its use in deuteronomistic Deuteronomy. With the expression "the land sworn to the fathers," the Deuteronomists reminded their hearers of their origins in Egypt, origins that are particularly eloquent, even transparent, for an exiled community. Are there not parallels between Egypt and Babylon? Cannot YHWH who intervened on behalf of the fathers in Egypt intervene again for the diaspora in Babylon?

71. It is principally the phrase *bwʾ wyrš* ⟦'go and take possession'⟧ that refers to the tradition of the war of YHWH (see A. de Pury, "La guerre sainte israélite: Réalité historique ou fiction littéraire?" *ETR* 56 [1981] 5–38 at 20ff.) and the verb *hdp* ⟦'drive out'⟧ (see Deut 9:4, Josh 23:5). Who is the subject in 6:19, YHWH or Israel? Perhaps this ambiguity is intentional, to show a certain "cooperation" between YHWH and Israel during the expulsion of the enemies.

72. See the fine article by the late Jacques Pons, "Confrontation et dialogue en Genèse 12–36," *ETR* 65 (1990) 15–26.

73. For this very important text, see esp. J. Lust, "Ez., XX, 4–26: Une parodie de l'histoire religieuse d'Israël," in *De Mari à Qumran: L'Ancien Testament* (J. Coppens Festschrift; ed. Henri Cazelles; BETL 24; Gembloux, 1969) 127–66; and recently Franz Sedlmeier, *Studien zur Komposition und Theologie von Ezechiel 20* (SBB 21; Stuttgart: Katholisches Bibelwerk, 1990).

74. The author of this text uses the phrase *nśʾ yd* 'raise the hand'.

If for the deuteronomistic editors of Deuteronomy the fathers evoke Egypt, the insertion of the names of the patriarchs at certain points must be attributed to a *post*deuteronomistic redaction. The identification "fathers = patriarchs" is facilitated from the moment Deuteronomy no longer functions as a prologue to the Deuteronomistic History, but as a conclusion to the Pentateuch. In order to have readers who have begun at Genesis think of Abraham, Isaac, and Jacob when they come to the "fathers" in Deuteronomy, practically all that was needed was to create a "patriarchal frame" around the book by inserting the names Abraham, Isaac, and Jacob at the beginning (1:8, 6:10) and end (30:20, 34:4).

Even so, certain passages in the corpus resist the suggested identification, especially Deut 9:5. In its present form, this verse reads as follows: "Not [[88]] because of thy righteousness or the uprightness of thy heart art thou going in to possess their land; but because of the wickedness of these nations YHWH thy God is driving them out from before thee, and that he may confirm the word which YHWH swore to thy fathers, to Abraham, to Isaac, and to Jacob." Curiously, not one of the patriarchal narratives contains a promise concerning the expulsion of peoples.[75] On the contrary, this tradition of a military conquest is closely connected to the Exodus. If the narrators wanted the reader to identify the fathers with the patriarchs, it was necessary to add their names explicitly. The same observation applies to Deut 29:12ff. The addition of the names of Abraham, Isaac, and Jacob in a context where the fathers appear in connection with the "covenant formula" (YHWH, the God of Israel–Israel, the people of YHWH), typical of the Sinai tradition,[76] already presupposes the reclaiming of this formula on behalf of Abraham by the Priestly school (Genesis 17).[77] Similarly, in the deuteronomistic intercessory prayer of Deut 9:26ff., which is constructed exclusively around the exodus, the addition of the names of the patriarchs to verse 27 "interrupts the perfect continuity of the motif of the exodus from Egypt in verses 26 and 28," as Jacques Vermeylen, for example, puts it.[78]

75. John A. Emerton, "The Origin of the Promises to the Patriarchs in the Older Sources of the Book of Genesis," *VT* 32 (1982) 14–32, at p. 30: "No such promise was made to the patriarchs. It may be agreed that this promise was made to the Israelites at the time of the Exodus."

76. Rudolf Smend, *Die Bundesformel* ([[ThStud]] 68; Zurich: EVZ, 1963).

77. So, among others, Alexander Reinhard Hulst, "Opmerkingen over de Kaʾašer-Zinnen in Deuteronomium," *NedTT* 18 (1963–64) 337–61 at 345.

78. Jacques Vermeylen, "Les Sections narratives de Dt 5–11 et leur relation à Ex 19–34," in *Das Deuteronomium: Entstehung, Gestalt und Botschaft* (ed. N. Lohfink; BETL 68; Louvain: Peeters, 1985) 175–207, at p. 201.

If the presence of Abraham, Isaac, and Jacob is due to a postdeuteronomistic redaction (in my opinion, the final redaction of the Pentateuch), does this mean that the deuteronomistic school was unaware of any patriarchal tradition; or, to put it another way, what existed for the Deuteronomists *before* Egypt? In Deuteronomy there are only two texts that explicitly mention a descent into Egypt, one of which (Deut 10:22), with its allusion to 70 fathers, who made the journey, seems to be late and even dependent on Priestly texts [[89]] (Gen 46:27, Exod 1:5).[79] In contrast, Deut 26:5, the beginning of the famous "historical credo," certainly belongs to the deuteronomistic edition of the book and probably goes back to an ancient tradition.[80] "A wandering Aramean was my father; and he went down into Egypt." We note first of all that this father (singular!) remains anonymous. And if this text is meant to allude to Jacob,[81] evoking such an Aramean ancestor corresponds rather badly with the Jacob cycle in Genesis or his descent into Egypt in royal chariots (Gen 49:19ff.). Albert de Pury has proposed an interpretation of this enigmatic text. He says, "The Deuteronomist intended to present the ancestor in an unfavorable light: this ancestor is a stranger and he is in distress. The Deuteronomist definitely did not want to know anything about the patriarchs, let alone Jacob!"[82] Egypt is the beginning of the history of *Israel*; the ancestor who descended there is still an *Aramean*.

This rejection of the tradition of Jacob (and of all patriarchal tradition?) is probably an inheritance from the prophet Hosea, the "spiritual father" of the deuteronomistic movement. Hosea 12 contains a ferocious criticism of a religious identity passed through the blood, namely by identification with an ancestor (Jacob). The listeners are exhorted to abandon this way and to turn toward YHWH, "God ever since Egypt" [[NJPSV]], whose relationship is mediated by a prophet (Hos 12:10[9], 14[13]).[83] Deuteronomy has clearly chosen this "vocational," exodus option: the importance

79. See Mayes, *Deuteronomy*, 211ff.; Preuss, *Deuteronomium*, 50.

80. Ever since Leonhard Rost ("Das kleine geschichtliche Credo," *Das kleine Credo und andere Studien zum Alten Testament* [Heidelberg: Quelle & Meyer, 1965] 11–25), vv. 5* and 10a have been considered an ancient formula enlarged later; see Lohfink, "Un exemple de théologie"; Briend, "Rite et parole," 90.

81. The identification of the father in Deut 26:5 with Jacob remains the current opinion; there are, however, several skeptical voices, such as, for example, Mayes, *Deuteronomy*, 334; and earlier, Kurt Galling, *Die Erwählungstraditionen Israels* (BZAW 48; Giessen: Alfred Töpelmann, 1928). 1 Sam 12:8 may be cited in favor of identification with Jacob.

82. A. de Pury, "Le Cycle de Jacob comme légende autonome des origines d'Israël," in *Congress Volume: Leuven, 1989* (VTSup 43; Leiden: Brill, 1991) 83.

83. For further details, see A. de Pury, "Osée 12 et ses implications pour le débat actuel sur le Pentateuque," in [[*Le Pentateuque: Débats et recherches* (Lectio Divina 151; Paris: Éditions du Cerf, 1992)]] 175ff.

of Moses in [[90]] Deuteronomy no longer needs to be demonstrated, and several times we have mentioned the fact that each generation is called to be responsible in relation to the divine demands. The role of the fathers in Deuteronomy is in keeping with this point of view. Contrary to the patriarchal narratives, which can be characterized as a "narrative genealogy,"[84] the fathers in Deuteronomy, despite all their importance, remain an anonymous, collective mass. They express the exodus origins of the addressees and the continuity of the history of Israel with YHWH. But at the same time the appeal to them shows that the present and the future can only succeed if the addressees "choose life," that is, the Torah and its Mosaic mediation.

The Importance of the "Fathers" for the Structure of the Deuteronomistic History

The exodus interpretation of the fathers in Deuteronomy is confirmed in the rest of the Deuteronomistic History, the books from Joshua through 2 Kings.[85]

In fact, the formula of the land sworn to the fathers is found from the beginning of the book of Joshua. Josh 1:6, "Be strong and of good courage; for thou shalt cause this people to inherit the land which I swore to their fathers to give them," is strongly reminiscent of the allusion to the oath in Deut 31:7. The close connection between the two books is thus underlined.

The oath addressed to the fathers appears for the last time in the [[91]] Deuteronomistic History in Josh 21:43ff.: the introduction to the covenant of Joshua in chapter 23 that signifies the end of the conquest.

> Thus YHWH gave to Israel *all* the land which he swore to give to their fathers; . . . And YHWH gave them rest on every side according to *all* he had sworn to their fathers; not one of *all* their enemies had withstood them, for YHWH had given *all* their enemies into their hands. Not one of *all* the

84. See E. Blum, *Die Komposition der Vätergeschichte* (WMANT 57; Neukirchen-Vluyn: Neukirchener Verlag, 1984) 484.

85. For the following, see my *Israels Väter*, 285ff.; these are the important texts for a "theology of the fathers" in Joshua to 2 Kings: The oath made to the fathers: Josh 1:6, 5:6 (Dtr^2), 21:43ff.; Judg 2:1 (post-Dtr). The land given to the fathers: 1 Kgs 8:34, 40, 48; 14:15; 2 Kgs 21:8. "Commanded the fathers": Judg 2:20, 3:4 (Dtr^2); 1 Kgs 8:58; 2 Kgs 17:23. The covenant concluded with the fathers: 1 Kgs 8:21; 2 Kgs 17:15. The God of the fathers: Josh 18:3 (post-Dtr?); Judg 2:12; 2 Kgs 21:22. The fathers and Egypt: Josh 24:6, 17 (post-Dtr); Judg 6:13; 1 Sam 12:6, 8 (Dtr^2); 1 Kgs 8:21, 53 (Dtr^2); 9:9; 2 Kgs 21:15. The fathers compared to the following generations: Judg 2:17 (Dtr^2), 19, 22 (Dtr^2); 1 Kgs 14:22; 2 Kgs 17:14, 41 (post-Dtr). Others: Josh 4:21 (Dtr^2?), 22:8; 1 Sam 12:7, 15 (Dtr^2); 1 Kgs 8:57; 2 Kgs 22:13.

good promises which YHWH had made to the house of Israel had failed; *all* came to pass. (Josh 21:43–45)[86]

Kôl 'all' is found six times in these three verses. All, really all, that YHWH promised was realized. At the level of the "chronology" of the deuteronomistic work, the book of Joshua is thus presented as the fulfillment of the promises to the fathers on which Deuteronomy had been so insistent, but at the same time these verses are intended for addressees who are deprived of this fulfillment. From this point of view, this proclamation is still effective on a new level, as summarized by Gerhard von Rad: "With the fulfillment of the history, the present reality of this ancient promise is not diminished. . . . The promise of the land remains in force for Israel despite its first fulfillment."[87]

The fathers who recall this promise in the book of Joshua, as in Deuteronomy, are the generation sojourning in Egypt, the generation of the exodus; in Joshua they are not identified with the patriarchs at all, and moreover the context shows that they are unfamiliar with the patriarchal traditions (see, for Josh 21:43ff., the theme of "rest," the extermination of enemies; for 5:6 "the milk and honey" and so forth).

After the text of Joshua 21, the relationship between the "fathers" and the "land" will be defined differently. Henceforth, one [[92]] no longer says "the land that YHWH *swore* to their fathers"[88] but "the land that YHWH *gave* to the fathers," and this is found for the first time in 1 Kings 8, during Solomon's dedication of the Temple[89] (1 Kgs 8:40: "that [the people Israel] may fear thee all the days that they live in the land which thou gavest to our fathers"). The appearance of the formula of the gift of the land to the fathers in 1 Kings 8 calls to mind the following remarks:

86. It is not necessary to divide these verses into two different layers as is done by, for example, G. Braulik, "Zur deuteronomistischen Konzeption von Frieden und Freiheit," in *Congress Volume: Salamanca, 1983* (ed. J. A. Emerton; VTSup 36; Leiden: Brill, 1985) 29–39 = G. Braulik, *Studien zur Theologie des Deuteronomiums* (Stuttgarter Biblische Aufsatzbände 2; Stuttgart: [[Katholisches Bibelwerk]], 1988) 219–30. The pervasiveness of *kôl* [['all']] is explained very well as the choice of a single author.

87. G. von Rad, "Typologische Auslegung des Alten Testaments," *EvT* 12 (1952–53) = *Gesammelte Studien zum Alten Testament* (TBü 8; Munich: Kaiser, 1971) 272–88 at 284.

88. This expression is found again in Judg 2:1, but this verse is part of a postdeuteronomistic insertion (Judg 2:1–5); see, e.g., A. D. H. Mayes, *Judges* (Old Testament Guides; Sheffield: JSOT Press, 1985) 60; Van Seters, *In Search of History*, 341ff.; Pierre Gibert, *Vérité historique et esprit historien: L'histoire biblique de Gédéon face à Hérodote* (Paris: Éditions du Cerf, 1990) 26.

89. In the deuteronomistic editing of the book of Jeremiah, the formula of the gift of the land likewise appears for the first time at the moment the Temple is spoken of (Jeremiah 7). And like 1 Kings 8, Jeremiah 7 immediately evokes the exile and the destruction of the Temple.

1. For the Deuteronomists, the land was not decisively given until the construction of the Temple. But as in Josh 21:43ff. and chapter 23, the "true" situation of the readers is taken into account. During the inaugural prayer, the exile and the destruction of the Temple are constantly present.

   If [the people Israel] sin against thee . . . so that they are carried away captive to the land of the enemy . . . if they repent . . . and pray to thee toward their land, which thou gavest to their fathers, the city which thou hast chosen, and the house which I have built for thy name; then hear thou in heaven. (1 Kgs 8:46–49*; cf. vv. 33ff.)

2. The fathers of the gift of land are thus the generation of the conquest, or to put it another way: they are the addressees of Deuteronomy (to whom the gift of land is frequently promised), who have become the "fathers" in 1 Kings 8 and elsewhere.

This transformation of the addressees of Deuteronomy into fathers appears also in the use of the verbs *krt* 'make (a covenant)' and *ṣwh* 'command'. These verbs, which in Deuteronomy are reserved for the hearers alone (see Deut 5:3, 6:1, and so on) are now related to the fathers; thus 1 Kgs 8:21 speaks of the "*bĕrît* ⟦'covenant'⟧ of YHWH which he made with our fathers, when he brought them out of the land ⟦93⟧ of Egypt," or 2 Kgs 17:13 of "all the Torah which I commanded your fathers."

"They forsook YHWH, the *God of their fathers*, who had brought them out of the land of Egypt"–this is how the deuteronomistic redactor summarizes his presentation of the period of judges in Judg 2:12. The same phrase, "forsake YHWH, the God of the fathers," reappears to characterize the reign of Amon, the predecessor of Josiah. The history of Israel from the period of judges to the reign of Josiah is thus framed by the theme of disobedience to YHWH, the God of the fathers. By using this phrase the Deuteronomists confirm once more the great esteem they had for Josiah and his reform: Josiah who walked "in all the ways of David his father" (2 Kgs 22:2); thus a relationship is established between the two kings who, along with Hezekiah (2 Kgs 18:3), constitute the exceptions to the negative history of Israel after the period of judges.[90] This negative view of history also becomes clear in texts that recall the disobedience of the fathers and their descendants, such as Judg 2:19: "But whenever the judge died, they turned back and behaved worse than their fathers." The period of Moses thus nearly looks like a "golden age." This is the period when the

90. Solomon is portrayed (1 Kgs 11:1ff.) more ambiguously. As for Hezekiah, his submission to the king of Assyria (2 Kgs 18:13ff.) introduces a small discordant note.

promises made to the fathers in Egypt were realized, which is why the exilic addressees of Deuteronomy must reappropriate the period of exodus and conquest.

The patriarchs have no place in this view of origins. In fact, the scarce references to Abraham, Isaac, and Jacob (Israel) in the books from Joshua to 2 Kings all belong to postdeuteronomistic contexts.[91] A postexilic [[94]] date also seems likely for Joshua 24.[92] This text, which exhibits many parallels with Nehemiah 9, integrates the three patriarchs into its recapitulation of history. It is interesting to note that of these only Abraham receives the title "father," whereas the *fathers* appear in Joshua 24, as in deuteronomistic texts, after Egypt, as shown by v. 6: "I brought *your fathers* out of Egypt." Apparently the postexilic authors knew and respected the difference between the patriarchs and the deuteronomistic fathers. In fact, many biblical texts retain a trace of the fact that these two types of ancestor reflect two different types of origin myth. For the deuteronomistic redactors, the true and only Israel was found in the Babylonian exile, and they presented them, for obvious reasons, with an origin myth of the "Exodus" type, with fathers in Egypt, outside the land. The patriarchs, by contrast, seem in the same period to have represented an origin myth that might be called "autochthonous," in the sense that they were apparently popular among the nonexiled population (in Ezek 33:24, those who remained in Palestine laid claim to the land by appealing to Abraham).[93] These patriarchs, of whom the Deuteronomists were not terribly fond, nonetheless found their way into Deuteronomy.

91. These are 1 Sam 12:8 (see A. D. H. Mayes, *The Story of Israel between Settlement and Exile: A Redactional Study of the Deuteronomistic History* [London: SCM, 1983] 101; 1 Kgs 18:31, 36 (see Immanuel Benzinger, *Die Bücher der Könige* [Kurzer Hand-Commentar zum Alten Testament 9; Fribourg-en-Breisgau: Mohr, 1899] 111); 2 Kgs 13:23 (see Martin Rehm, *Das zweite Buch der Könige: Ein Kommentar* [Wurzburg: Echter, 1982] 135); 2 Kgs 17:34 (see Rehm, p. 173).

92. Despite the impressive work of William T. Koopmans (*Joshua 24 as Poetic Narrative* [JSOTSup 93; Sheffield: JSOT Press, 1990]), who envisions a date around the seventh century (pp. 410ff.), a postexilic date recommends itself for good reasons to a considerable number of exegetes; see especially Mayes, *The Story of Israel*, 49ff.; J. Van Seters, "Joshua 24 and the Problem of Tradition in the Old Testament," *In the Shelter of Elyon* (G. W. Ahlström Festschrift; ed. W. Boyd Barrick and John R. Spencer; JSOTSup 31; Sheffield: JSOT Press, 1984) 139–58; Christoph Levin, *Die Verheißung des neuen Bundes in ihrem theologiegeschichtlichen Zusammenhang ausgelegt* (FRLANT 137; Göttingen, 1985) 114ff.; Blum, *Studien zur Komposition*, 363ff.; Uwe Becker, *Richterzeit und Königtum: Redaktionsgeschichtliche Studien zum Richterbuch* (BZAW 192; Berlin: de Gruyter, 1990) 69ff.

93. See Sara Japhet, "People and Land in the Restoration Period," in *Das Land Israel in biblischer Zeit: Jerusalem-Symposium 1981* (ed. Georg Strecker; GTA 25; Göttingen, 1983) 103–25.

Deuteronomy as the Conclusion to the Pentateuch

[[95]] It appears quite certain that the Torah as an official document first saw the light of day in the context of a Persian policy known as "imperial authorization."[94] The prospect of the publication of the Pentateuch, sanctioned by Persian authority, implies a search within Judaism for a compromise[95] between the various ideological currents, especially between the "Priestly" redactors and the "Deuteronomists."

This is the context in which the separation of Deuteronomy from the Deuteronomistic History and its attachment to the Pentateuch is probably situated,[96] perhaps initially with the intention of reinforcing the deuteronomistic position somewhat. But how could the integration of Deuteronomy into this new Torah corpus be further emphasized? This is what might be called the "final redaction," concerned for the harmony of the whole, which took on the task by inserting into Deuteronomy (and elsewhere)[97] the names of the patriarchs, in apposition to the deuteronomistic fathers. The theory that this identification is the work of a redaction of the Pentateuch is confirmed by the fact that neither in Joshua through 2 Kings nor in Jeremiah are the fathers assimilated in this way to the patriarchs. As we have already seen, the insertion of the names of Abraham, Isaac, and Jacob into Deuteronomy was carried out in a very considered way; it happened at strategic locations, such as the very beginning (Deut 1:8) and the end (34:4) of the book. The next insertion appears in 6:10, the first text mentioning [[96]] an oath to the fathers after the historical surveys in Deuteronomy 1–3 and 5 (and the first text belonging to "group II"); in 30:20 the insertion of the patriarchal triad marked the end of the great Mosaic discourse. Finally, the names of Abraham, Isaac, and Jacob were introduced into three "difficult" passages (9:5, 9:27, 29:12), where the context scarcely permitted an "automatic" allusion to the traditions of the patriarchs. By mentioning Abraham, Isaac, and Jacob seven times[98] and thence-

94. Frank Crüsemann, "Le Pentateuque, une Tora: Prolégomènes à l'interprétation de sa forme finale," in *La Pentateuque en question* (ed. A. de Pury; Le Monde de la Bible; Geneva: Labor et Fides, 1991) 339–60.

95. See ibid., 353ff., and the presentation by Blum, *Studien zur Komposition,* 345ff. (in my opinion, more convincing).

96. See Crüsemann, "Le Pentateuque, une Tora," 359.

97. Peter Weimar (*Die Berufung des Mose: Literaturwissenschaftliche Analyse von Exodus 2, 23 – 5, 5* [OBO 23; Fribourg: Éditions Universitaires, 1980] 341ff.) attributed the definition of the "God of the fathers" as the "God of Abraham, Isaac, and Jacob" in Exodus 3–4 to the final redactor of the Pentateuch.

98. The figure 7 in itself is not an argument for dating these texts. Rather, it reinforces the theory of a deliberate procedure; see G. Braulik, "Die Funktion von Siebenergruppierungen im Endtext des Deuteronomiums," in *Ein Gott, eine Offenbarung: Beiträge zur biblischen*

forth imposing the identification "fathers = patriarchs," the final redaction is manifestly striving to separate Deuteronomy from the Deuteronomistic History and reinforce the cohesiveness of the Pentateuch. In fact, the promises made to the patriarchs now function as a leitmotif covering the entirety of "Genesis to Deuteronomy" (see especially Gen 50:24; Exod 32:13, 33:1; Lev 26:42; Num 32:11; Deut 32:4). The last passage containing this promise is particularly interesting. Just before the death of Moses, YHWH shows him the land with the following comment: "This is the land which I swore to Abraham, to Isaac, and to Jacob, 'I will give it to thy descendants.'" This verse offers two major modifications with respect to the occurrences of the divine oath in Deuteronomy: the patriarchs are not called "fathers,"[99] and the oath is expressed by a direct quotation and not by an infinitive construction. These changes come from the fact that in this chapter, which reflects one of the "last stages of the redaction of the Pentateuch,"[100] v. 4 was composed entirely during the final redaction.[101] ⟦97⟧ In fact, the direct quotation in Deut 34:4 repeats the *first* promise of the land addressed to Abraham in Gen 12:7: "To your descendants I will give this land." The promise is thus reiterated[102] at the end of the journey and applied to all three patriarchs.[103] In the context of the Pentateuch, it will remain unfulfilled, which confers on the Torah a feeling of prologue. This nonfulfillment is perhaps to be explained initially by the constraints of Persian censorship; according to F. Crüsemann, a document recognized as imperial law "could not contain in any way a narrative of the violent conquest of important neighboring provinces,"[104] but afterward this prologue made it easier for each new generation to appropriate the divine

---

Exegese, Theologie und Spiritualität (N. Füglister Festschrift; ed. Friedrich Vinzenz Reiterer; Würzburg: Echter, 1991) 37–50.

99. Several versions have noticed this "irregularity" and added *lʾbtyk* ⟦'to your fathers'⟧; see BHS.

100. Buis and Leclercq, *Le Deutéronome*, 213.

101. This theory is corroborated by the observation that Deut 34:4 apparently presupposes 32:52. Deut 32:48–52 is as a rule generally attributed to "P" (see recently M. Rose, "Empoigner le Pentateuque par sa fin! L'investiture de Josué et la mort de Moïse," in *La Pentateuque en question* [ed. A. de Pury; Le Monde de la Bible; Geneva: Labor et Fides, 1991] 129–47 at 142). If we were to follow L. Perlitt ("Priesterschrift im Deuteronomium?" *ZAW* 100 [suppl.; 1988] 65–88 at 72ff.), who attributes Deut 32:48ff. to a post-Priestly, "deuteronomizing" redactor (the final redactor?), we could envisage the same author for both texts.

102. See also Gen 12:6: Abraham passed through (*ʿbr*) the land; and Deut 34:4: "Thou shalt not go over (*ʿbr*) there." The relationship between the two texts has been emphasized by Sven Tengstrom, *Die Hexateucherzählung: Eine literaturgeschichtliche Studie* (ConBOT 7; Lund: Gleerup, 1976) 146ff.

103. This explains the quotation in Deut 34:4 of a speech in the singular addressed to all three patriarchs. Some versions attempted to "correct" this; see BHS.

104. Crüsemann, "Le Pentateuque, une Tora," 359ff.

promises. If the Pentateuch is "framed" (the origins cycle aside) by the patriarchal traditions, the Exodus traditions nonetheless retain their relative importance. Let us simply recall that Genesis 12–35* in fact constitutes an autonomous "major unity"[105] that in its oldest weft furnishes an independent origins story.[106] The "rupture" between the story of the patriarchs and the story of the exodus is still visible in the tale of the calling of Moses (Exodus 3), where the land promised to the generation in Egypt is presented as completely unknown and without any reference to a patriarchal promise (Exod 3:8ff.).[107] In a compromise document it was inevitable to countenance a "cohabitation" of the two [[98]] origin myths. And it is Deuteronomy, functioning as the "link," that in its final form brilliantly reflects this cohabitation: reading Deuteronomy as the climax of the Pentateuch, the patriarchal origins have the last word; but taking Deuteronomy as the prologue to the Deuteronomistic History, the exodus origins regain their full importance. However we read this book, it confronts every individual and every generation with the eternally vital question of origins.[108]

105. For the phrase, see Rendtorff, *Das überlieferungsgeschichtliche Problem*, and *Introduction à l'Ancien Testament*, 273ff.

106. See the remarks of de Pury and Römer, "Le Pentateuque en question," 77ff.

107. For the problem, see Jean Louis Ska, "Un nouveau Wellhausen?" *Bib* 72 (1991) 253–63, at p. 258.

108. Recent events in Eastern lands, especially the Soviet Union, demonstrate once again that a crisis in a system provokes a crisis in its origin myths. The toppling of the statues of Lenin is a symbol of the rejection of a "founding father." The change of "Leningrad" to "St. Petersburg" is in this respect most eloquent.

The Succession of Joshua

J. ROY PORTER

The argument is that the succession of Joshua to Moses as depicted by Dtr reflects the practice and ideology of the Israelite monarchy. The essay builds on N. Lohfink's discovery of a formula of succession in Josh 1:1–9, which has strong echoes of the law of the king in Deut 17:14–20. Porter explores the possible location of a ritual of royal succession in the covenant ritual at Shechem, which was a widely accepted postulate at the time when he wrote (less fashionable now, but see Sperling in this volume [pp. 240–58]). He looked further for support to ancient Near Eastern practices as evidenced in royal treaty texts.

The idea that Joshua represents an ideal royal figure has been widely taken up in scholarship on the DH (cf. G. E. Gerbrandt, *Kingship according to the Deuteronomistic History* [*SBLDS* 87; Atlanta: Scholars Press, 1986] 116–23; M. Weinfeld, *Deuteronomy and the Deuteronomic History* [Oxford: Clarendon, 1972; repr. Winona Lake, Ind.: Eisenbrauns, 1992] 170–71; R. D. Nelson, "Josiah in the Book of Joshua," *JBL* 100 [1981] 531–40). Porter faces squarely the problem for the argument that Joshua is not, after all, Moses' son. In contrast, C. Schäfer-Lichtenberger (*Josua und Salomo* [VTSup 58; Leiden: Brill, 1995], especially p. 220) questioned whether similarities in certain respects entail similarities in all respects. The more fundamental question is whether the deuteronomic and Davidic concepts of kingship are the same, as Porter argues. Contrast Knoppers ("The Deuteronomist and the Deuteronomistic Law of the King," *ZAW* 108 [1996] 329–46), who contrasts the deuteronomic king-law sharply with what he sees as Dtr's positive portrayal of Solomon's wealth and power.

[[102]] In the Pentateuch and the book of Joshua, there are a number of passages which describe in different ways the designation of Joshua as Moses' successor, and the nature of the work he is appointed to perform.

Reprinted with permission from John I. Durham and J. Roy Porter (eds.), *Proclamation and Presence: Old Testament Essays in Honour of Gwynne Henton Davies* (London: SCM / Richmond: John Knox, 1970) 102–32.

The number and variety of such descriptions show that this was an important element in the Pentateuchal tradition about Joshua. Indeed, if Noth is correct, it is the oldest surviving element in that tradition in the Pentateuch as we have it–in contrast to at least some material in the book of Joshua–for he argues that only in the original form of Num 27:15–23 is the figure of Joshua genuinely and originally at home in a predeuteronomic and pre-Priestly passage.[1] The traditions dealing with [[103]] the appointment of Joshua as Moses' successor have been discussed in part by K. Möhlenbrink[2] and, as far as the specifically Deuteronomic material is concerned, by N. Lohfink.[3] Combining their discussions, two basic blocks of material may be distinguished:

1. Num 27:12–23[4] + Deut 34:9,[5] in connection with which Num 32:28 and 34:17 have also to be considered.
2. Deut 31:1–8,[6] 14f., 23 and Josh 1:1–9, with which Deut 1:38; 3:21f., 28 are clearly connected.

1. In his *Überlieferungsgeschichte des Pentateuch* (Stuttgart: W. Kohlhammer Verlag, 1948) 193, Noth holds that in its existing form Num 27:15–23 is part of the P narrative work, but that it must depend on older and predeuteronomic traditions, since it does not suit the interests of P, which was not concerned with any narrative of the conquest of Palestine, cf. also ibid., 16. That this passage indeed enshrines ancient conceptions will be argued in the following pages, but such a view can hardly be based on Noth's premises. In the first place, Num 27:15f. says nothing about the conquest and occupation of Palestine as Joshua's function, unlike, for example, Deut 21:1–8, which Noth describes, not quite correctly, as "parallel in content," ibid., 193: it is concerned solely with Joshua's leadership of the nation in succession to Moses. Indeed, Noth himself makes precisely this point in his *Überlieferungsgeschichtliche Studien* (Halle: Max Niemeyer Verlag, 1943) 1.191. Secondly, while Noth is certainly correct in stating that P's special interest is the statutes and ordinances which constituted Israel as a community at Mount Sinai, ibid., 205f., and even that these are 'timeless', ibid., 209, yet for P they are also embodied in *continuing* institutions, such as the priesthood. Thus the transmission of certain offices, for example, those of the priests and Levites, must be provided for. Num 27:15f. secures this in the case of the ruling authority of Moses, alongside whom stands the priestly Aaron, in P's view, and it is therefore in no way discordant with the overriding concern of the P complex.

2. K. Möhlenbrink, "Josua im Pentateuch," *ZAW* 59 (1943) 49–56.

3. N. Lohfink, "Die deuteronomistische Darstellung des Übergangs der Führung Israels von Moses auf Josua," *Scholastik* 37 (1962) 32–44. Cf. also his "Der Bundesschluss im Land Moab," *BZ* n.s. 6 (1962) 32–56.

4. The reasons for holding that the whole of this pericope is concerned with the appointment of Joshua as Moses' successor will be discussed below.

5. At this point, it does not greatly matter whether we see this verse as the direct continuation of Num 17:12–23, with many scholars, or, with Möhlenbrink, op. cit., 52, as an independent recapitulation of the original form of the passage in Numbers. Probably the first alternative is preferable, since, as will be argued later, the theme of the people's obedience forms an important element in the description of Joshua's succession.

6. It is frequently claimed, cf. Möhlenbrink, op. cit., 52; Noth, *Überlieferungsgeschichtliche Studien*, 1.39, that only vv. 2, 7, 8 and possibly v. 1 are original to this section. This is true

[[104]] We may begin by considering this second block, representing the Deuteronomic tradition. The important contribution made by Lohfink is his clear demonstration that the passages in question are not simply exhortations addressed to Joshua, but that they represent a regular formula for the installation of a person into a definite office. This formula has three members which receive a very distinct and precise shape in the linguistic usage of the Deuteronomic school:

(a) Encouragement of the person addressed, expressed by the phrase חֲזַק וֶאֱמָץ [['be strong and courageous']]; cf. Deut 31:7 (cf. v. 6), 23; Josh 1:6, 7, 9. Cf. also the related phrases אֹתוֹ חַזֵּק [['encourage him']] (cf. Deut 1:38) and וְחַזְּקֵהוּ [[also 'encourage him']] (cf. Deut 3:28). In close connection with this particular expression occur other pairs of words with similar meanings, such as ירא [['fear']] and חתת [['be terrified']] (cf. Deut 31:8); ערץ [['be afraid']] and חתת (cf. Josh 1:9); ירא and ערץ (cf. Deut 31:6); cf. לֹא תִּירָאוּם [['do not fear them']] (Deut 3:22).[7] [[105]]

(b) Statement of a task or function, introduced by כִּי אַתָּה [['for you']] (cf. Deut 31:7, 23; Josh 1:6). Cf. also כִּי הוּא [['for he']] (Deut 1:38; 3:28).

---

in the sense that the language properly belongs to the installation of an individual, i.e., Joshua, and is only secondarily transferred to 'all Israel'. But whether the passage ever actually existed without vv. 3–6 is much more doubtful. Noth argues that these verses are additions partly because some of them have the singular rather than the plural form of address, and partly because they anticipate vv. 7f. But the alternation of singular and plural verbs is too common a characteristic of Deuteronomy to provide any sound criterion for the division of sources; cf. the comments of A. R. Johnson, *The One and the Many in the Israelite Conception of God*, 2nd ed. (Cardiff: University of Wales Press, 1961) 12. With regard to the second point, the section is carefully constructed so that it refers both backwards, to earlier passages in Deuteronomy, and forwards, by transferring the words spoken to Joshua to the nation also. Thus v. 3b is not an anticipation of v. 7, as Noth holds, but a clear reminiscence of Deut 3:28 and indicated as such by the phrase 'as the Lord has spoken', while vv. 4f. follow on from the mention of Joshua with an adaptation of the words addressed to him at Deut 3:21f. Other instances in an installation ceremony of a closely similar address to the individual, on the one hand, and to a group, on the other, such as is represented here in v. 6 and vv. 7f., are found elsewhere, cf. especially 1 Chr 22:6–16, 17–19, and it thus seems advisable to treat the section as a unity.

7. Lohfink, cf. "Die deuteronomistische Darstellung . . . ," *Scholastik* 37 (1962) 37 n. 27, thinks that these further word-pairs indicate a Deuteronomic expansion of the original formula, under the influence of the well-known Deuteronomic *Gattung* [['literary type']] of the "war-sermon." This may be so, but it is noteworthy that similar twin verbs occur, along with the principal expression, in accounts of installations which, as Lohfink himself recognizes (cf. ibid., 39), do not derive from the Deuteronomic passages but reflect an actual current practice. So, ירא [['fear']] and חתת [['be terrified']] occur at 1 Chr 22:13; 27:20; 2 Chr 32:7. But in any case, as will become clear later, these installation formulae clearly varied in the exact details of their wording and we can no longer recover an "original" form, if indeed such a thing ever existed.

(c) Assurance of the divine presence and help, expressed either in a double-member statement, cf. Deut 21:8b (cf. v. 6); Josh 1:5, or in a single-member one, cf. Deut 31:23; Josh 1:9; Deut 3:22b.

Although this formula receives such clear expression in the Deuteronomic tradition, it is not itself confined to that tradition: this is shown by the fact that D. J. McCarthy, quite independently of Lohfink, has demonstrated that there exists elsewhere in the Old Testament a formula for 'investing an officer', in which he finds exactly the same three elements that have been discussed above.[8] Lohfink[9] also calls attention to this point and a combination of the references given by the two scholars produces the following additional list of passages as evidence for the formula in question: 2 Sam 10:12; Hag 2:4; Ezra 10:4;[10] 1 Chr 22:6–13, 16; 28:2–10, 20; 2 Chr 19:8–11; 32:6–8. To these may be added at least such passages as Josh 7:1; 10:24f.;[11] 1 Chr 22:17–19; 2 Chr 19:5–7. [[106]] It will be seen that the pattern of the formula is not exactly uniform and its distinctive wording in the Deuteronomic material represents only one variant of it. Sometimes (b) precedes (a),[12] and the elements of encouragement (a) and assurance (c) can be expressed in different ways, although it is worth noting that (a) almost invariably has the form of two imperatives joined together by *wāw* [['and']].[13] Nevertheless, the fundamental structure seems

8. D. J. McCarthy, *Treaty and Covenant* (Rome: Pontifical Biblical Institute, 1963) 143f., no. 6.

9. "Die deuteronomistische Darstellung . . . ," *Scholastik* 37 (1962) 39.

10. This is perhaps the weakest example and is hardly more than a somewhat distant adaptation of the formula.

11. Lohfink, "Die deuteronomistische Darstellung . . . ," *Scholastik* 37 (1962) 38, would not include this passage, because he considers it represents a speech of a leader in the Holy War, rather than a formula of admission to office: the two *Gattungen* [['literary types']] had features in common, which led to their confusion in the Deuteronomic circle. But Lohfink is not consistent here, for 2 Sam 10:12, which he takes as his basic instance of the formula, is just as much a war-speech. Nor is Josh 10:24f. addressed to the whole people, as he claims, but אֶל קְצִינֵי אַנְשֵׁי הַמִּלְחָמָה [['to the leaders of the warriors']] and the three basic elements are present in it, if not in the same order as in Deuteronomy and Joshua: so, (a) encouragement, v. 25a; (b) statement of function, v. 24b; (c) assurance of divine help, v. 25b. It is similarly instructive to compare 2 Chr 15:2–7, which could be described as admission to a task (the extirpation of idolatry), with 2 Chr 20:14–17, which could be described as a war-speech, for, in both of these, traces of the formula under discussion can be discerned, even though this does not constitute the *Gattung* for these passages in their existing form, cf. J. M. Myers, *II Chronicles*, AncB (New York: Doubleday and Company, 1965) 88, 115. Thus (a) encouragement is represented by 2 Chr 15:7a; 20:15b, 17b, (b) statement of task, by 2 Chr 20:16 and probably 2 Chr 15:7b, and (c) assurance of divine help, by 2 Chr 15:2, יהוה עִמָּכֶם [['Yahweh is with you']] and 2 Chr 20:17c. At this point, we are only concerned with indicating the formula and not with its *Sitz im Leben* [['setting in life']], a problem which will be considered later.

12. E.g., in the passages from 1 and 2 Chronicles.

13. A possible exception is Hag 2:4, cf. Lohfink, "Die deuteronomistiche Darstellung . . . ," *Scholastik* 37 (1962) 39 n. 33.

clear enough to permit us to speak of a definite form of installation to an office or function in this case.

If, then, the formula under consideration is not necessarily the creation of the Deuteronomic school, it is necessary to go on to enquire from where that school derived it and what are its original setting and background. As the survey of its occurrences has shown, it could be used on a variety of occasions and as a means of admitting to a number of different functions. Thus, to discover the background of its Deuteronomic usage, we have first to discover its purpose and occasion in Deuteronomy and Joshua and then to see what parallels to this can be found elsewhere in the Old Testament. The answer to the first question can hardly be in doubt: the formula is used on the occasion of the transfer of the leadership of the nation from Moses to Joshua and its purpose is to install Joshua into the same office that Moses had held.[14] [[107]] When the Deuteronomic version of the formula is examined from this point of view, there emerge other features in it, in addition to the ones already noted, which can be seen to be significant pointers towards its character and *Sitz im Leben*, not least because of their occurrence in what appear to be related passages elsewhere in the Bible. We may call attention to five such features.

I

First, the words of installation are described as a solemn charge, expressed by the *Piʿēl* of the root צוה [['command']].[15] The significance of this word is that, in this particular setting, it indicates admission to a clearly defined office, as its use in the description of the ceremony in Num 27:12f., where very interestingly it occurs twice, vv. 19, 23, clearly shows.[16] Thus it is found in conjunction with the installation formula when such a definite office is in question, the kingship,[17] judgeship,[18] or a position of

14. That Joshua is depicted in the canonical Old Testament tradition, which in this context is predominantly Deuteronomic, as the successor of Moses, is universally recognized: cf., e.g., R. Bach, "Josua," *RGG*³, vol. 3, p. 872 and, for convenient lists of biblical passages illustrating the point, cf. E. M. Good, "Joshua son of Nun," *IDB*, vol. E–J, p. 996 and B. D. Napier, *Song of the Vineyard* (New York: Harper and Row, 1962) 125f.

15. Cf. Deut 31:14, 23; Josh 1:9; Deut 2:21–28. Although the word צוה is not found in Deut 31:7, the use of the root קרא [['summon']] there, which occurs with צוה in similar contexts (cf. Deut 31:14; 1 Chr 22:6) probably indicates the same idea.

16. For the sense of the root in Numbers 27, cf. N. H. Snaith, *Leviticus and Numbers*, CentB, new ed. (London: Thomas Nelson and Sons, 1967) 311.

17. 1 Kgs 2:1; 1 Chr 22:6. The fact that in this latter passage Solomon is designated the temple-builder implies his succession to the throne, since to build the temple was one of the most important prerogatives of ancient Near Eastern kings. For this in Israel, cf. G. Widengren, *Sakrales Königtum im Alten Testament und im Judentum* (Stuttgart: W. Kohlhammer Verlag, 1955) 14–16. Thus the play on בַּיִת as meaning both 'temple' and 'dynasty' in 2 Samuel 7

authority in the [[108]] public works' system.[19] Elsewhere, when the installation formula is used with reference to less specific functions, the root צוה is not found with it. Further, this root suggests the action of someone in authority who transfers his power to another, either wholly in the case of his successor, or partly in the case of a subordinate.[20] Thus the occurrence of צוה in the passages under discussion indicates that the installation formula in them has its background in the royal practice and administration of the Judaean monarchy, with which the outlook of at least the Deuteronomic history, where the Deuteronomic presentation of Joshua really belongs, is closely linked.[21] More particularly, in view of the fact that it is the [[109]] transfer of authority from Moses to his successor that is in question, it is from the practice that marked the transmission of the royal office from one king to another that the Deuteronomic presentation would seem to be derived.

---

rests on a fundamental concept of the monarchical pattern and provides no evidence for a secondary transformation of an original text, as has been widely accepted since the basic study of the chapter by L. Rost, *Die Überlieferung von der Thronnachfolge Davids* (Stuttgart: W. Kohlhammer Verlag, 1926) 47–74. Similarly, if 1 Chronicles 22; 28–29 are to be understood as an account of the transmission of kingship from David to Solomon, there is no need to cut out from these chapters, as incompatible with their main concern, the sections in which Solomon is commanded to build the temple, as is proposed by K. Baltzer, *Das Bundesformular* (Neukirchen: Neukirchener Verlag, 1960) 79–84. Also in the light of these considerations, we should be cautious about regarding 2 Sam 7:13 as a later addition to the chapter, in spite of the majority of scholarly opinion, such as is recently represented, for example, by J. Schreiner, *Sion-Jerusalem Jahwes Königssitz* (Munich: Kösel Verlag, 1963) 98f.

18. Cf. 2 Chr 19:9.

19. Cf. 1 Chr 22:17. Since David's words are addressed to כָל שָׂרֵי יִשְׂרָאֵל [['all the leaders of Israel']] they can hardly mean that these men were to take part in the actual labor of building the temple. Rather, we should see here the appointment of these 'leaders' to supervisory positions over the public labor force, corresponding to the manner in which this was in fact organized during the reign of Solomon, for the construction of the temple, cf. 1 Kgs 5:13–18, especially v. 16; and 9:23.

20. This would be the situation with reference to the appointment of judges at 2 Chr 19:8f., for the king was the fount of justice in Israel, cf. E. R. Goodenough, "Kingship in Early Israel," *JBL* 47 (1929) 169–205. The point is clearly brought out in such passages as Exod 18:14–26 and Deut 1:9–18, where Moses, like the Israelite king, seems to represent the νόμος ἔμψυχος [['the law personified']].

21. Cf. Noth, *Überlieferungsgeschichtliche Studien*, 1.137; G. von Rad, "The Deuteronomic Theology of History in I and II Kings," *The Problem of the Hexateuch and other Essays*, trans. E. W. Trueman Dicken (Edinburgh and London: Oliver and Boyd and New York: McGraw-Hill, 1966) 214–21. Von Rad believes (p. 218) that the Deuteronomic history's 'messianic' view of King David represents a great change from the theological outlook of the book of Deuteronomy itself. But the dichotomy must not be pushed too far, in view of the considerable evidence that Deuteronomy depicts Moses as the prototype of the Davidic king, cf. J. R. Porter, *Moses and Monarchy* (Oxford: Basil Blackwell, 1963) 23–27.

II

Secondly, there is the close connection of the installation formula in its deuteronomic setting with an exhortation to keep the law of Moses and even with a reference to the actual book of the law. In particular, in Josh 1:7 the first element of the formula occurs, to be followed immediately by a warning to Joshua to act according to the law of Moses and a command to him, v. 8, to study continually סֵפֶר הַתּוֹרָה הַזֶּה [['this book of the law']]. Noth[22] holds that Josh 1:7–9 is a later addition to the original text and Lohfink[23] agrees that these verses are an intrusion in the formula proper, although he is compelled to make an exception for the last clause of v. 9, since this is necessary to provide element (c). Yet both these authors emphasize how fully these verses correspond to the deuteronomic theological interests and, in support of this observation, we may point to the fact that warnings about keeping the law and directions for reading and preserving the book of the law are found immediately following the descriptions of Joshua's appointment in Deuteronomy 31.[24] However, [[110]] it is by no means certain that we ought to view this feature simply as a specifically deuteronomic expansion of an originally predeuteronomic formula, for we have a mention of the need to observe the law in other passages in the Old Testament where the formula is found.[25] It can of course be argued that these passages are either in fact deuteronomic or are following a deuteronomic model: 1 Kgs 2:3f. is almost universally held to be deuteronomic and G. von Rad[26] has cogently argued that the speeches in the

22. Cf. *Überlieferungsgeschichtliche Studien*, 1.41 n. 4 and his *Das Buch Josua*, 2nd ed. (Tübingen: J. C. B. Mohr [Paul Siebeck], 1953) 28f.

23. Cf. "Die deuteronomistische Darstellung . . . ," *Scholastik* 37 (1962) 36–38.

24. Cf. Deut 31:9–13, 23–29; the evidence is all the clearer when it is recognized that vv. 16–22, which interrupt the original connection between v. 15 and v. 23, are a very late insertion, cf. Noth, *Überlieferungsgeschichtliche Studien*, 1.40. G. Widengren, "King and Covenant," *JSS* 2 (1957) 13, relying on the use of the second person singular in the verse, thinks that v. 11 may originally have been addressed to Joshua, in which case it would parallel the custom of the Israelite king's reading of the law. The suggestion is interesting but unfortunately the reason for it is untenable, cf. above, note (6): we have, e.g., exactly the same feature in the speech to the Levites in vv. 26, 27a, which can hardly be addressed to Joshua.

25. Cf. 1 Kgs 2:2–4; 1 Chr 22:11–13: cf. also 1 Chr 28:7. It may be noted that the first two of these passage contain a specific reference to the law given by Moses, and this leads one to ask whether כָל הַתּוֹרָה [['the whole law']] in Josh 1:7 may not be original, in spite of the opinion of the great majority of commentators, cf. most recently J. Gray, *Joshua, Judges and Ruth*, CentB, new ed. (London: Thomas Nelson and Sons, 1967) 50. The argument from the following מִמֶּנּוּ [['from it']] is not decisive in view of such passages as Exod 25:15; Lev 6:8; 7:18; 27:9; Judg 11:34. [[Note: The author's point is that the Hebrew term cited is a masculine form, though a feminine would be expected following the feminine noun 'law'. Ed.]]

26. Cf. "The Levitical Sermon in I and II Chronicles," op. cit., 268 and in general, his *Das Geschichtsbild des chronistischen Werkes*, BWANT 54 (Stuttgart: W. Kohlhammer Verlag,

books of Chronicles, of which 1 Chr 22:11–13 obviously forms part, are closely related to the sermonic hortatory material characteristic of the deuteronomic school. It may readily be admitted that the language and formulation of 1 Kgs 2:3f. are deuteronomic and even, though with much less certainty, that the speeches in Chronicles are in what von Rad has called 'the Deuteronomic-Levitical tradition'. But the possibility still remains open that the deuteronomic combination of the installation formula with an exhortation to keep the law springs from an actually existing and regular practice, just as we have seen the formula itself does. For we note that the passages outside Deuteronomy and Joshua, where the combination of installation formula and law occurs, are [[111]] concerned with the succession of a new king to the throne, and thus point in the same direction as the use of the root צוה discussed above. There is a good deal of evidence for the close association of the king and the law[27] and for the view that this connection was forged at his enthronement. Here we may refer to an important and much discussed verse, 2 Kgs 11:12. For our present purpose, it is not of great importance to decide whether the עֵדוּת [['witness; law']] referred to here are the Mosaic Tablets of the law or a royal protocol on the Egyptian model, for even von Rad,[28] who takes the latter view, emphasizes that the word is virtually synonymous with בְּרִית [['covenant']] so that thus the עֵדוּת would contain the provisions of the divine covenant with the dynasty. But the descriptions in the Old Testament of the Davidic covenant show that by it the king was bound to keep Yahweh's law and that the prosperity and even the continuance of the dynasty depended upon this, cf. especially Ps 89:29–38; 132:11f.[29] It is thus entirely appropriate that when Joshua succeeds he should be exhorted to keep the law and admonished that his success depends on his doing so:[30] this fits in perfectly with the use of the installation formula at the accession of a king, provides further evidence for the background of the deuteronomic presentation of the transfer of leadership from Moses to Joshua, and indicates how this should be understood.

1930). Cf. also W. Rudolph, *Chronikbücher* (Tübingen: J. C. B. Mohr [Paul Siebeck], 1955) xiv–xv.

27. Cf. the fundamental works of Widengren, cited above in nn. 17 and 24, and J. R. Porter, op. cit., 11–13.

28. Cf. "The Royal Ritual in Judah," *The Problem of the Hexateuch and other Essays*, 227f.

29. This reference is particularly significant in the present context if Psalm 132 is part of a liturgy to commemorate the inauguration of the Davidic dynasty, cf. J. R. Porter, "The Interpretation of 2 Samuel vi and Psalm cxxxii," *JTS* n.s. 5 (1954) 167–69. Cf. also H.-J. Kraus, *Worship in Israel*, trans. G. Buswell (Oxford: Basil Blackwell and Richmond: John Knox Press, 1966) 183–88.

30. Cf. Josh 1:7f. Cf. G. Östborn, *Tōrā in the Old Testament* (Lund: Hakan Ohlssons Boktryckeri, 1945) 65.

There are further considerations which support such an opinion. [[112]] It has often been noted, and it is indeed obvious, that by far the closest parallel to what Joshua is commanded to do in Josh 1:7f. is what the king is commanded to do in Deut 17:18–20[31] and this in itself is an indication that the Deuteronomist describes Joshua in royal terms. What has not generally been remarked is that, according to Deut 17:18, the king is to acquire a copy of the law immediately on his accession, for this is the meaning of the phrase כְשִׁבְתּוֹ עַל כִּסֵּא מַמְלַכְתּוֹ [['when he sits on the throne of his kingdom']].[32] Thus Joshua is pictured as [[113]] coming into possession of a copy of the law when he succeeded Moses, just as the king was to do when he succeeded to the throne. It may even be that there is some significance at Josh 1:8 in the use of the demonstrative pronoun זֶה, which also occurs similarly in Deut 17:18f. The expressions סֵפֶר הַתּוֹרָה הַזֶּה [['this book of the law']] or הַתּוֹרָה הַזֹּאת [['this law']] are otherwise confined to the book of Deuteronomy. Apart from Deut 1:5 and 4:8, where the הַזֹּאת is proleptic, referring, as the latter passage shows, to the הַחֻקִּים וְהַמִּשְׁפָּטִים [['the laws and statutes']] of either 5:1f. or 12:1f., these expressions indicate an actual document, usually a book written, or read, by the people[33] or the priests

31. That the 'law of the king' in Deut 17:14f. has in view a real situation, that it is not directed against the monarchical institution and that vv. 18–20 are an integral part of it have been shown by A. Caquot, "Remarques sur la 'loi royale' du Deutéronome," *Semitica* 9 (1959) 21–33. Cf. also the comments of Widengren, "King and Covenant," *JSS* 2 (1957) 15, and of J. R. Porter, *Moses and Monarchy*, 25. *Contra*, cf. E. W. Nicholson, *Deuteronomy and Tradition* (Oxford: Basil Blackwell and Philadelphia: Fortress Press, 1967) 93, who, however, does not appear to know the above-mentioned studies. The arguments tentatively put forward by G. von Rad, *Deuteronomy*, trans. D. Barton (London: SCM Press and Philadelphia: Westminster Press, 1966) 119, for regarding vv. 18f. as a later addition are extremely weak; (1) no doubt in these verses Deuteronomy is thought of as a literary document but it had become so in Judaean circles–and it is the practice of the *Judaean* monarchy which, we hold, these verses reflect–at least before the time of Josiah, as von Rad (ibid., 27f.) and Nicholson (op. cit., 101f.) both admit; (2) if it is stated that "v. 20 is better understood as the direct continuation of v. 12," we have to ask to what, in that case does the מִצְוָה [['command']] of v. 20 refer, and it should be noted that, in Deuteronomy, the word often indicates precisely the whole Deuteronomic law, cf., e.g., Deut 8:1; 15:5. O. Bächli, *Israel und die Völker. Eine Studie zum Deuteronomium* (Zürich: Zwingli Verlag, 1962) 187f., interprets Deut 17:18f. as showing the king having responsibility for reading and interpreting the law, a function which belonged to him throughout the monarchical period. In the course of his discussion, Bächli calls attention to the exercise of this function in the cases of Joshua and, significantly, Solomon, cf. especially 1 Kgs 8:14f. B. Lindars suggests that the word מצוה in Deuteronomy "is to be connected with the function of the king in promulgating law," cf. "Torah in Deuteronomy," *Words and Meanings*, D. Winton Thomas *Festschrift*, eds. P. Ackroyd and B. Lindars (Cambridge: University Press, 1968) 128.

32. For this interpretation, cf. especially 1 Kgs 2:12; 2 Kgs 13:13; also 1 Kgs 1:46; 3:6; 2 Kgs 11:19; 1 Chr 28:5.

33. Cf. Deut 27:3, 5f., 8, 26.

and elders[34] or Moses himself.[35] Possibly, then, behind Josh 1:8 lies the practice of handing over an actual document to the king at his accession, as at 2 Kgs 11:12, although it may well be the case that the deuteronomic writer has transformed this into סֵפֶר הַתּוֹרָה הַזֶּה in pursuit of his particular interest. As a further parallel between Joshua and the picture of the king in Deuteronomy 17 attention may be called to Josh 8:30–35. This passage is clearly deuteronomic and, indeed, from the literary point of view it is constructed from various passages in the book of Deuteronomy,[36] but there are important deviations from what is said in Deuteronomy,[37] and it is necessary to ask the reason and purpose of these. They cannot all be discussed here, but from the standpoint of the present enquiry, it may be observed that it is Joshua who builds the altar and writes out the law, while it is the whole people who are commanded [[114]] to do it in Deuteronomy;[38] and perhaps Joshua even offers the sacrifices.[39] Similarly it is Joshua who reads the law, while Deuteronomy envisages this as the function of the priests and elders.[40] It would now be widely accepted that the passage in Joshua 8 is based, however remotely in its present form, on an actual festival at Shechem,[41] which probably involved (as vv. 33f. suggest) a covenant-renewal ritual and which is to be connected with the ceremony described in Joshua 24. Possibly, therefore, the part played by Joshua here reflects the part played by the king in the festival during the monarchical period, while the presentation in Deuteronomy comes from the exilic period, when the kingship had come to an end.[42] For elsewhere, we find that

34. Cf. Deut 31:11f.

35. Cf. Deut 31:9, 24, 26; 32:46. Nothing is said as to who wrote the law in Deut 28:58, 61; 29:21, 29; 30:10, though probably we are to understand that it was Moses, but in any case it is a written book that is in question.

36. Primarily, Deut 27:4–8, but cf. also Deut 27:11–14; 29:10; 30:1; 31:9–13. For a valuable discussion of Josh 8:30–35, cf. S. Mowinckel, *Psalmenstudien* (Amsterdam: Verlag P. Schippers, 1961) 5.97f.

37. Some of these are listed in E. Nielsen, *Shechem: A Traditio-Historical Investigation*, 2nd rev. ed. (Copenhagen: G. E. C. Gad, 1955) 77.

38. Cf. Deut 27:3, 5f., 8.

39. LXX reads the singular in v. 31, ἀνεβίβασεν [['he sent up']]. If this is original, MT may represent an example of dittography, ויעלו [['they sent up']] being influenced by the following עליו [['upon it']]. The words וַיִּזְבְּחוּ שְׁלָמִים [['upon it']] would then be a gloss, when the change had taken place, perhaps added under the influence of Exod 24:5.

40. Cf. Deut 31:11.

41. Cf., e.g., W. Beyerlin, *Origins and History of the Oldest Sinaitic Traditions*, trans. S. Rudman (Oxford: Basil Blackwell, 1965) 43.

42. The chapters of Deuteronomy which contain the material under consideration are extremely difficult to analyze with respect to the date and character of the material in them. However, the edition–or editions–of "Deuteronomy" which they represent may well come from the exilic period. Cf. O. Eissfeldt, *The Old Testament an Introduction*, trans. P. Ackroyd (Oxford: Basil Blackwell and New York: Harper & Row, 1965) 233.

kings, in their capacity as head of the cult, build altars,[43] read the law,[44] and offer sacrifices.[45] Further, v. 32 says that Joshua inscribed a copy of the law of Moses אֲשֶׁר כָּתַב [['which he wrote']]. These last words [[115]] are usually omitted, following LXX, as a gloss, and their subject is considered to be Moses; but it could equally well be Joshua, referring to a book of the law which he himself had *already* written.[46] Joshua would thus be depicted as having done what the Israelite king was commanded to do in Deut 17:18. The case is somewhat different with Josh 24:25f., but once again a custom typical of ancient Near Eastern kingship lies in the background. Here Joshua inserts his own statutes and ordinances into the book of the law. This presents a close parallel to what is known of the ancient Mesopotamian law-codes, which were basically a promulgation of old traditional regulations by the sovereign, but to which he might add his own decrees designed to safeguard the traditional laws and to bring them up to date. There is evidence that Israelite kings did the same thing and thus Joshua's action in these verses represents his promulgation of the law in accordance with royal practice.[47]

The connection, then, between the installation formula and the law in Joshua 1 can be seen to be very close, once it is realized that the deuteronomic tradition is drawing on the particular type of installation ceremony represented by the accession of a king, and indeed this combination is itself a pointer to such a background. In concluding this part of the discussion, attention may be drawn to another possible example of the connection of law and enthronement, which also again suggests that the linking is not a creation of the deuteronomic school but a concept already extant which it adopted and adapted to its own outlook. It has been suggested that the position of Psalm 1, which invokes a blessing on the one who keeps the law, just before Psalm 2, which is part of a royal enthronement festival, is not fortuitous,[48] and that they [[116]] belong together as a part of the liturgy for the king's accession.[49] Psalm 1 certainly has mythological features,

43. Cf. 1 Sam 14:35 (Saul); 2 Sam 24:25 (David); 1 Kgs 6:20 and 9:25 (Solomon); 1 Kgs 12:33 (Jeroboam); 1 Kgs 16:32 (Ahab); cf. also 2 Kgs 16:10f. (Ahaz).

44. Cf. 2 Kgs 23:1–3.

45. Several of the passages cited above in n. 43 speak of the king sacrificing. For kings sacrificing עֹלוֹת וּשְׁלָמִים [['burnt-offerings and peace-offerings']] cf. also 1 Sam 13:9f.; 2 Sam 6:17.

46. Cf. the somewhat ambiguous translation of RSV.

47. For a discussion, which cannot be repeated here, of the significance of the promulgation of the law by Mesopotamian and Israelite kings, cf. J. R. Porter, *Moses and Monarchy*, 15, 24.

48. Cf. E. Nielsen, "Some reflections on the History of the Ark," *SVT* 7 (1960) 71.

49. Cf. M. Bič, "Das erste Buch des Psalters: Eine Thronbesteigungsfestliturgie," *La Regalità Sacra*, R. Pettazzoni *Festschrift* (Leiden: E. J. Brill, 1959) 316–32, especially p. 320.

especially the "tree" and the "streams of water," which appear elsewhere as part of a widespread royal ideology.[50] It might therefore have the function of setting before the new king an ideal of royal behavior,[51] which consisted in faithful obedience to the law, and of reminding him that only by so doing could he hope to prosper. It would thus correspond very closely to the words of David to Solomon and of Yahweh to Joshua, as they enter their new office,[52] and the combination of Psalms 1 and 2 would be exactly parallel to the pattern of exhortation to keep the law and installation formula in the passages we have been discussing. Another context in which the combination of law and enthronement appears is perhaps also significant. In Ps 93:5, one of the psalms celebrating the accession of Yahweh to his royal throne, occur the words עֵדֹתֶיךָ נֶאֶמְנוּ מְאֹד [['your laws are very sure']][53] and, if Weiser's view is correct,[54] the so-called Enthronement Psalms were part of the liturgy of a covenant-renewal [[117]] festival, which would include the reading of law. Of course, Yahweh here is the one who gives the law, not the one who keeps it, but, *mutatis mutandis* [['in all relevant respects']], the same pattern of law and installation is found in connection with the divine king as with the earthly monarch. Further, in another Enthronement Psalms, Ps 99:6f., there is a curious and not very clearly motivated reference to three great figures of the past who kept Yahweh's testimonies and statutes. In the light of the above discussion, this should perhaps be understood as an indirect exhortation to the congregation, and perhaps especially to the king,[55] to observe the law, by reminding them that this has been the distinguishing mark of their famous predecessors.

50. Cf. G. Widengren, *The King and the Tree of Life in Ancient Near Eastern Religion* (Uppsala: A.-B. Lundequistska Bokhandeln, 1959), and E. O. James, *The Tree of Life* (Leiden: E. J. Brill, 1966), especially pp. 1–31 and 93–128.

51. Cf. I. Engnell, "Planted by the Streams of Water," *Studia Orientalia Johanni Pedersen Dicata* (Copenhagen: Einar Munksgaard, 1953) 85–96.

52. Compare especially the mention of the observance of the law, followed by וְכֹל אֲשֶׁר־יַעֲשֶׂה יַצְלִיחַ [['and in all that he does, he prospers']], Ps 1:3, with the same feature followed by לְמַעַן תַּשְׂכִּיל אֵת כָּל־אֲשֶׁר תַּעֲשֶׂה [['so that you succeed in all that you do']], 1 Kgs 2:3, אָז תַּצְלִיחַ [['then you will prosper']], 1 Chr 22:13, and אָז תַּצְלִיחַ אֶת־דְּרָכֶךָ וְאָז תַּשְׂכִּיל [['then you will prosper in all your ways, and then you will succeed']], Josh 1:8. For the connection of ideas between Psalm 1 and Joshua 1, cf. also R. A. Carlson, *David, the Chosen King* (Uppsala: Almqvist and Wiksell, 1964) 243 n. 1.

53. עדות here, as frequently in the Psalter, means Yahweh's laws as forming a single corpus, cf. G. Widengren, *Sakrales Königtum . . .*, 94 n. 69.

54. Cf. A. Weiser, *The Psalms*, trans. H. Hartwell (London: SCM Press and Philadelphia: Westminster Press, 1963) 35–52.

55. For the special place of the king in the Enthronement Festival, cf. S. Mowinckel, *The Psalms in Israel's Worship*, trans. D. R. Ap-Thomas (Oxford: Basil Blackwell and New York: Abingdon Press, 1962) 1.128f., and for the probable influence of the enthronement of the earthly king on the festival of Yahweh's enthronement, cf. Weiser, op. cit., 63.

We may possibly also understand that this element was related to, if not derived from, the similar exhortation at the accession of the human king.

III

The examination thus far has tended to suggest that the features of the deuteronomic presentation of the succession of Joshua find their closest parallel in a passage not mentioned by Lohfink or McCarthy, namely in David's speech to Solomon in 1 Kgs 2:1ff., which, in view of the facts already discussed, is to be interpreted as a formal handing over of authority from the old king to the new. This passage may be analyzed as follows:

(a) Solemn charge, v. 1: *Piʿēl* of צוה [['command']].
(b) Encouragement, v. 2: חָזַקְתָּ וְהָיִיתָ לְאִישׁ [['be strong and act the man']].
(c) Exhortation to keep the law, v. 3.
(d) Assurance of divine help, v. 4. [[118]]
(e) Statement of task, v. 5, introduced by וְגַם אַתָּה [['You also']].[56]

Clear traces of the same pattern may be discerned in 1 Chronicles 22–23:1; 28–29, chapters which, as K. Baltzer has shown,[57] represent the transmission of the royal authority from David to Solomon, and are thus a parallel to, or an expansion of, 1 Kgs 2:1ff. Thus:

(a) 1 Chr 22:6: *Piʿēl* of צוה.
(b) 1 Chr 22:13b; 1 Chr 28:10b, 20b.
(c) 1 Chr 22:12, 13a. Cf. 1 Chr 28:7; 29:19a.
(d) 1 Chr 22:16b; 1 Chr 28:20c. Cf. 1 Chr 22:11a.
(e) 1 Chr 22:7–12, esp. v. 11, עַתָּה [['now']]; 1 Chr 28:10a, עַתָּה. Cf. 1 Chr 29:19b.

What is important in both these sets of passages is the appearance of the exhortation to keep the law, which seems to be a mark of the installation formula only when this is employed for a king, since it is not found when the formula is used for admission to another office. Hence the

56. Lohfink may be correct, "Die deuteronomistische Darstellung . . . ," *Scholastik* 37 (1962) 39, in thinking that element (b), encouragement, may sometimes consist of a single verb. He calls attention to Hag 2:4, where וַעֲשׂוּ [['work']] certainly appears to represent element (e), and to 2 Sam 10:12, where וְנִתְחַזַּק [['and let us be courageous']] may do so, although here it could be held that v. 11 represents the mention of the task. If Lohfink is to be followed, then, in the above analysis וְהָיִיתָ לְאִישׁ [['act the man']] should be considered as the statement of the task, so that the scheme would be confined to vv. 1–4. Whichever alternative is preferred does not seriously affect the argument for the presence of a definite pattern in 1 Kgs 2:1ff.

57. K. Baltzer, *Das Bundesformular,* 79–84.

occurrence of this element in Josh 1:1–9 is significant as indicating the original royal background of the account of Joshua's installation there.

At this point, we should notice a feature which also occurs both in the case of Solomon and in the case of Joshua, the fact that the successor assumes office immediately on the death of his predecessor[58] [[119]] and that this occurs without any break or interruption. This in itself constitutes a notable difference from the succession to the charismatic leadership, where, in the deuteronomic pattern of the book of Judges, there is always an interval between the death of one judge and the raising up of another.[59] It is, however, peculiarly characteristic of the monarchical institution in the Ancient Near East that it was dynastic, so that it was greatly concerned with securing a clearly regulated and uninterrupted succession in the royal office, especially of course from father to son,[60] and it was just this which distinguished it from other types of political organization, not least from the old charismatic rulership.[61] It need hardly be pointed out that the parallel is not exact since Joshua was not the son of Moses,[62] but

58. Cf. Deut 31:2, which, in view of Deut 34:7, implies Moses' imminent death; Josh 1:2; 1 Kgs 2:2a; 1 Chr 23:1.

59. 1 Sam 8:1 (cf. 12:2) is not deuteronomic but probably is based on an old local tradition, cf. Noth, *Überlieferungsgeschichtliche Studien,* 1.97. In any event, it represents an exceptional case and is commonly understood precisely to reveal an attempted advance from the genuinely old institution of the judgeship, cf., e.g., H. W. Hertzberg, *I & II Samuel,* trans. J. S. Bowden (London: SCM Press and Philadelphia: Westminster Press, 1964) 71.

60. To give a single example from the immediate environment of Israel, this concern is very prominent in the Ugaritic legends of Keret and Aqhat, cf. G. R. Driver, *Canaanite Myths and Legends* (Edinburgh: T. &. T. Clark, 1956), especially pp. 5, lines 28ff.; 8, lines 46ff. As for the Old Testament, this concern is basic in 2 Samuel 7, a passage which reveals perhaps more clearly than any other the nature of Israel's royal ideology, cf. vv. 11b–16, 25–29.

61. This is shown by the fact that it is precisely the question of regular hereditary succession that is at issue when the introduction of kingship in Israel is proposed, cf. Judg 8:22f.

62. On the other hand, the intimate association of Joshua with Moses during the wilderness period should be noted. It seems clear that Joshua did not belong originally in most of the traditions concerning this period in which he now appears (cf. Beyerlin, op. cit., 48f.). We may wonder whether he has not been introduced largely for the purpose of being designated as Moses' successor, cf. Beyerlin's comment on Exod 17:8f., op. cit., 16, so that his relationship to Moses is patterned on that of the king to the young heir-apparent. Thus he is described as a נַעַר [['young man, servant']] and he is associated in the direction of the community during Moses' lifetime (cf. Num 32:28; Deut 32:44) with what could be called "rights of succession," cf. Num 34:17, as was the case with Solomon and David, cf. 1 Kgs 2:35, Abijah and Rehoboam, cf. 2 Chr 11:22, and Jotham and Azariah, cf. 2 Kgs 15:5b. In this capacity Joshua is regularly designated as מְשָׁרֵת [['servant']], cf. Exod 24:13; 33:11; Num 11:28 and this word is used of him in connection with his installation as Moses' successor at Josh 1:1. First, it may be observed that this term, or the root, is most frequently used of servants in the royal administration, cf. 2 Sam 13:17f.; 1 Kgs 1:4, 15; 10:5; Prov 29:12; Esth 1:10; 2:2; 6:3; 1 Chr 27:1; 28:1; 2 Chr 9:4; 17:19; 22:8; interestingly, the noun is employed of heavenly agents in contexts where Yahweh is pictured in royal imagery, cf. Pss 103:21 (cf. v. 19); 104:4 (cf. vv. 1–3). But,

there is much [[120–21]] in the account of the transfer of office from one to the other which suggests features of the more properly dynastic succession and which leads to the conclusion that in this respect Moses and Joshua are depicted as prototypes of the Israelite King.

As further possible support for this contention, reference may be made to the narrative of the choice of Saul as king in 1 Samuel 9–10. Whatever may be said of the original background and significance of these chapters, their present setting in the Deuteronomic History is the succession of Saul to the office of Samuel,[63] in view of the latter's imminent decease.[64] The element of encouragement, (b), seems to be clear in 1 Sam 10:7a, and that of the assurance of divine help, (d), in 1 Sam 10:7b. We may find the statement of the task, (e), in 1 Sam 10:1b and the solemn charge, (a), in the words of 1 Sam 9:27.

---

secondly, the word is also used of Elisha's chief servant, cf. 2 Kgs 4:43; 6:15 and of Elisha himself in the same capacity *vis-à-vis* Elijah, cf. 1 Kgs 19:21, and it has therefore been suggested that the closest parallel to the relationship between Moses and Joshua is the one between Elijah and Elisha, so that Joshua's succession, like Elisha's, would be to the prophetic office (cf. M. de Buit, *La Sainte Bible: Le livre de Josué*, 2nd ed. [Paris: Editions du Cerf, 1958] 10). Certainly this was how the matter was viewed in later Jewish tradition, cf. Sir 46:1. But there is no indication in the canonical traditions about him that Joshua acted as a prophet. Further, it may be asked whether the legend of Elisha as the successor of Elijah, which has some curious features, has not itself been influenced by motifs which really belong to the royal sphere: (1) In the words of J. Gray, *I & II Kings* (London: SCM Press and Philadelphia: Westminster Press, 1963) 366, referring to 1 Kgs 19:16, "there is no other case of the conferring of prophetic authority by anointing." But before the exile the rite of anointing was confined to the installation of kings, and even if the expression is intended, in the case of Elisha, to be understood in a figurative sense (cf. O. Eissfeldt, *Könige*, HSAT 1, 4th ed. [Tübingen: J. C. B. Mohr, 1922] 329), it would still be necessary to give full weight to the background whence it is derived. (2) The "mantle" which plays so important a part in conferring his position on Elisha, cf. 1 Kgs 19:19b; 2 Kgs 2:13f., is properly a robe of state, commonly worn by kings (cf. for the evidence J. A. Montgomery and H. S. Gehman, *The Books of Kings*, ICC [Edinburgh: T. & T. Clark, 1951] 316). (3) The ascension of Elijah, cf. 2 Kgs 2:11, which also plays a vital part in the designation of Elisha as his successor, cf. v. 10, again probably has a royal background, cf. G. Widengren, "The Ascension of the Apostle and the Heavenly Book," *Uppsala Universitet Årsskrift* (Uppsala: A.-B. Lundequistska Bokhandeln, 1950) 7–24, and, especially in regard to the feature of the heavenly chariot, cf. H. P. l'Orange, *Studies on the Iconography of Cosmic Kingship in the Ancient World*, Inst. for Sammenlignende Kulturforskning (Oslo: H. Aschehoug & Co., 1953) 48–79. If this is so, the undoubted similarities between the two groups Moses-Joshua and Elijah-Elisha reflect a common royal pattern. For the general possibility of features borrowed from kingship in the call and appointment of prophets, cf. Widengren, "The Ascension of the Apostle and the Heavenly Book," *Uppsala Universitet Årsskrift*, 33 n. 3.

63. This is shown by the repeated use of the word שפט [['judge, deliver']] to describe the function of the new king in 1 Samuel 8, a feature rightly stressed by Hertzberg, op. cit., 72.

64. 1 Sam 8:1, 5; 12:2.

Again, the recurrence of several of the main features of the formula in the case of a king who is succeeding to the "judgeship"[65] of his predecessor confirms what has already been noted as the probable source of the same features in the succession of Joshua.

That the leadership of Moses, as this is pictured in Deuteronomy, was considered to involve a continued succession to the office he had held has recently been emphasized by M. G. Kline, who does not hesitate to use the adjective "dynastic" to describe [[122]] this succession.[66] But, as has already been seen, this concept really belongs to the sphere of royal ideology rather than to the charismatic leader, whom Moses and Joshua are usually supposed to exemplify. Indeed, Kline himself comments: "It may be observed in passing that Deuteronomy's interest in the perpetuity of Yahweh's rule and specifically its concern with the security of the dynastic succession is a mark of the profound unity between the Deuteronomic and Davidic covenants."[67] That is, the closest parallel to what we have in Deuteronomy with regard to the succession of Joshua is to be found in the royal Davidic covenant, where the security of the succession and the continuation of the royal house forever is one of the major concerns.[68]

Again, however, this depicting of the succession element in the office of Moses in terms of the Davidic covenant can be seen to be much older than the deuteronomic presentation. We may take as our starting-point some comments of M. L. Newman in his discussion of the "J" tradition in Exodus.[69] He refers to Exod 34:27 for Yahweh making a covenant with Moses, just as he did with the Davidic king,[70] and to the expression לְעוֹלָם [['forever']] in Exod 19:9a, which, together with the synonym עַד עוֹלָם, is used elsewhere at least twenty times in connection with Yahweh's promise of the continuation of the Davidic dynasty, and which, in Newman's view, suggests "the establishment of a dynastic office of covenant [[123]] media-

65. The extent to which Saul's kingship was viewed as the continuation of the old charismatic leadership of the "judges," of which Samuel was the last, has been stressed above all by A. Alt, cf. his *Essays on Old Testament History and Religion*, trans. R. A. Wilson (Oxford: Basil Blackwell and New York: Doubleday and Co., 1966) 188–92 and 243f., but he seriously underestimates the new, and distinctively monarchical features, in Saul's royal authority.

66. Cf. M. G. Kline, *The Treaty of the Great King* (Grand Rapids: W. B. Eerdmans Publishing Co., 1963) 35–40.

67. Ibid., 38. Möhlenbrink, op. cit., 54, had already noted how sharply the narratives of Joshua's succession distinguish him from the line of charismatic leaders.

68. Cf. especially Ps 132:11f. and the comments of Aubrey R. Johnson, *Sacral Kingship in Ancient Israel*, 2nd ed. (Cardiff: University of Wales Press, 1967) 23–25, and Ps 89:35–38 and the comments of G. W. Ahlström, *Psalm 89* (Lund: C. W. K. Gleerups Förlag, 1959) 50f.

69. Cf. M. L. Newman, *The People of the Covenant* (New York: Abingdon Press, 1962) 50f.

70. Further evidence for this is supplied by Exod 34:10a; 32:10b; Num 14:12b. For a discussion of these passages, cf. J. R. Porter, *Moses and Monarchy*, 17 n. 52.

tor." It is true that, in Newman's view, this was intended to refer to the establishment of a *priestly* dynasty, in which "the succession was traced from Moses to Aaron to Aaron's sons, Nadab and Abihu."[71] But to such an interpretation there are at least two cogent objections. First, Newman bases his view on the fact that Aaron, Nadab and Abihu share in the eating of the covenant meal, that is in the making of the covenant, at Exod 24:1f.; 9–11.[72] But so do the seventy elders, who can hardly be thought of as representing a priestly dynasty, and there seems no reason for importing the idea of the establishment of a priestly succession into the Exodus passage at all. Secondly, there seems no evidence in the biblical sources that Aaron was expected to succeed to the office of Moses and, according to tradition, he did not but died before him.[73] Still more is this true of Nadab and Abihu who, again according to tradition, died before Aaron[74] and were expressly excluded as the transmitters of the priestly line.[75]

As has been noted, the only successor to Moses known to the Old Testament is Joshua and it is significant that in Joshua 24, one of the passages where his figure seems to be rooted more firmly in the tradition,[76] he is found acting as the mediator of a covenant, and in this chapter there is even the suggestion of a particular covenant, as in the case of Moses, with Joshua and his family.[77] Thus the argument of Newman, with its emphasis on the parallels between the covenant with Moses and that with David, again points to Joshua as Moses' successor in the royal pattern.

Further, there is much evidence that the Israelite king was responsible for maintaining and renewing the covenant,[78] and [[124]] the influence of royal practice may even be discerned in Joshua 24. Behind the conclusion of the covenant in that passage seems to lie the formula of Deut 26:17–19, according to which, on the one hand, Yahweh declares that Israel is his people, and, on the other, the people declare that Yahweh is their God. On the basis of such passages as 2 Kgs 2:17; 23:3, G. Fohrer has concluded that this formula is a reflection of the terms of the covenant concluded

71. Newman, op. cit., 132.

72. Ibid., 51.

73. Cf. Num 20:28.

74. Cf. Lev 10:1–3.

75. Cf. 1 Chr 24:2.

76. This was first demonstrated by A. Alt, "Josua," *Kleine Schriften* (Munich: C. H. Beck, 1953) 1.191f.

77. This may be indicated by Josh 24:15b.

78. Cf., above all, Widengren, "King and Covenant," *JSS* 2 (1957) 1–32, and the suggestive comment of J. Bright, *A History of Israel* (Philadelphia: Westminster Press, 1959 and London: SCM Press, 1960) 300, that, in the account of Josiah's covenant in 2 Kings 23, we find "the king playing a role similar to that of Moses in Deuteronomy and Joshua in Joshua 24."

between God and his people by the king.[79] Thus, whatever the precise origin of the material in Joshua 24 in its present form, we again see Joshua fulfilling the same function that was ascribed both to Moses and to the Davidic king.

Evidence for the presence of a pattern derived from royal practice in the accounts of Joshua's succession may also perhaps be found in another direction. Royal features in the patriarchal legends have not infrequently been noted,[80] and recently B. J. van der Merwe has put forward the hypothesis that, in Genesis, Joseph is presented as succeeding Jacob as ruler.[81] He calls attention to several elements in the picture of Jacob which are found elsewhere in the Old Testament in connection with kings and in particular, with reference to the theme of the present study, he notes "the strong resemblance between Gen 47:29 and 1 Kgs 2:1."[82] The very fact that a succession narrative with so many royal characteristics appears in the case of Joseph and Jacob itself [[125]] makes it not improbable that similar considerations may apply to the account of two other great figures of the past, Joshua and Moses, where there is succession of rulership. It may be possible to go even further. Gen 48:22 seems to imply that Jacob bequeathed to Joseph, on the occasion of the latter's succession, the town of Shechem which he owned, as leader of his group, by right of conquest.[83] Involved in Joshua's succession to Moses, especially in the deuteronomic tradition, is his conquest of the Promised Land, which Moses had failed to accomplish;[84] further, he was to divide the territory among the different tribes,[85] which implies that he had the same sort of rights over the land as did the later Israelite king.[86] It is noteworthy that on three occasions material about the succession of Joshua is closely linked with the statement that Moses was to ascend a mountain to view Palestine, and in the case of at least two of these, Num 27:12ff. and Deut 3:23ff., the succes-

79. Cf. G. Fohrer, "Der Vertrag zwischen König und Volk in Israel," *ZAW* 71 (1959) 17–22, especially 21f.

80. Cf. especially the articles on the individual patriarchs in Engell-Fridrichsen, *Svenkst Bibliskt Upplagsverk,* vols. 1–2 (Gävle: Skolförlaget, 1948–52). Cf. also G. Widengren, "Early Hebrew Myths and Their Interpretation," *Myth, Ritual and Kingship,* ed. S. H. Hooke (Oxford: Clarendon Press, 1958) 183f.

81. Cf. B. J. van der Merwe, "Joseph as Successor of Jacob," *Studia Biblica et Semitica Theodoro Christiano Vriezen . . . dedicata* (Wageningen: H. Veenman en Zonen, 1966) 221–32.

82. Ibid., 225.

83. Ibid. For recent discussions of this difficult verse, cf. G. von Rad, *Genesis,* trans J. H. Marks (London: SCM Press, 1961 and Philadelphia: Westminster Press) 413f.; E. A. Speiser, *Genesis,* AncB (New York: Doubleday and Co., 1961) 358.

84. Cf. Deut 1:38; 3:21, 28; 31:3, 7; Josh 1:6.

85. Cf. Josh 13:7.

86. Cf. E. M. Good, op. cit., 992.

sion of Joshua seems to be virtually the consequence of the divine command to Moses.[87] But it has been shown that the episode of Moses' ascent of the mountain to survey the land in fact enshrines an ancient legal rule for the transfer of property, by which it was intended to indicate that Moses was given full possession of Palestine before his death.[88] We seem justified in assuming then that Joshua's succeeding Moses implied his inheriting the right of full ownership of the Promised Land which his great predecessor had not been able to [[126]] exercise. But such an absolute right was something that belonged only to the Israelite king, in sharp contrast to the older type of charismatic leader, as such a verse as 1 Sam 8:14 makes clear.[89] Once more, there would appear to be a feature in the accounts of the succession of Joshua which can best be explained as a reflection from an originally royal background.[90]

IV

The preceding remarks may serve to introduce a further consideration. Kline has called attention to the influence on the book of Deuteronomy of the form of the vassal treaty, common to much of the ancient Near

87. In the third example, Deut 34:1–9, the link is perhaps not quite as close.

88. Cf. D. Daube, *Studies in Biblical Law* (Cambridge: University Press, 1947) 25–39; "Rechtsgedanken in den Erzählungen des Pentateuchs," *Von Ugarit nach Qumran*, eds. J. Hempel and L. Rost, BZAW 77 (Berlin: Verlag Alfred Töpelmann, 1958) 35.

89. For the full implications of Samuel's speech in 1 Sam 8:10–18 for the nature of kingship in Israel, cf. I. Mendelsohn, "Samuel's denunciation of Kingship in the Light of the Akkadian Documents from Ugarit," *BASOR* 143 (1956) 17–22.

90. The foregoing argument attempts to suggest that Num 27:12–14 and 15–23 belong closely together, although most scholars consider them to be two originally distinct sections, cf. Möhlenbrink, op. cit., 49. But even if Noth, *Numbers*, trans. James D. Martin (London: SCM Press and Philadelphia: Westminster Press, 1968) 213, is right in thinking that vv. 15–23 only became linked with vv. 12–14 when the Pentateuch was united with the Deuteronomic History work, and that the linking reflects the typical deuteronomic coupling of Moses' death with Joshua's succession, this would only mean that the scheme "Moses' ascent of a mountain/installation of Joshua" is deuteronomic from the *literary* point of view, and we can still go on to consider what factors may have led to the formulation of this scheme. These, we have proposed, may be found in ideas connected with Israelite kingship. In any case, there are some grounds for holding, against Möhlenbrink and Noth, that the narrative of Joshua's installation is original to the Numbers narrative at this point. Möhlenbrink, op. cit., 51, claims that vv. 18–23 are entirely unconnected with any other material in Numbers 26–29. But the last verse, v. 65, of Numbers 26 mentions Joshua as one of the two survivors of an earlier census. Thus the account of his succeeding Moses, now found in Num 27:18–23, would have a certain appropriateness at this point and may even have followed 26:65 directly, if the pericope about the daughters of Zelophehad should be viewed as an independent piece of quite ancient legal tradition later added to the basic narrative, as is suggested by Noth, *Numbers*, 211.

Eastern world, and specifically to its influence on the material dealing with the succession of Joshua, while [[127]] Baltzer has noted a similar reflection of this treaty form in 1 Chr 22:28–29. It is noteworthy that the idea of the continuation of the overlord's dynasty figures prominently in such treaties: the vassal's oath of obedience is directed both to the reigning king and to his successors. The object of this was to secure the peaceful and orderly transmission of the royal office, since a change of ruler created a difficult situation, when disaffection and revolt might be expected to occur. This royal dynastic concern is clearly indicated in the statements, which round off the accounts of Solomon's accession, that the new king was firmly established on the throne and received the complete obedience of his subjects.[91] Very much the same kind of statements occur also in the case of Joshua. Kline refers particularly to the great vassal treaty of Esarhaddon, which had among its objects the securing of the succession of his son Ashurbanipal to the throne of Assyria, and it is not without interest to compare some of the obligations undertaken by the vassals in this treaty with what is said about the complete submission of the Israelites to Joshua. Thus,

> You will seize the perpetrators of insurrection . . .
> If you are able to seize them and put them to death,
> Then you will seize them and put them to death,[92]

may be compared with Josh 1:18a. Again,

> You will hearken to
> Whatever he[93] says and will do whatever
> He commands,[94]

may be compared with Deut 34:9b; Josh 1:16f.

[[128]] Further, similar statements about the people's awe of the monarch and the firm establishment of his kingdom occur in connection with Solomon's dream at Gibeon:[95] here, the exceptional wisdom given to

91. Cf. 1 Kgs 2:12; 1 Chr 29:23f. It might be argued that the former passage, with its emphasis on Solomon's firm grip on the throne, merely reflects the fact that his succession had been disputed, cf. 1 Kings 1. But the narrative in Chronicles, where the people's obedience is at least equally strongly stressed, omits all reference to this struggle for power, and this suggests that something more is involved.

92. The translation of D. J. Wiseman, "The Vassal-Treaties of Esarhaddon," *Iraq* 20 (1958) 39f. For the significance, in relation to the Old Testament, of the obligations assumed by the vassals in these treaties, cf. R. Frankena, "The vassal-treaties of Esarhaddon and the dating of Deuteronomy," *OTS* 14 (1965) 122–54, especially pp. 140–44.

93. I.e., Ashurbanipal.

94. Wiseman, op. cit., 43f.

95. Cf. 1 Kgs 3:28; 2 Chr 1:1, 13b.

Solomon on that occasion[96] is understood as a special sign of divine favor, which creates an abnormal terror among his subjects.[97] But, in Baltzer's words, *Der Offenbarungstraum Salomos in Gibeon ist der letzte Akt des Thronwechsels* [['The dream-revelation to Solomon at Gibeon is the last act in the transfer of the throne']],[98] a comment which applies as much to the narrative in Kings as to that in Chronicles. In precisely the same way, as soon as Joshua succeeds to the position of Moses, he is marked out by a sign of Yahweh's special favor, which is to make clear his continuity with his predecessor[99] and which produces awe and obedience in the people.[100] Interestingly enough, a parallel phenomenon is found in the nondeuteronomic, and possibly earlier, tradition of Joshua's succession where it would appear that it is his possession of the רוּחַ חָכְמָה [['spirit of wisdom']] which causes the Israelites to obey Joshua.[101] Noteworthy also is the considerable identity of language used, in the kind of statements under discussion, in the cases of Solomon and Joshua respectively.[102] The absolute obedience and the great awe which are envisaged in the passages just reviewed are surely most characteristic of the monarchy in Israel, as in the world of [[129]] the ancient Near East generally,[103] and, taken together with the other evidence adduced earlier, they provide a further pointer to the original setting of the description of Joshua's succession.[104]

96. Cf. 1 Kgs 3:12f.; 2 Chr 1:12.

97. This is especially clear from 1 Kgs 3:28, significantly following the story in 1 Kgs 3:16–27, which is to be taken as the practical evidence of Solomon's remarkable wisdom.

98. Baltzer, op. cit., 83. The point is brought out by such passages as 1 Kgs 3:6, 7a, 14; 2 Chr 1:8, 9a.

99. Cf. Josh 3:7.

100. Cf. Josh 4:14.

101. Cf. Deut 34:9. Wisdom in the Old Testament is closely associated with kingship, cf. N. W. Porteous, "Royal Wisdom," *SVT* 3 (1953) 247–61, and it is never mentioned in connection with the type of leadership represented by the pre-monarchical judges.

102. Thus שָׁמַע [['obey']] occurs at 1 Chr 29:23 and at Deut 34:9; Josh 1:17f. גָּדַל [['be, make great']] occurs at 1 Chr 29:25; 2 Chr 1:1 and at Josh 3:7; 4:14. יָרֵא [['fear']] occurs at 1 Kgs 3:28 and at Josh 4:14.

103. For a recent brief account of Canaanite kingship, which particularly stresses these aspects, cf. J. L. McKenzie, *The World of the Judges* (New York: Prentice Hall, 1966 and London: Geoffrey Chapman, 1967) 110.

104. In discussing the succession of Joshua, Lohfink, in line with the above discussion, notes ("Die deuteronomistische Darstellung . . . ," *Scholastik* 37 [1962] 44): *dass auch ein Element der Bestätigung durch den Erfolg und der Annahme der Führung durch die Untergebenen zu einem Amt gehört, steckte wohl im traditionellen Erzählungsmaterial* [['that also an element of confirmation through success, and of acceptance of the leadership by subordinates, belongs to an office was presumably contained in the traditional narrative material']]. He thinks, however, that these themes belong only to Joshua as commander-in-chief and not to the other office of Joshua which he distinguishes, the divider of the land. But the two cannot be clearly distinguished, since both have a common home in the figure of the Israelite king.

V

In the article referred to earlier, Lohfink demonstrates that in the deuteronomic tradition there is in fact a double installation of Joshua in his office, on the one hand by Moses, on the other hand by Yahweh himself,[105] and that this represents a deliberately intended and carefully constructed scheme. Lohfink discusses the reason for the double installation only in the most general terms, but once again this phenomenon is best understood when we see its original home in the practice and ideology of the Israelite monarchy. For there we find not infrequently both the designation of the new king by Yahweh himself and also his installation by some human agency. In the case of the accession of Solomon in 1 Chronicles, where, as has been noted, the parallels with Joshua seem particularly close, David appoints Solomon king,[106] but his previous divine election is clearly referred to in the words אֶחָד בָּחַר־בּוֹ אֱלֹהִים [['whom alone God has chosen']].[107]

Nor is the picture in Samuel and Kings fundamentally different, [[130]] for such a verse as 2 Sam 7:12[108] implies that Solomon was chosen by Yahweh before his appointment by David, narrated in 1 Kgs 1:30. The same pattern is apparent in the case of David, who in 1 Samuel is viewed as the successor of Saul, since the charisma of the spirit which Saul had passes to him;[109] thus, Yahweh designates David and Samuel anoints him[110] and, when the elders of Israel anoint David, it is recognized that he has already been designated by a divine oracle.[111] Very interestingly, the same feature occurs in at least two of the accounts of the accession of Saul. Saul is designated by Yahweh and then anointed by Samuel;[112] again, he is chosen by the sacred lot[113] and then accepted by the people in the cry

105. Ibid., 40, 43f.

106. Cf. 1 Chr 23:1.

107. Cf. 1 Chr 29:1. Cf. 1 Chr 28:5.

108. Cf. also 1 Kgs 2:4. For the divine choice of Solomon in 2 Samuel, cf. now G. W. Ahlström, "Solomon, the Chosen One," *History of Religions* 8 (1968) 100f.

109. Cf. on this point, J. L. McKenzie, "The Four Samuels," *Biblical Research* 7 (1962) 1–16, and A. Weiser, "Die Legitimation des Königs David," *VT* 16 (1966) 328.

110. Cf. 1 Sam 16:1–13. That this passage forms an integral part of the narrative of David's rise to the throne in 1 Samuel is shown by Weiser, "Die Legitimation des Königs David," *VT* 16 (1966) 326f.

111. Cf. 2 Sam 5:1–3. For this oracle, cf. J. Alberto Soggin, *Das Königtum in Israel*, BZAW 104 (Berlin: Verlag Alfred Töpelmann, 1967) 64–66, and his comment on 2 Sam 5:1–3, op. cit., 69: "Wiederum erkennen wir das Schema: göttliche Designation–Bestätigung durch die Versammlung–Krönung."

112. Cf. 1 Sam 9:17; 10:1.

113. Cf. 1 Sam 10:20–23. McKenzie, *World of the Judges*, 172, completely misunderstands this passage when he seeks to distinguish between choice by divine election and choice by lot, for the two are the same, as 1 Sam 10:24, at least in its present context, plainly shows.

יְחִי הַמֶּלֶךְ [['may the king live!']],[114] or perhaps "made" king by them.[115] Further, we find the same rhythm of divine designation and human installation in the case of at least three rulers of the northern kingdom.[116]

[[131]] That this pattern is a regular feature of royal ritual is indicated by a number of psalms which, it would now be widely accepted, formed part of an actual coronation ceremony, or the re-enactment of such a ceremony, but which also contain a reference to Yahweh's own appointment of the king. Reference may be made particularly to Pss 2:6f.; 21:4–6; 110:1f.; 132:11f., 17f.[117] The case is strengthened when it is observed that this double appointment of the ruler, by both divine and human agency, is not confined to Israel but is commonly found throughout the ancient Near East.[118] Once more, an interesting feature in the accounts of the transmission of the leadership of the nation from Moses to Joshua seems best explained as a reflection of specifically royal ideology and practice.

The present study has been mainly concerned with the deuteronomic tradition of the succession of Joshua, and space does not permit any extended discussion of the alternative tradition which is found mainly in the book of Numbers. However, we have had occasion to refer more than once to this second tradition in the course of the argument, from which it is clear that it presents an understanding of Joshua's succession which is basically similar to that of the deuteronomic outlook on this question.[119] Nor has it [[132]] been possible to consider the more general question of the extent to which the figure of Joshua as a whole is depicted in royal

114. Cf. 1 Sam 10:24. For the implications of this expression, cf. P. A. H. de Boer, "Vive le roi!" *VT* 5 (1955) 225–31, especially 231: "יחי המלך *signifie donc: le roi vit, il détient la puissance royale*" [["יחי המלך means therefore: 'the king lives, he holds royal power' "]].

115. Cf. 1 Sam 11:15.

116. Cf. 1 Kgs 11:29–39; 14:7 and 12:20 (Jeroboam I): 1 Kgs 19:16; 2 Kgs 9:1–6, 13 (Jehu): 1 Kgs 14:14; 16:2 (Baasha). We do not actually read of any human installation of Baasha, but it is legitimate to suppose that it occurred. Cf. also 2 Kgs 10:30; 15:12 (the four sons of Jehu). It may well be that the explicit mention of a divine designation only in the case of these particular rulers is dictated by the deuteronomic editors' theological and historical conceptions, as is stressed by T. C. G. Thornton, "Charismatic Kingship in Israel and Judah," *JTS* n.s. 14 (1963) 7. Thornton admits, however, that these editors may well be reflecting earlier ideas and the evidence adduced below strongly suggests that such is the case.

117. For a representative view, which sees all these Psalms as forming part of a coronation ritual, cf. the comments ad loc. of H.-J. Kraus, *Psalmen*, 2nd ed. (Neukirchen: Verlag der Buchhandlung des Erziehungsvereins, 1962).

118. Cf. the evidence summarized by Thornton, op. cit., 2–4.

119. The writer may perhaps be permitted to refer to his discussion of the key passage, Num 27:15–23, in *Moses and Monarchy*, 17–19. For the relation of this passage to the deuteronomic traditions, cf. the remarks of R. A. Carlson, op. cit., 241.

categories in the Old Testament tradition,[120] which would again tend to confirm the view that his succession to Moses is described in terms that have a similar royal background.

One further point may be made in conclusion. Since the fundamental work of Alt and Noth, it has become widely accepted that the historical Joshua had no original connection with the historical Moses. If this is so, it must be said that the process by which Joshua came to be viewed as the "second Moses" needs much further investigation than it has so far received. Such an investigation cannot be attempted here, but, in view of the preceding discussion, it may perhaps be suggested that the practice and ideology of the royal succession, which, as has been seen, was so vital a concern for the monarchical system in Israel and the ancient Near East, played an essential part in the entire development. Here was an existing pattern by which two great leaders of the nation could be brought together and the transfer of authority from one to the other could be explained and accounted for. It would then be no accident that the succession of Joshua to the office of Moses is most strongly emphasized, and its royal features most clearly discernible, in the scheme of the "deuteronomistic historical work," with its central preoccupation with the responsibility of the Israelite king for the maintenance of the Covenant and thus for the whole religious and social well-being of the nation.

120. Cf., e.g., E. M. Good, op. cit., 996; Östborn, op. cit., 65f.; Widengren, "King and Covenant," *JSS* 2 (1957) 15.

Gilgal: A Contribution to the History of Worship in Israel

HANS-JOACHIM KRAUS

The book of Joshua has had a somewhat special place in the scholarly discussion of the historical books, partly because, though it showed a convergence of priestly and deuteronomic concepts and language, the narratives in it (legends, or *Sagen*, according to Noth, following the older German work of Gressmann and Alt) could not be traced to the Pentateuchal sources. Kraus's essay played an important part in this discussion in the early aftermath of Noth's work. He agrees that Joshua cannot be traced to Pentateuchal sources but differs from Noth in looking for pre-Dtr material rather than post-Dtr additions to explain the special features of the book.

The present essay addresses the question of the relationship between the cultic history of Israel and the biblical text in the case of Gilgal and Joshua 3–4. Gilgal was an important cultic center in early Israel, as is clear from a number of texts (for example, 1 Sam 11:14–15). It remains unidentified but may have been at the site known as Khirbet el-Mefjir, not far from Jericho. Kraus argues that Joshua 3–4 is an etiological narrative from the sanctuary at Gilgal near Jericho, celebrating the memory of the exodus together with entry to the land, possibly in the context of the Feast of Passover (see Josh 5:10–12). The argument makes now outdated assumptions about an amphictyonic setting and also takes issue with von Rad's theory of the separate origins of the exodus and Sinai traditions, with the proposal that the ancient covenant renewal ceremonies centered on Shechem were moved at a certain point to Gilgal. These specific

Translated and reprinted with permission, from "Gilgal: Ein Beitrag zur Kultusgeschichte Israels," *Vetus Testamentum* 1 (1951) 181–99. Translation by Peter T. Daniels. The RSV has been used for all biblical quotations in this article.

arguments belong only to the history of interpretation of the historical books. However, the essay stands as a reminder of some of the fundamental options in interpreting these. The connection between texts and the ancient religious institutions remains to be explained. The parallel between the crossing of the Jordan and that of the Reed Sea is found also in Ps 114:3 (compare with Mic 6:4–5) and therefore seems in itself to belong to an ancient tradition. This kind of datum can be insufficiently dealt with in excessively "literary" theories of the composition of the books.

⟦181⟧ The place of worship called Gilgal is mentioned several times in the Old Testament. The role of this place is especially significant in the early history of Israel. Many legends and historical traditions in the book of Joshua cling to the holy place of Gilgal (Josh 4:19; 5:9, 10; 9:6; 10:6, 7, 9; 14:6). The significance this worship place comes especially to the fore during the time of Samuel and Saul (1 Sam 10:8; 11:14; 13:4, 7–8, 12, 15). And in the time of the prophets Hosea and Amos, the tribes of the Northern Kingdom of Israel were still making pilgrimages to Gilgal (Hos 4:15, 9:15, 12:12[11]; Amos 4:4, 5:5). It is thus beyond doubt that the place Gilgal, whose topographic identification will be taken up below, was a sanctuary of high rank. The present investigation therefore concerns the question whether any sort of worship observances can be recognized in the Old Testament tradition of Gilgal that might explain the great importance of the sanctuary, during the time of Samuel and Saul, for example. It does not suffice simply to assert that Gilgal was a worship place of high rank; rather, we must ask *which particular sacred ceremony* established the importance of the sanctuary. But first allow me to make a few comments on the location of the place of worship under discussion.

I

Where was the place of worship called Gilgal? In his article "Das byzantinische Gilgal,"[1] A. M. Schneider sought to prove that the Byzantine and Christian traditions ⟦182⟧, which can be traced into the Middle Ages, believed that the Gilgal mentioned in the Old Testament was located at Khirbet el-Mefjir, 2 km north of Eriḥâ ⟦the name of Jericho as cited in these sources⟧. This identification is suggested by the Madaba map and the medieval pilgrims' reports, as well as by Josephus (*Ant.* 5.1.11) and Eusebius (*Onomasticon* 64.24ff.). Granted, no traces of remains by which to demonstrate an exact location have been found. Consequently, for the time being we have accepted the locality identified by Schneider. Up to now, no

1. A. M. Schneider, "Das byzantinische Gilgal," *ZDPV* 54 (1931) 50ff.

other convincing means of locating Old Testament Gilgal in the environs of Jericho has presented itself. The more specific description "Gilgal on the east border of Jericho" in Josh 4:19 could therefore correspond to the location specified in the Byzantine and Christian tradition. According to the biblical tradition, the hallmark of the sanctuary was, more than anything else, the twelve sacred stones that certainly formed the sacred heart of the place of worship (see Josh 4:20).

All of the references to Gilgal in the Old Testament, however, including 2 Kgs 2:1 and 4:28 and probably also "Beth-gilgal" in Neh 12:29, refer to a Gilgal near Jericho, in the neighborhood of modern Khirbet el-Mefjir.[2] It is therefore not possible to prove there was a second Gilgal near Shechem, at Julejil[3] or, as attempted by E. Sellin in his book *Gilgal* (1917), to seek yet another solution. We have every reason to assume a single Gilgal near Jericho.

II

During the time of Samuel and Saul, Gilgal was already a recognized place of worship, famous throughout Israel. There is absolutely no other way to explain the significance the place assumes in 1 Samuel. Thus, for this investigation into the customary worship ceremonies at Gilgal, we must turn to the book of Joshua and look there for some footholds. In the book of Joshua, however, [[183]] a major difficulty appears. The Joshua 2–5 complex, where the traditions bearing on Gilgal are found, represents a notorious problem for literary criticism. Joshua 3–4 especially involves complicated layerings within the text that have yet to be explained satisfactorily. We might first consider the investigations of scholars who believe they have found the Pentateuchal sources J, E, and P also in Joshua. The complicated literary problem is solved by the separation of sources.[4] The textual difficulties are eliminated by the expedient of assignment to different source-documents. But it must be noted: not only do the theories of the various investigators diverge immensely, but in each of the source analyses every available possibility from J1 to P2 is appealed to, yielding even then only a partial understanding of the text. I concur with Martin Noth's judgment[5] that all attempts using source analysis to take the book of Joshua back to a number of continuous narrative strands have failed. As

2. K. Galling, *Biblisches Reallexikon* (Tübingen: Mohr, 1937) col. 197. We will return to Deut 11:30 later in this investigation.

3. A. Schlatter, *Zur Topographie und Geschichte Palästinas* (Stuttgart: Calwer, 1893) 246ff.

4. A. Wiesmann underestimates the difficulties of the text when he tries to recover an "original order" by rearrangement ("Israels Einzug in Kanaan," *Bib* [1930] 126ff.; [1931] 90ff.).

5. M. Noth, *Das Buch Josua* (HAT; Tübingen: Mohr, 1938) 11.

H. Gressmann[6] and Albrecht Alt[7] already recognized, Joshua 1–6 comprises a complex of etiological legends. The foci of these legends are the worship places of Jericho and Gilgal. In his commentary on Joshua as well as in his *Überlieferungsgeschichtliche Studien* 1, Noth provided convincing proof[8] that the legends of the book of Joshua cannot be derived from the Pentateuchal sources. They are instead old traditions, gathered by the Deuteronomist, slightly reworked, and inserted into a historical framework.[9] But how does Noth explain the complicated state of the text in Joshua 3–4? [[184]] Understandably, for him it is a matter of intervention in the first place by the deuteronomistic collector and editor but then of later insertions into the text of the Deuteronomistic History in various stages as well. In this way, the layerings in Joshua 3–4 can also be explained: first, by pointing to the deuteronomistic editor, who would be justifiably interested in such an important narrative as the passage of the Ark through the Jordan; and second, by noting later insertions at various stages, which testify to a lively literary prehistory of the modern text. The question then immediately arises whether such an explanation does justice to the other material that can be observed in the tradition of the Deuteronomistic History and whether the supposition of a lively *literary* history of the text is not a too hastily adopted way out of the difficulties. Would it not be possible to explain much of the unevenness of the text of Joshua 3–4 by means of a particular quality of the *worship* traditions of Gilgal already received by the Deuteronomist? While we ask this question, we agree with Noth that in Joshua 1–6 (and, furthermore, in the book of Joshua generally) *no* Pentateuchal sources are found and prepare ourselves to understand the complicated narrative in Joshua 3–4 in essence as arising out of predeuteronomistic worship traditions, admittedly without entirely excluding a literary reworking of the deuteronomistic text at a later time.

A glance at Joshua 3–4 shows immediately that a number of ideas, institutions, and customs rooted in worship influenced Joshua 3–4. If we ignore for a moment every understanding of the report of the passage through the Jordan that is oriented to the historical continuity of the Joshua narratives, then the following elements of the ritual can be ex-

6. H. Gressmann, *Die Anfänge Israels* (Die Schriften des Alten Testaments 1/2; Göttingen: Vandenhoeck & Ruprecht, 1922).

7. A. Alt, *Josua* (BZAW 66; Berlin: Töpelmann, 1936) 13–29.

8. M. Noth, *Überlieferungsgeschichtliche Studien*, vol. 1: *Die sammelnden und bearbeitenden Geschichtswerke des Alten Testaments* (Schriften der Königsberger Gelehrten Gesellsch.–Geisteswissensch. Klasse 18/2; Tübingen: Max Niemeyer, 1943) 40ff.

9. The "Deuteronomistic History" comprises the books of Joshua, Judges, 1–2 Samuel, and 1–2 Kings. By means of an introduction prefaced to Deuteronomy, it too was incorporated into the Deuteronomist's History as the foundation. See ibid.

tracted from the narrative. First, "levitical priests" appear (Josh 3:3). They bore the worship object, the holy Ark, according to a precisely prescribed order (Josh 3:5). Then twelve men from Israel step up (Josh 3:12). Twelve stones are brought together in a particular location and ultimately erected in Gilgal (Josh 4:20). What does all this mean? Are we really to suppose that, beginning with the Deuteronomist, editors ⟦185⟧ and correctors of the text made it their business to introduce details into a preexisting narrative that were as precise as possible and corresponded to the later liturgy? Even if we consider this possibility inevitable, we still cannot overlook the fact that (surely inseparably bound to the original version of the narrative) the passage talks about *twelve* stones. Did these twelve stones go back, as *maṣṣebot* ⟦'sacred stone pillars'⟧, to the Canaanite period?[10] In view of the occurrence of the characteristic number twelve, applied to the tribes of Israel, this is quite unlikely. On the other hand, we know nothing of any significance about Gilgal as a place of worship within the amphictyonic worship organization, such that the number twelve might find some sort of explanation in this context. And what about the Ark? Does it belong to the "original narrative" of the arrival of the Israelites? In that case, the Ark would have been Israel's traveling sanctuary–that in itself would not be too astonishing. But another question arises: could not the Ark also have been stationed in Gilgal at some earlier or later period than the occupation of the land, and would not one further have to suppose that the place of worship near Jericho was a central sanctuary of the amphictyony?[11] This question arises from the observation that in the report in Joshua 3–4 the Ark is surrounded by typical worship accoutrements. These accoutrements cannot so easily be ascribed to later accretions.

III

Josh 4:20 reports that Joshua erected twelve stones in Gilgal. Setting aside the question whether Joshua actually belongs in the original form of the narrative, let us note that the twelve stones were thought to be the specific feature of the place of worship in Gilgal (Josh 4:20). These stones represent the center of the holy place; they give factual substance to the image of a *circle of stones* called up by the very sound of the name *Gilgal*. In typical

10. Noth, *Josua*, 5.

11. Albrecht Alt raised a question that is very important for our investigation: does not the significance that Gilgal had as the scene of the tribes' first swearing of allegiance to Saul need to be ascribed to the fact that Gilgal during the time of Samuel and Saul was already the worship center of the league? (Alt, *Die Staatenbildung der Israeliten in Palästina* [Reformationsprogramm der Universität Leipzig; Leipzig: Edelmann, 1930] 27).

etiological form, this sentence is added to the report of the erection of the twelve stones:

> When your children ask their fathers in time to come, "What do these stones mean?" then you shall let your children know, "Israel passed over this Jordan on dry ground." (Josh 4:21–22)

On Josh 4:20ff., Noth comments: "The twelve stones are a memorial to the miraculous passage through the Jordan by which Yahweh cleared the way for the Israelites into the land west of the Jordan."[12] Accordingly, the sanctuary of Gilgal with its twelve stones would be the focus of the historical accounts of the entry into arable land. But here new questions immediately come to mind: What sort of "historical events" are transmitted in Joshua 3–4? Is it not striking that the passage through the Reed Sea is deliberately presented by the text as being *repeated* at the Jordan? What are vv. 23–24 in chap. 4 trying to say?

> For the LORD your God dried up the waters of the Jordan for you until you passed over, as the LORD your God did to the Red Sea, which he dried up for us until we passed over, so that all the peoples of the earth may know that the hand of the LORD is mighty; that you may fear the LORD your God for ever.

Is this simply one of those adaptations of old material so easily recognizable by the historical study of legends? What does it mean when the Reed Sea miracle is placed parallel to the Jordan miracle?

Thus, an investigation of the etiological high point of the narrative of the passage through the Jordan (Josh 4:20ff.) also brings up a series of questions. We will pass over Joshua 5 at present, a chapter containing very difficult problems, but we must return to it later.

IV

Now let us consider the narrative in Joshua 3–4 from an entirely different angle. Gerhard von Rad performed a great service by showing the way to a new understanding of the transmission of the Hexateuch from the perspective of literary-critical analysis of the Pentateuch.[13] His form-critical [[187]] investigations (in part building on S. Mowinckel)[14] have achieved

12. Noth, *Josua*, 5.

13. G. von Rad is of the opinion that the narrative layers of the Pentateuchal sources J, E, and P can also be followed through the book of Joshua ("Hexateuch oder Pentateuch?" *VF* [1947–48] 52ff.).

14. S. Mowinckel, *Le décalogue* (Études d'Histoire et de philosophie religieuses 16; Paris, 1927).

significant results.[15] Von Rad seeks the roots of the Hexateuch traditions in the ancient Israelite celebration of festivals and has identified two main traditions. First, in the Hexateuch, a "land-occupation tradition" is definitive and predominant. This tradition has left traces in, among other places, a "small historical creed"[16] that contains the story of the saving events of the prehistory of Israel from the exodus from Egypt to the occupation of the land and validates these events, as we shall see, in the sphere of worship (Deut 26:5ff.).

Alongside this "small historical creed," which appears in another version in Deut 6:20–24, a number of other similar texts can be identified in the Old Testament in which, surprisingly, only the Exodus from Egypt, the wandering in the wilderness, and the occupation of the land, but not the events at Sinai, are depicted.[17] Thus, concludes von Rad after intensive argumentation, there was once a tradition that existed in Israel's worship independently of the Sinai tradition. In the outline of the Hexateuch, the occupation tradition (which could also be called the "exodus tradition") is absolutely determinative, since the definitive holy deeds of Yahweh in the prehistory of Israel are communicated with clear continuity in this tradition. Second, in a later period the originally independent Sinai tradition[18] was added to the occupation tradition. The Old Testament includes texts that give an account of the events at Sinai without any reference to the occupation of the land. In the sphere of worship, the Sinai events were transmitted.[19] The course of a worship ceremony in which the events at Sinai were reenacted can be recovered from the Exodus 19–24 complex, and also from Deuteronomy. Von Rad has shown where this ritual procedure, which is also echoed in several psalms, was located. [[188]] He came to the realization that very early on a festival of covenant renewal was celebrated in Shechem, the central worship place of the ancient Israelite amphictyony.

Even if it is true that in the period after the conquest the twelve tribes commemorated the Sinai covenant at ancient Shechem, the central sanctuary of the ancient Israelite amphictyony, the question still remains to which place of worship and to which liturgical ceremony von Rad saw the land-occupaton tradition to be connected. The events in Gilgal are known to be the end-point of the land-occupation tradition. According to the tradition of the book of Joshua, Joshua supposedly apportioned the land

15. G. von Rad, *Das formgeschichtliche Problem des Hexateuchs* (BWANT 4/26; Stuttgart: Kohlhammer, 1938).

16. Ibid., 3ff.

17. Ibid., 8ff.

18. Ibid., 11ff.

19. Ibid., 18ff. Mowinckel, *Le décalogue*, 129.

among the individual tribes at Gilgal (Josh 14:6). From this fact, von Rad concludes that Gilgal must also have been the site on which the entire occupation tradition focused. There is much to be said for this point of view. Just as the tradition points to Gilgal as the terminus of the immigration, it also suggests that the sanctuary in the vicinity of Jericho was the center at which the entire occupation tradition was preserved. If we are willing to agree with this conclusion of von Rad's research, then another question immediately arises: which *liturgical ceremony* was it in which the occupation tradition was transmitted? What festival was celebrated at Gilgal? This question, the starting-point of our investigation, inevitably follows: If the occupation tradition was transmitted in a sacral context, then we are obliged to seek a corresponding worship ceremony. The Sinai tradition just referred to celebrates the coming of God to his people–the event of law-giving and covenant-making–in a liturgical enactment still recognizable to this day. The primeval events at Sinai are repeated in the worship event, and this at Shechem, as we have seen. If the occupation tradition was also transmitted at a sanctuary, then we must now seek to show the corresponding festival ceremony. Unfortunately, von Rad did not pursue the goal of his inquiries consistently at this point. He said: "Here [in researching the course of the occupation events] we encounter greater difficulties that partially have their basis in one simple fact, namely, that the ⟦189⟧ occupation tradition cannot be one theme a liturical enactment could encompass in toto, and therefore it was far from displaying many recognizable features that in turn pointed to historical analogies."[20] Certainly even a brief consideration will lead to this conclusion: an event as all-encompassing as the one contained in the occupation tradition and related in the "small historical creed" could not have been entirely performed within a worship ceremony. How can the passage through the Reed Sea and the taking of the land as such be comprehended in a single liturgical performance? This is the direction of our considerations. However, we must always remember that what seems highly improbable in modern thinking may have been possible in ancient times. In any case, I see the task as fundamentally not to rule anything out a priori. It is indeed strangely inconsistent that, after finding such a convincing explanation for the Sinai tradition in the liturgy in Shechem, von Rad pursued the taking of the land tradition simply in its expression in the "small historical creed" and then investigated the Sitz im Leben of this "creed" in worship. Since no liturgical performance *can* encompass the occupation tradition as a whole, von Rad limits himself to the creedal confession, which does include the entire extent of the saving event, from the exodus from Egypt

20. Von Rad, *Formgeschichtliche Problem des Hexateuchs,* 38.

to the occupation of the land, and thus in place of an unrealizable worship enactment such a confession could have had a liturgical importance. From the contexts in which the "creed" is found in Deuteronomy, von Rad infers that the occupation tradition was anchored in the Feast of Weeks and could be seen as the cult-legend of this festival. But in the end, von Rad felt the imbalance of his position: the occupation tradition on the one hand was supposed to be the cult-legend of the Feast of Weeks but on the other hand was supposed to have originated in Gilgal. In this result the inconsistency appears with full clarity, for what connects the time of the festival with the place of worship? *The question of the worship enactment of the occupation tradition must be taken up once again.* The "small historical creed" that von Rad observed must [[190]] now be cconsidered to be already something derivative, possibly a collection of the actual contents of the liturgy.

With von Rad's search for the focus in worship of the occupation tradition, we have arrived at another angle on the narratives in Joshua 3–4. We have realized that Gilgal as the terminus of the occupation tradition was the holy place at which the apportionment of land to the tribes once took place. If we now ask about the actual enactment in worship at Gilgal, we will have to recall the questions derived from the text of Joshua 3–4. At the heart of these questions stands the observation that the historical report of the entry of the Israelites west of the Jordan is shot through with elements from the sphere of worship—or to express it more concretely, with elements of a liturgical performance. We recall the striking fact that the passage through the Reed Sea, according to the explicit presentation of the narrative in Joshua 3–4, was *repeated* in the Jordan. This suggests to us that Joshua 3–4 may describe a liturgical performance that portrays the events of the occupation tradition in a sacred enactment. Without going into all the difficulties that arise with such an assumption even at a first close inspection of the text, let us first examine whether it makes sense to pursue such an assumption. Let us stay with the occupation tradition discovered by von Rad. It contains two highly significant themes: (1) the exodus from Egypt, with the central event of the passage through the Reed Sea; and (2) the entry into the land of Canaan. Would these two principal themes come to full expression in our hypothetical enactment? We can answer this question positively. If in fact a ritually enacted passage through the Jordan celebrated the passage through the Reed Sea (see Josh 4:23–24), then the reenactment would have commemorated the entry into the land west of the Jordan at the same time. It would then be possible that the occupation tradition was indeed one that was embraced entirely within a liturgical event. But in practical terms, how might we imagine such a passage through the Jordan? Now, this question is not hard to answer. There is a ford near Khirbet el-Mefjir (some 10 km from Gilgal) where one can walk across the Jordan.[21] [[191]] The only other question is at what point in time such a crossing can be made. At the end of April, the daily flow of the Jordan runs very high with the snowmelt from the Lebanon and Hermon, which makes crossing the ford impossible.[22]

V

There are still a variety of obstacles to our supposition that Joshua 3–4 is the deposit of a liturgical performance focused on Gilgal, and these must not be overlooked. To begin with, there are two points that require special attention. However, if these points are clarified, then the other difficulties are resolved as well.

The Joshua 3–4 narrative presents the passage through the Jordan as an activity of the *league of twelve tribes* and places the *Ark* at the heart of this activity, in the role of worship sanctuary. Now these two facts would at first glance indeed give good support to the supposition of a regularly practiced liturgical reenactment. However, we must ask when Gilgal ever was the central worship place of the league of twelve tribes and, thus, of the Ark-sanctuary of Israel. According to Noth's investigation, Shechem was probably the central sanctuary of all Israel in the period after the occupation of the land.[23] Thus, during the early period of Israel, which is the period under consideration for the liturgical performance of the occupation tradition, the Ark could not have been in Gilgal. It turns out from an investigation of the earliest sources "that the sanctuary at Shechem was probably once the amphictyonic midpoint of the Israelite league of tribes; and that appears to be the earliest state of affairs we are able to recover."[24] It is hardly possible to dismiss Noth's explanations convincingly; too many texts point to Shechem. The assembly at Shechem (Joshua 24) was the foundational event that legitimized the central place of worship immediately after the taking of the land. Thus, in spite of everything that has been presented so far, we must still pursue the question further: could Gilgal, the place [[192]] where the apportionment of the land among the twelve tribes was decided, actually have existed outside of the amphictyonic worship sphere—perhaps as a sanctuary with special traditions pertaining to a single tribe? Could not the Ark, if it was a traveling sanctuary, have played

21. N. Glueck, *The River Jordan* (Philadelphia: Westminster, 1946) 199.

22. G. Dalman, *Arbeit und Sitte in Palästina*, vol. 1: *Jahreslauf und Tageslauf* (Gütersloh: Bertelsmann, 1927) 206; F. M. Abel, *Géographie de la Palestine* (EBib; Paris: Gabalda, 1933) 1.123ff.

23. M. Noth, *Das System der Zwölf Stämme Israels* (BWANT 4/1; Stuttgart: Kohlhammer, 1930) 66.

24. Idem, *Geschichte Israels* (Göttingen: Vandenhoeck & Ruprecht, 1950) 81.

a significant role at the end of the period of wandering and hence in Gilgal? So we return to the hypothesis already introduced above, that the Ark, after it was originally stationed in Shechem, later came to Gilgal. Is it possible to pursue this theory any further?

First, we must continue to emphasize that it is *simply a hypothesis* that Shechem was the central worship place of the ancient Israelite amphictyony in the period after the taking of the land. Actually, if we investigate the earliest sources of the Old Testament for the sanctuaries where the Ark of Yahweh appeared prominently during the initial period after the taking of the land, then only Gilgal (Joshua 3–4) and Bethel (Judg 20:26–27) can be named. Admittedly, this does not mean that Shechem is ruled out. We cannot overlook a narrative as important as the one transmitted in Joshua 24. So we must ask what the relation of a sacred performance in Gilgal to the amphictyonic worship of the early history of Israel might have been. Two attempted explanations must be examined here.

(1) In his article "Die Landnahmesagen des Buches Josua," K. Möhlenbrink establishes that Joshua 3–4 contains a double narrative tendency. Möhlenbrink distinguishes in general in the book of Joshua between original "Gilgal traditions," which must be attributed to a "three-tribe amphictyony" located in Gilgal in an early period,[25] and "Ephraimitic traditions," which represent the concerns of the whole twelve-tribe league later centralized at Shiloh. The following conclusion relevant to our investigation could be drawn from Möhlenbrink's explanations: the worship festival that we have discovered at Gilgal was a sacred enactment belonging to a three-tribe amphictyony, whose cult-legend was later reworked and altered in light of the reality of the twelve-tribe league. But this assumption is impossible. The [[193]] Ark, setting up the twelve stones, the passage through the Jordan as repetition of the Reed Sea event—all of these elements belong structurally to the liturgical celebration assumed for Gilgal. If these elements are removed, then the point of the etiology that aims to explain the twelve stones of the stone circle (*Gilgal* = 'stone circle'; Josh 4:20ff.) is evacuated of its content. It is hardly possible to presuppose the existence of the twelve stones in Gilgal as early as the pre-Israelite period. There is much more reason to suppose that Gilgal, a stone circle sanctuary, which must have already been considered as such in pre-Israelite times, took on the character of a stone circle sanctuary with twelve stones through the ancient Israelite amphictyony. This would not only conform to the tendency of the text in Joshua 3–4 but also justify the significance that Gilgal had in Israel during the time of Saul.

25. According to Möhlenbrink, the "three-tribe amphictyony" would have comprised the tribes that entered early—Benjamin, Reuben, and Gad.

(2) It is more likely, however, that *Gilgal replaced Shechem as the central sanctuary very early on*. It can scarcely be doubted that the assembly at Shechem, mentioned several times (Joshua 24) together with the ancient descriptions of a liturgical enactment on Mount Ebal and Mount Gerizim (Josh 8:30ff. and Deuteronomy 27), represent the terminus a quo of the twelve-tribe league and its amphictyonic system of worship. But this is all we know concretely. However, there is a remarkable passage, which has long been considered problematic in Old Testament research and has been the starting point of many a literary-critical hypothesis, that can be adduced as evidence for a transfer of the Shechemite cultus to Gilgal. It is Deut 11:25ff., and it reads:

> No man shall be able to stand against you; the LORD your God will lay the fear of you and the dread of you upon all the land that you shall tread, as he promised you. Behold, I set before you this day a blessing and a curse: the blessing, if you obey the commandments of the LORD your God, which I command you this day, and the curse, if you do not obey the commandments of the LORD your God, but turn aside from the way which I command you this day, to go after other gods which you have not known. And when the LORD your God brings you into the land which you are entering to take possession of it, you shall set the blessing on Mount Gerizim and the curse on Mount Ebal. Are they not beyond the Jordan, west of the road, toward the going down of the sun, [[194]] in the land of the Canaanites who live in the Arabah, over against *Gilgal*, beside the oak of Moreh?

One thing is clear: this Gilgal "beyond the Jordan" can only be the place of worship near Jericho.[26] But since when are Ebal and Gerizim near Gilgal? The statements of our text can, if we take them seriously and do not regard them as "senseless glosses," only be understood if we consider a transfer of the Ebal-Gerizim ceremonies to Gilgal. The text therefore means something like this: Ebal and Gerizim, the two mountains on which blessing and curse are invoked, *now* lie (after the transfer of the worship arrangements) no longer near Shechem, but near Gilgal; there the old ceremony now takes place. Also if Deuteronomy 11 is a late text, it is quite possible that a very old testimony to a shift in ritual that took place in the early history of Israel has been preserved.

If Gilgal had now become the central sanctuary of the twelve-tribe league, then the Sinai tradition and the occupation tradition come closer together than von Rad supposed. This explains why the Sinai and occupation traditions already stood at the core of the ancient Israelite amphicty-

26. Schlatter's conjecture (*Zur Topographie und Geschichte Palästinas*, 246ff.) wrongly puts too much emphasis on Deut 11:25ff. in order to prove that there was a Gilgal near Shechem.

ony's belief. A tribal confederation residing together in a common land cannot be understood on the basis of a Sinai tradition alone.

VI

After the explanations just given, there is no further obstacle to considering Joshua 3–4 *a cultic legend of a festival of the Exodus from Egypt and the occupation of the land.* The Joshua 3–4 narrative that is so hard to understand in its existing form stands in a new light. If we attempt to reconstruct the individual acts of the celebration, the following picture emerges: the far side of the Jordan was the departure point of the common procession. Josh 3:4 indicates that this involved a solemn, orderly procession; a carefully measured interval is to be maintained. Before the procession begins, the people "sanctify" themselves (Josh 3:5)–they take the precautions [[195]] necessary for ritual purity (compare Exod 19:10, Num 11:18, Josh 7:13). The signal to begin is given when the Ark is lifted up by the priests and carried in front of the people, at the head of the procession (Josh 3:6). When the Ark comes to the bank of the Jordan, the priests stand still for a moment. Before fording the river, words are spoken regarding the supreme significance of the event. In Josh 3:10, we read the words of a brief address, and the significance of the liturgical performance emerges. With the Jordan's crossing, the people enter the arable land, and the occupation of the land is accomplished. Yahweh thus continually renews his gift of the land to his people by means of a sacral act. What this means and how this enactment affected the beliefs of Israel we can only begin to imagine now. Unfortunately, we cannot describe the far-reaching theological consequences here. Just one thing must be noted. We have the impression that the appellation of God, "Yahweh, the LORD of all the earth," in Josh 3:11, 13 is a name for Yahweh that was used especially in the worship at Gilgal. At the heart of the enactment was the passage through the Jordan, which in the cultic legend was described with strict reference to the events at the Reed Sea. The water stood "in one heap" (like a dam, Josh 3:13); the procession through the Jordan then also had the following significance:

> For the LORD your God dried up the waters of the Jordan for you until you passed over, as the LORD your God did to the Red Sea, which he dried up for us until we passed over, so that all the peoples of the earth may know that the hand of the LORD is mighty; that you may fear the LORD your God for ever. (Josh 4:23–24)

The Reed Sea miracle and crossing of the Jordan are compared with each other. But this was more than an abstract comparison; it was a concrete experience in worship. In the course of the sacral enactment, the passage through the Jordan *fulfilled* the event at the Reed Sea. This appearance of unity evoked by the liturgical act finds its highest expression as worship experience in Psalm 114 (see also Ps 66:6).

If we examine Joshua 3–4 in detail, we will be able to find a whole series of references to the event at the Reed Sea. Thus it emerges from Josh 3:17 that the Ark waits in the Jordan, [[196]] lets the people pass by and then takes over the role of the rearguard–that is, the protection of the people against the "Egyptians." There is no unified information in the text about the place of the erection of the twelve stones. It looks as though on this point there were two (or even three) different customs prevailing in the liturgy, perhaps at different times. Thus we would have to attribute the lack of coherence in the text here to the lively history of transmission within the worship sphere. In any case, it is clear that twelve stones were brought together and set up as a memorial. It is explicitly stressed that the enactment was carried out by the entire confederation of tribes. All twelve tribes of the covenantal people were brought through the water, and all twelve tribes took possession of the land west of the Jordan together. The setting up of the twelve stones was indeed a ritual act that, each time, brought the unified action of the twelve tribes to visible expression and established them as a memorial.

We should now delve into various motifs that are characteristic of a cultic legend and that, for example, seek to emphasize the miraculous character of the events. For the time being, however, these comments must suffice.

VII

When was the festival of the crossing and the occupation of the land celebrated at Gilgal? This question remains to be discussed. As we saw, von Rad concluded from the observations suggested to him by the context of the "small historical creed" in Deuteronomy that the occupation tradition is the cultic legend of the Feast of Weeks. This thesis deserves a thorough examination, to which end, in this context, at least a few points of view should be given. In Joshua 5, there are three different items that require our attention at this point: (1) The circumcision of Israel, which (who would not immediately perceive connections with our explanations thus far?) concludes with the sentence "This day I have rolled away the reproach of Egypt from you" (Josh 5:9); (2) the Passover celebration "at evening in the plains of Jericho" (Josh 5:10); (3) the appearance of the "commander of the army of Yahweh" (Josh 5:11). These three narratives are firmly connected [[197]] with Gilgal. Presumably the strange narrative of the appearance of the "commander of the army of the LORD" (Josh 5:13–15) is the oldest legitimation that the sanctuary at Gilgal can exhibit.

We will not go further into the circumcision (Josh 5:1–9), since here many unresolved questions remain (though these might gain some clarification in consequence of our discussion). For the question of the date of celebrating the occupation tradition in Gilgal, however, the narrative of the Passover festival (Josh 5:10–12) is probably decisive. This Passover celebration is very clearly marked as a festal conclusion to the wandering in the wilderness and ceremonial acceptance of the first produce of the arable land:

> And on the morrow after the passover, on that very day, they ate of the produce of the land, unleavened cakes and parched grain. And the manna ceased on the morrow, when they ate of the produce of the land; and the people of Israel had manna no more, but ate of the fruit of the land of Canaan that year. (Josh 5:11–12)

The eating of matzah obviously existed in Canaan as a celebration held by the original population of the land. According to the tradition of Josh 5:10–12, however, the feast celebrated in Gilgal was named "Passover" and celebrated as a *conclusion to the wandering in the wilderness and new beginning in the arable land*. A later addition to v. 10 dates the feast in Gilgal according to the Israelite calendar of feasts as "the Passover feast" on the 14th of Nisan (compare Josh 5:10 with Josh 4:19). It is natural, therefore, to bring the commemoration of the occupation into connection with the Passover festival; especially as in the Old Testament tradition the exodus from Egypt counts as the cultic legend of the Passover festival. But at this point one can only warn against unilinear reconstructions after the event. It is certain that the date in Josh 5:10 was added later. Above all, it is important to ignore as far as possible the later Passover festival and its dating. So then the surprising phrase "unleavened cakes and parched grain" (Josh 5:11) catches the eye. It diverges from the usual Priestly expression and points to the early period. On the one hand, we have here to do with eating matzah and, on the other, with the consumption of "grain." Which feast is in view in Josh 5:10–12? How is the text to be understood? These questions are hard to answer. We just know too little of the feasts of ancient Israel; the later festival calendars have overlaid the earlier texts with their developed regulations. So it will hardly be possible to ⟦198⟧ specify an exact date. But this much is certain: Josh 5:10–12 must have to do with a harvest festival. The barley harvest can already be ripe on the 16th of Nisan;[27] wheat is harvested in June. The first-named date, which would point to the matzah festival, is the most likely.[28] At that time a procession through the

27. Dalman, *Arbeit und Sitte in Palästina*, 3.9.

28. The "small historical creed" should probably be seen as a confession that summarizes the elements of the feast of the occupation of the land. In the delivery of the "firstfruits," etc., in the Feast of Weeks (von Rad) is the time when this confession is recited (Deut 26:1ff.).

Jordan would indeed be possible.[29] Thus, nothing would stand in the way of the twelve tribes of Israel coming to Gilgal during the old matzah festival in order to observe the festival of the occupation of the land.

VIII

At this point, allow me to note a few conclusions that follow naturally from what has been established in this investigation. With Noth, I see the Deuteronomist as the collector and editor of the sources of the book of Joshua. In this context it must be emphasized that the cultic legend of the occupation of the land came to the Deuteronomist from the amphictyonic cultus of Gilgal. The intervention of the Deuteronomist in the preexisting material will have consisted in inserting into the framework of his history texts that followed the worship practice of their own time. And it was just this insertion that did the most to mask the true form of the narratives in Joshua 3–4. Still other texts from the Deuteronomistic History could in fact also be mentioned (2 Samuel 6–7!), from which it becomes clear that the Deuteronomist has included cultic legends in the framework of his history.[30] But as soon as the true character of the narratives in Joshua 3–4 is recognized, then it finally becomes understandable why the Deuteronomistic History, which begins at the moment of the occupation of the land, excluded what presumably once existed, namely, the conclusion of the Pentateuchal sources. These (corresponding to the "small historical creed") must have continued as far as the event of the occupation of the land: the Deuteronomist ⟦199⟧ had available the *authoritative* source of the occupation of the land in the form of the amphictyonic cultic legend of Gilgal, and so we have here traditional material of the highest rank. All other narratives of the Pentateuchal sources on the event of the taking of the land receded in significance before this tradition that was available to the Deuteronomist.

Naturally, many other aspects could have been adduced here. We need only remember the significance that Gilgal had during the time of Samuel and Saul, which can be understood only if we consider Gilgal a place that already counted, along with Shechem, as the most important location in the early history of the twelve-tribe league. Consider further the stories of Elijah and Elisha and the miracle-narratives that are so uniquely reminiscent of the wilderness period. And think finally of the role that Gilgal played at the time of the prophets Amos and Hosea. Many questions remain open. Our investigation is indeed just a small contribution to the history of worship in one important sanctuary of ancient Israel.

29. Abel, *Géographie*, 123ff.

30. Cf. my book *Die Königsherrschaft Gottes im Alten Testament* (Tübingen: Mohr, 1951) 30ff.

The Role of the Priesthood in the Deuteronomistic History

RICHARD D. NELSON

In this essay, Nelson examines a series of related issues in the Deuteronomistic History: the relationship between priests and Levites, the priesthoods of Eli, Abiathar, and Zadok, and the priestly dimensions of Josiah's reforms. He argues that the Deuteronomistic History distinguishes between priests and Levites, even though the two groups overlap. The Deuteronomist considers priests to be drawn from the ranks of the Levites but without any regard for particular families. Nelson thinks that the oracles concerning Eli and Zadok (1 Sam 3:11–14, 1 Kgs 2:27) introduce important concepts for the later history of the monarchy such as the correlation between threat and punishment, the (dis)establishment of an enduring dynasty, and the legitimate overthrow of priestly and royal houses. As for the much-debated nature of Josiah's reforms, Nelson envisions a variety of groups being affected. But he finds little evidence to corroborate the view that the priests of the high places were admitted to the priesthood of the central sanctuary. Instead, Nelson thinks that nonsacrificing Yahwistic priests in Judah, not connected to the high places, were moved to Jerusalem and assigned priestly duties at the Temple.

Many scholars have thought that the Deuteronomist was uninterested in sacrifice and cultic affairs. Nelson admits that this judgment carries some weight but argues that the Deuteronomist was interested in the history of the priesthood insofar as the details of this record could serve larger aims. If the affairs of Levites, priests, and cult(s) could be used to make a larger theological point, the Deuteronomist shows no hesitation in discussing them.

Reprinted with permission from *Congress Volume: Leuven, 1989* (ed. J. A. Emerton; Vetus Testamentum Supplements 43; Leiden: Brill, 1991) 132–47. In this article, Dtr has been changed to DH when the siglum refers to the Deuteronomistic History.

⟦132⟧ Beneath the surface of the OT remain traces of competition among rival priestly families, but the Deuteronomistic History (DH) demonstrates little partisan interest in these controversies.[1] For example, Dtr makes no effort to produce complete genealogies for either the Elides or the Zadokites. The "father" of Eli's house remains mysteriously unspecified in 1 Sam 2:27. The genealogy offered for Zadok is notoriously problematic (2 Sam 8:17). Moreover, in spite of his ostensible concern with the "faithful priest" Zadok (1 Sam 2:35), Dtr fails to provide genealogical links between him and later Jerusalem priests.

Yet one ought not to exaggerate Dtr's lack of interest in priestly matters. Solomon's temple dedication, for example, includes some priestly theology within its predominantly deuteronomistic presentation (1 Kgs 8:10–11). The sacrifice list of 2 Kgs 16:15 shows some acquaintance with priestly lore. Priests appear throughout Dtr from beginning (Deut 31:9) to end (2 Kgs 25:18), and not always as completely peripheral figures.

It seems appropriate, therefore, to investigate Dtr's assumptions about priests and Levites, to re-examine the critical passages 1 Sam 2:27–36 and 2 Kgs 23:5–9, and to trace how Dtr used priests to shape his theological plot.

Priests and Levites

Dtr's assumptions about priests derived from reading Deuteronomy in the light of the institutions of his own day. It would be a mistake to assume that his viewpoints were simply identical with those of Deuteronomy or even that he properly understood ⟦133⟧ Deuteronomy's original meaning. Instead, we must ask how what Deuteronomy has to say about priests and Levites would have been understood by a Judahite of the Josianic period.[2]

The relationship between priests and Levites in Deuteronomy is disputed. Some insist that Deuteronomy simply equates Levites and priests.[3] Others find a distinction between priests who served at altars and Levites who did not.[4] The so-called *Identitätsformel* ⟦'formula making identical'⟧

1. On the distance between the deuteronomistic school and priestly concerns, M. Weinfeld, *Deuteronomy and the Deuteronomic School* (Oxford, 1972 ⟦reprinted, Winona Lake, Ind.: Eisenbrauns, 1992⟧) 182–89, 210–24, 227.

2. I am assuming a Josianic Dtr who had before him both the singular and plural strata of Deuteronomy 5–28.

3. J. A. Emerton, "Priests and Levites in Deuteronomy," *VT* (1962) 129–38.

4. G. E. Wright, "The Levites in Deuteronomy," *VT* 4 (1954) 325–30; R. Abba, "Priests and Levites in Deuteronomy," *VT* 27 (1977) 257–67. In partial agreement, A. H. J. Gunneweg, *Leviten und Priester* (Göttingen, 1965) 69–77, and J. Lindblom, *Erwägungen zur Herkunft der Josianischen Tempelurkunde* (Lund, 1971) 32–33.

("the priests, the Levites" [['the Levitical priests']]) is often assumed to imply a claim that all Levites are or ought to be priests.[5]

A review of the evidence suggests that Dtr understood Deuteronomy's separate use of "priest" and "Levitical priest" over against "Levite" to refer to two different but overlapping groups. In Dtr's opinion, priests were properly drawn from the ranks of the Levites, but without any particular limitation in regard to family. Priests were simply Levites who had been appointed to priestly office, sometimes but not always serving as sanctuary supervisors.

First, it is certainly possible to read Deuteronomy as implying two distinct groups, whatever Deuteronomy may have originally intended. The most natural reading of Deut 10:6 and 8 suggests the divine institution of Levites in general and the specific choice of one priestly family from with them. God set apart the tribe of Levi for altar service (here the non-specific phrase "stand to minister before Yahweh"), for blessing in Yahweh's name and for carrying the ark. The first two of these tasks were appropriate for these Levites designated priests (17:12, 18:5; cf. 21:5). Priests and Levites together shared responsibility for carrying the ark. Distinctions between priests and Levites must also have been suggested to Dtr when reading Deut 26:1–11 alongside 26:12 or comparing 27:9 with 14.

Second, the Levitical cities list in Joshua 21 indicates that Dtr would have known of Levites who were without appointments to priestly office. This list is generally accepted as a reflection of [[134]] historical reality, from the time of either Josiah or the United Monarchy.[6] The absence of important sanctuaries from the cities and their explicit purpose of providing pasture (Josh 21:2; cf. Num 35:2) indicate the settlement of substantial numbers of Levitical persons whose functions were something other than altar service.[7] Deut 28:8 also implies the existence of Levites supported by their "patrimony" rather than sacrificial revenues.

Third, Dtr himself distinguishes between priests and Levites. Consider Dtr's staging (in Josh 8:33) of the blessing and cursing event somewhat obscurely commanded in Deut 11:29, 27:11–14. While in Deuteronomy the Levites as a whole apparently perform their role of announcing the curses

5. Gunneweg, *Leviten*, 126–36, who traces four different nuances of the relationship between priests and Levites. Most helpful is U. Rüterswörden, *Von der politischen Gemeinschaft zur Gemeinde* (Frankfurt, 1987) 68–75. After literary-critical analysis, he concludes that Deuteronomy makes no distinction between priest and Levite in service, but does distinguish them in status.

6. Y. Aharoni, *Land of the Bible* (2nd ed.; Philadelphia and London, 1979) 301–5.

7. One thinks of Deuteronomy's reference to the "Levite within your towns" (12:12, etc.). On the basis of the terminology of the present form of Deuteronomy, Lindblom traced four Levitical categories, including two of cultically unattached rural Levites, *Erwägungen*, 22–41, 44.

while still in their assigned place among the other tribes on Gerizim, Dtr adds to the scene a separate group of Levitical priests to bless the people. That is, Dtr divides the Levitical priests from the rest of Levi, who presumably are standing with the remainder of the people in front of the mountains. This same distinction is clear in Deut 31:9, 25.[8] Two distinct groups are being addressed—the "priests the sons of Levi" in v. 9 and the "Levites" in v. 25. The priests are given the law and commanded to read it to assembled Israel. The Levites, in contrast, put the law by the ark once the task of writing it has been completed.

Finally, the way Dtr handles ark bearing indicates a clear distinction between priest and Levite. In agreement with Deut 10:8, carrying the ark was the task of all members of Levi and not the exclusive province of either group. Dtr clearly labels both priests and Levites as ark carriers in Deut 31:9, 25. As Abba has pointed out, Levites sometimes carry the ark in the DH and in his presentation of his sources (for example, 1 Sam 6:15), but priests tend to take over this task at important occasions such as the assault on Jericho or the dedication of the Temple.[9] Thus Zadok and Abiathar accompany the Levites carrying the ark up to David (2 Sam 15:24), but carry it back down themselves (v. 29). Although Dtr's [[135]] report of bringing the ark for the temple dedication (1 Kgs 8:3–4, 6) is confused in its present form, the role of ark bearing is preserved for both priests and Levites, at least by the MT.

One opinion of Dtr is clear—all genuine priests must be from the tribe of Levi. He scorns Jeroboam for violating this principle (1 Kgs 12:31, 13:33) for the high places and, by implication (12:32, 13:2), for Bethel. Perhaps Dtr includes a Levitical presence in the transfer of the ark (1 Kgs 8:4) in order to contrast the authenticity of Solomon's sanctuary to Jeroboam's. Whatever the facts about Zadok's lineage, Dtr would simply have taken his Levitical descent for granted, and in this he may actually have been correct.[10]

Yet the priesthood is certainly not limited in Dtr's view to the descendants of Aaron. Dtr must have picked up a distinctly anti-Aaronide attitude from Deuteronomy. While he would have read there that Aaron and Eleazar had been set apart for the priesthood (10:6), he would also have read 9:20, where God's anger is directed at Aaron because of the golden calf episode. Moses has to intercede to save Aaron, destroying the calf in

8. On the assumption that Dtr was not concerned with Levites, historical criticism has denied practically all these verses to Dtr. Once Dtr's views are understood, this is no longer reasonable.

9. Abba, p. 261; on the implications of 1 Sam 14:18 MT for this, see P. R. Davies, "Ark or Ephod in Sam. xiv 18?," *JTS* NS 26 (1975) 82–87.

10. F. M. Cross, *Canaanite Myth and Hebrew Epic* (Cambridge, Mass., 1973) 214–15.

a Josiah-like act of purification (9:21; 2 Kgs 23:6, 12, 15). Given the high probability that Bethel was staffed by Aaronic priests,[11] Dtr must have had clear reservations about that particular priestly family.

Although Dtr was willing to give Aaron his historical due (1 Sam 12:6, 8), he considered the priesthood open to anyone from the tribe of Levi. On the basis of Deut 10:6, Dtr apparently took the "father" of Eli to be Aaron (1 Sam 2:27). Yet Zadok replaces the Aaronic Abiathar without Dtr feeling any need to provide him with an Aaronic genealogy.

When it served no redactional purpose, however, Dtr made no issue of Levitical legitimacy. He let the potential problems of 1 Sam 7:1b and 2 Sam 6:3 slide, and blithely listed Ira the Jairite (2 Sam 20:26) and Zabud son of Nathan (1 Kgs 4:5) as priests.[12] Because for Dtr priesthood was primarily a matter of office rather than function, it did not bother him to report non-priestly sacrifices [[136]] (1 Kgs 18:30–38; Judg 6:19–24; 1 Sam 7:9).[13] Nor was he troubled by kings serving in priestly roles.[14]

Eli, Abiathar, and Zadok

The oracle of 1 Sam 2:27–36 is confusing because of its multiple focus. While there is widespread consensus that Dtr had a hand in the creation of this threat against Eli's house, there is controversy as to the extent of his redactional activity.

According to some, Dtr was totally responsible for the insertion of a prophetic oracle at this point in the narrative, although the oracle may have had a pre-history.[15] Others have taken the threat as an integral part

11. As the golden calf connection and Judg 20:27–28 imply. It is intriguing that the ill-fated oldest sons of Aaron and the sons of Jeroboam have similar names: Nadab and Abihu, Nadab and Abijah; L. Sabourin, *Priesthood: A Comparative Study* (Leiden, 1973) 124.

12. Dtr apparently assumed that Eleazar son of Abinadab, Ira, and Zabud were Levites. The Lucianic Greek ties Ira to the Levitical city Jattir (Josh 21:14). Zabud may have been the son of someone other than the prophet Nathan.

13. Although Dtr's sources indicated that Samuel wore an ephod and objected to Saul offering sacrifice, there is no reason to think that Dtr considered Samuel to be a priest. Saul's disobedience in 1 Sam 13:13 was to Samuel's command (10:8) and is not presented as an infraction of priestly privilege.

14. In 2 Sam 6:13, 17–18 David wears an ephod and blesses the people in Yahweh's name. The priestly privilege of "going up to the altar" (1 Sam 2:28; 2 Kgs 23:9) is something kings can do (illegitimately in 1 Kgs 12:33; legitimately in 2 Kgs 16:12). Although most cases of royal sacrifice should be understood as factitive (2 Sam 6:13; 1 Kgs 3:15), the dedication sacrifices of Solomon and Ahaz may be a different matter (1 Kgs 8:63–64; 2 Kgs 16:12–13). The question of David's sons as priests (2 Sam 8:18; 1 Kgs 4:5) is less clear; G. J. Wenham, "Were David's Sons Priests?," *ZAW* 87 (1975) 79–82.

15. Most recently P. K. McCarter, *I Samuel* (Garden City, 1980) 87–93, on the basis of an extensive reconstruction of the original text from the LXX and the Qumran materials.

of the source narrative, limiting Dtr to the addition of vv. 35–36 and perhaps v. 34.[16] In my opinion, Dtr's only major contribution was v. 35.[17]

Some sort of threat must already have been present in the narrative source. Its emphasis on the sins of Eli's sons (2:12, 22–25) must have led somewhere in the plot, most logically to an oracle of doom.

However, in v. 35 new interests become visible. The basic narrative prepares the reader for the punishment of Eli's house and the eventual pre-eminence of Samuel, but not for the introduction of a new priestly line. In other words, with v. 35 the focus on the punishment of Eli's family shifts suddenly to their subordination to a new priest.

[[137]] The distinctive language of Dtr concentrates in v. 35.[18] For example, the *hiphil* of *qwm* [['arise, raise']] is used in several deuteronomistic expressions.[19] The phrase in v. 35 is mirrored by Deut 18:15, 18; Judg 2:16, 18; 3:9, 15, but the oracle against Jeroboam in 1 Kgs 14:14 provides the most remarkable parallel: *whqymt ly khn nʾmn* [['And I will raise up for Myself a faithful priest']] / *whqym yhwh lw mlk* [['And the Lord will raise up for Himself a king']]. Although the topic of "house" permeates the entire oracle, the phrase *byt nʾmn* [['enduring house']] points directly to 1 Sam 25:28 and 2 Sam 7:16, both from Dtr's sources in reference to David. Dtr made this expression his own in 1 Kgs 11:38, using it to provide the content of God's promise to Jeroboam. The parallel to 1 Sam 2:35 is nearly exact: *wbnyty lk/lw byt-nʾmn* [['And I will build you/him an enduring house']].

Verse 36, in contrast, demonstrates no deuteronomistic features. Its idiosyncratic wording points to its being part of the source narrative,[20] into which it fits naturally. The original oracle has prepared us for the

---

This complex threat is often taken as a multiple reference by Dtr to the battle of Aphek, the atrocity at Nob, the sorry situation of Eli's house after the deposition of Abiathar, and the final degradation of the non-Jerusalem priests in Josiah's reform.

16. M. Tsevat, "Studies in the Book of Samuel, I," *HUCA* 32 (1961) 193–95, provides a source-critical analysis. For a summary of positions, see R. Gnuse, *The Dream Theophany of Samuel* (Lanham, Maryland, 1984) 189–93.

17. Verse 34, which connects the oracle to the Ark Story, is secondary and presumably also deuteronomistic.

18. "Heart" and "soul" are often found in deuteronomistic expressions although never in this precise usage (Weinfeld, *Deuteronomy*, 334). Note the similarity of *hthlk lpny* [['to walk before me' / 'to remain in my service']] (vv. 30, 35) to the expression used in 1 Sam 12:2; 1 Kgs 2:4; 3:6; 8:23, 25; 9:4 and in Dtr's source at 2 Kgs 20:3. The phrase is not exclusively deuteronomistic (Gen 17:1, etc.) however, and was used by Dtr's source as well (v. 30). On the phrase, see H. Kenik, *Design for Kingship: The Deuteronomistic Narrative Technique in 1 Kgs 3:4–15* (Chico, California, 1983) 72–82.

19. Weinfeld, *Deuteronomy*, 327, 350.

20. M. Noth, "Samuel und Silo," *VT* 13 (1963) 393–94.

topic of a survivor belonging to Eli's house but cut off from priestly prerogatives, as well as the topic of non-participation in Israel's prosperity. These concerns carry over into v. 36. Moreover, the source narrative as a whole had been preparing the reader to expect that Samuel would succeed Eli (vv. 11, 18, 21, 26), focusing on him as the prophet to whom Yahweh appeared (3:19–21). Once we have set aside v. 35, the one from whom Eli's descendants will seek favors must be Samuel.

By adding v. 35, Dtr supplemented an older threat of premature death, partial loss of priestly office, and economic distress with an additional prediction of replacement by a new priestly family. The perspective is expanded beyond the figure of Samuel, whose disobedient sons could make up no sure house (8:3, 5).[21]

Why did Dtr add v. 35? It can hardly be said that he saw the replacement of Eli's line by the Zadokites as a critical turning point in Israel's history. The following narrative, taken over by and large from earlier sources, demonstrates Dtr's basic disinterest in matters [[138]] of priestly lineage by presenting an extremely clouded picture of the course of Eli's house. Genealogical and narrative links are handled in a careless manner. Dtr seems completely unfazed by the consecration of a non-Elide, the intriguingly named Eleazar son of Abinadab, as guardian of the ark (1 Sam 7:1). Dtr lets 1 Sam 14:3 introduce Ahijah son of Ahitub, but Ahijah disappears after this chapter, his place being taken by Ahimelek son of Ahitub (1 Samuel 21, 22:9). Although one presumes that this is Ahijah's brother or perhaps Ahijah by a different name, Dtr makes no effort to clarify the matter. Of course, 2 Kgs 2:27 insists that Abiathar is of Eli's house, but again Dtr fails to close the genealogical link. 2 Sam 8:17 is usually thought to be corrupt, but if the MT is correct, then Zadok must be understood as son of yet another Ahitub unconnected with Eli's house. Only someone whose attention was completely off genealogy could let such a notice stand without some explanation.

To understand Dtr's reason for introducing Zadok's house, one must begin with Dtr's reference to this prophecy in 1 Kgs 2:27. Here Dtr reduces the oracle's complex threat to a simple expulsion from priestly office. Although this is a contradiction of 1 Sam 2:33, Dtr is reading the oracle with v. 35 as its center of gravity, ignoring much of the oracle's content: the absence of any old man, death "in the prime of manhood," the

21. Dtr refers again to this threat in 1 Sam 3:11–14 (most directly in vv. 12–13) in order to underscore Samuel's prophetic role and move the story on to the debacle at Aphek. 1 Sam 3:12 and 2 Kgs 2:27 use similar language in referring to this threat: "all that I have spoken concerning his house" and "the word of Yahweh which he had spoken concerning the house of Eli."

family's alienation from Israel's prosperity. As far as Dtr is concerned, Abiathar's loss of priestly place was sufficient fulfillment by itself.

Since all other prophecy-fulfillment pairs in Dtr focus on a single act of fulfillment, there is no reason to look beyond 1 Kgs 2:27 to Nob[22] or to the reformation of Josiah[23] for further incidents to which this prophecy might refer.

Therefore the fall of Eli's house was of no direct theological interest to Dtr, apart from its witness to the accuracy of God's word.[24] Since Dtr's opinion of the Aaronic line was presumably [[139]] guarded at best, he was quite happy to let stand an oracle against Eli, but made nothing further of it.

Nor was Dtr much interested in Zadok. Although he is the sole content of Dtr's addition in 1 Sam 2:35, Zadok plays no role in Dtr's notice of the fulfillment of this oracle. Mention of Zadok's appointment as priest is saved until 1 Kgs 2:35b, almost as an afterthought. The puzzle then is this. Whereas 1 Sam 2:35 is concerned with the house of the faithful priest, 1 Kgs 2:27 is concerned only with the house of Eli. Why bring Zadok the "faithful priest" into 1 Samuel only to ignore him in 1 Kings?

Zadok's priestly line can hardly be said to be a theme in the remainder of the history. Even after he is deposed, Abiathar remains beside Zadok in the list of 1 Kgs 4:4, after which Zadok himself disappears. Zadok's total absence from the temple construction and dedication is striking (contrast Jehoiada, Urijah, or Hilkiah). No priestly houses or lines are ever again mentioned in Dtr, only unconnected individual priests. The topic of the "faithful priest" is simply dropped once it has served its limited redactional purpose. But what was its purpose?

The key is recognizing the commentary these priestly houses offer on Jeroboam's dynasty. We have already noted how Dtr used nearly identical language in referring to Zadok and Jeroboam. About Zadok, the man of God says, "I will raise up for myself a faithful priest . . . and I will build him a sure house" (1 Sam 2:35).

To Jeroboam God promises through Ahijah, "I will build you a sure house" (1 Kgs 11:38), and when this promise is blocked by Jeroboam's dis-

22. The only suggestion of a connection with the Nob atrocity is provided by the LXX and 4QSam[a] addition of "sword" to 1 Sam 2:33. Yet this is most likely an attempt to clear up the difficult *ymwtw ʿnšym*, which ought to be understood as death "in the prime of manhood" so that there would never be an old man in the family; H. W. Hertzberg, *I & II Samuel* (London and Philadelphia, 1964) 34 = *Die Samuelbücher* (Göttingen, 1956) 21–22; H. J. Stoebe, *Das erste Buch Samuelis* (Gütersloh, 1973) 119.

23. The request for priestly places in v. 36 cannot refer to 2 Kgs 23:8–9, as recognized by Noth, "Samuel," 394.

24. One thinks of the rebuilding of Jericho (1 Kgs 16:34), about which Dtr certainly had no interest apart from its role in a prophecy-fulfillment pair.

obedience, Ahijah announces, "Yahweh will raise up for himself a king" (1 Kgs 14:14).

P. Buis has classified both 1 Sam 2:27–36 and 1 Kgs 14:7–16 as "simple indictments" on the basis of their structure.[25] Both refer to the undoing of previous election promises concerning a "house" because of cultic disobedience. Both represent the first half of a prophecy-fulfillment pair (1 Kgs 15:29 notes the fulfillment of 14:7–12).

Each begins (1 Sam 2:27–28; 1 Kgs 14:7–8a) with a review of a past election to office ("I chose from all the tribes of Israel; I exalted you from among the people") coupled with a divine gift (sacrificial offerings, the kingdom). Accusations of disobedience follow (1 Sam 2:29; 1 Kgs 14:8b–9), interpreted as a rejection of ⟦140⟧ Yahweh ("honor your sons above me; cast me behind your back"). Highly complex threats (1 Sam 2:30–36; 1 Kgs 14:10–16), initiated by *lkn* ⟦'therefore'⟧, have *krt* ('cut off') as their operative verb. In Eli's house there would be no old man and no increase; in Jeroboam's every male would be cut off. Limited exceptions to God's blanket punishment are allowed by both 1 Sam 2:33 and 1 Kgs 14:13, and Jeroboam's child plays a role similar to that of Hophni and Phinehas (1 Sam 2:34; 1 Kgs 14:12).

In conclusion, Yahweh announces that he will raise up replacements. The similarity between these two oracles is striking.

Thus, Dtr's mention of Eli's family and Zadok's house reflects no real interest in priestly matters. Rather the oracle, its reiteration in 1 Sam 3:11–14, and its fulfillment in 1 Kgs 2:27, serve to introduce concepts important to the story of monarchy—a sure house, the interplay of promise and punishment, the replacement of one dynasty by another, and the ambiguity of a promise made "forever." Eli points to both Solomon and Jeroboam; Zadok points to David.

One major axis of promise in the DH is that to David of a "sure house" (2 Sam 7:11b–16), a promise which would hold true in spite of his successors' spotty record of obedience (1 Kgs 11:36, 39; 15:4; 2 Kgs 8:19). This "promissory covenant" was based on David's record of fidelity (1 Kgs 11:34, 38; 15:5). Zadok as faithful priest points to this eternal promise to David. As though to guide our thoughts in this direction, Dtr associates Zadok directly with God's anointed king (1 Sam 2:35).

A second, more restricted promise plays a role in the presentation of Solomon, the retention of the "throne of Israel" (that is, rule over the Northern Kingdom; 1 Kgs 2:4; 8:20, 25–26; 9:4–5) by the Davidic house. This promise was conditional upon Solomon's obedience and, in view of

25. "Notification de jugement et confession nationale," *BZ* NS 11 (1967) 193–205. The other examples in the DH are Judg 2:1–5 and 2 Sam 12:7–14.

Solomon's failure, was passed on to Jeroboam (11:31, 37). Dtr prepares the reader for this move with a borrowed reference to the way the disobedience of Eli's sons undermined God's promise to his house.[26]

A dynastic promise was also offered to Jeroboam (1 Kgs 11:38). If he would be obedient like David, he would receive a promise like David's, a "sure house" to rule over the Northern Kingdom. Jeroboam could hope for an eternally binding dynastic promise like that given to David. Of course, Jeroboam turned out to be an arch-villain instead, and Dtr's editorial statement in 13:34 makes ⟦141⟧ it clear that the offer of such a promise was voided. Instead, Jeroboam's house would be "cut off," just as Eli's house had been (1 Sam 2:31, 33). The connection to Eli is made explicit in the oracle delivered by Ahijah to Jeroboam's wife, in which again the operative verb is "cut off" (1 Kgs 14:10, 14). Here Eli's house finds its counterpart in Jeroboam's house, and the elevation of Zadok as successor corresponds to that of Baasha. Thus Eli and Zadok serve as redactional pointers to what is really important to Dtr, namely, divine dynastic promise and royal obedience and disobedience.

Josiah's Reform

Many, beginning with Wellhausen, have concluded that Deut 18:1–8 reflects the struggle of Levites for priestly recognition[27] and link Deut 18:6–8 with 2 Kgs 23:9, suggesting that the latter verse reports Josiah's failure to implement Deuteronomy's proposed policy. The Levite of Deut 18:6 is equated with the high-place priests denied a role at the Jerusalem altar.

Whatever the original intent of Deut 18:6–8, it is hard to see how either Dtr or Josiah could ever have read it as a demand that the priests of the high places be admitted to the priesthood of the central sanctuary. Are we to imagine that Dtr would blithely report a violation of Deuteronomic law by his hero (2 Kgs 22:2, 23:3, 25)?

There is no reason to see any reference to Deut 18:6–8 in the event described by 2 Kgs 23:9.[28] If, as I have suggested above, the rural Levites

26. On the interplay of the dynastic oracles in the DH, see R. D. Nelson, *The Double Redaction of the Deuteronomistic History* (Sheffield, 1981) 99–118.

27. J. Wellhausen, *Prolegomena to the History of Israel* (Edinburgh, 1885) 121–52 = *Prolegomena zur Geschichte Israels* (2nd ed., Berlin, 1883) 125–57.

28. Gunneweg, pp. 119–23; Lindblom, pp. 30–33; J. G. McConville, *Law and Theology in Deuteronomy* (Sheffield, 1984) 132–35; E. Würthwein, "Die Josianische Reform und das Deuteronomium," *ZTK* 73 (1976) 417. Since Dtr knew priests and Levites as distinct groups, he would naturally have taken Deut 18:1–2 to apply to the whole of Levi, vv. 3–5 as referring to priests, and the subject of vv. 6–8 as any non-priestly Levite who might come to the sanctuary to serve in a role appropriate to his rank. The use of the term "fellow Levites" in v. 7 rather

served in non-priestly roles, they would not have been included in Josiah's general transfer of priests to Jerusalem. The relatively tiny number of Levites who returned from exile suggests that no transfer of Levites to Jerusalem ever took place.

⟦142⟧ The key to understanding 2 Kgs 23:5–9 is recognizing that not all Judahite rural priests sacrificed on the high places, but that some functioned only in those sorts of priestly service which could be performed apart from altar, sacrifice, and sanctuary. For example, there is no indication of any sanctuary in Anathoth for the priests located there to serve. Deuteronomy itself is the chief historical evidence for the existence of priests unconnected with sanctuaries. The book makes very little of sacrifice in its description of priests and emphasizes instead their instructional and judicial roles.[29] The existence of non-sacrificing priests would be in harmony with the common view that instruction and oracle were the core priestly functions in Israel and that the exclusive privilege to perform sacrifice was a later development.[30]

If one accepts this assumption, most of the puzzles of 2 Kgs 23:5–9 are solved. It becomes clear that five separate priestly groups are described. About the first three, there has never been any particular confusion:

(1) The *priests of the Jerusalem Temple* co-operated in the reform (v. 4).

(2) The *Northern Yahwistic priests* were slaughtered (v. 20). According to Dtr, at least some of these were non-Levitical priests (1 Kgs 12:31–32, 13:33). Their execution was foretold in 1 Kgs 13:2.

(3) The *Judahite idolatrous priests* (*kᵉmārîm*; Hos 10:5; Zeph 1:4) were deposed (v. 5). That these are non-Yahwistic priests is made clear by the context of vv. 4–6, especially v. 5b. They provide a clear parallel to the horses of the sun in v. 11, which were also blamed on the kings of Judah and "deposed." These idolatrous priests had "made smoke" (*qṭr*) at non-Yahwistic high places (cf. 22:17; 1 Kgs 11:8).

The other two groups are described in a way that has tended to confuse readers. Together these two groups make up "all the priests" brought to Jerusalem from the cities of Judah (v. 8):

---

than "priests" would certainly have blocked off any idea that this Levite would be seeking a priestly appointment. Dtr would have read the protasis of the conditional sentence as continuing through v. 7: "if he comes and serves, then he may eat." That is to say, the issue would not be whether the Levite might minister (so the RSV) but that he should receive his proper allowance (so the NEB).

29. H.-J. Kraus, *Worship in Israel* (Oxford, 1966) 97 = *Gottesdienst in Israel* (2nd ed., Munich, 1962) 117). Priests serve as judges (Deut 17:8–11, 19:17, 21:5), offer ritual instruction (24:8), and exhort before battle (20:2–4). Priests preserve the book of the law (17:18) and bless in Yahweh's name (21:5).

30. A. Cody, *A History of Old Testament Priesthood* (Rome, 1969) 11–14, 115–20.

(4) The *Judahite Yahwistic priests who served at high places* were moved to Jerusalem along with all the priests of Judah (v. 8). These priests had "made smoke" on the high places which Josiah defiled (v. 8; cf. 12:4; 14:4; 15:4, 35; 16:4; 1 Kgs 22:44). It is this group to which v. 9 refers. They did not receive priestly appointments but "ate [[143]] unleavened bread" with their brother priests who did.

(5) The *Judahite Yahwistic priests not connected with high places* also were moved to Jerusalem. Although they were not contaminated by involvement with the high places, Josiah presumably moved them to Jerusalem to prevent any resurgence of non-central sacrifice. Verse 9 implies that, in contrast to the high-place priests, they were assigned priestly duties in Jerusalem.

Once this distinction is understood, vv. 8–9 read quite smoothly. Josiah brought all Judahite priests to Jerusalem no matter what their previous service had been (8aα). Then in v. 8aβ Dtr repeats the pattern of mentioning a sanctuary linked to its personnel by an *ʾšr* clause (cf. v. 7: "the houses . . . where the women wove") to describe Josiah's desecration of the high places ("the high places where the priests made smoke"). After mentioning some specific high places (8b), Dtr then backtracks in v. 9 to clear up any potential confusion about the priests mentioned in 8aβ. Lest any reader imagine that these contaminated high-place priests served as Jerusalem Temple priests, Dtr adds a limiting sentence: "However, the priests of the high places [in contrast to the rest of the priests whom Josiah brought to Jerusalem] did not come up to the altar of Yahweh in Jerusalem [as the other Judahite priests did], but they [instead] ate unleavened bread among their brothers."

Josiah's exclusion of the high-place priests had nothing to do with any supposed disobedience to Deuteronomic law. It was the result of their association with the dubious religious practices of the Yahwistic high places to which the prophets witness.[31] Certainly, Dtr associated these high places with pagan practices (1 Kgs 14:23–24; 2 Kgs 16:4, 21:3).

There are several possibilities for understanding the unleavened bread of v. 9.[32] The most likely explanation is that it represents the bread of hospitality. Since it could be made quickly, unleavened bread was traditionally the fare offered to visitors (Gen 19:3; 1 Sam 28:24; perhaps Judg 6:19). This fits the situation perfectly. All priests lived in Jerusalem, but only a portion of them were actually employed as altar priests. As a result, the former high-place priests were forced to share the hospitality of their brothers who had priestly appointments.

31. Lindblom, *Erwägungen*, 31, 47–49.

32. D. Kellermann, "*maṣṣāh*," *TWAT* 4 (Stuttgart, 1984), cols. 1074–82 [[trans. "מַצָּה; מַצּוֹת," *TDOT* 8 (Grand Rapids: Eerdmans, 1997) 494–501]].

Once more we see that Dtr has no particular interest in priestly concerns. While this centralizing realignment of priestly office may have been critically important to the Zadokites, Dtr gives no hint of [[144]] any such significance. The interaction between the families of Eli and Zadok is not in view here at all. Dtr asserts nothing in v. 8 beyond Josiah's reforming zeal. He is content simply to imply that the rural non-high-place priests received appointments in Jerusalem, but makes no definite assertion about it. In v. 9, Dtr merely intends to prevent a misunderstanding.

Priests as Redactional Tools

Although he had no special interest in priests, Dtr uses them as redactional tools to drive home ideological truths. Thus, Eli and Zadok provide the raw material for one of Dtr's prophecy fulfillment pairs, as do the high-priests installed in Bethel (1 Kgs 13:2; 2 Kgs 23:20).

At critical turns in the story, Dtr uses priests as guarantors of legitimacy. For example, he added the Levitical priests as carriers of the ark to his source in Joshua 3, 4, 6.[33] Presumably this was done on the basis of Deut 10:8 in order to underline Joshua's scrupulous obedience to Deuteronomy (cf. Josh 1:7–8, 8:30–31, 11:15, 23:6).

Another example of this is the role played by Jehoiada in Joash's accession. In the light of 2 Kgs 11:1, Dtr has a crisis of dynastic legitimacy on his hands. Although he insists on Joash's Davidic descent in vv. 2–3, the figure of Jehoiada the priest serves to undergird it. The priest becomes the prime mover in the conspiracy, taking vigorous action, initiating the secrecy, giving orders, handing over weapons. Things go off without a hitch. The propriety of the revolution is shown by the care Jehoiada takes for the Temple's sanctity (vv. 15–16). The priest crowns the under-age king, hands him the "testimony" (apparently the book of the law, Deut 17:18–20) and then serves as his stand-in (cf. 23:3) as the covenant is initiated. Jehoiada becomes the king's teacher to ensure his righteousness. Everything happens "according to the custom" (v. 14), and Jehoiada is a redactional sign of that.

Urijah serves a similar function in regard to Ahaz's new altar (2 Kgs 16:10–16). As I have suggested elsewhere, Dtr presents this altar as a minor reform by Ahaz and intends the reader to view it in a positive light.[34] The legitimate priest Urijah is introduced to construct the altar without demur and to offer proper sacrifices upon it, all at the king's command

33. The original bare participle of the source is preserved in Josh 3:15a.

34. R. D. Nelson, "The Altar of Ahaz: A Revisionist View," *Hebrew Annual Review* 10 (1986) 267–76.

(vv. 11, 15–16). This goes some [[145]] way to overcome the reader's objections to an altar built on a foreign model.

Priests are also used to underline the propriety of Josiah's reform. However, because Dtr wants to make Josiah the chief actor of the reform, priests are only supporting characters. Josiah initiates all five narrative episodes (22:3, 12; 23:1, 4, 21) and is the subject of each reforming verb. Contrast, for example, Hilkiah's minor role with that of Jehoiada. Hilkiah carries out his proper role as outlined in 2 Kgs 12:9–16, but only under secondhand royal instigation (22:3). Hilkiah does find the book and recognizes it (v. 8; contrast Shaphan, v. 10). But his role in the plot is limited to putting it into proper administrative channels (v. 8). No priestly oracle is consulted. Instead, Hilkiah serves merely as one of a large delegation sent to inquire of a prophet (vv. 13–14), the size and prestigious composition of which is designed to indicate the seriousness of the situation (cf. 19:2). Again in contrast to Jehoiada, priests are merely part of the crowd for the covenant making (23:2; contrast 11:17). Their direct assistance is limited to a porter's role in a single reforming act (v. 4).

At other times, priests are used redactionally to evaluate kings and their policies. Jeroboam's non-Levitical priests (1 Kgs 12:31–32, 13:33) are a clear example. Dtr uses them for an indirect attack on the legitimacy of Bethel and more directly to excoriate Jeroboam, who "kept on installing" them (cf. the *waw* perfect of 12:32). His arbitrary intransigence is stressed by 13:33, and v. 34 raises the non-Levitical priests to the status of the major sin of Jeroboam's house, as a summary expression for Jeroboam's guilt.

Things are more subtle in regard to Joash's reform of Temple finances (2 Kgs 12:4–16). Joash's first attempt at reform (vv. 4–6) fails. The king then expresses policy change in general terms, but it is actually Jehoiada who works out the details of the new plan. Everything is done to present this plan positively. The silver is collected by one of the priests who guard the entrance and is put safely in a chest kept in open view. The counting is done by representatives of the crown and priesthood. The grammar of vv. 9 and 11 indicates that a new customary procedure has been established. On the one hand, the direct role of the priesthood is eliminated (8b), yet the perquisites of priests are not affected (v. 16). The narrative's focus is less repair of the temple than the importance of co-operation between priest and king, with the king taking the lead. This sets the stage for the reform of Josiah, characterized by royal assertiveness and priestly cooperation.

2 Kings 17 tells of the priest of Bethel sent by the king of Assyria [[146]] to instruct the newly-settled foreigners of Samaria. This priest is of no theological interest to the author (who here is Dtr^2, the exilic editor). Rather, he serves to introduce the real purpose of this chapter—the opportunity to

draw an invidious comparison between these syncretistic foreigners and the religious practices of Israel. He taught them to fear Yahweh (v. 28) and they did (v. 32), but not really, for they feared Yahweh and served their own gods at the same time (vv. 33–34, 41). Their actions illustrate Israel's earlier failed attempt to fear Yahweh and worship other gods simultaneously. The syncretism of these foreigners (vv. 19–34a, 41) encloses and comments on the tragedy of the Northern Kingdom (vv. 34b–40).

The exilic editor (Dtr^2) says nothing negative about this priest. He is not called a high-place priest; rather, he is a teacher. He is not connected with the altar of Bethel or anything that Josiah would later purge. He is not necessarily even from Bethel, but from Samaria (either the territory or the city). No judgment is made on his legitimacy because his function is purely narrational and redactional, to lead to the syncretism of the settlers which is itself introduced only to condemn the syncretism of Israel.

In a similar way, the appointment of non-Levitical priests by these settlers is used to condemn their religious behavior and thereby the earlier corruption of Israel. These foreigners "made gods" as Jeroboam had done (1 Kgs 14:9) and put them into his infamous "houses of the high places" (1 Kgs 12:31, 13:32; 2 Kgs 23:19) made by the citizens of the Northern Kingdom (2 Kgs 17:29; the "Samaritans" here refer to the citizens of Israel before the Assyrian takeover; cf. the use of Samaria in 1 Kgs 13:32, 21:1; 2 Kgs 17:24, 23:18–19).[35] Again like Jeroboam, the settlers installed non-Levitical priests to serve in these "houses" (v. 32; cf. 1 Kgs 12:31, 13:33). Thus, these resettled foreigners aped Israel in trying to fear Yahweh while worshipping other gods.

At the very end of the book of Kings, priests are again used redactionally by the exilic editor, this time to indicate the complete collapse of Judah's religious structures. 2 Kgs 25:18 marks the last item in the destruction of the Temple establishment (vv. 13–17). Seriah the head priest, Zephaniah the priest of the second rank, and the three "keepers of the threshold" are taken captive and presumably executed. This verse clearly refers to previous texts ⟦147⟧ from the DH, mostly to 2 Kgs 23:4 and less directly to 12:10 and 22:4. Personnel earlier connected with the repair and reform of the Temple have been wiped out. Representatives from all three orders of priesthood have been killed.[36] Once again, priests play a role in the narrative, not because the deuteronomistic author was especially concerned about them, but in order to make a theological point.

35. This accords with Assyrian usage; S. Talmon, "Polemics and Apology in Biblical Historiography: 2 Kgs 17:24–41," *The Creation of Sacred Literature* (Berkeley, 1981) 65–66 ⟦repr. in Talmon, *Literary Studies in the Hebrew Bible* (Jerusalem/Leiden, 1993) 134–59⟧.

36. For a similar redactional strategy, see P. R. Ackroyd, "The Temple vessels–a continuity theme," *VTSup* 23 (Leiden, 1972) 166–81.

The Deuteronomic Theology of the Book of Joshua

GORDON J. WENHAM

In Joshua Israel enters and conquers the land promised to it in earlier books. The narratives of Judges through Kings recount the experience of Israel within this land. Joshua's dual role as the continuation of the Pentateuch and the precursor to Judges raises a series of questions. Is the book of Joshua set apart from Genesis through Deuteronomy (a Pentateuch) as a separate work or does Joshua belong together with Genesis through Deuteronomy as one work (a Hexateuch)? Or does Joshua belong with Judges through Kings as part of the Deuteronomistic History, a work that has been edited in light of the standards pronounced in Deuteronomy? In a close comparison of prominent themes in Deuteronomy and Joshua, Wenham contends that the theology of Joshua is close to the theology of Deuteronomy on five major themes: holy war, the land, the unity of all Israel, Joshua as the successor to Moses, and the covenant. Wenham contends that this continuity between Deuteronomy and Joshua even extends to the chapters (Joshua 13–21) that other scholars have deemed to be Priestly in character. In this regard, his conclusions should be compared with others included in this volume (Noth, Porter, Rofé, Van Seters, Sperling). In the judgment of Wenham, the thematic parallels are so close that he does not deem it necessary to view Joshua 13–21 as the work of a secondary deuteronomistic editor. Yet Wenham refrains from seeing Joshua as part of a Hexateuch in contrast to a Deuteronomistic History. Although Joshua has close affinities with Deuteronomy, Wenham sees major differences between its perspective and the perspective of the rest of the Pentateuch, on the one hand, and the rest of the Former Prophets, on the other hand.

Reprinted with permission from *Journal of Biblical Literature* 90 (1971) 140–48.

⟦140⟧ The close relationship between the books of Deuteronomy and Joshua has long been observed. Linguistically Deuteronomy has closer links with Joshua than with any other part of the former prophets.[1] In content too Joshua forms a perfect sequel to Deuteronomy; the program of the holy war of conquest set out in Deuteronomy is successfully carried out in Joshua.[2] As is well known there have been two main theories to explain the relationship between these books. According to the Hexateuch theory, Joshua forms not only the conclusion of the Pentateuch, but was created out of the same four main sources J, E, D and P.[3] According to the Deuteronomic History theory, Joshua is the second part of the great historical work, comprising Deuteronomy and the former prophets, which was created by a Deuteronomist during the sixth century B.C., using earlier sources. The latter theory has commended itself to the majority of recent commentators on Joshua.[4] It is generally supposed that there were two stages in the deuteronomistic editing of Joshua and that chaps. 13–21 and 24 represent secondary additions by the Deuteronomist to an earlier deuteronomic book of Joshua. It is on the arrangement of the material that this hypothesis rests, and it is admitted that there is very little change in outlook between the two Deuteronomists. Therefore, for the purposes of the study of the theology of the book it is not really necessary to take into account the different stages of its redaction. But it will be argued here that the arrangement of the material is more subtle than at first appears, and that its theology is so close to the book of Deuteronomy that there is little need to postulate a secondary redaction by a later Deuteronomist who was responsible for editing Kings.

The books of Deuteronomy and Joshua are bound together by five ⟦141⟧ theological leitmotifs ⟦'leading motifs'⟧: the holy war of conquest, the distribution of the land, the unity of all Israel, Joshua as the successor of Moses, and the covenant. The opening chapter of Joshua not only provides a perfect link with the book of Deuteronomy, by its reference to the death of Moses (Josh 1:1; Deuteronomy 34), but concisely introduces the five main themes of the book of Joshua: holy war (vv. 2, 5, 9, 11, 14), the land (vv. 3, 4, 15), the unity of Israel (vv. 12–16), the role of Joshua (vv. 1–2, 5, 17), and the covenant (vv. 3, 7–8, 13, 17–18).

1. See S. R. Driver, *Deuteronomy* (3d ed.; ICC; Edinburgh, 1902) xci–ii.

2. Cf. A. C. Tunyogi, "The Book of Conquest," *JBL* 84 (1965) 374–80.

3. A similar type of approach is still advocated by G. Fohrer, *Introduction to the OT* (London, 1970) 197ff.

4. E.g., M. Noth, *Das Buch Josua* (2d ed.; Tübingen, 1953) 7ff. H. W. Hertzberg, *Die Bücher Josua, Richter, Ruth* (2d ed.; Göttingen, 1959) 8ff. J. Gray, *Joshua, Judges and Ruth* (London, 1967) 16ff. J. Bright, "Joshua," *Interpreter's Bible* (Nashville, 1953) 541ff., offers a hybrid theory combining features of the Hexateuch and Deuteronomic History hypotheses.

Holy War

According to G. von Rad, "Deuteronomy is by far the richest source in the Old Testament for the concepts and customs of the holy war,"[5] By means of explicit legal enactments (Deut 20:1–20; 23:10–15; 25:17–19) and militaristic speeches (7:16–26; 9:1–6) the book of Deuteronomy expounds the principles of the holy war. The book of Joshua illustrates these principles in some detail. Chaps. 1–11 contain four full-length statements of the holy war theme: the conquest of Jericho, the second attack on Ai, the Judean and the Galilean campaigns (chaps. 2, 6, 8, 10, 11). In addition, there are two stories of failure to carry out the holy war, the first attack on Ai and the treaty with the Gibeonites (chaps. 7 and 9).

Holy war begins with Yahweh's promise of success and an exhortation to fight bravely (Josh 1:6, 9; 6:2; 8:1; 10:8; 11:6). The narratives stress that it is God who takes the initiative in the conduct of the war. It is he who sends Israel into battle and ensures its success. Because God is fighting for it, Israel need only trust and be confident. That Yahweh directs the war is brought out vividly by the vision of "the commander of the Lord," who appears to Joshua with a drawn sword in his hand (5:13–15). While encouraging Israel, Yahweh strikes terror in the hearts of its enemies before the battle even begins (2:9, 24; 5:1; 9:24; 10:21). The function of the spies in Joshua 2 is not so much to bring back tactical information as to encourage Israel's faith:[6] they say, "Truly the Lord has given all the land into our hands; and moreover all the inhabitants of the land are fainthearted because of us" (2:24).

After God has given his instructions to Joshua, Joshua obeys; then he instructs the people, and they obey. The pattern of divine command–obedience of the people is central in the holy war stories. Verbal repetition is used to stress the fidelity with which the command is carried out (1:2, 11; 6:2ff., 6–8; 8:1–2, 3ff., 9ff.; 11:6–7, 9). So Israel goes out to battle in obedience to Yahweh's command. Then Yahweh fights for Israel. This is explicitly stated in the story of the battle near [[142]] Gibeon: "the Lord threw down great stones from heaven" (10:11), and "the Lord fought for Israel" (v. 14). Divine intervention is implicit in the sudden collapse of the walls of Jericho, and possibly in Joshua stretching out his javelin towards Ai (Josh 8:18; cf. Exod 14:16; 17:9–13). The enemy panics, and Israel pursues. Their cities are burnt to the ground, and all human beings are killed. Other valuables, such as gold, silver and cattle, are given to the treasury of the Lord. In the case of Jericho, the cattle were also killed, and at Hazor the horses were hamstrung (6:21ff.; 8:20ff.; 10:28ff. and 11:6ff.).

5. *Der heilige Krieg im alten Israel* (Zürich, 1951) 68. [[Trans. *Holy War in Ancient Israel* (Grand Rapids, Mich.: Eerdmans, 1991).]]

6. See S. Wagner, *ZAW* 76 (1964) 268.

We have two stories showing what happened when Israel failed to keep the rules of the holy war. In the first assault on Ai Israel was defeated because Achan had transgressed the ban at Jericho. But even if the narrator had not said that Yahweh was angry with Israel, it might have been expected that the attack would fail, because there is no mention of a word from Yahweh to start the battle (chap. 7). Similarly in the case of Gibeon, Israel "did not ask direction from the Lord," and so afterwards regrets its action (9:14).

We have seen how the principle of strict obedience to the command of Yahweh forms a leitmotif of the holy war stories. However, it is not confined to them. It runs through the whole book. Israel's prompt and exact obedience is stressed in chaps. 3–4 and 13ff. It binds together the large complex of stories in chaps. 1–4 and connects chap. 23 with chap. 1. It may further be noted that the form and themes of the holy war are used to relate the crossing of the Jordan; and, like the crossing of the Red Sea, it is a miraculous sign: "so that all the peoples of the earth may know that the hand of the Lord is mighty" (4:24).

The Land and Its Distribution

The purpose of the holy war was to take possession (*yrš*) of the land which Yahweh promised to the patriarchs (Deut 1:8; 6:10, 18; 7:8; 34:4).[7] Deuteronomy gives some indications of the borders of the promised land (1:7; 34:1–3) and describes how Moses made a start in conquering Transjordan and allotting it to the two and a half tribes (Deuteronomy 1–3). Israel is strictly enjoined to make no treaties with the inhabitants of Canaan, but to exterminate them (Deut 7:1–5). However, it is recognized that owing to Israel's small population the process of occupation will be slow (Deut 7:1–5, 22).

The completion of this task under the leadership of Joshua is described in two stages in the book of Joshua. First, in Joshua 1–12 the conquest of the land is described, and then in Joshua 13–21 how it was [[143]] distributed among the various tribes. Just as in Deuteronomy, the book of Joshua assumes that it is the duty of the Israelites to drive out or exterminate the native inhabitants of Canaan. Thus each battle ends with the ban (Josh 6:21; 8:24f.; 10:10, 28, 30, 35, 37, 39, 40; 11:11, 14, 21). The Gibeon incident shows that the Israelites intended to kill all who lived within the promised land (9:18). Because they thought that the Gibeonites lived afar off, they made a treaty with them (cf. Deut 20:10ff.). In Josh 13:6–7 Joshua

7. See G. von Rad, "The Promised Land and Yahweh's Land in the Hexateuch," *The Problem of the Hexateuch and Other Essays* (Edinburgh, 1966) 79ff.

is told to allot the land to the tribes, though the Canaanites are still in partial occupation. God promises, "I will myself drive them out (*hwryš*) from before you" (13:6). The land is, therefore, distributed among the tribes who are expected to carry on the work of eliminating the earlier inhabitants. Caleb offers to drive out the Anakim, if Joshua gives him their land (14:12). Joshua tells Ephraim and Manasseh to drive out the Canaanites from their areas, "though they have chariots of iron" (17:18).

In both sections of the book, chaps. 1–11 dealing mainly with the conquest, and chaps. 13–23 dealing with the allotments, it is recognized that the task of driving out the Canaanites is unfinished. Gibeon makes a treaty with Israel (chap. 9); of the major northern cities only Hazor was burned (11:13). Some Anakim remained in Gath, Gaza, and Ashdod (11:22). The passage at the end of chap. 11 requires careful study, for on first reading it looks as though the editor is guilty of crass self-contradiction. On the one hand, he says that he took (*lqḥ*, vv. 16, 23) all the land; yet some of the big towns were not burnt and some of the earlier population was left (vv. 13, 22). Though possibly in the early sources of Joshua the situation was seen differently, the deuteronomic editor probably understood the taking of the land to mean the gaining of control without eliminating all the opposition.[8] In chaps. 13ff. it is again observed several times that not all the Canaanites were driven out (13:13; 16:10; 17:13). In chap. 23 the expulsion of the remainder is apparently still the goal. Joshua promises that "the Lord your God will push them back before you and drive them out of your sight" (Josh 23:5), as long as Israel remains faithful to the covenant. However, the era of intense struggle is over. Twice it is said (11:23; 14:15) that the land had rest from war. More interesting is the usage of *hnyḥ* [['he gave rest']] in this connection. Twice it is used in Deuteronomy of Yahweh giving rest to Israel. In Deut 3:20 the Transjordanian tribes are told to help the others "until the Lord gives rest to your brethren as to you." In Deut 12:10 when Israel has settled in Canaan–and "when he gives you rest from all your enemies round about"–then it is to worship at the place which the Lord will choose. The first passage is quoted exactly in Josh 1:15 and the second [[144]] very closely in Josh 23:1. In three other passages (1:13; 21:44; 22:4) reference is made to the idea. In both Deuteronomy 12 and Joshua 23 the idea of Yahweh giving rest to Israel is closely associated with the allotment of the inheritance (*nḥlh*). Finally, as Y. Kaufmann has pointed out, the boundaries of the promised land in Joshua do not correspond either to those promised to the patriarchs or to the area subsequently occupied by Israel or to the ideas of later

8. See Y. Kaufmann, *The Biblical Account of the Conquest of Palestine* (Jerusalem, 1953) 84ff.

priestly writers. He, therefore, argues that the limits of the promised land in Joshua must correspond to the historical reality of the era of the conquest.[9] This may be too sweeping a conclusion, but at least the peculiar boundaries of the promised land in Joshua fit the hypothesis that the editor envisaged a decisive military campaign but only a partial settlement.

The Unity of Israel

Deuteronomy repeatedly addresses its message to all Israel (e.g., 1:1; 5:1; 11:6); and twice, as if to underline that every single Israelite is involved, there is the less common phrase, every man of Israel (*kl-ʾyš yśrʾl*, 27:14; 29:9). Deuteronomy recalls that the covenant was made with all Israel (5:3). Certain punishments are prescribed with a view to their deterrent effect on all Israel (13:12; 21:21). The concern that all Israel should be involved is seen in the assertion that each tribe sent a spy (1:23), in the summons to the Transjordanian tribes to help the other tribes acquire their land (3:18ff.), and in the listing of the individual tribes which participated in the covenant renewal ceremony near Shechem (chap. 27). Another facet of the Deuteronomist's preoccupation with the unity and total involvement of all Israel is seen in his stress that Israel must worship Yahweh alone and at the central sanctuary (Deuteronomy 12–18).[10]

A similar concern with the unity of Israel may be seen in Joshua. The expression "all Israel" is again frequent (3:7, 17; 4:14; 7:23f.; 8:21, 24; 23:2), together with the phrases, "the whole congregation of Israel" (18:1; 22:12, 18), "all the assembly" (8:35) and "all the tribes of Israel" (22:14; 24:1). As prescribed in Deuteronomy all Israel joins in stoning Achan the covenant breaker (Deut 13:10; Josh 7:25). All the fighting men of Israel take part in the military campaigns in Palestine (8:3; 10:7, 29, 31, 34, 36, 38, 43); the defeat at Ai coincides with Joshua's decision to send into attack only part of his forces (7:3ff.). The participation of the tribes of Reuben and Gad and the half-tribe of Manasseh in the Palestinian campaign is mentioned on various occasions (1:12ff.; 4:12; 22:1ff.). [[145]] The book of Joshua particularizes Israel as a union of twelve tribes (cf. 18:2), each of which receives an inheritance (Joshua 13–21). Israel's constitution is symbolized by the erection of twelve stones at Gilgal (chap. 4). Like Deuteronomy the book of Joshua is interested in national rituals and feasts, such as circumcision and passover (5:2ff.). Chap. 22 is concerned with the threat to the unity of Israel posed by the erection of an altar in the Jordan

9. *Biblical Account*, 47ff.

10. Deuteronomy seems to be concerned with a central, as opposed to a sole, sanctuary in these chapters, unless the altar on Mount Ebal (Deuteronomy 27; cf. 11:29ff.) is to be identified with the place which Yahweh will choose.

valley. The Palestinian tribes view the altar as schism from the only legitimate central sanctuary at Shiloh (22:18ff.). But the Transjordanian tribes plead that they have erected this altar as a testimony to their unity with the west-bank tribes (22:24ff.), so that their children will not forget that they are all one people.[11]

The Role of Joshua

The place of Joshua in both Deuteronomy and the Book of Joshua is one of the strongest links between the two books. It is clearly a fundamental concern of the editor to demonstrate that Joshua was the divinely appointed and authenticated successor to Moses. He does this in two ways: by means of the accepted legal terminology in describing Joshua's appointment, and by drawing parallels between the careers of Moses and Joshua.

N. Lohfink has shown that the appointment of Joshua as Moses' successor follows a carefully worked-out schema.[12] As leader of Israel, Joshua is given a twofold office, military commander and distributor of the land. His work as commander is denoted by the terms "come" and "cross over" (*bwʾ* and *ʿbr*); and his work as distributor of the land by "cause to inherit" (*hnḥyl*). His appointment is first mentioned in Deut 1:37–38 and is taken up again in 3:28. At the close of the great covenant ceremony recorded in Deuteronomy, Joshua is installed in his double office by Moses in 31:7: "You shall come (*bwʾ*) with this people into the land which the Lord has sworn to their fathers to give them; and you shall put them in possession of it" (*hnḥyl*). Divine confirmation of his appointment as commander is given in a theophany in 31:23. Only in Josh 1:2–5 is Joshua told to start exercising his role as military commander, and then in vv. 6–9 he is confirmed in his second office as distributor [[146]] of the land. But not until Josh 13:7 is he told to start exercising his second office and actually to distribute the land. Thus Joshua 1–12 is taken up with depicting Joshua in his office as commander and chaps. 13ff. with his work in allotting the land.

Furthermore, the editor of the book of Joshua points to him as Moses' true successor by comments attributed to actors in the story or by his own

11. This chapter contains a number of words characteristic of the pentateuchal source (P), and it is therefore generally regarded as a postdeuteronomic editorial insertion (see the commentaries of Noth and Gray). This is quite possible; but in view of this chapter's conformity with the overall scheme of Joshua, it might be better to suppose that the deuteronomic editor had access to P-like material that was independent of the documentary source. This explanation is adopted by S. R. Driver (*Deuteronomy*, iv ff.) to explain the P-like passages in Deuteronomy.

12. N. Lohfink, "Die deuteronomistische Darstellung des Übergangs der Führung Israels von Moses auf Josue," *Scholastik* 37 (1962) 32–44.

editorial remarks. Thus, the Transjordanian tribes tell Joshua: "Just as we obeyed Moses in all things, so we will obey you" (Josh 1:17; cf. 4:14). The narratives bring out parallels between the lives of Moses and Joshua, which can scarcely be accidental. In Joshua 3–4, Joshua has his own Red Sea crossing. The Jordan river stands in a heap and the tribes of Israel cross on dry ground (3:13 parallel to Exod 15:8; 3:17 parallel to Exod 14:21–22, 29 [P]). As Moses did, so Joshua celebrates the passover. He encounters the commander of the Lord's army and is told, as was Moses, "Put off your shoes from your feet, for the place where you stand is holy" (5:15 parallel to Exod 3:5 [E]). As did Moses, he intercedes for the people when they sin (7:7ff. parallel to Deut 9:25ff.). As God hardened the heart of Pharaoh, Moses' archenemy, so he hardens the heart of Joshua's enemies (Josh 11:20 parallel to Exod 9:12 [E]). Josh 12:1–6 lists Moses' victories; 12:7–24 lists Joshua's victories. Josh 13:8ff. lists Moses' allotments; 14:1ff. lists Joshua's allotments. And finally, as did Moses before his death, Joshua makes two speeches which follow the covenant form.[13]

The Covenant and the Law of Moses

One of the more important developments of recent scholarship has been the discovery that the OT writers were familiar with Near Eastern treaty forms. Indeed, it has been cogently argued that the present structure of the book of Deuteronomy is in large measure based on this form.[14] The similarities between this form and Joshua 23 and 24 has also attracted attention. Just as important for the understanding of the theological dependence of Joshua on Deuteronomy are the content and terminology used. From Deut 31:26 it appears that in Deuteronomy "the book of the law" is a technical term for the covenant document.[15] Without such a document no covenant or treaty was valid. We have seen how Joshua 1 takes up the ideas of Deuteronomy 31 in its treatment of Joshua as Moses' successor. It also takes over the phrase "book of the law" as a description of the covenant document (Josh 1:8). The [[147]] message of the book of Joshua seems to be that Israel was careful by and large to fulfill its covenant obligations and that this is why it enjoyed the blessings conditional on obedience and was able to conquer the promised land. Time and again explicit

13. See K. Baltzer, *Das Bundesformular* (Neukirchen, 1960) 29ff., 71ff. [[Trans. *The Covenant Formulary* (Philadelphia: Fortress, 1971).]]

14. Among the many discussions of this feature, see particularly Baltzer, *Bundesformular*, 76ff.; M. G. Kline, *Treaty of the Great King* (Grand Rapids, 1963) 27ff.; and D. J. McCarthy, *Treaty and Covenant* (Rome, 1963) 109ff.

15. N. Lohfink, *Biblica* 44 (1963) 284ff.

reference is made to "the law," "the word which Moses commanded," or some other expression for the covenant stipulations.

Often it is explicitly stated that something was done in accordance with the word of Moses. The words of Moses constitute the strategic plan for the whole conquest and the motive for distributing the land. Thus the Transjordanian tribes help in the campaign because of the word of Moses (1:13; 22:2). The crossing of the Jordan is in accordance with Moses' instructions (4:10). An altar is built on Mount Ebal as "Moses commanded" (8:30ff.). The Gibeonites know that Moses ordered the destruction of all the native inhabitants (9:24). At the end of the Galilean campaign there is this summary: "As the Lord has commanded Moses, his servant, so Moses commanded Joshua, and so Joshua did; he left nothing undone of all that the Lord commanded Moses" (11:15). The allotment of the land also follows Moses' instructions (11:23; 14:2, 5). In accordance with specific Mosaic promises, Caleb is allotted Hebron (14:6ff.), and the daughters of Zelophehad are given part of the west bank (17:3f.). Joshua 20 records the establishment of cities of refuge as Moses commanded, and chap. 21 the allocation of certain cities to the priests and Levites.

Besides these explicit references to Israel's conscious obedience to the Mosaic injunctions, it is possible that certain other incidents are included to show its punctilious regard for the deuteronomic law. Certainly the presuppositions of Deuteronomy appear to underlie the account of the treaty with Gibeon. It was because Israel thought that the Gibeonites had come from afar that it made a treaty with them. Later when they were discovered to be living within the promised land, Israel was very angry. Why should there have been this reaction? Deut 20:10ff. provides the answer. Israel was to make treaties only with those who dwelt outside the promised land. Its inhabitants were to be liquidated. Another possible allusion to Deuteronomy is found in the punishment of Achan, the covenant-breaker, who is stoned and whose property is burnt (Josh 7:25; cf. Deuteronomy 13). The five kings were hanged, "but at the going down of the sun, Joshua commanded, and they took them down from the trees and put them in the caves" (Josh 10:27). This detail suggests that the narrator had in mind the law of Deut 21:23, "the body (of a hanged man) shall not remain all night upon the tree, but you shall bury him the same day."

Joshua 23 sums up Israel's situation as viewed by the editor. In Joshua's day Israel was faithful in carrying out Yahweh's demands, and so enjoyed success in all its campaigns. "Not one thing has failed of all [[148]] the good things which the Lord your God promised concerning you." "But just as all the good things which the Lord your God promised concerning you have been fulfilled for you, so the Lord your God will bring upon you all the evil things . . . , if you transgress the covenant" (Josh

23:14ff.). As long as Israel remains faithful to Yahweh, it will enjoy success; but if it forsakes him, it will be driven from the promised land. Chap. 24, the account of the renewal of the covenant at Shechem, is the strongest evidence for supposing that Joshua underwent a secondary deuteronomistic redaction. Though such a hypothesis cannot be excluded, it may be pointed out that chap. 24 is a fitting climax to the whole book. The challenge to the people to consider whether they will serve Yahweh as Joshua did (vv. 19ff.) is in effect a challenge to the later reader to examine himself as to whether he will obey the Lord.

To sum up. The theology of the book of Joshua is largely dependent on the ideas to be found in Deuteronomy. So close in fact is the affinity of outlook between Deuteronomy and Joshua that it is reasonable to suppose that both books were edited by the same man or school. Chaps. 13–21 of Joshua are sufficiently integrated into the rest of the book that it seems unnecessary to postulate that they were inserted by a secondary deuteronomistic editor. However, the evidence of the theology of Joshua does not permit us to decide the larger question, whether the Hexateuch or the Deuteronomic History theory is the more adequate. On the one hand, Joshua appears at a few points to be dependent on P traditions. But it may be that the P-like passages in Joshua 22 merely represent an overlap of the vocabulary of P with that of D.[16] The Deuteronomic history theory, on the other hand, certainly has the advantage of economy. Yet, as has been pointed out by G. von Rad, the theological outlook of the various books in the so-called Deuteronomic History is less uniform than is sometimes supposed.[17] Perhaps more striking is the very different attitude toward Jerusalem in Deuteronomy and Joshua from that in Kings. Jerusalem is only mentioned in passing as an unconquered Jebusite city in Deuteronomy and Joshua (Josh 15:63), and the central sanctuary is evidently located elsewhere. In contrast, the editor of Kings appears to regard all worship outside Jerusalem as sinful (2 Kings 17). Thus, although the theology of the Book of Joshua allows us to affirm a close connection between it and Deuteronomy, it is less obvious how it is related to the rest of the Pentateuch, on the one hand, and to the former prophets, on the other.

16. See n. 11 above.

17. *Old Testament Theology* (Edinburgh, 1963) 1.346f. He points out, among other things, the different treatments of sin and judgment in Judges and Kings.

The Deuteronomist from Joshua to Samuel

JOHN VAN SETERS

As the chapters by Dietrich and Naumann, McCarter, Rofé, Sperling, Wenham, and Van Seters indicate, the nature and extent of the deuteronomistic contribution to Joshua, Judges, and Samuel is one of the most controverted issues in the study of the Deuteronomistic History. In line with his previous work on the traditions of the Pentateuch, Van Seters argues that Deuteronomy (D) and the Deuteronomistic History were written before the work of the Yahwist (J) and the Priestly composition (P). Because Van Seters considers both J and P to be later than D, he has no problem with seeing Yahwistic (e.g., Joshua 24) and Priestly contributions (e.g., Joshua 14–17) to Joshua. In this, his analysis differs dramatically from Noth's. The Deuteronomist is presented as a much more active author than previous scholars thought. The Deuteronomist, like other ancient historians, freely composed speeches and narratives when he wished to do so or when sources were lacking. Van Seters also argues for a whole series of later secondary additions to the text of Joshua, Judges, and Samuel. By allowing for Yahwistic and Priestly contributions, as well as numerous secondary interpolations, Van Seters preserves a high degree of internal coherence within the (original) deuteronomistic narrative.

[[322]] The literary problems of the books of Joshua and Judges are so numerous and complex that no comprehensive review of the present state of scholarly discussion can be attempted here. Nevertheless, this study would

Reprinted with permission from Van Seters, *In Search of History: Historiography in the Ancient World and the Origins of Biblical History* (New Haven: Yale University Press, 1983; repr. Winona Lake, Ind.: Eisenbrauns, 1997) 322–53.

not be complete without seriously considering Noth's proposal that a substantial amount of Joshua and Judges belongs to a Deuteronomistic History stretching from Moses (Deuteronomy) to the end of the monarchy (2 Kings). In these introductory remarks I shall focus upon the debate between those who advocate the continuation of the Pentateuchal sources into Joshua (and Judges 1)[1] and Noth, whose thesis is that such sources end in the Tetrateuch and that Joshua derives from a completely different literary corpus and process, namely, Dtr.[2]

The argument by those scholars in Old Testament literary criticism who still advocate the notion of a Hexateuch is simple but telling. Both the Yahwist and Priestly source of the Pentateuch contain the theme of the Promised Land, to which both accounts point forward. It would appear inconceivable that such sources did not conclude with a treatment of the conquest. Advocates of this view attempt to find Yahwist and Priestly versions of the conquest in Joshua and in Judges 1.

The argument for Noth's position, which many scholars have adopted, is that since Joshua is so closely integrated with Deuteronomy and follows it as its natural continuation, it is difficult to accommodate Joshua to the usual view about the growth of the Pentateuchal traditions. What earlier scholars regarded as overwhelming evidence of the Priestly source in Joshua [[323]] is set down by Noth as merely a few late glosses in the Priestly Writer's style. On the other hand, those who oppose Noth's thesis tend to limit the deuteronomistic influence in Joshua and Judges to some late deuteronomistic redaction of the Hexateuchal material. This view, however, still makes it difficult to understand how later material from an independent Priestly source could have been added to the work.

The problems that result from having to choose between these two positions are alleviated when it is understood that the need for the choice arises out of only two tenets of Pentateuchal criticism that are currently under attack.[3] The first is the view that the various Pentateuchal sources are independent of each other and were combined only by later redactors. Increasingly scholars are coming to view the Priestly source as both author and redactor, whose work supplements earlier sources of the Pentateuch.[4] The second tenet being criticized is the early date of the Yahwist. Some scholars now advocate a much later date than previously suggested, and J

1. Among the many advocates of this view, we note in particular the views of von Rad (1966: 1–78; 1949); Mowinckel (1964).

2. In addition to Noth's *Überlieferungsgeschichtliche Studien* (1981), see also idem, *Das Buch Josua* (1971). For a review of this issue, see Radjawane 1973–74; and Hayes and Miller 1977: 217ff.

3. See Van Seters 1975: 48–53; 1979.

4. See also Cross 1973: 293ff.

may, in fact, be postdeuteronomistic.[5] While this is not the place to deal with the whole discussion of Pentateuchal criticism, the implications of these two changes are great for resolving the debate between the advocates of a Hexateuch and the supporters of a DH. To accept these changes would mean to acknowledge that Deuteronomy and the DH were written first. The Yahwist and the Priestly Writer looked upon the conquest as portrayed in Joshua as the fulfillment of their land promise theme, and thus composed the rest of the Pentateuch (the Tetrateuch) in two stages as additions to the earlier history. There was consequently no need for them to produce their own accounts of the conquest-settlement tradition *de novo*. Of course it was still possible for the Yahwist and the Priestly Writer to supplement the deuteronomistic conquest narrative with additional material in their own style and perspective, and I hope to show that they did so.

I do not intend to solve here all the literary problems of the Pentateuch, although I believe that an analysis of Joshua is an important part of that solution. Instead I shall focus upon the Deuteronomistic History and its proper delineation in Joshua, Judges, and the early chapters of 1 Samuel. This task has been obscured by the debate over a Hexateuch as well as by the quest for early historical documents and a multiplication of deuteronomistic redactions. We will examine all these issues in the following pages.

Joshua 1–12

[[324]] Joshua[6] begins by establishing a continuation with Deuteronomy: "After the death of Moses, the servant of Yahweh. . . ." The divine speech that follows in vv. 1b–9 recapitulates the language and themes of Joshua's prior commissioning for leadership by Moses (Deut 31:14–15, 23–24; 32:44).[7] The dimensions of the Promised Land in v. 4 correspond to those given in Deut 11:24b, and the exhortations accompanying it in vv. 3 and 5 are similar in language to Deut 11:25. There are repeated references to God's commands and promises to Moses, and especially to the "law" (*tôrāh*) and to the "book of the law" (*sēper hattôrāh*), vv. 7 and 8, which clearly refers to Deuteronomy. It is the ruler's obligation to consult this law constantly (v. 8; see Deut 17:18ff.), and by doing so he will have great success (Deut 5:32ff.; 29:8 [ET 9]; also Josh 23:6–7).

5. In addition to works in n. 3 above, see also Schmid 1976; Vorländer 1978; Schmitt 1980; Rose 1981.

6. In addition to the works mentioned in n. 2 above, we should perhaps mention the recent commentary by Soggin, *Joshua* (1972). However, this work adds little in the way of original literary analysis beyond that proposed by Noth.

7. McCarthy 1971.

Joshua's command to the officers (vv. 10–11) sets the stage for the following action (3:2ff.) and provides the chronological framework for these events. The speech refers to both crossing the Jordan and taking possession of the land—the themes of the whole book. It also repeats the divine command of v. 2 and the subject of Joshua's commissioning in Deut 31:2ff. Joshua's further exhortation to the Reubenites, the Gadites, and the half-tribe of Manasseh in vv. 12ff. picks up on the theme and language of Deut 3:18–20, stating that the eastern tribes were to serve in the army of conquest with their western brethren. This theme is recapitulated at various points in Joshua.[8] One significant difference from the earlier account is that in vv. 16–18 the tribes make a reply to Joshua, whereas in Deut 3:18–20 no such response is given to Moses.[9]

From the evidence of heavy dependence upon Deuteronomy, it may be safely asserted that Joshua 1 is a thoroughly deuteronomistic introduction which does not include within it any other source. It is not just an editorial prologue attached to an otherwise independent story or series of stories but the true beginning of the whole basic account of the conquest. Without it, the rest of the story of Joshua would be badly fragmented. This realization puts the other pieces of the Joshua puzzle in proper perspective. Instead of taking the customary approach of considering deuteronomistic material as secondary and a redactional addition to an older substratum, I am suggesting that Dtr is the author of the conquest narrative.

⟦325⟧ The story of Rahab, the harlot, and the spies (in Joshua 2) presents a major literary problem. Apart from the many internal problems that the story contains, there is the special difficulty of how the story fits into its context. First, it does not agree with the chronology indicated in 1:11 and 3:2, since the time required would be more than three days. Second, in the story of the fall of Jericho in chap. 6 nothing that the spies could have learned from Rahab would in any way assist in the capture of the city. The exercise of spying was entirely unnecessary. To see this as some alternate tradition of the taking of the city is highly speculative and unconvincing.[10] The point of the episode is entirely theological, centering on the confession, by the non-Israelite Rahab, of faith in the God of Israel. Nothing of military significance is discussed or even suggested. Rahab's mention of the divine deliverance at the Red Sea and the defeat of Sihon and Og points to a strong connection with the Pentateuch and with the Yahwist in particular. This whole story is secondary and not part of the

8. Josh 4:12–13, 22:1–6.

9. On the other hand, the P account in Numbers 32 has developed the response into a lengthy dialogue between Moses and the tribes.

10. See Soggin 1972: 37ff. If this was an old source, as Soggin suggests, why did Dtr do such a poor job of integrating it into his overall chronology and scheme of events?

original deuteronomistic stratum. The episode was contrived and added in order to articulate a more universalistic perspective on Israel's religion. This leads me to my second principle in the study of Joshua: if Pentateuchal sources are to be found in Joshua, whether J or P, they are all secondary additions made directly onto the original deuteronomistic work.

The account of the crossing of the Jordan in Joshua 3 and 4 presents us with a text that has been greatly complicated by such secondary additions, which were probably made in two stages.[11] The original deuteronomistic presentation of the crossing begins in 3:2–3 as a direct continuation of chap. 1. The notation in 3:1 is an itinerary notice by the P source of the Pentateuch.[12] It disturbs the chronology of the "three days" and is thereby disclosed as an addition. The statement in v. 4a, "However, there is to be a distance between you and it [the Ark] of about two thousand cubits, do not come near it," is another addition, one that seems to contradict the whole point of the people following the Ark, namely, "in order that you may know the way you are to go, for you have not passed this way before" (v. 4b). The concern for a large space is the Priestly Writer's concern for the Ark's holiness. To this source also belongs the injunction in v. 5 to the people to sanctify themselves, since the reference to "tomorrow" is again out of keeping with the context: the crossing takes place the same day. The rest of the deuteronomistic account I would identify as found in 3:6–7, 9–11, 13–16; 4:10b, 11a, 12–14. The story thus reconstructed has Joshua indicate to [[326]] the people that the miracle of the dividing of the Jordan's waters is proof to them that Yahweh will give them victory over their foes. This is followed by a simple description of the miracle and the crossing of the people, including the eastern tribes. The reference to the eastern tribes makes the connection back to 1:12ff.[13] A second theme, the exaltation of Joshua (3:7; 4:14), rounds out the episode.

In Dtr's account, as set forth above, the author does not make any reference to a memorial of stones.[14] Since two such versions do occur, it is evident that they belong to two subsequent additions to the story. The first type of modification is in the activity and position of the priests. In the deuteronomistic account the priests carrying the Ark simply move to the edge of the river, at which point the waters are "cut off" upstream and the whole procession crosses the river. In the additions the priests bearing

11. For an entirely different division of the text in which deuteronomistic material is regarded as secondary, see ibid., 43–46; and Noth 1971: 26–39.

12. Coats 1972: 135–52.

13. Soggin (1972: 45) assigns 4:12–13 to the predeuteronomistic author, although he has previously attributed 1:12–18 to Dtr. This kind of source analysis is highly questionable.

14. Given the deuteronomic animosity toward standing stones, it would be surprising if Dtr made any mention of them. Both J and P, however, have a way of turning such *maṣṣēbôt* [['standing stones' or 'pillars']] into memorial stones.

the Ark remain standing in the river on dry ground while all the people cross, and then the stones are taken from the riverbed at the point where the priests stood. Here the two additions also part company. In the earlier addition the stones are taken from the river to the place where the people lodge for the night, namely Gilgal (3:8, 12, 17; 4:1–5, 8, 20–24). In the second addition a memorial is also set up in the river itself as a "memorial forever" (4:6–7, 9–10a, 11b, 15–19).[15]

A few observations may be made about these additions. First, they depend entirely upon the basic deuteronomistic account; in no way can they be viewed as the conflation or editorial combination of independent sources or traditions. Second, the additions suggest some continuity with the sources of the Pentateuch. The first addition makes a strong connection with the Red Sea event, as in Josh 2:10, with its emphasis upon the crossing on "dry ground," the characteristic motif of J. The setting up of twelve stones for the twelve tribes is also paralleled by Moses' action at Sinai in Exod 24:4 (J). The author of the second addition, when it is taken together with 3:4a, 5, would appear to be the Priestly Writer. He emphasizes the great sanctity of the Ark, the stones as a "sign" (*ʾôt*) and "memorial" (*zikkārôn*) in perpetuity (*ʿad ʿôlām*), and the precise dating of events (as is his custom with wilderness wanderings). It is also likely that it is he who portrayed [[327]] the division of the waters at the Jordan as a great wall of water, just as he represented it in his description of the Red Sea event.[16] The children's questions also have their closest parallels in the J and P sources.[17]

The various units of chap. 5 do not belong to Dtr. The opening verse, 5:1, is directly connected with the preceding J addition of 4:23–24 and is parallel as well to 2:9–11. It serves to make the response of the nations to the two miracles–the Red Sea and the Jordan crossings–similar, and to emphasize their greatness.[18] On the other hand, 5:1 is somewhat awkward in the present context because it does not serve to introduce any new event, as one would expect. Its only purpose seems to be to make a theological statement. The descriptions of the circumcision, vv. 2–9, and of the keeping of the Passover, vv. 10–12, are priestly texts. The episode in

15. It is possible that the second addition developed as a midrashic interpretation of 4:5b and understood the text to mean: "And you are to raise for yourselves each one stone upon *its* shoulder [i.e., one upon the other] according to the number of Israelite tribes." This would produce a column, not a row of stones, which would then be visible above the surface of the water.

16. The rather awkward phrases *nēd ʾeḥad* [['single heap']] (v. 13) and *qāmû nēd ʾeḥād* [['rose in a single heap']] (v. 16) may well represent explanatory glosses supplied by P. See especially the studies of Childs 1967; 1970; Coats 1967; 1969.

17. Exod 12:26–27 (P); 13:8–10 (J); cf. Deut 6:20–24.

18. Cf. also Exod 15:14–16.

vv. 13–15 dealing with Joshua's encounter with the "commander of Yahweh's host" looks like a parallel to Moses' theophany on Sinai in Exodus 3 and is probably the work of J.[19]

The conquest of Jericho in chap. 6 should be viewed as the direct continuation of the Jordan crossing in 4:12–14 (Dtr). This chapter also presents a number of points of confusion in the extant version of the story. The source of this confusion is that P has attempted to turn the rather simple procedure, set forth by Dtr, of marching around the wall seven days in silence with only a shout at the sign of the shofar, into an elaborate procession.[20] The addition of all the trumpet-playing priests has ruined the effect of the one blast on the horn and the great war cry. Connections have also been made with the spy story in vv. 17b, 22–23, 25.[21]

The story of the conquest of Jericho appears to end on a positive note: "Yahweh was with Joshua and his fame was throughout the land." It is surprising, therefore, to find in 7:1 that all was not well and that Yahweh was, in fact, angry with his people. The story of Achan concerns a matter of holiness, and there is much here that is reminiscent of such issues in the [[328]] Pentateuch, especially the rebellion of Korah in Numbers 16.[22] I would consider the story of Achan an addition by P with connections to the preceding account in 6:18, 19, 24b, where the reference to the "treasury of the house of Yahweh" seems to be an anachronism.

With the battle of Ai in chap. 8 we return again to the DH. The introduction in vv. 1–2 makes the story a sequel to the conquest of Jericho. Verses 3–9, however, are directly related to chap. 7 in that they refer to the previous attack upon Ai. The problem with these verses is that they form a doublet with those that follow and are unnecessary to the sense of the story. When they are removed as part of a later addition, there is no longer any suggestion of an earlier defeat.

The building of the altar at Ebal and the reading of the law in 8:30–35 seem to represent a digression that does not easily fit in with the geography of the campaign. The actions portrayed here are directly related to

19. As this episode now stands, it looks strangely incomplete. One solution would be to suppose that the rest of the account was lost (cf. Soggin 1972: 76–78). The other would be to see it as an introduction to the divine speech of 6:2, with 6:1 treated as a parenthetical statement. In this case 5:13–15 is regarded as a secondary addition to the divine speech of 6:2ff. in order to supply Joshua with a theophany parallel to that of Moses.

20. This can be seen by isolating 6:1–3, 4aβ, 5, 6a, 7 (omitting *wayyōʾmer ʾel hāʿām* "and he said to the people"), 10–11, 14–16aα, b, 17a, 20b, 21, 24a, 26–27.

21. The additions in vv. 18, 19, 24b will be dealt with below.

22. The story of the rebellion of Korah, Dathan, and Abiram has usually been divided between the J and P sources (see Noth 1968: 120–22), but I can find little justification for such a division. J is otherwise quite disinterested in the priesthood, and the story has as its main concern the controversies over the priesthood of the postexilic period.

the injunctions of Moses in Deut 11:29–30 and in chap. 27, but both of these passages are also secondary within Deuteronomy. The regulations concerning the altar in Deut 27:5–7 and Josh 8:31 correspond to the law given in Exod 20:25 (J). Likewise, the location given in Deut 11:30 as "beside the oak of Moreh" at Shechem recalls the same location sanctified with an altar by Abraham (in Gen 12:6) and the place where Jacob buried foreign gods under the oak (in Gen 35:4). These associations strongly suggest that the additions to Deuteronomy in 11:29–30 and chap. 27, as well as in Josh 8:30–35, were all made by the Yahwist.[23]

The treaty with the Gibeonites in chap. 9 is a story that presupposes the law of warfare in Deut 20:10ff.; this law is a completely artificial and ideological creation and was never an actual institution of Israel in this form. Consequently, there can be no doubt that the story as a whole is a thoroughly deuteronomic invention. Within the story, however, some literary complexity has been created by later additions. On the one hand, Joshua has the role of leadership and enters into an agreement with the Gibeonites (vv. 15a, 16, 22, 24–26, 27). This is the original version of Dtr. To it has been added the version that shifts the blame for the agreement with the Gibeonites onto the "leaders of the congregation," who did not take the trouble to inquire of Yahweh. This addition is to be found in vv. 14, 15b, 17–21, 23, and in some glosses in v. 27. The language [[329]] and the repetitious style of composition are characteristic of P,[24] but this is not a separate, self-contained version of the story. It is an addition that was primarily intended to shift the blame from Joshua to the "leaders."[25]

The story of Joshua's defeat of the "southern coalition" in chap. 10 presents no great problems. It continues on from chap. 9 and clearly presupposes the events there. The one interruption in the narrative is the unit about the sun standing still, along with a short poem in it said to have been derived from the "Book of Jashar."[26] Since Dtr again quotes from this source in 2 Sam 1:18ff., the verses in Josh 10:12–14 are probably from Dtr also. The reference in v. 15 to Joshua's return to camp, however, is

23. On these texts see Perlitt 1969: 248 n. 3, where he is quite critical about the suggestions that these texts contain early premonarchic covenant traditions. On Joshua 24, which many scholars associate with Josh 8:30–35, see below.

24. For a treatment of the priestly style, see McEvenue 1971.

25. It is, in this latest priestly addition to the story that some scholars like Soggin (1972: 113–14) want to find the *oldest* traditions and a historical background to the story. From the literary perspective, such a viewpoint is questionable.

26. On the meaning of the poem, see Holladay 1968: 166–78. As indicated by Holladay, the poem is based upon an omen of a rather common type in Near Eastern texts in which the position of the heavenly bodies was regarded as propitious (or unpropitious). Dtr, however, construed the text to mean a rather miraculous event. Whether the original poem was associated with Joshua, as Holladay suggests, is much more difficult to say.

clearly out of place, since the pursuit of the enemy is still in progress. The flight of the kings in vv. 16ff. really follows closely from v. 10. For the rest, there is no reason to see any other hand in the work.

The campaign against Hazor and the "northern coalition" in chap. 11 is also thoroughly deuteronomistic, with few, if any, later glosses. The presentation of the battle, preceded by the oracle of salvation to Joshua before the battle itself, is quite typical of deuteronomistic style. Deuteronomy envisages the complete success of the conquest and the use of the ban (*ḥerem*) against the inhabitants, and the summary statements in Joshua 11 indicate that these measures were successfully carried out. Also, the theme of God hardening the heart of the enemy so as to lead them into war in order to destroy them (11:20) is typical of Dtr, as in Deut 2:30.

The list of defeated kings on both sides of the Jordan in chap. 12 does not contain anything that is distinctive of the deuteronomistic source, and I agree with Mowinckel[27] that it is from the hand of P. It could be explained only as corresponding to P's love of lists, which he displays so prominently throughout the Pentateuch. At various points it does not entirely agree with the previous deuteronomistic account.

To sum up my observations about the first half of Joshua, I have suggested that the original version of the conquest was composed by Dtr. There is, to my mind, no evidence of an earlier *Sammler* [['compiler']] which constituted [[330]] a predeuteronomic source. This proposal by Noth[28] replaced the older critical position that the early Hexateuchal sources continued on into Joshua and were simply edited by Dtr. The fact is, as I have tried to show, that the sources J and P both made *post*deuteronomistic additions to the basic deuteronomistic presentation as supplements or modifications of the earlier work. Thus these Hexateuchal sources did not need to present their own conquest narrative as a completion of their Tetrateuchal compositions. They simply built onto the DH of the conquest and settlement their own prehistory of these events and modified the older DH where they felt it desirable to do so. If this analysis is correct, it accounts for the critical points in favor of a Hexateuch that have been raised against Noth by von Rad and Mowinckel, but it keeps intact Noth's fundamental observation that Dtr is not just a redactor of older sources but an author-historian in the full sense of the word.

The DH interpreted the tradition of the entrance into the arable land as a great military conquest along the lines of the frequent invasions that Israel and Judah had experienced at the hands of the Assyrians and Babylonians. In these cases Israel and Judah had often been party to coalitions that sought to resist the invader, usually to no avail. In the presentation of

27. Mowinckel 1964: 59–60.

28. Noth 1971: 13.

Joshua's invasion the coalitions of the native inhabitants, both the southern and northern groups of kings, are defeated and the various cities destroyed.

Furthermore, the deuteronomistic narrative has a basic similarity to the accounts of such military campaigns in the Near Eastern inscriptions, particularly those of the Assyrian annals and the "letters to the god."[29] The latter often given special attention to a few major battles or conquests of important cities while summarizing the overthrow of many others in a stereotyped series. They may also highlight at the outset of a campaign the overcoming of a special physical barrier, such as a river in flood or a mountain range. Before an important battle the king often receives an "oracle of salvation" from a deity who promises to deliver the enemy into his hand.[30] Sometimes envoys come from a great distance to sue for peace and submit to terms of servitude in order to avoid destruction. It is also not unusual during the course of a campaign to consult or rely upon omens in order to predict the ultimate outcome of the war. General descriptions of sieges or military stratagems; summary treatments of attack and flight of the enemy and the burning of cities; enumerations of participants of coalitions, kings [[331]] defeated, or cities taken; lists of casualties and the amount of booty; dedications of victory and of spoils to the god—all occur with great regularity. In the royal inscriptions of the Assyrians and Babylonians the native peoples of Syria-Palestine are all lumped together under the rubric of "Amorites" or "Hittites." Also, the borders given in these inscriptions for the "land of the Amorites/Hittites" correspond closely to those in Josh 1:4.[31] Once we isolate the basic deuteronomistic account of the conquest, without the stories of Rahab (chap. 2) or the sin of Achan (chap. 7) and the other additions of J and P (especially chap. 5), then it is remarkable how closely Dtr's work has been made to correspond with the literary pattern of military campaigns in the Assyrian royal inscriptions. Even the "installation" of Joshua as the leader who succeeds Moses suggests that the conquest is the first victorious campaign of the new regime.

This treatment of the migration into the land does not seem to be reflected in the "gift of the good land" theme in the prophetic tradition.[32] Instead it grows directly out of the militant "puritanical" reform of Deuteronomy, in which the obliteration of everything un-Israelite in Israel's religious practices is justified on the basis of an "original" command by

29. For a discussion of these texts, see Van Seters, *In Search of History*, 60–68.

30. See Weippert 1972.

31. Van Seters 1972.

32. The only exception to this would appear to be Amos 2:9–10, but 2:9–12 is suspect as a deuteronomistic addition. See Ward 1969: 67 n. 3.

God to obliterate the indigenous population and all their alien forms of worship. Israel's very right to the land requires its purification. The Dtr historian has turned this theological principle in Deuteronomy into a great invasion and campaign of victory under the leadership of Joshua. The continuity between Deuteronomy and Joshua seems to be firmly established at numerous points in the first eleven chapters of Joshua, and especially in the opening chapter of the book. This is not the place to debate the degree to which the Dtr historian edited Deuteronomy and made additions to it, especially in chaps. 1–4 and 29–34. Nevertheless, it seems reasonable to assume that if a DH did exist as an extended work of one author, then Deuteronomy was incorporated into it as its prologue and statement of guiding principles. Joshua's conquest is the initial carrying out of those principles by cleansing the land of Amorites.

The Land Division: Joshua 13–24

The designation of sources for the second half of Joshua is a hotly debated issue. Most scholars are willing to admit that the division of the land among the tribes is secondary to the original conquest narrative. However, [[332]] whereas Noth would attribute it to a second deuteronomistic redactor, Mowinckel and von Rad ascribe it to the Pentateuchal sources, because there is little evidence throughout most of the material of any deuteronomistic influence. Noth's counter to this is that the deuteronomistic redactor employed documentary source materials from various periods without altering them, only reworking them to fit them into his own general scheme. Several scholars have followed this proposal with their own suggestions about the time and function of such hypothetical documents.[33]

All this evidence of documents, however, has been created by scholars *ex nihilo* [['out of nothing']], because there are no such extant lists, nor is there any reason to suppose that such records ever existed. No comparable records can be produced from the ancient Near East such that the originals can be reconstructed out of what we have in these chapters. The artificial and idealized character of the lists has been frequently noted, and yet to attribute this to editorial reworking while at the same time using the theory of documents to explain the lack of a particular editorial hand is contradictory. The evidence by which to identify the author is abundant and cannot be easily ignored or explained away.[34]

First, let us consider what can be attributed with some certainty to Dtr. The unit in 21:43–45 contains a summary of the complete victory

33. See the discussion and bibliography in Hayes and Miller 1977: 235–36.
34. See Mowinckel's critique in 1964: 62–67.

that is very similar to 11:15, 23, and while it seems somewhat redundant, it is nevertheless thoroughly deuteronomistic in character. The following unit, 22:1–6, in which the eastern tribes are dismissed by Joshua and permitted to return home, completes a theme begun in Josh 1:12–18 and mentioned again in 4:12–13. The language also is typical of Dtr. What follows in 22:7–35 is quite different. The farewell speech by Joshua in chap. 23 is so clearly in the style of Dtr that there seems little need to demonstrate this fact. But the attribution of any other texts in this part of Joshua to Dtr, beyond these few, remains questionable.[35]

Most of the latter half of Joshua is dominated by the allotment of land to the various tribes. Von Rad, in his study of this theme, suggests an important distinction between the deuteronomic notion of the inheritance of the land and that used by P.[36] This distinction is that while Dtr "speaks almost exclusively of the inheritance of *Israel*" as a whole,[37] P refers to [[333]] the inheritance of the individual tribes and the families within the tribes.[38] This means that for Dtr it was enough to suggest that Joshua, through his leadership in the conquest of the land, had brought the people as a whole into their inheritance. The Priestly Writer, however, developed this theme to delineate the precise inheritance of each of the tribes and of the families within each tribe, and so greatly expanded the conquest/settlement theme in this direction. There is no reason to conjecture a second deuteronomistic redactor for this material (as Noth does) when it corresponds so closely with the Priestly program as laid out in Numbers. In this program P indicates first that the census of the tribes by families was undertaken with a view to the future division of the land by lot among the various tribes and the families within each tribe (Num 26:52–56; 33:54). Closely related to this is the description of the general boundaries of the land of Canaan, which is to be divided by lot (Numbers 34). This is followed by the injunction about the cities for the Levites, into which are incorporated the laws for the cities of refuge.

A comparison of the Priestly program with Joshua shows how it was carried out in the land of Canaan, and there is no need to suppose that it was put together by any other hand than P. This author was still

35. It will be shown below that the appointment of the cities of refuge in chap. 20 (with the exception of v. 6 and the last phrase in v. 9) also belongs to Dtr.

36. Von Rad 1966: 79–93.

37. Deut 4:21, 38; 12:9; 15:4; 19:10; 20:16; 21:23; 24:4; 25:19; 26:1.

38. Num 18:21, 24; 26:53–54, 56; 36:3. Based on the fact that Deut 10:6–9 is clearly a later P addition to Deuteronomy, I would also suggest that all the remarks about Levi having no portion or inheritance (*ḥēleq wᵉnaḥălâ*) in Israel in Deut 12:12; 14:27, 29; 18:1ff. are later P additions, so that the distinction in usage between D and P is even more consistent than von Rad had suggested.

confronted with the task of integrating his material into the original deuteronomistic text of Joshua. He did this partly by way of commentary. For instance, it has often been remarked that Josh 13:1a shows a close similarity to 23:1b, but this observation is never carried far enough. If we set down the parallel texts, we can make some observations about them.

Joshua 23:1–5 (Dtr)	Joshua 13:1–7 (P)
1. A long time afterward, when Yahweh had given rest to Israel from all their enemies round about, and Joshua was old [and] well advanced in years,	1. And Joshua was old [and] well advanced in years. And Yahweh said to him, "You are old [and] well advanced in years and there remains much land to be possessed.
2. Joshua summoned all Israel . . . and said to them, "I am now old [and] well advanced in years. . . .	2. (This is the land that remains . . .).
4. Behold I have allotted to [[334]] you as an inheritance for your tribes those nations that remain, along with the nations that I have already cut off, from the Jordan to the Great Sea in the west.	6b. I will dispossess them from before the Israelites. Only allot it to Israel as an inheritance as I commanded you.
5. Yahweh your God will push them back before you. . . . "	7. Now therefore divide this land for an inheritance to the nine tribes and the half tribe of Manasseh."

From this comparison we can observe that P has borrowed his introduction in 13:1 from 23:1b–2 (in spite of the chronological problem arising from 23:1a); but P's main concern is with 23:4. According to Dtr, Joshua is committing to the people all the territory within the idealized boundary, including what he has conquered for them; it remains for them gradually to realize this inheritance to the full by pushing these nations back the whole distance from the borders of Egypt to the Euphrates. P distinguishes quite carefully between the lands that remain to be conquered (which he defines by a long geographic digression in the middle of the divine speech) and the lands that are already conquered, which must be allotted. This then becomes the point of departure for his treatment of the specific allotments to the individual tribes, in which he uses his own terminology (13:7ff.).[39]

A brief comparison of the two versions of the division of the land among the eastern tribes, in Josh 13:8–33 and Deut 3:8–17, is instructive.[40] The version in Deuteronomy begins with a general description of the total area of the land taken in the defeat of the two kings (vv. 8–10). [[335]] This land is then distributed in two parcels corresponding to the two kingdoms (vv. 12–17). The northern parcel goes to the half-tribe of Manasseh, and the southern area is given to both the Reubenites and the Gadites, with no attempt to draw boundaries between them. There is, throughout this description, no reference to any method of division, such as the use of lots, or any indication of inheritance distributed to smaller subdivisions, such as families. By contrast, Josh 13:8ff., after repeating the general dimensions of the land for no apparent reason, divides up the land fairly precisely, according to the principle laid down in P—the division to be made according to the families of the tribes, with the boundaries and the cities clearly designated.[41] This sets the pattern for the rest of the land division from chap. 14 onward, in which the allotment for the western tribes is made.

The first general allotment of territory to the tribe of Judah and the house of Joseph, in chaps. 14–17, seems to be interrupted by, or to include, short narrative portions in a somewhat different style from the rest of the material.[42] These are the allotment of land to Caleb (in 14:6–15) and his conquest of it within the territory of Judah (in 15:13–19), and the

39. Smend has suggested that 13:7, along with v. 1abα, belongs to the original Dtr and that Joshua 23 is to be attributed to a later redactor, DtrN. Without going into detail on this proposal it may be pointed out, on the basis of von Rad's study of terminology in n. 36 above, that it seems most difficult to see how Smend can find any basis for 13:7 in the deuteronomistic corpus. Nor does 13:7 appear to me to follow very readily from v. 1abα. The land division does not finally come about because of Joshua's advanced age but as a result of the conquest. The *wᵉʿattāh* [['and now']] (v. 7) is a very imprecise editorial connective no matter how one views this pericope. Furthermore, Smend makes no attempt to show how the following division of the land to the nine and a half tribes can be so easily integrated into the original DH, which is what 13:7 implies. In fact, everything speaks against this, and Smend's suggestion fails on this account. It is more likely that those texts that contain an overwhelming preponderance of deuteronomic phraseology, such as Josh 1:1–9 and chap. 23, are part of the primary DH, and those that contain little or none are secondary (Smend 1972 [[the Smend essay has been translated in this volume as "The Law and the Nations: A Contribution to Deuteronomistic Tradition History" (pp. 95–110)]]). In this tribute to von Rad one might have expected Smend to pay more attention to von Rad's article on the subject, which he does not even mention!

40. For a recent discussion of these texts, see Wüst 1975. The traditio-historical method employed in this work is not compatible with the results of the literary analysis used here.

41. Note the reference to a specific P tradition in 13:21b–22 = Numbers 31.

42. See a similar digression in Deut 3:14.

tribe of Joseph's complaint about lack of space at the conclusion of their allotment (in 17:14–18). Also, parallels are drawn between these units and a similar case in Num 32:39–42. This type of narrative digression does not seem to me (as it does to most scholars) to signify a separate source, and the passages contain some features that are characteristic of P.[43] Consequently, I am inclined to see the entire allotting of territory in chaps. 14–17 as constructed by the hand of P.

The allotment in chaps. 18–19, which deals with the last seven tribes, is also the work of P.[44] The manner in which the assembly is convened at Shiloh and the procedures laid down for the land division are characteristic of the P style. This has long been recognized and there seems to be no good reason to dispute it.[45] The allotment of the cities of refuge in chap. 20 is a more complex matter. On the one hand, it seems to correspond to the instructions in Deut 4:41–43 and 19:1–13, rather than to the P provisions in Num 35:6–34. For this reason I would add it to the list of deuteronomistic texts in the second half of Joshua. Josh 20:6 and the final phrase in v. 9bβ, [[336]] however, are modifications by the Priestly Writer. The designation of the cities for the Levites in 21:1–42 corresponds only to the P injunction in Num 35:1–8 and so belongs to P.[46]

As noted above, 22:1–6 belongs to Dtr and fits well with the other statements about the eastern tribes. On the other hand, vv. 7ff. constitute a new beginning, and the whole story about the altar of witness of the eastern tribes, in which Phineas the priest and the "chiefs of the congregation" play a leading role, has much that is characteristic of P's style and vocabulary. The whole of 22:7–34 belongs to P, as do the final notations in 24:32–33.

The pericope in 24:1–27, however, is another matter.[47] It constitutes a second farewell speech by Joshua, and it hardly seems likely that both

43. Mowinckel (1964: 44ff.) ascribes all these texts to the Yahwist, but much in them is not compatible with this source designation. It also makes difficult an explanation of how such J fragments became scattered throughout the P source in chaps. 13–19.

44. Vink 1969: 63–73.

45. Noth's remarks (1943: 183ff. [[= *The Chronicler's History* (JSOTSup 50; Sheffield: JSOT Press, 1987) 112ff.—ed.]]), that we have to do only with some glosses in a priestly style and phraseology, are forced and unconvincing.

46. Noth's treatment of this chapter (1943: 189–90 [= *The Chronicler's History*, 118–19]) typifies the problem with his analysis. Since this is a Priestly addition to the deuteronomistic version of Joshua, it must belong to a P redactor and not to the P source itself, which Noth regards as an independent literary work. However, if P, even in the Pentateuch, was only a supplement to the other sources, then Noth's approach to the problem of P in Joshua suffers from a misunderstanding of the nature of this source.

47. See the study of Perlitt (1969: 239–84) for his critique of earlier approaches. Even so, his own solution to this chapter is not entirely convincing. It is not an "ur"-dt work but a postdeuteronomistic work.

would come from the same hand. I have considered chap. 23 as more likely the work of Dtr; but even though there are some deuteronomic phrases in chap. 24, it is a postdeuteronomistic addition. The historical recitation of events is a significant clue to its authorship. It seems to correspond to a summary account of J's version of the Pentateuch,[48] especially in the statements about the patriarchs, in the description of the Red Sea event, and in the Balaam story, while containing nothing that is distinctively P. The nature of Joshua's covenant making is also similar to the covenant ceremony of Moses in Exodus 24 and the witnessing scene in Gen 31:43–54. Josh 24:1–27 was added to chap. 23.

To summarize the source analysis of the latter half of Joshua (13–24), we would suggest as the original deuteronomistic text Josh 20:1–5, 7–9; 21:43–22:6; 23:1–16. To this, at the first stage of supplementation, the Yahwist added 24:1–27. P then added the rest in chaps. 13–19; 20:6, 9bβ; 21:1–42; 22:7–34; 24:28–33. The meaning of this analysis is that Dtr included within his story of the conquest only the setting up of the cities of refuge on the "west bank"–paralleling Moses' actions on the "east bank" in compliance with deuteronomic law–and the dismissing of the eastern tribes, which completes their original recruitment in Deut 3:18ff. The farewell speech in chap. 23 also parallels Moses' final admonitions and [[337]] provides the transition to the next period of history. This basic deuteronomistic account in Joshua has the appearance of a tightly composed, unified whole, with strong literary continuity to Deuteronomy on the one hand and to Judges on the other.

At the first stage of supplementation, what could be the purpose of the Yahwist's addition of Joshua 24 to Dtr's account? It cannot be just a conclusion to the story of Joshua, which was already provided in the earlier work. Joshua 24 is the summing up in credo form, after the model in Deut 26:5–9, of the Yahwistic presentation of the Pentateuch from Abraham to the conquest; it is thus the concluding chapter of the Yahwist's entire work. It also provides J's final challenge of faith to his own exilic audience–whether in the homeland or in the Babylonian exile–to serve Yahweh rather than the gods "in the region beyond the River, or the gods of the Amorites in whose land you dwell" (Josh 24:15). Each household must now make that decision for itself. A more fitting conclusion to the Yahwist's history could scarcely be proposed.[49]

The major addition by P to the conquest story is the precise but artificial and idealized division of the land to the tribes and clans, or families.

48. See the discussion by Childs (1967). Here Childs discusses the so-called credos as historical summaries–not as old liturgical texts, as von Rad had proposed.

49. Is it too much to suggest that in Joshua's second writing of the law one can see J's legitimation of his own second presentation of the law after Deuteronomy?

This shows a historiographic concern for geographic precision about the settlement of individual tribes and about the boundaries of the "Promised" Land as a whole, and it parallels P's concern for chronological precision in the Pentateuch, which is greater than J's. But we cannot fully appreciate the purpose of P's additions until we give some consideration to the literary problems of Judges.

Judges 1:1–2:5

The fundamental problem of the Hexateuch is, perhaps, how to view Judg 1:1–2:5 and its relationship to what comes before and after it.[50] Since the days of E. Meyer literary critics have commonly ascribed this unit to the early Pentateuchal sources, preferably J, and have viewed it as J's counterpart to the conquest narratives in the first half of Joshua.[51] They have considered it older because it seemed to represent a view of the [[338]] settlement as piecemeal and incomplete, and therefore closer to the actual facts than the deuteronomistic presentation of a single invasion, as in Joshua. This judgment, in turn, has had great implications for the assessment of the second half of Joshua, since the latter has parallels or excerpts that are almost identical to those in Judges 1. It therefore becomes necessary to assign at least some of the texts on the division of the land to J. The result is a highly fragmentary separation of sources for Joshua 13ff.[52]

The primary difficulty with this approach is the recognition by all scholars that Judg 1:1–2:5 is an intrusion in its present context. The literary mechanism for making this addition is the repetition of Judg 2:6ff. in Josh 24:28ff. This means that scholars have had to try to explain why Dtr set aside the Yahwist's version of the conquest and a later redactor reintroduced it. None of their proposals seems satisfactory. Noth, who opposed the notion of a Hexateuch, simply regarded the unit as a later redactional addition that made use of unspecified early sources—a conglomerate of various materials but not a Pentateuchal document.[53] In spite of Noth's view of the matter, scholars have persisted in finding a connection between Judg 1:1–2:5 and the Pentateuchal sources.[54] In my view the issue has not yet been resolved.

50. For a survey of the current literary discussion, see Hayes and Miller 1977: 236–69. Note also the commentaries of Burney 1930; Moore 1895. Special attention will be given to de Geus 1966; and Weinfeld 1967.

51. See Moore 1895: xxxii–xxxiii, 3–100; Mowinckel 1964: 17–33.

52. Mowinckel 1964: 67ff.

53. Noth 1943: 7–10 [[*The Deuteronomistic History* (2d ed.; JSOTSup 15; Sheffield: JSOT Press, 1991), here pp. 7–10. As a convenience to readers, references to Noth's work have been keyed to this recent English translation.—ed.]].

54. See Weinfeld 1967.

In analyzing Judges 1 the first point to observe is that, except for a few possible additions, the chapter is a unity.[55] The first part, vv. 1–21, deals with the settlement of the southern tribes, and the second part, vv. 22–35, with the northern tribes. Any traditions or other "sources" that may have existed behind the present account[56] are fully integrated into the perspective of the whole, and no redactional framework can be removed without destroying the sense of the individual elements. Second, any analysis must take seriously the close relationship between this chapter and the latter half of Joshua. Not only is the general time frame set "after the death of Joshua," but the unit presupposes the allotment of the land. Since the whole allotment scheme is also considered secondary to the DH, the question arises whether Judges 1 is part of the same supplemental source. Third, the work in Judges 1 shows the influence of a broad range of biblical texts. Its terminology and its specific historical allusions indicate familiarity with the Pentateuch, and it also contains information taken from the historical books. In its variety of style and use of literary genres, in the range of its sources, and in its use of editorial comment, the work represents [[339]] a rather advanced historiography. Let us consider some of these issues in greater detail.

As indicated above, Judges 1 presupposes the distribution of the land by lot (*gôrāl*). This is the terminology and perspective of the Priestly Writer, and there is no reason to suppose that any other author held such a view of the settlement.[57] It is further assumed in Judg 1:3, 17 that the allotments of Judah and Simeon were closely tied to one another, as set forth in Josh 19:1–9. The same close association is true of Judah and the Calebites. When it recognized that Judg 1:20 is out of place and should come directly after v. 10,[58] then the pericope of Judg 1:10, 20, 11–15 forms a sequel to the allotment scene in Josh 14:6–15, just as the parallel version does in Josh 15:13–19. There is no point in trying to decide which of the two almost identical versions is the original, because both are from the same hand. They merely serve slightly different functions in the two different contexts. P was never shy about repeating himself. The combination of the people of Judah with the Kenites (v. 16), on the other hand, does not go back to Joshua but to the Pentateuch, Num 10:29–32, where Hobab the Midianite (Kenite), Moses' father-in-law, receives a promise

55. See de Geus 1966: 43.

56. The notion of archival documents, so dear to many scholars, is highly speculative. Just what historical genre would correspond, in whole or in part, to the material in Judg 1:1–2:5?

57. See von Rad (1966: 82), where he presents a list of all the texts. Von Rad attributes some of the instances to JE, but all of these are in Joshua 13–17 or Judges 1, texts that we do not regard as part of the JE corpus.

58. See de Geus 1966: 37.

from Moses that he will be treated well and allowed to share the land with Israel. Furthermore, it would appear that the allotment of land in Joshua is treated by P only as an unfulfilled promise, so that the individual tribes must claim their land by their own military actions. This pattern of allotment before conquest can be seen in Josh 14:6–15 and 15:13–16, and it exemplifies the more general pattern of Judah's allotment in Joshua 14–15 before its conquest of the territory in Judg 1:1–21. Similarly, the "house of Joseph" receives its allotment in Joshua 16–17 before it conquers the region in Judg 1:22–26.

This brings us to the matter of the parallel texts, in which Judg 1:21 = Josh 15:63, Judg 1:27–28 = Josh 17:11–13, and Judg 1:29 = Josh 16:10. It is usual to assume that these texts are primary in Judges 1 and secondary in Joshua, since the series of unconquered territories continues with the other tribes as well in Judg 1:30–33, and these have no counterpart in Joshua.[59] Yet in Josh 13:13 we find a similar qualification—that the eastern tribes "did not drive out the Geshurites and the Maacathites, but Geshur and Maacath dwell in the midst of Israel to this day." The language and style of the statement are reminiscent of Judges 1. Yet this is hardly a stray Yahwistic text, as some have suggested, since it [[340]] fits well in its context and provides the pattern for the subsequent texts of this kind in Joshua. Furthermore, the remarks in Josh 19:47 about Dan losing its primary holdings and moving to the north complement the statement in Judg 1:34 that the Danites were not successful in conquering the Amorites in their southern allotment. Again, we cannot suppose that Josh 19:47 does not belong originally with the whole allotment pericope of vv. 40–48.

These facts are best explained by assuming that the same author, P, composed both the Joshua and Judges 1 texts. In his description of both the initial distribution of the land and the subsequent taking of it, the Priestly Writer wanted to stress that the promise was not entirely kept. The information about the cities that were not conquered comes partly from the DH, which provided information about the later conquest or acquisition of Jerusalem and Gezer, and about the local population being put to forced labor.[60] The presence of non-Israelites in the land could also represent the author's own experience in a later day, when the urban population in the northern region of Israel was an ethnic mixture of Israelite and non-Israelite.

59. Cf. de Geus 1966: 39–40; Mowinckel 1964: 15–16, 24.

60. 1 Kgs 9:20–21. This text is interesting for two reasons. It speaks of the Israelites' inability to destroy the remaining inhabitants, although in Dtr this inability is clearly the result of disobedience. Second, Dtr, following D, prefers the terminology of extermination, *ḥrm*, while the author in Joshua 13ff. and Judges 1 consistently uses the verb *yrš*, "to dispossess."

The antiquity of the particular events presented in the anecdotes in Judg 1:4ff. and 22ff. is rather questionable. The story about Adonibezek seems to have as its point of departure Joshua's campaign against Adonizedek of Jerusalem in Joshua 10.[61] The totally artificial character of the name Adonibezek, and his association with both Bezek and Jerusalem, give the show away as a rather ad hoc creation. The story of the capture of Bethel, like the Jericho story, combines such simple motifs as the use of spies, leniency to the informer, and the secret entrance to the city—but it is hardly convincing.[62]

It is not difficult to suppose that all of Judges 1 could be the work of P. If this identification is accepted, then it becomes clear that the account of Joshua's death was repeated in Josh 24:28ff. because that was the only way to fit the new material into its context. The reference to the burial of Joseph's bones in v. 32 draws on information from the Pentateuch, but it also creates a parallel to P's account of the burial of other patriarchs at ⟦341⟧ Hebron. The notation on the death and burial of Eleazar, the priest in v. 33, also fits well with P authorship. The rather full list of cities not taken by the Israelites, the love of antiquarian information about ancient peoples and place names, and the concluding geographic digression[63] are all characteristics of the Priestly style.

This brings us to a consideration of Judg 2:1–5. Here an angel of Yahweh accuses Israel of violating the command not to make a covenant with the inhabitants of the land but to expel and dispossess them; he warns that they will suffer the consequences. Because this theme has a number of precursors in different sources, it is not easy to identify the author. Primary among these thematic precursors is Deuteronomy 7, but since Deuteronomy nowhere mentions any "angel of Yahweh," it would be difficult to an author who used Deuteronomy to introduce such a figure without explanation. Another precursor of this text is Exod 23:20–33 (J).[64] Here the "angel of Yahweh" is introduced as a guiding and directing force but is never actually presented as a person.[65] Rather, he seems to represent

61. See de Geus 1966: 35–36.

62. Cf. de Geus 1966: 40–41. I am not convinced by de Geus's statement, "Het is duidellijk, dat de auteur van Ri. 1 in vv 22–26 weer een oudere overlevering heeft benut" ⟦'It is clear that the author of Judges 1 in vv. 22–26 has again availed himself of an older tradition'⟧. Saying so does not make it so, and why should all the signs of lateness, e.g., "the house of Joseph," be regarded as only editorial?

63. Note 1:36. Cf. Num 34:3–5; Josh 15:1–4 (P). See the discussion by Burney 1930: 33–35.

64. See also Exod 32:31; 33:2; 34:16; Num 20:16. Because I do not subscribe to a distinctive E source in the Pentateuch, I regard all these texts as J. Cf. the discussion by Burney (1930: 35–36). That this is not an early usage of the "angel" is evident from Mal 3:1ff.

65. The theophanic use of the "angel of God/Yahweh" in Genesis and in Exodus 3 and Joshua 5 is another matter.

the spiritual presence of Yahweh, as appears to be the case in Genesis 24, where divine providence is the activity of the "angel of Yahweh." If Judg 2:1–5 is dependent upon Exod 23:20–33, the author has made a rather literal interpretation of the angel's function of admonishing the people (vv. 21–22). It is unlikely that Judg 2:1–5 can be reconciled with the Yahwist's perspective.

The third text that is relevant here is Num 33:50–56 (P). In this passage Moses charges the people to take possession of the land, to dispossess all its inhabitants, and to destroy all their cult objects and places of worship. They are solemnly warned that leaving the task incomplete will have dire consequences. Nothing is said here about Yahweh (D) or the "angel of Yahweh" (J) going before the people to give them victory. Also, the task of dispossessing the inhabitants is closely combined with the process of distributing the land by lot, clearly implying that each tribe is responsible for taking possession of its own allotted inheritance.

The events described in Judg 1:1–2:5 seem to fulfill the threat of dire consequences in Numbers 33. The individual tribes attempt to claim their allotments, but they are only partly successful since many enclaves of indigenous inhabitants remain in the land. This leads to the reprimand by the angel of Yahweh that the people have not been obedient and therefore will [[342]] have to suffer the consequences. It seems reasonable to conclude that Judg 2:1–5 is the work of P. The reference to God establishing his covenant with the fathers "forever" (*lᵉʿôlām*) further confirms this, since it clearly employs P terminology. The suggestion in the admonition that the people also made a covenant with the inhabitants of the land likewise seems to point back to Joshua 9 and the P addition of vv. 14, 15b, 17–21, and 23, where the tribal leaders are clearly culpable for their actions. Finally, descriptions of the people weeping in response to bad news are also found in the testing stories of the wilderness journey, particularly in the P versions (Num 11:4ff.; 14:1). There seems little reason to doubt that Judg 2:1–5 belongs to P, along with chap. 1.[66]

Judges 2:6–16:31

Dtr continues his history in Judg 2:6ff. by moving from the life and activity of Joshua to the time of the judges in such a way as to make Joshua the first judge. He interprets the period of the judges as a cyclic repetition of events in which the people fall away from serving Yahweh to take up the

66. This also means that P was responsible for the repetition of Judg 2:6ff. in Josh 24:28–31 in order to allow for the addition of Judg 1:1–2:5. He also appended the special notices of Josh 24:32–33 at the same time.

worship of the gods of the nations around them. As a result, they are not able to continue their conquests by defeating these nations but instead become oppressed by them or subservient to them. Then, from time to time, Yahweh sends relief through a "judge" or "deliverer," but the people's renewed allegiance to Yahweh during the judge's rule is only temporary: they repeat their old ways after the judge's death, with the result that Yahweh vows not to complete the conquest of the land that was left upon the death of Joshua. Up to this point (2:6–21) the pattern is in agreement with the statements of warning found in Joshua 23. But 2:22–3:4 introduces a new element that is not consistent with what has gone before. It suggests that the remaining nations were intended even before Joshua's death to be a test of Israel's obedience to Yahweh; therefore, the fact that they remain unconquered does not represent a change in the divine plan (vv. 22–23; 3:1a, 4; cf. 2:21).[67] A second reason for the nations to remain in the land was so that the people might practice the arts of war (3:1b–2). Both reasons, which are compatible with each other, give an entirely positive purpose to the presence of the nations and mitigate the notion that they function as a punishment. The list of the nations that [[343]] remain (3:3) corresponds to the geography of the Promised Land as set forth in Josh 13:2–6—a section that we assigned above to P. For this reason I regard 2:22–3:4 as a further addition by P to the deuteronomistic prologue of his history of the judges.[68]

The recognition that Judg 1:1–2:5 and 2:22–3:4 are the work of P puts into perspective the priestly texts on the division of the land in Joshua. P is concerned not only with the ideal dimensions of the Promised Land but also with the problem of why these dimensions were never realized. This problem is considered on two levels. The first has to do with the peoples who remained within the allotted tribal boundaries. These were the responsibility of the tribes, who failed to carry out fully their assignment to dispossess these peoples. Within the larger idealized boundaries, however, were other nations purposely left by God as a means of testing and training for the Israelites. With these additions in Judges, the whole Priestly scheme of the settlement is complete and it is evident that P made no further additions to Dtr's work.[69]

67. See also Deut 7:22 and Exod 23:29–30, where a gradual conquest is suggested but not for the reason stated in Judg 2:23; 3:4. Therefore I cannot agree with Weinfeld's inclusion of 2:22–3:4 within Dtr (1967: 97ff.). The deuteronomistic language in 2:22–23 and 3:4 is borrowed primarily from the immediate context, so its presence is no surprise.

68. Josh 3:5–6 reverts back to the language of Dtr and is the continuation of 2:21, the original deuteronomistic prologue (cf. Weinfeld 1967: 98).

69. But see below, n. 79.

Dtr's introduction in 2:11–21 and 3:5–6 is used as the theological framework by which the various episodes of the "judges" or "saviors" are incorporated into the history. Dtr may speak of his heroes as judges who save the people from their enemies or saviors who judge the people. Efforts to reconstruct a predeuteronomistic "Book of Saviors," whom Dtr only later made into judges, cannot sustain such a distinction between these two uses in the text. The fact is that Dtr could even speak on occasion of the kings of Israel as saviors whom God provided for his people to deliver them from their enemies in response to their cry for help (see 2 Kgs 13:4–5; 14:26–27). Furthermore, we cannot separate the story of the first "savior," Othniel, from Dtr's introduction. The whole account is an artificially constructed model of deliverance made up of elements taken from the introduction with no ancient tradition whatever behind it.[70] The stories of the other judges in the DH are then made to correspond in their introductions and conclusions to this model.[71]

The rest of the stories of the judges or deliverers seem to derive a certain amount of their material from old folk legends, and various attempts have been made to reconstruct their earlier forms in order to reproduce a predeuteronomistic collection.[72] In most cases, however, the framework of Dtr has been so thoroughly integrated into the story itself that it is surely Dtr who is responsible [[344]] for the present collection. This can be seen, for instance, in the story of Ehud. The theological framework—the people's apostasy, the divine handing over of the people into the power of the enemy, their oppression and appeal for help, God's sending of a deliverer—is interwoven with the political background of the story so completely in 3:12–15 that it is difficult to extract an original literary stratum. The same is true for the story of Deborah and Barak, where the theological framework and the narrative setting are completely integrated in the introduction (4:1–4).[73]

In the case of Gideon too the political background to his exploits has been combined with the stereotyped themes of deuteronomistic theology (6:1–6). But, in addition to this, Dtr has introduced the words of a prophet (6:7–10) who recounts the sacred history and issues a warning against the worship of the "gods of the Amorites."[74] This also has an interesting parallel in Samuel's words to the people on the occasion of their

70. See Moore 1895: 84–85; Burney 1930: 64–65. Efforts to salvage some historical kernel in the story have hardly been convincing.

71. See Hoffmann 1980: 272–74.

72. See the studies by Richter 1966.

73. Hoffmann 1980: 273 n. 6.

74. For the deuteronomistic character of this text (contra Richter) see Hoffmann 1980: 275. Hoffmann regards the whole of Judg 6:1–8:35 as a carefully constructed work of Dtr.

election of a king (1 Sam 10:17–29). What happens in both instances is the subsequent divine election of a leader to rescue the people from their enemy.[75]

Gideon is responsible, early in his career, for a cultic reform (6:25–32). The description of pulling down the altar of Baal and cutting down and burning the Asherah so clearly follows the language and prescriptions of Deuteronomy and Dtr that Hoffmann is justified in viewing it as a purely deuteronomistic construction.[76] Later in his career Gideon introduces another cultic change by making an ephod from the golden objects taken in battle. But the ephod led to apostasy by causing the people to "play the harlot after it" so that it "became a snare" to Gideon's family (Judg 8:27). Again the language is thoroughly deuteronomistic and part of Dtr's larger history of cultic reform. Gideon represents a premonarchic example of both positive and negative cultic reform that anticipates the actions of the later kings of Israel and Judah. Further, the story of Gideon concludes with the people's apostasy and judgment (8:33–35), thus completing the cycle of the people's typical behavior as outlined in 2:11ff.

The theological framework introducing the story of Jephthah in 10:6–16 is much more extensive than in the previous stories.[77] Here Dtr elaborates on the theme of Israel's apostasy in the service of foreign gods, which results in Yahweh's anger and the Israelites' subsequent servitude to the Philistines and the Ammonites. Since these two powers dominate Israel's concerns until the time of David, the unit encompasses this larger history as well. Because of this oppression the people cry to Yahweh and in [[345]] response they receive a divine oracle, much as in the case of the prophet's word in 6:8ff. At the same time the unit serves as a recapitulation and reenforcement of the themes of 2:6–21, which again are part of the larger cult history of Dtr.

Yet it would be wrong to view the introduction in 10:6–16 as merely an editorial digression or late addition, for the author is careful in 10:7–9 to set forth the political situation of Ammonite supremacy. This state of affairs is again picked up in 10:17–18, which provides the bridge to Jephthah's election as the people's leader in 11:4ff. Furthermore, the device of narrating negotiations between the two warring parties in 11:12–28 allows Dtr to once again recapitulate the sacred history of the exodus and conquest and to fully integrate the exploits of Jephthah into his history.

In addition to the theological framework, the author, Dtr, also assumes a chronological framework, a forty-year generation of rest from

75. See also *In Search of History,* 250–64.

76. Hoffmann 1980: 275–78.

77. Hoffmann 1980: 280–87. Especially noteworthy are the comparisons that Hoffmann makes with 1 Samuel 12.

war after deliverance by a judge. Within this scheme are periods of various lengths, between the death of one judge and the "raising up" of another, during which the Israelites were under servitude to a foreign power. The analogy for such a chronological scheme is the chronological framework of the monarchy, so that Dtr had his chronological and theological framework for both the judges and the kings. We are reminded here of our earlier discussion of Herodotus and other early Greek historians, who, in the absence of a precise chronology for early Greek history, used an average length of 30, 33⅓, or 40 years per generation to complete their chronology.[78] Ouside the deuteronomistic scheme in Judges, and somewhat in tension with it, are the so-called minor judges of Judg 10:1–5 and 12:8–15. These are secondary and should not be allowed to confuse the pattern.[79] It has also long been recognized that chaps. 17–21 stand outside Dtr's work as later additions. They interrupt the continuity of the work from the time of Samson to the story of Samuel in 1 Samuel 1–7, and they will not be considered any further here.

Dtr created the period of the judges out of his collection of hero stories by suggesting that during this time, between Israel's entrance into the land and the rise of the monarchy, a succession of magistrates ruled the people. Dtr was familiar with a type of magistrate known as a "judge" (*šōpēṭ*), who was more than the one who presided in a court of law. During periods of interregnums some of the Phoenician cities had apparently been governed by a nonhereditary officeholder with this title.[80] The application [[346]] of such an institution to premonarchic Israel may be both anachronistic and artificial, since it presupposes a highly unified state, but it was Dtr's way of trying to come to terms with a little-known period of Israel's history. On the other hand, he made no effort to create any real uniformity among the rather broad diversity of persons who were thought to fill the ranks of the judges of this period, apart from the fact that they act in some way to deliver the people from their enemies—and even this needs qualification in some cases.

It is clear that for Dtr the story of Samson is not really the end of the line of judges, since both Eli and Samuel are to follow. These stories of heroes or deliverers were never intended as a self-contained collection. There would appear to be little point in such a collection since it is not the portrayal of a heroic age, such as we find in Homer. The so-called "prag-

78. See *In Search of History*, 8–18.

79. These additions may be the hand of P. See especially the remarks of Burney 1930: 289–90.

80. Josephus *Ag. Ap.* 1.156ff. See also Moscati 1968: 29, 132–33, 209–10. The fact that two judges were often appointed to one city may explain why both of Samuel's sons were associated with Beersheba (1 Sam 8:1–2).

matic" theme would have little relevance by itself in a later age of the monarchy. The period of the judges could have significance only as part of a larger history, and that larger history of Israel could not be written without the history of the monarchy. The history of the books of Kings is the intellectual prerequisite for the history of the judges. Individual stories about events and persons could exist in the past, but to construe these events as related to each other in both a chronological and an ideological way is to make a conscious effort to write history.

1 Samuel 1–7

The chapters in 1 Samuel 1–7 confront us once again with the question of the nature of Dtr's history. Was the material that he took up largely preformed, or did he extensively reshape the traditions for his own purposes? Is the hand of Dtr evident in only a few minor "redactional" additions, or does the material as a whole conform to his basic thematic concerns? How does this unit function as a bridge between the period of the judges and that of the monarchy?

It is easy to see how the subjects dealt with in these chapters fall into two blocks of material that can then be explained as separate sources or traditions having only a loose connection or secondary integration with each other.[81] One group of stories describes the birth and childhood of Samuel (1 Sam 1:1–2:11, 18–21, 26; 3:1–4:1a) and his career as deliverer and judge (1 Sam 7:3–16). A second set deals with the Ark of Yahweh and the fate of the priests who were in charge of it ⟦347⟧ (1 Sam 2:12–17, 22–25, 27–36; 4:1b–7:2). But these two subjects do not simply come together as two documents compiled and interwoven by an editor. They are not self-contained entities, and a different explanation is needed to understand their relationship to each other.

Let us first consider the story of Samuel. The narrative of Samuel's birth would certainly seem to be appropriate as a pious *vita* ⟦'life'⟧ of a famous holy man, telling about his dedication to Yahweh from birth.[82] The one disturbing detail in this story, however, is the etymology given for his name in v. 20, which appears to derive it from the verb *š'l*, "to ask." This is reinforced by the frequent repetition of the verb in vv. 27–28 and has led scholars to speculate that the birth story was originally about Saul, whose name is in fact derived from the verb *š'l*.[83] But since nothing in the

81. This is now the position of most of the recent commentaries. See Hertzberg 1964; McCarter 1980; Stoebe 1973. Cf., however, the earlier commentaries, such as Smith (1899), where no such division is observed.

82. On the *vita* ⟦'life'⟧ of a holy man, see Rofé 1970: 435–39.

83. Note especially *hû' šā'ûl lᵉyhwh* ⟦'he is loaned to YHWH'⟧, v. 28.

story in any way fits Saul the king, there is no reason to suppose that a tradition about Saul's birth lies behind it.

It seems better to follow McCarter's suggestion, that the author really finds the etymology of the name Samuel (*Šᵉmûʾēl*) in the phrase "from Yahweh" (*mē yhwh*), as if the name meant "the one who is from God" (*še mēʾēl*).[84] Such etymological mistakes and shifts in pronunciation are not at all uncommon in biblical name etiologies. The further play on the verb *šʾl* would then have to do, not with his name, but with his future destiny. The designation of a child's destiny is a common element in such birth stories.[85] Thus it is not necessary to see a connection with a possible Saul tradition.

There is therefore no need to separate Samuel's birth story on any literary or traditio-historical grounds from the subsequent account of his youth. The oath to dedicate Samuel is fulfilled in his subsequent employment under Eli in the temple (1 Sam 2:11, 18–21, 26; 3:1–4:1a). This immediately raises the problem of the relationship of the account of Samuel's boyhood in the temple to the other texts about the sons of Eli. The texts about Samuel, when put together, do not read like an independent source; rather, their interpretation depends heavily upon how one understands this second block of material.

According to L. Rost, the story of the capture and return of the Ark—often called the Ark Narrative—originally existed as a separate document.[86] Rost believes this work included not only 1 Sam 4:1b–7:2 but [[348]] also 2 Samuel 6, which tells of David bringing the Ark into Jerusalem. He considers this document an early source used by the author of the Succession Story, since the latter added 2 Sam 6:16, 20–23 in order to incorporate the Ark Narrative into his own work. For Rost this means that the Ark Narrative must have been a document of the early monarchy, since he dates the Succession Story to the Solomonic era. This early dating has caused any signs of lateness in all subsequent treatments of the Ark Narrative to be judged as editorial additions. In the previous discussion, however, I quest ioned the early dating of the Succession Story, which I called the Court History; this removes the major argument for viewing the Ark Narrative as an early source.[87]

A recent study by P. D. Miller and J. J. M. Roberts poses some serious questions about the limits of the Ark Narrative as defined by Rost.[88] The

84. McCarter 1980: 62.

85. Neff 1970.

86. Rost 1965: 122–59 [[trans.: *The Succession to the Throne of David* (Sheffield: Almond, 1982)]]. Other studies that use Rost's work as a point of departure for their own analysis are: Schicklberger 1973; Campbell 1975.

87. *In Search of History*, 277–91.

88. Miller and Roberts 1977.

basic issue for Miller and Roberts is whether or not the Ark Narrative could simply begin with 1 Sam 4:1b, without prior dependence on, or connection with, what has gone before. They correctly conclude that this cannot be the case. The events recounted in chap. 4 raise the obvious questions of why Israel suffered this great defeat at the hands of the Philistines and why special attention is given to the calamities of the household of Eli. For the reader, these questions have already been answered by the previous descriptions of the impious actions of the priests Hophni and Phinehas (the sons of Eli) in 1 Sam 2:12–27 and 22–25 and the subsequent prediction of disaster upon the household of Eli in 1 Sam 2:27–36.[89] Since the remarks about the sacrilegious behavior of the sons of Eli and the description of their ultimate fate fit so well together, it does not seem persuasive to attribute these two groups of texts to different sources.

The addition of these verses (2:12–17, 22–25, 27–36) to the Ark Narrative, however, does not entirely solve the problem, for some introduction to the figure of Eli is demanded not only by chap. 4 but also by 2:12ff. Miller and Roberts have responded to this problem by suggesting that some additional introductory material has been lost or displaced in the process of connecting the story of the Ark with the story of Samuel.[90] But this explanation seems unnecessarily complicated, since the preceding pericope [[349]] in 1 Sam 1:1–2:11 does provide a suitable introduction to the figure of Eli. In fact, 2:11 leads directly into 2:12. Furthermore, if we put together all the remarks about Eli—his age, his eyesight, his position as seated at the door of the Temple or the gate of the city—we find a remarkable consistency that goes beyond the necessity of redactional integration.[91] The major argument against the unity of the story of Samuel and the Ark Narrative is that Samuel does not figure in the action of 4:1b–7:1. Yet, given the circumstances described in the Ark Narrative, it is hardly suitable to him to have any place in the narrative at this point.

Where the Ark Narrative ends has also become a disputed issue. Rost views 2 Samuel 6 as the climax to the Ark Narrative, but this has recently been questioned by Miller and Roberts.[92] They point to an obvious break in continuity between 1 Sam 7:1 and 2 Sam 6:1, as indicated by a change in the name of the place where the Ark was kept, from Kiriath-jearim to Baalejudah, and a change in the names of those in charge of the Ark, from Eleazar to Uzzah and Ahio (although all three are called sons of Abinadab).

89. McCarter (1980: 26) concurs with the analysis of Miller and Roberts, with the qualification that 2:27–36 is a later deuteronomistic addition. But this has rather serious consequences for the basic thesis of Miller and Roberts, which McCarter too easily ignores.

90. Miller and Roberts 1977: 19. The technique of the "lost beginning" or "lost ending" is a frequently used, but quite dubious, method of literary criticism.

91. See 1:9, 12ff.; 2:22; 3:2; 4:13, 15, 18.

92. Miller and Roberts 1977: 22–26.

The alternative proposed by Miller and Roberts is that the Ark Narrative ends in 1 Sam 7:1. But this hardly seems an adequate ending to the story. The Ark is only temporarily housed, with one consecrated priest in attendance. This scarcely fulfills what they regard as the whole point of the story, the prophecy of the "faithful priest" and his "sure house" who "shall go in and out before my anointed forever" (2:35). This prediction must surely refer to the establishment of an important priestly family to be in charge of the Temple in Jerusalem.[93]

The problem with this debate is the assumption by all these scholars that the Ark Narrative is a self-contained story. If, however, this is no more the case for the end of the story than for the beginning, then the lack of direct continuity between 1 Sam 7:1 and 2 Samuel 6 is no difficulty. The latter text would take for granted that some time had elapsed between the two parts of the story, and this is just what is indicated in 1 Sam 7:2.[94] Furthermore, the similarities between the two parts of the Ark Narrative greatly outweigh the minor differences.

It has already been noted above at several points that the Ark theme played a vital role in the DH beginning with the crossing of the Jordan, which is the first miracle produced by the Ark. This is followed immediately by the conquest of Jericho, which results from the simple procession with the Ark around the city. Then the ark theme disappears from view until the episodes of the Ark Narrative. Immediately following the [[350]] restoration of the Ark and its location in Jerusalem is the divine promise to David, which is closely related to his wish to properly house the Ark in a temple.[95] But the climax for Dtr is not reached until the Ark finds its permanent resting place in the Solomonic Temple.[96] The Ark Narrative is just part of the wider theme of the Ark as the symbol of the divine presence; implicit in the one Ark are the notions of unification and centralization of worship.

It is widely recognized that Dtr often referred to the Ark as the "Ark of the Covenant of Yahweh/God" because he regarded it as the repository of the covenant laws of Deuteronomy.[97] Thus the term is used frequently in Dtr's story of the Jordan crossing along with the more abbreviated forms. When this deuteronomistic designation occurs in 1 Sam 4:3–5, however, it is dismissed as a redactional addition, although it is hard to explain, if this were the case, why this change was not made throughout. From the viewpoint of the story it makes sense to use the longer form at

93. See McCarter 1980: 91–93.
94. Miller and Roberts (1977: 20) regard this text as redactional.
95. 2 Sam 7:1ff.
96. 1 Kings 8.
97. Deut 10:1–5.

the beginning, and especially in conjunction with the Israelites' hope that the presence of the Ark will save them. In enemy territory the Ark would scarcely be recognized as "the Ark of the Covenant." Instead, the phrase "the Ark of the God of Israel" comes to the fore, especially in the months of the Philistines, revealing the author's sensitivity for the appropriateness of the terminology he employs.

Of special interest is the author's designation in 1 Sam 4:4—"the Ark of the Covenant of Yahweh who is enthroned on the cherubim." This designation is similar to the one in 2 Sam 6:2—"the Ark of God, which is called by the name of Yahweh of hosts who is enthroned on the cherubim"—and calls for special comment. The title of God as the one enthroned upon the cherubim is very likely derived from the liturgical tradition and refers to God as king upon the heavenly throne.[98] According to Dtr's description of the Temple, great cherubim were constructed in the holy of holies in such a way that the Ark could be placed under the outstretched wings; together they were regarded as the seat of the deity.[99] Thus Dtr is responsible for the juxtaposition of the Ark as the portable throne of the deity with the symbols of the cherubim and the special divine title of the one "enthroned on the cherubim." Dtr goes further and also associates the "glory," *kābôd*, with the Ark, both in 1 Sam 4:21–22 and in [[351]] the description of the placing of the Ark in the Temple in 1 Kgs 8:11.[100]

Furthermore, once it is admitted that 1 Sam 2:27–36 is part of the Ark Narrative, then the case for Dtr's authorship of the whole becomes very strong indeed.[101] There is no question that the notion of Yahweh's election of his people while they were in Egypt, and the special election of one place out of all the tribes as a place of worship, are deuteronomic themes. Here Dtr adds to these, using the same terminology, the special election of a priestly house. This is not the house of Aaron, of which Dtr knows nothing.[102] Instead it is the priestly office that continued from the time of

98. See Pss 80:2; 91:1; Isa 6:1–2.

99. 1 Kgs 8:6–7. The P version in Exod 25:10–22 seems to have taken the development a step further by actually making the cherubim and the "mercy-seat" a part of the Ark itself.

100. Cf. Isa 6:1–5 with its combination of Yahweh of hosts enthroned as king, winged seraphim, and the "glory."

101. See also McCarter's arguments (1980: 91–93) for Dtr's authorship. On the other hand, the arguments for associating this prediction in 2:27–36 with the outcome of events in chap. 4 are equally convincing. McCarter (1980: 98) is also forced to suggest that 3:11–14 has been revised to accommodate 2:27–36. All these problems would be solved by admitting that chaps. 2–4 were by the same author.

102. The reference to Aaron in Deut 9:20 appears to me to be secondary and presupposes the story in Exodus 32. The unit in Deut 33:48–52, in which the name of Aaron occurs (v. 50), is also secondary. In the rest of Deuteronomy Aaron and a special Aaronic priesthood play no role.

the Exodus through the period of the judges to the very beginning of the monarchy. This original priesthood, like the Davidic monarchy, had been assured a perpetual succession, but now through the disobedience of Eli's sons it is rejected, and the author has the deity declare: "I will raise up for myself a faithful priest, who shall do according to what is in my heart and in my mind; and I will build him a sure house, and he shall go in and out before my anointed forever." The pattern here is exactly the same as that used in the rejection of Saul and the election of David to replace him. It also parallels the promise to David of a "sure house" and clearly refers to the Zadokite priesthood established by David for the service of the Jerusalem Temple. A new era is marked not only by the election of David and the building of the Temple but also by the beginning of a new priestly line.[103] We cannot maintain that this unit contains only a few phrases of deuteronomistic editing. The whole conception suggests the same deuteronomistic hand that we have seen before, the same schematization of history, the same election and rejection dependent upon obedience to the law.[104]

⟦352⟧ If 1 Sam 2:27–36 is indeed the work of Dtr and is part of the larger Ark Narrative as well, then the question of the meaning of the Ark Narrative must be addressed anew. Miller and Roberts are correct in stressing that the Ark Narrative, at least in chaps. 4–6, is primarily concerned with the theological question of whether or not the capture of the Ark as the symbol of the divine presence really signaled the defeat of Yahweh. They bring forward a considerable body of comparative Near Eastern material to suggest that the capture and carrying off of one's gods was a common subject of religious texts among the ancients; such an event called forth a variety of responses, both on the occasions of defeat or victory and when the gods were returned to their rightful owner. From this they argue that the Ark Narrative represents a document written on the occasion of the actual return of the Ark from the hands of the Philistines as portrayed in this account. Yet at this point their argument seems rather

103. The notion of beggar priests (Levites), 2:36, who were disinherited, coming to the Jerusalem priesthood for employment is a direct allusion to the consequences of the Josiah reform. See also McCarter 1980: 93.

104. The reference in 1 Kgs 2:27, on the other hand, does not belong to Dtr but to the later Court History, as I have argued above (*In Search of History*, 277–91). The connection of Abiathar with the house of Eli is a weak one and may be entirely artificial and of late polemical intent. The genealogical line is traced back through 1 Sam 22:20 and 14:3, but this last reference is rather curious, because only by identifying Ahitub as Ichabod's brother is the line traced back to Eli. Yet why was it necessary to mention Ichabod at all, since the latter must have been a younger brother to Ahitub, if we are to believe this statement? The connection of Ahitub with the priestly family of Eli looks forced indeed, but it is hard to say who was responsible for it. It probably grew out of the postexilic controversies over priestly authority.

weak, especially since they exclude 2 Samuel 6 from consideration. It is difficult to believe that the occasion for the Ark Narrative may be found in the remarks about the return of the Ark to its temporary lodging in the house of Abinadab and to see in Eleazar the "faithful priest" (1 Sam 7:1; cf. 2:35).

Once the story is seen in its larger deuteronomistic context, however, another major concern immediately comes to mind—the exile. It is precisely at this time that "the glory has been *exiled* from Israel" (1 Sam 4:21, 22).[105] What happened to the Ark at the time of the fall of Jerusalem is unknown, but there is no reason to doubt that it was part of the booty taken from the Temple. Yet the larger question that was being addressed in this story about an earlier capture of the Ark was whether the deity was now subject to the foreign gods or still in control of the affairs of men. In somewhat different, though related, ways, Dtr and Ezekiel answer this question by affirming the latter.

This brings us to a consideration of 1 Sam 7:3–17.[106] This pericope, as we have it, presupposes the prior introduction of Samuel in the previous chapters. It also takes for granted that the Israelites have suffered defeat and are subservient to the Philistines, and that "all the house of Israel lamented after Yahweh" (7:2). This last verse is not just a transition to a new unit but a necessary introduction to what follows. In this chapter [[353]] Samuel fulfills the twofold role of prophet and deliverer-judge. In his capacity as prophet, he preaches to the people in Dtr's style to repent from their worship of foreign gods and to serve Yahweh alone, as in the prologue of Judges. In his role as deliverer-judge, Samuel rescues the people from the hand of the Philistines.[107] One cannot fail to see that Samuel is being presented as the last of the victorious judges who was able to subdue the enemy and bring peace to the Israelites during his period of office.[108] The victory at Ebenezer also provides a contrast to the earlier

105. The notion of the "glory" of Yahweh leaving the Temple and going into exile is also strong in Ezekiel 8–10.

106. Noth (1943: 54ff. [[= *Deuteronomistic History*, 76ff.]]) has identified this chapter as substantially the work of Dtr. Some recent studies have attempted to find some older traditional material within it. See Weiser 1962: 5–24; Birch 1976: 11–21.

107. Samuel's role in battle is not unlike Joshua's, especially in Joshua 10, where the victory is won through the prayer of the leader.

108. There is admittedly some inconsistency between 7:13 and the later suggestions of Philistine domination in chaps. 9ff. But 7:13 is so obviously stated in terms of the deuteronomistic formula that its lateness can hardly be doubted. The pattern of judgeships being quite separate from each other, as in Judges, breaks down with Eli, Samuel, and the careers of Saul and David. The pattern has thus been made to fit material that was not entirely suitable for it. The author (Dtr) really regards the "days of Samuel" as closed at the end of chap. 7 but must have a new situation of need to account for the rise of Saul.

Israelite defeat there, and so properly completes this series of episodes. At the same time Samuel's career brings to a close the era of the judges, since the story of Samuel would have followed from the end of Samson's career in Judges 16.[109]

1 Samuel 1–7 is the work of Dtr combining two themes, the story of Samuel and the Ark Narrative. These were never independent documents, and it is scarcely possible, in my view, to recover earlier stages in the tradition of these themes, if they ever existed. The way they are presented, however, provides not only a continuity with the age of the judges but also a strong link between the age of Moses/Joshua on the one hand and David/Solomon on the other, with the Ark serving as the primary connection. This means that we can affirm Noth's basic thesis that one continuous history runs through the period from Moses to the end of the monarchy.

109. I do not think that we can speak of 1 Samuel 7 as a prophetic story that has been supplemented and reworked by Dtr (see McCarter 1980: 149ff.). I find no evidence of an earlier stratum distinct from the work of Dtr, and unless this can be demonstrated more convincingly, I view it all as the work of Dtr.

Bibliography

Birch, B. C.

1976 *The Rise of the Israelite Monarchy: The Growth and Development of 1 Samuel 7–15*. Missoula, Montana.

Burney, C. F.

1930 *The Book of Judges, with Introduction and Notes*. 2d ed. London.

Campbell, A. F.

1975 *The Ark Narrative (1 Sam. 4–6; 2 Sam. 6): A Form-Critical and Traditio-Historical Study*. Society of Biblical Literature Dissertation Series 16. Missoula, Montana.

Childs, B. S.

1967 Deuteronomic Formulae of the Exodus Traditions. Pp. 30–39 in *Hebräische Wortforschung: Festschrift Walter Baumgartner*. Vetus Testamentum Supplements 16. Leiden.

1970 Traditio-Historical Study of the Reed Sea Tradition. *Vetus Testamentum* 20: 406–18.

Coats, G. W.

1969 The Song of the Sea. *Catholic Biblical Quarterly* 31: 1–17.

1967 The Traditio-Historical Character of the Reed Sea Motif. *Vetus Testamentum* 17: 253–65.

1972 The Wilderness Itinerary. *Catholic Biblical Quarterly* 34: 135–52.

Cross, F. M.

1973 *Canaanite Myth and Hebrew Epic: Essays in the History of the Religion of Israel.* Cambridge.

Geus, C. H. J. de

1966 Richteren 1:1–2:5. *Vox Theologica* 36: 32–53.

Hayes, J. H., and Miller, J. M. (eds.)

1977 *Israelite and Judaean History.* London.

Hertzberg, H. W.

1964 *I & II Samuel.* Philadelphia.

Hoffmann, H.-D.

1980 *Reform und Reformen: Untersuchungen zu einen Grundthema der deuteronomistischen Geschichtsschreibung.* Abhandlungen zur Theologie des Alten und Neuen Testaments 66. Zurich.

Holladay, J. S., Jr.

1968 The Day(s) the Moon Stood Still. *Journal of Biblical Literature* 87: 166–78.

McCarter, P. K.

1980 *1 Samuel.* Anchor Bible 8. Garden City, New York.

McCarthy, D. J.

1971 An Installation Genre? *Journal of Biblical Literature* 90: 31–41.

McEvenue, S. E.

1971 *The Narrative Style of the Priestly Writer.* Analecta Biblica 50. Rome.

Miller, P. D. Jr., and Roberts, J. J. M.

1977 *The Hand of the Lord: A Reassessment of the "Ark Narrative" of 1 Samuel.* Baltimore and London.

Moore, G. F.

1895 *A Critical and Exegetical Commentary on Judges.* International Critical Commentary. New York.

Moscati, S.

1968 *The World of Phoenicians.* London.

Mowinckel, S.

1964 *Tetrateuch-Pentateuch-Hexateuch: Die Berichte über die Landnahme in den drei altisraelitischen Geschichtswerken.* Beihefte zur Zeitschrift für die Alttestamentlich Wissenschaft 90. Berlin and New York.

Neff, R.

1970 The Birth and Election of Isaac in the Priestly Tradition. *Biblical Research* 15: 5–18.

Noth, M.

1971 *Das Buch Josua.* Handbuch zum Alten Testament 7. 3d ed. Tübingen.

1943 *Überlieferungsgeschichtliche Studien.* Tübingen. Partly translated as *The Deuteronomistic History.* Journal for the Study of the Old Testament Supplement Series 15. Sheffield, 1981.

Perlitt, L.

1969 *Bundestheologie im Alten Testament*. Wissenschaftliche Monographien zum Alten und Neuen Testament 36. Neukirchen-Vluyn.

Rad, G. von

1949 Hexateuch oder Pentateuch? *Verkündigung und Forschung* 1–2: 52–56.

1966 *The Problem of the Hexateuch and Other Essays*. Translated by E. W. Dicken. Edinburgh and London.

Radjawane, A. N.

1973–74 Das deuteronomistiche Geschichtswerk: Ein Forschungsbericht. *Theologische Rundschau* 38: 177–216.

Richter, W.

1966 *Traditionsgeschichtliche Untersuchungen zum Richterbuch*. Bonner biblische Beiträge 18. Bonn.

Rofé, A.

1970 The Classification of the Prophetical Stories. *Journal of Biblical Literature* 89: 427–40.

Rose, M.

1981 *Deuteronomist und Jahwist: Untersuchungen zu den Berührungspunkten beider Literaturwerke*. Abhandlungen zur Theologie des Alten und Neuen Testaments 67. Zurich.

Rost, L.

1965 Pp. 119–253 in *Das kleine Credo und andere Studien zum Alten Testament*. Heidelberg. Reprint of *Die Überlieferung von der Thronnachfolge Davids*. Beiträge zur Wissenschaft vom Alten und Neuen Testament 3/6. Stuttgart, 1926.

Schicklberger, F.

1973 *Die Ladeerzählung des ersten Samuelbuches: Eine literaturwissenschaftliche und theologiegeschichtliche Untersuchung*. Forschung zur Bibel 7. Würzburg.

Schmid, H. H.

1976 *Der sogenannte Jahwist: Beobachtungen und Fragen zur Pentateuchforschung*.

Schmitt, H.-C.

1980 *Die nichtpriesterliche Josephsgeschichte: Ein Beitrag zur neuesten Pentateuchkritik*. Beihefte zur Zeitschrift zür die Alttestamentliche Wissenschaft 154. Berlin and New York.

Smend, R.

1972 Das Gesetz und die Völker: Ein Beitrag zur deuteronomistischen Redaktionsgeschichte. Pp. 494–509 in *Probleme biblischer Theologie: Festschrift Gerhard von Rad*, edited by H. W. Wolff. Munich.

Smith, H. P.

1899 *The Books of Samuel*. International Critical Commentary. Edinburgh.

Soggin, J. A.

1972 *Joshua*. London.

Stoebe, H.-J.

1973 *Das erste Buch Samuelis*. Kommentar zum Alten Testament 8/1. Gütersloh.

Van Seters, J.
1972 The Terms "Amorite" and "Hittite" in the Old Testament. *Vetus Testamentum* 22: 64–81.
1975 *Abraham in History and Tradition*. New Haven and London.
1979 Recent Studies on the Pentateuch: A Crisis in Method. *Journal of the American Oriental Society* 99: 663–73.

Vink, J. G.
1969 *The Date and Origin of the Priestly Code in the Old Testament*. Oudtestamentische Studiën 15. Leiden.

Vorländer, H.
1978 *Die Entstehungszeit des jehowistischen Geschichtswerkes*. Europäische Hochschulschriften 13/109. Frankfurt.

Ward, J. M.
1969 Amos and Isaiah: Prophets of the Word of God. New York and Nashville.

Weinfeld, M.
1967 The Period of the Conquest and of the Judges as Seen by the Earlier and the Later Sources. *Vetus Testamentum* 17: 93–113.

Weippert, M.
1972 "Heiliger Krieg" in Israel und Assyrien: Kritische Anmerkungen zu Gerhard von Rads Konzept des "Heiligen Krieges im alten Israel." *Zeitschrift für die Alttestamenliche Wissenschaft* 84: 460–93.

Weiser, A.
1962 *Samuel: Seine geschichtliche Aufgabe und religiöse Bedeutung.* Forschungen zur Religion und Literatur des Alten und Neuen Testaments 81. Göttingen.

Wüst, M.
1975 *Untersuchungen zu den siedlungsgeographischen Texten des Alten Testaments, I: Ostjordanland.* Beihefte zum Tübinger Atlas des Vorderen Orients B/9. Wiesbaden.

Joshua 24 Re-examined

S. David Sperling

Joshua 24 is a controversial text in the debate about the DH. Its covenantal subject matter focuses the question of the role of the Deuteronomist in the creation of the parts of the history books. A number of modern writers have treated it as a deuteronomistic invention, placed at the end of the narrative of the conquest, in line with the deuteronomistic habit of marking important transitions with reports of covenantal acts. This approach goes back to Noth, and the article itself takes issue with the work of L. Perlitt and J. Van Seters (see pp. 218–20 in this volume), who date the chapter respectively to the Assyrian crisis and the exile. The alternative point of view on the chapter is represented by W. T. Koopmans, *Joshua 24 as Poetic Narrative* (JSOTSup 93; Sheffield: Sheffield Academic Press, 1990), who argues that it derives from a genuine covenant tradition at Shechem.

Sperling also thinks Joshua 24 recalls a covenant tradition at Shechem in which Yahweh became the God of the covenant with Israel (cf. Judg 9:4, 46). He argues that it is a unified work that is neither deuteronomistic nor derived directly from any Pentateuchal source. In a linguistic and stylistic analysis he shows that much of the language of Joshua 24 is not paralleled in Deuteronomy. Similarities with expressions on the ninth-century Mesha stele argue that the date of the chapter may be earlier than is often thought.

Sperling successfully highlights the difficulty of reducing individual texts to conformity with deuteronomistic patterns. Especially he shows

Reprinted with permission from *Hebrew Union College Annual* 58 (1987) 119–36.

Author's note: An earlier form of this paper was presented to the May 14, 1986 meeting of the Columbia University Seminar on the Hebrew Bible. I wish to thank the seminar members for their many helpful suggestions. I am especially grateful for the oral and written comments of Professors Morton Smith of Columbia and Murray Lichtenstein of Hunter College.

that the characterization of language and style as deuteronomistic is complex. His argument may sometimes overstate the individuality of the present chapter. It might be balanced by the observation that language resembling that of Dtr is found rather broadly in the treaty tradition, which is a slightly different angle on the argument (see K. A. Kitchen, "Ancient Orient, 'Deuteronomism,' and the Old Testament," in *New Perspectives on the Old Testament* (ed. J. B. Payne; Waco, Tex.: Word, 1970) 1–19, especially 16–19).

[[119]] The scholarly literature on Joshua 24 is voluminous. The chapter has been studied from the viewpoints of classical source criticism, form criticism, and tradition-history, but little consensus has emerged with regard to its authorship, the date of its composition, the antiquity of its traditions, its *Sitz im Leben* [['life setting']] or its historical value.[1] The present paper was written primarily in response to the analysis of Joshua 24 by Lothar Perlitt in his *Bundestheologie*[2] and the recent paper by John Van Seters in the Ahlström Festschrift.[3]

On the basis of his literary analysis, Perlitt attributes Joshua 24 to the Deuteronomist and traces its historical background to the Assyrian crisis of the seventh century. In contrast, it will be argued here that (a) Joshua 24:1–28[4] [[120]] is a unified literary work by a single author who is not to be identified with the Deuteronomist or any other Pentateuchal source;[5] (b) that author was able to utilize the sources of the Pentateuch and other parts of the Bible and at the same time to deviate from them for literary or ideological purposes; (c) the author of Joshua 24 differed with the Pentateuchal sources as well as with traditions preserved elsewhere in the Bible on significant points of history and ideology; (d) Joshua 24 preserves

1. For bibliography to 1970, see J. Soggin, *Joshua* (Philadelphia: Westminster, 1972) 222–23; and Y. Kaufmann, *Sepher Yehoshua* (Jerusalem: Kiryat Sepher, 1970) 248–56. Recent relevant studies include F. Cross, *Canaanite Myth and Hebrew Epic* (Cambridge: Harvard, 1973) 84, n. 15; A. van Selms, "Temporary Henotheism," in *Symbolae Biblicae et Mesopotamicae Francisco Mario Theodoro de Liagre Böhl Dedicatae*, (eds.) M. Beek and A. Kampen (Leiden: Brill, 1973) 341–48; D. McCarthy, *Treaty and Covenant* (Rome: Biblical Institute, 1978) 221–42, 279–84; R. Boling and G. E. Wright, *Joshua* (AB; Garden City, N.Y.: Doubleday, 1982) 527–45.

2. L. Perlitt, *Bundestheologie im Alten Testament* (Neukirchen-Vluyn: Neukirchener, 1969) 239–84.

3. J. Van Seters, "Joshua 24 and the Problem of Tradition in the Old Testament," in *In the Shelter of Elyon: Essays on Ancient Palestinian Life and Literature in Honor of G. W. Ahlström* (JSOTSup 31; Sheffield: JSOT, 1984) 139–58.

4. For the treatment of vv. 1–28 as the extant literary unit, see M. Noth, *Das Buch Josua* (2d ed.; HAT; Tübingen: Mohr, 1953) 135–40; Kaufman, op. cit., 248–55; H. W. Hertzberg, *Die Bücher Josua, Richter, Ruth* (ATD; Göttingen: Vandenhoeck & Ruprecht, 1959) 131–38; McCarthy, *Treaty*, 221–34.

5. Cf. Kaufmann, op. cit., 248.

pre-monarchic Shechemite traditions[6] but was written sometime in the eighth century before the fall of Samaria.

The setting of Joshua 24 is Shechem,[7] a city not connected with the conquest traditions of the books of Joshua and Judges. Joshua has summoned all of Israel to stand before God (האלהים). In their presence he relates the story of Israel's ancestors who "lived beyond the river . . . and served other gods."[8] Joshua speaks of Jacob's descent into Egypt, the dispatch of Moses and Aaron, the striking of Egypt, the drowning of the Egyptian army in the darkness, the sojourn in the wilderness, the conquest of Transjordan, the battle with Balaq aided by Balaam the curser,[9] the crossing of the Jordan, the battle at Jericho, the dispatch of the צרעה [['hornet']],[10] and God's gift of the land.

[[121]] After completing the narration, Joshua turns to the people, admonishing them to remove the "foreign gods" and serve Yahweh exclusively. He notes that they have the option of serving other gods if they do not wish to serve Yahweh. He and his household however will serve Yahweh. The people then affirm that they too will serve Yahweh. Joshua then warns them that Yahweh's service is "impossible" because as a jealous god Yahweh will not forgive them if they "sin in their rebelliousness" and serve the "foreign gods." The people protest that they are prepared to

6. On Shechemite traditions in general, see E. Nielsen, *Shechem, A Traditio-Historical Investigation* (Copenhagen: Gad, 1969); on the city itself, see E. Campbell, "Shechem (City)," *IDBSup*, 821–22; cf. idem, "Judges 9 and Biblical Archaeology," in *The Word of the Lord Shall Go Forth: Essays in Honor of David Noel Freedman in Celebration of his Sixtieth Birthday*, (eds.) C. Meyers and M. O'Connor (Winona Lake, Ind.: Eisenbrauns, 1983) 263–71.

7. LXX reads 'Shiloh' in v. 1 and v. 25. The Greek reading is secondary. 'Shiloh' may be an attempt at harmonization with 18:1 or the result of a later anti-Samaritan bias. See Nielsen, op. cit., 18:1; Boling, op. cit., 533.

8. The "other gods" of v. 2 recurs in v. 17. In vv. 20 and 22 they are replaced by "foreign gods." For the alternation of אחר 'other' and נכר 'foreign', cf. Exod 34:14 and Ps 81:10.

9. The reference to Balaam and Balaq is not significant for dating. The Deir ʿAllā texts show that Balaam was a character of folklore, who like Gilgamesh or Aḥiqar was popular in more than one culture. For recent studies of the Deir ʿAllā Balaam material with bibliography, see J. Hackett, *The Balaam Text from Deir ʿAllā* (Chico, Calif.: Scholars Press, 1984); A. Lemaire, "Les inscriptions de Deir ʿAllā et la littérature araméenne antique," *CRAIBL* (1985) 270–85. The reference in Mic 6:5 to Balaam and Balaq as ancient figures who would be known to Micah's listeners is probably older than the Deir ʿAllā text. According to Lemaire ("Deir ʿAllā," 272–73), the Deir ʿAllā text dates from ca. 750 B.C.E. but is based on an original a century or two older.

10. Aside from Joshua 24, צרעה is attested only in Exod 23:28 and in Deut 7:20 which is derived from it. On the relation between these passages, cf. G. Schmitt, *Du sollst keinen Frieden schliessen mit den Bewohnern des Landes* (BWANT; Stuttgart: Kohlhammer, 1970) 17–20. The traditional translation of צרעה as 'hornet' is supported by an Egyptian pun in an early text. See J. Wilson in *ANET* 477, n. 36. For a recent attempt to explain the significance of the צרעה, see O. Borowski, "The Identity of the Biblical *ṣirʿâ*," in *Essays Freedman*, 315–19.

serve Yahweh and to bear their own witness to their choice. Once the people have agreed to abandon all the "foreign gods," Joshua makes a covenant on their behalf. There in Shechem he provides them with a fixed rule. All these matters, he sets down in writing in a document of God's teaching (ספר תורת אלהים). Finally, Joshua erects a large stone under the oak in Yahweh's sanctuary which he designates as witness to Yahweh's words to the people.

The structural unity of Josh 24:1–28 is most obvious in the rhetorical progression of Joshua's argument. Speaking in Yahweh's name in the manner of a prophet,[11] Joshua begins with a recital of the *magnalia dei* ⟦'great acts of God'⟧ performed on the people's behalf. Inasmuch as Yahweh has always aided his people, fought for them, and given them unearned victories and unworked for prosperity, they must serve Yahweh alone and remove all other objects of worship. In 24:15 Joshua gives the people a "choice" of worshipping the gods "beyond the river" (left behind by their ancestors) or the local gods (whose people were delivered into Israelite hands). Here, Joshua of necessity speaks for himself and not Yahweh asserting that he and his household will serve Yahweh. The people respond appropriately, virtually summarizing the long account of Yahweh's saving acts. Joshua eggs on the people by telling them that they cannot possibly serve Yahweh, thus making His exclusive worship a goal to be attained. He is then able to reiterate the demand of v. 14 to remove all the other gods and to bring about the people's compliance. The actions of covenant and its accompaniments follow.

The logical structure of Joshua's rhetoric is heightened by the repetition of key words and phrases. Not surprisingly the name Yahweh ⟦122⟧ occurs eighteen times.[12] Forms of אלהים ⟦'God'⟧ occur sixteen times.[13] The verb עבד 'worshipped' also occurs sixteen times.[14] Other significantly repeated words are forms of אב 'ancestor' (eight times),[15] עבר 'crossed/ across' (seven times),[16] מצרים 'Egypt/Egyptians' (seven times),[17] ישב 'dwelt' (six times),[18] נתן 'gave, granted' (six times),[19] and שלח 'sent' (four times).[20] In addition, Giblin's important study has demonstrated how the

11. Kaufmann, *Yehoshua*, 251, terms the entire chapter "a prophetic story"; cf. McCarthy, *Treaty*, 239 and Van Seters, "Joshua 24," 147.

12. Verses 2, 7, 14^2, 15^2, 16, 17, 18^2, 19, 20, 21, 22, 23, 24, 26, 27.

13. Verses 1, 2^2, 14, 15^2, 16, 17, 18, 19, 20, 23^2, 24, 26, 27.

14. Verses 2, 14^3, 15^4, 16, 18, 19, 20, 21, 22, 24, 31.

15. Verses 2^3, 3, 6^2, 14, 15.

16. Verses 2, 3, 8, 11, 14, 15, 17.

17. Verses 4, 5, 6, 7^2, 14, 17.

18. Verses 2, 7, 8, 13, 15, 18.

19. Verses 3, 4^2, 8, 11, 13.

20. Verses 5, 9, 12, 28.

placement of significant words and the repetition of grammatical forms serve to tighten the structure of the chapter.[21]

When Perlitt wrote in 1969, he noted the great variety of earlier opinion regarding the source identification of Joshua 24,[22] but made the generally accurate observation that recent scholars, even those who maintained the antiquity of its traditions, acknowledged its deuteronomic/deuteronomistic language.[23] Proceeding from this literary 'consensus',[24] Perlitt attempted to show that the historical circumstances underlying the chapter fit the seventh century only.[25] More recently, John Van Seters has correctly noted that Perlitt's historical argument is flawed.[26] For his part, Van Seters[27] identifies the author of Joshua 24 with the Yahwist of the Pentateuch, whom he dates to the Exilic Period.[28] Our study begins therefore with a detailed analysis of the language of the chapter.[29]

24:1: As Nielsen[30] and Hertzberg[31] have noted, the leadership elements [[123]] enumerated here are characteristic of Deuteronomy. The phrase ויתיצבו לפני האלהים 'they stood themselves before God' is unique. Its closest parallel is התיצבו לפני יהוה 'stand yourselves before Yahweh' in 1 Sam 10:19.

24:2: בעבר הנהר 'beyond the river' recurs in vv. 14–15. From the Syro-Palestinian perspective, the expression means 'east of the Euphrates'. Cf. 2 Sam 10:16, 1 Kgs 14:15.[32] The claim that Israel's ancestors were 'settled beyond the river' contradicts Deut 26:5 in which the unnamed ancestor of Israel was a 'wandering[33] Aramean' whose ultimate origin was unknown.

21. C. Giblin, "Structural Patterns in Joshua 24:1–25," *CBQ* 26 (1964) 50–69; cf. Boling, *Joshua*, 533.

22. Perlitt, *Bundestheologie*, 238; cf. Nielsen, *Shechem*, 90–92.

23. Perlitt, ibid., 239; Kaufmann, *Yehoshua*, 248, whose work was not consulted by Perlitt, calls the writer of Joshua 24 "an independent author, writing in an archaic style containing linguistic ingredients from various 'sources'."

24. McCarthy refers to "the rather uncritical assumption that the text is Dtistic." See *Treaty*, 283, cf. ibid., 221–34.

25. See below.

26. Van Seters, "Joshua 24," 145–46; cf. my comments to v. 2 below.

27. Van Seters, ibid., 149.

28. Van Seters, ibid., 153.

29. The method followed here is similar to McCarthy's (*Treaty*, 221–34), whose treatment of the language is much less detailed.

30. Nielsen, *Shechem*, 79, 87.

31. Hertzberg, *Josua*, 133.

32. Cf. L. Toombs, "Beyond the River," *IDB* 1.405–6.

33. 'Fugitive' may be a better translation. Borger (BAL, 3.114) has compared Sennacherib's characterization of Marduk-Apla-Iddina as *aramê ḫalqu munnabtu* 'fugitive Aramaean runaway' (OIP 242 v 22); cf. G. Mendenhall, *The Tenth Generation* (Baltimore: Johns Hopkins, 1973) 137.

Perlitt makes much of this geographic datum: "Von jenseits des Stromes droht Israel Lebensgefahr! Jenseits des Stromes aber leben die Assyrer, deren Götter hier und heute mitten in Israel zur Anbetung aufgestellt sind. Dafür kommt nur eine Zeit in Betracht: die des 7 Jh.s, und das ist die Zeit, in und aus deren religiösen Nöten die dt Predigt erwuchs" ⟦'From beyond the river, mortal danger threatens Israel. But beyond the river dwell the Assyrians, whose gods have been set up for worship here and today in the midst of Israel. For this, only one time is possible–namely, the seventh century, and that is the time in–and out of–whose religious crises the deuteronomic paranesis developed'⟧.[34] There are a number of problems with this analysis. First, the danger from Assyria was not limited to the seventh century. Assyria's first incursion into Israelite territory was in the ninth century and continued for the next two.[35] Second, were Perlitt correct, some reference to the fall of Samaria, however veiled, would be expected. Third, Joshua 24 does not refer to any "mortal danger" from "beyond the river." Mortal danger, described in vague terms, comes from Yahweh if one chooses to worship gods from that region, or any other, along with Him (v. 20). Fourth, there is no evidence that Assyria demanded the adoration of its gods in its conquered or tributary territories.[36] In בעבר הנהר ישבו אבותיכם מעולם 'your ancestors had always dwelt beyond the river', the term מעולם ⟦'always]" connotes antiquity and permanence.[37] The closest ⟦124⟧ parallel[38] to this verse is in the ninth century Mesha inscription (KAI 181:10): ואש גד ישב בארץ עטרת מעלם 'the Gadites had lived in the land of Ataroth from of old'.

תרח אבי אברהם ואבי נחור 'Teraḥ, father of Abraham and father of Naḥor'. Neither the name Teraḥ, nor the name Naḥor is mentioned in Deuteronomy.

34. Perlitt, *Bundestheologie*, 251.

35. See P. Machinist, "Assyria and Its Image in the First Isaiah," *JAOS* 103 (1983) 720–21.

36. See M. Cogan, *Imperialism and Religion* (Missoula, Mont.: Scholars Press, 1974); cf. Van Seters, "Joshua 24," 146.

37. West-Semitic *ʿlm* is semantically equivalent to Akkadian *dārû* 'everlasting'. (For references to *dārû*, see *CAD D*, 115). Cf. Phoenician *šmš ʿlm* 'eternal sun', Ugaritic *špš ʿlm* and Amarna *šamaš darītum* 'from of old' attested at Amarna and Boghazköy (see *CAD D*, 114b) prove the antiquity of West-Semitic *mʿlm*. See also S. Gevirtz, "West-Semitic Curses and the Problem of the Origin of Hebrew Law," *VT* 11 (1961) 143 and n. 5; idem, "On Canaanite Rhetoric: The Evidence of the Amarna Letters from Tyre," *Or* 42 (1973) 177; H. Tawil, "Some Literary Elements in the Opening Sections of the Hadad, Zakir, and the Nerab II Inscriptions in the Light of East and West Semitic Royal Inscriptions," *Or* 43 (1974) 42, n. 10; F. Bron, *Recherches sur les inscriptions phéniciennes de Karatepe* (Geneva: Droz, 1979) 187–88.

38. 1 Sam 27:8 may be parallel. Note however that NJV a.1. translates מעולם as 'from the region of Olam'.

ויעבדו אלהים אחרים 'they served other gods'.[39] No other biblical tradition says explicitly that the immigration of Israel's ancestors was responsible for their rejection of the foreign gods and their adoption of Yahweh worship. According to J, Yahweh had been worshipped everywhere from earliest times.[40] In consequence, Abraham's departure from Haran did not represent a departure from previous religious practice. According to P, the god known to Abraham as *El Shaddai* was not distinct from Yahweh whose name was revealed first to Moses.[41]

בכל ארץ כנען 'in all of Canaan-land'. כל ארץ כנען occurs only in Gen 17:8 (P) but is not distinctive. Cf. Amarna *māt kinaḫḫi gabbaša* (EA 162:41).

וארב את זרעו 'I made his offspring numerous'. Cf. Gen 16:10, 22:17; Exod 32:13; Jer 33:22.

24:4: ואתן לעשו את הר שעיר לרשת אותו 'I gave Mt. Seir to Esau as his inheritance'. For the thought, cf. Deut 2:5. The closest linguistic parallels, however, are Lev 20:24 and Num 33:53.

24:5: ואשלח את משה ואת אהרן 'I sent Moses and Aaron'. Cf. the early tradition in Mic 6:4 and the late one in Ps 105:26. In Deuteronomy nothing is said of Aaron's mission. He is recalled only in connection with Yahweh's anger against him (9:20) and his death (10:6, 32:50).

ואגף את מצרים 'I struck Egypt'. The verb נגף [['strike']] appears in Deuteronomy only in the *nifʿal.*[42] Deuteronomy does not employ נגף for the smiting of the Egyptians, preferring instead the 'mighty hand' (6:21), accompanied [[125]] by the 'outstretched arm' (11:3, 26:8). The phrasing here is closest to Exod 7:27, 12:23.

כאשר עשיתי בקרבו 'as I did in its midst'. As Nielsen has noted, this looks like an abbreviation.[43] Cf. Exod 3:20, 10:1; Num 14:11.

ואחר הוצאתי אתכם 'then afterwards I brought you out'. The construction ואחר + verb immediately following does not occur in Deuteronomy. Cf. Deut 21:13 with Lev 14:8.

39. The notice about the service of other gods led later Jewish tradition to depict Teraḥ as the proprietor of an idol shop and Abraham as an idol smasher. Cf. L. Ginzberg, *The Legends of the Jews* (Philadelphia: Jewish Publication Society, 1937) 1.213–17; cf. Nielsen, *Shechem*, 87.

40. See Gen 4:1, 26.

41. See Gen 17:1; Exod 6:2–3. For a recent survey and discussion of the different modern theories about religion in the patriarchal narratives, see G. Wenham, "The Religion of the Patriarchs," in *Essays of the Patriarchal Narratives*, (eds.) A. Millard and D. Wiseman (Winona Lake, Ind.: Eisenbrauns, 1983) 161–95; to the bibliography add J. Van Seters, "The Religion of the Patriarchs in Genesis," *Biblica* 61 (1980) 220–23.

42. Deut 1:42; 28:7, 25.

43. *Shechem*, 88. He does, however, not rule out its originality.

24:7: ויצעקו אל יהוה 'they[44] cried out to Yahweh'. Cf. Exod 14:10.

וישם מאפל 'he put darkness'. This form of the word for 'darkness' occurs nowhere else in the Bible. In its version of this event Exod 14:19–20 refers to עמוד הענן 'the cloud-pillar' and הענן והחשך 'the dark cloud'. Deut 11:4 makes no mention of the darkness.

ויבא עליו את הים ויכסהו 'he brought the sea over him, covering him'. There is no exact parallel, but cf. Exod 15:10, Ps 78:53. Deut 11:4 has the interesting reading: הציף את מי ים סוף על פניהם 'He caused the water of the Red Sea to overflow them'.

ותראינה עיניכם את אשר עשיתי במצרים 'Your own eyes beheld what I did to Egypt'. The closest parallels are Exod 19:4, Deut 29:1.

ימים רבים 'many days'. The figure may be indeterminate. Cf. Deut 1:46, 2:1, and see Driver, *Deuteronomy*, 31–34. It is possible however that the writer is referring to the ancient forty-year wilderness tradition (Amos 2:10). In the Mesha stele the ימן רבן 'many days' (KAI 181:5) during which Omri humbled Moab are equivalent to the ארבען שת 'forty years' during which he occupied Medeba (KAI 181:8).

24:8: ואביאה אתכם אל ארץ האמרי היושב בעבר הירדן 'I brought you to the land of the Amorite who dwells on the far side of the Jordan'. Amos 2:9, 10 refer to the conquest of ארץ האמרי 'land of the Amorite' as a well-known tradition. According to Nielsen, "the word אמרי does not appear in any *ancient* [*emphasis his*—SDS] tradition"[45] about the Transjordanians. [[126]] Nielsen believes that אמרי [['Amorite']] was applied secondarily "to the Transjordanian population as a consequence of the policy of the house of Joseph, from the period of Judges until the kingdom of Jeroboam II, and more probably in the latter."[46] But see Num 32:39, Judg 10:8. J. Van Seters holds a more extreme view: "it is very difficult to date any Old Testament

44. In vv. 6–7 there is an alternation between third person (ancestors) and second person (present generation). Van Seters ("Joshua 24," 147) claims that "this is not a feature of early prophecy so that one must conclude that it is a special feature of the Dtr tradition." Naturally, this requires him (ibid., 157) to assign a late date to Amos 2:4:

על מאסם את תורת יהוה וחקיו לא שמרו ויתעום כזביהם אשר הלכו אבותם אחריהם.

[['Because they rejected the law of the Lord and did not keep his statutes, but have been led astray by the lies which their ancestors followed.']]

The late dating of Amos 2:4 is in agreement with a number of other scholars who assign the verse to the Dtr redaction of Amos. See, e.g., J. L. Mays, *Amos, A Commentary* (Philadelphia: Westminster, 1969) 40–42. It must be noted however that the similar כי מאסו את תורת יהוה צבאות [['for they have rejected the law of the Lord of Hosts']] occurs in Isa 5:24 and that כזב and תעה are unattested in Deuteronomy. But even if we grant the lateness of Amos 2:4, this so-called "special feature" of alternation between third person (ancestors) and second person (present generation) is found in Amos 2:6–15 and very prominent in Hosea 12–13.

45. Nielsen, *Shechem*, 94, n. 3.

46. Ibid.

source which uses the term 'Amorite' . . . for inhabitants of Palestine before the eighth century B.C."[47] Biblical sources, argues Van Seters, were influenced by the term *amurrû* 'Westerner' in cuneiform sources which began in the early eighth century to employ *amurrû* for "the kingdoms of Syria . . . Palestine, including Phoenicia, Israel, Moab, Ammon, Edom and the Philistine cities."[48] It must be replied first that the fluidity of Akkadian *amurrû* is much earlier than the eighth century;[49] that the use of biblical אמרי, however fluid, does not designate the same groups as Akkadian *amurrû*;[50] that it is unlikely that Hebrew writers learned from outsiders how to apply their own local designation.

וילחמו אתכם ⟨שני מלכי האמרי⟩ '⟨The two Amorite kings⟩[51] did battle with you'. The reference to the two Amorite kings must be moved here from v. 12 where it is difficult syntactically and contextually. The two kings are not named, in contrast to Josh 2:10; 9:10; 12:2, 4, 5; 13:10, 12, 21, 27.

ותירשו את ארצם 'you took possession of their land'. Cf. Moabite: וירש עמרי את כ[ל אר]ץ מהדבא 'Omri had taken possession of all Medeba-[La]nd' (KAI 181:7–8).

ואשמידם מפניכם 'I destroyed them on your behalf'. The phrase is very similar to Amos' description of the destruction of the Amorites (2:9). [[127]]

24:9–10: Mic 6:5 cites an exchange between Balaq, King of Moab, and Balaam, son of Beor, as a familiar tradition but mentions no battle between Israel and Moab. The narrative of Judg 11:25 explicitly says that Balaq did not engage Israel in battle. Accordingly, both differ with Josh 24:9–10. There is some linguistic resemblance between Josh 24:9–10 and Deut 23:5 which refers to Balaam as being called on to 'curse' קלל Israel

47. J. Van Seters, "The Terms 'Amorite' and 'Hittite' in the Old Testament," *VT* 22 (1972) 81.

48. Ibid., 66.

49. See *AHw*, 46a; *CAD A/2*, 93–95. There is a similar fluidity in early Egyptian sources. Rameses II, in a text ca. 1296 speaks of "the shore in the land of Amurru" with reference to the Phoenician coast. See *ANET*, 256, n. 9; contrast Van Seters, "Amorite," 65.

50. Note, for example, that Phoenicia and Edom are never called 'Amorite' in the Bible and that biblical 'Amorite' never means 'Westerner'. On the problems involved in the relation between the Hebrew and Akkadian terms, see N. Tur-Sinai, *The Language and the Book: Beliefs and Doctrines* [Hebrew] (Jerusalem: Bialik Institute, 1955) 134–39; H. Huffmon, "Amorites," *IDBSup*, 20–21; J. Luke, " 'Your Father was an Amorite' (Ezek 16:3, 45): An Essay on the Amorite Problem in OT Traditions," in *The Quest for the Kingdom of God: Studies in Honor of George E. Mendenhall*, (eds.) H. Huffmon and A. Green (Winona Lake, Ind.: Eisenbrauns, 1983) 221–37; A. Altman, "The Original Meaning of the Name Amurru 'Ha'emori'," in *Studies in Hebrew and Semitic Languages Dedicated to the Memory of Professor Eduard Yechezkel Kutscher*, (eds.) G. Sarfati and P. Artzi (Ramat-Gan: Bar-Ilan, 1980) 76–102 [Hebrew; English summary, lx].

51. LXX to v. 12 refers to 'twelve Amorite kings'.

and to Yahweh's (lack of) 'desire' אבה to comply. Nonetheless the phrase ויברך ברוך [['so he blessed (you) insistently']] is unique to Joshua 24. At the same time the derivative character of Deut 23:5 is apparent because the Deuteronomist cites the episode as a legal precedent to justify the exclusion of Ammonites and Moabites from the Israelite community.

וישלח ויקרא ל . . . 'he sent a call for . . . '. Not distinctive. Cf., e.g., Gen 27:42; Judg 4:6, 16:18.

24:11: וילחמו בכם בעלי יריחו 'the inhabitants of Jericho did battle with you'. The battle with the Jerichonians contradicts the narrative of chap. 6, which, as Soggin has noted, has "a completely ritual context [in which] there is hardly room for any kind of military action."[52]

בעלי יריחו 'the inhabitants of Jericho'. The plural of בעל for inhabitants of a place is confined to the books of Judges and Samuel. See, e.g., Judges 9 (passim); 1 Sam 23:11, 12; 2 Sam 21:12. There is a similar use in late Phoenician texts. See KAI 3:5. Deuteronomy employs **ישבי העיר** [['the inhabitants of the city']] (13:16), and **אנשי עירו** [['the men of his city']] (Deut 21:21, 22:21).

The list of the seven nations is apparently a gloss designed to mitigate the contradiction between the beginning of v. 11 and the tradition of chap. 6. It may be noted, however, that the sequence "Amorite, Perizzite and Canaanite" is unique.[53]

24:12: ואשלח לפניכם את הצרעה ותגרש אותם מפניכם 'I sent the hornet ahead of you and it drove them out before you'. Structurally this verse resembles Exod 23:28: ושלחתי את הצרעה לפניך וגרשה את . . . מלפניך [['And I will send the hornet ahead of you, and it will drive out . . . before you']]. The **צרעה** [['hornet']] is also mentioned in Deut 7:20. The idiom **גרש מפני** 'drove out before' recurs in v. 18. McCarthy correctly describes **גרש** as "un-Dtistic."[54] See, e.g., Exod 34:11; Judg 2:3. Once again there is a ninth century Moabite parallel: **ויגרשה כמש מפני** 'Chemosh drove him out before me' (KAI 181:19).

לא בחרבך ולא בקשתך 'Not by your sword nor by your bow'. The hendiadys 'sword and bow' means 'warfare'. Cf. Gen 48:22; 2 Kgs 6:22. [[128]]

24:13: ארץ אשר לא יגעת בה 'a land for which you did not toil'. The phrase is unique. But see, e.g., Isa 62:8; Ps 6:7.

וערים אשר לא בניתם ותשבו בהם כרמים וזיתים אשר לא נטעתם אתם אכלים '(I have given you) cities which you inhabit although you did not build them. You enjoy olive groves and vineyards which you did not plant'.

52. J. Soggin, "The Conquest of Jericho through Battle," *ErIsr* 16 (1982) *215.

53. The order differs in the versions. See Nielsen, *Shechem*, 89.

54. McCarthy, *Treaty*, 232. In Deuteronomy גרש 'expel' appears only in 33:27, in a poetic chapter whose relation to the rest of the book is questionable. Deuteronomy prefers forms of ירש [['dispossess']]. See, e.g., Deut 11:23; 12:2, 29; 18:14; 19:1.

This verse has a close parallel in Deut 6:10–11: והיה כי יביאך יהוה אלהיך אל הארץ אשר נשבע לאבתיך אברהם ליצחק וליעקב לתת לך ערים גדלת וטבות אשר לא בנית. ובתים מלאים כל טוב אשר לא מלאת וברת חצובים אשר לא חצבת כרמים וזיתים אשר לא נטעת ואכלת ושבעת. 'When Yahweh your god brings you into the land which He swore to your ancestors Abraham, Isaac, and Jacob to give you great prosperous cities which you did not build, and houses filled with every delight which you did not fill, and hewn cisterns[55] which you did not hew, and you enjoy to satiety olive groves and vineyards which you did not plant . . . '.

The Joshua passage is obviously primary. In Josh 24:13 the "land" and "cities" are the objects of ואתן [['And I gave']]. In Deut 6:10–11, the "cities" and "houses" stand without a governing verb (לתת [['to give']] complements נשבע [['he swore']]). In addition, Deuteronomy explicitly assigns the promises to the Patriarchs. The primacy of Joshua 24 is also reflected in its realistic picture of a victorious force occupying the territory of the defeated. This picture is elaborated by the Deuteronomist, who describes the cities as great and prosperous, populated with houses which are filled with delights and which contain private cisterns. The Israelites do not merely eat, but eat to satiety. The Deuteronomist apparently employed Joshua's words as part of Moses' prophetic warning.

24:14: ועתה יראו את יהוה 'Now then, fear Yahweh'. Cf. 1 Sam 12:24; Ps 34:10.

ועבדו אתו בתמים ובאמת 'and serve Him with wholehearted devotion'. The phrase occurs nowhere else. The pair is attested in reverse order in Judg 9:16, 19, likewise set in Shechem. In deuteronomic language the concept of wholehearted devotion is expressed by בכל לבבכ[ם] ובכל נפשכ[ם] [['with all your heart and with all your soul']]. See Deut 6:5, 11:13.

והסירו את אלהים אשר עבדו אבותיכם בעבר הנהר ובמצרים 'and remove the gods your ancestors served beyond the river and in Egypt.'[56] Cf. v. 23 below. [[129]] For similar removals of offending gods, see Gen 35:3; Judg

55. For these private cisterns, cf. Isa 36:16. Cf. also Moabite: ואמר לכל העם עשו לכם אש בר בביתה 'So I said to the entire people: Each of you make a cistern for yourselves in your own home' (KAI 181:24–25).

56. Pace Nielsen (*Shechem*, 102) and Van Seters ("Joshua 24," 149), there are no explicit statements in Joshua 24 that Israel served Egyptian gods in Egypt. Verse 14 refers to Israel's persistence in the service of its ancestral gods in Egypt. In v. 15 Joshua tells the people to choose between the ancestral gods from beyond the river and the local Amorite gods if they do not approve of Yahweh's service. The writer of the chapter believes that Joshua's contemporaries might continue in the service of their ancestral gods and that they might be drawn to the service of the local gods, but that they presumably would not be tempted to serve the gods of those who put them in the 'slave house' (v. 17). It was the Deuteronomist who first suggested that Israel might be tempted to worship the gods of Egypt (Deut 29:15–17). He was followed by Ezek 20:5–8 which explicitly attributes the worship of Egyptian gods to Israel in Egypt.

10:16; 1 Sam 7:3–4. A. van Selms refers to this action as "temporary henotheism" and cites parallel phenomena in other Near Eastern cultures.[57]

24:15: בחרו לכם היום את מי תעבדון 'choose now whom you will serve'. In Deuteronomy it is Yahweh who chooses, not the people. See Deut 4:37; 7:6, 7; 10:15; 14:2. For the people choosing gods, see Judg 5:8, 10:14; Isa 1:29.

היום 'now, right away, presently'. The form is common in Deuteronomy. See, e.g., Deut 1:10, 39; 4:4, 8; 5:1. It is also well attested elsewhere. See, e.g., Gen 19:37, 21:26, 22:14, 24:12, 30:32, 42:13, 47:23; Exod 2:18, 13:4; Lev 9:4; Judg 21:6.

אלהי האמרי אשר אתם ישבים בארצם 'the gods of the Amorite in whose land you dwell'.[58] Cf. Judg 6:10.

ואנכי וביתי נעבד את יהוה 'but I and my household shall serve Yahweh'. The phrase is unique.

24:16: חלילה לנו מעזב את יהוה 'far be it from us to forsake Yahweh'. The word חלילה [['far be it']] does not occur in Deuteronomy.

24:17: כי יהוה אלהינו הוא המעלה אתנו ואת אבתינו מארץ מצרים 'for Yahweh our god is the one who brought us and our ancestors up out of the land of Egypt'. The verb העלה 'brought up' is found in exodus traditions of all periods. For early examples, see Amos 2:10, 3:1, 9:7; Hos 12:14; Mic 6:4. Cf. Gen 50:24; Exod 32:4, 7, 8; 33:1; Lev 11:45; Num 14:13, 20:5; Deut 20:1; Judg 6:13; 1 Sam 12:6; 1 Kgs 12:28; 2 Kgs 17:36; Jer 16:14–15; Ps 81:11; Neh 9:18.

בית עבדים 'slave-house'. The term occurs in the Bible in texts of all [[130]] periods as an epithet of Egypt. See, e.g., Exod 13:3, 14; 20:2; Deut 5:6, 7:8, 13:6; Judg 6:8; Jer 34:13; Mic 6:4.

וישמרנו בכל הדרך אשר הלכנו בה 'who protected us throughout our entire journey'. Cf. Gen 28:20. See further Exod 18:20; Deut 1:31.

24:19: לא תוכלו לעבד את יהוה 'you will be unable to serve Yahweh'. The statement is unique.[59]

57. A. van Selms, "Temporary Henotheism," in M. Beck and A. Kampman et al. (eds.), *Symbolae Biblicae et Mesopotamicae Francisco Mario Theodoro de Liagre Böhl Dedicatae* (Leiden: E. J. Brill, 1973) 341–48. As far as the author of Joshua 24 was concerned, the removal of the foreign gods was supposed to be permanent. Most Israelites apparently accepted the notion that it was sinful to worship other gods in the presence of Yahweh (Exod 20:3). At the same time, however, the priesthood taught that all sins could be expunged (Lev 16:30). In consequence, it was popularly believed that a (temporarily) reformed thief, murderer, adulterer, liar under oath, or Baal worshipper could participate in the cult with a clear conscience. See Jer 7:9–10.

58. 'Amorite' clearly refers to the earlier Cisjordanian population as it does in v. 18. See Kaufmann, *Yehoshua*, 253, 254. The 'gods of the Amorite' are the Baals and Astartes. See O. Eissfeldt, "El and Yahweh," *JSS* 1 (1956) 31.

59. The notion is completely incompatible with the thinking of the Deuteronomist. See McCarthy, *Treaty*, 229, 240.

אלהים קדשים הוא 'He is a holy god'. The plural קדשים [['holy']] with אלהים [['god']] in reference to Yahweh is unique. It is more at home in polytheistic language. Cf. Dan 4:5, 6, 15.

אל קנוא הוא 'He is a jealous god'. The closest parallel in Nah 1:2. Cf. Exod 20:5, 34:14; Deut 5:9, 6:15.

לא ישא לפשעכם ולחטאותיכם 'He will not forgive your sins of rebelliousness'. For the language, cf. Gen 50:17; Exod 23:21, 34:7. The singular פשעכם [['your rebellions']] in hendiadys with חטאותיכם [['your sins']] is to be understood adjectivally. It must be emphasized that although פשע is already attested in Ugaritic[60] and very frequently in biblical Hebrew, it does not occur in Deuteronomy.[61]

24:20: ושב והרע לכם 'He will turn and do you harm'. The phrase is unique. For the construction, see Deut 23:14, 30:3; 1 Kgs 8:47; Isa 6:10, 12; Jer 18:4; Mic 7:9; Mal 3:18; Ps 78:34.[62]

וכלה אתכם 'he shall destroy you'. The verb כלה 'destroy, annihilate' occurs in all periods of Hebrew and is attested earlier as *kly*, in the same sense, in Ugaritic.[63] The threat is general and lacking in specific historical allusions.

אחרי אשר היטיב לכם 'after having dealt kindly with you'. For אחרי אשר [['after']] see Deut 24:4; Josh 7:8, 9:16, 23:1; Judg 11:36, 19:23; 2 Sam 19:31. For the thought of the passage, cf. Deut 28:63.

24:21: לא כי את יהוה נעבד 'Not so! We shall serve Yahweh'. For examples of the emphatic denial לא כי see Gen 19:2; Josh 5:14; 1 Sam 12:12; 1 Kgs 3:22.

24:22: עדים אתם בכם . . . ויאמרו עדים 'You are your own witnesses. . . . They replied, "We are."'[64] Cf. 1 Sam 12:5; see also Ruth 4:11. [[131]]

24:23: ועתה הסירו את אלהי הנכר אשר בקרבכם 'now remove those foreign gods that are among you'. Cf. v. 4 above; Gen 35:2–4; Judg 10:16; 1 Sam 7:3–4.[65]

60. CTA 17:VI: 83 // *gʾan* [['pride']]. The virtually identical parallelism is attested in Ben Sira. See Y. Avishur, *Stylistic Studies of Word-Pairs in Biblical and Ancient Semitic Languages* (Neukirchen: Neukirchener, 1984) 409–10.

61. This observation also argues against Perlitt's assignment of Hos 8:1b to the "dtr redigierten Hoseabuch [['the deuteronomistically redacted Book of Hosea']] (*Bundestheologie*, 147).

62. There are similar constructions in Akkadian and post-biblical Hebrew. See D. Sperling, "Late Hebrew *ḥzr* and Akkadian *saḫāru* [['turn']]," *JANES* 5 (1973) 404.

63. See J. Patton, *apud* Avishur, *Word-Pairs*, 46.

64. So, Hertzberg, *Josua*, 132, and see below at v. 27.

65. On the relation between the demand for removing the foreign gods in Joshua 24 and Gen 35:2–4, see A. Alt, "Die Wallfahrt von Sichem nach Bethel," in A. Alt, *Kleine Schriften zur Geschichte des Volkes Israel* (Munich: Beck, 1953) 1.79–89. Outside of Joshua 24, the demanded removal of the foreign gods is followed by an explicit statement of compliance. In Joshua 24, in contrast, that notice is absent because it is the only case in which the demand is not connected to a military threat. It appears that the writers of these other pericopes

והטו את לבבכם אל יהוה אלהי ישראל 'direct your heart to Yahweh, god of Israel'.[66] Despite the many attestations of לבב [['heart']] in Deuteronomy the idiom הטה לבב אל does not appear there. Deut 32:46 has שימו לבבכם אל for 'turning toward'. 'Turning/directing the heart (away)' is expressed by סור (Deut 17:20. The parallel in 1 Kgs 11:2–4 has הטה [['direct']]), and פנה [['turn']] (Deut 29:17).

24:24: את יהוה אלהינו נעבד ובקולו נשמע 'We shall serve Yahweh our god and obey Him'. The closest parallel is 1 Sam 12:14. For the reverse sequence of שמע בקול [['obey']] and עבד [['serve']], see Deut 13:5.

24:25: ויכרת יהושע ברית לעם ביום ההוא 'On that day Joshua made a covenant for the people'. Although כרת ברית ל־ [['make a covenant for']] has several meanings,[67] the appropriate sense here is 'in behalf of'.[68] Cf. Hos 2:20. Joshua acts as mediator in behalf of the people. He himself requires no covenant because he is already committed to Yahweh's service.

וישם לו חק ומשפט בשכם 'He established a fixed rule for them at Shechem'. See 1 Sam 30:25; cf. Exod 15:25; Ps 81:5; Ezra 7:10.[69] The hendiadys חק ומשפט [['statute and law']] is not attested in Deuteronomy. [[132]]

24:26: ויכתב יהושע את הדברים האלה בספר תורת אלהים 'Joshua wrote these words down in a document[70] **of God's teaching'.**[71] The expression ספר

---

wanted to demonstrate that obedience to the call for the physical removal of competing deities in wartime would result in Yahweh's full military cooperation.

66. Cf. Gen 33:20; see Noth, *Josua*, 139. The repetition of 'Yahweh, god of Israel' from v. 2 serves to frame the words of Joshua and the people and to provide a transition to the next series of actions.

67. Perlitt, *Bundestheologie*, 261–62.

68. L. Koehler, "Problems in the Study of the Language of the Old Testament," *JSS* 1 (1956) 4; cf. Soggin, *Joshua*, 225. The לעם [['for the people']] is balanced by לו [['for them']] in the next phrase. Both mean 'for, in behalf of'.

69. As Perlitt notes (*Bundestheologie*, 268, n. 3), in the first three passages חק ומשפט [['statute and law']] refers to a specific custom; 1 Sam 30:25 to spoils division; Exod 15:25 to water purification; and Ps 81:5 to sounding the ram's horn. In Ezra 7:10, however, חק ומשפט seems to have a more general sense of 'statutes and decrees' somehow associated with the written תורת יהוה [['law of Yahweh']] referred to in the same verse. Perlitt argues from the proximity of ספר תורת אלהים [['the book of the law of God']] in Josh 24:26 that חק ומשפט in v. 25 carries a meaning similar to חק ומשפט in Ezra 7:10, thus reflecting late usage. It is, however, much more natural to understand חק ומשפט in Josh 24:25 as a reference to the specific action of covenant making in the same verse. See NIV and Boling (*Joshua*, 529) a.1. In addition, the MT of Ezra 7:10 is uncertain. Both LXX and Peshitta indicate a plural חקים ומשפטים, which unlike חק ומשפט, is well attested in Deuteronomy (e.g., Deut 4:5, 8, 13; 5:1; 6:1; 7:11; 11:32; 12:1) and a sure sign of Deuteronomy's influence elsewhere. See, e.g., 2 Kgs 17:37; Mal 3:22.

70. *Spr* is the common West Semitic word for 'document'. For comparisons, see Y. Muffs, *Studies in the Aramaic Legal Papyri from Elephantine* (Leiden: Brill, 1969) 207. In biblical Hebrew ספר [['book']] can refer to a written document of any length. See Gen 5:1; Num 5:23; Deut 24:1; Josh 1:8; 2 Kgs 5:5, 22:8; Isa 29:11; Jer 32:11.

71. On the differences among MT, Peshitta, and LXX with regard to ספר תורת אלהים, see Nielsen, *Shechem*, 108.

תורת אלהים [['the book of the law of God']] occurs only here. The similar ספר תורת האלהים is found in Neh 8:18.[72] It is difficult to determine whether ספר תורת אלהים refers to an already existing document to which Joshua added or whether his record constituted that ספר תורת אלהים.[73] The Peshitta to this passage reflects the reading: ספר תורת משה [['the book of the law of Moses']]. Inasmuch as the historical summary earlier in the chapter makes no mention of Moses as lawgiver, it is likely that the Peshitta's reading was influenced by the better attested ספר תורת משה of Josh 8:31, 32; 23:6. No mention is made of the disposition of the document such as we might have expected from a comparison with 1 Sam 10:25 and similar passages.

ויקח אבן גדולה ויקימה תחת האלה במקדש יהוה 'he took a large stone[74] and stood it up at the foot of that oak[75] which is in Yahweh's sanctuary'. Joshua's action violates Deuteronomy's prohibition against dedicating standing stones (Deut 16:22). In addition, the Deuteronomist prohibits trees in the Yahweh sanctuaries.[76] [[133]]

24:27: הנה האבן הזאת תהיה בנו לעדה כי היא שמעה את כל אמרי יהוה והיתה בכם לעדה פן תכחשו באלהיכם 'This stone then shall be a witness in our midst for it has heard all of Yahweh's words. Indeed it will witness against you should you deny your god'. This is a pun on עד ב־ 'witness to' (see, e.g., 1 Sam 12:5) and עד ב־ 'witness against' (e.g., Num 5:13). For the stone as

72. Cf. Neh 8:8; 9:3. Neither the expression תורת אלהים [['the law of God']], nor the concept of written divine תורה are significant for dating. For early examples see Isa 1:10; Hos 4:6, 8:12. Perlitt (*Bundestheologie*, 270) takes ספר תורת אלהים as proof of the lateness of Josh 24:26 because it employs terminology similar to Neh 8:8, 9:3. Perlitt understands that usage to reflect the conceptions of Deuteronomy and those works composed under its influence. He is surely correct with regard to Nehemiah but in that book much more than the phrase ספר תורת אלהים is involved. The Nehemiah references are to some form of the Pentateuch, i.e., the same document referred to in Neh 8:1 as ספר תורת משה 'the book of the Law of Moses'; in Neh 8:2, 9 as התורה 'the Law', and in Neh 8:3 as ספר התורה 'the Book of the Law'. Unlike the author of Joshua 24, the writer of Nehemiah 8–9 describes the public reading of divine תורה. His heroes, however, do not write in that תורה or write a תורת אלהים of their own.

73. In either case, Joshua's action would be opposed to the ideology of Deuteronomy (4:2, 13:1) which views its teachings as complete and unalterable. Early Jewish sources attempted to resolve the contradiction. See Kaufmann, *Yehoshua*, 254, n. 7; note the Targum's translation: 'He secreted them in the Torah-book'.

74. The excavations at Shechem uncovered a great standing stone and its socket in the forecourt of the temple precinct there dated 1450–1100 B.C. See the discussion by E. Campbell, "Judges 9 and Biblical Archeology," in *Essays Freedman*, 263–71.

75. Cf. Gen 12:6, 35:4; Judg 9:6.

76. Deut 15:21. The medieval Jewish commentators were troubled by Joshua's violation of this law and attempted to mitigate the difficulty. The Targum, for example, translated אלה [['oak']] by Aramaic אלתא 'doorpost'. In contrast, Rashi and Qimḥi explained that Shechem had acquired temporary sanctity by serving as host to the Ark. As such, it could accurately be called a מקדש [['sanctuary']] without housing an altar.

witness, see Gen 31:52. The phrase אמרי יהוה [['words of Yahweh']] is unique. It must also be noted that the verb כחש does not occur in Deuteronomy in the sense 'deny'.[77]

24:28: וישלח יהושע את העם איש לנחלתו 'Joshua then dismissed the people, all of them, to their allotted portions'. Cf. the dismissal of the people in 1 Sam 10:25. For the expression איש לנחלתו [['to their allotted portions']], see Judg 2:6, 21:24; Jer 12:15. The writer of Judg 2:6ff. borrowed this verse in order to begin his tale of the people's infidelity after Joshua's death.

This detailed study of words, expressions and grammatical constructions in Josh 24:1–28 leads to the conclusion that Perlitt's attempt to link Joshua 24 to Deuteronomy on linguistic grounds has virtually no basis. The language of the chapter is not deuteronomic or deuteronomistic. Aside from the tribal leadership terminology of v. 1, in those passages in which genuine resemblances to Deuteronomy were observed, it was shown that the Deuteronomist was the borrower. Other elements were seen to have parallels in Deuteronomy as well as in other parts of the Bible and therefore are not distinctive. Indeed, several parallels to the ninth century Moabite inscription of King Mesha were noted. At the same time, we have found no words, phrases, grammatical constructions, or historical allusions which indicate a date later than the eighth century B.C.E.[78]

In his recent article, John Van Seters makes some observations on the form of Joshua 24, arguing that it is based on the deuteronomistic parenesis. He begins by citing similarities to 1 Sam 10:17ff. which also contains the formula "Thus says Yahweh, the God of Israel," and noting that it is followed by a (very brief) recital of saving history, which in turn is followed by Samuel's rebuke (v. 19) that the people have rejected Yahweh. But as Van Seters himself remarks, the order of elements in 1 Samuel 10 is not the same as in Joshua 24.[79] We may add that Joshua 24 in [[134]] contrast to 1 Samuel 10, contains no rebuke nor does it call for an array of Israel according to its tribal elements. In sum, 1 Samuel 10 and Joshua 24 share the motifs of divine speech and recital of sacred history. But these are also combined in prophetic speeches uninfluenced by the deuteronomistic parenesis such as Hos 12:1–13:10, Amos 6:1–5, and Mic 6:1–8.

To prove that 1 Sam 10:7f. is "thoroughly" deuteronomistic Van Seters compares that passage to Judg 6:8–10 which "contains the prophetic

77. The verb כחש in Deut 33:29 is probably related to post-biblical כחש 'was weak/meager'. For references, see Jastrow, 629a.

78. According to Campbell, "Shechem," 821. Shechem was continuously occupied from ca. 1000 B.C.E. until it suffered a major destruction in 724. Joshua 24 is set in a flourishing Shechem oblivious to any impending doom.

79. Van Seters, "Joshua 24," 146.

speech: 'Thus says Yahweh the God of Israel,' followed by a summation of the salvation history and a divine admonition against worshipping the 'gods of the Amorites in whose land you dwell.'" But as Van Seters himself observes, this pericope differs from both Joshua 24 and 1 Samuel 10 in lacking an assembly.[80]

Van Seters then turns for further proof to 1 Sam 12:7ff. "where a convocation is presupposed." Samuel calls on the people to "take their stand before Yahweh and then recounts to them God's acts of deliverance towards them and their forefathers. At the end of this is a warning against disobedience and disloyalty."[81] Van Seters is certainly correct to compare Joshua 24 with the Samuel pericope but that section is generally considered to belong to the early stratum of the Book of Samuel.[82]

According to Van Seters, all of the above texts and Joshua 24 are dependent on the deuteronomistic parenesis: "It is not just a question of some vague prophetic influence. . . . This reference back to the fathers, whether in terms of what God has done for them or how they sinned against Yahweh by serving other gods and the consequences for the present generation addressed in the second person by prophet or speaker, is found most frequently in Dtr preaching."[83] Indeed, Van Seters is correct with regard to frequency, but frequency does not mean invention. The technique is already found in Hosea[84] and Amos.[85]

Believing that he has demonstrated that the form of Josh 24:1–27, is derived from the deuteronomic parenesis, Van Seters turns to the contents of its historical summary. He draws the questionable inference that the historical summary in Joshua 24 must be "later than all the Dtr examples"[86] because it is so elaborate, and observes that vv. 24:2–13 depart radically in matters of detail from the deuteronomistic tradition [[135]] and agree substantially with the Yahwistic source of the Pentateuch. In consequence, Van Seters concludes, "the author of Josh 24:1–27 is none other than the Yahwist of the Pentateuch," whose work was composed during the exilic period as an addition to the Deuteronomic History.[87]

The exilic dating leads Van Seters to understand Joshua 24 as reflective of exilic concerns. The people assembled at Shechem are no longer a nation but simply individual households who are bidden to follow Joshua's

80. Ibid., 147.
81. Ibid.
82. See N. Gottwald, "Samuel, Book of," *EncJud* 14.792.
83. Van Seters, op. cit., 147.
84. See Hos 9:10–17, 10:9–13:10.
85. Amos 2:6–15. Cf. n. 44 above.
86. Van Seters, op. cit., 148.
87. Ibid., 149.

example. The references to the foreign gods must also be understood in this vein. "The theological crisis of the exile meant that the Jews in these regions of the diaspora were sorely tempted to worship the gods of these regions."[88]

We cannot enter here into the literary-critical problems involved in dating the Yahwist[89] and must be content with the following observations. First, that Jews, and earlier, Israelites, were tempted to serve other gods is no indication of date. Unless Yehezkel Kaufmann was correct in his radical view that biblical descriptions of Israel's worship of other gods than Yahweh are merely prophetic exaggerations,[90] there was always a "theological crisis" in Israelite Canaan. Second, there is an important ideological difference between the J source of the Pentateuch and Joshua 24. According to J, Yahweh worship was instituted during the first human generation.[91] Joshua 24 in contrast, and specifically that section which Van Seters views as the contribution of the Yahwist to the Deuteronomic History,[92] connects Yahweh worship with Abraham's immigration to Canaan. This tradition, by the way, would seem to be a bad lesson for the exile. Why cite a precedent which justifies the worship of the gods of the nations in the lands of the nations?[93] Third, Joshua 24 makes no reference to any earlier covenant or law associated with Moses at Sinai, Horeb, or the plains of Moab. In the exilic period, why stress a [[136]] covenant made in the land? A far better lesson for the exiles would have been the Horeb or Sinai covenant traditions in which Israel bound itself exclusively to Yahweh outside of Canaan. Fourth, the covenant to serve Yahweh alone is a monolatrous, not monotheistic, notion.[94] The consistent monotheism which began to assert itself in the exilic period preferred different religious imagery.[95]

88. Ibid., 153. Note, however, that the gods of the Amorites are local, the ancestral gods are traditional, and the gods of the Egyptians are not mentioned. In sum, the gods of the diaspora regions are not the concern of Joshua 24.

89. For a recent discussion with bibliography see W. Schmidt, "A Theologian of the Solomonic Era? A Plea for the Yahwist," in *Studies in the Period of David and Solomon and Other Essays*, (ed.) T. Ishida (Winona Lake, Ind.: Eisenbrauns, 1982) 55–73.

90. Y. Kaufmann, *The Religion of Israel* (Chicago: University of Chicago Press, 1960); for a recent critique see D. Sperling, "Israel's Religion in the Ancient Near East," in *Jewish Spirituality from the Bible to the Middle Ages*, (ed.) A. Green (New York: Crossroad, 1986) 16–21.

91. See n. 40 above.

92. Van Seters, op. cit., 148.

93. Note that Jeremiah's adversaries in Jer 44:17 justify their worship of the Queen of Heaven by citing ancestral precedent.

94. See Sperling, op. cit., 16.

95. See my forthcoming monograph, *No Other Gods*. [[The projected volume did not appear. But see the author's *The Original Torah: the Political Intent of the Bible's Writers* (New York: New York University Press, 1998) 61–74.]]

Joshua 24 clearly does not fit the conditions of the exile. At the other extreme, the chapter cannot be contemporary with the events it describes because it accepts the fall of Jericho to the Israelites as a real event and views Joshua as a full-fledged leader of all Israel. These traditions would have taken some time to develop. In addition, it seems as though the author of Joshua 24 had access to the JE literature in some form.[96]

By combining our analysis with the results of earlier scholarship and with what is known about Shechem from biblical and extra-biblical sources, we may draw certain conclusions about the dating of the chapter: Shechem was an important city with ancient religious traditions dating back well into the second millennium. The Israelites reinterpreted those traditions in the light of their own historical, mythical and cultic traditions. It is well known that the worship of a god El/Baal Berith is attested at Shechem. Joshua 24 is based on an early northern Israelite reinterpretation of that tradition in which Yahweh, the god of the exodus, became the covenant-god at Shechem.[97] The language of Joshua 24, however, points to the ninth–eighth centuries and this agrees with the historical perspective of the chapter. The people live in peace and comfort. We have noted that destruction is threatened only in general terms and that there is no reference to exile. The historical setting fits nicely with the conventional dating of JE as earlier than D. In consequence, we would date the composition of Joshua 24 to a period early in the long and prosperous reign of Jeroboam II (ca. 786–746).

96. See the Pentateuchal citations in the detailed comments above. There are no specific indications that the author of Joshua 24 had access to P.

97. See McCarthy, *Treaty*, 222.

Part 3

Samuel, Kings

The Apology of David

P. Kyle McCarter, Jr.

Much of historical-critical scholarship is concerned with isolating the sources used by biblical writers. In this study, McCarter explores the original setting and function of one of the sources thought to be embedded in the book of Samuel: "the history of David's rise." McCarter thinks that the limits of this source extended from 1 Sam 16:14 to 2 Sam 5:10*. The material in these chapters recounts in great, and in some cases graphic, detail Saul's tragic demise, David and Jonathan's friendship, Saul's persecution of David, and David's accession to the throne. Based upon a comparison with a Hittite historiographical document, entitled by modern scholars the "Apology of Ḫattušili," McCarter is inclined to see the occasion for 1 Sam 16:14–2 Sam 5:10* in terms analogous to those for the composition of this Hittite work. The history of David's rise or, in McCarter's terms, the apology of David, explains David's ascendancy to kingship over all Israel. McCarter thinks that this apology was written to defend King David against a variety of charges. Both an early date (the reign of David) and a setting in the Jerusalem court are suggested for the narrative.

[[489]] Among the ancient prose sources of the books of Samuel stand three major compositions. They are: (1) the ark narrative, found principally in 1 Sam 4:1b–7:1 but also including in the opinion of some scholars parts of 1 Samuel 2 or 2 Samuel 6; (2) the so-called history of David's rise, the delimitations of which are discussed below; and (3) the court history of David or, as it is often called, succession document of 2 Samuel 9–1 Kings 2. Of these it is the last mentioned that has received the most scholarly scrutiny and acclaim on account of its high literary quality and presumed homogeneity and historical value. The former two have been

Reprinted with permission from *Journal of Biblical Literature* 99 (1980) 489–504.

treated more or less as "poor relations" since the time of Leonhard Rost, who in his programmatic treatment of all three compositions gave most of his attention to the succession document while consigning the ark narrative to secondary status and providing only a cursory treatment of the history of David's rise.[1] Recently, however, the situation has begun to change. The ark narrative is the subject of a series of important new studies,[2] including a monograph by Patrick D. Miller, Jr. and J. J. M. Roberts which brings it very close to a definitive interpretation,[3] and the history of David's rise also is enjoying considerable scholarly attention.[4] It is to the [[490]] latter–the history of David's rise or, as I prefer to describe it for reasons given below, the apology of David–that the present paper is devoted.

The arrival of the young David at Saul's court is the subject of 1 Sam 16:14–23. The material that follows describes his early career as a servant of Saul, giving emphasis on the one hand to the popular acclaim of his martial exploits and on the other to the fluctuations in his relationship to the royal family, so that when finally compelled to flee out of fear of the jealous king, he is not only the popularly acclaimed military leader of Israel but also the husband of Saul's daughter Michal and the intimate friend of Jonathan, Saul's eldest son. The flight from court is described in 1 Sam 19:8–17, after which there follows a series of episodes depicting David first as an outlaw leader, then as a Philistine mercenary, but all the while as a fugitive from Saul, until at last the king is slain in battle with the Philistines in 1 Sam 31:1–13. The succeeding material in the early chapters of 2 Samuel describes the unsettled period following Saul's death. David, now king of Judah, finds himself at war with the house of Saul, a

1. *Die Überlieferung von der Thronnachfolge Davids* (BWANT 3/6; Stuttgart: W. Kohlhammer, 1926), reprinted in *Das kleine Credo und andere Studien zum Alten Testament* (Heidelberg: Quelle und Meyer, 1965) 119–253.

2. Monograph-length treatments include: J. J. Jackson, "The Ark Narratives: an Historical, Textual, and Form-Critical Study of I Samuel 4–6 and II Samuel 6" (unpublished Th.D. dissertation; Union Theological Seminary, New York, 1962); F. Schicklberger, *Die Ladeerzählung des ersten Samuel-Buches: Eine literaturwissenschaftliche und theologiegeschichtliche Untersuchung* (Forschung zur Bibel, 7; Würzburg: Echter, 1973); and A. F. Campbell, *The Ark Narrative (1 Sam 4–6; 2 Sam 6): A Form-Critical and Traditio-Historical Study* (SBLDS 16; Missoula: Scholars Press, 1975).

3. *The Hand of the Lord: A Reassessment of the "Ark Narrative" of 1 Samuel* (The Johns Hopkins Near Eastern Studies; Baltimore: Johns Hopkins, 1977).

4. Again there are several monograph-length studies: H.-U. Nübel, *Davids Aufstieg in der Frühe israelitischer Geschichtsschreibung* (Bonn: Rheinische Friederich-Wilhelms Universität, 1959); F. Mildenberger, "Die vordeuteronomistische Saul-Davidüberlieferung" (unpublished dissertation; Tübingen, 1962); R. L. Ward, "The Story of David's Rise: A Tradition-Historical Study of I Samuel xvi 14–II Samuel v" (unpublished Ph.D. dissertation; Vanderbilt: 1967); and J. H. Grønbaek, *Die Geschichte vom Aufstieg Davids (1. Sam. 15–2. Sam. 5): Tradition und Composition* (Acta Theologica Danica 10; Copenhagen: Munksgaard, 1971).

conflict that is resolved only with the death of Abner, Saul's general who has been ruling Israel in the name of Ishbaal, Saul's son, and of Ishbaal himself. In 2 Sam 5:1–10 David is proclaimed king over all Israel; he captures the city of Jerusalem to serve as his capital.

It was this large block of material in 1 Samuel 16–2 Samuel 5 that Rost first identified as an originally independent and unified narrative recounting the early part of David's career. Prior to Rost's work this section usually was analyzed as a composite product of interwoven narrative strands running through it and beyond into the preceding and succeeding sections, but since the appearance of his *Thronnachfolge Davids* those scholars who suppose that an originally independent and more or less unified composition underlies the story at this point have been in the majority.[5] No one has found in this material the unity and homogeneity generally accorded the succession document or even the ark narrative. As detailed below it betrays the marks of deuteronomistic expansion, and even in its predeuteronomistic form it is somewhat heterogeneous in appearance. Nevertheless it is possible in the opinion of most recent scholars to demonstrate that it has an overarching unity of theme and purpose. This unity is often explained [[491]] as the consequence of the work of an editor who assembled materials of diverse traditional background and impressed upon them his own point of view.[6] An alternative explanation, which is accepted in the present paper, is that the unity reflects the presence of an underlying, more or less unified composition by an author with a clear point of view, to which various secondary materials, some of them deuteronomistic, have accrued.[7]

5. The chief advocates of the minority position have been O. Eissfeldt (*Die Komposition der Samuelisbücher* [Leipzig: J. C. Hinrichs, 1931] 55 and passim; cf. *The Old Testament: An Introduction* [New York: Harper and Row, 1965) 271–80), G. Hölscher (*Geschichtsschreibung in Israel* [Lund: CWK Gleerup, 1952] 18–19 and passim), and most recently a student of Hölscher, H. Schulte (*Die Entstehung der Geschichtsschreibung im Alten Israel* [BZAW 128; Berlin/New York: de Gruyter, 1972] 105–80).

6. See especially Grønbaek, *Aufstieg Davids*, 16–18. I agree with Grønbaek that the narrator was working with a variety of independent and traditional materials (see below, especially n. 12), but Grønbaek's attempt to include the prophetic introduction to the story (1 Sam 15:1–16:13, especially 16:1–13) in the original narrative is, in my opinion, unsuccessful. We must reckon not only with a layer of underlying materials but also with a layer of appended materials of varying antiquity, including but not restricted to deuteronomistic supplementation.

7. What we know about the late development of the Books of Samuel suggests this explanation. A comparison of the MT and LXX texts of 1 Samuel 17 and 18 shows that traditional materials continued to be interpolated into the narrative up to and in this case beyond the time of the divergence of the ancestral texts of the versions we know today. Cf. A. Weiser, *The Old Testament: Its Formulation and Development* (New York: Association Press, 1961) 164.

Additions to the Original Narrative

I have discussed the literary history of the books of Samuel in detail elsewhere.[8] The following is a summary of that discussion as it pertains to the secondary additions to the original narrative of David's rise to power.

The First Book of Samuel, in which most of the material under discussion here is contained, is a part of the larger Deuteronomistic History that extends from Deuteronomy through 2 Kings. Deuteronomistic expansion and revision, however, are less conspicuous in Samuel than in Judges on the one hand or in Kings on the other and were not the major shaping forces of the book. Instead, in my opinion, 1 Samuel received its primary form from a pre-Deuteronomistic History of the establishment of monarchy in Israel and the transferal of the royal office from Saul to David. This history was composed from a prophetic perspective that was suspicious of monarchy in any form, committed to an ideal of prophetically-mediated divine selection of leaders, and thus opposed to hereditary succession and supportive of the prophetic office as an ongoing institution in the age of the monarchy. It is represented in 1 Samuel by the story of Samuel's career as a prophet in chaps. 1–7, which incorporates older material (especially the ark narrative), and the account of the inauguration of the monarchy in chaps. 8–15, which also incorporates older material. This prophetic [[492]] history accepted the story of David's early career that now stands in 1 Sam 16:14–2 Sam 5:10 and included it in more or less unrevised form except for the addition of an introduction in which David is anointed king by the prophet Samuel and some revision of the tale of the seance at En-dor, again introducing Samuel into a story in which he originally played no part. In short the author of the prophetic history has left his mark on the history of David's rise only in 1 Sam 15:35–16:13 and parts of 1 Samuel 28.[9]

The deuteronomistic supplementation of this prophetic history was, as just noted, light. The career of Samuel was recast in the deuteronomistic pattern for the careers of the so-called major judges, and the epoch as a whole was viewed, in accordance with Samuel's deuteronomistically revised speech in 1 Samuel 12, as a time of transition from the age of judges to the age of kings.[10] The history of David's rise itself was not significantly reshaped, but, as in the case of the retelling of the story of David's refusal

8. *I Samuel* (AB 9; Garden City: Doubleday, 1980) 12–30.

9. I regard the curious episode in 1 Sam 19:18–24 as neither a part of the original composition nor a contribution of the author of the prophetic history. It is a late accretion, written in the spirit of the prophetic history but inconsistent with it in detail (cf. the assertion in 1 Sam 15:35 that Samuel never saw Saul again before he died).

10. On these points see especially D. J. McCarthy, "The Inauguration of Monarchy in Israel: a Form-Critical Study of I Samuel 8–12," *Int* 27 (1973) 401–12.

to take Saul's life (1 Samuel 26) in a form that casts the merits of David's case in the best possible light (1 Sam 23:14–24:23; see below), some of the themes implicit in the history have been made quite explicit by rewriting that may have been deuteronomistic, and there is clear evidence of expansion that anticipates subsequent parts of the Deuteronomistic History and of the introduction of the fundamental deuteronomistic motif of the dynastic promise to David. Secondary material produced by this redactional activity can be recognized by its characteristic themes and language and/or its editorial function (i.e., linkage of material to other parts of the Deuteronomistic History). Application of these criteria to 1 Sam 16:14–2 Sam 5:10 produces the following tabulation of features probably or certainly of deuteronomistic origin.

1. *Revision of the account of the battle in the Valley of the Terebinth* (1 Samuel 17, passim). An older report of an Israelite victory in which David played a major role in the success of Saul's forces has been overlaid with a popular account of David's single combat with a Philistine champion.[11] [[493]]
2. *Additions to the story of David and Jonathan* (1 Sam 20:11–17, 23, 40–42). These verses are intrusive in the context and anticipatory of the Meribaal episode in 2 Samuel 9. They serve the editorial purposes of the deuteronomistic historian.
3. *The first account of David's refusal to take Saul's life* (1 Sam 23:14–24:23). Though considerable older material is incorporated into it, this unit as a whole is a tendentious retelling of the episode described in 1 Samuel 26. It presents David as a model of Yahwistic piety (cf. 24:6–7) and places in Saul's mouth an explicit acknowledgment of David's future kingship (24:21–22).
4. *Abigail's second speech* (1 Sam 25:28–31). The phrases look beyond the history of David's rise to the deuteronomistic presentation of the dynastic promise to David in 2 Samuel 7.
5. *Additions to the account of David's reign in Hebron* (2 Sam 2:10a + 11; 3:9–10, 18b; 5:1–2, 4–5). Both chronological formulae and thematic interpolations are included.

At the end of the older composition the deuteronomistic historian gathered certain other materials pertinent to David's establishment of his capital at Jerusalem (2 Sam 5:11–6:23). Finally, he appended as a capstone for the entire story of David's rise to power a long passage describing the giving of the dynastic promise to David (2 Samuel 7).

11. In the textual tradition that stands behind MT the story was revised and enlarged a second time with the interpolation of the material missing from the LXX.

Except for the prophetic and deuteronomistic additions just cited, therefore, 1 Sam 16:14–2 Sam 5:10 is an old, more or less unified composition[12] describing David's rise to power, which can be subjected to independent analysis.

The Character of the Original Narrative

In 1966 Artur Weiser, in a highly influential study of the history of David's rise,[13] was able to demonstrate that the purpose of the narrative is to show by a careful presentation of the events of the early part of David's career that his succession to Saul's throne was lawful. There is particular emphasis, as Weiser noted, on the legitimacy of the Davidic claim to the kingship of *all* Israel, north as well as south. Thus David, though a Judahite by birth, is shown to have been a favored [[494]] member of the court of the Benjaminite king; indeed he is presented to us as the successful suitor of the king's daughter (1 Sam 18:20–27) and the popularly acknowledged leader of the armies of both Israel and Judah (1 Sam 18:16). From this position, we are told, he eventually rose up to displace his father-in-law as king, and the intervening episodes as set forth in the narrative give no warrant for casting any blame upon David for the dark events that attended the transfer of power, including his estrangement from Saul, Saul's death, and the deaths of Jonathan and Ishbaal, the sons of Saul who might have stood in his way; David was even innocent of implication in the affair that led to Abner's assassination. In the end the northern tribes proclaimed him king as willingly and enthusiastically as Judah had earlier (2 Sam 5:3; cf. 2:4). His accession, in short, is shown by this history to have been completely lawful.

More recent studies, especially the important 1971 monograph of J. H. Grønbaek,[14] have emphasized the importance of the theological undergirding given this legitimation theme in the course of the history of David's rise. It is made completely clear in the narrative that the transfer of the throne from David to Saul was in accordance with the will of Yahweh.

12. Even with the secondary expansions stripped away the history of David's rise retains some of its heterogeneous appearance. Its author seems to have made use of a variety of materials available during David's lifetime. Many episodes, including the account of David's refusal to take Saul's life in 1 Samuel 26 and the story of the Abigail-Nabal affair in 1 Samuel 25, look as though they had an independent existence before their incorporation into the larger narrative. Others, such as the etiological tale of the incident at Sela-hammahlekoth (1 Sam 23:24b–24:1), appear already to have undergone some development in the tradition.

13. "Die Legitimation des Königs David: Zur Eigenart und Entstehung der sogen. Geschichte von Davids Aufstieg," *VT* 16 (1966) 325–54.

14. *Aufstieg Davids*, especially 271–73.

David is presented as a man generously blessed with divine favor, Saul as a man rejected by his god.[15] Indeed the theological *leitmotif* of the entire history is the assertion "Yahweh was with David," which appears first in 1 Sam 16:18 and is repeated often thereafter, while the corresponding assessment of Saul's situation is the narrator's introductory remark to the effect that "the spirit of Yahweh departed from Saul" in 1 Sam 16:14. The importance of the contrasting disposition of Yahweh toward the two antagonists is demonstrated subtly but unmistakably by the development of the story itself. David succeeds in everything he undertakes (cf. 1 Sam 26:25), and even things he does with no intention of personal gain often work to improve his situation. On the other hand Saul's undertakings, especially his plots against David's life, seem to be not only unsuccessful but cursed with a dark irony, frequently resulting in further successes for David and further grief for Saul himself.

The history of David's rise, then, is a narrative that promulgates a political point of view supported by theological interpretation of the [[495]] events it recounts. Its purpose is to show that David's accession to the throne was lawful and that the events leading up to his proclamation as king over all Israel were guided by the will of the god of Israel. A narrative with such a purpose might have arisen at any of several points in the development of the biblical text. In view of the fact that a leading concern is the legitimation by appeal to the divine will of a king whose right of accession might be questioned, we should probably think of a period when such a king was on the throne, such as the time (as at least one recent study has argued)[16] of the reign of Jehu in the northern kingdom. On the other hand, we must also reckon with the fact that the particular king whose legitimacy is defended here is David, a circumstance that seems strongly to favor a southern provenience for the narrative. Accordingly a number of recent treatments of the history of David's rise, including those of Grønbaek and T. N. D. Mettinger,[17] favor a date in the early years following the death of Solomon when the right of the Davidic king to sover-

15. This motif, especially the negative aspect of it that applies to Saul, seems to anticipate the theology of the larger prophetic history into which the history of David's rise was incorporated, but the similarity is no more than superficial. There is nothing in the older composition that corresponds to the prophetic criterion for acceptance or rejection, viz. obedience to the prophetically-mediated word of Yahweh (cf. 1 Sam 13:13–14; 15:23b, 24; etc.). I cannot agree, therefore, with those scholars who find it necessary to suppose that the history of David's rise was composed or substantially rewritten in prophetic circles (Mildenberger) or, more generally, in the north (Nübel). See further below.

16. Cf. J. Conrad, "Zum geschichtlichen Hintergrund der Darstellung von Davids Aufstieg," *ThLZ* 97 (1972) 321–32.

17. Grønbaek, *Aufstieg Davids*, 18–25, 273–77; Mettinger, *King and Messiah: The Civil and Sacral Legitimation of the Israelite Kings* (ConBOT 8; Lund: CWK Gleerup, 1976) 38–41.

eignty in the north was being challenged. This hypothesis is plausible in many ways, but it is difficult to imagine that a document defending the right of accession of a king who was not the natural successor to his kingship could have arisen in pro-Davidic circles at a time when Jeroboam I or one of his successors was asserting just such a right with regard to the northern claims of the Davidic kingship itself. I think we must look instead for a provenience that satisfies both of the requirements we have considered; that is, our document must have been composed in the south in pro-Davidic circles, and it must have been promulgated at a time when the throne had just been transferred from one house to another. Since all of David's successors in Judah were his descendants, it is obvious that the only provenience that can meet both requirements is Davidic Jerusalem, and we must consider the possibility that the history of David's rise in its earliest formulation dates to the reign of David himself.

The hypothesis of a Davidic date for the history of David's rise gains support from recent study of the literary genre to which it belongs. Harry A. Hoffner, Jr., has called attention to a special category of Hittite historiographical literature which, following E. H Sturtevant, he calls "apology."[18] In the strict sense of the term as Hoffner understands it an apology is "a document composed for a king who had [[496]] usurped the throne, composed in order to defend or justify his assumption of the kingship by force."[19] Of the surviving examples of Hittite apology, one–the so-called apology of Hattushilish III,[20] the thirteenth-century king–is especially instructive for the study of the history of David's rise. It tells the story of the early career of Hattushilish and his rise to power, describing his rebellion against his nephew and predecessor, Urhi-teshub. It may be summarized as follows.[21]

Hattushilish, after identifying himself and citing his royal lineage (1:1–4), begins his apology with an introductory acknowledgment of the decisive role of the goddess Ishtar in what is to follow, coupled with an expressed wish for a hearing by a human audience: "I tell Ishtar's power; let mankind hear it" (1:5). As the youngest child of Murshilish (II), he says, he

18. See "Propaganda and Political Justification in Hittite Historiography," in *Unity and Diversity: Essays in the History, Literature, and Religion of the Ancient Near East* (ed. H. Goedicke and J. J. M. Roberts; Baltimore/London: Johns Hopkins, 1975) 49–62.

19. Ibid., 49.

20. *CTH* (= *Catalogue des textes hittites*, ed. E. Laroche, in *Revue hittite et asianique* 58–62 [1956–58]) 81. To my knowledge the best readily available English translation is still that in E. H. Sturtevant and G. Bechtel, *A Hittite Chrestomathy* (Special Publications of the Linguistic Society of America, William Dwight Whitney Linguistic Series; Philadelphia: University of Pennsylvania, 1935) 42–99.

21. All quotations are from the translation of Sturtevant and Bechtel, *Hittite Chrestomathy*, 65–83.

was not expected to live and was assigned to the service of Ishtar; it was in this priestly role that he gained the divine favor that was responsible for his later success (1:9–21). His public career began with the death of his father and accession of Muwattallish, his brother, who appointed him to a high office and gave him the Upper Country, the northern part of the Hittite homeland, to rule (1:22–26). This early success provoked jealousy, especially on the part of a certain Armadattash, the previous ruler of the Upper Country, and malicious charges were made against him, eventually reaching the ears of Muwattallish (1:27–35). The crisis passed, however, when Muwattallish learned the truth of the matter (cf. 1:6–63), Hattushilish himself being sustained throughout the affair by Ishtar, who had brought him words of comfort in a dream and championed his cause (1:36–42), an episode that provides him an occasion for a long paean to the goddess (1:43–58). "My Lady Ishtar always rescued me," he says (1:43; cf. 1:50, 58).

Safely back in the good opinion of his brother, Hattushilish enjoyed success after success. He was now the chief military officer of the Hittites, building up a record of victories abroad while efficiently protecting the homeland from invasion (1:64–72). When Muwattallish retired to the Lower Country, a series of major rebellions and invasions began in the Upper Country, but Hattushilish, who was left in sole charge, thwarted them all (1:75–2:47), in each case, he says, [[497]] with Ishtar's help (2:24, 37, 45). He was appointed "king" or viceroy of a number of Hittite principalities (2:48–68), whose troops he led to battle alongside Muwattallish (2:69–72). He further consolidated his position at this time by a politically advantageous marriage to a priestess of Ishtar (3:1–4) and by a final legal victory over his old rival Armadattash (2:74–78; 3:14–27).

The critical series of events in Hattushilish's rise to power began with his brother's death. Muwattallish died without "a legitimate son," as Hattushilish puts it, and was succeeded by Urhi-teshub, the son of a concubine. Hattushilish stresses his own restraint: "I . . . firm in (my) respect for my brother, did not act selfishly" (3:38). He took his nephew's cause upon himself, he says, and installed him as great king of the Hittites, placing the entire army at his disposal and keeping for himself only those territories that had been lawfully assigned him in the past (3:38–45). Urhi-teshub, however, did not respond in kind. He was jealous of the favor of Ishtar, we are told, and soon deprived his uncle of all his possessions except a small home base (3:54–60). "And, firm in (my) respect for my brother," says Hattushilish, "I did not act selfishly. And for seven years I submitted" (3:61–62). But finally, when Urhi-teshub took away his remaining dominions and, as Hattushilish puts it, "tried to destroy me" (3:63), he could submit no longer and declared war. There is great emphasis placed upon the fact that this was no furtive palace rebellion: it was an openly declared contest, an ordeal at arms, which would decide by its outcome whose cause was just (3:65–72). Ishtar, who "had even before this been promising me the kingship" (4:7), marched with Hattushilish once again, and Urhi-teshub was defeated, captured, and banished (4:7–35). Hattushilish concludes his apology with a final rehearsal of Ishtar's role in his rise to power and an appeal to his descendants never to abandon her worship (4:41–86).

The apology of Hattushilish is a narrative testimony to the power of the king's patron deity, to whom he ascribes his success. It is addressed, however, not to a divine but to a human audience ("Let mankind hear it" [1:5]), and its purpose must be understood accordingly. It reviews the steps by which Hattushilish came to the throne, purporting to demonstrate thereby the legitimacy of his accession. The major themes of the document contribute to this end. First, the ability of Hattushilish to rule is shown by reference to his various administrative accomplishments and military successes. Second, it is made clear that he was the favorite of his brother, Murshilish, and his viceregent in the rule of the Hittite dominions. Third, he is shown never to have acted out of self-interest though presented with frequent opportunities to advance his own cause, but instead to have conducted himself in accordance with a deep respect for his brother's memory (". . . firm in [my] respect for my brother, I did not act selfishly" [3:39, 61; 4:29, 61]). ⟦498⟧ Fourth, he is exonerated from all blame in the incessant personal conflict that attended his rise to power, and the source of the antagonism is shown to have been the jealousy of his rivals, especially Armadattash, and the groundless suspicions of Urhi-teshub. Finally, as already mentioned, the decisive factor in his ascent at every stage is shown to have been the effective power of Ishtar's favor, by which he was protected from every danger ("Ishtar always rescued me" [1:43, etc.]) and given success in all his undertakings.

On the basis of an examination of this and other comparable compositions Hoffner makes a persuasive case for the existence of a Hittite tradition of apology literature with which he cautiously associates the biblical history of David's rise. "That such a piece of royal propaganda may have had independent existence before portions of it were incorporated into the present canonical Book of Samuel," he writes, "has been long suspected by Old Testament scholars. . . . But what needs to be stressed here is that, although it may be impossible at present to prove any formal link between the Apology of Ḫattušili and the royal propaganda of David and Solomon, it is not impossible to speak of a tradition of royal apologies in the Hittite kingdom or even of a certain loose literary form, which several of them seem to assume. More than this one should not expect, since one would after all not expect usurpations to occur often enough in a stable society to justify the development of an elaborate traditional format."[22] Hoffner's reluctance to define this "tradition of royal apologies" too strictly is, I think, prudent. Surely there is nothing distinctively Hittite or even ancient Near Eastern about the literary category of political self-justification with its accompanying claims for the legitimacy of the usurper, his ability to rule, his moral rectitude, and his divine election to office. Efforts to find more than "a certain loose literary form" shared by the several examples of the category would probably fail. On the other hand the apology of Hattushilish demonstrates the potential for an elaborate development of this genre in the general cultural milieu in which the history of David's rise was composed, and the striking similarity of themes in the two compositions is a clue to the original character of the Israelite document.

[[499]] The biblical history of David's rise in its original formulation was, we may suppose, an apology in the sense defined by Hoffner. It shares the basic themes of the Hittite apology of Hattushilish as enumerated above. First, David's ability to rule is illustrated by reference to his early military successes, the spontaneous loyalty of the people of Israel and Judah, and the skill and restraint with which he wages the long war with the house of Saul after his accession as king of Judah. Second, he is shown to have begun as Saul's trusted lieutenant and to have won the loyalty of the royal family. Third, he is depicted as thoroughly loyal to the king, never seeking out the power that steadily comes to him, and indeed refusing at least one opportunity to secure his position by slaying Saul. Fourth, he is shown to have been blameless in all his dealings with Saul, whose jealousy and groundless suspicions were responsible for the alienation of David and the conflict that ensued. Finally, it is made clear that David's rise to power was made possible, indeed inevitable, by the special favor of the god of Israel, "Yahweh is with him" being, as already noted, the leitmotif of the entire composition.

Thematic Analysis

A thematic analysis of the history of David's rise that is sensitive to the rhetorical posture of the author reveals the apologetic character of the com-

22. "Propaganda and Political Justification," 50. Herbert M. Wolf, in a 1967 Brandeis dissertation written under Hoffner's direction ("The *Apology of Hattušiliš* Compared with Other Ancient Near Eastern Political Self-Justifications," especially 99–117), concludes from a form-critical analysis of the Hittite composition that none of the parallel literature is comparable to the Hattushilish text in the careful development of its themes; its similarity to the history of David's rise is best explained, he believes, by assuming some kind of direct literary influence of the one upon the other. Although this last conclusion seems to go much too far, Wolf's study clarifies the provenience and character of the history of David's rise in a fundamental way and deserves more attention than it has received.

position most clearly. Apologetic literature by its very nature assumes a defensive attitude toward its subject matter, addressing itself to issues exposed to actual or possible public censure. This is precisely the posture of the history of David's rise. A careful reading leads to the conclusion that the author is speaking to one possible charge of wrongdoing after another in an attempt to demonstrate David's innocence in the series of events that led to his succession. This case for the defense is made by relating the events in question in a way intended to allay all suspicions, and though the author becomes quite explicit at times, as in his report of Abner's death (see below), he does not permit himself to step out from behind his narrative and comment directly on the issue at hand. Nevertheless, the charges against which he defends David are easily recognized; the following list shows how they are dealt with in the narrative.

Charge 1. *David sought to advance himself at court at Saul's expense.* The extraordinary attainments of the young Judahite at the Benjaminite court, especially in light of his subsequent fall from favor, might suggest that he acted out of a strong and perhaps unscrupulous self-interest while in Saul's service. The narrator, however, shows that David came to court at Saul's behest (1 Sam 16:19–22) and that as long as he was there he was completely loyal and indeed did much to help Saul's own cause (cf. 1 Sam 19:4–5). He did not seek out his [[500]] marriage to the princess Michal, the most conspicuous sign of his elevated position, but instead protested his unworthiness of the match (1 Sam 18:23), which was in fact Saul's idea (vv. 20–21a), until persuaded by the insistence of Saul's courtiers.

Charge 2. *David was a deserter.* The circumstances of David's departure from court might lead to the suspicion that he shirked his responsibilities to Saul and deserted. The narrator of the history of David's rise, however, takes special pains to show that David was forced to leave in order to save his life (1 Sam 19:9–17) and that he did so reluctantly, having first explored every possibility of remaining. In short, he was driven away from the place of his true loyalties by Saul's hostility (cf. 1 Sam 26:19). Moreover Saul's own daughter and his son, the crown prince, saw the rightness of David's side and aided his escape (1 Sam 19:11–17; 20:1–21:1).

Charge 3. *David was an outlaw.* The fact that David was known to have spent part of his life as leader of a band of outlaws–a fact that, we must assume, was too well known to be suppressed–would surely have inspired public disapprobation. The narrator is careful to show, however, that David at that time was a fugitive from Saul's unjust pursuit and that he earnestly sought reconciliation (cf. 1 Sam 26:18–20). Saul even recognized this state of affairs himself in his rare lucid moments (v. 21).

Charge 4. *David was a Philistine mercenary.* The public knowledge that David had served in the army of a king of the Philistines, Israel's most hated foe, would certainly have provoked objections. Again this must have been too widely known to be denied. The narrative, however, makes it clear that David was forced into Philistine service as a desperate last resort. "Any day now I might be taken by Saul," he says to himself in 1 Sam 27:1. "There is nothing better for me than to escape to the land of the Philistines. Then Saul will give up on me and no longer seek me throughout the territory of Israel, for I shall be safely out of his reach." It is scrupulously shown, moreover, that while he was in the Philistine army, he never led his troops against any Israelite or Judahite city, though he deceived Achish of Gath, his lord, into thinking so (1 Sam 27:8–12). Indeed he took advantage of the power of his position to attack Israel's enemies and thereby to enrich Judah (1 Samuel 30).

Charge 5. *David was implicated in Saul's death.* Some must have suspected, if only on the ground of *cui bono*, that David was involved in the demise of his predecessor, especially since Saul died fighting against the Philistines at a time when David was in the Philistine army. Indeed the forces of Achish were known, it seems, to have participated in the battle of Mount Gilboa (cf. 1 Sam 29:1–2)! Nevertheless, David was not, we are told, with Achish at Gilboa (1 Sam 29:11), and it is subtly but clearly implied that if he had been, he would have fought [[501]] *with* Saul rather than against him. In 1 Sam 29:8, having been told by Achish that he must quit the march north, David expresses a wish to "go out and fight against the enemies of my lord, the king." Though Achish assumes the reference is to him, the irony is not lost on the audience. Elsewhere in the story, moreover, David is shown to have been fastidious about the sanctity of the person of Saul, the anointed of Yahweh, refusing an opportunity to slay him when it is offered (1 Samuel 26) and strictly punishing the violator of his person (2 Sam 1:14–16).

Charge 6. *David was implicated in Abner's death.* Suspicion must have fallen on David in regard to the death of Abner, inasmuch as it was he who set Ishbaal on his father's throne (2 Sam 2:8–9) and seemed, therefore, to have been the major obstacle to David's kingship over the northern tribes. The narrative shows, however, that David and Abner had reached an accord before the latter's death, inasmuch as Abner, having quarreled with Ishbaal (2 Sam 3:7–11), had actually begun to champion David's cause in the north (vv. 17–18) and had offered him the kingship of Israel (v. 21a). In particular we are informed three times (!) that after their last interview Abner left David "in peace" (vv. 21b, 22, 23). In other words, the narrator means to show us that here as in the previous cases suspicion of David is groundless. Instead Abner died in consequence of a private quarrel with Joab, David's commander-in-chief (2 Sam 2:12–32; 3:22–30), and David knew nothing, as we are explicitly advised in 2 Sam 3:26b, of the deception that finally cost Abner his life. When he learned of Abner's death, we are told, David declared, "I and my kingship are innocent before Yahweh forever of the blood of Abner, son of Ner!" (2 Sam 3:28).[23] Furthermore, he pronounced a curse upon Joab's house (v. 29) and led the mourning for Abner himself (vv. 31–35), much to the approval of the people (v. 36). "All the people and all Israel knew at that time," says our narrator (v. 37), "that it had not been the king's will (*kî lōʾ hāyĕtâ mēhammelek*) to kill Abner, the son of Ner."

Charge 7. *David was implicated in Ishbaal's death.* As in the cases of the deaths of Saul and Abner, David must have been suspected of treachery in the murder of Ishbaal. The narrative shows, however, that Ishbaal was slain without David's knowledge by a pair of Benjaminites [[502]] (2 Sam 4:2–3), opportunists who hoped to gain David's favor by taking the life of their master (vv. 5–8). But David was not pleased by the news and indignantly condemned the assassins to death (vv. 9–12a). It was David, moreover, who arranged for the honorable burial of Ishbaal's remains.

In short, the history of David's rise or the apology of David, as we are now entitled to call it, shows David's accession to the throne of all Israel, north as well as south, to have been entirely lawful and his kingship, therefore, free of guilt. All possible charges of wrongdoing are faced forthrightly, and each in its turn is gainsaid by the course of events as related by the narrator. Some or all of these charges must actually have been made during David's lifetime. The issues they raise concern his personal behavior and would have been liveliest during his own reign. This reinforces the conclusion reached above on other grounds that the apology of David in its original formulation was of Davidic date. It must have been composed in the context of such events as the Shimei incident (2 Sam 16:5–14) and Sheba's revolt (2 Sam 20:1–22), when David's claim to the territory of the northern tribes was being seriously challenged and when he was being censured, at least by Shimei (2 Sam 16:8–9), for the blood of the house of Saul. It is to this censure that our document finally addresses itself.[24]

23. T. Veijola (*Die ewige Dynastie: David und die Entstehung seiner Dynastie nach der deuteronomistischen Darstellung* [Annales Academiae Scientarum Fennicae, B/193; Helsinki: Suomalainen Tiedeakatemia, 1975] 30–32) considers this verse (as well as vv. 29, 38–39) to be of deuteronomistic origin; but although David looks ahead here to the dynasty he hopes will succeed him, it is not necessary in my opinion to see in this a reflection of a developed theology of dynastic promise. Note that in any case—even if we strike vv. 28–29, 38–39 as secondary—the apologetic purpose of the passage is carried forward quite explicitly by what remains (especially v. 37).

24. The modern historian, who must try to adjudicate in this ancient controversy, is in a difficult position. He has only David's side of the story. The circumstantial evidence against David is extremely strong; yet the apology is an effective piece of rhetoric, and most of its claims are credible. It seems unlikely that David set out from the beginning to seize Saul's kingship for himself. It is difficult to believe, however, that he did not at least close his eyes to the political assassinations that in the end placed him on the throne.

Theological Claims

We have spoken already of the theological claims that buttress the narrator's purpose, and we may reconsider them now in light of our thematic analysis of the document. This subject has bearing, as we shall see, upon the question of the demarcations of the original composition.

The narrative opens with a negative claim. "The spirit of Yahweh departed from Saul," we are told in 1 Sam 16:14a.[25] This statement simply and immediately establishes the situation out of which the rest of the story will develop. Saul has been abandoned by Yahweh, and we [[503]] must therefore look ahead to his fall from power. In the same moment, moreover, we are prepared for the arrival of David, inasmuch as the "evil spirit" that rushes in to haunt Saul (v. 14b), as if filling a vacuum left by the departure of the other spirit, creates the need for a musician whose playing will comfort the king (vv. 16–17). Yahweh's choice of David and his abandonment of Saul, which in the later prophetic edition of the narrative will be explained as consequences of Saul's disobedience to the prophetically-mediated divine word (1 Sam 13:13–14; 15:22–23, 26; 28:18), are left without explanation in the original composition. As in the case of Ishtar's preference for Hattushilish in the Hittite document reviewed above, there is no attempt made here to explain Yahweh's attitude toward David or Saul; it is a matter of the mystery of a divine mind.[26] But Yahweh's attitude is made clear nonetheless. Throughout the narrative Saul is like a man living under a curse. He is caught up in something larger than himself, something from which he cannot extricate himself, and all his devices go wrong.

David, too, is presented to us as a man caught up in events he cannot control. In his case, however, everything seems inevitably to go well, and he advances step by step toward the kingship almost in spite of himself. It hardly needs to be said that this situation furthers the apologetic purposes of the narrator, who, as we have noted, is making a sustained effort to show that David did not connive to improve his own position at any point. The relevant assertion about David, which recurs throughout the compo-

25. The majority of scholars have located the beginning of the history of David's rise at this point (cf. for bibliography, Grønbaek, *Aufstieg Davids*, 25 n. 59), and their position has been reinforced recently by the detailed analysis of Veijola (*Ewige Dynastie*, 102 n. 156). As explained above, I agree with Veijola that 15:1–16:13 represents a secondary introduction of prophetic origin, but I assume it derives from a predeuteronomistic writer rather than a prophetic Deuteronomist (DtrP), as Veijola believes. Weiser ("Legitimation des Königs David," 325-26) considers 16:1–13 to have belonged to the original composition, and to this Grønbaek (*Aufstieg Davids*, 25–29; cf. 37–76, 261–62) would add chap. 15 as well (see also Mettinger, *King and Messiah*, 33–35).

26. It would be a mistake to interpret Hattushilish' reference to his childhood service as a priest of Ishtar (1:17–21) as an explanation for the goddess's subsequent favor. She had many faithful priests and did not make kings of them all. The document implies, moreover, that she had singled out Hattushilish even before his term of service (cf. 1:12–17).

sition, is "Yahweh was with him." It occurs first in 1 Sam 16:18 on the lips of one of Saul's attendants, striking the theological keynote of the drama even before David has actually set foot on stage. It is recapitulated in 1 Sam 18:14 (cf. MT's expansion in v. 12b), where its implications are made explicit: "David was successful in all his undertakings, for Yahweh was with him." We are told also that it was in bitter realization of these implications that Saul finally resolved to take David's life (1 Sam 18:28–19:1a). This expression, as we have already seen, is the theological *leitmotif* of the apology of David, and the decisive influence of Yahweh's special favor for David runs throughout the narrative, the end of which is marked [[504]] by a final repetition of the expression in connection with a glance ahead: "And David continued to grow greater and greater, for Yahweh Sabaoth[27] was with him."[28]

27. Reading *yahweh ṣĕbāʾôt* [['Yahweh Sabaoth']] on the basis of LXX and 4QSam[b]. MT is expansive: *yahweh ʾĕlōhê ṣĕbāʾôt* [['Yahweh, God of (the heavenly) armies']].

28. Mettinger (*King and Messiah*, 41–45) makes a case for extending the conclusion of the history of David's rise to include certain other materials in 2 Samuel 5–7. Most scholars still agree, however, on locating the conclusion at 2 Sam 5:10 (Grønbaek, *Aufstieg Davids*, 29–35; cf. 246–58, 271; Veijola, *Ewige Dynastie*, 98–99).

The David–Saul Narrative

WALTER DIETRICH AND
THOMAS NAUMANN

This is an excerpt from the volume on Samuel in the series Erträge der Forschung, which aims to present and evaluate the latest research on the biblical books. There is accordingly a mass of information here on recent scholarly work. The excerpt is highly methodological in orientation, however, the main problem faced being the relationship between diachronic and synchronic readings of Samuel. The latter includes both the theological interpretation of Karl Barth and the vast wave of the newer literary approaches to which the work of Robert Alter was an important stimulus. The essay poses difficult questions to proponents of synchronic and diachronic interpretations alike, arguing that, understood correctly, each needs and can help the other. The older questions about the books of Samuel–particularly the relationship between "blocks" (such as the "Rise of David" and the "Succession Narrative") and redaction, and the dating of the various parts–are thus put in a new context. The essay is interesting not least as a reflection from Germany on a great deal of modern English language work on Samuel.

The Biblical David–Saul Narrative

Preliminaries/Obstacles to Synchronic Contemplation

[[47]] Careful, serious work with the biblical text in its existing wording, canonized by synagogue and church, always comes before and after every historical-critical analysis. Professional exegetes, particularly those writing

Translated and reprinted with permission, from "Die David-Saul-Geschichte," in Dietrich and Naumann, *Die Samuelbücher* (Erträge der Forschung 281; Darmstadt: Wissenschaftliche Buchgesellschaft, 1995) 47–86. Translation by Peter T. Daniels. Cross-references to other sections of the book have been omitted from this reprint. The RSV has been used for quotations from the English Bible.

in German, bewitched by the spirit of the Enlightenment, kept far away from the centuries- or millennia-old exercise of simple or highly subtle, humble and pious or highly intellectual Bible reading for a good one hundred years. Jewish exegesis has remained much more true to the age-old pursuit of interpretation than has contemporary Christian exegesis. Thus impulses from both Jewish and pre-Enlightenment Christian (whether Church Fathers or Reformation) traditions as well as secular literary criticism have led to an entirely new, impartial, and fruitful reading also of the books of Samuel.

It was not by chance that what we may call the extra-critical, integral reading of the David and Saul stories bore fruit, not only and not originally in specialized publications by exegetes, but in works by nonexegetes. The first person to be discussed here is Karl Barth, a theologian whose in-depth familiarity with the Bible is well known. Within the exegetes' guild, however, he was not always highly regarded. In the second volume of his *Church Dogmatics,* under Theology, Karl Barth (1942, 2/2; 1959: 404–34) interpreted the juxtaposition of Saul and David as a paradigm for the relationship between "rejection" and "choice." In accordance with his understanding of scripture, he had little or no concern for historical-critical exegesis but confronted the final text of the Bible directly and with only apparent [[48]] naïveté. He was not concerned with its historical and literary-historical dimension but resolutely only with the theological. He argued that the portrait of Saul from the very beginning exhibited ambivalence: Saul was the king desired by the people in their short-sightedness and preserved by God in his generosity. God would bring about something good with him, and to this extent he was completely and in all seriousness his chosen one! On the other hand, Saul embodied the foolish will of Israel, and as soon as he himself (even only in "microscopically" tiny traces) showed a tendency to forsake God high-handedly, he was promptly discarded. Contrast David. In no way was he a pure, shining light; yet with him, even bloody sins could not negate his status as chosen! He is not the elected one from dubious motives but the one desired by God. He is not described as an accomplished superman and great king but as the one elevated by God from humble beginnings (shepherd, minstrel, refugee) who repeatedly humbles himself before God and the people, who achieves his successes not by his own means but with God's help, and who is led again and again beyond his personal limitations. So David, the perpetually chosen, has a "Saul side"–just as Saul, though brought down at the end, has a "David side." The truly accomplished man and king is thus neither of these two. They, like every other Old Testament ruler, are in the end surrogates–more negative or more positive–for the true king who will come after them. In the Cross of Christ, God takes the rejection upon himself and settles the account of the Saul side of the kingdom; in the resurrection of Christ he brings the David side of the kingdom to fulfillment. Because the history of the Israelite monarchy was the prehistory of Jesus Christ, election already outweighed rejection, and grace already outweighed judgment.

Specialized exegesis had every reason to be both astonished by and critical of this profound attempt at interpreting 1 Samuel. Barth's approach was so extremely broad, so imperious, the canvas brushed with such broad strokes, that he was perhaps far too unconcerned about numerous exegetical and historical problems with the result that he simply bracketed them and focused on the theological dimensions that had gone into the David and Saul stories.

⟦49⟧ Another approach unfamiliar to specialists came from a Jewish-American literary critic, Robert Alter. He should be seen as the one who triggered, or at least was the primary amplifier of, the method of "literary criticism" finding more and more acceptance, especially in American Old Testament scholarship. This literary criticism seems to be the exact opposite of *Literarkritik*. The (biblical) text under investigation is not dissected analytically, separated into various levels and smaller details, nor is it investigated form- or tradition-critically with regard to the social and intellectual historical conditions that influenced it; rather, it is approached as a whole exactly as it appears, with attention to its linguistic form and the intention of the statements expressed in it. In his 1981 book, Alter provides guidance in reading not just the books of Samuel but all of the narrative biblical books. In six chapters, he presents the most important techniques of Hebrew narrative art: the ever-recurring (yet never exactly the same) "type-scene," the alternation between report and dialogue, the mechanics of repetition (fully intentional and deliberately varied), the art of characterization and reticence, the finesse of consciously introduced contradiction, and finally the tension-rich play between the knowledge of the narrator and the (partial) ignorance of the actors and reader. Again and again, Alter takes the examples for his investigations from the David and Saul stories. Two examples must suffice: the juxtaposition of 1 Sam 16:14ff. (David comes to Saul's court as minstrel and becomes his adjutant) and 1 Samuel 17 (David enters the battle as a shepherd boy and Saul's court as the slayer of Goliath) has always been a stumbling block for critical exegesis. Alter (1981: 147ff.) sees the tension not as bothersome but as directly stimulating our understanding of what is intended. Comparable to a post-Cubist portrait, which depicts a face simultaneously from the front and from the side, David in 1 Samuel 16–17 is described as both personally winning and publicly imposing. Rash criticism is not offered or appropriate; instead, we should be sensitive to "the writer's binocular vision of David" (1981: 148). 1 Samuel 18 serves Alter (1981: 116ff.) as an example of the art of characterization: in direct description, much is said about David's success and favored status but nothing about his character. Then he becomes the king's [[50]] son-in-law. The narrative draws Saul as a fully transparent individual in his crass aggressiveness. Michal is transparent in only one point, that she is smitten by love ("It is the only instance in all biblical narrative in which we are explicitly told that a woman loves a man. But . . . Michal's love is stated entirely without motivated explanation"; Alter 1981: 118). David, on the other hand, remains completely opaque in regard to his feelings and intentions.

Alter teaches us to listen closely to what is quietly said, and it hardly seems an injustice to note that he sometimes seems to hear what is not said at all. The secret key word of his book is "artistry"; he conceptualizes the biblical narrator not as reporter or historian but as artist. And so it is perhaps not coincidental that time after time artists have been drawn to the stories of David and Saul. We are not speaking here of visual artists such as Michelangelo or Marc Chagall but of various contemporary writers. Four novelists have dealt with the biblical narratives of David and Saul, of Michal and Bathsheba: Stefan Heym, Joseph Heller, Torgny Lindgren, and Grete Weil. This is not the place to introduce their work; that has been done elsewhere (Dietrich 1976, 1989), and these literary efforts are enticing enough on their own. It suffices here to remark that each of these novels in its own way shows the liveliness and fruitfulness with which the biblical narratives depict characters and events from the earliest monarchy, how much they stimulate sensitive understanding and penetrating inquiry, and how much room they leave for imaginative rethinking and creative retelling. The biblical tale of David and Saul reveals itself not only to historical-critical analysis but also to a committed, holistic reading: this is what the artists, literary critics, and theologians can teach us exegetes.

The Rejected One: Saul

Recent exegesis has become increasingly involved with the final form of the biblical text, but it has not always penetrated to the deeper dimensions just mentioned.

[[51]] Edelman (1991; in shorter form, 1990) takes up the task of interpreting the portrait of Saul as it has been developed in the "historiography of Judah." She means by this the final deuteronomistic edition of the biblical text, which surely did not have its origin only in the exilic period but undoubtedly already existed in its early stages toward the end of the monarchy (Josiah). For her, the material was shaped according to conventional "patterns" that were well known to the "audience." Saul, like David (and for that matter, supposedly Jonathan too), had to undergo a tripartite coronation ceremony, consisting of designation (= anointing), probation, and crowning. For Saul (as for David), a sort of royal biography had to be prepared and transmitted to posterity. For Saul (as for David) this happened according to the simple plan "good beginning–bad end," signaled by the leitmotif of divine "spirit," which appears at the beginning and is lost at the end. This is the (albeit oversimplified) theoretical underpinning (Edelman 1991: 11–32) of a "close reading" of the Saul stories, which nevertheless hardly achieves any genuine profundity.

Berges (1989) has already prospected more deeply. He sees Saul depicted in 1 Samuel as an unjust, and in the end self-judged, judge. Especially in two court-like scenes in 1 Samuel 22, the king shows himself to be an incompetent judge: he accuses his own officers and the priests of Nob, unjustly, of conspiring with David. But the entire complex comprising 1 Samuel 19–26 is constructed as a "great court scene" (1989: 125). David is the defendant. Saul appears as

> prosecutor and judge: the charge is high treason. Jonathan is David's defense counsel. . . . On two occasions David produces evidence of his innocence. Although he could have killed Saul, he did not do so. He leaves judgment to YHWH and does not create his own law. In the encounter with Abigail he then learns precisely to refrain from arbitrary law, even though he is in the strongest position. The death of Nabal shows him that YHWH will also pass just judgment on Saul. In the last encounter between Saul and David, the king recognizes his guilt. The prosecutor publicly admits that he is in the wrong. So he himself will have to bear the punishment that he intended for David. (Berges 1989: 128)

The discussion of the character of King Saul has in recent years been oriented strongly toward the tragic dimension. Good in his book on irony in the Old Testament (1981) entitles his chapter on Saul "The Tragedy of Greatness." He begins by recounting how interpreters have already seen Saul's tragedy as justified.

> What makes Saul tragic? . . . Is it that Saul attempted the impossible–to unite two incompatible concepts of kingship? Is it the psychic degeneration brought on by Saul's knowledge of his rejection by Yahweh? Perhaps the tragedy lies in a fatal flaw, the undependability of his will, or in the gloomy inevitability of David's good fortune and Saul's bad? Is Saul's tragedy his personal alienation from Samuel on the one hand and David on the other? Did a disordered and [[52]] unstable personality and the political forces of the time conspire to make him incapable of coping with his task? (Good 1981: 56–57)

Each of these aspects captures something of the intention of the text. In particular, the texts have much to report about a "disordered and unstable personality"; again and again they note that Saul possessed a marked sense of inferiority, formulated explicitly in 1 Sam 15:17. This was previously described in, for instance, 9:21; 10:14–16, 21–22; 11:13; 13:11–14; 14:45 (according to Good [1981: 70–71], it may certainly be doubted that all of these passages actually express Saul's feeling of inferiority). Good continues in a somewhat different vein: "The theme is the theological ambiguity of the establishment of a monarchy and Saul's failure to fill the bill. . . . In a sense, he [the author] has told the story of a man not fitted for a job that should not have been opened. Yet Saul came close enough to being great that he emerges as tragic" (Good 1981: 58–59).

Humphreys (1978, 1980, 1982) thinks that he is able to bring out the tragic in Saul more clearly by trying to uncover, beneath the upper text-layer of 1 Samuel as we have it, a primeval epic whose theme was none other than "The Tragedy of King Saul." This epic was not freely designed but assembled from a series of individual narratives. In particular, these original individual narratives are *9:1–10:16; 11:1–15; 13:1–7a, 15b–23; 14:1–46; 15:4–9:13, 20–21, 24–26, 30–31, 34–35; 17:12, 14, 17–23a, 24–25, 30, 48, 50, 55–58; 18:2, 20, 22–25a, 26–27; 18:6–9a; 19:1–7, 11–17; 26:1–8, 10–14a, 17–22, 25b; 28:3–15, 19b–25; chap. 31. It is hard to fend off the impression that this selection of texts has been made primarily on the basis of their content.

As Humphreys sees it, what can be said about the Saul epic is similar to the sort of thing that may be said about the Greek heroic epics: "The emphasis is on the inner psychic development and deterioration of the man Saul and his personal relationship with others" (1980: 77). The old underlying narrative would have later been reworked in Northern Israelite prophetic circles and then again in the Judahite court (see below, pp. 293–305). In the process, the original tragic undertone was largely lost.

In contrast, Gunn (1980) stays with the final biblical text. In its current form, he finds a very specific, theologically deeply cryptic form of tragedy brought to expression. The interior motivating force of the entire story is the duality of rejection ⟦53⟧ and election. The reader already knows that Saul's rulership lies under an unlucky star; he soon learns that God rejected him, and shortly thereafter he learns whom God has selected as his successor. Saul, by contrast, knows only that he is rejected and that his throne is destined for another—but not for whom. So, all unsuspecting, he takes the elected one into his immediate circle and furthers his rise. With time he grows distrustful; out of love grows love–hate, and finally blazing hatred. Yet everything he attempts against David redounds to David's advantage and to Saul's disadvantage. As a result, Saul sinks into unquenchable fury and helpless impotence. In the end he breaks down, not because of David or the Philistines or even his own powerlessness, but because of–God! God has imposed the kingship on him formally, only then to lie in wait for an opportunity to rid himself of the unloved king. From the very beginning, he has loaded the dice against him–why else the strangely nonsensical order by Samuel in 10:8, just after the anointing? Why else the overly harsh and relentless reaction to Saul's initially only minimal transgression? Saul is God's "victim"; David is his "favorite." Saul is faced with "an uneven match" in David (Gunn 1980: 115). Determinedly, he defends himself against the fate hanging over his head and in the process brings about something worse–but can you blame him? It is not his jealousy of David that is the origin of all evil, but God's "jealous persecution of Saul" (1980: 129). It is not so much Saul but "God [who has] a dark side" (1980: 131).

Exum (1992) evaluates the recent work on Saul's tragedy as well. For her, the story of the first king is "the clearest example of biblical tragedy" (1992: 16). She attempts to prove this by extended comparisons of the Saul narrative with those of Samson and Oedipus. Her view corresponds closely with Gunn's, even though she criticizes him for making Saul far too much of a blameless sacrifice to divine willfulness (1992: 17–18)–whereas Saul, as least as much as God, is "a particularly complicated personality" (1992: 35). Thus, he suffers for two reasons: "his own turbulent personality and the antagonism of God toward human kingship" (1992: 41). This perspective is reminiscent of Good, but Exum takes it a step further: Saul is in fact literally the "scapegoat" (1992: 38) for the people's inappropriate longing for a king. As though [[54]] he had been "deputized," he took (or had to take) the punishment for this trangression upon himself and in so doing cleared the way for the Davidic dynasty. In God's economy, "predestination to evil" is allocated to him. God works toward his downfall–and finds in Saul himself his best agent. From the very beginning, Saul's character exhibits questionable sides, which (Exum 1992: 41) gain the upper hand at first under the "terror of divine enmity." It appears that "demonic forces" (1992: 40) lie behind this, but it is God himself; it is he who drains his spirit from Saul, who refuses him forgiveness for his (tiny) guilt, who propels him into embitterment and despair.

Such empathetic presentations give rise to an impressive portrait of Saul as a tragic figure. He, pitilessly hunting down David, is in truth the quarry. God drives him into disaster–and this for reasons that he himself in greatest part must answer for. It may be doubted, of course, that this is really the Bible's own message, rather than the expression of a particularly modern perspective on life. Fretheim (1985) disparagingly asks, with regard to the interpretations of Humphreys and Gunn, "whether that is actually an aspect of the God revealed in the text, or whether scholars have more personal theological problems with the way in which the God of the text speaks and acts" (1985: 599 n. 20). Fretheim prefers to defend God against the accusation that he had dealt underhandedly with Saul. Instead, God had not foreseen Saul's turn toward evil. Saul's first, still very minor transgressions had come as a surprise! He would have immediately recognized that this was just the beginning and that the experiment with Saul needed to be ended immediately, before irreparable harm ensued. It is in God's favor to say that he learned from his mistake: he did not place any particularly strong demands on David, but instead protected him from misdeeds and placed him and his entire dynasty under an unconditional promise (2 Samuel 7).

Is this the way it was? Probably the biblical authors portray God neither through groping historical experiments nor as dark, impenetrable fate. Instead, so complicated and ambivalent a process as formation of a state raises difficult historical and theological problems that do not have one-dimensional solutions. Should there be a king in Israel, and who and how should the king be? From [[55]] the very beginning there were distinct, even opposing points of view. The formation of the tradition proceeded in the same way, full of tension and contradiction. Nonetheless, the biblical authors were utterly convinced that this portion of the history of Israel, like every other, was thoroughly ruled by YHWH's guiding hand. Thus the ultimate downfall of Saul, just like the unstoppable ascendancy of David, must have had a meaning. It was reasonable to see the destinies of the two coupled together: as much as the one waxed, the other waned. If YHWH had chosen the one–and in the course of (traditional) history this became a rock-solid certainty–then he must have rejected the other. The biblical presentation certainty directs its principal attention, not toward the rejecting activities of YHWH, but toward the electing; not toward God's dark side, but toward the light. Yet divine light also casts shadows–and this is where Saul may be found. All who attempt to complete the portrait of the God of the David and Saul story solely on the basis of Saul and his fate are literally groping in the dark–and manage to reveal themselves as incompetent or cynical in the process. The biblical narrators at most hint at such a possibility; it is certainly not their own viewpoint, nor should it become the view of their readers and interpreters.

The Chosen: David

Even the title of Brueggemann's book *David's Truth* (1985) makes it clear that he places the accent elsewhere. The subtitle . . . *in Israel's Imagination and Memory* hints that it deals, not with the historical David and his merits (or the historical Saul with his supposed disadvantages), but with the portrait that the Bible paints of him. And for Brueggemann there is no doubt: the Bible is "naively enthusiastic for David" and "relentlessly polemical against Saul" (1985: 20). Contrary to the superficial impression (and the position of scholars that has often been put forward recently), however, this has nothing to do with Davidic court propaganda. The David and Saul stories are in fact not court literature but folk literature—more specifically, "survival literature"; even more precisely, ⟦56⟧ "political partisan narrative" (1985: 22). They are written not for the powerful but for the simple people. That a nobody, a *ḫapiru*, was able to evade the attacks of the king and finally become king of Israel himself is a revolutionary event. "One may then understand this narrative to be hopeful, because it tells, generation after generation, that the marginals can become the legitimate holders of power. . . . David is a model for the last becoming first" (1985: 23). What matters is simply for the Bible reader to put on the right eyeglasses: "tribal reading" is on call in reading the David and Saul narrative (1985: 30).

However, anyone who finds Brueggemann's approach and goal warmly sympathetic will not be able to avoid the fact that his interpretation shares the weakness of all works that treat the superficial layer of the text without historical-critical probing and remain there. The perspective on the text chosen, the traits emphasized, and the way they are evaluated largely depend on the discretion of the interpreter. The pictures that emerge promise to be quite lively, but they are subjective as well, and in their flatness and one-dimensionality do not always convince, sometimes appearing downright unbelievable. In the case of Brueggemann, it is striking that he flatly denies the readily available pro-Davidide dimension of the text and in place of it insinuates what might be called a premonarchic thought-pattern (which, incidentally, presupposes an extremely early dating). David in the process takes on a touching weakness and Saul a terrific evil—which in both cases corresponds only partly to the biblical portrait.

Knierim (1970) uncovers in 1 Samuel a differentiated, strongly theological basic plan. The occurrences of the root *mšḥ* ⟦'anointed, messiah'⟧, taken as a whole, yield a real "messiah-ology" that is developed in terms of the first two kings of Israel, both in positive description and in negative delimitation. According to Knierim, it must have been prophetic circles that took so much care to have Saul and David anointed by the prophet Samuel (and not "merely" by the people or the aristocracy), and thereby both of them were first endowed with the (prophetic) spirit before they achieved any mighty deeds in the military sphere (1 Sam 9:1–10:16, 16:1–13). Yet, in the future, only one of the two is able rightly to achieve this high distinction; ⟦57⟧ the other fails. The David and Saul narratives very effectively contrast Saul, no longer legitimate but still a powerful "messiah," with David, the legitimate but still powerless "messiah." The latter is borne through all external and internal danger; the former has "no other choice but to do what leads to his downfall" (Knierim 1970: 129).

Miscall (1983) considers it fundamentally mistaken to achieve a specific understanding of the text, especially of David's nature, be it one-dimensional or dialectical. He admits: "My mode of reading is a departure from the main ways of reading the Bible, particularly their desire for clear and definite meaning" (1983: 73). Accordingly, his favorite word is "ambiguity." Practically everything reported in the narratives about David in 1 Samuel 16–22 that he investigates is ambiguous. A few examples: When 1 Sam 16:7 says that man sees the external, but God sees into the heart, it does not mean at all that God has looked into David's heart and recognized it as pure but merely that God's motives for election (as well as for rejection!) cannot be observed (1983: 52–53). When in 17:28 Eliab speaks of David's "evil heart," we should not conclude that he might be somewhat on the right track—or that David is somewhat arrogant (1983: 66). In 17:45–47 an unusally pious speech by David rings out. "But is this a sincere or a self-serving speech?" (1983: 69). What Miscall asserts about 1 Samuel 17 holds for the entire presentation of David in 1 Samuel: "The narrative raises the questions of David's motivations and intentions . . . , but leaves them indeterminate. David is a cunning and unscrupulous schemer, and he is also an innocent 'man of destiny' for whom all goes right. The text supports a spectrum of portrayals of David and thereby does not support any one definite or probable portrayal" (1983: 83).

Miscall's idiosyncratic interpretation provoked a strong refutation by Payne (1984). For centuries, the portrait of David in Samuel has been felt to be positive, even radiant—how can it now all of a sudden be described as totally ambivalent! Both the psalmist and the narrator of 1 Samuel 17 had known and honored David as an exemplary and popular hero; otherwise they would not have been able to speak of him so enthusiastically. Shadows across the portrait of David are familiar—even that this king [[58]] could submit to criticism. Overall, the Bible trusts the historically positive portrait of David as well.

Perhaps all too clear apologetics wielded the pen in this riposte, and Miscall's exhortation deserved not to be interpreted rashly and one-dimensionally but to be taken to heart—not least by Miscall himself! His determination to find ambivalence everywhere in the text is also not exactly unforced. The same holds for the urge to parallel specific points in the David and Saul stories with points in other biblical narratives, despite all individual differences and literary-historical chasms. The fight with Goliath in 1 Samuel 17, for instance, according to Miscall should be compared with Jacob's fight at the Jabbok (Gen 32:23ff.)—a gross, if I may say so, overestimation of Goliath (Miscall 1983: 77ff.). David as Saul's son-in-law (1 Samuel 18) is supposedly connected with Jacob as Laban's son-in-law (Genesis 29–32): both fathers-in-law have two daughters, both sons-in-law are penniless and therefore must "pay" a most unusual bride-price, both families quarrel, in both cases the father of the daughter is deceived with the help of teraphim (Miscall 1983: 87–88). Fine. But what do we learn from this? Are not such coincidences to be expected in the structure of society at the time and therefore simply chance?

With explicit reference to Miscall but still more capriciously, Pleins (1992) throws up a bridge from the David and Saul stories to the narrative of the binding of Isaac: without reference to Genesis 22, the depiction of the conflict between Saul and David is "inexplicable" (1992: 35). "The Saul story reflects the Abraham story with terrible irony" (1992: 32). "Terrible irony"—the expression threatens to turn itself back on the author. What do the anecdotes of Saul's attacks on David and Jonathan have to do with the most densely compressed Jewish Passion narrative, Genesis 22? And how can David's renunciation of revenge in 1 Samuel 24 and 26 be compared with Isaac's sacrificial role?

What strange fruit a mania for parallelizing unchecked by historical-critical analysis can ripen into is seen in an older article from the Scandinavian Myth-and-Ritual school. Kapelrud (1974) lists traits belonging to David that he has also discovered in various members of the ancient Near Eastern world of the gods: his shepherding, say, or his lyre-playing, or the assertion of the "eternality" of his throne. "Is it only a coincidence or is there some common background?" (1974: 38). Unfortunately, Kapelrud opts for the latter choice and explains that David would have appeared to the narrators precisely as a bringer of salvation, as a divine shining light, and so they would have applied to him epithets from the primeval Near Eastern divine myths.

[[59]] Definitely to be taken seriously, by contrast, because it is also classified as (literary-) historical and thus made credible, is an analogy first perceived by Grønbaek (1971: 96–100) and then by Garsiel (1985: 120–21) and Berges (1989: 235–38): the analogy between the story of David and the story of Joseph (Genesis 37ff.).

David and Joseph were both youngest brothers, both worked in their youth as shepherds, both are described as exceptionally handsome and intelligent, both are quite early pictured in contrast to their future significance, both were sent by their father to their brothers and endured their enmity, both had to overcome deep experiences of both sorrow and exile, of both it is said that God is "with them," both made a fairytale-like ascent to the royal court, both married highly placed women, both were designated by God to save their people. None of the exegetes mentioned above offers a conclusive explanation for this amazing parallelism. Possibly it lies along the same lines as the relationship between the Ark and the Exodus stories. The Exodus and Joseph stories are of Northern, Israelite origin; the David and the Ark stories are Judahite. On the (very likely) supposition that the Israelite narratives are somewhat older, it is entirely possible that the Judahite, or more precisely, established Jerusalem narrators or writers, created a sort of Judahite national epic, undoubtedly with the use of older individual Judahite traditions. This was in conscious contrast to the corresponding Northern model. They created one national epic about the founder of the royal house of Jerusalem and one about the central ritual object of the divine house of Jerusalem.

Subsidiary Figures: Jonathan, Michal

The profound friendship between David and Jonathan has always worked a peculiar sort of magic on expositors, this being the only pair of friends described by the Bible (Kaiser 1990: 281; in striking comparison with Greek literature, in which friendship between men is frequently memorialized and celebrated). Is it failure of respect for the Bible, or is it a necessity of our time to consider whether Jonathan's love (which David in his touching lament for his fallen friend praised as "more wonderful than the love of women") was homoerotic love?

Gunn (1980: 93) thinks that the biblical authors had already thought about this. Supposedly, they intentionally took care to show David many times coupling with women and thus heterosexual. About Jonathan, [[60]] on the other hand, only love for David is mentioned. Thus, Saul's eldest son, the crown prince, appears to be homosexual and, consequently, unfit to continue the dynasty.

Horner (1978: 40–58), whose book on homosexuality in the Bible took its title from Jonathan's love for David, wishes to tackle the theme without false presuppositions. Working outside the attitudes of "homophobia in Western culture" (1978: 36) and the inhibited, apologetic defensiveness of exegetical specialists, he attempts to determine the true state of affairs and the thoughts of the biblical writers on the question. For him, on the basis especially of 1 Sam 20:30–31 and 2 Sam 1:26, it is absolutely certain that David in his youth had a homoerotic love affair with Jonathan; that he never strove to conceal this; and that nonetheless he "married eight times and had many children. . . . Above all, this type of homosexuality had nothing to do with effeminacy. Such men were warrior friends" (1978: 38). Among solid young men, then, (temporary) homosexual relationships were not considered reprehensible; they were only despised when they were combined with effeminacy, even "unmanliness," in the view of a patriarchally organized world.

Now Thompson had already in 1974 presented an investigation of the use of the verb *ʾahēb* 'love' in the David and Jonathan narratives and, beyond that, throughout 1 Samuel. (The examples: 1 Sam 16:21–Saul; 18:1, 3; 20:17; 2 Sam 1:26–Jonathan; 1 Sam 18:20–Michal; 18:16, 22, 28–Saul's surroundings/Israel.) The contexts (that is, the results) exhibit the concept not as an expression of personal inclination but as a political term that reaches into the realm of treaty language.

Doob Sakenfeld (1983) demonstrates something quite similar with respect to another main concept that is important in this context: *ḥesed*. In 1 Sam 20:8, David requests *ḥesed* of Jonathan, meaning, in context, protection for his endangered life; in 1 Sam 20:14–15 (and then in 2 Sam 9:1) "we find the roles reversed." In each case the word means "an act," or better, "an action" "of loyalty" (1983: 197); its occasional association with *bĕrît* makes it entirely clear that it has "political rather than personal overtones" (1983: 199). On *ʾahēb*, after practically repeating Thompson's argumentation, she goes on to refer to the analogous Akkadian concept *raʾāmu*, which goes as far as to mean 'show loyalty'; thus *ʾahēb* here might mean approximately 'to show reverence to a radiant hero, the future king'. Homosexuality could thus hardly be the matter at hand (1983: 201; one hopes this is an unexpected result and not the secret motive for the investigation!).

Exum (1992) stresses that in 1 Samuel David appears only as the object, not the subject, of 'love'. It also reports that Jonathan loved David; "nothing is said of the converse" (1992: 73). In the text, the entire movement is from Jonathan to David: Jonathan gives David not just "love" but solemn avowals of brotherhood (1 Sam 20:12ff.) and even his weapons (18:4). This symbolizes the transfer of power from Saul (and the Saulides) to David (and the Davidides). The chiastic arrangement of the [[61]] Jonathan scenes scattered through 1 Samuel is thought to point in the same direction: A/A′ Jonathan's victory over and defeat by the Philistines (1 Samuel 13, 31); B/B′ Jonathan's alliance with David (1 Sam 18:1–4; 23:15–18); C/C′ Jonathan's intervention on behalf of David's security (19:1–7; chap. 20). These assertions hardly further the exposition. How can they, when this "composition" was hardly assembled deliberately but is the result of a multistage textual growth?!

Perhaps the deepest insights into Jonathan's character are achieved by Jobling (1986). He recognizes that the narrative strategy of the biblical authors is such an important factor that he asks precisely "whether he is not a purely literary construction" (1986: 27–a suspicion that, in view of a passage such as 2 Sam 1:26, can hardly be substantiated). That is, Jonathan was no less than the personified solution of a difficult dual task that the biblical narrators believed had been set before them: to justify the legitimacy of dynastic rule in Israel and to prove the dependability of God. "The transition from Saul to David, otherwise theologically implausible, is by Jonathan made theologically plausible" (1986: 14). The narrator's technique is to show Jonathan first fully identified with Saul, then increasingly distanced from his father and progressively identified with David, and finally giving himself fully over to David's patronage. Basically, it is already clear in 1 Sam 18:1–5: "The kingship has passed from Saul to David by the mediation of Jonathan" (1986: 20). Taking up the structuralist actant model (Greimas, Lévi-Strauss, Leach), Jobling sees Jonathan as playing a double role in God's plan to save his people Israel from its enemies through David: as Saul's son and crown prince, Jonathan is first an "adversary"; as David's friend and through his own abdication, he becomes a "helper" toward the divine objective. But he cannot become the latter without having first been the former: "Jonathan's identification with . . . Saul provide[s] him with the royal authority to abdicate" (1986: 25)! In this way, yet another theological problem is solved: the contradiction between God's original pledge to Saul and his ultimate rejection. Is God unreliable? Far from it: "Yahweh's grace is utterly free, Yahweh's demand is utterly binding. Saul sins, and must be rejected. But Yahweh made him a promise, which must be kept. Therefore, the passing of Saul's [[62]] kingship must express the radical discontinuity caused by sin . . . , but also the radical continuity guaranteed by grace" (1986: 26). In the character of Jonathan it becomes possible that "the kingship passes by legitimate means to one who has become his heir" (1986: 26).

Another significant subsidiary role in the David and Saul stories is played by Michal, Saul's daughter, Jonathan's sister, and according to the tradition, David's first wife. According to the categories of Berlin (1983: 24ff.), she is an example of the "full-fledged character with opinions and emotions of her own," as distinct from the weakly limned "type" (for example, Abigail) and the mere "agent" (for example, Bathsheba). Bechmann (1988) sets all of the passages dealing with Michal in a series (1 Sam 18:20–29; 19:10–18; 25:44; 2 Sam 3:12–16; 6:16, 20–23; [21:8]) and sees her described there in a double role as "David's savior and sacrifice." Outside the Song of Songs, this is the only place in the Bible that discusses the love of a woman for a man—yet she remains just a pawn in the men's game of power and intrigue. "Here Saul succumbs because of Michal's decision" (1988: 75). It is she "to whom David owes his very life. Without Michal there would be no Davidic dynasty" (1988: 80). In remarkable contrast to this, there stands the fact that for broad stretches she appears, "never as subject, but always as object" (1988: 77) until in the end her "love . . . is inverted to contempt," and she "seeks and provokes the conflict with David" (1988: 79).

Exum (1992: 81ff.) on the whole offers a similar interpretation of this female character but introduces the category of the tragic as well: Michal loves David, but nothing indicates a return of love. She saves his life–and loses him in the process (Exum sees the escape through the window as a birth symbol; 1992: 89). She is given to another at the behest of her father and taken back from him at the behest of David–without any consultation of her in the process. She is called, according to whoever happens to have control of her, "Saul's daughter" or "David's wife"–making her recognizable as a personality striving for autonomy (1992: 84–85). In the end it remains open why Michal had no children: is it because David spurns her or she him (1992: 87)?

The synchronic analysis of the Michal pericopes [[63]] by Clines (1991) is vivid. He poses a series of questions that the careful reader gleans from the texts but that the texts do not answer clearly and unambiguously. Of course, the right answer (or are there several right answers?) as a rule is already determined; it must merely be discovered. The methodological principle must be that speculation is not freely indulged but that the text constitutes an "anchor" for the respective attempts at solution. It is then utterly pointless to inquire into the respective historical states of affairs (contrary to the efforts of Stoebe, for instance [1958] 1989); one reaches no further back than to the text or the narrator and his opinion on the question under consideration.

A couple of examples: Why does Saul wed David to Michal rather than Merab? (Answer: because the negotiated bride-price for Michal was of a clear–that is, verifiable–size; the bride-price for Merab was not; Clines 1991: 28ff.) Why did Michal love David? (The text offers no clue to an answer; 1991: 31ff.) Did David love Michal? (Answer: the reader may answer the question either yes or no; 1991: 37–38) How is Michal's lie to Saul in 1 Sam 19:17 to be judged? (Answer: more critically than the exegetes usually do; 1991: 38ff.) What feelings did Michal harbor toward Paltiel, 2 Sam 3:15–16? (Answer: this remains unclear, 1991: 47ff.; "the character of Michal becomes more than ever enigmatic," p. 52.) Why does Michal in 2 Samuel 6 react so indignantly to David's entrance? (The answer, given with a certain regret, but based unambiguously on the text: because she had "some definite views about . . . royal dignity," 1991: 59.)

The core of the recent book on "Queen Michal" (Clines and Eskenazi 1991) consists of a series of lectures given at a symposium on Narrative Research on the Hebrew Bible; alongside this, however, an entire palette of highly diverse older and newer interpretations are reproduced, beginning with a (!) historical investigation of insipid dictionary entries and popularized character studies down to sermons and poetic reworkings of the material. The result of such variety "is a more reader-involving book than most works of biblical criticism" (1991: 7). The emphasis is exclusively on the synchronic exposition of the Michal pericopes. This dominates naturally in the belletristic portraits of Michal, in part directly reprinted (1991: 145–56, 199–200) but for the most part reviewed in detail (1991: 157–74, 207–23). Yet even the specifically exegetical articles largely follow narratological methodology. The insights thus collected are extensive and stimulating—indeed, practically confusing in their variety and occasional contradictions. They impressively verify the high literary quality of the biblical narratives and justify their esthetic contemplation. Of course there are other aspects as well that must not be neglected.

The Michal (Merab) stories as they now appear, like the entire David and Saul story in general, are without a doubt [[64]] considered, artful constructions; yet, also without a doubt, there were preliminary oral stages underlying the extant form of the text, and in between there were various literary stages. Interpretations fixated on the final text are richly faceted and, once in a while, profound. Yet, in many respects they remain quite superficial, exhibiting a dubious capriciousness in choice of viewpoint, and are above all insensitive to the question of distinct settings of individual narratives and textual layers, each in its own time. Here and there one gets the feeling that the "literary analysis" and "close reading" methods of interpretation are skating on the thin ice of a superficial text, frozen relatively randomly and unevenly in the course of the processes of recording and canonization, scarcely perceiving the deep and very turbulent waters of biblical tradition—and literary-history beneath.

The Historiography of David and Saul

The Necessity of a Diachronic Approach

Research did not in the past, nor can it in the future, limit itself to apprehending the biblical narrative on David and Saul as it now appears—as an integrated unit, so to speak—and to investigating its structural markers and communicative intent. This is not a meaningless venture, as the impressive examples in the previous section make clear. The biblical authors who brought the text into its final form and all the tradents and expositors who transmitted it in this form and continually pondered it understood it as a meaningful whole. What they did was self-evident, somewhat right, and remains to this day quite successful.

The question arises, however, whether what the latest editors of the biblical text—sometime between the exile and the period of canon formation—thought they could recognize as the truth about David and Saul is the only or even the entire truth. The very fact that there are a variety of sometimes highly divergent yet equally canonical text versions (for instance, [[65]] versions of 1 Samuel 17–18 [[in the LXX and the MT]]) awakens doubts about whether it is truth. Various traces in the books of Samuel—such as the sometimes highly differentiated text versions, or dogmas and mnemonics like 1 Sam 16:7 ("Man looks on the outward appearance, but YHWH looks on the heart") or 17:47 ("YHWH saves not with sword and spear; for the battle is YHWH's"), and especially psalms by which the congregation could respond to the message of God's activity in history (1 Sam 2:1–10; 2 Samuel 22; 23:1–5; see Mathys 1994: 126–64)—indicate that even very late in the postexilic period particular lines of interpretive comments were registered and interpretive comments inserted.

It is undisputed that the books of Samuel underwent a (or several) deuteronomistic editing(s); what is disputed is only how extensively the text was reshaped. In any case the research into deuteronomistic activity carried forward by Martin Noth (1943) and others after him has made clear that this school of deuteronomistic scholars did not propagate just any truths indiscriminately but only the one(s?) that could be made consistent with the teachings of the book of Deuteronomy. In order to gain a hearing, they resolutely intervened, where necessary, in the traditions transmitted to them—in the case of the books of Samuel with comparative restraint, but far from negligibly. It is not reasonable, however, just to wish to read the David–Saul stories more "deuteronomistically" (as some of the works discussed in the previous section decidedly do), because the Deuteronomists (even according to Jewish tradition) permitted perspectives other than their own to remain; more precisely, they let them stand.

The Deuteronomistic History, which spans Deuteronomy to 2 Kings, is nowhere more clearly a "work of tradition" (Noth [[1943]]) than in the books of Samuel. Samuel's authors did not merely decide, out of their own free will, following only their own intentions, and using only a few formulations, to write down a thoroughly deuteronomistic history of Israel. They reworked diverse, virtually disparate source materials, which in some cases ran directly counter to their own interests (so, with Noth, emphatically Dietrich 1995). They wished to transmit to their readers and to posterity, not only their own truth, but also what was already in their possession or had been made known to them.

Now truth is always concrete—or else it is not truth. It is no accident that the Bible unfolds the truth about God and Man [[66]] mostly not by abstract theology but by concrete examples, such as David and Saul. Nor is it by chance that this truth was not settled once and for all but was pondered over generations and rewon ever anew. In the case of David and Saul, this was not only going on during their lifetimes or shortly thereafter but in ever new attempts, down to the exile and even in the postexilic period. In principle, every epoch had to determine the truth about David and Saul for itself—both with regard to the past and to the respective present moments. The results had to come out extremely differently, for it makes a big difference whether Saul and David were being considered in Benjamin or in Judah, whether during the United Monarchy or the divided kingdom, whether after the fall of Israel or not until after the fall of Judah. (To determine this in no way means to posit the biblical witnesses as slaves to their respective world views; quite the opposite. How else would a way of looking at life, if it became passé, be combated if not with timebound, timely truth?)

Scholarship has the task, and very likely also the means, of ascertaining as exactly as possible the various facets of the truth about David and Saul that were recorded as they were perceived during the course of Israelite-Judahite (intellectual) history. It is methodologically sensible to begin by carefully distinguishing the respective stages—diachronically—from each other, to describe each by itself, and then to observe—synchronically—their biblical juxtaposition and interpenetration and to reflect on the whole. This gives rise to a temporally and theologically historically differentiated concord. This will not be cacophanous but, with all of its richness, uncommonly harmonious; the biblical tradents and writers and, most recently, the Jewish people have provided for this by deciding on the oneness of a God who encompasses all contradictions, as well as the truth.

The Rise of David Narrative

After scholarship gave up the search for a continuation of the Pentateuchal sources in the portion of the canon known as the Former Prophets and before Martin Noth had claimed these books of the Bible for the Deuteronomistic History, hypotheses [[67]] developed about several smaller historical works within the compass of the books of Samuel. Leonhard Rost began, in 1926, with an article on the "tradition of David's succession." Rost also added the Ark narrative (1 Samuel 4–6, 2 Samuel 6) to this "source," which he saw stretching from 2 Samuel 7 to 1 Kings 2. The traditions of Samuel and of Saul's elevation and rejection (1 Samuel 1–3, 7–15) clearly stand apart. The textual complex from 1 Samuel 16 to 2 Samuel 5 remains.

Now, 1 Samuel 16 tells of David's anointing and 2 Samuel 5 of his enthronement; in between there is all sorts of chaos and confusion, through which the son of a nobody rose to be ruler of Israel, Judah, and Jerusalem. What could be more natural than the notion of an independent history of "David's rise," a counterpart to that of "David's enthronement"? Rost (1926: 133ff. = 1965: 238ff.) formulated the hypothesis, Alt adopted it ([1930] 1964: 15, 36). After a considerable delay, perhaps due to the war years, scholarship since the 1950s has once again taken up the problems it entails. The work did not turn out to be simple. Even the basic question about the beginning and end of the postulated history caused (and still causes) considerable difficulties. A natural way in, as it were, is the story of David's anointing, 1 Sam 16:1–13 (so Weiser 1966). But in 16:1 God orders Samuel no longer to mourn the rejected Saul but to anoint another in his place, a beginning point that unambiguously attaches David's narrative to the narrative in 1 Samuel 15. So the following possibilities for establishing a beginning point emerge:

- We count 1 Samuel 15 with the Rise of David Narrative (so Grønbaek 1971: 26–27; Mettinger 1976: 34–35); but 15:1 in turn seems to refer back to the anointing of Saul in 1 Sam 9:1–10:16 and, moreover, the entire chapter was only inserted by a deuteronomistic hand into its present context.
- We take the reference to the Saul story seriously and postulate a historiography not just of the Rise of David (and the Fall of Saul) but also of the prior Rise of Saul. This would have included, according to Campbell (1986: 125ff.), 1 Sam *9:1–10:16; chaps. 11, *15, and 16ff.; and according to Dietrich (1987: 89ff.; 1992: 63ff.), 1 Sam *9:1–10:16; chaps. 13–14, and 16ff.
- We accept that the attachment between 1 Samuel 15 and 1 Sam 16:1–13 was carried out only belatedly, perhaps deuteronomistically (Weiser 1966: 326; Mommer 1991: 178: "verse 1a$\alpha_2\beta$ can be neatly snipped out"). [[68]]
- We consider 1 Sam 16:1–13 secondary, as well as 1 Samuel 15, and have the old Rise story begin in 16:14 (Veijola 1975: 102; McCarter 1980a: 493; Kaiser 1990); but 1 Samuel 15 and 16:1–13 are hardly on the same plane tradition-historically or in purpose. Additionally, 16:14 mentions the "spirit of YHWH" that moved Saul, and 16:13 says that it fell on David; this is certainly a secondary connection, but hardly one first made by a deuteronomistic hand.

The end of the narrative in 2 Samuel 5 is likewise not clearly marked.

A finale appropriate to the theme of the Rise of David would be the conquest of Jerusalem, with the concluding pious summary in 2 Sam

5:6–10 (vv. 11–12 could be deuteronomistic; so Grønbaek 1971: 158; Veijola 1975: 98–99; and McCarter 1980b: 493). Yet a list of the names of David's sons follows in 5:13–16, which is presented as the continuation of the similar list in 2 Sam 3:2–5. Should the two be separated from each other? If not, are both of them really integral components of the Rise of David? Or are they actually preparation for the battle between David's sons for the Succession?

Furthermore, the fact that David makes an end of the Philistines (2 Sam 5:17–25) might be taken as a sensible conclusion to the many reports of confrontations with the Philistines in the Rise story. On the other hand, this passage now appears to be a bridge to the one in 2 Samuel 6 about the bringing in of the Ark, which earlier had actually fallen into Philistine hands. Should this also belong to the Rise of David—even, from a pious point of view, constituting its very climax? Corresponding to this and contradicting it at the same time is the fact that 2 Samuel 6 ends with a fight between David and Michal. Was it not the Rise story that previously again and again illuminated the developed relationship between these two (1 Sam 18:20ff., 19:11ff., 25:44; 2 Sam 3:12ff.)? Or was Rost right in the claim that the Michal scenes prove precisely that the Ark story is part of the Succession Narrative? Rost saw the actual starting point of the Succession Narrative to be the famous Nathan prophecy of 2 Samuel 7—which, however, Weiser (1966: 245ff.; followed by Mettinger 1976: 43–44) explained precisely as the crowning conclusion to the Rise story. More militant dispositions might perhaps plead that the impressive (others might prefer to say shocking!) list of "battles and victories of David" in 2 Samuel 8 is the triumphant finale of David's Rise—especially since here again, as so often previously, the Rise narrator speaks of "accompaniment by YHWH" (Nübel 1959: 77, who admittedly assumes that 2 Samuel 7 originally followed 2 Samuel 8).

What to do? Should we simply accept that the beginning and end of the History of the Rise of David cannot be determined with any more certainty but simply lie somewhere in 1 Samuel 15–16 and 2 Samuel 5–8? But does not such a crucial uncertainty demand an examination of the entire hypothesis?

If we look into the inner consistency of the textual complex 1 Samuel 16–2 Samuel 5 (or 8), a double impression is formed. On the one hand, we can hardly imagine that we are dealing with the self-contained product of a freely working, methodical writer. It must [[69]] have been a loose collection, assembled with difficulty from disparate individual narratives. On the other hand, we can observe throughout it the features of a well-considered ordering of materials as well as of a purposeful linking of individual pieces into larger contexts and these in turn into a meaningfully structured whole.

The second impression, of relative unity, is the basis for the scholars' works discussed above (on pp. [[276–91]]), which consider the biblical presentation of David and Saul as a whole. They sometimes suffer from the fact that they ignore the first impression, of considerable disparity.

Other scholars, now to be introduced, direct their attention primarily to the tensions, contradictions, and doublets in the text and strive for literary-critical [[in the older sense of the term]] explanations. Their goal is primarily the restoration of an "original" text that is as pure as possible and that can be read as a continuous history and plausibly be considered the creation of a single author.

They attempt to distinguish exactly two such works or authors, thinking they can capture the classic pentateuchal sources in the books of Samuel as well (Schulte 1972; North 1982). Why does David come twice into Saul's court (1 Sam 16:14ff., 17:55ff.), why does the fugitive David twice spare the life of Saul pursuing him (1 Samuel 24, 26), why does Saul fall once by his own hand and once by the hand of an Amalekite (1 Samuel 31, 2 Samuel 1)? Well, because both the "Yahwist" and the "Elohist" reported these things. But these sources peter out, at the latest (since Noth 1943), in the Former Prophets, or even (more recently) in the Tetrateuch itself.

Just as for the books of Moses, so also for the books of Samuel, literary criticism offers the possibility of a theory of supplementation as well as sources. An old, pristine, "basic document" was later newly edited by an "editor," who was the "originator of the confusion" in the present text (so Nübel [1959: 33], full of regret over the current state of 1 Samuel 20; the narrative originally had the following sequence, satisfying the literary taste of the exegetes: "20:7a, 8a, 7b, 8b, 9, 11, 12a aa, 13a aa bb, 12a cc–end, 13a cc–end, a, 16b, 14, 15, 16a, 17, 10").

If we relate this approach to the questions posed previously, [[70]] we have this: originally David made his court debut as a lyre-player and only later as Goliath-slayer (Kaiser 1990); Saul was originally spared in the cave of En-gedi and then later in the midst of his military retinue (Koch 1967: 175; the other way around for Mildenberger 1962: 111–12; Nübel [1959: 47ff.] again confidently takes a path that can hardly be followed, by reconstructing a basic narrative out of fragments of both stories, which would then have been expanded into the two versions); Saul died originally by his own hand, and only later did he receive suicide assistance from the Amalekites (so Grønbaek [1971: 217ff.], who admittedly takes the Rise of David narrator to be the second narrator).

Meanwhile, scholarship gave rise to a whole series of variants of the "basic document" plus "expansion layer" in the David and Saul historiography. For Nübel (1959), the present text is quite essentially the work of the supplementer; the individual components of the basic document can only be filtered out of it by meticulous detective work and must be carefully reconstructed in their original order. Its starting point is 1 Sam 16:1ff.; its ending point is 2 Samuel 7. "The generative factor and aim of the presentation of the history . . . is Yahweh's promise" (1959: 141). It should become clear that "the 'meaning of history' " is "trust" in God (1959: 144). The work was "written down before the momentum by which David established his great realm began to ebb" (1959: 124). Historically, the basic document still shows that "David had achieved a more friendly relationship to the amphictyony than Saul" and therefore was more successful (1959: 139). The revision, which far exceeded the bounds of the David and Saul material and comprised a history of the kingdom through good times and bad, was based in Elijah's antimonarchic traditions and also was leaning toward the outlook of Deuteronomy. It blackens the portrait of Saul as king and in its portrait of David sketches "a new royal ideal" of a pious, pure ruler who sheds no blood (1959: 147).

Mildenberger also (1962) declares the reviser to be inclined toward the prophets and to be a "forerunner of the Deuteronomist"; more precisely, to be rooted in Israelite prophetic circles. These prophets fled to Judah when the Northern Kingdom fell in 722 and operated in Jerusalem. "We see in our reviser a theologian who attempted to explain the fall of the North and at the same time to recognize God's salvific power in the continuation of the Davidic monarchy, a power that also to a great extent remained turned toward his people" (1962: 58). The basic document, for Mildenberger as for Nübel, has a fairly uncomplicated form, the center portion being something like this: 1 Sam 22:1–2, 6–8; 23:14–15, 19–24a; 26:1–20; 24:17b; 26:21; 24:18–23a; 26:22–25; 27:1–28:2; 29:1–11; 31. Overall, the work comprises the foundation of 1 Samuel 13–2 Samuel 7. Aside from 1 Samuel 13–14 and 2 Sam 1:17ff., it is not assembled [[71]] from individual prior narratives available to the author but freely composed by him. His intention is to prove, after the division of the kingdoms in 926, the legitimacy of Davidic rule over all Israel, North and South (1962: 164). Additionally, according to Mildenberger, there was a final priestly revision (for example, in 1 Sam 22:5, 9–23; 23:1–13; 30:1–26a).

Kaiser (1990), who investigates only part of the David and Saul story, arrives at quite similar results. The basic layer came from the period shortly after the division of the kingdom and comprised [. . .] 1 Sam 14:46; 16:14–23; 18:1aβb, 5; 19:8; 18:*6, 7, *8, 9; 19:9, 10a; 20:1b–7, 9–10, 18–22, 24–39; 21:1 [. . .]. The revision layer arose after 722 but is predeuteronomistic; one can see that it includes not "genuine" (that is, handed down from of old) but "constructed" (self-written) narratives:

1 Sam 16:1–13; 17:1–18:4, *6, *8, 10–30; 19:1–8, 10b–24. Last, there is a deuteronomistic textual layer in 20:11–17, 23, 40–42. Kaiser himself states, "Some of the operations suggested here . . . might at first glance appear far too violent," but the tensions in the text might be better explained this way than by accepting single authorship (1990: 287). This can be discussed.

Humphreys (1980, 1982) takes an entirely different path, uninfluenced by German-language scholarship, when he isolates out of the existing text an old Saul tragedy (see pp. 279–83, above). It is basically equal to a large part of the individual narratives dealing with Saul in 1 Samuel 9–31, which Humphreys reads and interprets as an ongoing unity. This basic layer underwent two revisions afterward, in each case being extended: first (probably before 722) by Northern prophetic circles (1 Samuel 1; 3:19–4:1; 7:5–12, 16–17; 8:1–7; 9:15–17, 20–21; 10:1, 5–8, 10–13, 17–26; 11:14, 16–17; 12:1–5; 13:7b–15a; chap. *15; 16:1–13; 17:1–11, 32–40, 42–48a, 49, 51–54; 18:10–11; 19:8–10, 18–24; 28:16–19a [note that this includes many texts with deuteronomistic insertions!]); then by Judahite court circles (1 Samuel *18, *19–21, *23–27, 29, 30; 2 Samuel 1–5—thus basically the pure David stories). At the very end, there was one more (very minor) deuteronomistic revision.

Van der Lingen (1983) tries to reconstruct an actual "B-document" that in some respects recalls Humphreys' Saul tragedy. It would provide an answer to the question troubling the Northern tribes about how so outstanding a man as Saul, at one time filled with the spirit of God, could sink so far and end in darkness. At the same time it clung to the idea of a Saulide monarchy. It would be found in 1 Samuel 11; *13–14; 16:15–23; *17–22; chaps. 26, 28, 31. Distinct from it would be an "A-document," with David at core, and would especially comprise 1 Samuel *17–19, 23, 24–25, 27, 29, 30; 2 Samuel *1–5. A non-cultically oriented, ardently pro-Davidic redactor, R II, from Abiathar's circle, would have combined the two works, idealizing David and turning Saul into a villain. A further redactor, R III, in the protodeuteronomistic period (that is, before 640 B.C.) shaped a theological epic from the whole.

McCarter (1980a) distinguishes an "original narrative" that would encompass the major part of the text from 1 Sam 16:14 to 2 Sam 5:10 and would be a "more or less unified composition" (1980a: 491), containing some "secondary materials" (1 Sam 13:13–14; chap. 15; 16:1–13; and chap. *28), [[72]] and deuteronomistic editing (to which would go back the parts of 1 Samuel 17 missing from the LXX version, as well as 1 Sam 20:11–17; 23:40–42; chap. 24; 25:28–31; 2 Sam 2:10a, 11; 3:9–10; 5:1–2, 4–5, 11–12; finally, the appending of the materials in 2 Sam 5:13ff.; chaps. 6–7).

This overview of the literary-critical models shows that only with deep incisions into the present text and after complicated surgery is it possible to maintain a relatively smooth text that would make it possible to satisfy the modern idea of a logically progressing historiography, focused in its subject matter. Such a text, obviously, can now be said to exist only in a very qualified way in the Bible. Moreover, scholarship is in no position to really come to an agreement on a single text. To be sure, there are striking coincidences between the various attempted solutions, which indicates that the approach is not fundamentally flawed, but the available apparatus is not suitable or not precise enough to achieve a result that is convincing in all of its details. Thus, in the course of research there has emerged a lowering of expectations: whereas in the beginning even quarter-verses were meticulously dissected, later work featured larger blocks. The outcome is that the basic layers arrived at are no longer considered pure and rigid in themselves in the former sense, but instead are composed of individual traditions; furthermore, we no longer see the revision(s) as minimal insertions into the work but as large, extensive ones.

In the process, the literary-critical approach has lost considerable rigor. In any case, if a seamless continuous text can no longer be achieved with certainty but "only" a "more-or-less unified composition," then it is appropriate wherever possible to apply diligence and intuition, not to distinguishing several textual layers, but to the question of whether the entire existing text (at least approximately) can be understood as a single large composition.

In fact, in the latest research, the accent is shifting more and more from pure literary criticism to composition and redaction criticism. In the process, the hiatus between synchronic and diachronic thinking is visibly narrowing. Nonetheless, it does not fully disappear. Diachronic thinking is distinct [[73]] from synchronic in three ways: the distinguishability of individual traditional units that existed before the compilation; the distinguishability of the work of the compiler (or even of a freely creating author!) from what was supposedly transmitted to him; and last, the distinguishability of a predeuteronomistic composition from the state of the text achieved primarily by insertions into the Deuteronomistic History.

Holding to this difference does not mean stressing it unduly. On all three levels–the individual traditions, the predeuteronomistic composition, and the Deuteronomistic History–the methodology of synchronic textual study can and should be brought more strongly into operation. This can (and often does) happen on the (deuteronomistic) final level of the text, but recent research pursues similar tendencies throughout, even on the level of what is called the Rise of David Narrative.

It was Artur Weiser who in a fairly brief article (1966) directed attention in this direction. He makes it clear that the author "used various individual traditions" and that his work therefore has a peculiarly "mosaic-like character" but that he gave it a thoroughly self-contained character (1966: 330–31). In that the author selected from preexisting tradition, carefully organized and combined what he selected, and cautiously commented on the resulting whole, he created a self-coherent, remarkable work literarily and theologically.

The picture sketched by Weiser was broadly painted in by Grønbaek in his detailed 1971 monograph. He analyzes the entire text, considers to what extent traditional material has been reworked, and what alterations were carried out during installation into the larger context. In this respect he accomplishes the basic work, his book looking to a great extent like a commentary on 1 Samuel 15–2 Samuel 5. He also arrives at the conclusion that in the Rise of David Narrative "predominantly oral traditional material" is reworked (Grønbaek 1971: 17). Occasionally, though, especially toward the end of his presentation, the author formulates larger sections independently (see 1 Sam 16:1–13; 18:17–19; 19:1–7, 18–24; 23:7–13, 2 Samuel 1–5). There are quite marginal supplementary traces of deuteronomistic revision; they may be found in 1 Sam 15:2, 6; 30:21–25; 2 Sam 1:17–27; 2:10–11; and 5:11–12 (Grønbaek 1971: 271).

⟦74⟧ Significant are the linguistic and structuring devices discovered by Grønbaek (and in part already by Weiser and later by others) with which the Rise of David narrator has shaped his materials into a major whole, despite all of the discrepancies in the transmitted material—and most recently this brings us very close to the synchronic approach, and we have even, in this context, been able to adopt direct observations, which have been achieved via highly sophisticated methodology.

Only a few examples of deliberate compositional practice within the David and Saul tradition need be named here.

- The statement that Yhwh is "with David" is very common in the Rise story, used practically as a central theme; this accompaniment formula hardly ever occurs as a component of an older narrative but is always a summarizing evaluation by the overall editor (Grønbaek 1971: 91; also Mildenberger 1962: 119; and Weiser 1966: 334–35).
- The frequent employment of the verb *ʾhb* 'love' in 1 Samuel 18–19, as well as *qšr* 'commit oneself' or 'conspire', used in 1 Sam 18:1 and 22:8, 13, appears to be a redactional device for connecting distinct narratives (Ackroyd 1975).
- The narratives gathered in 1 Samuel 19ff. are connected by a sort of flight itinerary and the formula "and David fled and escaped" (*mlṭ* and *brḥ*; Grønbaek 1971: 135).

- In 1 Samuel 18ff., a relatively regular alternation of lively narratives and abstractly summarizing compendia or brief notices can be observed; according to Rendtorff (1971), the Rise of David narrator deliberately organized his work according to such themes.
- On several occasions the author has bound materials together by inserting "comprehensive anticipatory redactional joints" (Willis 1973, with respect to 18:5, 9ff., 28–30); note also the use of two traditions of similar content but divergent transmission histories (1 Samuel 24 / 26; 21:1ff. / 27:1ff.) or the doubling of a particular piece of information at the opening of a long narrative (1 Sam 18:7 / 21:12; 23:19 / 26:1), according to Dietrich 1977: 51.

Several apparently disparate individual episodes are actually related to each other artistically. Gunn (1980) has a keen sense for this. "David controls madness. Madness controls Saul," he asserts about the contrast between 1 Sam 19:18ff. and 1 Sam 21:11ff. Thus, it is a matter of (not) being pierced by Saul's spear in 1 Sam 18:10–11 and 1 Sam 26:8. The curse that Saul would not cast on the right "object" (the Amalekites, 1 Samuel 15) he then casts on the wrong one (the priests of Nob, 1 Samuel 22)—while David does it twice, rightly (1 Sam 27:8ff., 30:17ff.).

Contrasting with such productive observations is the painful step backward that the latest major German-language commentary on Samuel, Stoebe's (1973), has taken, determinedly contributing nothing to the clarification of the literary composition of the David–Saul [[75]] historiography. Stoebe declares that 1 Samuel 16–31 is compiled from all sorts of heroic court epics and popular traditions (1973: 59), yet they were not strung together by some writer or composer. They grew together "in circles" during preliterary stages into thematically centered larger formations (1973: 59–62), when a possible final editor assumed a subsidiary role. One may certainly ask whether prefabricated narrative cycles might have found a place in the Rise of David Narrative, but this process does not explain the pervasive individual details or the features of deliberate literary activity that span entire thematic cycles. In conclusion, the place, time, and purpose of the postulated History of the Rise of David must be investigated.

A most extraordinary consensus about the place of origin of the Rise of David Narrative has been achieved by scholarship: Jerusalem—more precisely, the Davidic royal court. Admittedly, Humphreys (1980) thinks his "Saul tragedy" and van der Lingen (1983) thinks his "B-document" (see above) came into existence in the North and only afterward were worked together with the unambiguously Judahite-colored David narratives. But this in any case took place in Jerusalem.

On the question of dating, too, relative unanimity prevails. The vast majority of scholars are prepared to accept a very early date of origin:

either the time of David himself (Nübel 1959: 124, for the "basic document"; McCarter 1980a: 495; van der Lingen for both "B-document" and "A-document"; Brueggemann 1985) or the time of Solomon (Weiser 1966: 354; Mommer 1987: 60–61) or shortly after the division of the kingdom (Mildenberger 1962: 164, for the "basic document"; Grønbaek 1971: 35–36; Schicklberger 1974: 262–63; Mettinger 1976: 41; for the "basic document," again Kaiser 1990: 293). All in all, the tenth century is obviously taken to be the period in which the postulated Rise of David Narrative can best be accommodated, whether the story is discerned to be celebrating the founder of the Davidic–Solomonic kingdom or castigating the separation of the North from that same kingdom.

For several reasons, however, this early dating is not entirely beyond doubt. On the one hand, not all of the traditions reworked in 1 Samuel 16–2 Samuel 5 (or 8) make a particularly archaic impression; some are definitely "constructed narratives" (such as 1 Sam 16:1–13). These point to a noticeable distance between the narrator [[76]] and the period narrated. The same can be said for the abstract summaries that are distributed between the narratives and indeed belong to the skeleton of the composition as a whole. Most of all, the exalted level of theological reflection and the strongly theologizing language of other passages in the so-called Rise of David Narrative do not point to a totally archaic period of origin. For just this reason, some of the exegetes mentioned do not date all of the textual material between 1 Samuel 16 and 2 Samuel 5 (or 8) early, but only a basic structure, while they date parts of other portions much later.

On the other hand, interest in the stories of David and Saul by the people of Israel and Judah was hardly limited to the tenth century. J. Conrad suggests, for instance (1972: 329), that the bloody revolution of Jehu in 845 B.C. could have been the trigger for the drafting of the Rise of David Narrative. The author would have been contrasting the ruthless usurper in Samaria to the powerless David, patiently awaiting his opportunity. In the process, he was desiring to renew, in an underground manner, the old claim of the Judahite South to supremacy over the Israelite North. Perhaps links with contemporary history were here being rather boldly forged?

Scholars have also considered even later points in time, the years after the fall of the Northern Kingdom in 722 B.C. and the era of Josiah (640–609), particularly in connection with the proposal of later "editings" of the Rise of David Narrative (see above). In both periods, relations between North and South must have been crucial in people's thinking. The end of the kingdom of Israel unleashed a flood of refugees from the North into the South. Many traditions seem to have reached Judah at this point and were amalgamated with the Judahite heritage, alongside legal and poetic material, and even narrative material–the Jacob, Joseph, Moses, conquest, Judges, Elijah, Elisha, and Jehu stories–so why not also the Saul stories? According to current opinion, Josiah was encouraged by the downfall of Assyrian supremacy to encroach into the territory of the former Northern Kingdom from Judah and attempt to restore the Davidic United Kingdom. Might not David have represented or been presented to him as the model?

In this matter, the last word has not been spoken. Hopefully, the last word will not end up being the resigned statement by Seidl: "The time, place, and political situation respecting the drafting of the Rise story and its editing cannot be decided unambiguously" (1986: 44).

⟦77⟧ Several times above, the question of the intention of the so-called Rise of David Narrative has been broached. Weiser's article (1966) marked a milestone. According to him, it was "the tendency to legitimize David by Yahweh" that constituted "the linchpin" that held the entire composition together (1966: 327). This assessment of the Rise story as firmly pro-Davidic has been generally accepted in historical-critical scholarship.

McCarter (1980a ⟦pp. 260–75 in this volume⟧) further strengthened the trend by drawing a parallel to the so-called Apology of the Hittite King Hattushilish III. Its principal themes are (a) the qualifications of the ruler for his office, (b) his favored status with the goddess Ishtar, (c) his blamelessness, (d) his exculpation from bloody deeds that occurred, (e) and the praise of Ishtar. The Rise story is the "Apology of David," originating in David's time, aimed against a series of unsavory rumors about the king: he wormed his way into Saul's presence with dishonorable intent, he became a deserter, he sank to outlaw, he became a mercenary for the Philistines, he was involved in the rather obscure deaths of Saul, Abner, and Ish-bosheth. He considers the "Apology" to be, not just a detailed narrative argument, but a statement of divine will. Even the very first clauses (1 Sam 16:1–2!) are a fundamental assertion (analogous to Ishtar's preference for Hattushilish) that it had occurred to YHWH "in the mystery of a divine mind" (1980a: 503) to choose David–and not Saul!

McCarter is so overcome by the analogy that he overlooks some minor differences: how little the stories of Saul and David are painted in black and white; how very precisely in critical passages (2 Samuel 3–4!) God remains in the background; and especially how the Hittite Apology exhibits a clear, consistent, stereotypical style. It is formulated in the first-person style of royal self-presentations, whereas the supposed Israelite version is a narrative composition full of open questions and hidden traps.

Notwithstanding, Whitelam too calls the Apology of Hattushilish "the most striking parallel" to the Rise of David story (1984: 71), although the latter is of incomparably greater "literary artistry" (1984: 72). The books of Samuel as a whole are "responses . . . by the royal scribes to rumours, suspicions or charges circulating among the court or urban élite" (1984: 71). This is court propaganda–Whitelam takes care to keep this concept free of distorted understandings (1984: 66–67). Clearly enough, the texts reveal how much room for a "Defence of David" there would have been in the "élite power struggles" of the early Monarchic period (1984: 68). Certainly it would again have proved useful later, after the division of the kingdom or in Josiah's time, in the confrontation with the Israelite North; only after the fall of the Judahite monarchy did the work (with its sometimes very realistic traits) become obsolete. This is clear in the idealized late-deuteronomistic view of David in 1 Kgs 15:5 and particularly in the Chronicler's presentation (Whitelam 1984: 69–70).

⟦78⟧ The effect of the oversimplified classification of the Rise story as having a pro-Davidic bias or being tendentiously propagandistic is not unproblematic. The problem first flares up in Stefan Heym's novel *The King David Report* ⟦London: Hodder & Stoughton, 1973⟧, where a single great cover-up attempt rumbles behind the biblical presentation and David is designated without further ado as a "great murderer" (and Solomon even as a "little cutthroat"). Critical exegetes have arrived at similar judgments. Lemche (1978) evaluates the Rise of David story in view of its supposed propagandistic intent as simply historically unreliable. As soon as you wipe away the glossing-over of things, then the David traditions present the sobering portrait of a man who "deliberately worked his way up to the highest positions" (1978: 8). What shimmers through 1 Samuel 21–22 is that he cold-bloodedly delivered the priests of Nob up to the knife, 1 Samuel 25 shows him "frightening a man to death and stealing his wife" (1978: 12), 1 Samuel 27 exposes him as an unscrupulous turncoat to the Philistines–indeed, it is even possible that (contrary to the explicit but equally slanted protestation in 1 Samuel 29) he might have been present at the battle of Gilboa and thus might have borne responsibility for the defeat of Israel and the death of Saul. Basically, he was nothing but a politician and indistinguishable in this respect from Abdi-aširta (a demi-mondain ruler of the city of Jerusalem appearing in the Amarna Letters)–or Caesar (Lemche 1978: 18)!

VanderKam (1980) piles on even more. The whole time, the Rise of David story does nothing but incriminate Saul and exonerate David. Saul's (all too justified) action against David is represented as despotic caprice. The vow of friendship between Jonathan and David, of utmost significance politically, is an expression of purely personal affection. David's "ambitious maneuvers in the South" and his coldly calculated defection to the Philistines are presented as forced flight before the raging Saul. The only conclusion possible after close examination of the two murders, of Abner and

Ish-bosheth, is that David carried out the one single-handedly (1980: 529) and most likely caused the other. The fact that the Rise of David story behaves so vehemently as David's witness for the defense serves not to commend but to condemn the accused: "Precisely the zeal of the editor to exonerate David . . . leads one to suspect him as a conspirator" (1980: 533).

This is, to get to the heart of it, a hermeneutic of suspicion. The more decisively one asserts the opposite of what the biblical text seems to say, the more [[79]] certainly one believes one has scored the historical bull's-eye. Here Payne's criticism (1984: 59), that it is not permissible on the basis of a positive biblical statement to insinuate a negative historical state of affairs, is fully justified. For then what Lemche (1978: 2–3) laments about current presentations of the history of Israel would happen, with the polarity reversed: historical hypotheses all too rashly erected on textual witnesses—only this time, in contradiction to their plain meaning. Even assuming that hypercriticism is entirely or at least partly correct, it still remains to be established that the Bible did *not* intend the story of David exactly as it is presented and understood. In the story, David is not some sort of historical figure but a symbolic character. He portrays the incredible rise of someone marginalized to power, his story represents the off-chance that a powerful ruler might remain pure (or become pure again), it is a metaphor for the miraculous and yet goal-directed way of God with His own, and undoubtedly also for much more (so Brueggemann 1985; see pp. 283–87, above). Under no circumstances could the Bible paint the founder of the royal dynasty of Jerusalem and the prototype of the coming Messiah as a bloody and cynical despot. And it still remains probable that he was no such thing, for the biblical truth about David would hardly be without any clue to historical reality. And not without reason does the Bible *not* tell Abdi-Aširta's or Caesar's story—but David's!

The Rise of David in Broader Context

Scholarship has been attentive to a series of connections from the David and Saul story backward to the Samuel–Saul story and forward to the Succession Narrative. Some of the more conspicuous situations or observations about these links, in part already touched on above, are as follows:

- The postulated Rise of David story has no clear beginning; Saul, and Jonathan as well (see 1 Sam 18:4), are not introduced in a way that fits the style; for Saul this happens in 1 Sam 9:1–2 (see Dietrich 1992: 64–65), for Jonathan in 1 Sam 14:1.
- 1 Sam 16:1–13 follows directly from 1 Samuel 15 (see pp. 293–305, above).

- 1 Sam 16:1–13, Samuel's anointing of David, appears to be a deliberately constructed [[80]] counterpart to 1 Sam 9:1–10:16, Samuel's anointing of Saul (Dietrich 1992: 50–56).
- 1 Sam 18:1, 3 strikes up the theme of friendship between Jonathan and David for the first time; this theme runs through not only the David and Saul stories but on through the character of Jonathan's son Mephibosheth and through the Succession Narrative (see 2 Samuel 9, 16:1ff., 19:25ff.; prepared by 1 Sam 20:12–17, 42b; 23:16–18; 24:18–23a; 2 Sam 4:2b–4). Veijola has dedicated a separate article to these circumstances (1978) and claims that Mephibosheth was actually Saul's son (see 2 Sam 21:8). Only through redactional retouching (DtrH!) was he made Jonathan's son and thus a human symbol of the transfer of power from the Saulides to the Davidides.
- 1 Sam 19:18–24 is deliberately structured as a corresponding story to 1 Sam 10:10–12: Saul's prophetic experiences, marveled at in chapter 10, are disavowed in chapter 19 (Dietrich 1992: 57–62).
- 1 Sam 22:20–23 tells of the flight of the sole survivor of Saul's massacre of the priests of Nob to David; it turns out to be the very Abiathar who proves himself one of David's most trusted followers in the Succession confusion (2 Sam 15:24ff., 17:15ff.) but then goes over to Adonijah's side and becomes Solomon's enemy (1 Kgs 1:7, 42; 2:46–47).
- 1 Sam 26:14–16, a statement of David's directed against General Abner, exhibits connections not only with Abner's death in 2 Samuel 3 but with a secondary textual layer in the Succession Narrative (Cryer 1985). In 1 Kgs 2:5 the liquidation of General Joab is justified by Joab's murder of Abner—and thus is an allusion in the Succession Narrative back to the Rise of David story. The redacting visible here was not deuteronomistic in origin (contra Veijola 1975) but older and in fact identical with the redaction discovered by Würthwein (1974). It would thus reach back into 1 Samuel and comprise not only the Abner texts but also other scenes in which Joab and his brother Abishai, the "sons of Zeruiah," are shown in an unfavorable light (e.g., 1 Sam 26:6–8, 2 Sam 2:18–23).
- 2 Samuel 1–5 makes less of a mosaic-like impression than the preceding David and Saul stories; it operates in a much more unified way, building scene upon scene, similar to the following Succesion Narrative. Flanagan objects to the exclusive elevation of the Succession theme in 2 Samuel. The book as a whole deals, rather, with the questions about the consolidation of David's dynasty as against Saul's dynasty (Flanagan 1971) and the rise of Jerusalem to be the political and religious center of the young monarchy (Flanagan 1988: 236);
  2 Samuel 1–5 is an integral component of this presentational context. Ficker in turn postulates a small independent historical work (2 Sam

2:1–4a, 8–9, 12–32; 3:1, 6–13a, 17–39; 4:1–2, 5–12; 5:3) as the core of 2 Samuel 2–5, which would then have been interwoven into the whole of the emerging books of Samuel (Ficker 1977: 266).

- 2 Sam 3:2–5, 5:13–14, the lists of the sons of David born in Hebron and Jerusalem, are nearly indispensable, in each case preparing for the struggle between the sons of David to succeed their father, in 2 Samuel 10–19, 1 Kings 1–2.
- 2 Sam 3:12–16, the scene of Michal's return to David's side, not [[81]] only recalls the earlier references to Michal (1 Sam 14:49, 18:20ff., 19:11ff., 25:44) but also provides the background for Michal's exit in 2 Sam 6:16, 20ff.
- 2 Samuel 5, with information about the conquest of Jerusalem and the siege of the Philistines, is a very consistent consequence of the previous course of events and again prepares for the narrative of the transportation of the Ark into the City of David.
- 2 Samuel *6 falls back somehow on the Ark narratives in 1 Samuel 4–6 and at the same time explains David's desire to build the Temple (2 Sam 7:1ff.) and the reason that the Ark was carried along on David's field campaigns (2 Sam 11:11, 15:24ff.).
- 2 Sam 6:16, 20ff. offers an etiology for the fact that Michal bore no children to David, whereupon an obvious possibility for an alliance between the Davidide and Saulide royal lines slipped away. A whole series of episodes in the context of the Succession Narrative is dedicated to this theme: 2 Samuel 9, 16:1–4, 19:25–31 (the fate of the Saulide Mephibosheth and his servant Ziba); 2 Sam 16:5–13, 19:17–24; 1 Kgs 2:8–9, 36–46 (the conduct and fate of the Saulide Shimei); perhaps also 2 Samuel 20 (the revolt of the Benjaminite Sheba) and 2 Sam 21:1–13 (the killing of seven Saulides).
- 2 Samuel 7 explicitly takes up the previous story of David in vv. 1–2, 8–9 and anticipates the Succession theme by means of the Succession oracle (vv. 11ff.).
- 2 Samuel 8 provides a summary of David's wars that not only recalls the style and purpose of the Rise story but once again reports his victory over the Philistines (v. 1—referring to 2 Sam 5:17ff.?) and great victory over the Arameans (vv. 3–8—in anticipation of 2 Samuel 10?).

How should these findings be handled? Expositors working primarily with synchronic techniques naturally do not find them troublesome at all and offer a whole series of clues to viewing them integrally. Exegetes reckoning with the diachronic origin of the books of Samuel generally work with two explanatory models (partly combinable as well). They lead back across the narrative threads emerging from the Rise story either to the final deuteronomistic revision, for which the rise of David was just one building block in its overall historiographic structure, or to a predeuteronomistic history that already comprised more than the Rise of David.

The classic opinion on this question was formulated by Noth.

> For the story of Saul and David, Dtr had access to an extensive collection of Saul–David traditions, compiled long before Dtr from different elements—the old tradition on Saul and, in particular, the story of the rise of David and the story of the Davidic succession. As in the occupation story, the existence of this traditional material absolved Dtr from the need to organize and construct the narrative himself. Once he has stated his fundamental position on the institution of the monarchy in no uncertain terms (1 Sam-uel 8–12), he has little need to interpose in the traditional account his own judgments and interpretations. (Noth 1957: 61–62 [[ET: *The Deuteronomistic History* (2d ed.; JSOTSup 15; Sheffield: JSOT Press, 1991) 86]])

There would accordingly have been a pre-Deuteronomistic History, extending approximately from 1 Samuel 1 to 1 Kings 2, not really organized into a unit, but simply assembled out of several individual sources—among them the Rise of David story. The "Deuteronomist" must not have intervened too seriously here (except in 1 Samuel 8–12) but was able to insert the entire text block nearly unaltered into his work. The two dossiers have been considerably differentiated by recent scholarship.

It was Timo Veijola (1975) whose assessment of the deuteronomistic editorial activity in the books of Samuel set new benchmarks. For his starting point he chose the end of the Succession Narrative. In 1 Kings 1–2 he isolated extensive secondary passages that served "to prove Solomon's innocence and divine satisfaction with the Davidic dynasty" (1975: 25) and that are to be classified as deuteronomistic on the basis of their linguistic usage, their broad literary horizon, and particular formal properties (1975: 26ff.). From there he looked back to the books of Samuel and discovered preparations for those insertions in 1 Kings 1–2 (1975: 29–46), further statements on the divine legitimation of the "eternal dynasty" (1975: 47–80), connecting links between the great predeuteronomistic blocks of tradition (1975: 81–105; this is where the observations listed above come from) and, finally, indications of a deuteronomistic interpolation of 2 Samuel 21–24 within the course of the succession events (1975: 106–26).

According to this model, predeuteronomistically there was no connection between the Rise of David Narrative and the Samuel and Saul story or the Succession Narrative; only with the deuteronomistic editing were the major traditions of the first kings brought together. Of course, the books of Samuel did not attain their present form all at once. Veijola counts three deuteronomistic redactions: a fundamental one that set down the course of events in all important aspects, with primarily "historic" interests (DtrH); and two succeeding ones, adding a "prophetic" (DtrP) and a "nomistic" (DtrN) accent.

[[83]] According to Veijola (1975), the deuteronomistic text is apportioned as follows:

- DtrH: 1 Sam 2:27–36; 4:4b, 11b, 17bα, 19aγ, 21b, 22a; 14:3, *18; 20:12–17, 42b; 22:18bγ; 23:16–18; 24:18–23a; 25:21–22, 23b, 24b–26, 28–34, *39a; 2 Sam 3:9–10, 17–19, 28–29, 38–39; 4:2b–4; 5:1–2, 4–5, 11, 12a, 17a; 6:*21; 7:8b, 11b, 13, 16, 18–21, 25–29; 8:1a, 14b, 15; 9:1, *7, *10, 11b, 13aβ; (14:9;) 15:25–26; 16:11–12; 19:22–23, 29; 21:2b, 7; 24:1, 19b, 23b, 25bα; 1 Kgs 1:*30, 35–37, 46–48; 2:1–2, 4aαb, 5–11, 15bγ, 24, 26b, 27–31b, 37b, 42–45.
- DtrP: 1 Sam 3:11–14; 22:19; 28:17–19aα; 2 Sam 12:*7b–10, 13–14; 24:3, 4a, 10–14, 15aβ, 17, 21bβ, 25bβ.
- DtrN: 1 Sam 13:13–14; 2 Sam 5:12b; 7:1b, 6, 11, 22–24; 22:1, 22–25, 51; 1 Kgs 2:3, 4aβ.

All three levels of redaction, according to Veijola, not only were formulated freely but sometimes also were a reworking of preexisting material. Clearly this is the case primarily—and in general foundationally for the books of Samuel—in DtrH and to a limited extent also in DtrP and DtrN. The Deuteronomists pursued dual goals: to hand down and preserve the preexisting traditional material and at the same time to show it as illuminating the present-day circumstances of their exile. Regarding the David stories in particular, DtrH (going to work not long after the fall of the state of Judah) proves to be remarkably pro-Davidic/prodynastic; DtrP (beginning somewhat later) is sharply critical of David; and DtrN (late exilic or even postexilic) is again rather friendly to David, interested primarily, however, in the identity of Israel as the people of YHWH and in the Torah.

Much of Veijola's presentation is immediately convincing. Some of the bridges that connect the Rise of David story with its literary context (obviously in, say, 1 Samuel 2 or 2 Samuel 7; also in 2 Samuel 21 and 24) were built by deuteronomistic redactors in order to tame the great quantity of material and to interpret it in a particular direction. Of course, several of Veijola's assumptions also cause trouble, such as that of a pronounced dynastic posture on the part of DtrH. The basic author of the Deuteronomistic History is thus said to have represented this view in the middle of the exilic period, just after the complete deposition of the royal house of Jerusalem. This is not unlikely. It would not be advisable to see the biblical witnesses flatly reflecting only their contemporary circumstances and not also inveighing against them (see Dietrich 1995). Yet, the figure of David in the books of Samuel still bears so little of the prophetic-messianic or cultic-pious patina that made him so popular in Israel's belief in the postexilic period that it must be asked whether many of the passages Veijola attributes to DtrH do not much rather belong to a preexilic/predeuteronomistic impression of ideology about David than to an exilic/deuteronomistic one.

Regarding the above list of texts, this question of the preexilic Deuteronomist arises, in my [[Dietrich's]] opinion, especially for 1 Sam 24:18–20; chap. 25 (all the listed verses); 2 Sam 3:28–29, 38–39; 5:1–2; 8:14b, 15; chap. 9 (all the listed verses). This means two things: the problem of the transfer of power from Saul's dynasty to David's was primarily handled predeuteronomistically, and the materials of the Rise of David story and the Succession Narrative were already connected predeuteronomistically.

The discussion of the the Succession Narrative is resumed in later chapters. [[84]] But let us note at this point that Langlamet (1976) argues that the layer in 1 Kings 1–2 proved by Veijola to be secondary is not deuteronomistic but predeuteronomistic and part of a prodynastic editing of the Succession Narrative. Langlamet would ascribe to the same hand the so-called Benjaminite episodes in the Succession Narrative–among others, those dealing with Mephibosheth (Langlamet 1979, 1980, 1981).

Meanwhile, Veijola has also let it be known that he considers a predeuteronomistic editing of the Succession Narrative to be probable and has worked on profiling it (already 1978 = 1990: 58ff.; and especially 1979 = 1990: 84ff.). But he has not pursued this redaction beyond the bounds of the Succession Narrative (thus leaving this well enough alone!).

We arrive at the other possibility for explaining the lines of connection between the Rise story and its larger context: the assumption of predeuteronomistic redactions whose horizon extends beyond the stretch of text between 1 Samuel 16 and 2 Samuel 5 (or 8).

The most far-reaching proposal has been set forth by Campbell (1986). He proceeds from the observation that not only in the Rise of David Narrative but also in the Samuel and Saul stories, then again in the Succession Narrative, and further on in the biblical presentation of the history of Israel down to the time of Jehu, not only are stories of prophets told again and again, but decidedly prophetic points of view come to light. This leads him to his basic hypothesis: "It stakes a claim to be able to bring together features in the text of both Samuel and Kings, and to reconcile them in identifying a ninth-century text, covering 1–2 Samuel and extending deeply into 1–2 Kings. This Prophetic Record, in its own way, anticipates and prepares for the Deuteronomistic History" (Campbell 1986: 14).

In the books of Samuel, according to Campbell, the following passages (sometimes only in an original state) belong to this prophetic historiography: 1 Samuel 1–4; 7; 9:1–10:16; 11; 15–23; 25–31; 2 Samuel 1–5, 7, 8, and the Succession Narrative–in other words, the prophetic section excludes only the supposedly late, "anti-monarchical" texts in 1 Samuel *8–12, the Ark story 1 Samuel 5–6 + 2 Samuel 6, and the appendix in 2 Samuel 21–24. Everything else, at least at core, forms the beginning of a prophetic history from the ninth century. This is not really a history of Israel, definitely not the early royal period and certainly not just Saul or David, but is really a history of prophecy. Thus, the first main part (1 Samuel *1–7) is entitled "The emergence of the prophetic figure in Israel" and the second (1 Samuel 9–2 Kings 10) "The record of prophetic guidance of Israel's destiny under the institution of monarchy" (Campbell 1986: 101–2). Saul and David no longer really function as founders of the state–but, like Jeroboam I, Ahab, and Jehu also–as examples of good and bad attitudes to prophetic counsel. ⟦85⟧ The books of Samuel are basically made into prophetic books; however, only relatively brief passages in them are recognizably prophetic, and extensive ones make quite a different impression: for example, priestly (1 Samuel 1ff.) or courtly (1 Samuel 16ff.) or antidynastic (2 Samuel 11ff.). The obviously prophetic texts in turn come from very diverse realms of the prophetic movement (from the ecstatic groups to the Jerusalem court prophets to the opposition prophets of doom; see Dietrich 1992), and all of these are furthermore to be distinguished from a phenomenon already found in the books of Samuel (more so in Kings), historical prophecy, which works exclusively in writing and is deuteronomistically colored (see Dietrich 1972, despite the detailed criticism of Campbell 1986: 3–11). Campbell's hypothesis, then, threatens to shatter into pieces on numerous historical and literary circumstances.

In his monograph (1986), Campbell was still certain about counting 2 Samuel 8 and the Succession Narrative as part of the "Prophetic Record" (1986: 81–84, 102). In a still unpublished paper of 1993, he revised this opinion for the following reasons:

> The details of David's reign [that is, in 2 Samuel 8] are more likely to have been of interest to Judean sources. . . . It is also possible but unlikely that the so-called Succession Narrative . . . belonged within The Prophetic Record. . . . 2 Samuel 11–12 may have been edited within these prophetic circles. If the Succession Narrative had formed part of the Prophetic Record, it would have been to depict sin and its consequences within David's kingdom and the working out of the prophetic word (2 Sam 12:7b–10) in David's later years. It is unlikely, however, that so extensive a document with so little prophetic edition formed part of The Prophetic Record. (Campbell 1993: 32–33)

Here Campbell shows himself a prisoner of his hypothesis: because it is not prophetic, the Succession Narrative does not belong to the oldest, supposedly prophetic, historiography; consequently, the presumed oldest nucleus of crystallization of the books of Samuel disappears into the incomprehensible spheres of later revision. It would be wiser and more appropriate to the possible literary context of the Rise of David Narrative either to refer to the Deuteronomistic History as a whole or else to limit oneself to the distinctly observable connections within the books of Samuel, especially connections to the Succession Narrative. Recent research seems to be moving principally in this direction.

Mildenberger (1962) already saw the field of activity of the "editor," whom he postulated and dated after 722, to be limited to the text of the Rise of David Narrative and the Succession Narrative. For instance, he assigns 1 Kgs 2:5–9 to him, a passage that Veijola considered secondary but still deuteronomistic (Mildenberger 1962: 187ff.). It was finally "in the dynastic idea that his conception culminated" (1962: 24); he wished to legitimize the rule of David and the Davidides. What Mildenberger does not see is that extended passages of the Succession Narrative did [[86]] not meet this goal and, therefore, when they were to be united with the Rise of David Narrative, were revised prodynastically.

Ficker (1977: 266ff.) sketched a relatively complicated model of the history of the origin of the books of Samuel: it appears as if it had grown, so to speak, from an ancient kernel step by step. It did not happen in the exilic period but immediately, in the early monarchic period.

The starting point is the Succession Narrative (with Würthwein 1974, evaluated as anti-Solomonic at the core). This was immediately reworked prodynastically (in the redaction established by Würthwein) but also–and here is Ficker's contribution–introduced at a previous point in the text. If they meant to absolve David, as Würthwein supposes, while incriminating Joab (in 2 Sam 14:2ff., 18:10ff., 20:8ff.; 1 Kgs 2:5ff.), then their prior history, including its dark sides, must be told at the outset. This happened via the pre-placing of 2 Samuel 2–5. These chapters were already available to the editor in an older kernel (see above), and he expanded them to their present state. But this extension "immediately dragged additional extensions after it for practical reasons" (Ficker 1977: 277), and the respective expanders once again could fall back on already preformulated pieces. Thus 2 Samuel 1 and 1 Samuel 27–31 (David's seizing of power in 2 Samuel 2–5 finally presupposes the death of Saul) first crystallized onto 2 Samuel 2–20 + 1 Kings 1–2, then in turn 1 Samuel 23, 24, 26 (David's defection to the Philistines in 1 Samuel 27ff. must have been motivated by his fear of Saul), and then in the end 1 Samuel 18–19 (Saul's hatred for David could not remain unexplained). Into the resulting sequence of texts, something like the Jonathan episodes in 1 Samuel 20 (to prepare 2 Samuel 9 and, especially, the Mephibosheth scenes) or the story of the murder of the priests of Nob in 1 Samuel 21–22 (to explain why the priest Abiathar later plays an important role; see 2 Samuel 15, 17; 1 Kings 1–2) were inserted. This entire, multilayered process would already have been brought to a conclusion in the early part of Solomon's time (Ficker 1977: 278).

The extremely early dating, in particular, is far from convincing, but so is fragmenting things into numerous accreted events and fragmenting the text corpus from 1 Samuel 16 to 2 Samuel 5 into many slices. In principle, however, Ficker saw something highly important and right, which future research will overlook only at its own peril. This was that the so-called Rise of David Narrative probably never existed as a single work on its own but was conceived as an additional layer to the Succession Narrative. Or, more carefully, it was conceived together with a secondary textual layer in 2 Samuel 10–20 + 1 Kings 1–2 not least in order to shed more favorable light on gloomy memories and messages that were detrimental to the dynasty of David.

Bibliography

Ackroyd, P. R.

1975 The Verb Love–*ʾāhēb* in the David-Jonathan Narratives: A Footnote. *VT* 25: 213ff.

Alt, A.

1930 Die Staatenbildung der Israeliten in Palästina. Pp. 1–65 in vol. 2 of *Kleine Schriften zur Geschichte des Volkes Israel*. Munich. [3d edition, 1964.]

Alter, R.

1981 *The Art of Biblical Narrative*. New York: Basic.

[[Barth, K.]]

1942 *Die kirchliche Dogmatik II: Die Lehre von Gott, 2*. Zollikon/Zurich: Evangelischer Verlag. [4th impression, 1959] [[ET: *Church Dogmatics II.2: The Doctrine of God*. Edinburgh: T. & T. Clark, 1957/1987.]]

Bechmann, U.

1988 Michal: Retterin und Opfer Davids. Pp. 71–80 in *Zwischen Ohnmacht und Befreiung*, ed. K. Walker. Biblische Frauengeschichten. Freiburg.

Berges, U.

1989 *Die Verwerfung Sauls: Eine thematische Untersuchung*. Forschung zur Bibel 61. Stuttgart.

Berlin, A.

1983 *Poetics and Interpretation of Biblical Narrative*. Bible and Literature Series 9. [[Sheffield: Almond. Reprinted, Winona Lake, Indiana: Eisenbrauns, 1994.]]

Brueggemann, W.
1985 *David's Truth in Israel's Imagination and Memory.* Philadelphia.
Campbell, A. F.
1986 *Of Prophets and Kings: A Late Ninth-Century Document (1 Samuel 1–2 Kings 10).* CBQMS 17. [[Washington, D.C.: Catholic Biblical Association.]]
1993 The Prophetic Record: The Complete RSV Text of a Late Ninth-Century Document (1 Samuel–2 Kings 10). Forthcoming.
Clines, D. J. A.
1991 Michal Observed: An Introduction to Reading Her Story. Pp. 24–63 in *Telling Queen Michal's Story: An Experiment in Comparative Interpretation.* JSOTSup 119. [[Sheffield: Sheffield Academic Press.]]
Cryer, F. H.
1985 David's Rise to Power and the Death of Abner: An Analysis of 1 Samuel XXVI 14–16 and Its Redaction-Critical Implications. *VT* 35: 385–94.
Dietrich, W.
1972 *Prophetie und Geschichte: Eine redaktionsgeschichtliche Untersuchung zum deuteronomistischen Geschichtswerk.* FRLANT 108. Göttingen: [[Vandenhoeck & Ruprecht.]]
1976 Von einem, der zuviel wusste: Versuch über Stefan Heyms "König David Bericht." Pp. 41–67 in *Wort und Wahrheit: Studien zur Interpretation alttestamentlicher Texte.* Neukirchen-Vluyn: Neukirchener Verlag.
1977 David in Überlieferung und Geschichte. *VF* 22: 44–64.
1987 *David, Saul und die Propheten: Das Verhältnis von Religion und Politik nach den prophetischen Überlieferungen vom frühesten Königturn in Israel.* BWANT 122. [[Stuttgart: Kohlhammer.]] [2d edition, 1992.]
1989 Gott, Macht und Liebe: Drei neue Romane über die Davidszeit. *Reformatio* 38: 301–8.
1995 Martin Noth and the Future of the Deuteronomistic History. [[Pp. 153–75 in *The History of Israel's Traditions: The Heritage of Martin Noth,* ed. S. L. McKenzie and M. P. Graham. JSOTSup 182. Sheffield: Sheffield Academic Press.]]
Doob Sakenfeld, K.
1983 Loyalty and Love: The Language of Human Interconnections in the Hebrew Bible. *Michigan Quarterly Review* 22: 190–204. [[Rerinted in *Backgrounds for the Bible,* ed. M. P. O'Connor and D. N. Freedman. Winona Lake: Eisenbrauns, 1987.]]
Edelman (Vikander), D.
1990 The Deuteronomistic Story of King Saul: Narrative Art or Editorial Product. Pp. 207–20 in *Pentateuchal and Deuteronomistic Studies,* ed. C. Brekelmans and J. Lust. BETL 94. [[Leuven: Leuven University Press.]]
1991 *King Saul in the Historiography of Judah.* JSOTSup 121. [[Sheffield: Sheffield Academic Press.]]

Exum, J. C.
1992 *Tragedy and Biblical Narrative: Arrows of the Almighty.* Cambridge: Cambridge University Press.

Ficker, R.
1977 *Komposition und Erzählung: Untersuchungen zur Ludeerzählung (1 S 4–6; 2 S 6) und zur Geschichte vom Aufstieg Davids (1 S 15–2 S 5).* Th.D. Dissertation, University of Heidelberg.

Flanagan, J. W.
1971 *A Study of the Biblical Traditions Pertaining to the Foundation of the Monarchy in Israel.* Ph.D. Dissertation, University of Notre Dame.
1988 *David's Social Drama: A Hologram of Israel's Early Iron Age.* JSOTSup 73 / SWBA 7. [[Sheffield: Almond.]]

Fretheim, T. E.
1985 Divine Foreknowledge, Divine Constancy, and the Rejection of Saul's Kingship. *CBQ* 47: 595–602.

Garsiel, M.
1985 *The First Book of Samuel: A Literary Study of Comparative Structures, Analogies and Parallels.* Ramat Gan: Bar-Ilan University Press.

Good, E. M.
1981 Irony in the Old Testament. 2d ed. Bible and Literature Series 3. [[Sheffield: Almond.]]

Grønbaek, J. H.
1971 *Die Geschichte vom Aufstieg Davids (1.Sam.15–2.Sam.5): Tradition und Komposition.* Acta theologica danica 10. [[Copenhagen: Munksgaard.]]

Gunn, D. M.
1980 *The Fate of King Saul: An Interpretation of a Biblical Story.* JSOTSup 14. [[Sheffield: JSOT Press.]]

Horner, T. M.
1978 *Jonathan Loved David: Homosexuality in Biblical Times.* Philadelphia.

Humphreys, W. L.
1978 The Tragedy of King Saul: A Study of the Structure of 1 Samuel 9–31. *JSOT* 6: 18–27.
1980 The Rise and Fall of King Saul: A Study of an Ancient Narrative Stratum in 1 Samuel. *JSOT* 18: 74–90.
1982 From Tragic Hero to Villain: A Study of the Figure of Saul and the Development of 1 Samuel. *JSOT* 22: 95–117.

Jobling, D.
1986 *The Sense of Biblical Narrative II: Structural Analysis in the Hebrew Bible.* JSOTSup 39. [[Sheffield: JSOT Press.]]

Kaiser, O.
1990 David und Jonathan: Tradition, Redaktion und Geschichte in 1 Sam 16–20—Ein Versuch. *ETL* 66: 281–96.

Kapelrud, A. S.
1974 The Ugaritic Text RS 24.252 and King David. *Journal of Northwest Semitic Languages* 3: 35–39.
Knierim, R.
1970 Die Messianologie des ersten Buches Samuel. *EvTh* 30: 113–33.
Koch, K.
1967 *Was ist Formgeschichte? Neue Wege der Bibelexegese.* 2d ed. Neukirchen-Vluyn: Neukirchener Verlag.
Langlamet, F.
1976 Pour ou contre Salomon? La rédaction prosalomonienne de 1 Rois I–II. *RB* 83: 321–79, 481–528.
1978 Ahitofel et Houshaï: Rédaction prosalomonienne en 2 Sam 15–17? Pp. 57–90 in *Studies in Bible and the Ancient Near East: FS S. E. Loewenstamm,* ed. Y. Avishur and J. Blau. Jerusalem: Rubinstein.
1979 David et la maison de Saül: Les épisodes "benjaminites" de II Sam. IX; XVI, 1–14; XIX, 17–31; 1 Rois II, 36–46. *RB* 86: 194–213, 385–436, 481–513.
1980 David et la maison de Saül: Les épisodes "benjaminites" de II Sam. IX; XVI, 1–14; XIX, 17–31; 1 Rois II, 36–46. *RB* 87: 161–210.
1981a David et la maison de Saül: Les épisodes "benjaminites" de II Sam. IX; XVI, 1–14; XIX, 17–31; 1 Rois II, 36–46. *RB* 88: 321–32.
1981b Affinités sacerdotales, deutéronomiques, élohistes dans l'Histoire de la succession (2 Sam 9–20; 1 Rois 1–2). Pp. 233–46 in [[*Mélanges bibliques et orientaux: En l'honneur de M. Henri Cazelles.*]] AOAT 212. [[Neukirchen-Vluyn: Neukirchener Verlag.]]
Lemche, N. P.
1978 David's Rise. *JSOT* 10: 2–25.
Lingen, A. van der
1983 David en Saul in I Samuel 16–II Samuel 5: Verhalen in politik en religie. 's Gravenhage.
Mathys, H. P.
1994 *Dichter und Beter: Theologen aus spätalttestamentlicher Zeit.* OBO 132. [[Freiburg: Presses Universitaires.]]
McCarter, P. K.
1980a The Apology of David. *JBL* 99: 489–504.
1980b *1 Samuel.* AB 8. [[Garden City, New York: Doubleday.]]
Mettinger, T. N. D.
1976 *King and Messiah: The Civil and Sacral Legitimation of the Israelite Kings.* ConBOT 8. [[Lund: Gleerup.]]
Mildenberger, F.
1962 *Die vordeuteronomistische Saul-Davidüberlieferung.* Th.D. Dissertation, University of Tübingen.

Miscall, P. D.
1983 *The Workings of Old Testament Narrative*. Semeia Studies. Philadelphia: Scholars Press.
1991 Michal and Her Sisters. Pp. 246–60 in *Telling Queen Michal's Story: An Experiment in Comparative Interpretation*, ed. D. J. A. Clines and T. C. Eskenazi. JSOTSup 119. [[Sheffield: Sheffield Academic Press.]]

Mommer, P.
1987 Ist auch Saul unter den Propheten? Ein Beitrag zu 1 Sam 19,18–24. *BN* 38/39: 53–61.
1991 *Samuel: Geschichte und Überlieferung*. WMANT 65. [[Neukirchen-Vluyn: Neukirchener.]]

North, R.
1982 David's Rise: Sacral, Military, or Psychiatric? *Bib* 63: 524–44.

Noth, M.
1943 *Überlieferungsgeschichtliche Studien, I: Die sammelnden und bearbeitenden Geschichtswerke im Alten Testament*. SKGG 18. Tübingen. [2d ed., 1957. 3d ed., 1967]

Nübel, H.-U.
1959 *Davids Aufstieg in der Frühe israelitischer Geschichtsschreibung*. Diss. ev. theol. Bonn.

Payne, D. F.
1984 Estimates of the Character of David. *Irish Biblical Studies* 6: 54–70.

Pleins, J. D.
1992 Son-Slayers and Their Sons. *CBQ* 54: 29–38.

Rendtorff, R.
1971 Beobachtungen zur altisraelitischen Geschichtsschreibung anhand der Geschichte vom Aufstieg Davids. Pp. 428–39 in [[*Probleme biblischer Theologie*:]] *Festschrift Gerhard von Rad*. Munich: Kaiser.

Rost, L.
1926 *Die Überlieferung von der Thronnachfolge Davids*. BWANT 42. [[Stuttgart: Kohlhammer.]] Reprinted, pp. 119–253 in his *Das kleine Credo und andere Studien zum Alten Testament*. Heidelberg, 1965. [ET: *The Succession to the Throne of David*. Sheffield: JSOT Press, 1982.]

Schicklberger, F.
1974 Die Davididen und das Nordreich: Beobachtungen zur sog. Geschichte vom Aufstieg Davids. *BZ* 18: 255–63.

Schulte, H.
1972 Die Entstehung der Geschichtsschreibung im Alten Israel. BZAW 128. [[Berlin: de Gruyter.]]

Seidl, T.
1986 David statt Saul: Göttliche Legitimation und menschliche Kompetenz des Königs als Motive der Redaktion von I Sam 16–18. *ZAW* 98: 39–55.

Stoebe, H.-J.

1958 David und Mikal: Überlegungen zur Jugendgeschichte Davids. Pp. 224–43 in *Von Ugarit nach Qumran: FS O. Eissfeldt*. BZAW 77. [[Berlin: Töpelmann.]] Reprinted, pp. 91–110 in his [[*Geschichte, Schicksal, Schuld und Glaube*.]] BBB 72. [[Frankfurt am Main: Athenäum, 1989.]]

1973 Das erste Buch Samuelis. KAT 8/1. [[Leipzig: Scholl.]]

Thompson, J. A.

1974 The Significane of the Verb 'Love' in the David-Jonathan Narratives in 1 Samuel. *VT* 24: 334–38.

VanderKam, J. C.

1980 Davidic Complicity in the Deaths of Abner and Eshbaal: A Historical and Redactional Study. *JBL* 99: 521–39.

Veijola, T.

1975 *Die ewige Dynastie: David und die Entstehung seiner Dynastie nach der deuteronomistischen Darstellung*. AASF B 193. [[Helsinki: Suomalainen Tiedeakatemia.]]

1978 David und Meribaal. *RB* 85: 338–61. Reprinted, pp. 58–83 in *David: Gesammelte Studien zu den Davidüberlieferungen des Alten Testaments*. Helsinki/Göttingen, 1990.

1979 Salomo: Der Erstgeborene Bathsebas. Pp. 230–50 in *Studies in the Historical Books of the Old Testament*. VTSup 30. [[Leiden: Brill.]] Reprinted, pp. 84–105 in *David: Gesammelte Studien zu den Davidüberlieferungen des Alten Testaments*. Helsinki/Göttingen, 1990. [[See the English translation in this volume, pp. 340–57.]]

Weiser, A.

1966 Die Legitimation des Königs David: Zur Eigenart und Entstehung der sogen. Geschichte von Davids Aufstieg. *VT* 16: 325–54.

Whitelam, K. W.

1984 The Defence of David. *JSOT* 29: 61–87.

Willis, J. T.

1973 The Function of Comprehensive Anticipatory Redactional Joints in 1 Samuel 16–18. *ZAW* 85: 294–314.

Würthwein, E.

1974 *Die Erzählung von der Thronfolge Davids: Theologische oder politische Geschichtsschreibung?* Theologische Studiën 115. [[Zurich: Theologischer Verlag.]] Reprinted, pp. 29–79 in *Studien zum Deuteronomistischen Geschichtswerk*. BZAW 227. [[Berlin: de Gruyter,]] 1994.

David's Rise and Saul's Demise

Narrative Analogy in 1 Samuel 24–26

ROBERT P. GORDON

Gordon's essay brings the modern study of narrative, still in its youth in 1979, into the story of the historical books. The early doyens of the new branch of the discipline, J. Muilenburg, R. Alter, and H. Frei, feature here. And the narrative dimensions of plot, characterization, style, vocabulary, narrator and author compose the substance of the argument. The contention is that the story of Nabal in 1 Samuel 25 functions in relation to the similar narratives concerning David and Saul in the chapters that flank it, in such a way as to give pointers to the outcome of the larger narrative of David's Rise. There is an interesting engagement with D. Jobling's early work on the matter of plot development versus redundancy.

But the essay is not narrowly narratological. Its interest, rather, is properly hermeneutical, bringing about an engagement between narrative and historical studies. In this respect it shares a concern with that of Dietrich in the present volume (pp. 276–318). Gordon takes seriously questions concerning the genesis of the narrative in its historical matrix, taking an orientation, for example, to Rost's classic work on the Succession Narrative. In that context the very modern matter of authorial intention versus multiple readings arises (see Gunn's article in this volume, pp. 566–77), as does the fundamental question of the possibility of real history being written with all the means usually associated with literature.

[[37]] The narrative segment which is the subject of this paper belongs to the so-called "Story of David's Rise," to use Leonhard Rost's title for the second of the three major compositional units which he detected in the

Reprinted with permission from *Tyndale Bulletin* 31 (1980) 37–64.

books of Samuel.[1] In the event, the world of Old Testament scholarship was much more interested in Rost's arguments for the existence of an originally independent Narrative of Succession—2 Samuel 9–1 Kings 2, according to the classic formulation. When, in the late 1950s, the unitary potential of David's *Vorgeschichte* [['early history']] began to be recognized (witness the monographs by Nübel 1959; Mildenberger 1962; Ward 1967; and Grønbaek 1971)[2] [[38]] Rost's starting-point was advanced to 16:14, or, with Grønbaek, to 15:1, and his fragmentary approach gave way to a more positive evaluation of the canonical material thus delimited.[3]

Even so, "David's Rise" does not represent the same homogeneous blending of sources as is the case with the Narrative of Succession.[4] As we read we are more conscious of the individual narrative blocks making up the whole, and of the tensions which their conjoining has imposed on the composite work.[5] But this is not the whole story. For whether or not we subscribe to the theory of a large narrative unit separable from the rest of 1 and 2 Samuel, we have to reckon with a high degree of interplay among the various sub-units contained in these chapters. J. T. Willis's study of

1. L. Rost, *Die Überlieferung von der Thronnachfolge Davids* (BWANT 3, 6. Stuttgart, 1926) 133–35 (= *Das kleine Credo und andere Studien zum Alten Testament* [Heidelberg, 1965] 238–41). It is now of no more than antiquarian interest that Rost himself excluded 1 Samuel 24–26 from his hypothetical source, even though it comprised various pericopae and fragments from 1 Samuel 23 through 2 Samuel 5.

2. H.-U. Nübel, *Davids Aufstieg in der Frühe israelitischer Geschichtsschreibung* (diss. Bonn, 1959); F. Mildenberger, *Die vordeuteronomistische Saul-Davidüberlieferung* (diss. Tübingen, 1962); R. L. Ward, *The Story of David's Rise: A Traditio-historical Study of I Samuel xvi 14–II Samuel v* (diss. Vanderbilt, 1967; Ann Arbor: Univ. Microfilms); J. H. Grønbaek, *Die Geschichte vom Aufstieg Davids (1 Sam. 15–2 Sam. 5)* (Copenhagen, 1971). Cf. also A. Weiser, "Die Legitimation des Königs David. Zur Eigenart und Entstehung der sogen. Geschichte von Davids Aufstieg," *VT* 16 (1966) 325–54; R. Rendtorff, "Beobachtungen zur altisraelitischen Geschichtsschreibung anhand der Geschichte vom Aufstieg Davids," in *Probleme biblischer Theologie* (Fest. G. von Rad), ed. H. W. Wolff (München, 1971) 428–39; J. Conrad, "Zum geschichtlichen Hintergrund der Darstellung von Davids Aufstieg," *TLZ* 97 (1972) cols. 321–32; F. Schicklberger, "Die Davididen und das Nordreich. Beobachtungen zur sog. Geschichte vom Aufstieg Davids," *BZ* 18 (1974) 255–63; N. P. Lemche, "David's Rise," *JSOT* 10 (1978) 2–25.

3. Weiser, *art cit.* 344, claimed further territory for the *Aufstiegsgeschichte*, arguing that 2 Samuel 6 functions *ad majorem gloriam* [['for the greater glory of']] David. He also regarded 2 Samuel 7 as the keystone of the whole narrative, noting in particular the interaction between 1 Sam 25:28, 30 and 2 Samuel 7 (art. cit., 348).

4. At the same time we note Conroy's conclusion that "the current state of research no longer justifies an automatic and uncritical acceptance of 2 Samuel 9–20; 1 Kings 1–2 as a fully rounded literary unity with a clearly defined theme": C. Conroy, *Absalom Absalom! Narrative and Language in 2 Sam 13–20* (Rome, 1978) 3.

5. Ward, op. cit., 197f., suggests that, to some extent, the state of the narrative reflects David's circumstances while on the run from Saul; there was "no order or pattern in David's existence."

"comprehensive anticipatory redactional joints" in 1 Samuel 16–18 neatly illustrates the point: even 16:14–23, which has stoutly defied attempts at harmonization with 17:1–18:5, can be shown to function programmatically in [[39]] relation to the larger context of the struggle between Saul and David.[6] Some of the principal elements in the story are passed in review before the account proper gets under way.

Since agreement about the existence of an independent, self-contained account of David's early career is not crucial for our study we shall use "David's Rise" simply as a convenience-term. It is in any case indisputable that the second half of 1 Samuel is focused principally on David: "the stories of Saul and David are really stories about David."[7] Humphreys's portrayal of 1 Samuel 9–31 as a three-part story about Saul highlights a subsidiary theme, but makes a useful point at the risk of distorting the image which the section seems more naturally to project.[8] The motif to which all else in these chapters is subservient is that of David's progress towards the throne. And, in the way of biblical narrative, the question is not whether he will become king, but how he will become king.[9] He is from the outset God's nominee, and therefore the rightful claimant; Jonathan early acknowledges the fact and so, eventually, does Saul.

The "how" of David's accession comes to the fore at that point where the initiative seems to be passing from Saul to his fugitive servant. From chap. 24 on the narrator [[40]] is at pains to show that, despite the opportunities given, David did not take the law into his own hands. He emphatically was not implicated in Saul's death, nor in the deaths of Abner and Eshbaal. And it is not difficult to discover a likely reason for this emphasis. Sympathy for Saul and his house did not die easily in Israel, and certainly not during David's reign. The Gibeonite episode recounted in 2 Samuel 21 did not help matters, and there must have been many who agreed with Shimei's denunciation of David as a "man of blood": "Begone, begone, you man of blood, you worthless fellow! The Lord has avenged upon you all the blood of the house of Saul, in whose stead you have reigned" (2 Sam 16:7f.). As late as 2 Samuel 20 we read of a revolt of the men of Israel

6. J. T. Willis, "The Function of Comprehensive Anticipatory Redactional Joints in 1 Samuel 16–18," *ZAW* 85 (1973) 294–314 (especially 295–302).

7. G. von Rad, *Old Testament Theology* 1 (ET, London, 1962) 324. Cf. idem, "Zwei Überlieferungen von König Saul," in *Gesammelte Studien zum Alten Testament* 2 (München, 1973) 202.

8. W. L. Humphreys, "The Tragedy of King Saul: A Study of the Structure of 1 Samuel 9–31," *JSOT* 6 (1978) 18–27.

9. Cf. P. D. Miscall, "The Jacob and Joseph Stories as Analogies," *JSOT* 6 (1978) 32. Miscall distinguishes in this connection between divine word and human; the latter does not necessarily achieve fulfilment.

under the leadership of the Benjaminite Sheba ben Bichri. That this was an attempted coup by the pro-Saul faction seems more than likely.[10] At a later stage Solomon's maladministration can only have given credibility to the Saulide cause. It is small wonder, then, that David's non-complicity in the deaths of Saul and his family has been given such coverage in these chapters,[11] and still less wonder if "David's Rise" was produced under royal auspices and "represents the official interpretation of the Jerusalem palace.[12] Nowhere is this question of David's avoidance of blood-guilt addressed more directly than in 1 Samuel 24–26.

The Narrative Unit

I began by referring to 1 Samuel 24–26 as a "narrative segment," though strictly speaking the "wilderness cycle," as the "segment" may fairly be called,[13] begins at 23:14. It is a beginning which, to quote Klaus Koch, "is not markedly typical of the start to a Hebrew story,"[14] but that need not detain us. The [[41]] issue of blood-guilt is first raised at 24:1ff. and it is from this point on that the narrator applies his skills to the development of his all-important theme. On almost any analysis of these chapters 26:25 marks the closing bracket; Saul, having blessed David, "returned to his place."[15] 27:1 reports David's decision to take refuge with the Philistines and we enter a new phase in his story. Further justification for treating 23:14 (effectively 24:1)–26:25 as a narrative unit would therefore appear unnecessary.

Hitherto most treatments of 1 Samuel 24–26 have concentrated on the question of the relationship between chapters 24 and 26, usually to demonstrate that these are sibling accounts of a single incident. Literary criticism attributed the accounts to separate written sources.[16] Form criticism, on the other hand, envisages a period of separate development within the oral tradition.[17] But whereas Koch, who holds that we have

10. Sheba was perhaps even a kinsman of Saul; cf. J. Bright, *A History of Israel*[2] (London, 1972) 205.

11. Cf. Conrad, art. cit., 325; Lemche, art. cit., 12–13, 15.

12. Ward, op. cit., 216. Ward thinks that "David's Rise" was composed as early as Solomon's reign, when the hope of reconciliation between the Davidides and Saulides was still alive.

13. So Ward, op. cit., 50.

14. K. Koch, *The Growth of the Biblical Tradition: The Form-Critical Method* (ET, London, 1969) 137.

15. Grønbaek, op. cit., 183, is an exception.

16. Cf. K. Budde, *Die Bücher Samuel* (Tübingen/Leipzig, 1902) 157; H. P. Smith, *The Books of Samuel* (ICC; Edinburgh, 1912) 216.

17. Cf. Koch, op. cit., 132–48.

"two versions of the same story," appeals to oral tradition in order to account for the *differences* between them,[18] Grønbaek maintains that we are dealing with two originally independent traditions whose *similarities* are best explained as having arisen during a period of parallel development within the oral tradition.[19] The similarities certainly call for some explanation, though, it need hardly be said, this is but one aspect of a more general problem of parallel accounts in 1 Samuel. In what follows we shall not be discussing the origin or life-setting of the individual units, but rather their function within the narrative composite of "David's Rise."

Narrative Analogy

[[42]] At some point the traditions relating to David's early career were brought together to form a connected narrative corresponding *grosso modo* [['broadly']] to what we have in the MT. In this connection we can hardly avoid talking of a "narrator," however we envisage his role. By his shaping and deploying of the material available to him this narrator has infused his own spirit into the stories which he recounts. It is to him that we owe the overarching themes and dominant emphases which give the narrative its connectedness, and not just at the lowly level of topical or chronological arrangement. Current interest in "the Bible as literature," with attention being paid to the larger narrative unit, the development of plot, characterization and the like, has ensured for the narrator a more honourable status than heretofore. And rightly so, even if we do not subscribe to the view that the Old Testament is "a large chiasmus constructed one New Year's Day in the Exile."[20]

One of the outstanding features of biblical narrative, and perhaps the one which is most open to misrepresentation, is its tendency to laconicism, just as those points where the modern reader looks to the narrator to spell out his intention or, maybe, to moralize on the action of the story.[21] Where the reader's sensibilities are offended this taciturnity may be put down to moral indifference on the part of the narrator, or simply—and this has special relevance to "David's Rise"—to undisguised hero-worship. But Hebrew narrative is much more subtle than that, using a wide range of narrative techniques to perform the functions of the explicit commentaries in the more transparent narrative types. Prominent among these techniques is that of narrative analogy. Narrative analogy is

18. Ibid., 143.

19. Op cit., 169 (cf. 180f.).

20. If the author may be permitted to quote himself from somewhere in the oral tradition!

21. Cf. R. Alter, "A Literary Approach to the Bible," *Commentary* 60 (1975) 73.

a device whereby the narrator can provide an internal commentary on the action which he is describing, usually by means of cross-reference to an earlier action or speech.[22] [[43]] Thus narratives are made to interact in ways which may not be immediately apparent; ironic parallelism abounds wherever this technique is applied.

Narrative analogy, we submit, provides an important clue to the relationship between 1 Samuel 25, which tells the story of Nabal, and the contiguous chapters, which treat David's sparing of Saul. The point can be expressed in the simple equation: Nabal = Saul. Saul does not vanish from view in 1 Samuel 25;[23] he is Nabal's *alter ego.*

Predisposing Factors

Why should Nabal serve as a narrative function of Saul? Several predisposing factors are suggested by a surface reading of 1 Samuel 24–26, but by far the most important is the shared motif of David's magnanimity towards his enemies: "In each case, David perceives a powerful advantage in killing, but is restrained by a theological consideration."[24] Nabal, no less than Saul, poses the question, Will David incur blood-guilt on his way to the throne? Considerations such as that Nabal is not "the Lord's anointed" and that to kill him would not be a violation of royal sacrosanctity are temporarily set aside. The point is made in Abigail's speech that blood-guilt for anyone–even for a Nabal–could cast a shadow over David's throne at a later stage (25:30f.).

Time and place are also enabling factors in the role-identification of Nabal with Saul. While the Nabal story is in its proper setting inasmuch as it recounts an episode from the period of David's outlawry in the Judaean wilderness,[25] it is also significant that the [[44]] two places mentioned in 25:2 in connection with Nabal have strong associations with Saul. Maon is named three times in 23:24f. as the area where David hid and where Saul came within an ace of apprehending him. Carmel, where Nabal had his estate, was the place where Saul erected his stele in celebration of his victory over the Amalekites (15:12).[26]

22. Cf. Alter, loc. cit.

23. Pace Humphreys, art. cit., 19. A rough parallel is provided by Jobling's suggestion of role identification between David and Jonathan earlier in 1 Samuel: D. Jobling, *The Sense of Biblical Narrative* (SJSOT 7. Sheffield, 1978) 4–25.

24. J. D. Levenson, "1 Samuel 25 as Literature and as History," *CBQ* 40 (1978) 23.

25. W. Caspari, *Die Samuelbücher* (KAT 7; Leipzig, 1926) 311, thought that the Nabal story belonged with chapters 27–30 and David's stay at Ziklag, but there is little or nothing to commend this view.

26. Cf. Grønbaek, op. cit., 172.

Then there is Nabal's social status. He was a wealthy individual whose style of life could even have been the envy of Saul; he is therefore fit to stand as a narrative surrogate of Saul. Levenson, in declaring him "no commoner," ventures the opinion that he was "the *rōʾš bêt ʾāb* [['head of family']] or the *nāśîʾ* [['chief']] of the Calebite clan, a status to which David laid claim through his marriage to Nabal's lady."[27] And were we to indulge Levenson a little further in his speculations we should discover that the correspondence between Saul and Nabal does not end there, for Levenson surmises that the Ahinoam mentioned in 25:43 is none other than Saul's wife, the only other bearer of the name in the Old Testament. But perhaps it is too much a flight of fancy to imagine that "David swaggered into Hebron with the wife of a Calebite chieftain on one arm and that of the Israelite king on the other"![28]

Depiction

Psychologically Saul and Nabal are geminate. They refuse to know, in particular to acknowledge David for what he is, and they are alienated from those about them. Jobling brings out well this epistemological aspect of Saul's "rebellion" as it is depicted in earlier chapters of 1 Samuel.[29] Saul has it on the authority of no less than Samuel that he and his house have been rejected by God, but he will stop at nothing in order to frustrate the divine purpose. Jonathan, by way of contrast, "receives no revelations, and yet he knows."[30] As for alienation, it is not only Saul and Jonathan who are polarized in their attitudes to David (cf. 20:30–34). [[45]] Michal, Saul's daughter become David's wife, works against her father to prevent David's arrest; she would rather lie to Saul than see David fall into his hands (19:11–17).

At best, too, there is ambiguity about the attitude of Saul's servants to their master. On one occasion he complains because they withhold intelligence about David's movements: "You have all conspired against me, and no one informs me when my son makes a covenant with the son of Jesse, and none of you feels sorry for me or informs me that my son has stirred up my servant against me to lie in wait, as at the present time" (22:8). Only by appealing to their self-interest–would David exercise his powers of patronage in favour of Benjaminites as Saul had done?–can he hope to obtain information. But even then it is the Edomite Doeg, described as

27. Art. cit., 26f.
28. Ibid., 27.
29. Op. cit., 20f.
30. Ibid., 21.

"standing with the servants of Saul," who steps forward. Later, when Saul orders his servants to put the priests of Nob to the sword, their refusal means that Doeg again has to oblige (22:17–19).

Nabal reads like a diminutive Saul when viewed in this light. In his eyes David is just a fugitive slave, and there are far too many of them about the countryside these days. However, his acid dismissal seems to be more than an expression of contempt for a local *condottiere*: "Who is David? And who is the son of Jesse?" (25:10) sounds like an echo of Sheba's rebel-cry in 2 Sam 20:1: "We have no portion in David, and we have no inheritance in the son of Jesse." Nabal even talks like a Saulide sympathizer.[31]

In his relations with his wife and his servants Nabal again reads like a reflex of Saul. Abigail has no confidence in him: "But she did not tell her husband Nabal" (25:19); "she told him nothing at all until the [[46]] morning light" (25:36). Nor is it just that she acts independently of her husband: she is unable to say anything positive about him. For her he is a paradigm of reprobation, and her desperate errand is, not to save his life, but to save David from catching a blot on his escutcheon. And nowhere is the difference between "the lady and the fool" so marked as in their respective attitudes to David; Abigail is as perspicacious as Nabal is obstinately blind.

If Abigail cannot speak well of her husband it is not surprising that his servants think ill of him. There is no denying his cantankerousness, so that one of the servants can remind his mistress–apparently with impunity–that Nabal is "so much a man of Belial that one cannot speak to him" (25:17).

David's hot-blooded response to Nabal's incivility was to mobilize his entire band of six hundred followers, deploying them exactly as he did later in the recovery operation against the Amalekites: four hundred go into attack and two hundred stay by the baggage (cf. 1 Sam 30:9f., 21–25). On this occasion the scale of the operation certainly encourages us to see Nabal in larger-than-life terms. Perhaps, too, there is *double entendre*–a hint at the fate of the Saulide house?–in the servant's warning to Abigail in 25:17: "evil is determined against our master and against all his house." Be that as it may, when Abigail returned from entreating David she found her husband celebrating the wool-clip in right royal manner. His symposium is said to have been "like the feast of a king" (25:36), which may be

31. Levenson, art. cit., 24, links 1 Sam 25:10 with Sheba's revolt: "1 Samuel plants an ominous seed, which sprouts in the doomed rebellion of Sheba, but matures in the days of David's grandson Rehoboam, when the Northern tribes raise the identical cry, with a momentous effect on David's 'secure dynasty' (1 Kgs 12:16–17)."

an unsubtle way of drawing attention to the role-identification with which the narrator has been operating.[32]

Word-Reprise

[[47]] For specificity and directness Hebrew narrative, particularly in the aspect of narrative analogy, relies heavily on word-repetition. It is through "the repetitive use of key verbal stems"[33] that the narrator lays the hermeneutical markers which impart some measure of objectivity to our attempts to understand his viewpoint. The study of word-repetition therefore has an assured place in narrative analysis; for even our present fascination with multiple readings and open-ended analyses must leave us free to regard as our primary hermeneutic objective the elucidation of the meaning which the writer himself intended to convey.[34] The beauty of this device is that it enables the narrator to make his point with an absolute economy of words, whether it be to highlight parallelism, contrast, or development, across the contextual divide. There are instances of the phenomenon in 1 Samuel 24–26 which help to lay bare the narrator's intention in these chapters: chap. 25 contains verbal echoes of chap. 24 and is in turn echoed, briefly but distinctly, in chap. 26.

Chapters 24//25. In 25:8 David instructs his young men to go to Nabal and ask him to "give whatever you have available to your servants and to *your son David.*" David, in fact, makes a show of being deferential to Nabal, and it is important [[48]] for the narrator, in view of the sequel, that there is no excuse for Nabal's rudeness. However, "your son David" may also be seen as a deliberate echo of 24:16, where Saul addresses David as "my son David." The latter expression occurs three times in the parallel narrative in chap. 26 (vv. 17, 21, 25) and is peculiar to Saul in the books of Samuel.[35]

32. The same expression occurs in 4QSam[a], LXX at 2 Sam 13:27, possibly "suggested by a reminiscence of I 25, 36": S. R. Driver, *Notes on . . . the Books of Samuel* (Oxford, 1913) 302. Driver also allows the possibility that the words may have been omitted from MT 2 Sam 13:27 by *homoioteleuton*. Cf. E. C. Ulrich, *The Qumran Text of Samuel and Josephus* (Missoula, 1978) 85.

33. M. Fishbane, "Composition and Structure in the Jacob Cycle," *JJS* 27 (1975) 21; cf. R. Alter, "Biblical Narrative," *Commentary* 61 (1976) 63. For word-reprise as a poetic device see J. Muilenburg, "A Study in Hebrew Rhetoric: Repetition and Style," *SVT* 1 (1953) 97–111.

34. "It is what the author wants to get across to his readers or listeners that should be the concern of every teacher of the Old Testament": J. F. A. Sawyer, *From Moses to Patmos* (London, 1977) 9. For further discussion of authorial intention see H. W. Frei, *The Eclipse of Biblical Narrative. A Study in Eighteenth and Nineteenth Century Hermeneutics* (New Haven/London, 1974) 73–85, 250–66, 301f.

35. Cf. also David's use of "father" in his address to Saul in 24:11.

The second instance of significant word-repetition involves the contrasting pair "good" and "evil"—and it is noteworthy that of the approximately eighty occurrences of the roots יטב/טוב [['good'/'do good']] and רע [['evil']] in 1 Samuel fully one third are to be found in chaps. 24–26. In 24:17 (18) Saul is in a repentant mood and confesses to David, "You are more righteous than I; for *you have repaid me good, whereas I have repaid you evil.*" This point is developed in vv. 18ff. (19ff.) with further occurrences of the root טוב. When we pass on to the Nabal story and to David's meditation on the insult to his men the parallel with Saul is hard to miss: "Surely in vain have I protected all that belongs to this fellow in the wilderness, with the result that nothing has been lost of all that belongs to him; *and he has returned me evil for good*" (25:21). And with this the servant's report to Abigail is in agreement: "the men were very good to us and we suffered no harm" (25:15).

Thirdly, the figure of the ריב [['lawsuit']] makes its appearance in chaps. 24 and 25. In his exchange with Saul outside the cave David expresses his confidence that God will interpose on his behalf: "May the Lord be judge and give sentence between me and you, and *may he* see and *plead my cause*, and deliver me from your hand" (25:15[16]). The metaphor is picked up again in 25:39 when David receives the news of Nabal's death: "Blessed be the Lord *who has pleaded the cause of my reproach* at the hand of Nabal and has kept back his servant from evil." These are the only occurrences of the root ריב, in its forensic sense, in 1 Samuel.[36]

Chapters 25//26. [[49]] The most striking case of word-repetition comes in 26:10 in David's rebuttal of Abishai's suggestion that he finish Saul off with one thrust of his spear. Said David, "As the Lord lives, the Lord will smite him; either his day will come and he will die, or he will go down into battle and perish." This seeming vagueness as to the manner in which Saul would die is deceptive, for two of these statements have a direct bearing on Saul's fate. At the purely historical level it is a fact that Saul went into battle against the Philistines and perished on Gilboa (1 Sam 31:6). But, seen from the perspective of the wider narrative context, it is the first clause which carries the accent: "the Lord will smite him." The possibility of Saul's death at the hand of someone other than David does not arise in chap. 24, yet it forms the *point d'appui* [['foundation']] of David's argument against Abishai in chap. 26. Whence, therefore, this conviction that Saul's death would come as an act of divine judgment? We need only look back to the Nabal story for the answer. When Nabal heard from Abigail about the fate which she had so narrowly averted the shock

36. The verb is used in 1 Sam 2:10 ("those who oppose the Lord will be shattered"). וירב in 1 Sam 15:5 represents a defective spelling of the verb ארב [['lie in wait']].

was too great for him, with the result that "his heart died within him and he became like a stone" (25:37). About ten days after this "the Lord smote Nabal and he died" (v. 38). "Smote" here, as in 26:10, translates the verb נגף, the mere repetition of which is sufficient to point up the comparison between Saul and Nabal. The manner of Nabal's death provides the key to David's confident assertion in 26:10 and herein, as we shall presently suggest, lies also a pointer to the whole narrative thrust of 1 Samuel 24–26.

This adumbration of Saul's death in the judgment on Nabal may also be significant for the interpretation of 25:26, here Abigail expresses the hope that David's enemies will "be as Nabal." Since Nabal appears to have been fit and well when Abigail set out, her words can only amount to an imprecation of wrong-headedness on those who sought David's life—unless, that is, verse 26 anticipates Nabal's untimely demise.[37] The obvious difficulty with [[50]] this interpretation is that it assumes prophetic powers for Abigail and does little for the verisimilitude of the story. This, however, has to be balanced by the consideration that the whole of Abigail's speech portrays her as a woman of uncommon, even prophetic, powers of discernment. Since on other grounds the connection between the deaths of Nabal and Saul has been established we may the more confidently interpret 25:26 as a wish that Saul—for who else seeks David's life?—may suffer the same fate as Nabal (cf. 2 Sam 18:32).

Word-Play

The role-identification of Nabal with Saul is, arguably, canonized in Saul's final exchanges with David in 26:21–25, where we find Saul at his most conciliatory: "I have done wrong; come back, my son David, for I will never again harm you, because my life was precious in your eyes this day; behold, *I have played the fool* (הסכלתי) and have erred exceedingly" (v. 21). On any reckoning הסכלתי is a loaded word.[38] This is the verb with which Samuel launches into his denunciation of Saul at Gilgal: "You have acted foolishly (נסכלת); you have not kept the commandment of the Lord your God which he commanded you" (1 Sam 13:13); now in the presence of the successor to whom Samuel's speech makes allusion Saul pronounces judgment on himself.

But it is also worth considering whether הסכלתי has special significance within the more immediate context. In other words, does the

37. Cf. W. McKane, *I and II Samuel* (TC. London, 1963) 151; J. Mauchline, *1 and 2 Samuel* (NCB. London, 1971) 170; H. J. Stoebe, *Das erste Buch Samuelis* (KAT VIII/I. Gütersloh, 1973) 449.

38. R. A. Carlson, *David the Chosen King* (Uppsala, 1964) 207f., regards the use of this verb as characteristic of the deuteronomistic group.

admission "I have played the fool" point back to chap. 25 and the figure of Nabal? A definitive answer would require an excursion into the semantic field of 'folly' in Biblical Hebrew, and, in particular, a discussion of the merits of 'fool' as a translation of BH נבל.[39] S. R. Driver favoured the [[51]] translation 'churl' in 25:25 and this is the way of NEB: "'Churl' is his name, and churlish his behaviour."[40] James Barr, on the other hand, opts mediatingly for 'churlish fool', though he does not regard this as the original meaning of the actual name 'Nabal'.[41] There is indeed strong versional support for locating BH נבל within the semantic field of 'folly', evidence which extends to the Hebrew-Greek equivalences in Ecclesiasticus.[42] If 'Nabal' has some connotation of 'folly' then, as Gemser has noted, there is a handy Akkadian analogue in the personal name Saklu ('foolish').[43] It is also a matter of some relevance that the Hebrew root סכל denotes more than folly if by that we mean stupidity or imbecility. The folly in the moral realm which *BDB* associates with the root brings it within striking distance of BH נבל and נבלה.[44]

Word-play on Nabal's name is in any case a feature of 1 Samuel 25. It comes explicitly in v. 25 already quoted: "נבל is his name and נבלה is with him." There would seem to be another instance of play on the name in v. 37 which, in talking about the wine "going out of Nabal," seems momentarily to think of him as a נֵבֶל, a wine-skin. (The commentators' silence at this point could be attributable to myopia or to powers of restraint which this writer obviously lacks!) Finally, when the narrator describes Abigail as 'of good understanding' (טובת־שכל, v. 3) is he not saying that she was all that her husband, so aptly named, was not?

Function of Nabal Interlude

[[52]] A more exact statement of the function, or, perhaps more correctly, of one of the functions, of 1 Samuel 25 can now be undertaken. It is unlikely that the Nabal incident has been included merely to show us how David and his men fared in the wilderness,[45] or even to relate how David acquired Abigail as wife. Nor are the mines of authorial intention ex-

39. See the studies by W. M. W. Roth, "NBL," *VT* 10 (1960) 394–409, and T. Donald, "The Semantic Field of 'Folly' in Proverbs, Job, Psalms, and Ecclesiastes," *VT* 13 (1963) 285–92.

40. Driver, op. cit., 200.

41. "The Symbolism of Names in the Old Testament," *BJRL* 52 (1969–70) 21–28.

42. E.g., Ecclus. 4:27; 21:22.

43. B. Gemser, *De Beteekenis der persoonsnamen voor onze kennis van het leven en denken der oude Babyloniërs en Assyriërs* (Wageningen, 1924) 192f. I owe the reference to Prof. Barr's article.

44. *BDB*, 614f.

45. Cf. Mauchline, op. cit., 171, on chap. 25 as only incidentally a source of sociological information.

hausted, if they are touched at all, by Miscall's proposal to read the chapter as an oblique commentary on chap. 14, in virtue of the fact that it is also concerned with a vow rashly uttered: "1 Sam. 25, the Abigail and David episode, stresses the rashness of Saul's vow and his obstinacy in needlessly trying to fulfill it."[46]

In fact most are agreed that the centre of gravity in the Nabal story lies in Abigail's speech and the main issue which it confronts, namely the necessity of David's avoiding blood-guilt. 1 Samuel 25 is therefore of a piece thematically with the adjacent chapters which tell of David's avoidance of blood-guilt for Saul. This is not journey's end, however, for we must look more closely at the way in which Nabal contributes to the exposition of the theme. And first we shall take issue with Levenson who, while agreeing that there is a thematic relationship between chap. 25 and the adjoining chapters, nevertheless sees its main function in another direction.

> The difference between 1 Samuel 25 and its neighbors is that in the latter, David seeks out Saul solely in order to demonstrate his good will, whereas in our tale, only the rhetorical genius of Abigail saves him from bloodying his hands. In short, the David of chaps. 24 and 26 is the character whom we have seen since his introduction in chap. 16 and whom we shall continue to see until 2 Samuel 11, the appealing young man of immaculate motivation and heroic [[53]] courage. But the David of chap. 25 is a man who kills for a grudge. The episode of Nabal is the very first revelation of evil in David's character. He can kill. This time he stops short. But the cloud that chap. 25 raises continues to darken our perception of David's character.[47]

Levenson then sums it up in a sentence: "1 Samuel 25 is a proleptic glimpse, within David's ascent, of his fall from grace." So, for Levenson, the shadow of Bathsheba and Uriah, and of all the ugly entail of that episode, falls over this chapter.

The attractions of Levenson's thesis notwithstanding, there are good grounds for thinking that the Nabal story functions nearer home. In the first place, Levenson's exposition betrays a doubtful interpretation of David's behaviour in the cave at En-gedi. This is a point to which we shall return; suffice it to say just now that it is very doubtful whether the narrator would have viewed chap. 25 as giving "the very first revelation of evil in David's character." It is even more to be doubted that it was the narrator's intention that this chapter should discord with his otherwise "tendentious"—so Weiser[48] and most—account of David's rise. According to

46. Art cit., 30 (narrative analogy "is not limited to texts in close proximity").
47. Art. cit., 23.
48. Art. cit., 354.

another, and perhaps more satisfactory, reading, the account of David's honourable acquisition of Abigail stands self-consciously in contrast with the sordid matter of 2 Samuel 11–12. "Honourable" is, of course, a relative term here, though not necessarily as relative as Lemche implies when he accuses David of "frightening a man to death and stealing his wife."[49]

All this, however, is only to disregard the function of 1 Samuel 25 within its immediate narrative setting. For from 24:1 to 26:25 we have a three-part plot in which there is incremental repetition of the motif of blood-guilt and its avoidance.[50] [[54]]

Scene One (24:1–22[23]): David, incited to avenge himself on Saul, performs a symbolic act which is of sufficient gravity to cause him immediate remorse. He then berates his men and states the theological grounds for not striking Saul down.

Scene Two (25:2–42): David outraged by Nabal's rudeness to his men, sets out with the intention of destroying him and every male belonging to him. His anger is assuaged by Abigail's intervention; Nabal comes under divine judgment.

Scene Three (26:1–25): David is again incited against Saul, this time by Abishai. Saul and his men are in a deep sleep, as helpless before David as was Nabal when "his heart died within him and he became like a stone" (25:37). David unhesitatingly rejects Abishai's suggestion; Saul is "the Lord's anointed" and God will deal with him (vv. 9f.).

"Incremental repetition," in the sense in which I use it here, means the development or modification of a motif through repetition in separate narrative sequences. The changes and variations thus introduced "can point to an intensification, climactic development, acceleration of the actions and attitudes initially represented, or, on the other hand, to some unexpected, perhaps unsettling, new revelation of character or plot.[51] In the setting of 1 Samuel 24–26 we have to do with the maturation of an idea in David's mind, the progress being unfolded in three episodes each of which has its own point of resolution without prejudice to the coherence of the larger narrative unit.

Manifestly, the suggestion that there is incremental repetition in these chapters assumes that David's actions in relation to Saul in the first and third scenes are qualitatively different. Koch does not agree: [[55]]

49. Art. cit., 12.

50. For comment on ternary structure in biblical narrative see Humphreys, art. cit., 19; Miscall, art. cit., 31f.

51. Alter, "Biblical Narrative," 63.

> In both narratives David takes a token with him. Yet in chapter xxiv he only removes the skirt of Saul's robe, whereas in chapter xxvi he also (*sic*) takes Saul's weapon. Here also B (i.e., chap. 26) must be the later version. The story is lent a more soldierly aspect of the adversary is robbed of his weapon and not merely of a piece of his apparel.[52]

Koch, like most, regards chaps. 24 and 26 as variant accounts of the same incident. But this monistic view need not lead automatically to the conclusion that David's actions are meant to be accorded the same status. (Of course, if the accounts answer to two separate occasions when David spared Saul there is even less reason to force the parallel.)

On a straightforward reading of 24:1–7[8]—and I am not among those who hold that the MT is in need of reordering in this section[53]—David's excision of a piece of Saul's robe stands for more than the procuring of a token in proof of his goodwill toward the king. The fact that attempts have been made to illuminate the act from this and that source is immaterial, for in each case it emerges with an impressive, if not altogether uniform, symbolism.

Symbolism there certainly is if 24:4–5 is meant to be read in the light of 15:27f., where the tearing of a robe—whether Samuel's or Saul's is disputed[54]—signifies the forfeiture of his kingdom: "And Samuel turned to go, and he seized the skirt of his robe and it tore. Samuel said to him, The Lord has torn the kingdom of Israel from you this day, and will give it to your neighbour who is better than you." According to this interpretation, then, David, the "neighbour" in question, staked his claim to the kingdom that day in the cave when he [[56]] removed a piece from Saul's robe. The narrative complementarity of the two passages is also suggested by the occurrence in both of the expression כנף מעיל [['hem of (the) robe']] (15:27; 24:5), since it is not found elsewhere in the Hebrew Bible.[55]

52. Op. cit., 143. R. C. Culley, *Studies in the Structure of Hebrew Narrative* (Philadelphia, 1976) 49–54, represents a similar evaluation of David's behaviour in the two accounts.

53. Reasons were given in a short paper ("1 Samuel 24:7 (8) and the Dichotomized Servant in Q") read at the joint meeting of the British and Dutch Old Testament Societies in Cambridge, July 1979 (not yet published). [[This appeared as "Word-Play and Verse Order in 1 Samuel xxiv 5–8," *VT* 40 (1990) 139–44.]]

54. Grønbaek, op. cit., 164, thinks that it is Samuel's cloak which is torn—in which case compare Ahijah's tearing of his own robe in 1 Kgs 11:30–31. Cf. also R. A. Brauner, "'To Grasp the Hem' and 1 Samuel 15:27," *Journal of the Ancient Near Eastern Society of Columbia University* 6 (1974) 35–38. According to Brauner, Saul took hold of Samuel's cloak—an act symbolic of supplication—but inadvertently tore it; Samuel thereupon attached the symbolism to the *tearing* of the robe. 4QSam^{a}, LXX read '(and) Saul laid hold' for MT '(and) he laid hold'; cf. Ulrich, op. cit., 54.

55. Grønbaek, op. cit., 164f.

References to Akkadian texts from Alalakh and Mari illustrate the possibility that David's was a calculatedly symbolic act at En-gedi. Since grasping the hem of a superior's cloak was a common expression of submission it has been surmised that David's cutting of Saul's hem amounted to a declaration of revolt.[56] Actual cutting of a garment is mentioned in the Mari texts in connection with the immobilizing of a "prophetess." In one letter Baḫdi-Lim, administrator of the Mari palace, informs Zimri-Lim that "Aḫum the priest has removed the hair and the hem of the cloak of the *muḫḫutum* ⟦'female ecstatic, prophetess'⟧."[57] This evidently was thought to bring the *muḫḫutum* under the control of the king to whom the hair and hem were forwarded. The parallel with 1 Sam 24:4f.(5f.) is sufficiently close for Noth to conclude that "David, by cutting off the hem of the garment, does evil to Saul."[58]

⟦57⟧ Without committing ourselves to any of these explanations, we can still admit the probability that David's act was symbolic, and even grave in its implications. Some corroboration of this view comes in the statement in v. 5(6) that "*David's heart smote him* because he had cut off Saul's skirt." This is a strong statement which is used on only one other occasion—that of the census in 2 Samuel 24—to describe David's feelings of remorse (2 Sam 24:10). Now one of the outstanding features of the census narrative is that David's action had deeper implications than were at first apparent. Such, it would seem, is the case in 1 Sam 24:5(6).

If our interpretation of the incident in the cave is correct then the contrast with the similar-sounding episode in 26:1–12 is not to be missed. David, having once violated the sanctity of the king's person—to put it no higher—shows not the slightest sign of weakness on the second occasion. Standing between these two accounts is chap. 25, in which the whole issue of grievance, revenge and blood-guilt is played through to its conclusion. Thus David is given a preview of what will happen if he commits his case to God and leaves Saul unharmed. 1 Samuel 25 is therefore "proleptic"—it has "an inner significance which runs ahead of the external appearances"[59]—not so much in relation to the more distant events of 2 Samuel[60] as to its immediate context.

56. D. J. Wiseman in *Archaeology and Old Testament Study,* ed. D. W. Thomas (Oxford, 1967) 128. For text, see idem, "Abban and Alalaḫ," *JCS* 12 (1958) 129; see also *CAD* 16, 223.

57. *ARM* VI, 45, 7ff.; cf. VI, 26, rev. 8–9. Cf. E. Noort, *Untersuchungen zum Gottesbescheid in Mari: Die "Mariprophetie" in der alttestamentlichen Forschung* (AOAT 202; Neukirchen-Vluyn, 1977) 84–86.

58. M. Noth, "Remarks on the Sixth Volume of Mari Texts," *JSS* 1 (1956) 330.

59. Thus Jobling, op. cit., 12, on the function of 1 Sam 14:1–46 and 18:1–5 within the story of Saul. Cf. also Fishbane's remarks, art. cit., 22f., on proleptic elements in the Jacob cycle in Genesis.

60. Pace Levenson (vid. supra).

Redundancy versus Development

This positive appraisal of 1 Samuel 24–26 as narrative is greatly at variance with Jobling's verdict on the same chapters. [[58]]

> The attempt is made . . . to show Saul *both* as the rejected one *and* as willingly abdicating to David. In chap. 24, he begins by seeking David's life, and ends by confessing David's future kingship (v. 20). Their next encounter, in chap. 26, is a "redundant" repetition of this cycle, though without the specific confession. . . . But in the very next verse (27:1) David complains of the continuing danger to his life from Saul. The attempt fails; the theological aim is here pursued at the cost of narrative coherence, and even of psychological conviction; at no level does the account make sufficient sense.[61]

For Jobling the "theological aim" of 1 Samuel 13–31 is to "make theologically acceptable the transition from Saul's kingship to David's,"[62] an aim which he regards as capable of fulfilment only with Jonathan's mediation, and this pivotally in 18:1–5 where, according to Jobling, we have Jonathan's virtual abdication in favour of David.

If this be the yardstick then 1 Samuel 24–26 must indeed be judged a failure in narrative terms. However, as we observed at the outset, the legitimacy of David's claim to the throne is not the issue in this section; it is, rather, a question of how David is to appropriate what is legitimately his by divine decree: blood-guilt for Saul or not? Jobling, more than most, should have recognized this in view of the fact that Jonathan, on whom he pins so much, makes his most explicit statement about David's future kingship in 23:17, i.e., just as the "wilderness cycle" gets underway. Far from being a "redundant" repetition of chap. 24, chap. 26 builds on the earlier account and, through its speeches, points forward to the next phase of David's life on the run. 27:1, instead of destroying the coherence of the narrative, as Jobling alleges, strikingly emphasizes David's determination not to lift his hand against Saul; his magnanimity puts him in danger, so that he has to take refuge with the Philistines. Jobling is looking for a narrative coherence which makes no concessions to historical reality, for Saul never did deliver his [[59]] kingdom to David on a plate–of that much we may be certain. In short, Jobling has imposed his own stereotype on the narrative and castigated it for vacuity.

61. Op. cit., 22.
62. Ibid., 21.

Narrative and Speech

The discussion so far has scarcely begun to do justice to the fact that each of the component narratives in chaps. 24–26 climaxes in an exchange of speeches,[63] and if we were attempting a final analysis of the section–as if there could be such a thing–this would undoubtedly be a serious defect. It could be argued, on the other hand, that our approach will help to correct a prevailing imbalance. Certainly, if the narrative is judged solely in terms of the ideology of the speeches, chap. 26 falls flat on its face. Such is the criterion usually applied, which explains why Koch is not the only one to have expressed puzzlement about the present function of the chapter.[64] Saul's speeches in chap. 26 *are* anti-climactic when set alongside his affirmations at En-gedi. The most that he can manage is, "Blessed be you, my son David! You will do many things and will have success" (26:25). There may be hints of David's future regal status when he pronounces Abner and the rest worthy of death (v. 16), or when Saul confesses to him that he has "sinned" (v. 21),[65] but none of this matches the full-blooded affirmation of 24:20(21): "I know that you will certainly be king, and that the kingdom of Israel will be established in your hand." Indeed, it is hard to imagine how chap. 26 could have capped this, if that had been the intention.

But to judge the speeches of chap. 26 by the canons of chap. 24 is to fail to recognize that they are animated by other considerations, namely, the irreconcilability of David and Saul, and David's imminent withdrawal to Philistia. Chap. 26 recounts the last confrontation between the two, and the narrator makes the most of the [[60]] fact:[66] "Then David went over to the other side, and stood on the top of the hill at a distance, a great space being between them" (v. 13). The "distance" and "space" are surely not just physical here; in outlook and destiny the two are poles apart and already, even before the speeches, the gulf is fixed. Nothing that Saul can say will change the situation. To his invitation–or is it a plea?–to come back David merely replies, "Here is the spear, O king!" (v. 22).[67] David knew, and Saul knew, the significance of the spear in their relationship (cf. 18:10f.; 19:19f.).

In 26:13–25, then, the way is being paved for David's initiative announced in 27:1, the initiative which brought him into vassalage to the Philistines and saw him far from Gilboa when his people were deep in

63. Cf. von Rad, *Theology* 1, 54 ("the dialogues between David and Saul are the highlights to which the external events lead up"); so also Koch, op. cit., 150.

64. Op. cit., 147.

65. Cf. Koch, op. cit., 141n., 142.

66. Cf. Humphreys, art. cit., 24.

67. So the *K^{e}tîb* [['written']]; the *Q^{e}rê* [['read']] is "Behold the king's spear."

trouble. The subject is introduced by David in vv. 19f. ("they have driven me out this day so that I should have no part in the heritage of the Lord, saying, Go, serve other gods"), Saul's invitation to return (v. 21)–not paralleled in chap. 24–has to be read in the light of it, and David's committal of his future into God's hands in v. 24 probably has it in view.

In its own way the altercation between David and Abner, who does not figure in chap. 24, also contributes to the forward thrust of chap. 26. There is just a hint of historical allegory about David's upbraiding of the man who was to survive Gilboa and become the mainspring of Saulide resistance to David's rule over a unified kingdom of Israel: "Abner you cannot even guarantee the king's safety, and how are you going to ensure the survival of his house?" (cf. 26:15f.).

So then, the speeches in chap. 26 are oriented to the future, and herein lies their justification. The narrator who used the action of chaps. 24–26 to put across a theological point now uses speech to fuel the development of the next stage in his story.

Characterization

[[61]] Small slice of narrative though it is, 1 Samuel 24–26 does permit us to speak of character development in connection with David. As the action unwinds we can see the evidence of an inward change. But, according to Scholes and Kellogg, "characters in primitive stories are invariably 'flat,' 'static,' and quite 'opaque.' "[68] This applies as much to the Old Testament as to the rest of ancient literature: "The inward life is assumed but not presented in primitive narrative literature, whether Hebraic or Hellenic."[69] And for good measure the story of David and Bathsheba is cited for its opaqueness: situations are described in a detached, impersonal way, and without reference to the mental processes of those involved.

The "wilderness cycle" in 1 Samuel certainly does not fit so comfortably into this pre-Christian mould of Scholes and Kellogg. At a crucial point early in the story we have a very clear indication of David's state of mind: "And afterwards David's heart smote him because he had cut off Saul's skirt" (24:5[6]). Thereafter the inward change is expressed in plot rather than in overt character formulation. Plot formulation, if I may now quote approvingly from Scholes and Kellogg, "involves seeing the character at long range, with limited detail, so that his change against a particular background may be readily apparent."[70] This could have been written

68. R. Scholes and R. Kellogg, *The Nature of Narrative* (New York, 1966) 164.
69. Ibid., 166.
70. Ibid., 168.

with the "wilderness cycle" in mind. It is precisely because the stage-settings in chaps. 24 and 26 are so similar that we are able to perceive the difference in the actor.

Narration–History

Theology, narration–but how fares "David's Rise" as history? Some "concluding historical postscript" seems called for.

[[62]] For most of the modern period, and especially since Rost's work in the 1920s, the Succession Narrative has enjoyed recognition as the earliest, and also the foremost, example of Hebrew historiography. The lot of "David's Rise" was to endure regular comparison, inevitably unfavourable, with its prestigious rival. The Succession Narrative was "history" in the strict sense, "David's Rise" was not. It was its transparent theological-propagandist slant even more than the thorny problem of the duplicates–though the two may not be unconnected–which decided the fate of "David's Rise."

Koch's use of "saga" in connection with 1 Samuel 24 and 26 would also seem to reflect a negative view of the Davidic *Vorgeschichte* [['source narrative']]: "Sagas are reality poeticised."[71] But Koch's position is just a little more complicated than this. He regards chap. 24 ("account A") as deriving from a written source which described David's rise to kingship. "The complex literary type to which A belongs is therefore *historical writing*, for only a writer of history has as his theme the rise of a monarch's power over a particular nation and its persistence in face of external and internal danger."[72] He does not see the presence of heroic sagas in this earlier account as diminishing its status as history-writing, inasmuch as the historian has to make the best of the sources available to him. The compiler of "A" was no less a historian than Herodotus or Thucydides who make frequent use of saga.

A question of more direct relevance to the bulk of this paper is whether literary artistry and narrative technique are compatible with the interests of history-writing. In his highlighting of themes and causal relationships is the narrator not taking us ever further away from the original events and circumstances–assuming that such there generally are–and should we not be going in that other direction in any case? The short [[63]] answer to the first part of the question is that it is doubtful whether any self-respecting historian could operate without adopting a viewpoint or

71. Op. cit., 156.

72. Ibid., 145. For further discussion and interaction with Koch see H. J. Stoebe, "Gedanken zur Heldensage in den Samuelbüchern," in *Das Ferne und Nahe Wort* (BZAW 105; Fest. L. Rost; ed. F. Maass; Berlin, 1967) 208–18.

without introducing theme(s), with all that this implies for the selection and arrangement of material. Obviously the extent of our sympathy with the viewpoint may be influential in our evaluation of the work as "history," "story," or something else.

As for the second part of the question: I cannot see that we have any choice but to be interested in the historical dimension of Scripture, however great the strains such an interest may impose at times. Of course we must appreciate the significance and value of "the tradition," with proper regard for the metamorphosis of history in tradition, and of tradition as history. Nevertheless, it is hopelessly and unnecessarily reductionist to conclude that our study of the Old Testament can only produce a history of ideas.[73] Even to produce a "history of ideas" requires that we know when the ideas came into vogue and when they were superseded. And what is that but to treat the Old Testament as a document which bears witness to history?

It may be that at some point we shall take refuge in analogy; if so, we must select with care. Is it to be Shakespeare, with R. J. Coggins?

> We should laugh out of court anyone who approached *Hamlet,* primarily with a view to improving his knowledge of Danish history, or *Henry V* as a source of knowledge of fifteenth-century England; yet a very similar approach to many an Old Testament book is regarded as entirely natural and proper.[74]

There are indeed better sources for an understanding of Danish history and of fifteenth-century England, but the analogy could easily mislead. *Hamlet* and *Henry V* are [[64]] not even history-*like* in the sense in which Coggins himself would apply the term to Old Testament narrative. To many the analogy of Herodotus and Thucydides may be no more satisfactory, though I am bound to say that I think it somewhat nearer the truth. To be sure, there is a danger that immersion in the quest for "historicity" may actually cut us off from the thought-world of the Old Testament, but the danger is in the excess. The peril of the opposite extreme is the unwarranted assumption that Israel's self-understanding was a self-*mis*understanding. And that is a conclusion fraught with consequences for us all.[75]

73. As is suggested by N. Wyatt, "The Old Testament Historiography of the Exilic Period," *STh* 33 (1979) 66n.

74. R. J. Coggins, "History and Story in Old Testament Study," *JSOT* 11 (1979) 43; in similar vein D. Robertson, *The Old Testament and the Literary Critic* (Philadelphia, 1977) 5.

75. Cf. M. H. Woudstra, "Event and Interpretation in the Old Testament," in *Interpreting God's Word Today,* ed. S. Kistemaker (Grand Rapids, 1970) 58–59.

Solomon: Bathsheba's Firstborn

T. Veijola

Veijola offers a study of the narrative of David's affair with Uriah's wife, Bathsheba, that is a good illustration of a conventional literary- and historical-critical approach. Broadly, the historical assumptions follow the well-established view of the Succession Narrative as a separate composition (Rost). The specific thesis, not new in itself but presented with forceful new arguments, is that Solomon was actually the first son born to David and Bathsheba, not the second, and therefore the offspring of the adulterous encounter. The insertion between 2 Sam 11:27a and 12:24b was made by a writer who wanted to provide a more acceptable beginning for Solomon.

Veijola draws attention to strict illogicalities, unexpected features, and on their basis reconstructs a history of the text. It is interesting to consider that the same features (including the absence of a naming formula for the first child; the penitence of David *before* the child dies; the insufficient time for Bathsheba to give birth to a second child within the time frame of the Ammonite War) might lead to a different kind of treatment according to the modern literary approaches.

Dedicated to the memory of Uriah the Hittite

[[230]] The genealogy of Jesus at the beginning of the First Gospel (Matt 1:6) includes the notice "David was the father of Solomon by the wife of Uriah." What is peculiar about this notice is that instead of "Bathsheba" it

Translated and reprinted with permission from "Salomo: Der Erstgeborene Bathsebas," in *Studies in the Historical Books of the Old Testament* (Vetus Testamentum Supplements 30; Leiden: Brill, 1979) 230–50. Translation by Peter T. Daniels. The RSV has been used in this translation for all English scripture quotations.

speaks of "Uriah's wife," thus calling to mind the scandalous story behind Solomon's birth. Indeed, one might at first glance take from the notice the undertanding that Solomon was the adulterously conceived first child of David and Bathsheba—which could hardly have been the original intent of the genealogical notice. But quite aside from that, this possibility stimulates closer examination of the circumstances of Solomon's birth.

I

Recently, in an excursus in his book *Die Erzählung von der Thronfolge Davids,*[1] E. Würthwein touched on the question whether the narrative of the death of the first child of David and Bathsheba and the birth of the second (2 Sam 12:15b–24a) belonged to the original Succession Narrative at all; that is, whether Solomon was not really Bathsheba's *first*born. He begins by quoting some older authors who had already expressed their doubts on the passage[2] and then mentions two observations that could cast doubt on the originality of the narrative of the death of the first child: "(1) The story [[231]] of the birth of the adulterously conceived child is not carried through to the end; the expected name-giving, such as can be found in 12:24b, is missing. (2) The narrative of the birth of Solomon as second son precedes what follows by a long period of time."[3]

Nonetheless, Würthwein is not fully persuaded by these arguments but suggests that in the end the matter cannot be fully resolved.[4] Now it is in the very nature of things that one can never be absolutely certain, but it seems to me that Würthwein's observations, along with a few new ones, allow something more to be said.

II

It is in fact quite striking that, in the narrative of the birth of the adulterously conceived child, the name-giving is omitted. An impartial reader with some feel for Hebrew narrative art, after the present concluding sentence "and she bore him a son" (11:27a), would ask instinctively, "And what did she call him?"—because normally stories reporting the birth of a

1. E. Würthwein, *Die Erzählung von der Thronfolge Davids: Theologische oder politische Geschichtsschreibung?* (Zurich, 1974). More recent literature on this theme will be found in W. Dietrich, "David in Überlieferung und Geschichte," *VF* 22 (1977) 44–64.

2. J. Marquart, *Fundamente israelitischer und jüdischer Geschichte* (Göttingen, 1896) 26; S. A. Cook, "Notes on the Composition of 2 Samuel," *AJSL* 16 (1899–1900) 156–57; E. Auerbach, *Wüste und Gelobtes Land* (2d ed.; Berlin, 1938) 1.228 n. 1.

3. Würthwein, *Die Erzählung von der Thronfolge Davids*, 32.

4. Ibid.

child also include the name-giving.[5] This name-giving—corresponding to the meaning of the name[6]—appears to be an especially important feature for the Hebrew narrator to include. When the name-giving is omitted (which is extremely rare), there must be special circumstances.

In the narrative about Solomon as judge (1 Kgs 3:16–28), a prostitute reports that she and another had both recently brought children into the world (vv. 17–18) but does not give their names. But who would expect this in these circumstances? This is a *paradigmatic* narrative about the judicial wisdom of the king to which any *biographical* interest is foreign (similar to the New Testament paradigms),[7] so much so that the king, whose identity (Solomon) can be [[232]] determined from the wider context, remains anonymous in the narrative itself.[8]

The report of the miracle of Elisha and the Shunammite woman (2 Kgs 4:8–37) is similar. Through Elisha's miraculous power (v. 16), the woman becomes pregnant and bears a son,[9] whose name is not mentioned for transparent reasons: in the place where one would expect the name-giving (v. 17), there is an announcement, which is much more important in this context, that the son was born precisely at the time prophesied to the woman by Elisha (v. 16). This is the point of the narrative. Furthermore, throughout the long story, the names of the mother and father of the child remain unknown. Only the principal characters in the prophet's legend, Elisha and his servant Gehazi, are named, and they are already known from other passages; other than this, biographical questions do not concern this narrative at all.[10]

Things are quite different in the Succession Narrative, which is also called David's Family History.[11] There, biographical interest is generally characteristic and is especially pronounced in relation to the Davidic royal

5. Aside from the many genealogical stories in Genesis, cf. passages that, like 2 Sam 11:27a, read "and she bore him a son/daughter," with the name-giving appended: Judg 8:31, 13:24; 1 Sam 1:20, 4:19–21; Isa 8:3; Hos 1:3–4, 6, 8–9; Ruth 4:13, 17.

6. J. Pedersen, *Israel*, vols. 1–2 (2d ed.; Copenhagen, 1934) 190: "The name is part of the soul."

7. Cf. M. Dibelius, *Die Formgeschichte des Evangeliums* (5th ed.; Tübingen, 1966) 46–47.

8. This is a recurring traditional tale, the material of which is not genuinely Israelite; see M. Noth, *Könige* (Neukirchen-Vluyn, 1968) 47; E. Würthwein, *Die Bücher der Könige* (Göttingen, 1977) 36–37.

9. 2 Kgs 4:17; *wtld bn* [['and she bore a son']], as in 2 Sam 11:27 and 12:24.

10. Just as little biographical material is found in the corresponding narrative in the Elijah tradition (1 Kgs 17:17–24).

11. See, e.g., Cook, "Notes on the Composition of 2 Samuel," 155; A. F. Puukko, *Vanhan Testamentin johdanto-oppi* (Helsinki, 1945) 100; E. Sellin and G. Fohrer, *Einleitung in das Alte Testament* (10th ed.; Heidelberg, 1965) 241; F. Langlamet, "Pour ou contre Salomon?" *RB* 83 (1976) 345.

house. It is all the more remarkable that the firstborn of David and Bathsheba in *this* tradition remains nameless.

One might attempt to justify the missing name-giving *historically*, appealing to the New Testament tradition (Luke 1:59, 2:21), in which the name-giving occurs together with the circumcision on the eighth day, and combining it with the statement in 2 Sam 12:18 that the child died on the seventh day. Accordingly, the child could not yet have received a name. However, against this argument is the name-giving of the "second" child (12:24), which does not allow for an eight-day delay, and especially the lack of evidence for the currency of this New Testament practice in earlier times.[12] [[233]] Rather, from Old Testament reports of name-giving,[13] one gains the impression that a child received its name directly after birth.[14] If, in any case, the custom presupposed by the New Testament was valid for a time so much earlier–which as a possibility is very hypothetical anyway–one could hardly avoid the suspicion that the child had to die on the seventh day just so that a name need not be given it. In both cases, the report betrays its own historical improbability.

Both historical and form-critical considerations thus suggest that the firstborn child received a name. There is also the literary argument, which has already been advanced by S. A. Cook and E. Würthwein.[15] The clause *wyqrʾ ʾt šmw šlmh* [['and he called his name Solomon']] (2 Sam 12:24bβ) would constitute a perfect continuation of the abrupt ending of the narrative of the birth of the first child in 11:27a.[16] The directly preceding clause, *wtld bn* [['and she bore a son']] (12:24bα), would then be a repetition of the same clause in 11:27a, skillfully fitted to the context, which shows that everything within this enclosure (11:27b–12:24a) is a secondary insertion.

12. The Priestly tradition does in fact know circumcision on the eighth day (Gen 17:12, 21:4; Lev 12:3) but without name-giving. Gen 21:3–4 suggests instead that the boy received a name before circumcision.

13. Cf., e.g., the naming of the children of Jacob in Gen 29:32–30:24, also Gen 19:37–38, 35:16–18; Judg 13:24; 1 Sam 4:19–21, etc. While Moses, exceptionally, received his name (Exod 2:10) a long time after his birth (v. 2), this is closely connected with the peculiarity of the tradition: Moses had an Egyptian name that he could not have gotten from his Hebrew parents.

14. So also M. Noth, *Die israelitischen Personennamen im Rahmen der gemeinsemitischen Namengebung* (Stuttgart, 1928) 56; and R. de Vaux, *Les Institutions de l'Ancien Testament* (Paris, 1958) 1.74.

15. Cook, "Notes on the Composition of 2 Samuel," 156–57; Würthwein, *Erzählung von der Thronfolge Davids*, 31–32.

16. A significant sign that 11:27a is not felt as a satisfying narrative conclusion is Budde's attempt to place 12:25aβb after 11:27a (K. Budde, *Die Bücher Samuel* [Tübingen, 1902] 257), which is nothing but a rescue operation without either literary or factual basis.

I do not need to say anything further about the first part of this insertion, the Nathan–David scene (2 Sam 11:27b–12:15a), since its secondary character in this place has been long and widely recognized.[17] All the same, this scene too provides a [[234]] notable argument in this connection. Most notably, the punishment pronounced on David by Nathan (vv. *10–12)[18] mentions not one word about the death of the adulterously conceived child; only the introduction added later by the Deuteronomist (vv. 13–14) introduces the fate of the child into the word of judgment, in this way making it consistent with the succeeding narrative.[19] The question arises, then, whether the old Nathan–David scene might have arisen in a time or place where the story of the death of the firstborn was unknown.[20]

If we now return more closely to the resumption in 2 Sam 12:24bβ, we are bound to feel the identification of David as the subject of the clause *wyqrʾ ʾet šmw šlmh* as a little disturbing, since until the ninth century it apparently was customary for the mother to name the child,[21] as would also be considered normal on the basis of 2 Sam 11:26–27a. But there is a solution for this problem as well. In 2 Sam 12:24, as well as the Kethiv *wyqrʾ* [['and he called']], the feminine form *wtqrʾ* [['and she called']] has also been preserved as a Qere. This is also supported by several manuscripts and some versions (BHS). There is no doubt that the Qere represents the older reading,[22] which comes from a period when it was still customary for the mother to name the child, while the masculine form *wyqrʾ* reflects the later, altered patriarchal state of affairs with respect to naming.

[[235]] Furthermore, it appears that the later, masculine reading is closely connected with the tale of the death of the first child. In this nar-

17. See F. Schwally, *ZAW* 12 (1892) 153–55; Cook, "Notes on the Composition of 2 Samuel," 156; Budde, *Die Bücher Samuel*, 254; W. Nowack, *Richter, Ruth u. Bücher Samuelis* (Göttingen, 1902) 194; H. Gressmann, *Die älteste Geschichtsschreibung und Prophetie Israels* (2d ed.; Göttingen, 1921) 156–57; H. P. Smith, *A Critical and Exegetical Commentary on the Books of Samuel* (4th ed.; Edinburgh, 1951) 322; cf. also W. Dietrich, *Prophetie und Geschichte* (Göttingen, 1972) 132; and Würthwein, *Erzählung von der Thronfolge Davids*, 24.

18. These verses also have been reworked by the Deuteronomist (see Dietrich, *Prophetie und Geschichte*, 127–31), but that is irrelevant here.

19. T. Veijola, *Die ewige Dynastie* (Helsinki, 1975) 113.

20. L. Rost seeks to account for the existence of 2 Sam 12:15bff. with the Nathan–David scene: "Only with the incorporation of Nathan does the otherwise only loosely connected tale of the death of the child become an important component of the whole" (*Die Überlieferung von der Thronnachfolge Davids* [Stuttgart, 1926] 97). But what becomes of the "only loosely connected tale" if the account is incorrect?

21. The material is collected in S. Herner, "Athalja," *Vom Alten Testament: Festschrift für K. Marti* (BZAW 41; Berlin, 1925)137–41; cf. also Noth, *Die israelitischen Personennamen*, 56; de Vaux, *Les Institutions*, 1.74; J. J. Stamm, "Hebräische Ersatznamen," *Studies in Honor of Benno Landsberger on His Seventy-Fifth Birthday, April 21, 1965* (AS 16; Chicago, 1965) 414.

22. So also J. J. Stamm, "Der Name des Königs Salomo," *ThZ* 16 (1960) 287, 295.

rative, all attention is concentrated on David, to whom, according to the narrative, it is very important that he should have a second child in place of the one that died. Bathsheba plays no role at all here–she only does what David is not capable of: she gives birth (v. 24). For all the rest, including the name-giving, David alone is responsible. Thus the older, feminine reading *wtqr'* obviously refers to the birth, not of the second, but of the first child, in which Bathsheba's role is circumscribed, certainly, but nonetheless somewhat more active than in the second (compare 11:26–27a with 12:24abα). For David, on the other hand, the birth of the first child cannot have been a particularly joyful event, since the background of the child was somewhat too dark. Consequently, one could expect him to have no particular desire to participate in the name-giving, which according to prevailing usage was in any case the province of the mother.

What, then, did Bathsheba call her son? It was usual in ancient Israel for a child to bear a symbolic name,[23] which could allude to circumstances in the mother's life.[24] The name *Šĕlōmô* [['Solomon']] according to J. J. Stamm belongs to the class of so-called substitute names[25] and describes the result of the activity expressed by the Piel of the verb *šlm* 'replace, make whole'. Thus it means 'his wholeness'[26] or (with G. Gerleman,[27] building on Stamm) perhaps better, 'his replacement'. Stamm and Gerleman see in the name a reminiscence of the deceased child.[28] But was the first child with its dubious pedigree really still so important after the birth of the "second" that Bathsheba (still less David, according to the present text) would want to keep its memory alive?

Everything looks entirely different if we completely disregard the death of the [[236]] first child and simply recognize that Bathsheba gave him the name "Solomon" in memory of her recently deceased husband, Uriah. For in this case Bathsheba had every reason to name her firstborn son 'his replacement', namely the replacement of Uriah, whom she had recently lost in the war in what *she* must have believed was an entirely natural way. Joab could hardly take the principle "the sword devours now one, now the other" (11:25) seriously in Uriah's case (cf. 11:15), but for Bathsheba, on the other hand, it was the only possible explanation of her husband's fate. The gravity of Bathsheba's situation lies in the fact that she as a childless[29] widow was threatened with an extremely uncertain social

23. Cf. J. Barr, "The Symbolism of Names in the Old Testament," *BJRL* 52 (1969) 11–29.

24. So, e.g., Gen 4:1, 29:31–30:24. It is less common for circumstances in the father's life to affect the name-giving (Exod 2:22); cf. de Vaux, *Les Institutions*, 1.75.

25. On which, see Stamm, "Hebräische Ersatznamen," 413–24.

26. Stamm, "Der Name des Königs Salomo," 297.

27. G. Gerleman, "Die Wurzel *šlm*," *ZAW* 85 (1973) 13; cf. idem, "*šlm*," *THAT* 2.932.

28. Stamm, "Der Name des Königs Salomo," 296; Gerleman, "Die Wurzel *šlm*," 13.

29. At least, nothing is said of any previous children of Bathsheba.

situation.[30] At this moment it was especially lucky for her that she was expecting a child, a child of the king, no less. This opened a most unusual opportunity to be saved from the penurious state of a widow. As king's consort and the mother of a son, she was completely justified in giving her son the thanksgiving-name[31] 'his replacement', with Uriah in mind, since that is what Solomon really represented to her. On the other hand, with this name she could also save the honor of her royal spouse. She could imply to the neighbors, who could not know the intimate details, that the child was fathered by her previous husband, Uriah. That is, by a clever choice of name she could achieve what David failed to achieve when he ordered Uriah to Jerusalem.[32] Anyone with a moral objection to this sort of name-giving must first dispense with later judgments (or prejudices) and then also recall that moral scruples were obviously not a terrible burden on Bathsheba's character (cf. 1 Kings 1).

It goes without saying that later umbrage could be taken at a name for the great King Solomon that contained a reminiscence of Bathsheba's murdered husband. An eloquent sign of the unease felt here as well as of the [[237]] consciousness of the original meaning of the name "Solomon" among later readers of the Succession Narrative is the strongly gloss-like continuation of Solomon's naming (12:24bγ–25),[33] where God's love for this child is highlighted and he is renamed with the new, entirely orthodox name *Jedidiah* 'beloved of Yahweh'.

All sorts of questions arise in connection with the current reading. L. Delekat, for example, asks why in fact Yahweh publicly declared Bathsheba's second son his favorite; and Delekat adds: "The narrator does nothing to explain it. The impression given is: Yahweh has shown his displeasure, but then quickly gives in for his chosen one's sake."[34] But it is unfair and also unnecessary to accuse the original author of such meanness, since Solomon's renaming by Nathan is an utterly transparent, secondary[35]

30. On the place of widows, see, for example, de Vaux, *Les Institutions*, 1.69. In Bathsheba's case, levirate marriage probably did not apply, since her deceased husband was a foreigner.

31. The name "Solomon" also was a thanksgiving-name; see Stamm, "Hebräische Ersatznamen," 421.

32. On the other hand, it was not unusual for David to marry a recently widowed woman without an urgent reason (cf. Abigail, 1 Sam 25:39).

33. On the passage, see Würthwein, *Erzählung von der Thronfolge Davids*, 29–30; it is also secondary in the opinion of Langlamet ("Pour ou contre Salomon?"136, 506).

34. L. Delekat, "Tendenz und Theologie der David-Salomo-Erzählung," *Das ferne und nahe Wort: Festschrift für L. Rost* (BZAW 105; Berlin, 1967) 32.

35. The secondary character of the passage also becomes clear in that the name-giver, in accordance with the later, patriarchalized custom, is Nathan (cf. Herner, "Athalja," 139). The Masoretic reading of v. 25a, which thus deserves preference over the many attempts at corrections, can in fact only mean: "and he (Yahweh) sent (an order) by the prophet Nathan,

attempt to provide the king with an untainted new name, an attempt that was actually unable to succeed. The same goal was also served—with much greater sucess—by the preinserted narrative of the sickness and death of the first child, since afterward Solomon could actually be regarded as '*his* replacement'.[36]

III

The foregoing observations and considerations have already raised a number of doubts about the authenticity of the narrative of the death of the first child and the birth of the second (12:15b–24a). The *chronological* difficulty [[238]] with two births during the siege of Rabbah of Ammon adduced by Würthwein[37] has not even been mentioned yet.

According to 2 Sam 11:1, the mobilization of the army took place "at the turn of the year, at the time when kings would go campaigning." This (and parallels: 1 Kgs 20:22, 26; 1 Chr 20:1; 2 Chr 36:10) makes us think that this was a normal campaign, such as ancient Near Eastern rulers undertook more or less regularly at a particular season.[38] It could of course happen that a campaign might last longer than planned for unexpected reasons. But could the Israelites have been besieging Rabbah of Ammon for the nearly two years it would take to bring two pregnancies to term?

If we had only the report of the siege (2 Sam 11:1a, 12:26–31) without the Bathsheba story, no one would imagine so long a duration. Nor does the corresponding presentation by the Chronicler (1 Chr 20:1–3), from which the Bathsheba affair is omitted on moral grounds, give the impression of such a long siege. It must further be taken into account that the Ammonite War was not waged only by David's mercenaries (2 Sam 10:7; 11:1, 11, 24). The entire Israelite levy had marched out with the holy Ark (11:1, 7, 11; 12:28, 31) and submitted to the pledge of sexual abstinence (11:11, 13; cf. Josh 3:5; 1 Sam 21:6).[39] So the question arises whether such

---

and he called his name Jedidiah" (cf., e.g., Stamm, "Der Name des Königs Salomo," 287; *Jerusalemer Bibel* [German], and *Traduction Ecuménique de la Bible*).

36. T. N. D. Mettinger writes in true emulation of the supplementer: "The death of the child implies that the Davidic dynasty does not bear the blame in the matter of Bathsheba. The author of the SN (Succession Narrative) is also anxious to make it clear that Solomon is not to be mistaken for the illegitimate child" (*King and Messiah* [Lund, 1976] 30).

37. Würthwein, *Erzählung von der Thronfolge Davids*, 32.

38. The time designation 'turn of the year' (*tšwbt hšnh*) probably refers to the turn from winter to summer, thus to the spring, which also appears in the Assyrian annals as the normal time for an army to set out; see J. Begrich, *Die Chronologie der Könige von Israel und Juda und die Quellen des Rahmens der Königsbücher* (Tübingen, 1929) 88–89; de Vaux, *Les Institutions*, 1.289–90.

39. Cf. G. von Rad, *Der Heilige Krieg im alten Israel* (5th ed.; Göttingen, 1969) 7, 35–36.

a war of Yahweh, which was a common obligation of every conscriptable man in Israel, could last nearly two years, either on practical or theoretical grounds.[40]

K. Budde had already clearly seen the foregoing chronological difficulties when he said: "It goes without saying that ⟦239⟧ not everything so far narrated, conception and birth of two children, not to mention handing the second over to an educator,[41] took place before the end of the Ammonite War."[42] Budde claims to find the solution to the problem in the fact that the author spun out each of the narrative threads to its end and then returned to events that happened earlier (12:26–31).[43] But it is not easy to ascribe such a forced solution to the highly accomplished narrator of the Succession Narrative. If he had intended a recapitulation in Budde's sense, he would probably have made this apparent to the reader in some way. Instead, the impartial reader naturally thinks that the Bathsheba story is played out to the end during the siege of Rabbah of Ammon.

On the other hand, the chronological problem appears in a somewhat different light if we follow Budde's interpretation,[44] according to which the Ammonite War report (2 Samuel *10; 11:1; 12:26–31) represented an independent source that was only secondarily combined with the Bathsheba story. Even then, the situation is not wholly clear, since two followers of this version, S. A. Cook and L. Rost,[45] are of different opinions regarding Solomon's origin: for Cook he was the first son of Bathsheba; for Rost the second. But one could argue for Rost's viewpoint (Rost does not go into our particular problem, however) and say that the author has brought two entirely different materials into relationship here, and as a result chronological inconsistencies could easily arise. Rost himself admits, however, that the Bathsheba story presupposes the Ammonite War report as *context*. Therefore, even in his view, the two traditions were not simply juxtaposed mechanically.[46]

40. Interpreting the story as a long-lasting siege would be *petitio principii* ⟦'begging the question'⟧ for a theory of war in which Yahweh's decisive intervention was an integral element (cf. von Rad, ibid., 12–13; F. Stolz, *Jahwes und Israels Kriege* [Zürich, 1972] 187–91). By way of qualification, however, I question whether at the time there was any theory of "holy war" at all (cf. G. H. Jones, "'Holy War' or 'Yahweh War'?" *VT* 25 [1975] 642–58).

41. Budde (*Die Bücher Samuel*, 257–58) made Wellhausen's emendation of 2 Sam 12:25 popular: *wyšlm* ⟦'and made whole, completed'⟧ in place of *wyšlḥ* ⟦'and sent'⟧ (J. Wellhausen, *Der Text der Bücher Samuelis* [Göttingen, 1871] 185).

42. Budde, *Die Bücher Samuel*, 258.

43. Ibid.

44. Ibid., 250.

45. Cook, "Notes on the Composition of 2 Samuel," 156–57; Rost, *Überlieferung von der Thronnachfolge Davids*, 74–80, 97–98.

46. Ibid., 92.

If we tentatively accept the correctness of Rost's theory of the independence of the Ammonite War report *in principle*,[47] we must nevertheless make a correction [[240]] to it. 2 Sam 11:1 cannot be part of the campaign report alone, since this verse introduces not only the events of the war but also the sinister happenings in Jerusalem. At a time when kings are supposed to be campaigning in the field, David sends Joab out with the mercenaries and the Israelite conscripts, while he himself remains in the city. In this way, the course of the following story is set, and the alertness of the reader, who now waits with curiosity to see what might happen in a capital city empty of able-bodied men, is awakened. Yet at the same time, this very verse, in a literary sense, is the place at which the Ammonite War and the Bathsheba story overlap in time, which shows that, at least for the author of this verse (which is to say, the author of the Succession Narrative), the simultaneity of the events at the front and in the city was very important.

We could, of course, go a step further and object that, despite the synchronization in the Succession Narrative, from a *historical* point of view there were two different wars, as Rost explicitly observed.[48] This is a very bold hypothesis, however, which will require special proof, for the extant version of the narrative contains no clues to its correctness. Both according to the Ammonite War report (12:26, 27, 29) and the Bathsheba story (11:16–25), the siege of a city is in view, which, according to the introduction (11:1) and the War report (12:27, 29), was called Rabbah.[49] In both reports David does not personally participate in the war; the conduct of the war is in Joab's hands (11:6, 7, 14, 17, 18, 22, 25; 12:26, 27), as the author also states in the introduction (11:1). In both places it is a common endeavor of mercenaries and conscripts (11:7, 11, 24; 12:28, 29, 31), as the introduction assumes as well (11:1). Under these circumstances, the onus of proof is on those who, nevertheless, would find two different wars. Until such proof [[241]] is provided, there remains the chronological discrepancy between the Ammonite War and the Bathsheba story, with its two births, that cannot be explained away.

47. Rost (ibid., 80) argues that the extent of the "source" is 2 Sam 10:6–11:1, 12:26–31 and justifies its independence with stylistic arguments (pp. 75–76) which, given the state of modern literary criticism, will hardly persuade anyone.

48. Ibid., 77: "We do not know whether the war during which the Uriah story transpires was actually the Ammonite War of 12:26ff." The reason is: "In 11:2ff. we never encounter (aside from 12:9) the name of David's opponent, let alone the name of the besieged city" (p. 77). Cook apparently thinks similarly ("Notes on the Composition of 2 Samuel," 157).

49. The partition of the material into into three parts—"War report," "Bathsheba story," and "Introduction"—is simply an attempt to look at it from Rost's point of view.

IV

All the indications that we have so far assembled suggest that "the narrative of the first deceased child of Bathsheba" was actually "a legend that would remove Solomon's stain of having been born of an adulterous relationship."[50] This certainly requires us to provide an explanation for the peculiar character of the legend (2 Sam 12:15b–24a) as well.

According to this legend, David behaves *before* the child's death in the way that one usually behaves *after* a death (vv. 16–17, 21) and gives an explanation for his behavior that sounds remarkably rational(ized) (vv. 20–23). The passage has naturally always stood out and has found any number of interpretations, some of them quite comical. For K. Budde,[51] David's behavior is "proof of healthy human understanding and manly conduct." For A. Schulz,[52] on the contrary, it evidences "will power in surmounting unnecessary sorrow." However, for W. Caspari,[53] the king, "considering the current state of war," did without the customary obsequies. L. Rost[54] argues that, in David's answer to his servants, "the recognition of the uncompromising righteousness of God" is visible. For H. W. Hertzberg,[55]on the other hand, the "overriding recognition" is that "the matter between God and him (David) is henceforth really settled." It is J. Pedersen's explanation[56] that has been most influential. For him, David's behavior reveals an entirely new, liberal attitude toward death and toward the ancient Israelite funeral customs. David showed through his conduct that he did not know the consequences, according to traditional thinking, of impurity caused by death. "He judged behavior only according to its results." E. Würthwein,[57] too, adopted [[242]] Pedersen's interpretation; in contrast to Pedersen, however, he placed greater stress on the role of the author, who provided us with this character sketch of David with *critical* intent. The episode contains implicit criticism of David by the author of the Succession Narrative. But it is not easy to recognize this sort of critical intent in the presentation, as the quite different interpretations cited above show,[58] and Würthwein himself is also not fully persuaded of the

50. Auerbach, *Wüste und Gelobtes Land,* 1.228 n. 1.

51. Budde, *Die Bücher Samuel,* 257.

52. A. Schulz, *Die Bücher Samuel* (Münster, 1920) 2.135.

53. W. Caspari, *Die Samuelbücher* (Leipzig, 1926) 534.

54. Rost, *Überlieferung von der Thronnachfolge Davids,* 98.

55. H. W. Hertzberg, *Die Samuelbücher* (4th ed.; Göttingen, 1968) 259.

56. J. Pedersen, *Israel,* vols. 3–4 (Copenhagen, 1936) 345.

57. Würthwein, *Erzählung von der Thronfolge Davids,* 26.

58. Still another explanation is offered by G. Gerleman, "Schuld und Sühne," in *Beiträge zur Alttestamentlichen Theologie: Festschrift für W. Zimmerli* (Göttingen, 1977) 132–39. He says that the disagreement between David and his courtiers rests on their different points of departure: "David knew that the death of the newborn was an expiation by which Yahweh

correctness of his own interpretation.[59]

The solution of the problem is much simpler in my opinion, as long as we recognize the secondary character of the episode. Special significance then adheres to the statement in 12:18 that the child died on the seventh day. This announcement hardly arose purely by chance, since the period of seven days as the life-span[60] of the child fits better in this context than the other. On the one hand, the normal mourning period lasts seven days (Gen 50:10; 1 Sam 31:13; Jdt 16:24; Sir 22:12); on the other, according to the purity regulations, every woman during menstruation was in a state of uncleanness (*ṭmʾh*) for seven days, during which she could not be touched (Lev 15:19–24, 18:19, 20:18); the same also held for a mother who had borne a son (Lev 12:2), while the mother of a daughter was impure for twice as long (Lev 12:5).

Before we can proceed to draw some conclusions, we must consider one more thing: that, according to a notice in 2 Sam 11:4, Bathsheba had in fact already "purified herself of her impurity (*mṭmʾth*)"[61] when David first had her brought to him. Her bath thus signified the necessary purification after her just-completed period, and at that time she immediately became pregnant. [[243]] Now the later author, who introduced the death of the child on the seventh day, wished to make it capable of being understood in two ways. On the one hand, he wished to suggest to the reader the thought that after seven days, when David came to her (v. 24), Bathsheba again found herself in the same state as the first time and in this case also could immediately become pregnant. On the other hand, the seven-day lifetime of the child gave the narrator the opportunity to demonstrate that David was a pious man who did not hesitate to save the child through intensive prayer and fasting. At the same time, David could carry out the usual funeral rites in advance, which thus came about, not for "unenlightened" reasons but for chronological reasons. For if David had begun the funeral rites only *after* the death of the child, in the opinion of the author the favorable time for Bathsheba to conceive would have passed, something that he could no longer accept.

---

lifted an evil that had come into effect" but that the king wished to disguise from his servants (p. 138). This interpretation, unfortunately, builds on the untenable presupposition that 2 Sam 12:15bff. knows the Nathan–David scene (12:1–15a); the deuteronomistic vv. 13–14 are even made the key to the interpretation (pp. 133–36), but see nn. 17 and 19 above.

59. Würthwein, *Erzählung von der Thronfolge Davids*, 32.

60. Nothing in the style of the presentation keeps us from interpreting the seventh day as the seventh *day of life* of the child.

61. The late placement of the note (its proper place would be in v. 2) as well as its pedantic character suggest that it was conceived as a preparation for the legend in 12:15b–24a by the author of that passage.

Admittedly, several questions remain open here. From a purely biological point of view, it would be most improbable that a woman could become pregnant again seven days after giving birth.[62] Moreover, our narrator says nothing about how Bathsheba completed her mourning period after the death of her child. In any case, she observed the mourning period after the death of her husband (11:27). These problems naturally are no objection to the correctness of our thesis. Rather, they too speak for the legendary character of the narrative and must be reckoned as the concession the narrator had to make for wanting to accommodate two births during the Ammonite War. He could not wait until the following month, since he knew that his interference was already extending the Ammonite campaign to a questionable length anyway. The biological improbability of the matter, on the other hand, was scarcely noticed by the (male) narrator,[63] and Bathsheba's feelings were probably of little concern to him. [[244]] It is enough that David "consoles" her (12:24); after that, David can go to her and cohabit with her.

It was much more important in the eyes of the narrator to make the reader understand *psychologically* how David could go to Bathsheba directly after the death of the child. Here he also shows an especially delicate sensitivity. After he has shown how David carried out the funeral rites in advance and the child died (12:16–19), he describes in detail–in much more detail than would really be necessary–how David rises from the ground, washes and anoints himself, changes his clothes, goes to Yahweh's house to pray, returns home, and eats (v. 20). All that, which astonishes his courtiers (v. 21), is a sign that the king has found consolation and is ready for normal intercourse with other people–as well as for intercourse with his wife, Bathsheba. The measures just described, more or less fully enumerated, commonly indicate preparation for a sexual act as well.[64] Some of them even appear in the emergency measures with which David endeavors to bring Uriah, summoned home from the front, into sexual contact with Bathsheba. He says to him: "Go into your house and wash your feet" (11:8).[65] To the question why he had not gone home,

62. The Priestly legistlation too, which in its content must be older (see M. Noth, *Das dritte Buch Mose* [3d ed.; Göttingen, 1973] 82), takes into consideration a longer-lasting period for the recently delivered, during which she may not participate in the cult (Lev 12:4–5); sexual congress with her, however, is not forbidden by this rule.

63. It is equally unlikely that we can expect him to know that the greatest receptivity for conception in the woman is fourteen, not seven, days after the start of her period. For him, what was most important was to show on both occasions Bathsheba's pregnancy began at the same time, which also sounds entirely believable biologically.

64. Qoh 9:7–9; Ruth 3:3; Ezek 16:9ff.; cf. also Gen 29:22; Judg 14:10; Cant 1:3; 4:10; Esth 2:12, 18.

65. The word *rglym* [['feet']] here perhaps contains a sexual innuendo (cf. Exod 4:25; Isa 6:2; 7:20; Ruth 3:4, 7); so Hertzberg, *Die Samuelbücher*, 254.

Uriah answers, among other things: "Should I go home to eat and drink and sleep with my wife?" (11:11). A second time David tries to achieve his goal by inviting Uriah to eat and drink with him in order to get him drunk (11:13). We thus see that the author, who has David restore himself with all suitable means after the death of the child (12:20), was a sensitive man who knew "how fluid the boundary between physiology and psychology is"[66] and how the difficult task he had set himself could be carried out with tact and finesse.

V

In order to find out something about the intellectual and spiritual background of the narrator, we would be well advised to go briefly into the way in which [[245]] he introduces his narrative. He accounts for the death of the child with an irrational intervention by Yahweh: "And the LORD struck (*wygp*) the child . . . and it became sick" (12:15b). The expression used here, according to which a person is suddenly struck dead (*ngp*, Qal) by Yahweh, has two parallels in the David tradition–both, however, occurring in contexts that are suspected of being additions.

In the Nabal story (1 Samuel 25), the statement "and about ten days later, Yahweh *smote* Nabal; and he died" (v. 38) appears as a factually superfluous theological correction to the declaration in the previous verse: "his heart died within him, and he became as a stone." Nabal was then, in my opinion even according to Hebrew anthropology, already dead enough and needed no further smiting.[67]

The other passage that reports Yahweh smiting is 1 Sam 26:10, in a speech where David forbids Abishai to kill the sleeping Saul, because David expects that "the LORD will *smite* him; or his day shall come to die; or he shall go down into battle and perish." But this too is not an original context, as is very clearly shown by the unnecessary doubling of the introduction to the speech (vv. 9/10), the repetition of an entire clause spoken by David (vv. 9b/11a), and the discrepancy with the following context (vv. 11b/12a).[68]

These observations about vocabulary[69] are another confirmation that the narrative of the death of Bathsheba's firstborn is editorial. Admittedly,

66. R. Smend, "Essen und Trinken: Ein Stück Weltlichkeit des Alten Testaments," in *Beiträge zur Alttestamentlichen Theologie: Festschrift für W. Zimmerli* (Göttingen, 1977) 448.

67. H. W. Wolff, however, manages to diagnose this as a stroke due to cerebral hemorrhage (*Anthropologie des Alten Testaments* [Munich, 1973] 69).

68. The solution of H.-U. Nübel, who also attributes v. 9 to the editor, is a bit too strong (*Davids Aufstieg in der Frühe israelitischer Geschichtsschreibung* [Th.D. diss., Bonn, 1959] 54).

69. The substantive *mgph*, in the sense of a plague decreed by Yahweh, also has exclusively secondary attestation in the David traditions: 2 Sam 24:21, 25 (see my *Ewige Dynastie*, 109).

there are no statements in the Succession Narrative itself that correspond literally with the introduction to this narrative. But there are a few passages that come very close in theological content. Especially worth mentioning here are the three notices comprising a theology of history, on the basis of which [[246]] G. von Rad[70] supposed that he could grasp the real intention of the Succession Narrative, but which later (in part already earlier) were shown to be secondary insertions.

The first of these notices, the deuteronomistic commentary at the end of the old Bathsheba story (11:27b),[71] with its moral-theological character is perhaps still somewhat distant from the statement in 12:15b, which stresses the irrational side of the fateful work of Yahweh. But corresponding to it quite closely is the second of the theologically interpretive passages highlighted by von Rad, which stands at the end of our episode, 2 Sam 12:24bγ ("and the LORD loved him").[72] This passage, according to von Rad,[73] testifies "to the entirely irrational love of God for this person." It goes especially well with the beginning of the same narrative ("and the LORD struck the child . . ."). The third notice comprising a theology of history, 2 Sam 17:14b (for von Rad the most important),[74] shows in the context of the Absalom revolt how Yahweh's interference negates wise human counsel: "for the LORD had ordained to defeat the good counsel of Ahithophel so that the LORD might bring evil upon Absalom." No one will deny that this statement's content is in line with 2 Sam 12:15b ("and the LORD struck the child . . .").

Now Würthwein[75] has proved (as already supported by F. Langlamet)[76] that this third theologically interpretive passage is not an isolated intrusion but a component of an extensive editorial layer that wishes to portray Ahithophel in an unfavorable light as adviser.[77] Würthwein sums up this systematic editorial work by saying that "the hand of a man who

70. G. von Rad, "Der Anfang der Geschichtsschreibung im alten Israel" (1944); *Gesammelte Studien zum Alten Testament* (Munich, 1958) 181–86.

71. Dietrich, *Prophetie und Geschichte*, 132; see, in agreement: Würthwein, *Erzählung von der Thronfolge Davids*, 24; and Langlamet, "Pour ou contre Salomon?" 136; in disagreement: H. Seebass, "Nathan und David in II Sam. 12," *ZAW* 86 (1974) 210 n. 18; and Mettinger, *King and Messiah*, 30.

72. On the secondary character of the passage, see Cook, "Notes on the Composition of 2 Samuel," 157 n. 31; Budde, *Die Bücher Samuel*, 257; Würthwein, *Erzählung von der Thronfolge Davids*, 29–30; cf. also Wallis, *TWAT* 1.122.

73. G. von Rad, *Gesammelte Studien*, 183.

74. Ibid., 183–84.

75. Würthwein, *Erzählung von der Thronfolge Davids*, 33–42.

76. Langlamet, "Pour ou contre Salomon?" 350–56.

77. Würthwein (*Erzählung von der Thronfolge Davids*, 34–42) assigns 2 Sam 15:16b, 31; 16:21–23; 17:5–14, 15b, 23; 20:3 to this layer. Mettinger's conclusion (*King and Messiah*, 29), that 2 Sam 17:5–14 is of deuteronomistic origin, is rash.

proceeds very consistently and capably is at work."[78] This can also be said without exaggeration of whoever conceived the narrative of the death of Bathsheba's [[247]] firstborn. Würthwein also claims that the editing he discovered "is thoroughly in favor of the dynasty" and so "must be attributed to the court." It could hardly be otherwise with a narrator who fabricates a blameless origin for the most powerful member of the Davidic dynasty. Moreover, Würthwein emphasizes the "wisdom influence," which in the editing of the Ahithophel scenes "is clearly perceptible."[79] This influence also explains the "enlightened" aspects of David's behavior after the death of the first child (12:20–23).[80]

What emerges unambiguously from all of these different connections is that the legend of the death of the first child exhibits a considerable intellectual relationship with another, broader editorial layer within the Succession Narrative. The idea of deriving these two layers from one and the same hand is very attractive.[81] Before this can be decided definitively, however, the Succession Narrative must be worked through in terms of redaction history more thoroughly than it has been so far.[82]

78. Würthwein, *Erzählung von der Thronfolge Davids,* 42.

79. Ibid. Langlamet also postulated a "theological-wisdom" editing, which is both pro-David and pro-Solomon ("Pour ou contre Salomon?" 117, 128, 135–36, et al.). Earlier, especially R. N. Whybray emphasized the combination of the Succession Narrative with wisdom literature (*The Succession Narrative* [London, 1968] 56–95). However, because of insufficient literary-critical differentiation, Whybray without realizing it appears to have regarded the editorial layer as the original version of the Succession Narrative.

80. Compare especially 12:23 with the simile, typical of wisdom literature, in 2 Sam 14:14a (Whybray, ibid., 81) in the episode of the wise woman of Tekoa (2 Sam 14:2–22), which Würthwein considers as a whole to be a "wisdom intrusion" (*Erzählung von der Thronfolge Davids,* 46; cf. also Langlamet, "Pour ou contre Salomon?" 136).

81. In this connection it must be mentioned that Bathsheba was Ahithophel's granddaughter (compare 2 Sam 11:3 and 23:34). It is certainly possible that Bathsheba's marriage into the royal family caused friction with her old clan, after the circumstances of Uriah's death became known to the relatives. As a result, Ahithophel was attempting, through his anti-Davidic activity during Absalom's uprising, to avenge the assassination of Uriah who, like his own son, belonged to "the thirty" (2 Sam 23:39). As retaliation, Solomon's literary court propaganda would—probably only later—distance the unpleasant memory of Bathsheba's past and at the same time kill off the most dangerous member of her clan, the adviser Ahithophel, both physically and as to his way of thought. In these circles, death appears to have represented the appropriate solution to the problem of inconvenient personalities (2 Sam 12:18, 17:23).

82. A promising start appears in Langlamet, "Pour ou contre Salomon?" 349–79, 481–528. Langlamet himself emphatically stresses the preliminary character of the results he achieved, ending his brilliant work with the sentence: "But this is nothing but a working hypothesis that only a detailed study of the 'pro-Davidic' redaction in Samuel could confirm or refute" (p. 528).

VI

⟦248⟧ I come now to my conclusions. (1) For the question with which we began, the observations and considerations presented above indicate that Solomon's position as Bathsheba's firstborn no longer belongs in the realm of pure speculation. Instead, it appears to me to be historically most probable.

One could admittedly take the criticism a step further and say that the old story of Solomon's birth was recorded with such malicious intent that we cannot trust it historically. In reality, on that view we could know absolutely no details of Solomon's birth. There is, however, one firmly anchored historical statement that speaks against this radical scepticism: the name of King Solomon. If the meaning of the name is "his replacement" and if the historical basis is withdrawn from the predecessor of Solomon, then the name can only make sense as an allusion to Bathsheba's fallen husband, Uriah the Hittite.

At most it can be asked whether Solomon was only apparently "his replacement" or was so in reality. A positive answer to this question would presume that the story of David's adultery was a historically worthless anecdote[83] that arose from folk tradition, and it would mean that Bathsheba had in reality placed Uriah's son on the throne of the united monarchy. This possibility cannot be dismissed entirely out of hand, but neither can it be proved.

(2) In regard to the manner of representation and intention of the old Succession Narrative, the removal of the legendary insertion brings with it more unity of narrative and sharpness of content.[84] The Bathsheba affair with all of its horrors is described with well-known subtlety. In the end, the Succession Narrator states realistically: "But after the mourning period was over, David sent and took her into his house. So she became his wife and bore him a son and gave him the name Solomon" (11:27a, 12:24bβ). He does not include a single word of commentary–either theo-

83. On form-critical grounds, Gressmann called the Bathsheba story a "legend" but suggested that "it would be difficult to accuse David of something so defamatory without any basis" (*Die älteste Geschichtsschreibung und Prophetie Israels*, 156). But is his argument still valid, in view of modern insight? Cf. Würthwein, *Erzählung von der Thronfolge Davids*, 32.

84. Needless to say, the result achieved does not in the least support the goal assumed by Rost (*Überlieferung von der Thronnachfolge Davids*, 128) for the Succession Narrative that it was written *in majorem gloriam Salomonis* ⟦'for the greater glory of Solomon'⟧ (so still Mettinger, *King and Messiah*, 31). But J. Blenkinsopp's "pattern," for example, also suffers serious damage in that the adultery and its punishment (the death of the child) appear in different literary layers ("Theme and Motif in the Succession History [2 Sam. xi 2ff.] and the Yahwist Corpus," *Volume du Congrès International pour l'étude de l'Ancien Testament: Genève, 1965* [VTSup 15; Leiden, 1966] 47–48).

logical or moral—on the outrageous incident but passes on to the last act of the Ammonite War (2 Sam 12:26–31) in complete silence, which is more eloquent than a thousand words.

The Succession Narrator then says nothing about Solomon for a considerable time. He returns to that stage only in 1 Kings 1,[85] with Solomon's ambitious mother and the scheming prophet Nathan organizing a counterrevolution against Solomon's older brother Adonijah and his supporters.[86] With a masterly trick, Nathan and Bathsheba dupe the age-enfeebled David (a case of the "Pope's being deceived by the Curia")[87] by persuading him to fulfill a vow he is said to have made, thus securing the the throne for Bathsheba's son (1 Kgs 1:*11–49). On these events, too, the narrator makes no comment but continues calmly to the next phase, the portrayal of the purges that put an end to Solomon's political opponents (1 Kgs 1:*50–53; 2:*13ff.). One after another the opponents are executed, even violating the asylum of the sanctuary (2:28–31a, 34),[88] [[250]] but again the Succession Narrator declines explicit comment, merely stating laconically after the last execution, "so the kingdom was established in the hand of Solomon" (1 Kgs 2:46b). He has left it to us to draw our own conclusions about the theological and moral value of the events that are described.

85. For a detailed interpretation of 1 Kings 1–2, see my *Die ewige Dynastie*, 16–29; Langlamet agrees in the main, "Pour ou contre Salomon?" 323–79, 481–528 (with bibliography); and Würthwein, *Das Erste Buch der Könige*, 2–28.

86. Langlamet too emphasizes the connection between the presentation of 2 Samuel *10–12 and 1 Kings *1–2 ("Pour ou contre Salomon?" 522, 525). He suggests, however, that the Succession Narrator has different attitudes toward David and Solomon: "Despite his bitterness, he does not call David's authority into question. He opposes neither David nor the Davidic monarchy. He is not unaware of the faults and weaknesses of the deceased king: he himself seems to have evoked them in editing the first chapters of his 'Succession History,' where he details, in his own way, the circumstances of Solomon's birth" (p. 525). Dietrich also writes along the same lines: "The narrator in my opinion makes David no worse than in this case he really was" ("David in Überlieferung und Geschichte," 53). Can these judgments be maintained legitimately? Solomon's birth as a result of adultery was certainly not *his* sin, and who was in a position to know *how* David in this case *really* was? Cf. Würthwein, *Erzählung von der Thronfolge Davids*, 22.

87. Langlamet, "Pour ou contre Salomon?" 525.

88. In Adonijah's case Solomon also violates the law of asylum (1 Kgs 1:50, 51abα, 53 and vv. 51bα [*lʾmr* [['to say']]], 51bβγ, and 52 are secondary; see Langlamet, "Pour ou contre Salomon?" 500–502), although Adonijah is only executed later (2:25).

1 Kings 8:46–53 and the Deuteronomic Hope

J. G. McConville

The essay is concerned with how to evaluate differing points of view within the DH. After reviewing various approaches to the literature (all represented in the present volume), and taking issue with their accounts of the topic, it takes a cue from Wolff's identification of the key passages on hope for the future (also in the present volume, pp. 62–78). Like Wolff, and in contrast to Noth (pp. 20–30), it finds hope for a future for the people of Judah beyond the exile. There is agreement with Wolff too that the hope in Kings is somewhat muted. Wolff, however, did not distinguish strongly between the orientations of 1 Kgs 8:46–53 and Deut 30:1–10, attributing both to his second Deuteronomist. The essay tries to show that the former consciously articulates a more modest kind of hope from that of both Deut 30:1–10 and Jeremiah. It thus occupies a middle position between the positions of Noth and Wolff. The argument rests largely on comparative studies of vocabulary and style, one result of which is to urge caution against too readily labeling phraseology as "deuteronomistic." Individuality in such use may also have implications for authorship, and there is a suggestion that the books of the DH may have been separately edited.

⟦67⟧ The present article is intended as a contribution to the question what kind of hope is held out to Judah by the Deuteronomistic History (DH). There is a large measure of agreement on the identification of the most important texts for such a discussion. Prominent among them are Deut 4:25–31, 30:1–10, and the part of Solomon's prayer found in 1 Kgs 8:46–53. The agreement generally extends, furthermore, to the belief that

Reprinted with permission from *Vetus Testamentum* 42 (1992) 67–79.

these are in some way related to the main deuteronomistic programme of the exilic period.[1]

There is much less agreement, however, on the precise relationship of each of the texts to each other and to that programme. The diversity of opinion on this is related both to the complexity of the wider question of the nature of hope in the deuteronomic literature and to the fact that the texts in question manifest certain important differences from each other. Most notably, 1 Kgs 8:46–53 differs from Deut 30:1–10 at the crucial point of a hope of return to the historic promised land, which it refrains from offering (contrast Deut 30:3). In order to provide a context for the discussion of the texts in question, I shall consider briefly the main prevailing approaches to the question of hope in the deuteronomic literature.

Deuteronomic Hope in Contemporary Debate

Contemporary debate on deuteronomic hope stems from the thesis of M. Noth that Deuteronomy–Kings (DH) was the work of [[68]] a single author who lived in the exilic period.[2] Noth's view, however, that the finished work intended only to explain the downfall of the kingdoms of Israel and Judah was generally abandoned in favour of new attempts to account for those parts of the corpus which appeared to contain elements of hope for the future. Most influential in recent discussion have been the two contrasting approaches of F. M. Cross on the one hand, and R. Smend and his disciples on the other.

Cross, followed by R. D. Nelson, postulated a first, Josianic edition of the DH, which expressed hope for the future of Judah, focussed on the reforming king, whose righteousness engendered hope that the dynastic promise to David (2 Sam 7:8–16) was now being fulfilled in a new and exciting way. This Dtr^1, however, was soon confounded by events, and was revised by an exilic author rather in the mould of Noth's Dtr, whose intention was to explain the fall of the kingdom.[3] Cross's answer, therefore, to the elusive relationship between hope and judgement in the DH, is firmly in terms of separate redactions, which, though beginning from a

1. See, for example, E. W. Nicholson, *Preaching to the Exiles* (Oxford, 1970) 76–77, 118–19; H W. Wolff, "Das Kerygma des deuteronomistischen Geschichtswerks," *ZAW* 73 (1961) 171–86.

2. *Überlieferungsgeschichtliche Studien* 1 (2nd edn., Tübingen, 1957) 1–110. The first edition appeared as *Schriften der Königsberger Gelehrten Gesellschaft: Geisteswissenschaftliche Klasse* 18 (Halle, 1943) 43–266.

3. F. M. Cross, *Canaanite Myth and Hebrew Epic* (Cambridge, Mass., 1973) 274–89 [[pp. 79–94 in this volume]]; R. D. Nelson, *The Double Redaction of the Deuteronomistic History* (Sheffield, 1981). Wolff (n. 1) had also postulated a second Deuteronomist.

fundamentally similar ideology, took different views on the matter in question because of their different standpoints.

A distinct development from Noth's idea of a single Deuteronomist was that initiated by R. Smend,[4] and taken further by W. Dietrich and T. Veijola among others. Smend identified two distinct redactional layers in the DH, both exilic, and differing in the manner of their expression of hope for the future. DtrG [[later called DtrH]], the basic history, is optimistic and confident, characterized by a belief that the land is given, the conquest an established fact; DtrN, on the other hand, is a legalistic (*nomistisch*) expansion, in which land is held only in consequence of scrupulous adherence to law.

Disciples, notably Dietrich, uncovered an intermediate, "prophetic" layer (DtrP), characterized by unalleviated threats of judgement. These threats were directed mainly against northern [[69]] kings, whose wickedness is thus made to explain the ultimate fall of the kingdom of Israel. The blaming of Manasseh for the fall of Judah, however (2 Kgs 21:10–16), is also attributable to DtrP.[5] The pattern of three deuteronomistic redactional layers was also adopted by T. Veijola, who explained them primarily in relation to their understanding of the future of the Davidic dynasty (or lack of it),[6] and, with variations, by H. Spieckermann and E. Würthwein.[7]

The approach of Smend, Dietrich and others to the problem, therefore, differs from that of Cross in locating the whole redactional process in the exilic period. It has in common with it, however, the attempt to account for the presence of hope along with passages which are not overtly hopeful in terms of different redactions.

In my view, neither of these approaches is satisfactory. I have argued elsewhere[8] that Cross's idea of the transformation of an, *ex hypothesi* [['in terms of the hypothesis']], crudely triumphalist work into a wholly pessimistic one, by a few alterations and the addition of an appendix, is improbable, and fails to understand the ironies and ambiguities of the work.

The view of Dietrich and others is also vulnerable to important objections. No less than that of Cross, it depends on improbable polarizations,

4. "Das Gesetz und die Völker: Ein Beitrag zur deuteronomistischen Redaktionsgeschichte," in H. W. Wolff (ed.), *Probleme biblischer Theologie: G. von Rad zum 70* (Munich, 1971) 494–509 [[translated in this volume, pp. 62–78]].

5. W. Dietrich, *Prophetie und Geschichte: Eine redaktionsgeschichtliche Untersuchung zum deuteronomistischen Geschichtswerk* (Göttingen, 1972) 39. In his analysis, DtrP texts relating to the northern kingdom are 1 Kgs 14:7–11, 16:1–4, 21:20bβ–24 and 2 Kgs 9:7–10a, 17:21–23.

6. *Die Ewige Dynastie* (Helsinki, 1975).

7. H. Spieckermann, *Juda unter Assur in der Sargonidenzeit* (Göttingen, 1982); E. Würthwein, *I Könige, II Könige* (Göttingen, 1977, 1984); cf. idem, "Die josianische Reform und das Deuteronomium," *ZTK* 73 (1976) 395–423.

8. "Narrative and Meaning in the Books of Kings," *Biblica* 70 (1989) 31–49.

in an over-schematic system which, in the nature of the case, lacks external controls.[9] It has, furthermore, serious difficulty in accounting for the highly favourable portrait of Josiah. In Veijola's work, for example, both DtrG [[DtrH]] and DtrN (but not DtrP) [[70]] are in principle favourable to the Davidic monarchy (pp. 127–38, 141–42). Yet even an enthusiastic dynast, especially a "nomistic" one, can hardly explain the failure of the righteous king *par excellence* to produce better results than those which followed upon the life and work of Josiah.

In my view the interrelationships among the parts of the deuteronomic literature have been wrongly understood by the disciples of both Cross and Smend. The idea of the deuteronomistic literature as a series of redactions within a tradition that is, as regards both thought and language, essentially homogeneous, has distracted them from certain important characteristics of it. The point is exemplified by the failure of any of the works mentioned to give a satisfactory account of the relationship between the texts indicated above, which, as I have said, are among the most important in a discussion of deuteronomic hope.

Among the scholars I have mentioned, explanations of the difference between 1 Kgs 8:46–53 and Deut 30:1–10 on the point of a return to the land are various. Noth, for whom 1 Kgs 8:46–53 was the surest guide to the view of the DH on the future, did not even treat Deut 30:1–10, saying merely: "Dtr clearly knew nothing about the additions to the deuteronomic law which postulate a new future."[10] Wolff attributed Deut 30:1–10 (with Deut 4:25–31) to his second Deuteronomist ([n. 1] p. 182). Cross likewise attributed the passages in Deuteronomy to Dtr^2, along with 1 Kgs 8:46–53.[11] Nelson, however, saw the difficulty of attributing all three passages to the same hand (which Wolff had also felt), and thus ascribed Deut 4:29–31(40), 30:1–10, not to his Dtr^2, but to a later contributor, whom he identified with Wolff's "second hand" ([n. 3] p. 94). E. W. Nicholson, in

9. Cf. N. Lohfink's critique of Spieckermann's treatment of 2 Kings 22–23 in Lohfink (ed.), *Das Deuteronomium: Entstehung, Gestalt und Botschaft* (Leuven, 1985) 42–47; for example: "Meine erste Frage an Spieckermann lautet, ob er mit den drei Smendschen Deuteronomisten dem Befund vor allem in der zweiten Hälfte von Kapitel 23 wirklich gerecht wird oder nicht doch ein vorgegebenes System in den Text einträgt" [['My first question to Spieckermann concerns whether he has really done justice to the material—especially in the second half of chap. 23—with Smend's three Deuteronomists, or whether he has in fact read a preconceived system into the text']]. He goes on to express his doubts whether a serious attempt to come to terms with the failure of Josiah's Reform and the downfall of Judah should be made neither by DtrG nor by its reviser DtrP, both allegedly exilic, but only by the still later DtrN (p. 44).

10. Noth, cited in E, tr., *The Deuteronomistic History* (Sheffield, 1981) 98 = p. 109 of the German.

11. (N. 3), p. 278. Cf. A. D. H. Mayes, *Deuteronomy* (London, 1979) 367–68.

contrast, regarded Deut 30:1–10 as part of an addition to the deuteronomic law which lay before the Deuteronomist.[12]

The advocates of Smend's view arrive at no greater clarity. Dietrich does not even mention either 1 Kgs 8:46–53 or Deut 30:1–10, Veijola has no systematic treatment of any of the passages in question, and alludes to verses in 1 Kgs 8:46–53 only as evidence ⟦71⟧ for deuteronomistic terminology.[13] C. Levin, furthermore, alluding to 1 Kgs 8:46–53 and Deut 30:1–10 in the context of a discussion of deuteronomistic style, lumps them together vaguely as belonging to the "spätesten Schichten der deuteronomistischen Literatur" ⟦'the latest layers of the deuteronomistic literature'⟧.[14]

The scholars reviewed, especially those in the tradition of Smend, have attempted to explain the differences within the deuteronomic literature regarding hope for the future in terms of redactions which have different standpoints. These redactions, however, share a basic style of expression, so that phraseology and vocabulary are a sure guide to deuteronomic/deuteronomistic provenance.[15] This approach is in contrast to the idea that the individual books that make up the DH (including Deuteronomy) may have their own individuality, that they should be examined in the first instance to see whether they have an individual tendency and theme, and indeed that, while having stylistic similarities, they may actually use language in distinctive ways. I have argued elsewhere that the books of Kings should be read in precisely this way.[16] My present purpose is to make a further contribution to that argument by showing in detail how 1 Kgs 8:46–53 relates to Deut 30:1–10.

1 Kings 8:46–53 and Deuteronomy 30:1–10

My thesis in the remainder of the article is that 1 Kgs 8:46–53 stands consciously over against Deut 30:1–10. Furthermore the passage is best understood, I believe, in terms of the wider interests of the books of Kings, rather than abstracted from its context as one of a group of broadly similar "deuteronomistic" texts about the future. Indeed, I think that 1 Kgs

12. *Deuteronomy and Tradition* (Oxford, 1967) 36.

13. *Das Königtum in der Beurteilung der deuteronomistischen Historiographie* (Helsinki, 1977) 32, 76.

14. *Die Verheissung des neuen Bundes* (Göttingen, 1985) 100 n. 106.

15. So Veijola (n. 13) 13; cf. M. Weinfeld, *Deuteronomy and the Deuteronomic School* (Oxford, 1972) vii; W. Thiel, *Die deuteronomistische Redaktion von Jer. 1–25* (Neukirchen, 1973) 36.

16. See n. 8. I have argued similarly for Jeremiah, in a forthcoming study: *Judgment and Promise: An Interpretation of the Book of Jeremiah* (Leicester: IVP/Winona Lake, Ind.: Eisenbrauns, 1993).

8:46–53 deliberately distances itself from Deut 30:1–10, and that this is comprehensible in terms of the theology of Kings.

It is now time to show how this distancing–which also implies a degree of agreement–is achieved. The method of proceeding will [[72]] be to observe close similarities and differences of both thought and expression between the passages. However, I shall argue that 1 Kgs 8:46–53 knows not only the Deuteronomy passage, but also parts at least of its wider context, namely Deut 29:17–27, weaving together motifs from both. The effect is both to adopt the thought of the Deuteronomy passages (basically a message of judgement followed by pardon), and to adapt it, by means of small but significant variations. We begin by comparing and contrasting 1 Kgs 8:46–53 with Deut 29:17–27, first of all in tabular form.

Echoes of Deuteronomy 29:17–27 in 1 Kings 8:46–53

Deut 29:17–27 (18–28)	*1 Kgs 8:46–53*
1. Beware lest there be among you a man (*ʾîš*) or woman or family or tribe whose heart turns away this day from the LORD our God . . . (v. 17[18]).	If they sin against thee–for there is no man (*ʾādām*) who does not sin– . . . (v. 46).
2. . . . he blesses himself in his heart (*bilᵉbābô*) . . . though I walk in the stubbornness of my heart (*libbî*, v. 18[19]).	. . . if they lay it to heart . . . (*ʾel-libbām*), v. 47).
3. . . . the LORD would not pardon him (*lōʾ . . . yhwh sᵉlōaḥ*, v. 19[20]).	. . . and forgive thy people (*wᵉsālaḥtā*, v. 50).
4. And the LORD would single him out (*wᵉhibdîlô*) from all the tribes of Israel for calamity (v. 20[21]); cf. v. 15(16): You know how we dwelt in the land of *Egypt* and how we came through the midst of the *nations* through which you passed.	For thou didst separate them (*hibdaltām*) from among all the *peoples* of the earth, when thou didst bring our fathers out of *Egypt* (v. 53).
5. . . . he brought them out of the land of Egypt . . . and cast them into another land, as at this day (vv. 24, 27[25, 28]).	. . . for they are thy people and thy heritage which thou didst bring out of Egypt, out of the iron furnace (v. 51).

Cf. also the uses of the verb *šāmaʿ* [['hear']] in Deut 29:18[19], 1 Kgs 8:49; and of *šēm* [['name']] and *šāmayim* [['heaven']] in Deut 29:19[20], 1 Kgs 8:48–49.

This set of parallel ideas by no means exhausts the close relationship between the two pericopes. In general, of course, they belong within a similar framework, concerning as they do the fate of the people of Yahweh among, and in the eyes of, the nations, as a result of breach of covenant and expulsion from the land. This observation about basic similarities has to be qualified by noticing that the Kings passage is informed by the dynastic idea and a theology of the Temple, absent in Deuteronomy. My arrangement of pairs of [[73]] ideas, however, shows that there is a shift in thought between the two, which both goes beyond these differences and helps accentuate them.

Only the first pair of ideas is in a relationship of direct correspondence. Deut 29:17–27 pictures the nation falling into sin initially through the sin of an individual, or individual family (*mišpāḥâ*) or tribe (*šēbeṭ*). The idea is familiar in Deuteronomy (cf. chap. 13), and is developed in the present passage explicitly in v. 18b(19b), and then by what looks like a non sequitur between vv. 20 and 21(21 and 22). Verse 20(21) envisages the individual being singled out from the tribes for punishment according to the curses of the covenant, while v. 21(22), with the following verses, returns to the idea of the whole nation being led into sin and consequent punishment. The juxtaposition, perhaps with some irony, assumes Israel's failure to "purge the evil from the midst of you" (13:5). A similar train of thought is initiated by the opening words of 1 Kgs 8:46. The correlation between nation and individual is present in the juxtaposition of the plural and the singular: "If they sin . . . for there is no man who does not sin. . . ." The parenthesis, furthermore, is ominous, virtually turning what is formally a conditional sentence into a certainty. The Kings passage has its own irony. The most prominent individual-corporate relationship in the books of Kings is between king and people. The words "there is no man who does not sin," in the mouth of Solomon, are pregnant, foreshadowing their egregious fulfilment in himself, and hinting at the momentous consequences for the nation of the sin of the king in particular.

In the remaining pairs of ideas, a negative connotation in Deuteronomy 29 is turned into a positive one in 1 Kings 8. Where the sinful man of the former passage thinks only stubborn and complacent thoughts "in his heart," Solomon envisages the people "laying their sin to heart" in the sense of repenting. Where Deuteronomy 29 declares Yahweh unwilling to forgive the sinful man, Solomon appeals to him to do just that for the people.

The "separation" idea undergoes a more dramatic shift. In Deuteronomy it refers to a separating of the sinful man from the people for judgement; in Kings, with judgement on the whole people an accepted fact, the old idea of election is now expressed as "separation" from the peoples of the earth and becomes a ground of appeal to Yahweh for mercy.

Finally, the manner of allusion to the exodus from Egypt is [[74]] handled differently in each. In Deut 29:17–27 it functions first (vv. 15–16[16–17]) as a warning against idolatry, and ultimately (vv. 24, 27[25, 28]) in bitter irony to pronounce the sentence of a return to the desolation of the time before deliverance. In 1 Kings 8, in contrast, it is joined with the "separation" idea, and belongs to the appeal for mercy on the grounds of Israel's election.

With these comparisons I have tabulated the most obvious and important interchange of ideas between the passages. There are, however, further verbal echoes which form a secondary order of allusion, but which may strengthen the thesis about the conscious interplay of ideas, and may help point up its nature. The most striking of these echoes concern the nouns *šēm* [['name']] and *šāmayim* [['heavens']], which occur in close proximity in each passage, furnishing in each some of the assonance which characterizes both (Deut 29:19[20]; 1 Kgs 8:48–49). The Kings passage also draws in the verb *šāmaʿ* [['hear']] to its immediate play on these words featuring the letters *šin* and *mēm*, and the same verb occurs in Deuteronomy 29, albeit in somewhat less proximity to *šēm* and *šāmayim*. The relationship between the usage of this verb in the two passages, moreover, fits into the sort of pattern which we have already observed. The first (Deut 29:18[19]) is a hearing by the sinful individual of the words of the law, which produces the wrong response; the second, 1 Kgs 8:49, is an appeal for Yahweh to hear, in the hope that the hearing will lead to the positive response of forgiveness.

Šēm and *šāmayim* also function differently in each place. In the first the *name* of the sinful individual is blotted out from under *heaven*; in the second, prayer is made towards the house "which I (Solomon) have built for thy (Yahweh's) *name*," and answered from *heaven*. (The usage of *šāmaʿ* is drawn into this context, the *disobedience* being first–i.e., in Deut 29:18[19]–a ground for the blotting out from under heaven, and the *hearing*, conversely–i.e., on Yahweh's part in 1 Kgs 8:49–the consequence of the establishment of Yahweh's name in Jerusalem.)

These shifts in 1 Kings 8 vis-à-vis Deuteronomy 29 are consistent with the line of thought being developed in 1 Kings 8. The effect of the comparison of this cluster of assonant vocabulary in the two passages is to highlight a transformation from a train of thought which focusses on disobedience and destruction into one which focusses on forgiveness and restored relationship, based on ancient promise. To put these observations in the context of 1 Kings 8, they [[75]] fit well with the argument there that Yahweh, though he has put his name at Jerusalem, nevertheless dwells in heaven, and that therefore he can both hear prayer and act beyond the exile, and the end of the institutions of monarchy and Temple.

We proceed now to notice the echoes of Deut 30:1–10 and 1 Kgs 8:46–53. Here, I think, there are even more significant parallels between the two passages, for Deut 30:1–10 is like 1 Kgs 8:46–53 in that it expresses hope for the future of Israel beyond the exile. There are, however, important differences between the two, the chief of which lies in the expectation in the former passage of a return to the historic land. A comparison of the two passages, however, like that of 1 Kgs 8:46–53 with Deut 29:17–27, shows more differences. Once again, we begin by tabulating the most important of them.

Echoes of Deuteronomy 30:1–10 in 1 Kings 8:46–53

		Deut 30:1–10	*1 Kgs 8:46–53*
Usages of *šûb* [['return']]:	i.	Repent (vv. 1–2); note *šûb* hiphil and *ʾel-lēbāb* [['to heart']]; *šûb*: cf.	Of repentance only (vv. 47–48: *šûb* hiphil and *ʾel-lēb*; *šûb*).
		bᵉkol-lᵉbābᵉkā [['with all your heart']] . . . *napšᵉkā* [['your soul']] (v. 2).	Same phrase, v. 48.
	ii.	Restoration to land (v. 3)	
Usage of *šābâ* [['take captive']]:		Once, in phrase *šûb šᵉbût* [['restore']], of return to land, v. 3.	Frequently, of captors (*šōbêhem*) and of taking captive (vv. 46–48, 50).
Use of *rḥm* [['show compassion']]:		Yahweh exercises compassion (v. 3).	Yahweh grants that *the enemies* show it (v. 50).
Enemies:		Are cursed (v. 7).	Appear in neutral light.

The relationship between the two passages consists not only in the fact that they contain different expressions of hope for the exiled community, but also in the fact that in style, and otherwise in content, they are remarkably similar. The stylistic affinities consist to a large extent in plays on the verbs *šûb* and *šābâ* (to return, to carry into exile). These, however, are not used in quite the same way in the two passages. In Deut 30:1–10 the wordplay focusses on *šûb*, qal and hiphil, and connotes in turn Israel's *repentance* (vv. 1, 2) and Yahweh's *restoration* of their fortunes, in the sense of returning the people to their land. The only occurrence in these verses of a form related to *šābâ* is the noun *šᵉbût*, in the phrase: [[76]]

> *wᵉšāb yhwh ʾᵉlōhekā ʾet-šᵉbûtᵉkā*
> [['then the LORD will restore your fortunes']] (v. 3)

The situation in 1 Kgs 8:46–53 is different. There is still the basic use of *šûb* meaning 'repent', together with phrases incorporating it which are similar to some which were found in Deut 30:1–10: viz., *w^e^hēšîbû ʾel-libbam* [['take it to heart']], 1 Kgs 8:47; cf. Deut 30:1; *napšām . . . l^e^bābām* [['their soul . . . their heart']], 1 Kgs 8:48; cf. *napš^e^kā . . . l^e^bāb^e^kā* [['your soul . . . your heart']], Deut 30:2. However, there is no corresponding use of *šûb* to denote Yahweh's restoration of Israel's fortunes. Instead, the verb *šābâ* is more prominent, with the frequent use of *šōbêhem* 'their captors' and further occurrences in the phrases *šābûm šōbêhem* [['their captors take them captive']] (v. 46) and *nišbû sām* [['where they have been taken captive']] (v. 47). These last show that the verbal dexterity which centred on *šûb* [['repent']] in Deut 30:1–10 focusses here on *šābâ* [['take captive']] instead.

The relationship between the two passages appears, already from the above linguistic observations, to reflect a self-conscious reading of the one by the other. There is an identification yet a distancing. The point is confirmed by a closer look at what the passages are saying. Most notably, the position of the adversaries of Israel is different. In Deut 30:1–10 they are "enemies," upon whom the curses that have fallen on Israel will come in turn (v. 7). In 1 Kgs 8:46–53, though they are "enemies" here too (vv. 46, 48) they are also described several times merely as "captors," a word which carries less value-judgement. Moreover, they are not envisaged as falling victim to the curses of the covenant. Rather, the improved fortunes of Israel are seen as coming to pass under their auspices (v. 50). This is indeed the most significant shift between the passages. In Deut 30:3 Yahweh himself 'has compassion' on Israel (*w^e^riḥ^a^mekā*); in 1 Kgs 8:50, in contrast, Solomon merely beseeches Yahweh to 'grant them compassion in the sight of those who carried them captive, that *they* might have compassion on them' (*ûn^e^tattām l^e^raḥ^a^mîm lipnê šōbêhem w^e^riḥ^a^mûm*). It follows that the subtle shift that was already suggested by the focus on *šābâ* rather than *šûb* characterizes the relationship between the two passages in a profound sense. Deut 30:1–10 anticipates a dramatic new act of Yahweh, involving restoration of the exiles to the land, whereas 1 Kgs 8:46–53 thinks rather of Israel's surviving as a community in exile.

Before drawing conclusions from the foregoing, it is important to notice that the comparison between 1 Kgs 8:46–53 and the passages in Deuteronomy cannot be isolated from the question of [[77]] the relationships of each with the other Old Testament literature. Deut 30:1–10, first of all, has clear connexions with passages from the prophetic literature, notably Jeremiah 30–33; Ezekiel 36. The affinities are greater with Jeremiah. Once again, linguistic usage signals the link. Jeremiah knows both a circumcising of the heart (Jer 4:4; cf. Deut 30:6—with 10:16) and a 'restoration of fortunes' (*šûb š^e^bût*: Jer 29:10; 30:3, 18; 31:23; 32:44; 33:7, 11, 26). The latter motif clearly clusters round the so-called Book of Consolation. Its association with Deut 30:1–10 is strengthened by its occurrence twice in collocation with the verb *rḥm* [['have compassion']], where Yahweh is subject and said to have compassion on his people (30:18, 33:26). The Book of Consolation also develops the idea connoted both in Deut 30:6 and Jer 4:4 by "circumcising the heart." The essence of that idea is Yahweh's initiative in producing Israel's repentance, present in Jeremiah in the New Covenant theology of 31:31–34 and 32:39–40, and in Ezek 36:26–27, where it is also in collocation with the idea of a return to the land, v. 28. This feature of Deut 30:1–10 is quite as important a factor in the novelty and individuality of that passage as its introduction of the hope of restoration to the land. The two features together, therefore (i.e., return to land and Yahweh's initiative in the deliverance), characterize both Deut 30:1–10 and the prophetic passages cited; and neither is to be found in 1 Kgs 8:46–53.

Conclusion

I have tried to show that the enquiry into the Deuteronomist's theology of hope gains much from a study of Solomon's prayer, especially 1 Kgs 8:46–53. This passage shares motifs and expressions from parts of Deuteronomy 29 and 30, not unnaturally, perhaps, since both passages deal with the future of Israel in the light of the possibility (or certainty) of exile. The relationship with each (and both together) is of a special sort, however. In relation to Deut 29:17–27, the Kings passage echoes the language of curse found there, but does so, it seems, so as to alleviate the idea of curse and move the thought in the direction of hope. Vis-à-vis Deut 30:1–10, it also borrows motifs. That passage, in contrast to 29:17–27, concerns blessing for Israel, and is expressed in terms of return to the land. 1 Kings 8, however, does not want to go this far in its expression of hope. Here too, therefore, it seems to echo the language of the [[78]] Deuteronomy passage, but so as to modify it, allowing a hope that falls short of return to the land. By comparison with Deuteronomy 29–30 as a unit, therefore, it is like it in affirming hope beyond the exile, and unlike it in refraining from expressing that hope in terms of return.

One consequence of my observations concerns the source-criticism of the deuteronomic literature. I have supposed throughout that 1 Kings 8:46–53 is more likely to have read the passages in Deuteronomy than vice versa. This seems to follow from the fact that motifs from both the latter are interwoven in the Kings passage, in the framing of a particular theological perspective that seems to be in dialogue with them. It seems to follow also that the author of 1 Kgs 8:46–53 found Deut 29:17–27 and 30:1–10 already more or less juxtaposed before him.[17]

A more important consequence of our study, however, concerns our understanding of the nature of the deuteronomic literature. It is clear already from the problem posed by the varying texts which I have discussed that some kind of differentiation must be recognized among texts which have been broadly classed as deuteronomic. The tendency has been to resolve theological differences in terms of separate redactions. On the basis of the present study, two points may be made in this connexion. First, a question is placed against the undistinguishing use of vocabulary as a diagnostic tool in the identification of deuteronomic literature. Too often, similar vocabulary or phraseology is taken, without further ado, to imply similar origin and meaning. The case I have examined shows that the writer's use of vocabulary may be self-conscious, and intend both to express a measure of identity with a tradition and to criticize it.

Secondly, redaction-criticism in the OT should pay more attention to the context of a text in the book in question as a whole. I have tried to show elsewhere that the ending of the books of Kings is at best ambivalent about the future (see n. 8). Solomon's prayer can be well understood in the light of that assessment. Indeed, [[79]] Kings may be saying that hope for the future should not be reposed in any institution or mode of government. This would explain the non-royal terms of the hope contained in 1 Kgs 8:46–53, and finds a pregnant echo in Solomon's words: "there is no man who does not sin."

The view of Kings on the future is best expressed as one of openness. Its message about the failure of the dynasty and the consequent, immediate reality of exile is not ready to hold out a hope of return to the land (let alone a Messianic kingdom). While the prophetic texts briefly alluded to above may have taken a different cue from Deuteronomy, Kings rests content with its message that even in exile God will not abandon his people.

17. Contrast Wolff (n. 1) 181, who thought Deut 30:1–10 connected directly with Deut 28:45ff., and omitted Deuteronomy 29 from the context on the grounds of the criterion of number in the second person address. Others, however, have regarded Deut 28:69–30:20 as a unity, because of its apparent features of a covenantal liturgy; see Nicholson (n. 12) 21–22.

Prayer and Propaganda

Solomon's Dedication of the Temple and the Deuteronomist's Program

GARY N. KNOPPERS

That Solomon's prayer at the dedication of the Temple (1 Kings 8) is a pivotal composition in the Deuteronomistic History is a proposition held to by virtually all scholars. Yet commentators avidly disagree on the compositional history and import of this royal prayer. Over against those who contend for up to eight layers of composition in this passage, Knoppers argues that there is substantial literary evidence for its unity. Hitherto unrecognized correspondences exist between the liturgies of Temple dedication (1 Kgs 8:1–21, 55–66) surrounding King Solomon's prayer (1 Kgs 8:22–54). These parallels lend a sense of balance and symmetry to the proceedings. The correspondences extend to the prayer, which also manifests internal signs of literary unity. The Deuteronomist portrays the Temple dedication as the culmination of Israelite history after the exodus and the dawn of a new era for king, cult, and people. The author actively promotes the unity of his state by arguing for the Temple's centrality to the fate of his people. In the view of Knoppers, the deuteronomistic emphasis on popular prayer is best understood as a part of a preexilic program that links king, city, Temple, and people. If the deuteronomic code empowers a cultic center by centralizing sacrifice, the Deuteronomist bolsters the power of this center by centralizing prayer. Rather than indicating a devaluation or demythologization of the Temple, the Solomonic blessings, invocations, and petitions expand the Temple's role in Israelite life. By portraying the enthusiastic endorsement of the Temple by all Israelites in the time of Solomon, the Deuteronomist underscores the need for such enthusiastic support by all sectors of the people in his own day.

Reprinted with permission from *Catholic Biblical Quarterly* 57 (1995) 229–54.

[[*Author's note*: In this essay, a scripture reference with a star indicates the original form of the passage.]]

[[229]] A half century ago Martin Noth demonstrated that the Deuteronomist unifies his history through a series of speeches, prayers, and summarizing reflections.[1] Noth's argument that Solomon's prayer belongs to these major deuteronomistic orations has been almost universally accepted by scholars.[2] Despite this all too rare example of agreement among commentators, scholars continue to disagree about the compositional history and significance of this pivotal text.[3] Some follow Noth in viewing most of 1 Kings 8 as a unified pericope composed mainly, if not totally, by the (exilic) Deuteronomist.[4] Some scholars follow Cross in considering Solomon's [[230]] prayer to stem from a preexilic Deuteronomist (Dtr^1), whose work is supplemented by an exilic editor (Dtr^2).[5] Those scholars who adopt the redactional theory of Smend posit a series of exilic deuteronomistic editions and postdeuteronomistic additions.[6] Finally, O'Brien

1. M. Noth, *The Deuteronomistic History* (JSOTSup 15; Sheffield: JSOT, 1981) 4–11.

2. Ibid., 6–9, 93.

3. E. Talstra, *Het Gebed van Salomo: Synchronie en diachronie in de kompositie van I Kon. 8,14–61* (Amsterdam: VU Uitgeverij, 1988) 13–65, and M. A. O'Brien, *The Deuteronomistic History Hypothesis: A Reassessment* (OBO 92; Göttingen: Vandenhoeck & Ruprecht, 1989) 151–59, provide helpful surveys.

4. O. Plöger, "Reden und Gebete im deuteronomistischen und chronistischen Geschichtswerk," *Festschrift für Günther Dehn zum 75. Geburtstag* (ed. W. Schneemelcher; Neukirchen: Buchhandlung des Erziehungsvereins, 1957) 35–49 [[translated in this volume, pp. 31–46]]; M. Weinfeld, *Deuteronomy and the Deuteronomic School* (Oxford: Clarendon, 1972) 35–36, 195–98; H.-D. Hoffmann, *Reform und Reformen: Untersuchungen zu einem Grundthema der deuteronomistischen Geschichtsschreibung* (ATANT 66; Zurich: Theologischer Verlag, 1980); J. Van Seters, *In Search of History* (New Haven: Yale University Press, 1983) 310–11. B. O. Long (*1 Kings* [FOTL 9; Grand Rapids: Eerdmans, 1980] 94–108) contends that the (exilic) Deuteronomist has brought some order to the material in 1 Kings 8. Nevertheless, Long also believes that 1 Kings 8 evinces a complicated history of redaction. J. Levenson ("From Temple to Synagogue: 1 Kings 8," *Traditions in Transformation: Turning Points in Biblical Faith: Essays Presented to Frank Moore Cross, Jr.* [ed. B. Halpern and J. Levenson; Winona Lake, IN: Eisenbrauns, 1981] 143–66) believes that 1 Kgs 8:22–61 stems from the exilic Deuteronomist whom F. M. Cross calls Dtr^2.

5. F. M. Cross, *Canaanite Myth and Hebrew Epic* (Cambridge, MA: Harvard University Press, 1973) 274–89 [[pp. 79–94 in this volume]]; R. E. Friedman, *The Exile and Biblical Narrative* (HSM 22; Chico, CA: Scholars, 1981) 1–43; R. D. Nelson, *The Double Redaction of the Deuteronomistic History* (JSOTSup 18; Sheffield: JSOT, 1981) 69–73; S. L. McKenzie, *The Chronicler's Use of the Deuteronomistic History* (HSM 33; Atlanta: Scholars, 1985) 199–205; idem, *The Trouble with Kings: The Composition of the Book of Kings in the Deuteronomistic History* (VTSup 42; Leiden: Brill, 1991) 137–40. B. Halpern (*The First Historians: The Hebrew Bible and History* [San Francisco: Harper & Row, 1988] 168–71) ascribes all of 1 Kings 8 to the Josianic Deuteronomist.

6. R. Smend, "Das Gesetz und die Völker: Ein Beitrag zur deuteronomistischen Redaktionsgeschichte," *Probleme biblischer Theologie: Festschrift Gerhard von Rad* (ed. H. W. Wolff; Munich: Kaiser, 1971) 494–509 [[translated in this volume, pp. 95–110]]; idem, *Die Entstehung des Alten Testaments* (Stuttgart: Kohlhammer, 1978) 111–34; W. Dietrich, *Prophetie und Geschichte* (FRLANT 108; Göttingen: Vandenhoeck & Ruprecht, 1972) 73–74; E. Würthwein, *Die Bücher der Könige 1: Könige 1–16* (ATD 11/1; Göttingen: Vandenhoeck & Ruprecht, 1977) 84–103;

contends for a series of preexilic, exilic, and postexilic deuteronomistic redactions of a preexilic source.[7] Virtually all scholars recognize the presence of both a preexilic source and some priestly editing in 1 Kgs 8:1–13.

Aside from diverging on the composition and date of 1 Kings 8, commentators also disagree about its meaning, specifically the trope: Solomon's royal shrine as a house of prayer. The imperative in Deuteronomy 12 for one "place for Yhwh's name" has explicitly to do, of course, with sacrifice, the main form of worship in the ancient Near East (Deut 12:4–18, 26–27). Why, then, does the Deuteronomist have Solomon utter a lengthy prayer at the dedication of "the place that Yhwh shall choose to make his name dwell there?" According to Kaufmann, the replacement of sacrifice with prayer results from the Israelite understanding of worship as "dependence upon and submission to the one, omnipotent God."[8] For Noth, Solomon's prayer indicates deuteronomistic [[231]] devaluation of the temple.[9] The Deuteronomist, writing after the temple's destruction, purportedly recasts the temple's significance, "For him the temple is little more than a place towards which one turns in prayer."[10] Similarly, Weinfeld sees Solomon's prayer as evincing the deuteronomic demythologization of worship.[11]

Upon close scrutiny, none of these explanations is compelling. Prayer does not seem inherently to be any less mythological or any more clearly a sign of submission than sacrifice. If an exilic deuteronomist wished to downplay the temple's importance, why would this writer stress that the temple was the focal point of Israelite life and insist that people use the temple in all sorts of predicaments to supplicate Yhwh "at this house" or "toward this place"? Nor should prayer in an ancient context be disassociated from sacrifice. Halpern, McKenzie, and Miller point to a number of

---

G. H. Jones, *1 and 2 Kings* 2 vols.; NCB; Grand Rapids: Eerdmans, 1984) 191–209. T. N. D. Mettinger (*The Dethronement of Sabaoth: Studies in the Shem and Kabod Theologies* [ConBOT 18; Lund: Gleerup 1982] 38) follows the typology of DtrH, DtrP, and DtrN but admits that DtrH could have been written in the wake of either 597 or 586 B.C.E.

7. O'Brien, "*Deuteronomistic History Hypothesis*, 151–59. A. F. Campbell, S.J. (*Of Prophets and Kings: A Late Ninth-Century Document (1 Samuel 1–2 Kings 10)* [CBQMS 17; Washington, DC: Catholic Biblical Association of America, 1986] 207) pioneered the redactional model employed by O'Brien, but he assigns all of 1 Kgs 8:14–66 to the Josianic Deuteronomist.

8. Y. Kaufmann, *The Religion of Israel from Its Beginnings to the Babylonian Exile* (Chicago: University of Chicago Press, 1960) 269.

9. Noth, *Deuteronomistic History*, 93–95; idem, *Könige* (BKAT 9/1; Neukirchen-Vluyn: Neukirchener Verlag, 1968) 168–93.

10. Noth, *Deuteronomistic History*, 94. His views have recently been defended and extended by S. E. Balentine, *Prayer in the Hebrew Bible: The Drama of Divine-Human Dialogue* (OBT 20; Minneapolis: Fortress, 1993) 80–88.

11. Weinfeld, *Deuteronomy*, 195–209.

ancient Near Eastern texts that mention both prayer and sacrifice.[12] In this regard, the deuteronomistic presentation of Solomon's dedication of the temple is no different, for it depicts both royal sacrifice (1 Kgs 8:5, 62–64) and royal prayer (8:31–51).[13] Hurowitz documents the claim that the Deuteronomist's temple narrative contains similar components to those found in many ancient Near Eastern narratives of the construction of a temple or a palace.[14] Hence, in many respects, the sequence of events in 1 Kings 6–9 is not unusual.

Yet some problems remain, despite the affinities between Kings and the written remains of other ancient Near Eastern cultures. Solomon's prayer repeatedly promotes the temple as a place of prayer, not as a place of sacrifice. Moreover, Solomon wishes his sanctuary to function specifically as a place of popular prayer. To be sure, Solomon, like a number of other ancient Near Eastern monarchs, is also concerned about the role of his dynasty [[232]] (8:15–21) and the efficacy of his prayers (8:28–30, 52–53), but most of his attention is devoted to popular prayer (8:31–51). Solomon clearly encourages Israelites to journey to the temple and offer petitions there. Such prayer is an event of public worship.[15] Moreover, as Long observes, "the literary architecture [of 1 Kings 8] suggests a centering on the prayers offered to Yahweh."[16] Hence, we return to the question, Why does the Deuteronomist champion the temple as a site for Israelite prayer?

To address issues of interpretation one should first address literary issues.[17] In my judgment, there is substantial literary evidence for the unity

12. Halpern, *First Historians*, 179. McKenzie (*Chronicler's Use*, 208–9) calls attention to the appearance of both prayer and sacrifice in RS 24.266, noting the casuistic treatment of subjects as in 1 Kgs 8:37, 42, 44. See also the comments of P. D. Miller, "Prayer and Sacrifice in Ugarit and Israel," *Text and Context: Old Testament and Semitic Studies for F. C. Fensham* (JSOTSup 48; ed. W. Claassen; Sheffield; JSOT, 1988) 139–55.

13. See also the mention of Solomon's temple sacrifices in 1 Kgs 9:25 and 10:5.

14. (1) Decision and divine approval, (2) preparations, (3) description of building process, (4) building dedication, (5) prayer or blessing, (6) blessings and curses directed toward future monarchs (V. Hurowitz, *I Have Built You an Exalted House: Temple Building in Light of Mesopotamian and Northwest Semitic Writings* [JSOTSup 115; Sheffield: JSOT, 1992] 109–311).

15. As G. A. Anderson points out ("The Praise of God as a Cultic Event," *Priesthood and Cult in Ancient Israel* [JSOTSup 125; ed. G. A. Anderson and S. M. Olyan; Sheffield: JSOT, 1991] 15–33), such supplication is an act, not merely an interior attitude.

16. Long, *1 Kings*, 94–95.

17. My interest is specifically focused on the deuteronomistic version of 1 Kings 8. Hence, in this study I will neither delve into the larger literary context of Solomon's temple dedication nor explore the nature and number of predeuteronomistic strata in 1 Kings 8. For issues of context and deuteronomistic redaction, see G. N. Knoppers, *Two Nations under God: The Deuteronomistic History of Solomon and the Dual Monarchies 1: The Reign of Solomon and the Rise of Jeroboam* (HSM 52; Atlanta: Scholars, 1993) 91–112, and for issues of sources,

of 1 Kings 8. Hitherto unrecognized correspondences exist between the liturgies of temple dedication (8:1–21 and 8:55–66) surrounding King Solomon's prayer. These parallels lend a sense of balance and symmetry to the proceedings. The correspondences extend to the prayer, which also manifests internal signs of literary unity. This is not to deny the existence of scattered later additions to 1 Kings 8. The differences between the MT and the LXX point toward some fluidity in the development of the text.[18] Nevertheless, the placement of these rings suggests that the depiction of events preceding and succeeding Solomon's prayer are integral to the deuteronomistic presentation and function structurally as an interpretive key to the prayer itself.

The major movements in 1 Kings 8—the *mise en scène* [['the scene-setting' or 'introduction']], the elevation of the ark, the appearance of the (divine) cloud, the offering of thousands of [[233]] sacrifices, the Solomonic discourses on the Davidic promises and the Torah of Moses, and the celebration of the festival—all serve to integrate the temple and Solomon's prayer itself into Israel's corporate life. The Deuteronomist portrays the dedication of the temple as the culmination of Israelite history since the exodus and as the dawn of a new era for king, cult, and people. The author actively promotes the unity of his state by arguing for the temple's centrality to the fate of his people. The deuteronomistic emphasis on popular prayer is best understood as a part of a preexilic program that links king, city, temple, and people. If the deuteronomic code empowers a cultic center by centralizing sacrifice, the Deuteronomist bolsters the power of this center by centralizing prayer. Solomonic blessings, invocations, and petitions expand the temple's role in Israelite life. Solomon's prayer becomes both the model and the means for offering efficacious petitions to the deity. I wish to demonstrate the literary unity of 1 Kings 8 and, in turn, the coherent ideology toward which such unity points.

---

see Noth, *Könige*, 174–82; M. Görg, "Die Gattung des sogenannten Tempelweihespruchs (1 Kgs 8:12f)," *UF* 6 (1974) 55–63; O. Loretz, "Der Torso eines kanaanäisch-israelitischen Tempelweihespruches in 1 Kgs 8,12–13," *UF* 6 (1974) 478–80; Talstra, *Het Gebed*, 84–101.

18. D. Shenkel, *Chronology and Recensional Development in the Greek Text of Kings* (HSM 1; Cambridge, MA: Harvard University Press, 1968); J. Trebolle Barrera, *Salomón y Jeroboán: Historia de la recensión y redacción de 1 Reyes 2,12–14* (Institución San Jerónimo 10; Valencia: Institución San Jerónimo, 1980; distributed by Edilva, Valencia); idem, "The Text-Critical Use of the Septuagint in the Book of Kings," *Seventh Congress of the International Organization for Septuagint and Cognate Studies, Leuven, 1989* (SBLSCS 31; ed. C. Cox; Atlanta: Scholars, 1989) 285–99; S. L. McKenzie, "1 Kings 8: A Sample Study into the Texts of Kings Used by the Chronicler and Translated by the Old Greek," *BIOSCS* 19 (1986) 15–34; E. Tov, *Textual Criticism of the Hebrew Bible* (Minneapolis: Fortress, 1992) 155–97; R. Pennoyer, "The Textual and Editorial History of 1 Kings 8" (unpublished paper).

The Literary Unity of 1 Kings 8

The Deuteronomist portrays the dedication of the temple as a complex series of actions and discourses. The major players in this public liturgy are Solomon, the assembly of Israel, the elders, the priests, and the people. Despite the diversity of participants, recurring actions and speeches unify the proceedings. The correspondence between earlier and later events in the narrative represents deliberate authorial strategy on the part of the Deuteronomist. In what follows I am not arguing that 1 Kings 8 constitutes an exact chiasm. To press the case for ring composition so rigidly that every element within 1 Kings 8 would have to fit into a tightly defined schematic pattern would distort the evidence.[19] There are both complementary events, such as the offering of sacrifices (8:5, 62–64), and unparalleled events, such as the elevation of the ark into the temple (8:3, 6–9). In my judgment, both the correspondences between events and the actions which have no corollaries are important for understanding the Deuteronomist's broader narrative designs. Since 1 Kings 8 is often considered disunified, I will first make the case for unity and then address the significance of those components in 1 Kings 8 which do not appear to fit within this overall schema.

Symmetry and Balance, Part 1: The Dedication of the Temple

Seven literary frames can be discerned in 1 Kings 8. These literary rings extend to Solomon's prayer itself. There are also, as we shall see, some verbal parallels between petitions within Solomon's prayer and the literary rings which surround this prayer. [[234]]

1. Assembly (8:1–3)
    2. Sacrifice (8:5)
        3. Blessing (8:14–21)
            4. Solomon's Stance (8:22)
                5. Invocation (8:27–30)
                    6. Three Petitions (8:31–36)
                        7. Generalizing Petition (8:37–40)
                    6′. Three Petitions (8:41–51)
                5′. Invocation (8:52–53)
            4′. Solomon's Stance (8:54)
        3′. Blessing (8:55–61)
    2′. Sacrifice (8:62–64)
1′. Dismissal (8:66)

19. See the well-argued cautions of J. Kugel, "On the Bible and Literary Criticism," *Prooftexts* 1 (1981) 217–36.

The first (outermost) set of frames–containing Solomon's convocation of the Israelites (8:1–2) and his dismissing them (8:66)–provides a clear introduction and conclusion to the account of Solomon's dedication of the temple. In the second literary frame, "the king and all Israel" offer great numbers of sacrifices as the priests carry the ancient palladium into the temple,[20] and then, after Solomon's second blessing, "Solomon and all Israel" again offer sacrifices to honor the dedication of Israel's central sanctuary (8:62–64).

Before his first invocation and after his second invocation, Solomon blesses both God and people (8:14–21 and 8:55–61). The blessings begin with almost identical introductions: ויברך את כל ישׂראל ⟦'and blessed all Israel'⟧ (8:14);[21] ויברך את כל קהל ישׂראל ⟦'and blessed the whole congregation of Israel'⟧ (8:55). The two blessings also contain virtually identical introductions: ... ויאמר ברוך יהוה אלהי ישׂראל אשר ⟦'and he said, "Blessed be the Lord, the God of Israel, who . . .'⟧ (8:15); ... לאמר ברוך יהוה אשר ⟦'saying, "Blessed be the Lord, who . . .'⟧ (8:55b–56). Finally, each blessing contains statements alluding to the period of exodus and Sinai (8:16, 21, 56, 57, 58, 61).

The fourth set of frames describes Solomon's physical stance as he begins the first invocation and ends the second invocation.

> 8:22 ויעמד שׁלמה לפני מזבח יהוה נגד כל קהל ישׂראל ויפרשׂ כפיו השמים
> ⟦'Then Solomon stood before the altar of the LORD in the presence of the whole community of Israel; he spread the palms of his hands toward heaven'⟧
>
> 8:54 [22]קם מלפני מזבח יהוה מכרע על ברכיו וכפיו פרשׂות השמים
> ⟦'he rose from where he had been kneeling, in front of the altar of the LORD, his hands spread out toward heaven'⟧

⟦235⟧ The Deuteronomist's presentation is, thus, carefully arranged and is strikingly consistent: the descriptions of Solomon's physical stance frame his invocations, which, in turn, envelop his prayer.[23]

20. In 8:5, I read with the LXX^{B} (*lectio brevior* ⟦'shorter reading'⟧). The MT is expansionary: "and King Solomon and all the council of Israel." On the comparable movement of the ark in 2 Sam 6:13–19, see P. K. McCarter, "The Ritual Dedication of the City of David in 2 Samuel 6," *The Word of the Lord Shall Go Forth: Essays in Honor of David Noel Freedman in Celebration of his Sixtieth Birthday* (ed. C. L. Meyers and M. O'Connor; Winona Lake, IN: Eisenbrauns, 1983) 273–77.

21. I read with the LXX (maximum variation). The MT expands to the equivalent of 8:56, כל קהל ישׂראל ⟦'the whole congregation of Israel'⟧.

22. Whereas the MT of 8:54 reads, "he rose," the LXX has "and he rose." I read with the MT (*lectio difficilior* ⟦'more difficult reading'⟧).

23. I agree with the arguments of Levenson ("1 Kings 8," 155–56) that the contrast between the standing Solomon of 8:22 and the kneeling Solomon of 8:54 need not indicate multiple authorship.

There are also verbal parallels between the two invocations (1 Kgs 8:27–30 and 8:52–53). Levenson observes that both contain a plea to the deity found nowhere else in the Bible:[24] להיות עינך פתחות [['may your eyes be open']] (8:29); להיות עיניך פתחות [[same]] (8:52). Each invocation concludes with a request that Yhwh attend to the prayer of the king, and of both king and people, respectively: לשמע אל התפלה אשר יתפלל עבדך [['may you heed the prayers which your servant will offer']] (8:29); לשמע אליהם בכל קראם אליך [['may you heed them whenever they call upon you']] (8:52).[25] Although in this instance there is no exact verbal repetition in the two statements, apart from לשמע [['heed']], both depict Solomon interceding for prayers associated with the temple.

We have seen that Solomon's prayer is more integrated within its literary setting than scholars have previously recognized. There are additional indications of unity. The Deuteronomist incorporates the sevenfold prayer within the setting of Solomon's temple dedication by drawing a number of links between the petitions in this prayer, especially the fourth petition, and the frames which envelop the prayer. Of the seven supplications, the first three and the last three engage specific situations–adjudication of imprecatory oaths before the temple altar (vv. 31–32), defeat in war (vv. 33–34), drought (vv. 35–36), the plight of foreigners (vv. 41–43), military campaigns (vv. 44–45), and exile (vv. 46–51). The fourth and central petition (vv. 37–40) begins with specific difficulties but becomes more general. Solomon progresses from listing specific agrarian disasters and enemy raids to imploring Yhwh to consider "any plague or any disease" and to answer "any person's prayer or supplication" (8:37b–38). This comports with the invocations in 8:27–30* and 8:52–53:

8:28d ופנית אל תפלת עבדך ואל תחנתו
[['yet turn to the prayer of your servant and to his supplication']]

8:38 כל תפלה כל תחנה אשר תהיה לכל האדם[26]
[['any prayer or supplication offered by any person']]

8:52 אל תחנת עבדך ואל תחנת עמך ישראל
[['to the supplication of your servant and the supplication of your people Israel']]

Solomon's two invocations and central petition, therefore, engage more general situations and the efficacy of prayer itself.

24. Ibid., 156.

25. If 8:30 is original, it provides an even stronger parallel to 8:52, because 8:30 speaks of the supplications of both king and people. But I am inclined to think that the first half of 8:30 is an addition to the text, inserted by repetitive resumption of the phrase "to this place" from the end of 8:29. The insertion brings the first invocation more into line with the second.

26. A few manuscripts in the LXX and Syriac traditions have the equivalent of וכל תחנה [['any supplication']].

[[236]] There is also a resonance between Solomon's seven petitions and his first invocation (1 Kgs 8:27–30). All of them speak of the deity as residing in the heavens.

> ואתה תשמע אל מקום שבתך אל השמים[27]
> [['and you listen in the place of your heavenly dwelling']]
> ושמעת השמים [['and you hear from heaven']] (or) ואתה תשמע השמים[28] [['and you hear from heaven']]

Solomon's first invocation qualifies his earlier claim that he built a residence for Yhwh, "a place for your dwelling forever" (8:13), by asserting that the deity does not reside in the temple: "the heavens and the highest heavens cannot contain you, much less this house which I have built" (8:27). The ensuing request–that Yhwh respond from the heavens–establishes a pattern, which is followed in all seven petitions. The people are to appeal to their heavenly deity by recourse to the house built for his name on earth.

There is also a partial parallel between Solomon's behavior in prayer and his intercession on behalf of Israelite conduct in prayer. Solomon prepares to begin his first invocation when he 'spreads his palms toward the heavens' (ויפרשׂ כפיו השמים, 8:22). Similarly, at the end of the second invocation, Solomon rises from the place where he had been kneeling, 'his palms spread toward the heavens' (וכפיו פרשׂות השמים, 8:54). These two actions partially resemble a plea within Solomon's fourth, generalizing, petition. Solomon intercedes for anyone among God's people who 'spreads his palms toward this house' (ופרשׂ כפיו אל הבית הזה, 8:38). In this regard, those Israelites who use the temple for prayer–as Solomon hopes they will–emulate not only Solomon's words but also his conduct.

Symmetry and Balance, Part 2: The Structure of Solomon's Prayer

The case for unity includes the internal organization of Solomon's prayer.[29] I would argue that the components within each petition are more numerous, and their sequence more regular, than scholars have previously recognized. The Deuteronomist shapes each of Solomon's peti-

27. Here in 8:30 the LXX has καὶ ποιήσεις [['and act']] where the MT has ושמעת [['and you hear']].

28. While 8:32, 34, 36, 43 have ואתה תשמע השמים [['hear thou in heaven']], 8:45, 49 have ושמעת השמים [['hear in heaven']]; 8:39 reads ואתה תשמע השמים מכון שבתך [['then hear in your heavenly abode']].

29. A. Gamper ("Die heilsgeschichtliche Bedeutung des salomonischen Tempelweihegebets," *ZKT* 85 [1963] 55–63) and Levenson ("1 Kings 8," 153–57) demonstrate that most of the evidence for disunity in Solomon's prayer (e.g., stylistic and grammatical variation) is insignificant when compared with the overall evidence for unity.

tions according to a standard six-part (or seven-part) pattern. In my judgment, each of the seven petitions within this prayer (vv. 31–32, 33–34, 35–36, 37–40, 41–43, 44–45, 46–51)[30] contains at least six basic components: (1) hypothetical situation, ⟦237⟧ (2) cause, (3) repentance or prayer, (4) place, (5) supplication, (6) request that Yhwh act or forgive.

Three of the petitions (those of vv. 37–40, vv. 41–43, and vv. 46–51) also contain a seventh element, a rationale justifying a favorable divine response to the request (the sixth element). The reason for one petition (vv. 31–32) containing only five of six components is readily transparent. For the guilty party in a judicial dispute to repent (no. 3) would obviate the need for the deity to validate a purgatory oath at the temple altar. The variations in terminology in the location of petitions: בבית/הבית הזה ⟦'in this house/this house'⟧ (vv. 31, 33, 38, 42, 43), אל המקום הזה ⟦'toward this place'⟧ (v. 35), or דרך [ארצם] . . . העיר . . . והבית אשר בניתי לשמך ⟦'in the direction of their land . . . the city . . . the house that I have built to your name'⟧ (vv. 44, 48) can also be explained largely on the basis of context. The sixth petition (vv. 44–45) finds the people away from home while at war, imploring Yhwh to act on their behalf. Since the people are "along the way," they cannot pray "at this temple" or "toward this place." Provision for prayer "in the direction of the city which I have chosen and the house which I have built for your name," therefore, is not an indication of secondary authorship but is intrinsic to the particular situation addressed. Given the exilic plight of the people in the seventh petition (vv. 46–51), to suggest that the phraseology of location (component 4) conforms to that of the first five petitions is unreasonable.[31]

Summation of Symmetry and Balance

We have seen that the Deuteronomist carefully orders and unifies his presentation of Solomon's dedication of the temple by setting up seven sets of literary frames. The number of these rings is too many, and their usage too consistent, to be accidental. Whatever sources the Deuteronomist may have had at his disposal for the composition of this chapter, he has

30. I disagree with Halpern (*First Historians*, 168–69) that 8:44–45 and 8:46–51 represent one petition. Both 8:44 and 8:46 begin with similar protases: כי יצא עמך ⟦'if your people go out'⟧ and כי יחטאו לך ⟦'if they sin against you'⟧, and both 8:44–45 and 8:46–51 contain the standard sequence of components. I would also maintain that 8:44–45 and 8:46–51 engage different predicaments (military campaigns and deportations, respectively).

31. There may well be some exilic retouching in this last petition. Note the elaborate plays on שׁוב ⟦'turn back'⟧ and שׁבה ⟦'take captive'⟧ (J. Levenson, "The Paronomasia of Solomon's Seventh Petition," *HAR* 6 [1982] 135–38) and the differences between 1 Kgs 8:50–53 and 2 Chr 6:39–40 (McKenzie, *Chronicler's Use*, 204–5). But I see no reason on the basis of location to deny the existence of a preexilic substratum of this final petition (see below).

clearly put his own stamp on them. The rings create a well-balanced, well-organized, and well-focused liturgy. The appearance of six regular components within each of Solomon's seven petitions contributes to the unity of the prayer itself. The generalizing conclusion to Solomon's fourth petition, occurring halfway through his prayer, in turn, complements the two invocations framing the prayer. Solomon's prayer, therefore, is more than a well-unified composition: it is structurally well integrated within its literary setting.

⟦238⟧ The intricate literary architecture of 1 Kings 8 militates against removing entire sections of this chapter as the work of later redactors and glossators simply on the basis of a shift in style or a change of topic.[32] For instance, excising vv. 62–66 as the latest addition to 1 Kings 8 removes literary frames corresponding to, and complementing, two literary frames at the beginning of the chapter.[33] The exclusion of vv. 62–66 from primary, secondary, and tertiary composition means that in these earlier levels the people, once assembled, never go home. Similarly, to attribute 8:14–21 to an author different from the author of 8:55–61 because of variation in content—the Davidic promises as opposed to the relation of Solomon's prayer to the commandments of Moses—ignores the formal similarities between these two sections of the text.[34] We have seen that both pericopes appear as blessings, that both occupy similar positions in the text, and that both have similar introductions and conclusions. If one wants to argue that each blessing stems from a different author, one has to concede that the editor responsible for the second blessing has integrated his interpolation rather well into his *Vorlage.* This is a more labored explanation, however, than that of simply viewing both blessings as the work of a single author who is demarcating the bearing of a new edifice upon two different institutions.

By depicting Solomon's dedication of the temple as a complex but largely balanced series of movements and discourses, the Deuteronomist

32. G. Braulik ("Spuren einer Neubearbeitung des deuteronomistischen Geschichtswerkes in 1 Kön 8,52–53,59–60," *Bib* 52 [1971] 20–33) sees 8:52–53, 59–60 as material stemming from a level of composition later than the main deuteronomistic redaction. Dietrich (*Prophetie und Geschichte,* 74) staes that 8:28–30a, 53–61 stem from DtrN, but that 8:27, 30b–43 stem from a later author. Jones (*1 and 2 Kings*, 201–5) basically follows Würthwein (*Bücher der Könige*, 95–97) in viewing 8:27 as secondary, 8:29 as an attempt to integrate the interpolation of Solomon's prayer, and 8:54–61, 62–66 as later additions. O'Brien (*Deuteronomistic History Hypothesis*, 157–59) views 8:14–21, 23aα, 24*, 25–26, 28–29a, 55–56 as the work of the Deuteronomist, and 8:29b–30, 52–53 as the creation of a later author who purportedly inserted Solomon's prayer (8:29b–51). Putatively, 8:57–58, 61 stem from a nomistic Deuteronomist.

33. Contra A. Jepsen, *Die Quellen des Königsbuches* (2d ed.; Halle: Niemeyer, 1956) 102, and Würthwein, *Bücher der Könige*, 100–102.

34. Contra Würthwein, *Bücher der Könige*, 100–101, and Jones, *1 and 2 Kings*, 205–6.

engages various subjects while focusing attention, nonetheless, on his main subject: the centrality of this new sanctuary to Israelite life. The participation of the elders and the priests, as well as the innumerable sacrifices by king and people alike, commend Solomon's royal chapel as a truly national shrine. The first four frames envelop the royal prayer, making it the focal point of the Deuteronomist's presentation. The frames immediately surrounding Solomon's prayer—the blessings and invocations—communicate the significance of the prayer, integrating the innovation of a central sanctuary into Israel's [[239]] traditional cultic and political life. The petitions within Solomon's prayer dramatize the temple's role as the site at which Yhwh makes himself accessible to his people through prayer.

Asymmetry and Imbalance in 1 Kings 8

There are unique features in 1 Kings 8 as well as variations on earlier actions and motifs. These too are important for understanding the structure and meaning of Solomon's dedication of the temple. The elevation of the ark (8:1, 3, 6), the description of the ark's contents and placement (8:7–9), the appearance of the cloud in the temple (8:10–11), and Solomon's first speech (8:12–13) have no parallels in the material following Solomon's prayer.[35] Conversely, the celebration of the festival (8:65) seems to have no parallel in the proceedings preceding Solomon's prayer.[36]

Moreover, the supplicants in Solomon's discourses vary. In the king's first invocation, he speaks on behalf of himself (8:28, 29), but in his seven petitions he intercedes for the people (8:31–51).[37] In his second invocation, he speaks on behalf of both himself and the people (8:52); similarly, in his second blessing he speaks either of the people (8:56, 61) or of both king and people (8:57, 58, 59). Whence do the variations in subject come? If one author is responsible for most of 1 Kings 8, how does one explain the shifts in supplicants? To do justice to the literary complexity of 1 Kings 8, one should explain both the unity and the diversity, the symmetry and the asymmetry.

The Temple and Traditional Institutions

The largest block of unparalleled material occurs near the beginning of 1 Kings 8. The Deuteronomist provides generous coverage to the elevation

35. In the LXX^B, Solomon's initial speech (8:12–13) occurs between 8:53 and 8:54.

36. 4QKgs^a and the MT of 1 Kgs 8:2 and 2 Chr 5:3 mention the festival, but this reference is not found in the LXX^B, which probably represents the earliest reading (McKenzie, "1 Kings 8," 26).

37. The usage is consistent throughout all seven petitions, with the exception of 8:36. There Solomon asks of Yhwh, "Forgive the sin of your servants [plural in the MT] and people Israel." A few Hebrew manuscripts and the LXX read "your servant."

of the ark, its contents, and its placement within the adytum of the temple.[38] Since the Deuteronomist normally does not evince great interest [[240]] in the details of Jerusalem's established religious institution, his conscious attention to the many connections between king, temple, and ark must be explained on more than simply historical grounds.[39] Most commentators agree that the Deuteronomist incorporates a source into his narrative, but why does he choose to do so? The great attention the Deuteronomist accords to the ark might initially lead one to believe that his approach is essentially conservative. But does the appearance of the assembly of Israel, the priests, and the elders signify the triumph of traditional institutions in the midst of wholesale changes during the united monarchy?[40]

In my view, it is not accidental that the assembly, the elders, and the priests endorse an innovation in Israelite worship. Such a distinction enhances the prestige of the new temple. The transfer of the ark to the temple appears not as a revolution but as the culmination of one era and the beginning of another. For the Deuteronomist, the dedication of Solomon's temple marks the high point of Israel's history since the exodus. The consecration of a central sanctuary, in turn, becomes the point of a new departure in Israelite history. The temple, not the ark, is now the central, unifying cultic institution in Israelite life. The temple thus encompasses and supersedes the previous cultic symbol.

"A Place for the Ark"

In 1 Kgs 8:1–11 the Deuteronomist projects an image of Solomon as a curator and guarantor of one of his nation's most sacred cultic artifacts. As Noth and Würthwein observe, Solomon is not even that much of a factor

38. Hurowitz (*I Have Built*, 263) points out parallels in P to certain expressions in vv. 1–6. Even though many scholars view this priestly language as postdeuteronomistic, Friedman (*Exile and Biblical Narrative*, 48–60) vigorously defends its being original to the preexilic Deuteronomist. But 1 Kgs 8:4 is partially absent from the LXX and from 4QKgs[a] (McKenzie, "1 Kings 8," 27). I would attribute ויעלו את ארון יהוה ואת אהל מועד ואת כל כלי הקדש אשר באהל [['And they brought up the ark of the Lord, the tent of meeting, and all the holy vessels that were in the tent']] to a priestly writer, who elaborates upon the view of the Deuteronomist that the temple maintains and fulfills traditional cultic arrangements. Pennoyer ("Textual and Editorial History") argues the contrary position: that 1 Kings 8 underwent a priestly redaction before it underwent a deuteronomistic redaction.

39. Pace Noth, *Deuteronomistic History*, 95.

40. On the nature of these institutions, see H. Tadmor, "Traditional Institutions and the Monarchy: Social and Political Tensions in the Time of David and Solomon," *Studies in the Period of David and Solomon, and Other Essays* (ed. T. Ishida; Winona Lake, IN: Eisenbrauns, 1982) 239–57, and H. Reviv, "Popular Assemblies in the Bible," *Proceedings of the Seventh World Congress of Jewish Studies: Studies in the Bible and the Ancient Near East* (Jerusalem: Perry Foundation for Biblical Research, 1981) 95–98 (Hebrew).

in this section of the narrative.[41] Instead, the assembly (קהל ישׂראל), the elders, and the priests take center stage. I would argue, however, that the continuity between institutions–the ancient palladium and the temple, [[241]] the assembly of Israel and the king–lends authority to the new arrangements.[42] Solomon accords the ark profound respect by convening the elders of Israel at Jerusalem and offering countless sacrifices, as the priests elevate the ark into "the shrine of the temple."[43] The leaders of Israel's traditional institutions thereby authorize a major shift in Israel's worship. What is new gains clout through its association with what is old.

If the involvement of elders, priests, and the assembly of Israel ratifies the new arrangement from a human standpoint, a magisterial theophany ratifies the new arrangement from a divine standpoint. The Deuteronomist observes that at the temple's dedication "the priests were unable to stand to serve on account of the cloud, for the glory of Yhwh filled the house of Yhwh" (8:11).[44] This theophany leads Solomon to exult, in 8:13:

> Yhwh established the sun in the heavens,[45]
> he said that he would dwell in a thick cloud.
> I have built you a princely house,
> a dais for your eternal enthronement.[46]

41. Noth, *Könige*, 174–82; the source which Würthwein (*Bücher der Könige*, 84–91) reconstructs within vv. 1–13 hardly mentions Solomon at all.

42. Hence, the point is not Solomon's lack of interest in the ark, as opposed to his keen interest in the cherubim (Würthwein, *Bücher der Könige*, 86–91), but the endorsement by traditional leaders of Solomon's innovation.

43. The MT and the LXX differ significantly in 8:1–6, but these elements are common to both.

44. If the Priestly account of divine presence at the tabernacle is based upon an older tradition, the Deuteronomist may be drawing an implicit analogy between God's manifestation at the tent of assembly and his manifestation at the temple. Compare Exod 33:7–11 with Exod 40:33–38, and see the discussions of R. J. Clifford, "The Tent of El and the Israelite Tent of Meeting," *CBQ* 33 (1971) 221–27; M. Haran, *Temples and Temple-Service in Ancient Israel: An Inquiry into the Character of Cult Phenomena and the Historical Setting of the Priestly School* (Oxford: Oxford University Press, 1978 [[reprinted, Winona Lake, Ind.: Eisenbrauns, 1985]]) 194–204; F. M. Cross, "The Priestly Tabernacle in Light of Recent Research," *Temples and High Places in Biblical Times* (ed. A. Biran; Jerusalem: Nelson Glueck School of Biblical Archaeology of Hebrew Union College/Jewish Institute of Religion, 1981) 169–80; Friedman, *Exile and Biblical Narrative*, 48–60.

45. Reading with the LXX. The MT lacks ἥλιον ἐγνώρισεν (the LXX^{L} has ἔστησεν) ἐν οὐρανῷ [['established (LXX^{L} set) the sun in the heavens']]. I follow J. Gray's reconstruction (*I and II Kings* [OTL; 2d ed.; Philadelphia: Westminster, 1970] 195–96).

46. In 8:13 I read בנה בניתי בית זבל לך [['I have built for you a stately house']] with the MT. The LXX of 8:53 has οἰκοδόμησον οἶκόν μου οἶκον ἐκπρεπῆ σεαυτῷ [['build my house, a preeminent house for yourself']], while 2 Chr 6:2 reads ואני בניתי בית זבל לך [['I have built a stately house for you']].

Even though the Deuteronomist later (in 8:27) distances himself from the immanentization of divine presence proclaimed by his source, his very inclusion of this affirmation underscores the sanctity of the new sanctuary. The transition from one era in Israel's cultic history to another is successful. The manifestation of Yhwh's glory constitutes public proof of a divine *imprimatur* ⟦'stamp of approval'⟧. Although the Deuteronomist privileges the ark with copious coverage, he ⟦242⟧ subordinates its status to that of the temple which is its permanent abode. Simply by (re)presenting the roving ark as something needing a fixed home, the Deuteronomist implies that the ark served only a penultimate role, until a "place for the ark" could be built (8:21). The portable ark plays no continuing role, except as part of its permanent home. Conversely, by presenting the temple as enduring, the Deuteronomist portrays worship at the temple of Jerusalem as definitive for succeeding generations.

The Deuteronomist's supersessionist view of the temple elucidates why he makes no attempt to draw a parallel to the movement of the ark later in 1 Kings 8. The transfer of the ark is a unique event, consummating one era and inaugurating another. The ancient palladium has fulfilled its purpose. Hence, after 1 Kgs 8:21, the ark is never again mentioned in the Deuteronomistic History.[47] Instead, Solomon and the people celebrate "the festival" and offer thousands of sacrifices to honor Israel's permanent new shrine (8:62–64).

The First Blessing: The Temple and the Davidic Promises

If 1 Kgs 8:3–13 reflects the Deuteronomist's concern to integrate the temple into Israel's cultic history, Solomon's two blessings reflect the Deuteronomist's concern to integrate the temple into the framework of Israel's political and legal history.[48] It is certainly revealing that the Deuteronomist

47. The omission does not seem accidental. See, for instance, 2 Chr 35:3; Jer 3:16.

48. On the deuteronomistic clichés in 8:14–21, see Weinfeld, *Deuteronomy*, 324 (no. 1a), 326 (nos. 5, 6), 354 (no. 3). I regard parts of 8:25–26 as a later addition inserted by repetitive resumption from 8:25 ("and now Yhwh, God of Israel, observe to your servant David, my father") to the beginning of 8:26 ("and now Yhwh, God of Israel, may the promise about which you spoke to your servant David my father be fulfilled"). The author of this resumption stresses that the dynastic promise to David is unfulfilled and, for that reason, is contingent upon the continuing fealty of the Davidids. I would attribute 8:25–26 to the same exilic (or, less likely, postexilic) author who wrote 1 Kgs 2:4 and 9:4–5. Such additions (cf. 1 Kgs 6:11–14, present in the MT but missing from the LXX^{B}) are aimed less at criticizing the Davidids or the temple itself than they are at conditioning the inviolable divine promises to these institutions (pace L. Eslinger, *Into the Hands of the Living God* [JSOTSup 84; Sheffield: Almond, 1989] 155–81). Because the additions underscore the need for Davidic or Israelite fidelity and do not impugn the temple, they defend the reputation of the temple. See Knoppers, *Two Nations under God 1*, 99–112.

incorporates the relations of the newly completed temple to the Davidic promises (8:14–21) and to the Mosaic laws (8:55–61) under the rubric of blessing, and that in both cases the blessing extends to God and people.[49] [[243]] The dedication of Solomon's shrine confirms both David and Moses, the two most dominant figures in the Deuteronomistic History.

In coordinating the temple with the promises of David and the words of Moses, the Deuteronomist does not attempt to eradicate the differences between them. The rise of David, the Deuteronomist acknowledges, was relatively recent. Yet, such a historic event as the dedication of the long-awaited temple by an upstart royal house could not have occurred without the active involvement of Yhwh in Israel's history. In this regard, Solomon's first blessing resembles a concern with dynastic legitimacy found in a number of ancient Near Eastern royal dedicatory inscriptions and prayers.[50] The successful completion of the temple effects a bond between king and deity, confirming the king's right to rule.[51] For the Deuteronomist, the successful dedication of the central shrine validates Nathan's dynastic oracle (2 Sam 7:5–16) as well as David's prayer (2 Sam 7:18–29).[52]

> From the day I brought my people Israel from Egypt I never chose any city from any of the tribes of Israel[53] to build a house for the presence of my name [and I never chose any man to be ruler over my people Israel, but I chose Jerusalem for the presence of my name][54] and I chose David to be[55] in charge of Israel. (1 Kgs 8:16)

49. J. Levenson ("The Davidic Covenant and Its Modern Interpreters," *CBQ* 41 [1979] 204–19) summarizes the two dominant scholarly attempts to articulate the relationship of the Davidic covenant to the Mosaic covenant as integrationist on the one hand and segregationist on the other. If my analysis is correct, the relation of these two covenants was already debated among the intelligentsia of ancient Israel.

50. Hurowitz (*I Have Built*, 32–128) provides an extensive overview.

51. B. Halpern, *The Constitution of the Monarchy in Israel* (HSM 25; Chico, CA: Scholars, 1981) 31.

52. For a detailed study of the relations between the prayers of David, Solomon, and Hezekiah in both the Deuteronomistic History and the Chronicler's history, see R. L. Pratt, *Royal Prayer and the Chronicler's Program* (diss., Harvard University, 1987; Ann Arbor, MI: University Microfilms International).

53. Instead of the MT's מכל שבטי ישׂראל, the LXX[B] reads ἐν ἑνὶ σκήπτρῳ.

54. I read the bracketed clauses with 2 Chr 6:5–6 and 4QKgs[a] (see Trebolle Barrera, "Text-Critical Use," 287). The MT of 1 Kgs 8:16 omits through haplography (*homoioteleuton*) [['accidental omission by scribe because of consecutive words or phrases with same final letter(s)']] ולא בחרתי . . . להיות שמי שם [['I did not choose . . . that my name might be there']] (from להיות שם שמי [['that my name might be there']] to להיות שמי שם [['that my name might be there']]). See also the LXX[B] of 8:16. The MT as it stands contains a *non sequitur.* Yhwh responds to his previous history of never electing a city by electing David.

55. The Syriac and the targum of 2 Chr 6:6 add the equivalent of נגיד [['ruler']] here. I read with the MT of Kings and Chronicles (*lectio brevior* [['shorter reading']]).

Hence, the Deuteronomist actually champions the novelty of the deity's choice of ruler and city. This divine election benefits Israel. In the deuteronomistic construction of a new epoch, chosen people, chosen city, and chosen king belong together. That each choice is unprecedented paradoxically magnifies its importance.

The rest of Solomon's blessing explains how two of the Davidic promises have been fulfilled. In the *traditio* [['reworking of tradition']] of 1 Kgs 8:17–21 Solomon commends [[244]] the intentions of his father.[56] David "did well" in wishing to build a house for the name of Yhwh (8:18). What David was proscribed from doing, his son was divinely called to do.

> When your days are complete and you rest with your fathers, I will establish your seed after you, who stems from your own loins, and I will establish his kingship.[57] He shall build a house for my name and I shall establish his throne forever.[58] (2 Sam 7:12–13)

According to Solomon, Yhwh has confirmed his pledge to David by providing him with dynastic succession (1 Kgs 8:17–18). David's royal son, for his part, has realized his function in Nathan's prophecy by building the temple (8:19–21). Hence, Solomon twice refers to the fulfillment of Nathan's promises: אשר דבר בפיו אל דוד אבי ובידו מלא [['who with his hand has fulfilled what he promised with his mouth to David my father']] (8:15);[59] אשר שמרת לעבדך דוד אבי ותדבר בפיך ובידך מלאת כיום הזה [['You have kept the promises you made to your servant, my father David; you spoke with your mouth, and with your hand you have fulfilled it this day']] (8:24).[60] In the deuteronomistic presentation, history is providential. The divine choice of a particular city and ruler have coalesced in Solomon's tenure to secure a permanent place for the ark of the covenant (8:21). The dedication of the temple, therefore, confirms not only Solomon but David as well (8:15, 24, 66).

56. In the *traditum* [['tradition']] of 2 Sam 7:1–7 Nathan rebuffs David's initial plan to build the temple but later qualifies this disapproval by merely delaying the construction of the temple until the reign of David's successor and son; see M. Fishbane, *Biblical Interpretation in Ancient Israel* (Oxford: Clarendon, 1985) 396–97.

57. Reading with the MT and the LXX^{B}. The LXX^{A} adds "forever."

58. In 2 Sam 7:13 I read with the LXX^{BLMN}. The MT adds ממלכתו [['of his kingdom']]. See further P. K. McCarter, *II Samuel* (AB 9; Garden City, NY: Doubleday, 1984) 194.

59. Pennoyer ("1 Kings 8") points out that the apparatus of *BHS* for 8:15 is in error. I read אל [['to']] before "David" (with the Vg and a few Hebrew manuscripts) rather than the MT's את [[definite object marker]] (*lectio facilior* [['easier reading']]). The LXX has περί (= על [['concerning']]). Later in the verse I read בידו [['his hand']] with the MT rather than the בידיו [['with his hands']] reflected by the LXX and the Syriac.

60. In 8:24 the MT reads את אשר דברת לו [['what you told him']] after דוד אבי [['David my father']]. I read with the LXX, which lacks this phrase (*lectio brevior* [['shorter reading']]).

A Prayer for Prayer: Solomon's First Invocation

Like Solomon's two blessings, Solomon's two invocations integrate the newly completed temple into Israelite life. Having blessed Yhwh for actualizing past promises, Solomon draws the deity's attention to "the prayer of your servant" (1 Kgs 8:28). In his invocations Solomon requests that the deity heed his prayer, and he offers reasons why the deity should do so. Solomon's first invocation is specifically focused on why Yhwh should consider "the prayer your servant is praying at this place" (8:29). Solomon's rationale trades on deuteronomic "name" theology. The authors of Deuteronomy champion a single sanctuary as essential to Israel's duty, once the people find [[245]] their promised rest in the land.[61] This shrine is to play a critical role, in fact the only legitimate role, in Israel's sacrificial life.[62] When Solomon has fulfilled the deity's command to build this central sanctuary, he asks, in turn, that Yhwh his god pay heed "day and night" to the prayer and supplication offered there. Hence, Solomon justifies his request on the basis of Yhwh's own mandate for a center of worship, "the place of which you said, 'my name shall be there' " (8:29).

Solomon's first invocation sets a pattern for his petitions by affirming the deity's residence in the heavens. In the deuteronomistic schema, Yhwh resides in the heavens, and Israel resides on its land, but the temple is the place for Yhwh's name.[63] Given the gap between the heavens and the earth, Solomon is concerned with the deity's answering "the cry and the prayer which your servant prays before you this day" (8:28). Such terminology centered on royalty need not indicate, however, one of the oldest layers in 1 Kings 8.[64] While it is true that Solomon later prays only for the people, in his invocation he makes no request except for divine attentiveness to his prayer. In other words, Solomon prays that his prayer may open a channel of communication between a transcendent God and his earthly temple. In the present context, the prayer offered "this day" is the

61. Deut 12:10. The Deuteronomist promotes Solomon's reign as the realization of this rest (1 Kgs 5:15–26; 8:59); see G. von Rad, *The Problem of the Hexateuch and Other Essays* (New York: McGraw-Hill, 1966) 94–98, and chaps. 2–3 in Knoppers, *Two Nations under God 1.*

62. A. D. H. Mayes, *Deuteronomy* (NCB; Grand Rapids: Eerdmans, 1979) 220–30; M. Weinfeld, *Deuteronomy 1–11* (AB 5; Garden City, NY: Doubleday, 1991) 37–53, 74–78.

63. Even as commentators agree that the Deuteronomist's "name" doctrine is an important component of his theology, they debate the precise significance of the doctrine; see G. von Rad, *Studies in Deuteronomy* (SBT 9; London: SCM, 1953) 38–39; G. E. Wright, "The Temple in Palestine-Syria," *BA* 7 (1944) 66–77; M. Metzger, "Himmlische und irdische Wohnstatt Jahwes," *UF* 2 (1970) 139–58; S. Terrien, *The Elusive Presence: Toward a New Biblical Theology* (Religious Perspectives 9; San Francisco: Harper & Row, 1978) 161–98; Mettinger, *Dethronement of Sabaoth*, 19–37, 46–52.

64. Contra Dietrich, *Prophetie und Geschichte*, 74; Würthwein, *Bücher der Könige*, 97–100; Jones, *1 and 2 Kings*, 201; O'Brien, *Deuteronomistic History Hypothesis*, 157.

prayer which follows, addressing the various predicaments in which the people may find themselves (8:31–51).[65] Solomon's invocation is actually altruistic. The prayer he offers exploits his special position, as king, to intercede in behalf of his people.

The Temple as a Place for Prayer

The transfer of the ark, the theophany, the blessing, and the invocation establish the context within which the Deuteronomist wishes the temple's [[246]] function to be understood. Solomon's seven petitions actively promote the temple as a site of popular prayer. In the disparate circumstances which Solomon portrays, Israelites are to journey to Jerusalem and to pray "at this house." In this manner, Solomon's prayer becomes a unifying symbol in Israel's worship.

Solomon's Sevenfold Prayer

Solomon's prayer directs Israel's attention in various situations–in famine, drought, war, pestilence, injustice, defeat, and exile–to his royal shrine. Justice is contingent upon divine attention to proceedings at the temple (1 Kgs 8:31–32). Droughts can end, if the people "pray toward this place, praise [Yhwh's] name, and repent from their sins" (8:35–36). Military defeats caused by Israelite sin are reversible, if the people turn back to Yhwh, confess his name, and pray "at this house" (8:33–34).[66] Conversely, military campaigns can succeed, even at some distance from the temple, if the Israelite combatants pray in the direction of the city and temple and implore Yhwh for his aid (8:44–45). Even in the case of deportees sent to a land "far or near," the Deuteronomist suggests prayer in the direction of their land, city, and temple, so that they may find "compassion in the sight of their captors" (8:46–51).

The Deuteronomist also promotes an international role for the temple. In the ancient Near East palace-temple complexes communicated the power of a king (and his gods) to his people, his vassals, and foreign emissaries.[67] Recognition of the temple-palace's role in advancing royal

65. Hence, this is a "prayer *about* prayer" (G. Savran, "1 and 2 Kings," *The Literary Guide to the Bible* [ed. R. Alter and F. Kermode; Cambridge, MA: Belknap, 1987] 157). See also the comments of Balentine, *Prayer in the Hebrew Bible*, 80–81.

66. Jepsen (*Quellen*, 15–17) and Noth (*Könige*, 174) contend that the exilic predicament of vv. 46–51 repeats the putative exilic predicament of vv. 33–34, but, as Gray demonstrates (*I and II Kings*, 226–29), these passages address different situations.

67. A. S. Kapelrud, "Temple Building, a Task for Gods and Kings," *Or* 21 (1963) 56–62; G. W. Ahlström, *Royal Administration and National Religion in Ancient Palestine* (Studies in the History of the Ancient Near East 1; Leiden: Brill, 1982) 10–26; K. W. Whitelam, "The Symbols

propaganda clarifies one of the Solomonic petitions. Solomon intercedes for those foreigners who, having heard of Yhwh's "great name, . . . mighty hand, and . . . outstretched arm," journey to Jerusalem to pray at the temple. When Yhwh does according to all that the foreigner bids, all the peoples of the earth will come [[247]] to know Yhwh's name and fear him, recognizing that Yhwh's name is invoked at this house (8:41–43).[68]

The various predicaments addressed by Solomon present the temple as foundational to national security and well-being. The resonance between Solomon's two invocations and his central petition underscores this point. The temple is the appropriate site for any prayer and any supplication. By the end of Solomon's seven solicitations, it becomes clear that the Deuteronomist intends Solomon's prayer to function as a model for popular intercession with Yhwh. Considering the programmatic function of Solomon's prayer, it is highly unlikely that this deuteronomistic composition was authored during the Babylonian exile. Why would an exilic writer extend and expand the function of a temple that had been destroyed? The deuteronomistic trope of the temple as a site for prayer promotes the temple's value rather than devalues it.[69] Moreover, why would an exilic author list in such detail the various circumstances–purgatory oaths, famine, drought, blight, pestilence, military defeat–in which the temple could be a channel of blessing and justice to people in the land?[70]

The programmatic nature of Solomon's blessing, invocation, and prayer is most easily understood in the context of the late preexilic period, the time in which the Deuteronomist likely wrote his work. This writer enhances the temple's prestige in Jerusalem, Judah, and beyond by presenting the temple as pivotal to the livelihood of present and future generations. The Deuteronomist does not deny the existence of other Yahwistic sanctuaries in the time of Solomon (see, e.g., 1 Kgs 3:4), but he champions Solomon's sanctuary as central to Israel's well-being. Many of

---

of Power: Aspects of Royal Propaganda in the United Monarchy," *BA* 49 (1986) 166–73; C. Meyers, "The Israelite Empire: In Defense of King Solomon," *Backgrounds for the Bible* (ed. M. P. O'Connor and D. N. Freedman; Winona Lake, IN: Eisenbrauns, 1987) 181–97; G. A. Anderson, *Sacrifices and Offerings in Ancient Israel* (HSM 41; Atlanta: Scholars, 1987); S. Lackenbacher, *Le palais sans rival: Le récit de construction en Assyrie* (Paris: La découverte, 1990).

68. I grant that this concern for the plight of foreigners is unusual in the Deuteronomistic History, but I would not attribute 1 Kgs 8:41–43 to a late hand for that reason (pace C. Westermann, *Isaiah 40–66* [OTL; Philadelphia: Westminster, 1969] 412–13; Würthwein, *Bücher der Könige*, 96, 99; Jones, *1 and 2 Kings*, 202–4; and Balentine, *Prayer in the Hebrew Bible*, 85). The concern is consistent with the imperialistic tenor of Solomon's reign. A similar international role for the temple is envisioned in Solomon's second blessing (1 Kgs 8:59–61).

69. Contra Noth, *Deuteronomistic History*, 94.

70. Gray, *I and II Kings*, 222–27; Friedman, *Exile and Biblical Narrative*, 21; Halpern, *First Historians*, 168–74.

Solomon's petitions uphold the temple as a source of hope by advancing its role in addressing perennial problems, such as war, disease, plagues, and famines. Other petitions, however, have particular programmatic value in the context of the late preexilic period. As Gray observes, Solomon's intercession for Israelites dispossessed from their land by war, for example (1 Kings 8:33–34), would be particularly relevant for those Northerners who immigrated south to Judah following the [[248]] Assyrian exile.[71] They could use "this house" to plead for restoration to their land. The petition would also have value, however, for many Judaeans. After all, the Assyrian conquests of the eighth century did not affect Israel alone.[72] Even the petition concerning exile need not be exilic.[73] By the late seventh century, exile was an obvious possibility for the remaining inhabitants of Jerusalem and Judah.[74] To these people the Deuteronomist wrote a *plaidoyer* [['speech for defense']] on behalf of the Davidic king and his sanctuary. The temple is not simply a royal chapel or the sole legitimate place for sacrifice; it is also the divinely approved channel of blessing and forgiveness secured through prayer.

71. Gray, *I and II Kings*, 223–24; M. Broshi, "The Expansion of Jerusalem in the Reign of Hezekiah and Manasseh," *IEJ* 24 (1974) 21–26. Hence, J. Wellhausen's objection (*Die Composition des Hexateuchs und der historischen Bücher des Alten Testaments* [4th (= 3d) ed.; Berlin: de Gruyter, 1963] 270–71) that the Northerners did not acknowledge the sanctity of the temple of Jerusalem is misguided on two fronts. First, there is evidence that at least some northern Israelites supported the temple (e.g., Jer 41:4–5; 2 Chr 11:13–17; 30:4–11). Second, Solomon's prayer is programmatic, and it need not be historically descriptive.

72. The impact of the Assyrian conquests upon the outlook of the elite in Judah should not be underestimated, even though Jerusalem survived Sennacherib's campaign. The Assyrian campaigns caused tremendous political and demographic changes in Palestine; see A. Mazar, *Archaeology of the Land of the Bible, 10,000–586* B.C.E. (AB Reference Library; New York: Doubleday, 1990) 544–47; H. Tadmor and M. Cogan, *II Kings* (AB 11; New York: Doubleday, 1988) 223–51; B. Halpern, "Jerusalem and the Lineages in the Seventh Century BCE: Kingship and the Rise of Individual Moral Liability," *Law and Ideology in Monarchic Israel* (JSOTSup 124; ed. B. Halpern and D. W. Hobson; Sheffield: JSOT, 1991) 11–107; D. W. Jamieson-Drake, *Scribes and Schools in Monarchic Judah* (JSOTSup 109; Social World of Biblical Antiquity Series 9; Sheffield: Almond, 1991) 48–80; B. Becking, *The Fall of Samaria: An Historical and Archaeological Study* (Studies in the History of the Ancient Near East 2; Leiden: Brill, 1992). Given the detail which the Deuteronomist devotes to agrarian, legal, and martial predicaments, one would expect him to address an event which terminated the Northern Kingdom and left many of its inhabitants in other lands.

73. Given the record of other deportations in the ancient Near East, it seems plausible that the Deuteronomist would address this sort of predicament; yet, as H. W. Wolff ("The Kerygma of the Deuteronomic Historical Work," *The Vitality of Old Testament Traditions* [ed. W. Brueggemann and H. W. Wolff; Atlanta: John Knox, 1975] 91–93 [[pp. 62–78 in this volume]]) remarks, this petition offers exiles only a muted hope.

74. Hence, one need not look only to the events of 597 or 586 B.C.E. for catastrophes which had a decisive impact on the development of the deuteronomistic "name" theology (contra Mettinger, *Dethronement of Sabaoth*, 46–52).

A Prayer for Prayers: Solomon's Second Invocation

Having popularized Solomon's royal chapel as a national site for prayer, the Deuteronomist has Solomon again invoke the deity's attention. But Solomon's second invocation is different from his first invocation in that Solomon prays for the supplications of both king and people. The reason for the change is patent. If Solomon's prayer is influential, ordinary Israelites will [[249]] have recourse to his sanctuary. It would be inappropriate, therefore, for Solomon to continue speaking only of *his* petitions. The expansion of supplicants–from king in 1 Kgs 8:28–29 and people in 8:31–51 to king *and* people in 8:52–indicates deliberate authorial strategy. Israel is to adopt Solomon's prayer as its own.

But if the temple is to function as a channel to the deity for both monarch and laity in all kinds of predicaments, it is vitally important that Yhwh be responsive to their requests. Hence, Solomon asks that Yhwh's "eyes might be open to the supplication of [his] servant and to the supplication of [his] people Israel, listening to them whenever they call upon [him]" (8:52). Yhwh's transcendence need not impede his availability to either king or people. When the deity appears to Solomon following the dedication of the temple, he responds thus to the repeated Solomonic plea: "I have consecrated this house which you have built to place my name there forever; my eyes and heart will be there in perpetuity (9:3)."[75]

The popularization of the temple achieves a number of related ends for the Deuteronomist. Solomonic example and participation in public worship strengthen the status of the Davidids. The promotion of the temple as a place where all Israelites have a stake in their future, in turn, enhances the position of the central shrine, its *realia* [['objects']], and its priesthood. Even the recourse to Israel's election in the exodus (8:53) as grounds for divine attention to Israel's petitions (8:52) buttresses the stature of Solomon's sanctuary. Yhwh's election of one people from all the peoples of the land as his inheritance (נחלה) becomes a rationale for the appropriateness of his heeding petitions offered at this particular site. The orchestration of royal prayers with popular prayers reinforces the bond between God, king, temple, and people.

Solomon and Moses: The Second Blessing

According to G. H. Jones, this blessing "contains a number of strange elements."[76] Recognition that the Deuteronomist uses Solomon's blessings to address the relation of the temple to major institutions–the Davidic

75. Compare 8:29, 53.
76. Jones, *1 and 2 Kings*, 205.

promises and the Mosaic stipulations–elucidates the composition of 1 Kgs 8:55–61. Like the first blessing, Solomon's second blessing begins with a historical retrospect. He exalts the deity for the correspondence between the dedication of the temple and Israel's national beginnings. Solomon blesses Yhwh because he has given his promised rest to his people (8:56). The Deuteronomist thus draws a line from the Israel encamped upon the Plains of Moab to the Israel of the united monarchy.

⟦250⟧ The stress on continuity and fulfillment honors the past by relativizing it. Solomon makes the astounding claim that "not one word has fallen from every good promise he [Yhwh] spoke by the hand of his servant Moses" (8:56). The Deuteronomist thus implies that the words of Moses are incomplete without the Solomonic temple. The allusions to Deuteronomy are ingenious, because the Deuteronomist employs Deuteronomy's own mandate for centralization to ratify the construction of a central sanctuary by a Davidic king. In Solomon's second blessing, Deuteronomy speaks with a new royal voice.

Solomon's second blessing moves beyond the notion that the dedication of the temple represents a new beginning for Israel. The plea "may Yhwh our God be with us as he was with our fathers, may he not abandon us or forsake us" (8:57) reflects a periodization of history. The dedication of the temple inaugurates a new epoch, different from the epoch which began with Israel's ancestors, hence the need for the deity's presence. To be sure, the Deuteronomist does not leave the past behind. The temple's dedication enables Israel to refocus its attention on following divine commands. Solomon prays that Yhwh "might incline our hearts toward him, to follow in all of his ways, to observe his commandments and statutes, which he commanded our fathers" (8:58).[77] Similarly, Solomon concludes this blessing with the hope that "our heart might be at peace with Yhwh our God to follow in his statutes and to observe his commandments as at this day."[78] The temple functions as an inducement toward obedience.[79]

Hence, Israel's situation in the present is not identical to its situation in the past. Solomon prays that his royal prayer may also inspire obedi-

77. Reading לבבינו ⟦'our hearts'⟧ with some Hebrew MSS, the LXX, and the Vg. The MT has לבבנו ⟦'our heart'⟧. Later in the verse I follow the LXX^{B} in omitting the MT's משפטיו ⟦'his ordinances'⟧ (*lectio brevior* ⟦'shorter reading'⟧).

78. In 8:61 I read לבבינו ⟦'our hearts'⟧ (see the LXX and the Vg). The MT has לבבכם ⟦'your (pl.) heart'⟧.

79. J. D. Levenson ("The Jerusalem Temple in Devotional and Visionary Experience," *Jewish Spirituality from the Bible through the Middle Ages* [World Spirituality 13; ed. A. Green; New York: Crossroad, 1988] 33) calls attention to the rabbinic association (e.g., in *m. ʾAbot* 3.3) of God's tabernacling presence (שכינה ⟦'shekinah'⟧) with those who envelop themselves in Torah. The Deuteronomist adumbrates this trope by drawing a connection between the Solomonic temple and one's inclination to observe Yhwh's commandments.

ence, that his requests be near Yhwh day and night to uphold the cause of his servant and the cause of his people Israel (8:59).[80] In the deuteronomistic construction of history, Solomon's petitions have become in and of themselves grounds for hope. Now that the temple has become a constituent part of Israelite life, Solomon's prayer takes on a life of its own. Solomon's petitions are not only a model for Israelites' prayer in diverse circumstances but also a means to blessing and forgiveness.

⟦251⟧ Echoing his earlier concern for foreigners who might hear about Yhwh's great name, Solomon implores Yhwh to tend to the needs of his (royal) servant and people so that all the peoples of the earth may know "that Yhwh alone is God, there is no other" (8:59–60). This, then, is an additional incentive for Yhwh to respond to the exigencies of his people. The knowledge people in surrounding states gain about Yhwh and his incomparable status is linked to Yhwh's treatment of his own king and people.

Festival and Dismissal

Even as the dedication of the temple inaugurates a new era in Israel's history, it begins and ends with cultic institutions of the Sinaitic era. While 1 Kings 8 begins with Solomon convoking the assembly of Israel, overseeing the transfer of the ark to the temple, and offering thousands of sacrifices, 1 Kings 8 ends with Solomon offering thousands of sacrifices, leading "the great assembly" in the commemoration of "the festival," and dismissing an Israel gathered "from Lebo-hamath to the Wadi of Egypt" (8:66). The repeated mention of sacrifice is in itself significant. First, the temple is a place of sacrifice, a point which the Deuteronomist has no interest in denying.[81] Second, the temple dedication is a spectacle not of measure but of imbalance and excess. To assign 8:62–64, or for that matter 8:5, to a late hand, because of the great number of sacrifices, completely misses the point.[82] Third, in 8:5 and 8:62 both Solomon and the people offer sacrifices.[83] Together they also dedicate the temple (8:63). The solidarity between monarch and people is consonant with the prominent role the Deuteronomist accords the people in Solomon's prayer, in his second invocation, and in his second blessing. The sacrifices of king

80. I read 3d sg. suffixes with the MT, rather than the 2d sg. suffixes of the LXX (*lectio difficilior* ⟦'more difficult reading'⟧).

81. Contra Noth, *Deuteronomistic History*, 94.

82. See, for example, Würthwein, *Bücher der Könige*, 101, and O'Brien, *Deuteronomistic History Hypothesis*, 152.

83. The MT of 8:5 mentions Solomon and the עדת ישׂראל ⟦'council of Israel'⟧ offering sacrifices together, but reference to the council of Israel is lacking in the LXX^{B}.

and people not only glorify Yhwh but also endorse Solomon's interpretation of the temple as a national house of prayer.

Like the transfer of the ark, the celebration of the festival legitimates the temple. Conjoining Israel's major festival with the temple's dedication lends an aura of respectability to the latter. Consistent with the pan-Israelite emphasis in other major deuteronomistic compositions, 1 Kings 8 underscores the unanimity and commitment of all sectors of the people to deuteronomistic ideals.[84] The enthusiastic and widespread participation in this feast confirms the success of the temple. King, city, and temple all signify divine [[252]] benevolence to his chosen people. It is no wonder, then, that they "bless the king" as they return to their tents, "rejoicing and glad of heart for all the good which Yhwh did for David his servant and for Israel his people" (8:66).[85]

Conclusions

The efforts of Hezekiah in the eighth century, and especially of Josiah in the seventh century, to eliminate sanctuaries rivaling the temple of Jerusalem must have been controversial and subject to a variety of interpretations.[86] Temples played vital economic and administrative functions in the ancient Near East. Any attempt to destroy an array of cults or to centralize a given cult would have profound economic, social, political, and religious consequences. Supporters of other shrines and their attendant cults would undoubtedly view such reforms with disapprobation. The proscription of high places amounted to "the denial of religious experience to the majority of the population and the creation of a religious vacuum in their midst."[87] Allowing secular slaughter (Deut 12:15) as a way to manage the consequences of having only one site for sacrifice would in itself constitute a direct challenge to the practices of many traditional Yahwists.[88]

84. See Deut 1:1; Josh 23:2; 24:1–2; 2 Kgs 23:1–3; Reviv, "Popular Assemblies," 95–98.

85. I read with the MT. The LXX^B has καὶ εὐλόγησεν αὐτόν (= ויברכהו [['and he blessed him']]).

86. B. Oded, "Judah and the Exile," *Israelite and Judaean History* (OTL; ed. J. H. Hayes and J. M. Miller; Philadelphia: Westminster, 1977) 435–69; J. A. Soggin, *A History of Israel from the Beginnings to the Bar Kochba Revolt, AD 135* (London: SCM, 1984) 231–47; H. Spieckermann, *Juda unter Assur in der Sargonidenzeit* (FRLANT 129; Göttingen: Vandenhoeck & Ruprecht, 1982) 17–160, 307–81; F. J. Gonçalves, *L'expédition de Sennachérib en Palestine dans la littérature hebraïque ancienne* (EBib n.s. 7; Paris: Lecoffre, 1986); R. H. Lowery, *The Reforming Kings: Cult and Society in First Temple Judah* (JSOTSup 120; Sheffield: JSOT, 1991) 142–61, 190–209.

87. M. Weinfeld, "Cult Centralization in Israel in the Light of a Neo-Babylonian Analogy," *JNES* 23 (1964) 202–3.

88. J. Milgrom, "Profane Slaughter and a Formulaic Key to the Composition of Deuteronomy," *HUCA* 47 (1976) 1–17.

In the light of probable resistance to Josiah's actions, it is understandable that the Deuteronomist makes a literary effort to convince his audience of the temple's intrinsic value and its centrality to his people's fate. The Deuteronomist's highly positive depiction of the temple's dedication attempts to fill "the religious vacuum" created by centralization. From its inception Solomon's royal chapel plays the role of a national shrine, the divinely sanctified site for divine-human communication. At its dedication the temple not only was enthusiastically endorsed by all Israelites but also was endorsed by Yhwh himself. The temple, therefore, is vitally important to the people's livelihood. ⟦253⟧ Sacrificial practices may be abolished, curtailed, or redefined in the wake of the deuteronomic reforms, but such wholesale changes in cultic observance do not entail—at least not in the Deuteronomist's view—a movement toward secularization.[89] The temple of Jerusalem, the chief beneficiary of the Josianic reforms, has a crucial cultic and spiritual role to play in the life of Israel.[90] This role, as it is portrayed in Solomon's prayer, is highly benevolent. Human transgression of divine commands may be common, even inevitable (1 Kgs 8:46), but such transgression can be overcome. The temple is the place where people may appeal to the deity for justice and the revocation of calamities caused by their own sins. The range of cases in which such appeal may be made is not limited to any one dimension of life. Natural disasters, military defeats, and human disease are not obstacles to divine compassion and action.

By presenting such a flattering image of the temple in the tenth century, the Deuteronomist attributes seventh-century problems to the era of the two monarchies. If Judah and Israel decline, the fault lies not with their central sanctuary but with other sanctuaries. When Solomon and subsequent kings stray from the standard established during his reign, the ignominy they bring to their people only validates the standard they violate. The decadence of succeeding generations becomes an argument in favor of kingship, temple, and Jerusalem. For Judaeans in the eighth century, Hezekiah's trust in these verities is confirmed by the survival of both

89. Pace Weinfeld, *Deuteronomy*, 191–243, and E. W. Nicholson, "Deuteronomy's Vision of Israel," *Storia e tradizioni di Israele: Scritti in onore di J. Alberto Soggin* (ed. D. Garrone and F. Israel; Brescia: Paideia, 1991) 191–203. See also the cautions voiced by J. Milgrom, "The Alleged 'Demythologization and Secularization' in Deuteronomy," *IEJ* 23 (1973) 156–61.

90. As Levenson ("Jerusalem Temple," 57–58) points out, the spiritual role played by the second temple after its destruction both continued and developed the role it had played in Jewish devotional experience. M. Haran ("Cult and Prayer," *Biblical and Related Studies Presented to Samuel Iwry* [ed. A. Kort and S. Morschauser; Winona Lake, IN: Eisenbrauns, 1985] 87–92) discusses the substantial differences between the nature and role of the temple and the nature and role of the synagogue in the development of early Judaism. In my judgment, the Deuteronomist's emphasis on the first temple as a place of prayer abetted this long process of adaptation.

the Davidic monarchy and Jerusalem in the Assyrian crisis.[91] When Hezekiah is confronted by the Assyrian siege of Jerusalem, he travels to the temple and prays there (2 Kgs 19:14–19), citing Davidic and Solomonic petitions.[92] Yhwh responds to these petitions by delivering the king and the city.

For Judaeans in the seventh century, Josiah's refurbishing the temple, his extirpation of alien cults, and his centralization of official Yahwistic worship [[254]] attempted to reclaim the heritage of the united monarchy. The Josianic abolition of rival cults appears not as a revolution in the history of Israelite worship but as a reform honoring Israel's pristine commitment to its own central sanctuary. The relevance in the seventh century of the Deuteronomist's pan-Israelite emphasis at the temple's dedication is readily apparent. By portraying the enthusiastic endorsement of the temple by all Israelites in the time of Solomon, the Deuteronomist underscores the need for such enthusiastic support by all sectors of the people in his own day. Given the temple's status as a divine-human nexus, Judaeans neglect this shrine at their own peril.

91. McKenzie, *Trouble with Kings*, 108–9; G. N. Knoppers, "'There Was None like Him': Incomparability in the Book of Kings," *CBQ* 54 (1992) 418–25; idem, *Two Nations under God: The Deuteronomistic History of Solomon and the Dual Monarchies 2: The Reign of Jeroboam, the Fall of Israel, and the Reign of Josiah* (HSM 53; Atlanta: Scholars, 1994).

92. Pratt, *Royal Prayer*, 77–90; Knoppers, "There Was None," 421–23.

Dog Food and Bird Food:
The Oracles against the Dynasties in the Book of Kings

Steven L. McKenzie

In recent scholarship, the prophetic speeches against a sequence of Northern kings are regarded as important markers in the deuteronomistic account of the Israelite kingdom. Although some have contended that a major prophetic source or history may be recovered from these texts, McKenzie thinks otherwise. In his study of these prophetic addresses and their narrative contexts, McKenzie argues that these speeches, couched in stereotypical formulae, are heavily edited by the (Josianic) Deuteronomist. The Deuteronomist is fully capable of composing speeches and narrative out of whole cloth. McKenzie also argues that the prophecy and fulfillment notices stem from the Deuteronomist's hand. He concedes that the Deuteronomist have had access to disparate sources, such as individual prophetic stories and official royal annals, but he is disinclined to believe that an earlier prophetic history underlies any of the oracles. In McKenzie's view, the deuteronomistic editing of the monarchical period is more substantial than many scholars, following Noth, have allowed.

[[61]] The book of Kings contains a series of oracles against the first three Israelite royal houses (1 Kgs 14:7–16; 16:1–4; 21:21–24; 2 Kgs 9:6–10). Each of the oracles is accompanied by one or more fulfillment notices (cf. 1 Kgs 15:27–30; 16:11–13; 2 Kgs 9:25–26, 36–37; 10:10, 17).

Reprinted with permission from Steven L. McKenzie, *The Trouble with Kings: The Composition of the Book of Kings in the Deuteronomistic History* (Vetus Testamentum Supplements 42; Leiden: Brill, 1991) 61–80, 153–64.

Against the House of Jeroboam (1 Kings 14:7–18; 15:27–30)

Ahijah's oracle against Jeroboam's house in the context of the consultation concerning his sick son is the first of these anti-dynastic oracles. The judgement portion of the oracle (14:10–11) utilizes a gruesome curse that is also found in the oracles in 16:1–4 and 21:21–24: "The one belonging to Jeroboam who dies in the city the dogs will eat, and the one who dies in the open country the birds of the sky will eat." The curse is leveled against every male (משתין בקיר), 'bond or free' (עצור ועזוב) of the house of Jeroboam (cf. 1 Kgs 16:11, 21:21; 2 Kgs 9:8).

The uniqueness of the curse and the rarity of the expressions משתין בקיר and עצור ועזוב have led some scholars to contend that the language of these verses is not typical of the Deuteronomist and therefore betrays the existence of a predeuteronomistic version of the oracle (cf. Campbell 1986: 24–25; O'Brien 1989: 187). This is an idea that requires examination.

The idiom for males, משתין בקיר [['he that pisses against a wall']], occurs outside of the oracles against the dynasties only in the Abigail story in 1 Samuel 25 (vv. 22, 34). There also it is used in the context of the annihilation of a (royal?) household and could be Dtr's addition or inherent to an older story. The enigmatic expression, עצור ועזוב, occurs outside of the oracles against the dynasties only in Deut 32:36 and 2 Kgs 14:26.[1] The latter passage is clearly from Dtr's hand. Thus, while the possibility that both expressions are predeuteronomistic cannot [[62]] be ruled out there is no concrete evidence that this is the case. Since their few occurrences are all in the DH, it is fair to conclude that Dtr at least imported both expressions and adapted them to his account and that he may have coined them.

The curse itself, in precisely this form, is unique to the oracles against the royal houses in Kings. But similar curses involving unburied corpses are found in Deut 28:16, 26 and in vassal treaties from the ancient Near East (Hillers 1964: 68–69; Wallace 1986: 34–35). It is, then, specifically a curse of non-burial that is drawn from or based on a curse for treaty violations. But in 1 Kgs 14:11 its thrust has been altered. There it is used as part of a prophecy of the annihilation of a royal family or at least of its male members; hence its connection with משתין בקיר. The reference to the boy's burial in vv. 13, 18a also serves to connect the curse of non-burial with the real focus of the oracle–the demise of Jeroboam's house. The same is true of this series of oracles in general. Except for the association of the curse with the story of Jezebel's death in 2 Kings 9, there is no real

1. The exact meaning of the expression remains uncertain in spite of many attempts to solve it. The most recent treatment is that of Talmon and Fields (1989). See also Gray (1963: 307–8), Noth (1968: 316), Saydon (1952), and Würthwein (1985: 177).

concern in these narratives with the burial or non-burial of the royal family. The real interest is in the end of the current dynasty.

It is the downfall of Jeroboam's dynasty, of course, that is exactly Dtr's concern in 14:1–18. The language surrounding the judgement in vv. 7–16 is deuteronomistic, as H. Wallace (1986: 23) has shown.[2] Indeed, the basis in vv. 7–9 for the judgement in vv. 10–11 comes from the same ideology presented by Dtr in the earlier oracle by Ahijah (11:29–39*). Yahweh tore the kingdom from the Davidids and gave it to Jeroboam. But unlike David, Jeroboam was faithless and committed idolatry. There does not appear, then, to be an earlier oracle underlying 14:7–11. Dtr had an older treaty curse of non-burial, but he used it to describe the obliteration of Jeroboam's house because of his failure to be faithful to Yahweh as was David.

It is possible that Dtr used an older prophetic legend, a "consultation of a prophet in the case of illness," as the basis for the story in 14:1–18. Again, Wallace (1986: 22–23) points to the lack of deuteronomistic language in vv. 1–6 and suggests that those verses plus vv. 12, 17, and 18a formed the original legend. He may be correct, but a word of caution is in order. As mentioned in chap. one [[of McKenzie's book]], the original story of the boy's death must have been accompanied by an oracle explaining the reason for it. That reason is now supplied by the Deuteronomist's oracle in vv. 7–16 which has displaced any earlier explanation. [[63]] Hence, if an earlier prophetic story does underlie 1 Kings 14 it can no longer be recovered.

There are three fulfillment notices for the oracle in 14:7–16. The first in 14:18 tells of the death of Jeroboam's son as predicted by Ahijah. The reference to Ahijah the prophet as Yahweh's servant is a deuteronomistic expression. This verse and the similar one in v. 13 serve as Dtr's link between the curse of non-burial and the destruction of Jeroboam's house as punishment for his sins. The boy is blessed with a peaceful death and burial. But the other members of Jeroboam's dynasty are slated for violent overthrow without burial because they were not pleasing to Yahweh.

The notice concerning the fulfillment of Ahijah's words against the dynasty is found in 15:27–30. Dietrich (1972: 59–60) shows that the accounts

2. The passage in 14:14–16 deserves special comment. Verse 14 accords with the foregoing oracle from Ahijah and seems appropriate as it looks forward to Baasha's demolition of Jeroboam's house. Verse 16 also fits well with Dtr's theme concerning the sin of Jeroboam. Along with 2 Kgs 17:21–23 it forms an *inclusio* [['framing through repetition of words or phrases']] for Dtr's scheme tracing the downfall of Israel as the result of Jeroboam's sin. However, v. 15 may be a later gloss. It undercuts the case which Dtr builds against Israel in the series of oracles against the dynasties. It ascribes the fall of Israel to the idolatry of its citizens (cf. 2 Kgs 17:7–18). But this accusation is unprecedented in the previous treatment of Jeroboam.

of conspiracy and succession for Northern kings, based on official records, regularly consist of the elements in 15:27–28. But, 15:29 is an editorial addition giving the fulfillment of Ahijah's word against the house of Jeroboam in MT 14:10–11. It describes the violent end of Jeroboam's family members and points out that this fulfilled Ahijah's prophecy. Dietrich assigns it to his DtrP [[see introduction]]. He also argues (1972: 37) that one expects the fulfillment notice to conclude, like v. 29, with a clause beginning כדבר יהוה [['according to the word of the Lord']] referring back to the prophecy which it fulfills. This is the case with other fulfillment notices (1 Kgs 12:15, 22:38; 2 Kgs 10:17). Verse 30 then specifies the theological reason for the destruction of Jeroboam's house. Its language, especially its use of כעס [['provoke, anger']] is deuteronomistic: "the sins of Jeroboam which he both sinned and caused Israel to sin in his provocation with which he provoked Yahweh." Hence, Dietrich assigns 15:30 to another Deuteronomist, his DtrN.

Dietrich's literary case is well founded. Verses 27–28 contain source materials from official records.[3] Verse 29 is the Deuteronomist's fulfillment notice. But I see no need to take v. 30 as a later addition, as does Dietrich. The notice in 15:30 is very similar to the notice for Zimri in 16:19, which is from the Deuteronomist. The language and thought of 15:30 were drawn from the Deuteronomist's condemnation of Jeroboam for provoking Yahweh with idolatry in Ahijah's oracle (1 Kgs 14:7–9, 10b, 14–16). A similar comment also occurs in regard to the fall of Baasha in 16:13.

In sum, Ahijah's oracle against the dynasty of Jeroboam is the work of Dtr. He used an older treaty curse as the basis for the judgement oracle. But he completely changed the *Sitz im Leben* [['setting in life']] of the curse to refer to the demise of the Northern royal house. The Deuteronomist may have had a prophetic legend about the consultation of Ahijah for Jeroboam's sick son which he used as the setting for his oracle. But that legend cannot be recovered. The Deuteronomist composed the fulfillment notices regarding the boy's death in 14:18 and the fall of Jeroboam's [[64]] house in 15:29. The additional theological explanation in 15:30 is also the Deuteronomist's addition.

Against Baasha (1 Kings 16:1–4, 11–13)

Noth (1967: 82) saw Jehu's oracle in 16:1–4 as the Deuteronomist's composition drawn on the "annalistic" reference to Jehu (16:12) and elements of Ahijah's oracle (14:7, 10–11). Analysis of this passage confirms Noth's

3. On the nature of such official records, see n. 37 in chap. two [[of McKenzie's book]].

basic position. This oracle follows the same structure as the one by Dtr in 14:7–11 (cf. Wallace 1986: 24). A causal clause beginning with יען אשר [['because']] (v. 2; cf. 14:7) introduces the oracle. Then judgement is announced with a non-verbal clause, הנני [['behold']] plus participle (v. 3; cf. 14:10), although the לכן [['therefore']] before הנני [['behold']] as in 14:10 is lacking.

Campbell (1986: 39–41) observes several differences between Jehu's oracle against Baasha's house and the oracles against the houses of Jeroboam and Ahab. (1) Unlike the oracles in 1 Kings 14 and 21, the passage in 1 Kgs 16:1–4 is simply a report of Jehu's oracle without an accompanying narrative. (2) There is no story illustrating how Baasha was "exalted out of the dust" (16:2) and no parallel for the use of that expression in such a context. Campbell calls the expression a "rhetorical flourish" designed to compensate for the lack of an associated story. (3) The accusation in 16:2b consists of elements from judgement formulas which are not represented in the material Campbell assigns to his Prophetic Record. (4) The threat to 'cut off every male bond or free in Israel' (הכרתי משתין בקיר ועצור ועזוב בישׂראל), found in the oracles against Jeroboam and Ahab, is lacking in 16:1–4. (5) There is no general statement ("I will bring evil upon . . .") following "behold" as there is in the oracles against other dynasties. Rather, the "behold" in 16:3 introduces a particular aspect of judgement. Also, the stereotypical curse in 16:4 has לו [['to him']] in its second half, which may betray Dtr's pleonastic style. (6) Baasha's would have been the only Northern dynasty not explicitly rejected by Yahweh in 1 Kings 14–2 Kings 9.[4]

These differences lead Campbell to conclude that the Deuteronomist composed the oracle in 16:1–4. He had no oracle against Baasha in his *Vorlage* [['older text underlying the text in question']]. He was forced, therefore, to write one in order to balance the tradition in 16:11 about the destruction of Baasha's house and to conform to the pattern for the other dynasties. He wrote Jehu's oracle in imitation of the oracles of Ahijah and Elijah against Jeroboam and Ahab respectively.

Campbell's conclusion that 16:1–4 is the Deuteronomist's composition is certainly correct. His sense that 16:2 reflects a deuteronomistic "rhetorical flourish" to compensate [[65]] for the lack of a story is attractive. The second half of that verse consists entirely of favorite deuteronomistic expressions: "you have walked in the way of Jeroboam," "you have caused my people Israel to sin," and "provoking me to anger with their sins."

4. Another difference not noticed by Campbell is the use in 16:3 of the *hiphil* participle (מבעיר אחרי [['I am going to consume utterly']]) in the expression where 14:11 and 21:21 have the *piel* perfect, ובערתי אחרי [['and I will consume']].

But the differences cited by Campbell between the oracles against Jeroboam and Ahab and the one in 16:1–4 are not very significant and do not support his conclusion that only the latter is the Deuteronomist's composition. The lack of an accompanying story for 16:1–4 does suggest that the Deuteronomist had no *Vorlage* for Jehu's oracle. But our treatment of 14:7–18 indicates that even where he may have had an earlier story he still composed the oracle. Indeed, the similarities between 14:7–11; 16:1–4; and 21:21–24 are more striking than the minor differences that Campbell notices. Only the absence of the expression, "I will cut off every male bond or free in Israel," from 16:1–4 is noteworthy. Even so, a very similar expression, משתין בקיר וגאליו ורעהו [['male or his kinsman or his friend']], occurs in the fulfillment notice in 16:11.

The fulfillment notices for Jehu's oracle in 16:11–13 match perfectly the fulfillment notices in 15:29–30 for Ahijah's oracle against Jeroboam. Just as 15:27–28 seem to derive from an official record of Baasha's usurpation, so 16:9–10 contain an official report of Zimri's *coup*. Then vv. 11–12 are Dtr's addition. We have seen that the idiom משתין בקיר in 14:10 reflects Dtr's use of the curse of non-burial (14:11) against Jeroboam's house. Its occurrence in 16:11 also betrays Dtr's hand. As in 15:29, 16:11–12 tell of the destruction of the royal house in accord with a prophetic oracle and end with a כדבר יהוה [['according to the word of the LORD']] clause. Finally, the theological explanation in 16:13, like the one in 15:30, is also probably Dtr's addition. The two verses are nearly identical.[5]

15:30	*16:13*
על חטאות ירבעם	אל כל חטאות בעשא
[['because of the sins of Jeroboam']]	[['all of the sins of Baasha']]
	וחטאות אלה בנו
	[['and the sins of his son Elah']]
אשר חטא	אשר חטאו
[['which he committed']]	[['which they committed']]
ואשר החטיא את ישׂראל	ואשר החטיאו את ישׂראל
[['and which he caused Israel to commit']]	[['and which they caused Israel to commit']]
בכעסו אשר הכעיס את יהוה	להכעיס
[['thereby vexing the LORD']]	[['vexing']]
אלהי ישׂראל	את יהוה אלהי ישׂראל
[['the God of Israel']]	[['the LORD, the God of Israel']]
	בהבליהם
	[['with their false gods']]

Since 16:1–4 is so clearly Dtr's composition there can be no question of an underlying, prophetic oracle matched by a fulfillment notice in

5. The line "and the sins of Elah his son" in 16:13 is superfluous and may be an even later gloss. The same thing may also be true of the reference to "their idols" at the end of the verse.

16:11–12. Both must be Dtr's. This poses a difficulty for Campbell's reconstruction of [[66]] a Prophetic Record in the book of Kings. He never explains why his Prophetic Record had a gap in its treatment of the house of Baasha. It is hard to imagine a running prophetic account of the Israelite monarchy that would not include an oracle against one of its dynasties.[6]

A further illustration of Dtr's use of these fulfillments notices can be seen in the account of Zimri's death (1 Kgs 16:18–19). The account of Omri's victory over Zimri and Tibni in 16:15b–18, 21–24 seems to draw on official Israelite records. Verses 15a, 19–20, 25–28 are evident deuteronomistic additions. The addition of v. 19 is particularly significant. The story of Zimri's rebellion and brief reign ends perfectly appropriately with his death in v. 18. Verse 19 is Dtr's theological explanation for Zimri's demise. Zimri fell because of the sins he committed and because he walked in the way of Jeroboam and in "the sin which he caused Israel to sin," even though he only reigned seven days. This explanation is similar to those used for the destruction of the houses of Jeroboam and Baasha, and may have motivated them. In addition to his own sins, however, Dtr explains that Zimri "walked in the way of Jeroboam and in his [Jeroboam's] sin which he did to make Israel sin." Dtr composed no oracle regarding Zimri's death as he had for Baasha's house, perhaps because of the brevity of Zimri's reign. Consequently, there is no fulfillment notice, and Dtr's theological remark in 16:19 is added directly to his official source.

Against Ahab (1 Kings 21:20–24; 2 Kings 9:1–10:17)

The oracle against the "house of Ahab" occurs in the context of the story of Naboth's murder (1 Kings 21) and is fulfilled in Jehu's rebellion (2 Kings 9–10). The two stories were originally unrelated but have been linked by secondary additions. The signs of literary reworking that abound in both passages have exercised scholars considerably for years.[7]

6. The doublet in 16:7, as Dietrich (1972: 10, n. 2) puts it, *hat viel Kopfzerbrechen gemacht* [['has generated much perplexity']]. Most scholars have discounted the verse as a late corruption of vv. 1–4 (Dietrich 1972: 10, n. 2). However, Seebass (1975: 175–79) has argued for taking v. 7 as the original report of Jehu's word and seeing vv. 1–4 as a secondary interpretation of it. The location of v. 7 is secondary, of course, because it lies outside of the regnal formulas for Baasha. But, Seebass contends that a brief notice like 16:7 would fit much better between 15:34 and 16:5 than does the more detailed version in 16:1–4. He posits that Jehu's oracle against Baasha originally consisted of 16:7 plus 16:3a but that it was displaced with 16:1–4. O'Brien (1989: 193) describes 16:7 as an addition in two stages to emphasize that Jehu's oracle was against Baasha and his house and to clarify the nature of Baasha's sin. I find O'Brien's explanation more attractive than Seebass's.

7. For a review of the literature see Bohlen (1978: 23–31).

1 Kings 21:20–24

[[67]] The Naboth narrative proper in 21:1–16 is markedly different in some respects from the report of Elijah's oracle in vv. 17–29. Jezebel is primarily responsible for Naboth's death in vv. 1–16, but Ahab is the one condemned in vv. 17–29. This and other tensions have led scholars to see in vv. 1–16 a distinct and usually later level of composition or redaction from the original word of Elijah beginning in v. 17.[8] A. Rofé (1988b) has recently buttressed this viewpoint by observing late linguistic features within the narrative in vv. 1–16.

Our focus here is on Elijah's encounter with Ahab in 21:17–29. There is wide agreement that these verses betray more than one hand but very little agreement when it comes to separating various levels of writing within them. I would hazard the opinion that the oldest remaining segment of chap. 21 is in vv. 17, *18, 19a, and perhaps 20abα.[9] These verses introduce an individual condemnation of Ahab. The original content of this condemnation has been supplanted by insertions in v. 19b and vv. 20bβ–29. A portion of the original condemnation may be preserved in 2 Kgs 9:25–26 (see below).

A new level of editing is found in vv. 20bβ–24. Here there is more unanimity among scholars. There is a break in v. 20b beginning with יען [['because']], and the יען clause is a doublet to the introduction of the oracle in v. 19a. Deuteronomistic language is present in the rest of v. 20b, "you sold yourself to do what is evil in Yahweh's sight," and in v. 22, "because of the anger to which you provoked (הכעס אשׁר הכעסת) Yahweh, causing Israel to sin" (cf. Bohlen 1978: 202–5). The structure of this oracle parallels that of the oracles against the houses of Jeroboam (14:7–11) and Baasha (16:2–4), which we determined to be Dtr's work. A causal clause beginning with יען introduces the oracle and is followed by the announcement of punishment, which starts with הנני [['behold']] plus the *hiphil* participle (מביא [['I am bringing']]) in v. 21 (cf. Wallace 1986: 31). Most scholars agree, therefore, in assigning vv. 20bβ–22, 24 to Dtr (Bohlen 1978: 25). As with the previous oracles against the Northern dynasties Dtr has utilized the treaty curse of non-burial in the composition of an oracle detailing his theological reasons for the demise of the royal house.

[[68]] Verses 21b, 24 contain the same judgement as the oracle against Jeroboam in 1 Kgs 14:10–11: והכרתי לאחאב משׁתין בקיר ועצור ועזוב בישׂראל [['I will cut off from Israel every male belonging to Ahab, bond and free']]

8. E.g., Steck (1968: 40–43); Würthwein (1978: 376–77). Otherwise, Baltzer (1965: 76–77); Welten (1973: 24–26). For further bibliography see Campbell (1986: 96, n. 77).

9. Cf. Steck (1968: 43). Others, such as Noth (1967: 83n), contend that v. 20 is secondary because it interrupts the speech of God.

and the same curse leveled against the royal houses of Jeroboam and Baasha: המת לאחאב בעיר יאכלו הכלבים והמת בשׂדה יאכלו עוף השׁמים [['All of Ahab's line who die in the town shall be devoured by dogs, and all who die in the open country shall be devoured by the birds of the sky']]. But two important differences in Elijah's oracle surface in comparison to the other oracles against the royal houses. First, Elijah's oracle is not directed against the founder of the dynasty, Omri, as are the oracles against Jeroboam and Baasha, but against the "house of Ahab." Noth's explanation is that the Deuteronomist changed an individual word against Ahab into an oracle against the royal house in accord with 1 Kgs 14:10–11 (and 16:3–4). But this does not adequately explain why Dtr broke the pattern of the previous oracles against royal houses. The anomaly is best explained with T. Ishida (1977: 177–78) as tendentious, reflecting the view that Ahab's iniquity was the cause of the dynasty's fall, although he was not its founder. Ishida finds a parallel in Amos' designation of the Jehu dynasty as the "house of Jeroboam" (Amos 7:9).[10] Thus, Dtr directed the curse against Ahab because he viewed Ahab as the worst king of Israel.

Secondly, the oracle against Ahab contains the prediction of Jezebel's grisly death in 21:23. Such a prediction is anomalous in the oracles against the dynasties, and v. 23 have evidently been inserted, in rather clumsy fashion with וגם [['and also']], into the oracle against Ahab's house. Again, scholars are nearly unanimous in taking v. 23 as a post-Dtr insertion (e.g., Barré 1988: 10–11; Dietrich 1972: 27; Minokami 1989: 53).

Noth (1967: 83) assigned 21:25–26 to Dtr, and most scholars have continued to affirm their deuteronomistic origin (Bohlen 1978: 28). Verse 25a repeats the expression of v. 20b about Ahab selling himself to do what was evil in Yahweh's eyes, and v. 26, following Dtr's introduction to Ahab's reign (16:29–34), describes Ahab as the worst of Israel's kings. However, the two verses appear intrusive, and it is striking that they do not mention Naboth but focus instead on Ahab's idolatry. They are, therefore, best seen as a late summary of Ahab's reign based on Dtr's account (cf. O'Brien 1989: 203; Würthwein 1984: 252).

The postponement of the judgement against Ahab's house in vv. 27–29 is odd. The contrast between the description of Ahab as Israel's worst king in vv. 25–26 and that of his piety in vv. 27–29 jars the reader. These verses also do not fit the pattern of the oracles against the royal houses.

10. Miller (1967b: 320–24) saw the condemnation of the "house of Ahab" as the result of a conflict over royal ideology in which the prophetic tradition subscribed to the amphyctionic ideal of charismatic leaders and, thus, condemned the "house of Ahab," because Ahab and his sons were the first to succeed at dynastic monarchy. This view is undercut, however, by recent studies showing the dynastic nature of the Northern monarchy (Buccellati 1967: 200–208; Ishida 1977: 171–82; Wallace 1986: 37).

The curses [[69]] leveled at the houses of Jeroboam and Baasha are both enacted against their sons. Why, then, is this delay specifically noted for the curse against Ahab?

Some (e.g., Eissfeldt 1967b: 51 n. 2; Fohrer 1957: 26, 42; Hentschel 1977: 18–20; O'Brien 1989: 203–4; Steck 1968: 45) have tried to explain this anomaly by finding a predeuteronomistic tradition, which linked the Naboth episode with the account of Jehu's revolt, behind these verses. But the deferment in v. 29 of "the evil" (cf. v. 21) until the days of Ahab's son presumes the oracle which Dtr placed in Elijah's mouth in vv. 20bβ–22, 24 (Kittel 1900: 158; Jepsen 1970: 147–48). Also, as Jepsen (1970: 150–52) in particular has observed (cf. Minokami 1989: 35–36) the humbling of oneself, expressed with the verb נכנע is a late theological *topos* [['motif']] which appears elsewhere in the Bible primarily in Chronicles and P (Lev 26:41; 2 Chr 7:14; 12:6, 7, 12; 30:11; 32:26; 33:12, 19, 23; 34:27; 36:12; cf. 2 Kgs 22:19).[11] Therefore, 2 Kgs 21:27–29, are best taken as a postdeuteronomistic addition to this passage by an editor who is already aware of the claim that Elijah's oracle against Ahab was fulfilled in Jehu's revolt.

Two other postdeuteronomistic glosses in Elijah's oracle are worthy of note (cf. Miller 1967b: 312–13). The first is the reference to Samaria (אשר בשמרון [['who is in Samaria']] in v. 18, which stands in tension with the references throughout 1 Kings 21 and 2 Kings 9–10 to Naboth and his property being from Jezreel.[12] The second is the prophecy in v. 19b that the dogs would lick Ahab's blood in the same place where they licked Naboth's blood. The latter is signaled as an addition by the repetition of the command, "and you shall say to him, 'Thus says Yahweh. . . .'" The purpose of both of these glosses was to set the scene for the story of Ahab's death in the following chapter: "And they washed the chariot by the pool of Samaria, and dogs licked up his blood, . . . according to the word of the Lord which he had spoken" (22:38). But, Dtr was unaware of the account of Ahab's death in battle in 1 Kings 22. In his account Ahab died in peace (22:40). Both of these glosses in chap. 21 probably came from the editor who added the story of Ahab's death in 1 Kings 22 to the DH (cf. O'Brien 1989: 201–2).

11. O'Brien's response that the focus of these verses is not upon Ahab as an individual but upon his house (1989: 203) misses the point of the argument regarding the late use of נכנע [['to humble oneself']].

12. All the references to Samaria in chap. 21 are probably glosses. Napier (1959: 366–69) has shown that Jezreel was the original setting for the narrative about Naboth. As he points out, Naboth's "inheritance from his fathers" could hardly have been in Samaria which Omri purchased and built (1 Kgs 16:24). Jezreel is also the setting for the original narrative of Jehu's revolt in 2 Kings 9–10. For a different view see Timm 1982: 118–21.

2 Kings 9–10

[[70]] In the present account, Elijah's word against Ahab's house is fulfilled in Jehu's revolt (2 Kings 9–10). There is general agreement that the narrative upon which these two chapters are based was a straightforward "historical" account, written close to Jehu's reign, later used to justify Jehu's bloodletting.[13] The narrative in 2 Kings 9–10 is sprinkled with references which link it to 1 Kings 21. These references are all secondary additions to the story of Jehu's revolt and provide important hints about the composition of the MT's accounts of that story and the one about Naboth. The recent studies by L. Barré (1988) and Y. Minokami (1989) are particularly helpful for isolating and evaluating these secondary additions.

2 Kings 9:7–10a. Jehu's actions are impelled by a prophetic envoy sent by Elisha to anoint Jehu (9:1–13). The prophet follows his instructions to the letter, as the narrative makes clear:

v. 1 -	לך רמת גלעד [['go to Ramoth-gilead']]	v. 4 -	וילך . . . רמת גלעד [['and went to . . . Ramoth-gilead']]
v. 2 -	ובאת שׁמה וראה שׁם יהוא [['When you arrive there, go and see Jehu']]	v. 5 -	ויבא . . . ויאמר דבר לי אליך השׂר [['When he arrived. . . . "Commander, I have a message for you" ']]
v. 2 -	ובאת והקמתו מתוך אחיו והביאת אתו חדר בחדר [['get him to leave his comrades, and take him into an inner room']]	v. 6 -	ויקם ויבא [['he arose and went']]
v. 3 -	ויצקת על ראשו [['and pour some on his head']]	v. 6 -	ויצק השמן אל ראשו [['and poured the oil on his head']]
v. 3 -	ופתחת הדלת ונסתה [['Then open the door and flee']]	v. 10 -	ויפתח הדלת וינס [['and he opened the door and fled']]

The gap between notices of the prophet's execution of his instructions in vv. 6 and 10 indicates that the extended oracle in vv. 7–10a is secondary, and this has been widely accepted among scholars (cf. Barré 1988: 9). There is nothing about this oracle in Elisha's instructions, and the prophet's elaboration violates Elisha's order not to delay (ולא תחכה v. 3).

13. Wellhausen (1963: 285–87) derived 9:1–10:27 from a literary source which also included 1 Kings 20; 22; 2 Kgs 3:4–27; 6:24–7:20. We have already observed that Noth (1967: 80) derived 2 Kings 9–10 from a cycle of stories, including 1 Kings *11; *12; *14; (20); and 22, which dealt with prophetic intervention in the succession of Israelite kings. However, Noth recognized that these stories were simply similar in subject matter and were not specifically linked: "aber zu beweisen ist das nicht, da es an speziellen Beziehungen dieser Geschichten untereinander fehlt und nur das Thema und die Vorstellung vom Prophetenwort und seiner Wirkung ihnen gemeinsam sind" [['but it cannot be proved since these sections are not specifically linked with each other and they have in common only the subject and the idea of the word of the prophet and its effect', *The Deuteronomistic History*, 109]].

Dietrich (1972: 48; also Barré 1988: 10; Bohlen 1978: 293) notes a further indication of the secondary nature of vv. 7–10a in v. 12b where Jehu reports to his companions what the prophet said to him. He reports verbatim the instructions given by [[71]] Elisha to the prophetic messenger in v. 3: כה אמר יהוה משחתיך למלך אל ישׂראל [['Thus said the Lord: I anoint you king over Israel']] but says nothing about the speech in vv. 7–10a.

This passage has obvious affinities with Dtr's oracles against the royal houses. In vv. 8b–9 it forecasts the destruction of Ahab's house in the same terms as those earlier oracles: והכרתי לאחאב משׁתין בקיר ועצור ועזוב בישׂראל ונתתי את בית אחאב כבית ירבעם בן נבט וכבית בעשׁא בן אחיה [['and I will cut off every male belonging to Ahab, bond and free in Israel. I will make the House of Ahab like the House of Jeroboam son of Nebat and like the House of Baasha son of Ahijah']]. At the same time, 2 Kgs 9:7–10a differs from the previous oracles against the dynasties in form and purpose. Unlike the oracles in 1 Kings 14, 16, and 21, 2 Kgs 9:7–10a is not a judgement oracle. The structure common to the oracles against Jeroboam, Baasha, and Ahab—(לכן) הנני + יען (אשׁר) [['(therefore) behold + because (who)']] + *hiphil* active participle is absent from the prophet's word in 2 Kgs 9:7–10a. The previous oracles against the dynasties are all delivered to the king whose house is condemned years before the dynasty actually falls. But the prophet in 2 Kgs 9:7–10a addresses the usurper, Jehu, and impels him to lead his revolt. The word of the prophet in 2 Kings 9 is intended not as a prophecy against the royal house but as a commission for Jehu to begin his revolution (cf. Barré 1988: 109).

The two references to Jezebel within 2 Kgs 9:7–10a are probably later additions. Barré (1988: 11) perceives v. 7bβ (ודמי כל עבדי יהוה מיד איזבל [['and the blood of the other servants of the Lord by the hand of Jezebel']]) as an expansive gloss and prefers to read on the basis of the LXX in v. 8a "And I will avenge the blood of my servants the prophets . . . [which was shed] at the hand of the whole house of Ahab." But v. 7bα may also be an addition. The only previous references to the murder of Yahwistic prophets under Ahab are in 1 Kgs 18:12; 19:10, which I believe to be parts of postdeuteronomistic additions. While the expression "my servants the prophets" is deuteronomistic it could be an imitation in this instance.

The prophecy in v. 10a that "the dogs shall eat Jezebel in the territory of Jezreel, and none shall bury her" also occurs in 1 Kgs 21:23 and 2 Kgs 9:36. In both of these other cases it is secondary. All three passages, therefore, appear to be the work of an "anti-Jezebel" editor (so Barré 1988: 10–11 and Minokami 1989: 59) who may also be the one responsible for revising the story in 1 Kgs 21:1–16.

Thus, the oracle in 2 Kgs 9:7a, 8–9 is Dtr's composition. It draws on the oracles against the royal houses but serves a different purpose, that of commissioning Jehu. It is one of the links that Dtr provides in his prophecy-fulfillment scheme between Elijah's oracle against Ahab in the Naboth incident and the narrative of Jehu's revolt. However, the reference in v. 7b to Jezebel killing all of Yahweh's servants, which alludes in part to the murder of Naboth, is a later addition, along with v. 10a, to the commission composed by Dtr.

2 Kings 9:14–16. Another recent monograph by Trebolle (1984) focuses on these difficult verses and helps to clarify their origin. Trebolle argues (1984: especially 110–25) [[72]] that the "plus" in the LXX^{L} and the Old Latin at 10:36 preserves an Old Greek reading and represents the original form and placement of the notice of Jehu's conspiracy against Ahaziah:[14]

> LXX^{L}: και επορευθη Οχοζιας επι Αζαηλ βασιλεα Συριας εις πολεμον τοτε συνηψεν Ιου υιος Ναμεσσει επι Ιωραμ υιον Αχααβ βασιλεα Ισραηλ και επαταξεν αυτον εν Ιεζραηλ και απεθανεν και ετοξευσεν Ιου και τον Οχοζιαν βασιλεα Ιουδα επι το αρμα και απεθανεν και ανεβιβασαν αυτον οι παιδες αυτου εν Ιερουσαλημ και θαπτουσιν αυτον μετα των πατερων εν πολει Δαυιδ
> [['Ochozias [Ahaziah] went to war against Azael [Hazael] king of Syria. At that time Jou [Jehu] son of Namessei [Nimshi] conspired against Ioram [Joram] son of Achaab king of Israel and he wounded him in Jezrael [Jezreel] so that he died. And Jou shot (with an arrow) Ochozias king of Judah upon a chariot so that he died. His servants brought him into Jerusalem and buried him with his fathers in the City of David.']]

> OLD LATIN: *Cum enim abiiset Ocazias conuictus dolore regis Israel in pugna aduersus Azahel regem Syriae et in uerbo Domini comprehendisset Ieu filium Namessi Hyoram regem Israel filium Ahab et interfecisset eum factum est ut in eodem bello sagittaret Ochoziam regem Iuda in curru quem cum retulissent mortuum pueri eius in Hyerusalem et sepelissent eum cum patribus eius*
> [['So when Ochazias [Ahaziah], smitten with grief for the king of Israel, went out into battle against Azahel [Hazael], king of Syria, and, in accord with the word of the Lord, Ieu [Jehu] son of Namessus [Nimshi] captured and killed Hyorum [Joram], king of Israel, son of Ahab, it was accomplished in the same battle he shot with an arrow Ochozias in his chariot, whose dead body his servants brought back to Jerusalem and they buried him with his fathers.']]

14. The LXX^{B} at this point reflects the καιγε recension [[a recension of the Old Greek identified, in part, by its peculiar use of καιγε]]. However, the Lucianic family of manuscripts and the Old Latin preserve the earlier level. Whether this level is a proto-Lucianic recension, as Cross argued, or the OG as Barthélemy contended, it is the closest extant witness to the OG and frequently preserves OG readings. On this issue and the Greek recensions in general see Shenkel (1968: 5–21) and the bibliography that he cites.

The notice has been fragmented in the MT and the pieces dispersed in the narrative in 8:28–29 and 9:14–15a, which are, in part, duplicates. Since it is unlikely that a later redactor or translator would have reassembled the dispersed elements into a conspiracy notice in its original form, the original conspiracy notice for Ahaziah was probably broken up when it was fused with the narrative about Jehu's revolt in the process of the composition of the MT book of Kings. The original conspiracy notice was a continuation of the formula for Ahaziah begun in 8:25–27. Another "plus" in the LXX^{BL} at 9:16a represents the original placement of the material about Joram's return to Jezreel now paralleled in the MT at 8:29a, 9:15a, which has once again been displaced as a result of the addition of the narrative about Jehu's revolt in this chapter.

Hence, Trebolle identifies the following two insertions relating to 2 Kgs 9:14–16 (cf. 1984: 122–25, 185–89). First, part of the original conspiracy notice (now in LXX^{L}, VL 10:36*) was transferred to 8:28 and used to introduce the narrative about Jehu's revolt. The editor responsible for this transfer [[73]] also added two statements in 8:28 which are not paralleled in the "plus": את יורם בן אחאב [['with Joram son of Ahab']] and ברמת גלעד [['at Ramoth-gilead']]. The same editor also took the reference to Joram's wounding from 9:16a (LXX^{BL}), moved it to 8:29aβ, and composed 8:28b. This juxtaposition created the contradiction currently in the MT regarding the location (Ramot or Jerusalem) from which Ahaziah went to visit Joram. Secondly, the reference to Jehu's conspiracy against Joram was transferred from its original place (LXX^{L}, VL 10:36+) to 9:14a. In order to fit this statement into its context, the composer added 9:14b and moved 9:16a (as in LXX^{BL}) to 9:15a. Then, 9:16aβ ("for Joram lay there") was added to provide a transition.

Thus, in Trebolle's view, the text behind 9:14–16 originally read, "Now King Joram had returned to be healed in Jezreel of the wounds which the Aramaeans gave him when he fought with Hazael, king of Aram. Then Jehu mounted his chariot and went to Jerusalem." The present text in the MT is the work of a later editor who segmented and dispersed the original conspiracy notice throughout the narrative of Jehu's revolt.

2 Kings 9:25–26. In v. 26 Jehu asks Bidkar to recall a threat from Yahweh in response to the murder of Naboth. However, Jehu's recollection differs in several ways from the Naboth story in 1 Kings 21 (Bohlen 1978: 288, 300; Hentschel 1977: 36–37; Miller 1967b: 307–17; Rofé 1988b: 95–97; Steck 1968: 33–34). Jehu does not mention Elijah, who bore the oracle in 1 Kings 21. There is no reference to the presence of Jehu and Bidkar at the encounter between Elijah and Ahab in 1 Kings 21. Also, 1 Kings 21 contains no reference to the execution of Naboth's sons as implied in 2 Kgs 9:26. According to the latter verse, Naboth was killed the day before

(אמש) Yahweh delivered the oracle against Ahab,[15] but 1 Kgs 21:17 does not tell how much time elapsed between Naboth's death and Yahweh's word to Elijah. The oracle attributed to Yahweh in 2 Kgs 9:25–26 sounds nothing like any of 1 Kgs 21:17–29.

The two verses contain inserted material, as a large number of scholars have observed (Barré 1988: 13–14; Bohlen 1978: 282–84; Minokami 1989: 34–39; [[74]] H.-C. Schmitt 1972: 26–27; Schmoldt 1985: 42; Timm 1982: 140–41; Trebolle 1984: 163). Verse 25 disrupts the link between vv. 24 and 27. Ahaziah is impelled to flee (v. 27) by his observation of Joram's assassination (v. 24). The narrative's depiction of the quickness and secrecy of Jehu's revolt would hardly allow Jehu pause to give instructions regarding Joram's corpse while Ahaziah flees (Barré 1988: 14). The secondary nature of these verses is also indicated by the repetition of Jehu's instruction to cast Joram's corpse into Naboth's field:

v. 25a	v. 26b
שׂא השלכהו חלקת	ועתה שׂא השׂלכהו בחלקה
[['Pick him up and throw him into the plot of ground']]	[['So pick him up and throw him unto the plot of ground']]
שדה נבות היזרעאלי	כדבר יהוה
[['the field of Naboth the Jezreelite']]	[['in accordance with the word of the LORD']]

Some scholars (Bohlen 1978: 282–84; DeVries 1978: 90n; H.-C. Schmitt 1972: 26–27; Steck 1968: 33–34, 44–45) suggest that Yahweh's oath in v. 26 was an early prophetic oracle against Ahab (v. 26). They believe that it was applied to the situation under Joram by an apologist for Jehu. This would explain the variation between the references to Naboth in 9:25–26 and the account in 1 Kgs 21:17–26. S. Olyan (1984: 658n) believes that v. 26 was the original word to Ahab following Naboth's murder. It would be appropriate after 1 Kgs 21:17–19a, and we have already observed that 21:19b is a secondary interpolation anticipating the story of Ahab's death in 1 Kings 22. Barré (1988: 14), on the other hand, attributes 9:25–26 to the Deuteronomist. He argues that they display the Deuteronomist's tendency throughout 2 Kings 9–10 to relate Jehu's deeds to Elijah's oracle

15. Miller (1966: 308–11) contends that the word אמשׁ ('yesterday') in 2 Kgs 9:26 indicates that Naboth was killed immediately before the end of Joram's reign and not years before in Ahab's reign. This proposal is ingenious, but Miller does not provide enough evidence to prove it. The word אמשׁ occurs within Jehu's quotation of Yahweh's word when he and Bidkar "were riding behind Ahab." The editor who inserted Jehu's recollection of this word of Yahweh clearly has Ahab's reign and not Jehoram's in mind. Miller needs to show that Yahweh's oath ("As certainly as I saw the blood of Naboth and his sons *yesterday*") was once completely separate from its present context recalling Ahab's day or to produce independent evidence of a connection between Joram and Naboth.

against Ahab. Both Olyan and Barré may be correct. Perhaps Dtr appropriated Elijah's word to Ahab from the original Naboth story and inserted it in 9:25–26 as a fulfillment notice. This would account for the differences between 9:25–26 and the Naboth story in 1 Kings 21 as well as the lack of deuteronomistic language in vv. 25–26.

2 Kings 9:27b–29. Verse 29 contains a variant version (cf. 8:25) of Ahaziah's initial formula. It follows the OG chronology and may come from the same portion of the text reproduced in the LXX^{L} and Old Latin at 10:36+ (Trebolle 1984: 124), but it is clearly out of place here. What is more interesting is the account of Ahaziah's death and burial in vv. 27b–28. Trebolle shows that the reference to the transfer and burial of Ahaziah's body in v. 28 is a third insertion of information from the original conspiracy notice in 10:36+ (see under 9:14–16 above). But Barré (1988: 15) also points out that 9:27bβ–28 are dependent on the account in 2 Kgs 23:30 of Josiah's death at Megiddo and transfer to Jerusalem and burial there: [[75]]

9:28abα	*23:30a*
וירכבו אתו עבדיו [['His servants conveyed him in a chariot']]	וירכבהו עבדיו מת ממגדו [['His servants conveyed his body in a chariot from Megiddo']]
ירושלמה [['to Jerusalem']]	ויבאהו ירושלם [['and brought him to Jerusalem']]
ויקברו אתו בקברתו [['and they buried him in his grave']]	ויקברהו בקברתו [['and they buried him in his grave']]

Since he dates the Deuteronomist to the reign of Josiah, Barré sees both passages as the work of a postdeuteronomistic editor.

On the basis of the observations by Trebolle and Barré we may conclude that a late editor inserted 9:27bβ–28. This insertion borrowed partly from the original conspiracy notice for Ahaziah preserved in the Old Latin and LXX^{L} at 10:36+ and partly from the account of Josiah's death and burial in 23:30. This editor was probably the same one who inserted most of 9:14–16 into the MT.

2 Kings 9:36–37. These two verses are the fulfillment notice for the prediction against Jezebel in 1 Kgs 21:23. They have been secondarily attached to the story of Jezebel's death. That story climaxes in 9:35, so that vv. 36–37 are anticlimactic (cf. Dietrich 1972: 60).

Verse 36a (up to לאמר [['saying']]) belongs to the Deuteronomist (cf. Dietrich 1972: 37–38). The expression in 9:36a, 'it was the word of Yahweh which he spoke by his servant Elijah the Tishbite' (הוא דבר יהוה אשר דבר ביד עבדו אליהו התשבי), is similar to the notice in 2 Kgs 15:12, which is certainly deuteronomistic (הוא דבר יהוה אשר דבר אל יהוא [['it was the word that the LORD had spoken to Jehu']]). Verse 37 is also deuteronomistic, as Barré (1988: 15) and Rofé (1988a: 84) have recently contended. The scatological image in v. 37, 'like dung upon the surface of the ground' (כדמן על פני השׂדה) is deuteronomistic. It occurs elsewhere only in Jer 9:21, with a similar expression, לדמן על פני האדמה [['as dung upon the surface of the field']], found in deuteronomistic portions of Jeremiah (8:2; 16:4; 25:33; Bohlen 1978: 299; cf. H.-C. Schmitt 1972: 22). This verse accords both with the curse of non-burial leveled by Dtr against the house of Ahab and with the account of Jezebel's death in vv. 33–35. "These animals crushed Jezebel's corpse until it became unidentifiable, thus fulfilling the prophecy" (Rofé 1988a: 84).

However, v. 36b (+ לאמר [['saying']] in v. 36aβ) is a postdeuteronomistic insertion, since it presupposes Elijah's prediction in 1 Kgs 21:23. That verse, as we have seen, was inserted into the oracle composed by Dtr for Elijah in 21:20bβ–22, 24. The details concerning Jezebel's death in 9:36b do not correspond with those of the narrative that precedes. Verses 33–35 mention only that Jezebel's body was trampled by horses; they do not refer to the dogs that ate her corpse according to v. 36b (Steck 1968: 36; Bohlen 1978: 297). The addition in 2 Kgs 9:36b fulfills the prediction of 1 Kgs 21:23 that is reiterated in 2 Kgs 9:10a [[76]]. The three verses, along with 2 Kgs 9:7b and perhaps the current Naboth story in 1 Kgs 21:1–16, form a late, "anti-Jezebel" retouching to these stories. The addition in 2 Kgs 9:36b is the strongest expression of this anti-Jezebel sentiment. It gives a grotesque change of meaning to Dtr's scatological image in 9:37. Because her corpse is eaten by dogs, what is left of Jezebel is not simply *like* dung on the ground but actually is dung.

2 Kings 10:1a. Recent commentators (Barré 1988: 17; Minokami 1989: 55–56) have observed that this half verse is a tendentious gloss. It is a doublet of v. 6b except that the king with seventy sons in the latter is Joram. The attribution of the seventy sons to Ahab in 10:1a reflects Dtr's programmatic effort to describe Jehu's complete destruction of Ahab's house (with Barré).

2 Kings 10:10–17. Long ago B. Stade (1885: 276–78) advanced the view that 10:17 represented the original continuation of 10:12 and that the intervening material was secondary. Stade was on the right track but did not go far enough. There is good reason to believe that all of vv. 10–17 are a secondary addition to the deuteronomistic narrative.

Most scholars agree that 10:10 is typically deuteronomistic (Barré 1988: 17). Dietrich (1972: 24) says that the verse is *im typisch dtr Predigtstil* [['in typically Dtr preaching style']]. The verse interprets Jehu's massacre of the seventy princes (10:1–9) as an act of piety on his part as he sees to it that Yahweh's condemnation of Ahab's house is fulfilled in detail.

Verses 11 and 17 are very much alike and are best treated together.

10:11	*10:17*
ויך יהוא את כל הנשראים	ויך את כל הנשארים
[['And Jehu struck down all that were left']]	[['and he struck down all the survivors']]
לבית אחאב ביזרעאל	לאחאב בשמרין
[['of the House of Ahab in Jezreel']]	[['of [the house of] Ahab in Samaria']]
וכל גדליו ומידעיו וכהניו	עד השמדו
[['and his notables, intimates, and priests']]	[['until he wiped it out']]
עד בלתי השאיר לו שׂריד	
[['till he left him no survivor']]	

These two verses form an *inclusio* and suggest that the intervening materials, Jehu's murder of Ahaziah's kinsmen (10:12–14) and Jehu's encounter with Jehonadab (10:15–16), are secondary additions to the Jehu narrative. Other considerations confirm this indication. According to 10:1–9, Jehu sent to Samaria to have Ahab's seventy sons killed. There was no need for him to go there in v. 17. Also, a group of princes from Judah would hardly be found, unsuspecting, a day's journey north of Samaria two days after the revolt began in Jezreel (chap. 9) and one day after the massacre in Samaria (10:1–11; Benzinger 1899: 149).

[[77]] Verses 11 and 17 both share the perspective of v. 10 that Yahweh is fulfilling his word against the house of Ahab through Jehu. In fact, the statements in vv. 11 and 17 regarding Jehu's destruction of the members of Ahab's house are very similar to the fulfillment notices for the oracles against the previous two dynasties.

1 Kgs 15:29	*1 Kgs 16:11–12*	*2 Kgs 10:11, 17*
ויהי כמלכו	ויהי כמלכו	
[['As soon as he became king']]	[['As soon as he became king']]	
	כשבתו על כסאו	
	[['and ascended the throne']]	
הכה	הכה	ויך (יהוא)
[['he struck down']]	[['he struck down']]	[['And (Jehu) struck down']]
את כל בית ירבעם	את כל בית בעשא	את כל הנשארים
[['all the House of Jeroboam']]	[['all the House of Baasha']]	[['all that were left']]
לא השאיר	לא השאיר לו	ל(בית) אחאב
[['he did not spare']]	[['he did not spare of his']]	[['of the (House of) Ahab']]
כל נשמה	משתין בקיר	
[['a single soul']]	[['a single male']]	
		(בשמרון)
		[['(in Samaria)']]
		ביזרעאל
		[['in Jezreel']]

לירבעם ⟦'belonging to Jeroboam'⟧	וגאליו ורעהו ⟦'nor any kinsman or friend'⟧	וכל גדליו ומידעיו וכהניו ⟦'and all his notables, intimates, and priests'⟧ (עד בלתי השאיר ⟦'(till he left'⟧ לו שׂריד) ⟦'him no survivor)'⟧
עד השמדו ⟦'until he destroyed it'⟧	וישמד זמרי ⟦'Thus Zimri destroyed'⟧ את כל בית בעשא ⟦'all the House of Baasha'⟧	עד השמדו ⟦'until he destroyed it'⟧
כדבר יהוה ⟦'in accordance with the word of the LORD'⟧	כדבר יהוה ⟦'in accordance with the word of the LORD'⟧	כדבר יהוה ⟦'in accordance with the word of the LORD'⟧
אשר דבר ⟦'that he had spoken'⟧	אשר דבר ⟦'that he had spoken'⟧	אשר דבר ⟦'that he had spoken'⟧
	אל בעשא ⟦'to Baasha'⟧	אל אליהו ⟦'to Elijah'⟧
ביד עבדו אחיה ⟦'through His servant, Ahijah'⟧ השלני ⟦'the Shilonite'⟧	ביד יהוא הנביא ⟦'through the prophet Jehu'⟧	

Since the fulfillment notices in 1 Kgs 15:29 and 16:11–12 are Dtr's, 2 Kgs 10:11, 17 should also be assigned to him. The perspective on Jehu shared by 10:11, 17 with v. 10 also indicates this. The concern of vv. 12–14 for the fate of members of the Southern royal house betrays the hand of a writer from Judah, likely the writer who situated the story of Jehu's revolt within the literary boundaries for Azariah's reign, namely Dtr.

Barré (1988: 18–19) has pointed to indications within the stories in vv. 12–16 that Dtr did not compose them but drew them from sources available to him. The statement in v. 14b that Jehu's men slaughtered the party from Judah seems to contradict his order in v. 14a to take them alive. It betrays the editorial concern expressed in v. 11 to have Jehu kill all who are in any way related to Ahab. Also, the story in vv. 15–16 presupposes the previous acquaintance of Jehu and Jehonadab. But since no word about their former acquaintance is forthcoming the episode here is probably a fragment.

Dtr edited the story of Jehu's revolt to describe how he annihilated the royal family in fulfillment of Elijah's oracle against Ahab's house (v. 11). He then had Jehu move to Samaria so that he could include the stories in vv. 12–16 ⟦78⟧ as encounters between Jezreel and Samaria, and he enclosed those stories within another fulfillment notice (v. 18) after Jehu reached Samaria.

2 Kings 10:18–28. The account of Jehu's destruction of Baal worship from Israel is very different from the foregoing narrative, as several scholars in recent years have noticed (Minokami 1989: 96–97; Würthwein 1984: 242). The section from 9:1–10:17 is concerned solely with Jehu's overthrow of the royal house in fulfillment of Elijah's prophecy and ends perfectly appropriately with 10:17. It says nothing about Baal worship, but that becomes the focus in 10:18–27. In 10:18–27 Jehu acts essentially alone. He does not have the army with him as in the chapter's previous narrative.

The remark in v. 19b and the mention of Jehonadab in v. 23 are editorial (Barré 1988: 20–21). The entire account has been attached by v. 28 to the deuteronomistic summary of Jehu's reign beginning in v. 29. The editor responsible for 10:18–27 may have been Dtr, but a postdeuteronomistic editor seems more likely. The story in 10:18–27 bears similarities to the one in 1 Kings 18, which I believe to be part of a postdeuteronomistic addition to Kings. For instance, the prophets of Baal, who play a large role in 1 Kings 18, are mentioned in 2 Kgs 10:19. It is also striking that the deuteronomistic summary of Jehu's reign in 10:29–31 says nothing about Jehu's destruction of the Baal cult. What is more, while 10:26–27 detail the destruction of the temple of Baal and the מצבות [['pillars']], they say nothing about him destroying the altar of Baal or the Asherah mentioned in Dtr's introduction to Ahab in 1 Kgs 16:32–33 (against Barré 1988: 120).

2 Kings 10:29–36. These verses are widely held to be Dtr's work. Despite Jehu's faithful execution, in Dtr's portrayal, of Yahweh's wrath against the house of Ahab, he was still an Israelite king. As such, he received the same judgement as Dtr gave to every other Israelite king—he persisted in the sin of Jeroboam. But Dtr included something extra in the evaluation of Jehu. Because of his actions against the house of Ahab his dynasty would last to the fourth generation (v. 30). This obvious *vaticinium ex eventu* [['prophecy after the fact']] fits very well with Dtr's interpretation of Jehu's revolt as a whole. Jehu's bloodshed was the faithful execution of Yahweh's word against the evil house of Ahab (Barré 1988: 119–20).

Synthesis

In sum, I assign the following verses from the passages just surveyed in 2 Kings 9–10, at least in their present placement, to Dtr: 9:7a, 8–9, 15a, 16aα, 25–26, 36a, 37; 10:1a, 10:17; 29–36. [[79]] Other additions to the story appear to be from postdeuteronomistic writers: 9:7b, 10a, 14, 15a, 16aβ, 27b–29, 36b; 10:18–28. There is little in the Jehu story outside of these additions to indicate a prophetic origin or editing in the Jehu story. The additions make it clear that it was the Deuteronomist who used the Jehu story to illustrate the fulfillment of prophecy. He linked it with the Naboth episode as the fulfillment of Elijah's oracle against Ahab's house and incorporated the product within his prophecy-fulfillment scheme. There is nothing to indicate that the two stories were connected before Dtr. He followed the same scheme as with the previous oracles against Jeroboam and Baasha, illustrating how the prophetic curse repeated against each dynasty was effected in that dynasty's annihilation. The only difference in the case of Ahab's house was that Dtr had access to a lengthy narrative about Jehu's *coup* which he incorporated within his scheme as the fulfillment of Elijah's word which he set in the context of the Naboth incident.

Conclusions

We began this chapter in search of a running prophetic narrative underlying Dtr's version of the book of Kings. Our results in this quest have been decidedly negative. The Deuteronomist seems to have used individual prophetic stories as the bases for his accounts in 1 Kings 14 and 21. But others of his sources (e.g., 2 Kings 9–10) were not prophetic. Moreover, there is no evidence that the stories about prophetic activity during the reigns of Jeroboam, Baasha, and Ahab were connected with each other at a level underlying Dtr's composition.

The scheme that currently links the oracles against royal houses in 1–2 Kings is Dtr's. He probably borrowed the curse of non-burial from a set of treaty curses. But he applied it to a different context and used it to forecast the fall of the successive Israelite dynasties. He had no prophetic *Vorlage* for any of the oracles against the dynasties. The fulfillments for those oracles were also Dtr's doing, although he drew upon official reports for the details about the downfall of each dynasty. Thus, neither the curse employed by Dtr nor the prophecy-fulfillment scheme offers evidence of a predeuteronomistic prophetic narrative. Nor is there evidence for a scheme of anointings or royal designations in a predeuteronomistic prophetic document as Campbell contended. Some kings and heads of dynasties receive no prophetic designation (Nadab, Baasha, Elah, Zimri, Omri, Ahab), and there is a good deal of variation among the stories of those who do receive some prophetic endorsement (Saul, David, Solomon, Jeroboam, Jehu). All of these materials were first brought together by Dtr within a rubric which he imposed upon them.

The Deuteronomist's creative hand has been involved in every aspect of the development of the narratives analyzed. He has restructured the narratives, revised the oracles, and composed new imitative oracles in order to present a theology of history. This illustrates how Dtr was both an author and an editor. In the [[80]] case of Dtr these two enterprises are not mutually exclusive. This, as we have seen, was Noth's original understanding (1967: 11).

The Deuteronomist obviously had sources which he edited to form his narratives (e.g., 2 Kings 9–10). On occasion he also composed narratives out of whole cloth (e.g., 1 Kgs 16:1–4). By both processes he created a new work of history. He shaped all of his narratives with his own theological perspective. His purpose in the book of Kings was to offer a comprehensive theological explanation of the history of Israel and Judah in the divided monarchy.

Bibliography

Baltzer, K.
1965 Naboths Weinberg (1. Kön. 21). Der Konflikt zwischen israelitischem und kanaanaischem Bodenrecht. *WuD* 8:73–88.
Barré, L. M.
1988 *The Rhetoric of Political Persuasion. The Narrative Artistry and Political Intentions of 2 Kings 9–11.* CBQMS 20. Washington, DC.
Benzinger, I.
1899 *Die Bücher der Könige.* KHC 9. Leipzig.
Bohlen, R.
1978 *Der Fall Nabot. Form, Hintergrund und Werdegang einer alttestamentlichen Erzählung (1 Kön 21).* Trier Theologische Studien 35. Trier.
Buccellati, G.
1967 *Cities and Nations of Ancient Syria.* Rome.
Campbell, A. F.
1986 *Of Prophets and Kings: A Ninth-Century Document (1 Samuel 1–2 Kings 10).* CBQMS 17. Washington, DC.
DeVries, S. J.
1978 *Prophet Against Prophet: The Role of the Micaiah Narrative (1 Kings 22) in the Development of Early Prophetic Tradition.* Grand Rapids, MI.
Dietrich, W.
1972 *Prophetie und Geschichte.* FRLANT 108. Göttingen.
Eissfeldt, O.
1967a 'Bist du Elia, so bin ich Isebel' (1 Kon xix 2). Pp. 65–70 in *Hebräische Wortforschung.* Fs. W. Baumgartner. VTSup 16. Leiden.
1967b Die Komposition von 1. Reg 16, 29–2. Reg 13, 25. Pp. 49–58 in *Das Ferne und Nahe Wort.* Fs. L. Rost. BZAW 105. Berlin.
Fohrer, G.
1957 *Elia.* ATANT 31. Zurich.

Gray, J.
1963 *I & II Kings.* OTL. Philadelphia.
Hentschel, G.
1977 *Die Elijaerzählungen.* Erfurter Theologische Studien 33. Leipzig.
Hillers, D. R.
1964 *Treaty Curses and the Old Testament Prophets.* BibOr 15. Rome.
Ishida, T.
1977 *The Royal Dynasties in Ancient Israel. A Study on the Formation and Development of Royal-Dynastic Ideology.* BZAW 142. Berlin.
Jepsen, A.
1970 Ahabs Buße. Ein kleiner Beitrag zur Methode literarhistorischer Einordnung. Pp. 145–55 in *Archäologie und Altes Testament.* Festschrift K. Galling, eds. A. Kuschke and E. Kutsch. Tübingen.
Kittel, R.
1900 *Die Bücher der Könige.* HAT. Göttingen.
Miller, J. M.
1966 The Elisha Cycle and the Accounts of the Omride Wars. *JBL* 85:441–54.
1967a Another Look at the Chronology of the Early Divided Monarchy. *JBL* 86: 276–88.
1967b The Fall of the House of Ahab. *VT* 17:307–24.
Minokami, Y.
1989 *Die Revolution des Jehu.* Göttinger Theologische Arbeiten 38. Göttingen.
Napier, B. D.
1959 The Omrides of Jezreel. *VT* 9:366–78.
Noth, M.
1967 *Überlieferungsgeschichtliche Studien: die sammelnden und bearbeitenden Geschichtswerke im Alten Testament.* 3rd ed. Tübingen.
1968 *Könige* I. *I. Könige 1–16.* BKAT 9/1. Neukirchen-Vluyn.
O'Brien, M. A.
1989 *The Deuteronomistic History Hypothesis: A Reassessment.* OBO 92. Göttingen.
Olyan, S.
1984 *Haššalom*: Some Literary Considerations of 2 Kings 9. *CBQ* 46:652–58.
Rofé, A.
1988a *The Prophetic Stories.* Jerusalem.
1988b The Vineyard of Naboth: The Origin and Message of the Story. *VT* 38:89–104.
Saydon, P.
1952 The Meaning of the Expression עצור ועזוב. *VT* 2:371–74.
Schmitt, H.-C.
1972 *Elisa. Traditionsgeschichtliche Untersuchungen zur vorklassischen nordisraelitischen Prophetie.* Gütersloh.
Schmoldt, H.
1985 Elijas Botschaft an Ahab. Überlegungen zum Werdegang von I Kön 21. *BN* 28:39–52.

Seebass, H.

1975 Tradition und Interpretation bei Jehu ben Chanani und Ahia von Silo. *VT* 25:175–90.

Shenkel, J. D.

1968 *Chronology and Recensional Development in the Greek Text of Kings.* HSM 1. Cambridge, MA.

Stade, B.

1885 Miscellen 10. Anmerkungen zu 2 Kö. 10–14. *ZAW* 5:275.

Steck, O. H.

1968 *Überlieferung und Zeitgeschichte in den Elia-Erzählungen.* WMANT 26. Neukirchen-Vluyn.

Talmon, S., and W. W. Fields

1989 The Collocation משתין בקיר ועצור ועזוב and its Meaning. *ZAW* 101:85–112.

Timm, S.

1982 *Die Dynastie Omri. Quellen und Untersuchungen zur Geschichte Israels im 9. Jahrhundert vor Christus.* Göttingen.

Trebolle Barrera, J. C.

1984 *Jehú y Joás. Texto y composición literaria de 2 Reyes 9–11.* Institución San Jerónimo 17. Valencia.

Wallace, H. N.

1986 The Oracles against the Israelite Dynasties in 1 and 2 Kings. *Bib* 67:21–40.

Wellhausen, J.

1963 *Die Composition des Hexateuchs und der historischen Bücher des Alten Testaments.* 4th ed. Berlin.

Welten, P.

1973 Naboths Weinberg (1. Könige 21). *EvT* 33:18–32.

Würthwein, E.

1978 Naboth-Novelle und Elia-Wort. *ZTK* 75:375.

1984 *Die Bücher der Könige. 1. Kön. 17–2. Kön. 25.* ATD 11/2. Göttingen.

1985 *Die Bücher der Könige. 1. Könige 1–16.* ATD 11/1. 2nd ed. Göttingen.

Which Oracle Granted Perdurability to the Davidides?

A Textual Problem in 2 Kings 8:19 and the Function of the Dynastic Oracles in the Deuteronomistic Historical Work

Norbert Lohfink

Lohfink disagrees with the scholars who view the Davidic promises (2 Sam 7:5–16) as a composition heavily edited, if not written, by the Deuteronomist. Nevertheless, Lohfink recognizes that the Deuteronomist regularly cites the promises to David in his account of Judahite history. This raises the question posed by the chapter's title: which Davidic promises are cited in Kings? Lohfink pursues a detailed text-critical and exegetical study of one particular text in Kings that bears on this issue (2 Kgs 8:19). He concludes that the conditional dynastic oracles of 1 Kgs 2:4a, 8:25a, and 9:5b, which revise Nathan's dynastic oracle (2 Sam 7:5–16), provide the best insight into the perspective of the Deuteronomist (Dtr^1) on the validity and import of the Davidic promises. Since Solomon fails to live up to the conditions stipulated in these oracles and the Northern Kingdom secedes, one could conclude that the Davidic promises are completely null and void. But Lohfink thinks that there is another dimension to the Deuteronomist's coverage of the divided monarchy. The dynasty founded by David successfully built the Temple in Jerusalem, the city in which God chose to make his name reside. In Lohfink's judgment, the

Reprinted and translated with permission from "Welches Orakel gab den Davididen Dauer? Ein Textproblem in 2 Kön 8,19 und das Funktionieren der dynastischen Orakel im deuteronomistischen Geschichtswerk," in *Lingering over Words: Studies in Ancient Near Eastern Literature in Honor of William L. Moran* (ed. T. Abusch, J. Huehnergard, and P. Steinkeller; Harvard Semitic Studies 37; Atlanta: Scholars Press, 1990) 349–70. Translation by Peter T. Daniels. The NJPSV has been used in this essay for English biblical quotations.

oft-cited pledge of YHWH to grant the sons of David a continuing 'lamp' (*nîr*) in Jerusalem is a new promise that supports their right to rule in Jerusalem and Judah. But in the work of the second Deuteronomist (Dtr^2), the promises to Jerusalem and the Temple are themselves conditioned on the obedience of the kings and people.

[[349]] In the exegetical climate in which I grew up, the language of the deuteronomistic literature, shot through with clichés and stereotypes, was considered cluttered and inexact, the verbiage of epigones. Only under William L. Moran did I learn to pay attention also to the details within this seeming word goulash and to draw conclusions from the tiny differences in formulation and phrasing that the authors often deliberately used because of their view of history and their theology, often with far-reaching consequences. Thus I would like to offer an essay to my honored teacher and "doctor-father" that for once investigates with somewhat more exactitude an apparently very small, hitherto barely noticed, textual problem. It appears in one of the typical, exhaustingly recurring deuteronomistic notices in the books of Kings and involves questions that are all but too wide-ranging.

I

The report in Kings about Joram of Judah (mid-ninth century) occupies just nine verses (2 Kgs 8:16–24), of which six comprise the usual schematic frame (vv. 16–19, 23–24). In the evaluation of the king required by this schema, Joram is characterized negatively in v. 18: "He did what was evil in the sight of YHWH." In v. 19 there follows an explanation of why YHWH did not cause the downfall of the state of Judah at that time, despite this bad king. On the face of it, a downfall was clearly to be expected. First of all, the Masoretic Text reads as follows in BHS:

wĕlōʾ-ʾābâ YHWH *lĕhašḥît ʾet-Yĕhûdâ*
lĕmaʿan Dāwid ʿabdô
kaʾăšer ʾāmar-lô
lātēt lô nîr lĕbānā(y)w kol-hayyāmîm

The English rendition of this text in the NJPSV, which is meant to be a faithful translation of the "traditional Hebrew text," reads: [[350]]

However, the LORD refrained from destroying Judah,
for the sake of his servant David,
in accordance with His promise
to maintain a lamp for his descendants for all time.

This translation prompts me to make three comments.

(a) The key word *nîr* is rendered 'lamp' in accordance with a tradition going back to antiquity (often with messianic overtones) and is thus equated with Hebrew *nēr*. The word first resounds in the divine order regarding the succession of the descendants of the sinful Solomon in Ahijah's oracle to Jeroboam in 1 Kgs 11:36 and then recurs in two evaluations of kings—namely, 1 Kgs 15:4 and 2 Kgs 8:19. But this is actually a loanword distinct from *nēr*. Compare it with Middle and Neo-Assyrian *nīru* 'yoke, imposed rule'[1] and perhaps also Egyptian *nīr-w* 'power, royal scepter'.[2] Thus the Hebrew word *nîr* in the three passages could be translated abstractly, 'power, rule'. This finding of recent biblical scholarship should be readily accepted, since it is simply a return to what was known to a part of the Septuagint, the targums, and the medieval commentator Rashi.

(b) The content of the oracle on which the text plays is: *lātēt lô nîr lĕbānā(y)w*[3] *kol hayyāmîm*. The textually secure *lô* 'for him', referring to David, is left untranslated by the NJPSV. For another possible translation, see C. F. Keil: "*lĕbānā(y)w* serves to clarify *lô nîr*: a light with respect to his sons, i.e., by which he maintains sons (descendants) [[351]] on the throne."[4] So the Masoretic Text. Further considerations take us further back. The textual structure of Kings refers to Ahijah's oracle by means of the word *nîr*. But this suggests that *lbnyw* [['for his descendants']] is a corruption of *lpnyw* [['before his face']].[5] This must certainly be very old, for

1. J. W. Wevers, "Exegetical Principles Underlying the Septuagint Text of 1 Kings ii 12–xxii 43," *OTS* 8 (1950) 300–322, at 316 n. 13; P. D. Hanson, "The Song of Heshbon and David's *nîr*," *HTR* 61 (1968) 297–320; K. Seybold, *Das davidische Königtum im Zeugnis der Propheten* (FRLANT 107; Göttingen: Vandenhoeck & Ruprecht, 1972) 59 n. 7; R. D. Nelson, *The Double Redaction of the Deuteronomistic History* (JSOTSup 18; Sheffield: JSOT Press, 1981) 109; G. Vanoni, *Literarkritik und Grammatik: Untersuchung der Wiederholungen und Spannungen in 1 Kön 11–12* (ATSAT 21; St. Ottilien: EOS, 1984) 179 n. 620; M. Görg, "Ein 'Machtzeichen' Davids 1 Könige xi 36," *VT* 35 (1985) 363–68. It seems to me less justified when B. Halpern (*The Constitution of the Monarchy in Israel* [HSM 25; Chico, Calif.: Scholars Press, 1981] 36 et al.) and R. E. Friedman (*The Exile and Biblical Narrative: The Formation of the Deuteronomistic and Priestly Works* [HSM 22; Chico, Calif.: Scholars Press, 1981] 9 et al.) simply use 'fief' for *nîr* (in the sense "fief of God"). Their reference to Hanson is not justified. In the context of *nîr* he understands David as a human overlord, not as a vassal of Yahweh.

2. Görg ("Ein 'Machtzeichen' Davids," 366–67) introduces this possibility alongside the Assyrian, without considering either of them exclusively.

3. It is correct to reject the reading *ûlĕbānā(y)w* [['and for his descendants']] of some 60 medieval manuscripts (including: "pre-Lucianic" LXX, Hexaplaric LXX, Vulgate, Tiberian targum tradition): however old it might be in 2 Kgs 8:19, it is a secondary harmonization to the parallel in 2 Chr 21:7. Cf. D. Barthélemy, *Critique textuelle de l'Ancien Testament* (OBO 50/1; Fribourg: Éditions Universitaires / Göttingen: Vandenhoeck & Ruprecht, 1982) 1.*81 and 391.

4. C. F. Keil, *Biblischer Commentar über das Alte Testament* (2d ed.; Leipzig: Dörffling, 1876 [[English: *Commentary on the Old Testament*; repr., Peabody, Mass.: Hendrickson, 1996]]) ad loc.

5. First recognized by A. Klostermann, *Die Bücher Samuelis und der Könige* (Kurzgefasster Kommentar zu den heiligen Schriften A/3; Nördlingen: Beck, 1887) ad loc.; since then Klostermann's view has been accepted by many commentators and translators.

it was already found in the version of Kings underlying the parallel in 2 Chr 21:7. There is, moreover, the text-critical possibility that *lbnyw* is not original at all.[6] The promise referred to here probably read, in its original wording: YHWH intended "to preserve for him [= David] rule ⟨before His face [= in Jerusalem]⟩ for all time."

(c) A bit earlier in the text, an additional *lô* ⟦'to him'⟧ remains untranslated in the NJPSV. The MT reads: *lĕmaʿan Dāwid ʿabdô kaʾăšer ʾāmar-lô* 'for the sake of his servant David, in accordance with His promise to him [= David]'. Since the oracle that follows alludes to Ahijah's oracle to Jeroboam by means of the key word *nîr*, there must be a problem with the content here. It is understandable that the NJPSV smoothed out the text by not translating this *lô* as well. However, a contradiction has also been avoided: according to 1 Kings 11 the oracle referred to Jeroboam, but with *lô* 'to him' in 2 Kgs 8:19, it would refer to David. The omission of $lô_1$ ⟦= the first occurrence in v. 19⟧ calls for a text-critical discussion, but this would require going into the history of the text behind the MT, which is contrary to the principles of the NJPSV. Every witness to the MT contains the $lô_1$.

However minor this last problem appears, since it concerns the oracle promising that the dynasty of David would not be deposed from the throne by God, despite its sins, it takes on great significance. Therefore, a purely text-critical discussion comes first below (part II). The resulting text-critical hypothesis is plausible if we accept a secondary adaptation of the text to the Chronicler's theory of the historical validity of Nathan's oracle (part III). Recent writers on the Deuteronomistic History have not recognized this original theory of the rightly limited role of Nathan's oracle and consequently have interpreted the secondary form of ⟦352⟧ 2 Kgs 8:19 in terms of Chronicles (part IV). I shall therefore briefly demonstrate how the theory of the functioning of the dynastic oracle in history must have originally looked in Kings (part V).

II

Text-critically, regarding 2 Kgs 8:19, lw_1, here are the facts: Something corresponding to lw_1 ⟦the consonantal transliteration of $lô_1$⟧ of the MT of

6. The Vaticanus contains nothing at all corresponding to *(w)lbnyw*, but it is the only such witness to the LXX, aside from the asterisk in the Syrohexapla. Does this preserve the original LXX? Its Hebrew forerunner again could have lost the word via homoioteleuton (assuming similarity of *r* and *w*). Or else it could represent the oldest state of the Hebrew text. Then the relatively early (*Vorlage* of 2 Chr 21:7!) insertion *lbnyw* might never have supplanted *lpnyw*. The continuation would perhaps be a supplement harmonizing with "son" and "sons" in 1 Kgs 11:36 and 15:4. Thus J. Trebolle Barrera of Madrid (private correspondence, 13 December 1985), to whom I am deeply indebted for this and other important suggestions. A determination on this matter is not necessary for the present inquiry.

2 Kgs 8:19 is found in the targum, the Vulgate, the witnesses to Origen's LXX recension, and the "Lucianic" LXX manuscripts boc$_2$e$_2$ (including 3 Vetus Latina witnesses). No *lw*$_1$ is presupposed by the Vaticanus or the principal group of LXX manuscripts. The parallel in 2 Chr 21:7 has no *lw* in the MT; the Vulgate agrees. On the other hand, the LXX of 2 Chr 21:7 has this *lw* everywhere.

Thus, the situation is complicated. Between 2 Kings and 2 Chronicles we have found a criss-cross arrangement. The normal LXX appears to translate Kings with Chronicles and Chronicles with Kings.[7]

Since the main text of the LXX in the section including 2 Kgs 8:19 is not considered the Ur-LXX but the *kaige* recension (and thus a Greek version already harmonized with a proto-Masoretic text),[8] the *lw*$_1$ was certainly absent in the proto-Masoretic text of the first century B.C. Since the MT has *lw*$_1$ and the Hexaplaric recension already reflects this, the *lw*$_1$ must have been inserted within the proto-Masoretic text transmission between the *kaige* recension and Origen.

This does not mean that it was that recent, however, for it is witnessed in the "Lucianic" manuscripts. If their reading corresponds with those of the Vetus Latina and the LXX of Chronicles, then in all probability it was the reading of the Ur-LXX—or, for those who prefer such a formulation, a proto-Lucianic recension or another very early Greek translation.[9] That is [[353]] the case here. For the Hebrew tradition this means that in some other textual tradition of the books of Kings than the proto-Masoretic the *lw*$_1$ must have been present relatively early.

This is as far as we can come with the help of the external witnesses. But such means can do no more to clarify which of the two texts, the one with *lw*$_1$ or the one without it, is the original. We must weigh the internal probabilities. Let us follow both possibilities through.

7. A list of all 16 "textual criss-crosses" is given in M. Rehm, *Textkritische Untersuchungen zu den Parallelstellen der Samuel-Königsbücher und der Chronik* (AA 13/3; Münster: Aschendorff, 1937) 99. Rehm considers the phenomenon to be random. The phrasing would be the same whether the object was "included or omitted" (p. 101). He does not seem to have any feel for what is at stake here.

8. D. Barthélemy, *Les devanciers d'Aquila* (VTSup 10; Leiden: Brill, 1963) 34–41, 89–143; J. D. Shenkel, *Chronology and Recensional Development in the Greek Text of Kings* (HSM 1; Cambridge: Harvard University Press, 1968) 8, 20.

9. Cf. R. W. Klein, "New Evidence for an Old Recension of Reigns," *HTR* 60 (1967) 93–105; J. D. Shenkel, "A Comparative Study of the Synoptic Parallels in 1 Paraleipomena and I–II Reigns," *HTR* 62 (1969) 63–85; for the Vetus Latina: B. Fischer, "Lukian-Lesarten in der Vetus Latina der vier Königsbücher," in *Miscellanea Biblica et Orientalia R. P. Athanasio Miller O.S.B. completis LXX annis oblata* (ed. A. Metzinger; SAns 27–28; Rome: Herder, 1951) 169–77; overall especially also E. Tov, "Lucian and Proto-Lucian: Toward a New Solution of the Problem," *RB* 79 (1972) 101–13.

If we take lw_1 in 2 Kings as original, then we must deal with deliberate deletion–twice, no less. One deletion would have been the work of the author of Chronicles. He would have left the word found in his source out of his own text. The other deletion would have taken place at or after the origin of a special proto-Masoretic form of the text. That this could have happened in light of Chronicles is not entirely out of the question but also not certain for, generally, expansive harmonizations with parallel texts are easier to accept than shortenings. Also, in Chronicles there is no way one can point to a tendency toward shortening to match the pattern in the books of Kings. In the very same verse, a corrupt or difficult formulation of the pattern (*lw . . . lbnyw* ⟦'for him . . . for his descendants'⟧) was made understandable not by shortening but by extending (inserting *w* ⟦'and⟧ before *lbnyw*). From the Chronicler's point of view, there would have been no reason to omit the *lw*, for it will indeed refer to an oracle to David (see below).[10]

If we take the opposite view, that lw_1 was *not* originally present in 2 Kgs 8:19, then the situation at the beginning would still be reflected in the Hebrew text of Chronicles and even in the *kaige* text of the LXX. The proto-Masoretic text, presumably first century A.D., would have preserved the original state. The lw_1 would have first been introduced in a non-proto-Masoretic text family (assuming local texts: Egyptian or Palestinian) (phase 1) and then under its influence, relatively late (but before Origen) also in authoritative exemplars of the proto-Masoretic text of 2 Kings (phase 2). Phase 1 would be reflected in the Chronicles of the LXX, the Vetus Latina, and the "Lucianic" manuscripts; phase 2 in the post-Origen recensions and translations.

The second hypothesis is the more plausible. It places the shorter text at the beginning, manages with a single, independent, text-altering insertion, and corresponds better to the rest of the context of Chronicles. It is therefore already preferable at the level of purely text-critical argumentation.

At least one text-altering insertion, small though it may be, is certainly also ⟦354⟧ to be assumed here, since a mechanical scribal error is improbable. Naturally it would be good if we could suggest a reason why a *lw* was introduced into 2 Kgs 8:19 in an early text tradition. And as a matter of fact, a reason is available. It lies in the historical conception of Chronicles, even though 2 Chr 21:7 does not in fact contain the *lw* of 2 Kgs 8:19. If we read 2 Kgs 8:19 from the Chronicler's perspective and try to clarify a bit what we then understand, the insertion of the lw_1 suggests itself. But it is

10. I dispense with our assumption in the framework of the Hebrew Old Testament Text Project; see Barthélemy, *Critique textuelle*, 1.*83, 391.

known of the "Lucianic" text form and its forerunners that explicit objects ⟦of verbs; where other versions use pronouns only⟧ were likely to be introduced for clarification.[11]

It will thus have to be shown how the Chronicler's view of 2 Kgs 8:19 could cause David to be seen as the addressee of the *nîr* oracle, contrary to an original sense of the text, which in any case has yet to be proved. We therefore come to a second, wider level of inquiry.

III

The oracle to which 2 Kgs 8:19 refers consists of the following elements: (1) *ntn* ⟦'give'⟧ + (2) *nîr* ⟦'rule'⟧ + (3) *lĕdāwid* ⟦'for David'⟧ + (4) (in case this is the original reading) *lipnê* YHWH ⟦'before YHWH'⟧ + (5) *kol hayyāmîm* ⟦'forever'⟧. All five elements are found in the text of Ahijah's oracle to Jeroboam in 1 Kgs 11:36: (1) *wĕlibnô ʾettēn*[12] ⟦'to his son I will give'⟧ (2) *šēbeṭ ʾeḥād lĕmaʿan hĕyôt nîr* ⟦'one tribe, so that there may be rule'⟧ (3) *lĕdāwid ʿabdî* ⟦'for My servant David'⟧ (5) *kol hayyāmîm* ⟦'forever'⟧ (4) *lĕpānāy* ⟦'before Me'⟧.[13] None of the oracles addressed to David in the books of Samuel and Kings contains this linguistic combination, particularly not Nathan's oracle (2 Samuel 7). Thus, within the text of Samuel and Kings, the allusion to Ahijah's oracle is unambiguous. On the basis of the characteristics of the oracle, no reader could get the idea that an allusion was being made to an oracle previously addressed to David.

Furthermore, the reader would not be inclined on the basis of any *preceding text* to expect a corresponding oracle to David to be introduced when the narrator needed to establish why, despite the evil-doing of David's descendants, YHWH did not depose them from the throne. The individual examples of this are as follows:

(a) The first disaster case is Solomon. Solomon is punished in that *mamlākâ/mĕlûkâ* ⟦'kingdom/kingship'⟧ over "Israel" (more on this below) is taken away from his son Rehoboam. Only the tribe of Judah and the city of Jerusalem are left to his son Rehoboam. ⟦355⟧ For our theme it is significant that (1) the punishment was postponed until Solomon's death

11. Cf. Fischer, "Lukian-Lesarten," 175–76, nos. 4, 6.

12. The combination *lātēt nîr* . . . ⟦'to give rule . . .'⟧ arose by shortening by contraction of the first verb with the second object of *ntn šēbeṭ* . . . *lĕmaʿan hĕyôt nîr* ⟦'give a tribe . . . so that there may be rule'⟧. The *ntn* ⟦'give'⟧ of 2 Kgs 8:19 thus corresponds everywhere to the *ntn* of 1 Kgs 11:36.

13. The transposition of elements (4) and (5) is stylistically determined. In 1 Kgs 11:36 element (4) is at the end because it is to be developed much further. In 2 Kgs 8:19 element (4) is represented by only the single word **lĕpānā(y)w* ⟦'before him'⟧. Then element (5) (*kol hayyāmîm* ⟦'forever'⟧) supplies the suitable sentence-final cadence.

and that (2) then the House of David does not simply come to an end but retains rule over part of a realm. The solution to both problems is found in two passages, one a prophetic word to Solomon (1 Kgs 11:11–13) and the other Ahijah's oracle to Solomon's later, principal successor, Jeroboam, proclaimed during Solomon's lifetime (11:31–39). On the postponement of the punishment (#1), 1 Kgs 11:12 reads, "for the sake of your father David," and 11:34, "for the sake of my servant David, whom I chose, and who kept My commandments and My laws."[14] On the long-lasting rule of the Davidic dynasty in Judah (#2), 1 Kgs 11:13 reads "for the sake of My servant David and for the sake of Jerusalem[15] which I have chosen"; 11:32, "for the sake of My servant David and for the sake of Jerusalem, the city that I have chosen out of all the tribes of Israel"; and 11:36, "so that there would be rule (*nîr*) for My servant David forever before Me in Jerusalem–the city where I have chosen to establish My name." While in the answer to the first problem only David (and the choice of him) is mentioned, in the answer to the second problem the choice of Jerusalem is added. A reference back to an earlier oracle is not given anywhere, let alone an oracle to David. Above all, the most independent formulation among the five statements, the one with *nîr* in 11:36, is not marked as a quotation in any way. The reader encounters it here for the first time. The word *bḥr* with which the 'choice' of David is introduced in 11:34, which is strongly reminiscent of the narrative of his anointing in Bethlehem in 1 Samuel 16, is absent from Nathan's oracle in 2 Samuel 7, and precedes Nathan's oracle in the small historical summary in 1 Kgs 8:16–19. For the reader, then, 11:36 can contain no allusion to Nathan's oracle. It may be necessary in the discussion of the choice of Jerusalem ("to establish YHWH's name there," 1 Kgs 11:36) to see a vague reference to the statement in Nathan's oracle that Solomon would "build a house for YHWH's name" (2 Sam 7:13).[16] But this still does not connect the *nîr* saying to Nathan's oracle–just the choice of Jerusalem. Even the choice of Jerusalem cannot be specifically pinned to Nathan's oracle. The reader has known the exact formula in 1 Kgs 11:36 ever since Deuteronomy. It thus refers him to an act of YHWH that from the time of Moses had been projected. It reached its climax with the Temple dedication, and thereafter the more exact parallel to the formulation of 1 Kgs 11:36 is the oracle to Solomon in 1 Kgs 9:3 ("to set the name"). [[356]]

14. The text beginning with "because" is missing in the Ur-LXX.

15. The LXX has "Jerusalem, the city which." Probably a harmonization with 11:36.

16. Here in fact the text-critical question arises as to whether "name" itself is original. Cf. F. M. Cross, *Canaanite Myth and Hebrew Epic: Essays in the History of the Religion of Israel* (Cambridge: Harvard University Press, 1973) 243 n. 104.

(b) The second disaster case is Rehoboam. He "did what was evil in the eyes of YHWH" (1 Kgs 14:22; compare 15:3).[17] This judgment is not followed by any justification for the fact that YHWH did not administer any consequences for his bad behavior. The one place where we could most easily see a justification is earlier, in an elaboration not usually found elsewhere concerning the general king schema. This is 14:21, which does not read, as is usual later on, that the king reigned so-and-so-many years "in Jerusalem" but much more solemnly: "in Jerusalem, the city which YHWH had chosen out of all the tribes of Israel to put his name there." This is the narrator's text. There is no trace of reference to an oracle. Certainly it is an allusion to an oracle, for talk of "putting YHWH's name" occurred back in 1 Kgs 11:36. The reader is thus reminded of Ahijah's oracle. If the reader looked carefully, she or he would notice that the entire statement is assembled from elements of the two justifications for the limited continued existence of the Davidic dynasty in 1 Kgs 11:36 (regarding "put my name there") and 11:32 ("out of all the tribes of Israel"). This is thus at least an allusion to an oracle, except it is not an oracle delivered to David but to Jeroboam by Ahijah.

(c) Rehoboam's son and successor, Abijah, was a bad king as well (1 Kgs 15:3). For him, 15:4 gives explicit justification for YHWH's failure to intervene punitively: "For the sake of David, YHWH his God[18] gave him rule (*nîr*) in Jerusalem,[19] by raising up his descendant[20] after him and by preserving Jerusalem." Again no explicit reference is given to an oracle, but it is a clear allusion—precisely again to Ahijah's oracle, not to an oracle to David. As in Ahijah's oracle itself (see 11:32), reference to David is made in order to account for the behavior of YHWH. The explanation is given in 15:5.[21] It is interesting that the elements of Ahijah's oracle that are included here are different from the ones included in the case of Rehoboam.

(d) Two good kings follow: Asa and Jehoshaphat. But then comes the bad king, Jehoram, on whose assessment our entire discussion turns. For the first time, Ahijah's oracle is not just alluded to [[357]] but is introduced as a quotation of a previously pronounced oracle: *kaʾăšer ʾāmar* [['as he

17. The MT has "Judah" for the subject in 14:22, while the Ur-LXX has "Rehoboam." The parallel, 2 Chr 12:14, in the MT ought to reflect the original state, which has an unexpressed singular subject and thus objectively speaks of Rehoboam. The variants agree that in 1 Kgs 14:22b a continuation by Dtr[2] (see below) begins, which carelessly proceeded in the plural, since Dtr[2] was thinking of the people as a whole. The MT and LXX represent different kinds of attempts at leveling.

18. "His God" is absent from the Ur-LXX.

19. "In Jerusalem" is absent from the Ur-LXX.

20. Ur-LXX: "his descendants." Aural leveling to *ʾḥryw* in the Hebrew original?

21. The exception at the end regarding the matter with Uriah is absent in the LXX.

said']]. A certain climax of historical significance is achieved in the process, for in what follows there are several more kings whose evaluation is negative: Ahaz, Manasseh, and Amon. But in these cases, no justification is given (the previously observed technique) for YHWH's nonetheless allowing the Davidides to continue to rule and Jerusalem to continue to exist.[22] Obviously the principle by which YHWH operates regarding the Davidides has been sufficiently clarified.[23]

The text of 2 Kgs 8:19 without lw_1 [['for him']] fits the historical trend best so far. The text with lw_1, however, comes of all things at the moment when the connection with Ahijah's oracle (already long intimated) is made explicit. Now suddenly lw_1, marking this reference as an oracle to David, comes as a splash of cold water. The entire presentation of the books of Kings so far has given us no reason to expect a rebuke to be based on an oracle to David, not even on Nathan's oracle to David.

If the saying's reference to Nathan's oracle was obvious and self-explanatory to those who introduced the lw_1, then it must have been because that is exactly the *opinion of Chronicles*.[24] Its conception must now be sketched, at least briefly, as a counterpart to the view of the books of Kings, which has been dealt with so far.[25]

(a) In Nathan's oracle itself, in 1 Chr 17:11–14, the promise is tailored to Solomon alone. Eternal existence is promised to his throne. The passage in [[358]] 2 Sam 7:14 about possible sins and punishment is excised. Thus the reader is not prepared for the possibility that Solomon himself

22. We could perhaps also refer to 2 Kgs 19:34, 20:6, both in the sphere of the Isaiah–Hezekiah legends. But they are not "nevertheless-statements" about a sinful king in the framework of king evaluations. The name-formula in 2 Kgs 21:4, 7 has a completely different function: it demonstrates the monstrousness of Manasseh's sins.

23. We must here also take into account the proclamation by a man of God in 1 Kgs 13:2 about the Davidide Josiah, who was to return to Bethel. Until this appears, the reader has no reason to be concerned about the existence of the Davidides in Jerusalem for all time. Since all of the texts treated so far come from Dtr[1], at least the Manasseh story must have been greatly reworked by Dtr[2] (on the distinction between Dtr[1] and Dtr[2], see below), and a corresponding notice could have been deleted there or become unrecognizable. However, the absence of such notices for Ahaz and Amon probably speaks against this opinion.

24. "Above all": of course we must also reckon with the influence of presumptions that are liturgical, folkloric, and found in the already existing canon (Psalter!) about Nathan's oracle and its eternal validity, indeed with the presence of the word *nîr/nēr* in such contexts (cf. Ps 132:17; 2 Sam 21:17). If Chronicles has reduced the much subtler construction of the books of Kings entirely to the lasting validity of Nathan's promise, the reason must be in part due to influences from the general consciousness.

25. Much work has been done recently on the theology of Chronicles; see the bibliography in B. S. Childs, *Introduction to the Old Testament as Scripture* (Philadelphia: Fortress, 1979) 263–66. Of course, there are also problems of literary layering in Chronicles. However, since our context concerns the impression that the completed book produces in the consciousness of the reader, the following overview is confined to the canonical text.

could sin (and later the story of his sins is also omitted from the books of Kings).

(b) When David provides the impetus for the building of the Temple and thereby commemorates the promise granted to him in 1 Chr 28:2–7, we must certainly have the Chronicler's genuine version of the oracle. Everything is attuned to the "selection" of Solomon and to the building of the Temple. In fact, there is also a conditional element (28:7; compare 28:9), but in the same breath it is certified that, so far, no problem has arisen with Solomon ("if he keeps . . . as he does now"). Thus Solomon is not a problem case. It is not expected that a problem will yet develop. Nathan's oracle can operate without restraint.

(c) After taking the throne, Solomon asks YHWH to allow the oracle to be fulfilled (2 Chr 1:8–9). So once again the reader has no fear that something could go wrong.

(d) In the framework of the Temple dedication, the oracle is mentioned three times in a similar sense (2 Chr 6:10, 16, 42). In the accompanying vision, which corresponds to the apparition in 1 Kings 9, YHWH repeats the oracle. If in 1 Kgs 9:5 the talk was of the "royal throne over Israel," referring to Solomon's successors, it is now "your royal throne" (2 Chr 7:17–18). This is an important alteration, especially since Chronicles (in contrast to Kings) would not think of connecting the word "Israel" with Judah and Jerusalem after the division of the monarchy (see below).

(e) Next, there is no mention of Solomon's sin or of Ahijah's prophecy to Jeroboam (though Ahijah's prophecy is mentioned in the fulfillment notice of 2 Chr 10:15 for those who know the books of Kings). The Northern tribes indeed fall away, but it is as a sort of traffic accident due to Rehoboam's youth (13:6–7). The note about the reign of Rehoboam from 1 Kgs 14:21–22 is in fact reproduced in 2 Chr 12:13–14, but since Ahijah's oracle has not previously been introduced, despite the identical wording it does not allude to it as the source does. Through the preceding Shishak narrative, at the end of which Rehoboam repents (12:12), there is no occasion to suspect that YHWH had too great a problem with this king. Nathan's oracle thus continues to function unimpaired.

(f) The deeper theological clarification of the state of affairs then ensues with Rehoboam's son Abijah, who in Kings was a bad king like his father. It was because of him that Kings had therefore again alluded to Ahijah's oracle. Chronicles includes no information about his malfeasance. In fact, it constructs the presentation of Abijah around a holy war between North and South (13:2–20). Abijah's speech to his opponents from the North (13:4–12) is an important element within this narrative. It emerges from this that YHWH is on the side of the Davidides, since: [[359]] YHWH "gave David kingship over Israel forever—to him and his sons—by a covenant of salt for all time" (13:5). "A covenant of salt"[26] cannot refer to anything but the covenant with David in the promise of Nathan. We should note one more particular in looking at 2 Chr 7:17–18. Here the key word "Israel" remains connected with the Davidides, Judah, and Jerusalem. The rebellious tribes of the North have fallen out of the sacred reality referred to by "Israel." Therefore their history no longer needs to be recounted.

(g) A situation in which YHWH really needed to intervene against the Davidides, but for David's sake did not, appears in Chronicles for the first time with Jehoram [[2 Chr 21:7]]—thus exactly parallel with 2 Kgs 8:19. And here the model for the first time explicitly refers to an earlier word of YHWH (even if not a word to David). Here for clarification of the situation the Chronicler deliberately replaces the omitted oracle of Ahijah with Nathan's oracle. He does this quite explicitly, though with subtle caution, by a slight alteration of the text. The texts may be presented synoptically.

Kings	*Chronicles*
However, YHWH refrained from destroying Judah,	However, YHWH refrained from destroying the House of David
for the sake of His servant David	for the sake of the covenant he had made with David, and
in accordance with His promise	in accordance with his promise
to maintain rule for him	to maintain rule for him
for his descendants[27]	and his descendants
for all time.	for all time.

Remarks: (1) In Chronicles, Judah is replaced by "house of David." For the Chronicler "Judah" must not have been different from the "Israel" of the ten tribes, and "house of David" also introduces more appropriately the emphasis in what follows. (2) "Because of His servant David," which is an allusion to Ahijah's oracle that is meaningless in Chronicles, is changed into an unambiguous reference to the dynastic covenant in Nathan's oracle. (3) The ensuing text, de facto reproducing Ahijah's oracle, is not formally marked in any way as the text of the covenant with David. The connection *wĕka'ăšer* [['and in accordance with']] is so vague that someone knowing the text could go beyond it and recognize Ahijah's oracle, known from somewhere else. But the naïve, uninformed reader would naturally accept that what he or she found communicated here was the significant content of the covenant with David, thus Nathan's oracle—though in dif-

26. For "covenant of salt," see Lev 2:13, Num 18:19, Ezra 4:14. The Chronicler may have found justification in 2 Sam 23:5 for using the concept of *bĕrît* [['covenant']].

27. Here the Kings text is presented as it must have appeared to the Chronicler: with *lbnyw* [['for his descendants']].

ferent words, since the reader also knows the content from the narrative about David in Chronicles.

(h) Later in Chronicles, there is yet another passage referring back, by way of Kings, to Nathan's oracle. It is when the [[360]] Davidide succession is endangered in the story of Athaliah and Joash. The enthronement of Joash is based on the oracle to Nathan in 2 Chr 23:3.

So—contrary to the theory that the books of Kings served as the principal source—in Chronicles, Nathan's oracle is the sole guarantor of the perdurability of Davidide rule in Jerusalem. The same oracle, in fact, since throughout it is understood as a conditioned statement, is also the basis of the (premature?) end of Davidide rule and the Babylonian Exile. Notice that the reference to 1 Chr 17:14 ("David") and 2 Chr 7:16–22 ("Solomon") in the section on Manasseh (2 Chr 33:7–8) is based on 2 Kgs 21:7–16, which is repeated in highly compressed fashion, but accurately. There is no allusion to Nathan's oracle there. But this does not change the fact that (in the mind of the Chronicler) Nathan's oracle always operates where, despite the sins of the Davidides, no catastrophe ensues or that Nathan's oracle certainly represents the true divine principle of action for the entire history, from David onward.

We must reckon with the fact that in the fourth and third centuries, to which we can assign the introduction of lw_1 into one family of the Hebrew manuscripts of the books of Kings, the historical theology of Chronicles imbued the consciousness. Its very simple concept overlay the thoroughly subtler one of Kings. It is understandable then that, in a circle of tradents who did not conscientiously object to expanding their manuscripts a little when clarification seemed necessary, this little operation took place in 2 Kgs 8:19 and that later it affected even the MT and therefore also all of our present-day Hebrew Bible editions and nearly all [[of our modern]] translations.

IV

The introduction of lw_1 [['for him']] affects not only our texts but also distinct stages of the latest scientific *theory about the books of Kings and the entire "Deuteronomistic History."* This can be briefly introduced at this point.[28]

One of the most prominent reactions to Martin Noth's 1943 theory of the "Deuteronomistic History"[29] was a 1947 article by Gerhard von Rad,

28. What follows is in no way a review of the literature, for which see H. Weippert, "Das deuteronomistische Geschichtswerk: Sein Ziel und Ende in der neueren Forschung," *TRu* 50 (1985) 213–49.

29. M. Noth, *Überlieferungsgeschichtliche Studien: Die sammelnden und bearbeitenden Geschichtswerke im Alten Testament* (2d ed.; Tübingen: Niemeyer, 1957) [[in English, *The Deuteronomistic History* (2d ed.; JSOTSup 15; Sheffield: JSOT Press, 1991]].

"Die deuteronomistische Geschichtstheologie in den Königsbüchern" [['The Deuteronomistic Theology of the Books of Kings']].[30] [[361]] According to Noth, the (exilic) editor of the History was concerned "to present"[31] the actual end of the order of things "as divine ordinance" that had already been sketched in Deuteronomy. This happened when Jerusalem fell. Von Rad, however, thought that for the Deuteronomist YHWH's word operated "in double form" in creating history: on the one hand (as Noth alone had seen) "as a law, ordaining or denying"; on the other hand as "a 'gospel', a continually self-fulfilling promise to David, which brings salvation and forgiveness."[32] And in fact it is the promise of Nathan that "runs through the history of Judah, warding off the long-deserved judgment from the kingdom 'for David's sake.'"[33] Even though "in the later days of the monarchy the deuteronomist no longer speaks of the saving efficacy of the promise made by Nathan,"[34] in his very last notice, the pardon of Jehoiachin in 2 Kgs 25:27–30, "a carefully measured indication is given" that "the line of David has not come to an irrevocable end."[35] He could not believe "that the promise of Yahweh might fail, and that the lamp of David would be finally extinguished."[36]

No doubt about it: von Rad discovered in Kings the conception that we have identified as Chronicles' conception. Nathan's promise regulates the entire course of history, and the talk of the *nîr* of David belongs in this context. If we look closely, everything in von Rad's argument depends on our passage, 2 Kgs 8:19—in particular on its Masoretic reading *with* the lw_1 [['for him']].[37] For proof concerning the "divine restraint," the "divine patience" in the "history of the kingdom of Judah," von Rad simply provides a list of texts.[38] He begins with 1 Kgs 11:13; next are 1 Kgs 11:32, 36; 15:4;

30. G. von Rad, *Deuteronomiumstudien* (FRLANT 40; Göttingen: Vandenhoeck & Ruprecht, 1947) part B. Reprinted in idem, *Gesammelte Studien zum Alten Testament* (TBü 8; Munich: Kaiser, 1958) 189–204 [[translated as: "The Deuteronomic Theology of History in I and II Kings," *The Problem of the Hexateuch and Other Essays* (New York: McGraw-Hill, 1966) 205–21]].

31. Noth, *Überlieferungsgeschichtliche Studien*, 109.

32. Von Rad, *Gesammelte Studien*, 202 [["Deuteronomic Theology of History," 219]].

33. Ibid. [["Deuteronomic Theology of History," 219]].

34. Ibid. [["Deuteronomic Theology of History," 219]].

35. Ibid., 203 [["Deuteronomic Theology of History," 220]].

36. Ibid. [["Deuteronomic Theology of History," 219]].

37. Von Rad cites the verse in his own translation (ibid., 198 [["Deuteronomic Theology of History," 215]]). He puts "for his sons" in parentheses. He is thus clearly aware of the absence of these words in Vaticanus. On the other hand no awareness of the text-critical problem with respect to the lw_1 appears in his translation. This is probably a result of the dual apparatus in BHK^3, since there the first problem is noted in the second, principal apparatus, but the second problem only in the first apparatus, which indicates the variants that the editor considered less noteworthy.

38. Ibid., 198 [["Deuteronomic Theology of History," 214]].

and finally, 2 Kgs 8:19. Thus he cites all of the passages we investigated above (and no others) with entirely different results. With 2 Kgs 8:19, von Rad then calls a halt with a summary explanation: "In speaking of the 'lamp' which Yahweh promised to David, the Deuteronomist is of course referring to Yahweh's promise to establish and uphold the Davidic dynasty, given in the prophecy of Nathan in *II Sam.* VII."[39]

This article by von Rad not only attracted wide attention but clearly provided the impetus for the most important correction Noth's theory has received: the distinction between a preexilic, Josianic History (Dtr^1) and its exilic extension and editing (Dtr^2).[40] This happened in 1968 with [[362]] F. M. Cross's article "The Structure of the Deuteronomic History."[41] In fact Cross considers the "handling of this theme" by von Rad as "unconvincing" but takes the "persistence of the deuteronomistic stress upon the eternal decree of Davidic kingship"[42] to be so strong that here we have to see a kernel of the deuteronomistic historical theology. It is one of the two themes of Dtr^1, whose work peaks with Josiah and represents a "propaganda work of the Josianic reformation and imperial program."[43] When Cross develops the theme further,[44] he cites generally the same material as von Rad, although in a different order. Nathan's prophecy, YHWH's trust in the Davidides based on David's trust in him, and the series of *nîr*-statements relating to Ahijah's oracle form for him a single complex. The formulations in 1 Kgs 11:36, 15:4; and 2 Kgs 8:19 are a byform, an "alloform"[45] of the principal form of the statements. The text-critical problematic of 2 Kgs 8:19 is not mentioned when the verse is translated fully according to the Masoretic version of the text.[46] Consequently, we are unable to establish whether Cross also regarded the function of Nathan's oracle for the conception of the history of the books of Kings as the Chronicler saw it or whether (and how) he thought that the secondary text

39. Ibid., 199 [["Deuteronomic Theology of History," 215]].

40. The other development of Noth's hypothesis, proceeding from R. Smend's Göttingen School (details in, for example, Weippert, "Das deuteronomistische Geschichtswerk"), I consider less promising. Despite many good individual observations and the use of theoretical elements usable elsewhere, it has one major flaw: it never made a critical examination of Noth's exilic dating of the oldest version of the entire work.

41. In *Perspectives of Jewish Learning: Annual of the College of Jewish Studies* 3 (Chicago: College of Jewish Studies, 1968) 9–24; reprinted later in F. M. Cross, *Canaanite Myth and Hebrew Epic: Essays in the History of the Religion of Israel* (Cambridge: Harvard University Press, 1973) 274–89 [[in this volume, pp. 79–94]]).

42. Ibid., 278 [[84]].

43. Ibid., 284 [[89]].

44. Ibid., 281-85 [[86–90]].

45. Ibid., 281 [[87]].

46. Ibid., 283 [[88]].

expansion in 2 Kgs 8:19 was introduced into Kings. He naturally does not consider either the text or the concept to belong to a pre-Josianic "Dtr[1]."

Now here we must not throw the baby out with the bath water. Both von Rad and Cross (unlike Noth) correctly recognized that, in Kings' history of Judah, YHWH's will to save (for Josiah) was at work and allowed the Davidides, together with Jerusalem and Judah, to endure through history, even if they failed YHWH. Further, this will to save had to do with David, and oracles played a role in the process. This will to save is in fact a principal theme. The only thing they did not demonstrate was that all of the passages adduced constituted a unified complex and that the text on which they depended was Nathan's oracle. The *nîr*-oracle of Ahijah and the later references to it are, as I hope I have shown, an independent quantity. Furthermore, the references to David's faithfulness, not discussed in detail above, must be separated from Nathan's promise. For this purpose, mere reference to the (probably) deuteronomistic [[363]] formulation in Solomon's prayer, 1 Kgs 3:6, should suffice:

> You dealt "most graciously" with Your servant my father David, (A)
> because he walked before You in faithfulness and righteousness and in integrity of heart. (B)
> You have continued this "great kindness" to him by giving him a son to occupy[47] his throne, as is now the case. (C)

"Great kindness" must refer to Nathan's oracle. The presumed actual and causal series of events is, unquestionably:

> (B) David's faithfulness, righteousness, and integrity of heart
> (A) YHWH's pronouncement of a dynasty, via Nathan
> (C) YHWH's fulfillment of his pronouncement by the enthronement of Solomon.

But this means that David's faithfulness and devotion have a certain prior integrity in Yhwh's eyes, in themselves.[48] Not only are they the basis of Nathan's oracle but, if the oracle should some day no longer be in force, David's faithfulness would itself then yet again determine YHWH's actions

47. The Ur-LXX presumes a text without "occupying" [[so the MT]], probably even with an infinitive construction: "since you have put his son on his throne." This could be the older version.

48. According to H. Gese ("Der Davidsbund und die Zionserwählung," *ZThK* 61 [1964] 10–26; now also in idem, *Vom Sinai zum Zion: Alttestamentliche Beiträge zur biblischen Theologie* [BEvTh 64; Munich: Kaiser, 1974] 113–29), an older foundational relationship between David's actions on behalf of founding a sanctuary in Jerusalem and the dynastic statement (attested in Psalm 132) is deliberately denied in 2 Samuel 7. If the supposition is correct, then Dtr[1] already corrects this.

in history. If in the later representation of the history of Judah YHWH's acts are thus founded on David's faithfulness and devotion, it does not directly follow that Nathan's promise still held and operated there. History could be played out, yet YHWH could nonetheless, in view of David, still act graciously. This certainly does not fit very well with the categories of "law and gospel," which to all appearances secretly drove von Rad's analysis. But in literary criticism it must first be established how a literary work itself views things.

The differentiation between a "Dtr^1" and a "Dtr^2" is not called into question by these critical considerations of the function of Nathan's oracle. It was—although not yet bound up with the idea of a unified work of history in Noth's sense—already fairly well established by Kuenen and Wellhausen by means of individual observations on the text. Since the time of the article by Cross, further arguments have been produced (in Cross's school and elsewhere too) that lend it even greater weight.[49]

[[364]] In the area of investigations inspired by Cross, R. D. Nelson probably goes into the questions considered here in most detail, first in his 1973 dissertation (available on microfilm), and published in reworked form as *The Double Redaction of the Deuteronomistic History.*[50] He appears not to have noticed the text-critical problem of the lw_1 in 2 Kgs 8:19 at all.[51] But he has further radicalized the thesis of the major significance of Nathan's oracle for the construction of the history of Dtr^1.

In Solomon's story there are three places in which the duration of David's dynasty is based on the condition of observance of the law: 1 Kgs 2:4, 8:25, and 9:4–5. Usually one supposes that here an (exilic) Deuteronomist indicated his own interpretation (not attested in 2 Samuel 7) of Nathan's promise in that he, so to speak, formulated it anew. Only in this way could he make the end of his story understandable. Nelson sees it differently. Here a Deuteronomist speaks, but it is Dtr^1. Further, Dtr^1 concerns himself with a separate oracle, distinct from Nathan's. This separate oracle, even though it was not related in the story about David, was originally pronounced to David regarding Solomon and the rule of the Davidides over all twelve tribes ("throne of Israel"). The oracle is repeated by YHWH after the Temple dedication—again concerning Solomon. After

49. The fine analysis of the last portion of 2 Kings by G. Vanoni seems to me to be the most important analysis: "Beobachtungen zur deuteronomistischen Terminologie in 2 Kön 23,25–25,30," in *Das Deuteronomium: Entstehung, Gestalt und Botschaft* (ed. N. Lohfink; BETL 68; Leuven: Leuven University Press / Peeters, 1985) 357–62.

50. R. D. Nelson, *The Double Redaction of the Deuteronomistic History* (JSOTSup 18; Sheffield: JSOT Press, 1981). Cited from this edition.

51. He goes into the textual criticism of 2 Kgs 8:19 (in ibid., 148 n. 59). But he considers only the problem of *lbnyw*.

Solomon sinned and his successor (based on this oracle) lost the Northern tribes, his goal is reached. Nathan's oracle can–though now only in the realm of Judah–again operate at full strength. Nathan's oracle is for this purpose identical with the *nîr*-oracle of Ahijah, in whose form it is now cited.

It appears to me that the Deuteronomistic History is being read from the perspective of Chronicles in this oracle as well, and in the end the uninvestigated Masoretic reading in 2 Kgs 8:19 is the only basis on which the entire construction can be erected. Therefore I conclude that the various oracles in "Dtr[1]"–dealing with its text in general–regulate the progress of the story told, if one bases oneself on the textual criticism of 2 Kgs 8:19 worked out above. Some of Nelson's observations and theories are helpful, although they will now appear in a different context.

V

[[365]] I must begin with the opinion–contra Nelson–that the conditional dynastic oracle in 1 Kgs 2:4, 8:25, 9:4–5[52] is a deuteronomistic *reformulation of Nathan's oracle itself.*

Dtr[1] has barely touched 2 Samuel 7.[53] Probably only 2 Sam 7:1b and 11aβ, which he uses to connect to the previous history,[54] and 13a, where he adds the founding of the Temple (albeit only under Solomon) to the dynastic oracle, come from him.[55] The text was probably so set and so fa-

52. Does 1 Kgs 6:12 also belong in this set? The word could relate to the building of the Temple and would lead to the dynastic promise. But first, *ʾtk* is not entirely certain text-critically, and second, v. 12 leads uniquely to the Temple theme. T. N. D. Mettinger (*King and Messiah: The Civil and Sacral Legitimation of the Israelite Kings* [ConBOT 8; Lund: Gleerup, 1976] 277) adds 1 Sam 13:13–14 and 1 Kgs 11:38. But these two passages refer to Saul and Jeroboam.

53. Among the authors discussed here, F. M. Cross is the principal dissenter (*Canaanite Myth*, 251–55). A. L. Laffey (*A Study of the Literary Function of 2 Samuel 7 in the Deuteronomistic History* [Rome: Pontifical Biblical Institute, 1981]; published from the Ph.D. dissertation only in part) retains only 5 of the 24 typically deuteronomistic formulations listed by Cross. My own analysis of 2 Samuel 7 mentioned below differs from E. Kutsch's only in details and in the acceptance of two deuteronomistic hands. Cf. E. Kutsch, "Die Dynastie von Gottes Gnaden: Probleme der Nathanweissagung in 2 Samuel 7," *ZTK* 58 (1961) 137–53; now also in idem, *Kleine Schriften zum Alten Testament* (ed. L. Schmidt and K. Eberlein; BZAW 168; Berlin: de Gruyter, 1986) 129–45.

54. On the system of statements considered here, see G. Braulik, "Zur deuteronomistischen Konzeption von Freiheit und Frieden," in *Congress Volume: Salamanca, 1983* (ed. J. A. Emerton; VTSup 36; Leiden: Brill, 1985) 29–39.

55. 2 Sam 7:10 (11a), like 7:23–24, must belong to a very late deuteronomistic hand. Dtr[2] has left no traces in 2 Samuel 7. The text of Nathan's oracle in Dtr[1]'s version must thus have included vv. 1–9, 11a–17.

miliar that Dtr[1] would not have dared comprehensive alterations. Consequently, it was all the more important for him, in later references to the oracle, to provide his own version of it.

This purpose is served by the "conditional dynastic oracle" under discussion here, which occurs three times in the story of Solomon. It is relevant that it is found, referring to the Davidides, exclusively before the death of Solomon. If the condition was introduced in view of the catastrophe of the sixth century, one would expect it also to occur after Solomon. Clearly, it had achieved its goal by the end of the story of Solomon.

These three texts from the story of Solomon do not take up any of the typical formulations of 2 Samuel 7. On the other hand, in the third text there is a clear reference to a word of YHWH about and to David in which YHWH applies the promise anew to Solomon: see 1 Kgs 2:4a, 8:25a (earlier, in v. 24, the fulfillment of the Temple-building pronouncement of Nathan's oracle was already referred to), 9:5b. When we evaluate these [[366]] sections of the text, we note a building of expectation and the author's leading of the reader in a carefully thought-out literary work. Ancient Israelite narrative art sometimes held back information and only later surprised the reader with it. But the question is, which technique did Dtr[1] develop in the context of oracles and their fulfillment? As far as I can see, Dtr[1] tends not to mark the fulfillment of an oracle explicitly. He leaves this exercise for the reader. He can also simply allude to a previously proclaimed oracle, without explicitly referring to it. But when he uses oracles, he customarily situates them in their place in history and not necessarily in a form that anyone would expect of an oracle that had not yet been told.[56] Is it then imaginable that within the deuteronomistic text system of Samuel and Kings a threefold reference could appear in regard to such an important matter if the oracle referred to had not been previously narrated? I think not. But then, nothing but Nathan's oracle was available as a reference point.

In what sense is Nathan's oracle interpreted in the three passages? (1) Only the dynastic proclamation is picked up. The promise that a biological son will follow David on the throne is taken up in other passages (1 Kgs 2:15, 24; 3:6–7; 8:20; without explicit citation, probably also 1:48, 5:21). The promise for the construction of the Temple is mentioned in all

56. On citation technique in deuteronomistic literature, see D. E. Skweres, *Die Rückverweise im Buch Deuteronomium* (AnBib 79; Rome: Pontifical Biblical Institute, 1979). T. Veijola (*Die ewige Dynastie: David und die Entstehung seiner Dynastie nach der deuteronomistischen Darstellung* [Annales Academiae Scientiarum Fennicae B/193; Helsinki: Suomaleinen Tiedeakatemia, 1975] 133) claims that the legitimation of David is a "promise whose basis however is never communicated." It appears to me that the relevant passages make reference to the narrative of the anointing of David in 1 Sam 16:1–13.

relevant passages (1 Kgs 5:19; 6:12; 8:16–21, 24; later references must come from Dtr^2). (2) As a condition for the fulfillment of the dynastic proclamation, a virtuous life on the part of the king is introduced. The yardstick is David's virtuous life. (3) "Israel" is named as the realm of the Davidides. "Israel" means all twelve tribes. As Nelson has shown, the proclamation is formulated so that when the Northern tribes secede as a result of Solomon's sins, the reader knows that the oracle is being fulfilled.[57]

From this it now follows—and this conclusion is unfortunately almost never drawn by interpreters when the three passages are considered to be the deuteronomistic version of Nathan's oracle—that in the mind of Dtr^1 Nathan's promise, insofar as it was a dynastic and pan-Israelite proclamation of rule for the Davidides, [[367]] *lost its historical authority with the death of Solomon and the division of the kingdom.* As a proclamation to David that he would receive a son and as a proclamation of the construction of the Temple by this son, it had already been fulfilled. As an eternal proclamation of rule over Israel for David's dynasty, it is now abrogated because of Solomon's failure to meet the condition. For this reason, it no longer applies. This was certainly not the popular, cultic meaning of Nathan's promise or of one of the sources used by Dtr^1. But it was Dtr^1's own opinion.

This is also why, after Solomon, there is no further reference to 2 Samuel 7, despite the amount of the book of Kings that is attributed to Dtr^1. Everything after Solomon's apostasy from YHWH must be reorganized. This happened via Ahijah of Shiloh's oracle to Jeroboam son of Nebat, recorded in 1 Kings 11.[58] In what follows, the only elements that interest Dtr^1 are the ones concerning the new organization of [[both kingdoms and their]] power relations.

"*The* kingdom," and hence authority "over Israel," is handed over to Jeroboam. Thus for Dtr^1 *the* successor to Solomon is Jeroboam, not Rehoboam. In 11:38* Jeroboam receives a dynastic proclamation that—in accordance with the understanding of Dtr^1—corresponds exactly to the proclamation of an eternal dynasty to David: the proclamation of a "lasting dynasty, as I did for David." The condition is the same, too: to observe the law of YHWH "as My servant David did." One is simply not taking such

57. Nelson, *Double Redaction,* 99–105. R. E. Friedman ("From Egypt to Egypt: Dtr^1 and Dtr^2," in *Traditions in Transformation: Turning Points in Biblical Faith* [ed. B. Halpern and J. D. Levenson; Winona Lake, Ind.: Eisenbrauns, 1981] 167–92, at 175–76) offers a similar analysis—perhaps without knowing Nelson's, since he does not cite it.

58. The most recent (but so far incomplete) literary-critical analysis is found in Vanoni, *Literarkritik und Grammatik.* I believe vv. 31, 33 (except the last four words), 34, 36–37, 38 (except the last four words) can be shown to have been present in the version of the text available to Dtr^1, but I cannot justify this here. It represents a reedited source. Thus the text is already quite complicated in this version. Perhaps, therefore, Dtr^1 at a few important points refers to an oracle to Solomon, ascribable to Solomon only: 11:11–13.

sayings seriously if one does not see that it is a sort of second oracle of Nathan. Chronicles has, not without good reason, passed over it in silence. Jeroboam will play out his oracle just as Solomon did, only faster. The history of the North will be given reprieves by YHWH for various reasons. But ultimately, because of the "sins of Jeroboam," it will come to its early demise. But this is not what we are treating here.

There is definitely a limitation in this "second oracle of Nathan." Jerusalem and Judah should remain with the Davidides. For us everything depends on the reason for this. Is Nathan's promise being quoted? No, it is *a new promise that is now being issued for the first time*: the above-cited *nîr* proclamation (11:36).[59] If it had been meant as a kind of actualizing interpretation of Nathan's promise [[368]] or of an element of that promise, then doubtless some sort of reference would be found here. Dtr[1] employs this technique too often to assume that he omitted it here. It is thus a new arrangement of YHWH that now appears. Of course, it relates to Nathan's promise. For the Davidides, it replaces it. Without it they would now have no promise at all. Second, it is based on two realities, to which Nathan's promise also was closely related. The *nîr* proclamation originated "because of my servant David" (see 11:13, 32). This refers to YHWH's fidelity and David's perfect conduct. As stated in 1 Kgs 3:6, these two factors were also the basis for the promulgation of Nathan's promise in the mind of Dtr[1], and they were always mentioned later as the basis for YHWH's patience with Judah and the Davidides. The *nîr* proclamation further states "because of Jerusalem, the city that I chose . . ." (see 11:13, 32, 36). In the opinion of Dtr[1], the election of Jerusalem had indeed become an irrevocable reality as a result of Solomon's Temple building and Temple dedication. The choice of Jerusalem and the building of the Temple were precipitated by Nathan's oracle (at least in the mind of Dtr[1], who expanded the oracle accordingly and later created corresponding references). Here too the Davidides did not fail, which may be why they remained connected with Jerusalem and why no new dynasty arose there. That power in Jerusalem continues to be left to them comes out of a prior history, in which Nathan's oracle played a role. Yet it does not bear on this new situation, insofar as it is an oracle. The provision of a new oracle (that of Ahijah) reflects a decision by YHWH to stress the gravity of the prior history.

59. A question incidental to our context is whether Dtr[1] created it or found it already in his source. I prefer the latter. J. Trebolle Barrera (private correspondence, 13 December 1985) suggests that the following elements existed previously: *ltt/hywt – lw/ldwd ʾbyw – nyr kl hymym*. If one concludes that it was a new composition, then the *nîr* could connect with the *nēr yiśrāʾēl* [['lamp of Israel']] of 2 Sam 21:17 (cf. Veijola, *Ewige Dynastie*, 118–19)—which does not necessarily mean that *nîr* existed there at the time.

In 1 Kgs 14:21, 15:4; 2 Kgs 8:19, Dtr[1] creates a scheme, which presents in an exemplary manner how the *nîr* promise will carry the Davidides and Judah through all of their failures. The passages have already been analyzed in detail above. Then, the presentation of history continues with hardly any further comments (on the *nîr* promise) up to Josiah. He "did what was pleasing to Yhwh and he followed all the ways of his ancestor David; he did not deviate to the right or to the left" (2 Kgs 22:2). Dtr[1] has told the entire history of Israel for the sake of Josiah's reform and rule. It was not a matter of recalling an oracle that gave light to a dark future. Nathan's oracle had its effect in a specific hour of history. At the time when Dtr[1] is writing his work, the situation was no longer acute—at least not as far as dynastic problems were concerned. Within Jerusalem, YHWH's splendid Temple, established as the one sanctuary under Josiah, testified to the oracle's force in previous history.

Perhaps it makes sense to explain how Dtr[2] dealt with Nathan's oracle later, in the period of the exile. He blamed this catastrophe on the "sins of Manasseh" (2 Kgs 21:10–16, 23:26–27, 24:3–4). Yet the catastrophe [[369]] included the destruction of the Temple, and the Temple was one reason in Dtr[1] why YHWH let the Davidides survive despite their sins. Would not Dtr[2] have reasoned that the destruction of the Temple now placed Nathan's oracle in question, just as Dtr[1] reasoned that it had been placed in question by the division of the kingdom? To solve the problem, Dtr[2] invoked the same technique that Dtr[1] had used in the Solomon story to explain the nonfulfillment of the eternal rule of the Davidic dynasty over "Israel." Dtr[2] also introduced a condition, this time for the existence of the Temple and the holy city. It is clearly stated in his expansion, 1 Kgs 9:6–9 (and this text itself is already anticipated in Deut 29:21–27, albeit without yet specifying the Temple). From Manasseh on, Dtr[2] invokes three prophetic utterances that increasingly show that the condition for the further existence of the Temple and the city can no longer be met: 2 Kgs 21:11–15 (relating to Manasseh); 22:15–20 (the reworking of the Huldah oracle); 23:27 (following the evaluation of Josiah, a justification for why, despite Josiah's positive life-style, the wrath of YHWH did not subside). The third utterance explicitly names the Temple as an object of YHWH's wrath and formally cancels Nathan's oracle—only now with reference to the Temple.

* * *

Because von Rad considered Nathan's promise to have history-determining power (which for him appeared irrevocable until the end of Kings), he ascribed to the Deuteronomistic History a somewhat restrained "messianism."[60] How much more sober the picture of what seemed to be an insignificant text-critical question in 2 Kgs 8:19 looks in light of the above discussion. It is all but shocking. How the theme of Nathan's oracle must have influenced not only the tradition but also the consciousness of the people in Jerusalem and Judah in the waning period of the monarchy! How it also later influenced postexilic messianic expectations! Is it inconceivable that a writer would have relativized an oracle in this way? Or that "Dtr[1]" had the entire history of his people march to its theme, in order to provide sympathy for His Royal Highness Josiah, from the House of David, who ruled gloriously and finally put the world right? As our research into the most recent biblical scholarship has shown, even today veils of new interpretation over this intellectual boldness remain—also legitimized by the MT of 2 Kgs 8:19. How deeply the shock of the rule of Assyria must have shattered the traditional world of meaning in Judah. How little reliance there must have been during that historic hour on everything that the highest institutions of society had taken for granted before. And what courage this writer [[370]] must have had, on the one hand to hold fast to Israel's one God YHWH at the heart of his tradition, and on the other hand to take immense liberties with the facts of history and stand the hitherto long-received interpretive model on its head. With great realism he measured the sacred claim of legitimacy of his earthly king and lord itself against the actual course of history. If we look more closely, this even fits together precisely with other peculiarities of the deuteronomistic phenomenon. One only needs to think of something so unheard of in the ancient world as the centralization of ritual and sacrifice in a single sanctuary, which made the rest of the region sacrifice-free and turned its meat-eating into secular slaughter.

The longer I deal with this world, the more fascinating I find it. And with thanks I recall that the gateway to this world was opened for me by him to whom these pages are dedicated [[referring to William L. Moran, the honoree of the Festschrift in which this article was first published]].[61]

60. [[Von Rad, "The Deuteronomic Theology of History," 218.]]
61. Completed June 1986.

Part 4

New Directions

Toward a Redactional History of the Book of Kings

André Lemaire

Lemaire is one of a number of scholars who speak of multiple preexilic editions of the Deuteronomistic History and of at least one exilic edition. He views the preexilic editions as substantial and the exilic edition(s) as minor. Lemaire bases his case on variations in the regnal formulas of Northern and Southern kings. The judgment formulas of Northern and Southern kings, which exhibit by far the most variation among all of the regnal formulas, nevertheless fall into characteristic patterns. Since these variations do not seem random, Lemaire argues that they are pivotal to unraveling the compositional history of Kings. On the basis of his analysis, he comes to a number of conclusions. He agrees with Helga Weippert that a protodeuteronomistic composition, dating to the time of Hezekiah, predated the Josianic and exilic editions advocated by Cross. In addition, Lemaire posits a composition written during the reign of Jehoshaphat (ca. 850 B.C.E.). Hence, Lemaire argues for a centuries-long development of the Deuteronomistic History already prior to the exile. This rolling corpus model of the deuteronomistic work is quite different from the one-edition model proposed by Noth, the block model proposed by Cross, and the three-edition model proposed by Smend. Rather than imagining a work that underwent one, two, or even three major editions, Lemaire conceives of a series of books being constantly updated and expanded over hundreds of years.

Translated and reprinted with permission, from "Vers l'Histoire de la Rédaction des Livres des Rois," *Zeitschrift für die alttestamentliche Wissenschaft* 98 (1986) 221–36. Translation by Samuel W. Heldenbrand. The RSV has been used in this essay for English biblical quotations.

Author's note: This article is the reworked and completed version of a paper read on the August 16, 1984 at Strasbourg (Society of Biblical Literature, 1984 International Meeting).

[[221]] Since the classic essay by Martin Noth, *Überlieferungsgeschichtliche Studien,*[1] most contemporary exegetes attribute the redaction of the books of Kings to the work of a Deuteronomist redactor who is assumed to have compiled, adapted, composed, and finally edited the books of [[222]] Deuteronomy, Joshua, Samuel, and Kings during the exile, toward the middle of the sixth century B.C. This simple and perhaps simplistic interpretation has little by little almost completely replaced[2] earlier ones, such as in works written by I. Benzinger, G. Hölscher, and O. Eissfeldt,[3] who attempted to recover the hand of the Yahwistic and Elohistic redactors on into the books of the Kings. However, a certain number of problems remain to be explained, and it seems to me impossible to content ourselves with the thesis put forward by M. Noth, which he himself qualified in his unfinished commentary on 1 Kings.[4]

In fact, if one investigates contemporary studies[5] and commentaries more closely, it quickly becomes apparent that a deuteronomistic interpretation of Kings is rarely[6] adopted in the fashion proposed by Noth. In fact, while Noth had insisted that only one redaction/edition and one historian were evident in Kings, many contemporary exegetes see multiple hands and revisions in the mix:[7]

1. M. Noth, *Überlieferungsgeschichtliche Studien:* [[*Die sammelnden und bearbeitenden Geschichtswerke im Alten Testament*]] (Halle, 1943; 2d ed. Tübingen, 1957). This book has been translated into English: *The Deuteronomistic History* (2d ed.; JSOTSup 15; Sheffield: JSOT Press, 1991). [[As a convenience to readers, references to Noth's work have been keyed to this recent English translation.]]

2. Cf. J. R. Porter, "Old Testament Historiography," in *Tradition and Interpretation* (ed. G. W. Anderson; 1979) 125–62; see especially p. 148: "the possible continuation of the Pentateuchal sources in any part of Joshua–2 Kings has come to something of a dead end."

3. I. Benzinger, *Jahwist und Elohist in den Königsbüchern* (1921); G. Hölscher, "Das Buch der Könige, seine Quellen und seine Redaktion," in *Eucharisterion: Festschrift H. Gunkel I* (1923) 158–213; and especially idem, *Geschichtsschreibung in Israel: Untersuchungen zum Yahwisten und Elohisten* (1952); O. Eissfeldt, *The Old Testament: An Introduction* (1965) 281–301; see especially pp. 297–99. However, Eissfeldt recognizes the probable existence of two deuteronomistic redactions (see also pp. 284 and 299–300).

4. M. Noth, *Könige I* (BKAT 9/1; 1968) with allusions to deuteronomistic redactors, pp. 12, 46–48, 133–34, 174–75, 208, 310, 312.

5. See especially the *status questionis* of E. Jenni, "Zwei Jahrzehnte Forschung an des Büchern Josua bis Könige," *TRu* 27 (1961) 1–32, 97–146; A. N. Radjawane, "Das deuteronomische Geschichtswerk: Ein Forschungsbericht," *TRu* 38 (1973) 177–216; E. Cortese, "Problemi attuali circa l'opera deuteronomistica," *Rivista biblica italiana* 26 (1978) 341–352.

6. Cf. H. D. Hoffmann, *Reform und Reformen: Untersuchungen zu einem Grundthema* (1980); M. Rehm, *Das zweite Buch der Könige* (1982) 266–270.

7. Cf. Radjawane, "Das deuteronomische Geschichtswerk," 212: "Mit seiner These von dem *einzigen Verfass* des DtrG hat Noth mehr Widerspruch als Zustimmung gefunden" [['Noth's thesis of the single authorship of the Deuteronomistic History has been met with more disagreement than approval']].

- Thus, as is the case with R. Smend, W. Dietrich, and T. Veijola,[8] some contemporary exegetes see three stages in deuteronomistic redaction, DtrH, [[223]] DtrP, and DtrN in a fairly short lapse of time, between 580 and 560;
- Thus also, following the lead of F. M. Cross[9] and many others[10] who took up the view already argued at the end of the last century (particularly by A. Kuenen, J. Wellhausen, and W. Nowack),[11] other exegetes have distinguished a first preexilic edition of Kings under the reign of Josiah and a second exilic edition appearing around 560.

This last position has recently been systematically argued by Richard Nelson in *The Double Redaction of the Deuteronomistic History* and by N. Lohfink.[12] It seems to be largely accepted[13] today, while the view distinguishing three deuteronomistic stages of revision in twenty or so years of exile has been greeted with a certain skepticism and seems rather unlikely.[14]

8. R. Smend, "Das Gesetz und die Völker: Ein Beitrag zur deuteronomischen Redaktions-geschichte," in *Probleme biblischer Theologie: Festschrift G. von Rad* (ed. H. W. Wolff; 1971) 494–509 [[translated in this volume as "The Law and the Nations," pp. 95–110]]; idem, *Die Entstehung des A.T.* (1978) 114–25; W. Dietrich, *Prophetie und Geschichte: Eine Redaktionsgeschichtliche Untersuchung zum deuteronomistischen Geschichtswerk* (1972); T. Veijola, *Die ewige Dynastie* (1975); idem, *Das Königtum in der Beurteilung der deuteronomistischen Historiographie* (1977).

9. See F. M. Cross, "The Structure of the Deuteronomic History," in *Perspectives in Jewish Learning* 3 (Annual of the College of Jewish Studies; Chicago, 1968) 9–24; idem, *Canaanite Myth and Hebrew Epic: [[Essays in the History of the Religion of Israel* (Cambridge: Harvard University Press, 1973)]] 274–89.

10. Cf., for the whole of Dtr history, W. Richter, *Traditionsgeschichtliche Untersuchungen zum Richterbuch* (1963); idem, *Die Bearbeitungen des "Retterbuches" in der deuteronomischen Epoche* (1964); I. Schlauri, "W. Richters Beitrag zur Redaktionsgeschichte des Richterbuches," *Bib* 54 (1973) 367–403; and, from a more general standpoint, Cortese, "Problemi attuali," 343–47.

11. A. Kuenen, *Histoire critique des livres de l'A.T. I* (Paris, 1866; trans. of: *Historisch-kritisch Onderzoek naar het ontstaan en de verzameling van de boeken des Ouden Verbonds* [1861]) 407–424; cf. also I. Benzinger, *Die Bücher der Könige* (1899) xiii; J. Wellhausen, *Die Komposition des Hexateuchs und der historischen Bücher des A. T.* (1963) 263–301, especially pp. 298–99; W. Nowack, "Deuteronomium und Regum," in *Festschrift K. Marti* (BZAW 41; 1925) 221–31.

12. R. Nelson, *The Double Redaction of the Deuteronomistic History* (JSOTSup 18; Sheffield: JSOT Press, 1981); see especially N. Lohfink, *Rückblick im Zorn auf den Staat, Vorlesungen zu ausgewählten Schlüsseltexten der Bücher Samuel und Könige* (1984).

13. See, for example, J. A. Montgomery, *The Book of Kings* (ICC; 1951) 44–45; J. Gray, *I and II Kings* (2d ed.; 1970) 6–9; R. E. Friedman, "From Egypt to Egypt: Dtr^1 and Dtr^2," in *Traditions in Transformation: Turning Points in Biblical Faith* (F. M. Cross Festschrift; ed. B. Halpern and J. D. Levenson; Winona Lake, Ind.: Eisenbrauns, 1981) 167–192; idem, *The Exile and Biblical Narrative: The Formation of the Deuteronomistic and Priestly Works* (1982); H. G. M. Williamson, "The Death of Josiah and the Continuing Development of the Deuteronomic History," *VT* 32 (1982) 242–47, especially pp. 242–43; P. Buis, "Rois," *SDB* 9 (1982) cols. 695–740, especially cols. 728–31.

14. Cf. already F. Langlamet, *RB* 81 (1974) 605–6; Cortese, "Problemi attuali," 349; F. Langlamet, *RB* 85 (1978) 277–300; H. Weippert, *ZAW* 95 (1983) 365–66. Note that J. A.

The hypothesis of a double deuteronomistic redaction, first under the reign of Josiah, then again around 560, seems to be corroborated and extended by an interesting study by Helga Weippert, entitled "Die 'deuteronomistischen' [[224]] Beurteilungen der Könige von Israel und Juda und das Problem der Redaktion der Königsbücher."[15] According to Weippert, an analysis of the formulas used to evaluate the kings of Judah and Israel appears to support three different redactions:

I The first, under Hezekiah, would evaluate the kings of Judah from Jehoshaphat to Ahaz and the kings of Israel from Joram to Hoshea;

II The second, under Josiah, would evaluate the kings of Israel from Jeroboam I to Ahaziah and the kings of Judah from Rehoboam to Asa, then from Hezekiah to Josiah;

III The third, during the exile, would bring a negative evaluation to bear on the last kings of Jerusalem: Jehoahaz, Jehoiakim, Jehoiachin, and Zedekiah.

If the second and third redactions proposed by Weippert seem to align themselves with the deuteronomistic double-redaction theory of the books of Kings, preexilic (under Josiah) and exilic (around 560), it also seems to bring to light a new redaction, *pre-* or rather *protodeuteronomistic*, during the reign of Hezekiah, a redaction that would be connected with Hezekiah's religious reform and an effort at centralizing worship in Jerusalem.

These conclusions have met a certain amount of opposition and should probably be slightly revised, particularly in light of some refinements from W. B. Barrick and some criticisms from E. Cortese, J. Van Seters, and S. Timm.[16] This is what we will attempt to do here by briefly

---

Soggin ("Problemi di storia e di storigrafia nell'antico Israele," *Henoch* 4 [1982] 1–16, especially p. 7) has proposed a harmonization of the two positions by associating DtrH and DtrP to the preexilic era (under Josiah) and DtrN to the postexilic.

15. H. Weippert, "Die 'deuteronomistischen' Beurteilungen der Könige von Israel und Juda und das Problem der Redaktion der Königsbücher," *Bib* 53 (1972) 301–39; cf. also idem, "Der Ort, den Jahwe erwählen wird, um dort seinen Namen wohnen zu lassen: Die Geschichte einer alttestamentlichen Formel," *BZ* 24 (1980) 76–94, especially pp. 86–87; idem, "Die Ätiologie des Nordreiches und seines Königshauses," *ZAW* 95 (1983) 344–75, especially pp. 365–69; idem, "Das deuteronomistische Geschichtswerk," *TRu* 50 (1985) 213–49; see also M. Weippert, "Fragen des israelitischen Geschichtsbewußtseins," *VT* 23 (1973) 415–42, especially pp. 437–38.

16. W. B. Barrick, "On the Removal of the 'High Places' in 1–2 Kings," *Bib* 55 (1974) 257–59; E. Cortese, "Lo schema deuteronomistico per i re di Giuda e d'Israele," *Bib* 56 (1975) 37–52; J. Van Seters, "Histories and Historians of the Ancient Near East: The Israelites," *Or* 50 (1981) 137–85, especially p. 169 n. 103; S. Timm, *Die Dynastie Omri* (FRLANT 124; Göttingen: Vandenhoeck & Ruprecht, 1982) 28–40.

examining the primary historical and stylistic elements of each of the redactions, beginning with redactions III and I, which appear the most obvious.

(1) The existence of an exilic deuteronomistic redaction of the books of Kings following a redaction/edition during the reign of Josiah seems [[225]] clearly supported by the homogeneous nature of the evaluations of the last four kings of Judah:

> Jehoahaz: *wayyaʿaś hāraʿ bĕʿênê yhwh kĕkōl ʾăšer-ʿāśû ʾăbōtāyw.* (2 Kgs 23:32)
> [[And he did what was evil in the sight of Yhwh according to all that his fathers had done.]]
>
> Jehoiakim: *wayyaʿaś hāraʿ bĕʿênê yhwh kĕkōl ʾăšer-ʿāśû ʾăbōtāyw.* (2 Kgs 23:37)
> [[And he did what was evil in the sight of Yhwh, according to all that his fathers had done.]]
>
> Jehoiachin: *wayyaʿaś hāraʿ bĕʿênê yhwh kĕkōl ʾăšer-ʿāśâ ʾābîw.* (2 Kgs 24:9)
> [[And he did what was evil in the sight of Yhwh according to all that his father did.]]
>
> Zedekiah: *wayyaʿaś hāraʿ bĕʿênê yhwh kĕkōl ʾăšer-ʿāśâ yĕhôyāqîm.* (2 Kgs 24:19)
> [[And he did what was evil in the sight of Yhwh according to all that Jehoiakim had done.]]

From the redactors' point of view, the completely negative judgment proffered explains the fall of Jerusalem and the exile in 597 and especially in 587. Since this analysis of the text only confirms the existence of an exilic deuteronomistic redaction[17] that is accepted as true by most commentators, we will not elaborate on it here any further.

(2) In spite of the fact that several commentators had previously made allusions in one way or another[18] to the existence of a pre- or protodeuteronomistic redaction of the books of Kings under Hezekiah, H. Weippert's discovery of its existence seems to be the most original contribution

17. Although M. Noth disagrees (*Überlieferungsgeschichtliche Studien,* 110 n. 1 [[*The Deuteronomistic History,* 145 n. 1]]), this redactor was probably an exile and likely part of Jehoiachin's entourage in Babylon (cf. K. E. Pohlmann, "Erwägungen zum Schlußkapitel des deuteronomistischen Geschichtswerkes . . . ," in *Textgemäß: Aufsätze und Beiträge zur Hermeneutik des A.T.: Festschrift für E. Würthwein* [1979] 94–109).

18. Cf. A. Jepsen, *Die Quellen des Königsbuches* (2d ed.; 1953) 38; Eissfeldt, *The Old Testament,* 297–299; J. Schüpphaus, *Richter- und Prophetengeschichten als Glieder der Geschichtsdarstellung der Richter- und Königszeit* (Ph.D. diss., Bonn, 1967), as cited in *ZAW* 81 (1969) 143–44; cf. also G. Garbini, "Le fonti citate nel 'Libro dei Re'. . . ," *Henoch* 3 (1981) 26–46, especially 37–38, 46.

to the study that has recently come to light. Among the various ideological and literary aspects of this redaction, perhaps the most characteristic, as Barrick[19] has pointed out, seems to be the condemnation of the kings of Judah for their attitude toward the *bāmôt* or 'high places'. Thus, after a brief comment, *wĕhabbāmôt lōʾ-sārû* [['and the high places were not taken away']] (1 Kgs 15:14a), which was probably inserted and is aimed at Asa, we find, for Jehoshaphat:

> *ʾak habbāmôt lōʾ-sārû ʿôd hāʿām mĕzabbĕḥîm ûmĕqaṭṭĕrîm babbāmôt* (1 Kgs 22:44)
> [[yet the high places were not taken away, and the people still sacrificed and burned incense on the high places.]]

And as [[226]] for Joash (2 Kgs 12:4), for Amaziah (14:4), for Azariah (15:4) and for Jotham (15:35), in what seems to be a refrain,[20] the text has:

> *raq habbāmôt lōʾ-sārû ʿôd hāʿām mĕzabbĕḥîm ûmĕqaṭṭĕrîm babbāmôt*
> [[Nevertheless the high places were not removed; the people still sacrificed and burned incense on the high places.]]

This reference to the *bāmôt* [['high places']] that had not disappeared can be also be found in reference to Ahaz under a different form, for he himself took part in their cult worship:

> *wayĕzabbēaḥ wayĕqaṭṭēr babbāmôt wĕʿal-haggĕbāʿôt wĕtaḥat kol-ʿēṣ raʿănān* (2 Kgs 16:4)
> [[And he sacrificed and burned incense on the high places, and on the hills, and under every green tree.]]

Finally this long series of negative[21] evaluations ends with Hezekiah, of whom it is explicitly said,

> *hûʾ hēsîr ʾet-habbāmôt* (2 Kgs 18:4a)
> [[He removed the high places.]]

19. Barrick, "On the Removal"; cf. also H. Weippert, "Der Ort, den Jahwe erwählen wird," 86–87.

20. Only Joram and Ahaziah of Judah (H. Weippert's pattern IS2) do not enter into this pattern and do not appear, at first blush, to be associated with the same redactor as IS1 (cf. H. Weippert, "Die 'deuteronomistischen' Beurteilungen," 309–12, especially 312; idem, "Der Ort, den Jahwe erwählen wird," 86). This apparent exception probably is to be explained by the use of a previous Judean document justifying the coup d'état against Athaliah during the first years of the reign of Josiah (see below, n. 42).

21. Note that the building of the *bāmôt* [['high places']] is also held against the Israelites in 2 Kgs 17:9–11 in very similar terms, which may hint at the same redactor.

The redactional unity of the evaluations of the kings of Judah from Jehoshaphat to Hezekiah is not only characterized by the reference to the *bāmôt* but also by the use of the verb *sûr* 'to turn away, disappear'. The verb *sûr* is characteristically preceded by a term of negation and followed by the preposition *min* in the evaluations of the kings of Israel beginning with Joram (2 Kgs 3:3), all of whom are judged negatively. Slight variations to the formula may be found (Joram, 2 Kgs 3:3; Jehu, 10:29; Jehoahaz, 13:2, 6) but it is found most often in the form

> (*wayyaʿaś hāraʿ bĕʿênê yhwh*) *lōʾ-sār mē/min/mikkol/mēʿal ḥaṭṭōʾ(w)t yārobʿām* (*ben-nĕbāṭ*) *ʾăšer heḥĕṭîʾ ʾet-yiśrāʾel*
> [[(and he did what was evil in the sight of Yhwh) he did not turn aside from (all) the sins of Jeroboam (son of Nebat), which he made Israel to sin]]

used for Jehu (2 Kgs 10:31), Joash (13:11), Jeroboam II (14:24), Zechariah (15:9), Menahem (15:18), Pekahiah (15:24), and Pekah (15:28). This series of negative judgments[22] culminates in the final judgment on the whole kingdom of Israel in 2 Kgs 17:22:

> *wayyēlĕkû bĕnê yiśrāʾel bĕkol-ḥaṭṭōʾwt yārobʿām ʾăšer ʿāśâ lōʾ-sārû mimmennāh*
> [[and the people of Israel walked in all of the sins which Jeroboam did; they did not depart from them]]

and, in apposition to this judgment, the judgment of God:

> *hēsîr yhwh ʾet-yiśrāʾel mēʾal pānāyw.* (2 Kgs 17:23a; cf. 17:18a)
> [[Yhwh removed Israel out of his sight.]]

The redactional unity of the judgments on the kings of Judah, from Jehoshaphat to Ahaz, and on the kings of Israel, from Joram to the fall of Samaria, is thus [[227]] quite clear and distinguishable by the use of the verb *sûr* with the negative. Apparently this redaction, following the fall of Samaria in 722, was connected with the religious reforms of Hezekiah[23]

22. Note the inclusion [[of a qualifying phrase]] when comparing the judgment of Joram, *wayyaʿăśeh hāraʿ bĕʿênê yhwh raq lōʾ kĕʾābîw ûkĕʾimmô* [['and he did what was evil in the sight of Yhwh, though not like his father and mother']] (2 Kgs 3:2a), with that of Hoshea: *wayyaʿaś hāraʿ bĕʿênê yhwh raq lōʾ kĕmalkê yiśrāʾēl ʾăšer hāyû lĕpānāyw* [['and he did what was evil in the sight of Yhwh, yet not as the kings of Israel who were before him']] (2 Kgs 17:2).

23. H. Weippert suggests an Israelite redactor who may have taken refuge in Jerusalem and speculates that he may have been previously in the service of Hoshea, a fact that might explain the slightly modified judgment of this king (2 Kgs 17:2). On this point, see A. van der Kooij, *ZAW* 96 (1984) 109–12. However, the criticism of the sins of Jeroboam may result just as well from a Judean attached to the court of Hezekiah (cf. Cortese, "Lo schema deuteronomistico," 48).

(2 Kgs 18:4–6), a period also characterized by important literary activity (see Prov 25:1) and a desire for national reconciliation between the Northern and Southern Kingdoms.

It should be noted that the beginning of this series of judgments concerns the reigns of Jehoshaphat of Judah (ca. 871–846) and Joram of Israel (852–841)—that is, it begins toward the middle of the ninth century B.C. This dating for the beginning of the proto-Deuteronomic redaction remained a mystery to H. Weippert and was difficult for J. Van Seters to accept.[24] I will propose a fairly simple explanation linked to a better understanding of what Weippert called redaction II.

(3) Weippert joins what she calls redaction II, performed under Josiah, to:

- on one hand, the judgments rendered on the following kings of Judah: Rehoboam, Abijah, and Asa, and on the kings of Israel from Jeroboam I to Ahaziah; that is to say, on the kings of both kingdoms, from the division until 850;
- on the other hand, the judgments rendered on the kings of Judah: Hezekiah, Manasseh, Amon, and Josiah.

For this double period, Weippert distinguishes a pattern, which she calls IIS, describing the judgments on the kings of Judah, and a pattern IIN for the kings of Israel. However, she herself notes that the IIS pattern seems to apply to Jeroboam I as well, while the IIN pattern is "weitaus kompliziert" ⟦'very complicated'⟧ and that its structure "läßt sich nur schwer erfassen" ⟦'is difficult to grasp'⟧.[25] Hence, it is not surprising that Cortese, Van Seters, and Timm[26] have highlighted the weaknesses of this view.

In order to understand better the redaction of these judgments, one ought rather to distinguish the two periods that Weippert sought to join in her redaction II, separating on one hand the kings of Judah and Israel from the divided kingdom until around 850, and on the other the kings of Judah from the seventh century until Josiah: ⟦228⟧

(A) The judgments rendered on Manasseh, Amon, and Josiah were probably written during the reign of Josiah, in harmony with the conclusions of the exegetes who popularized the notion of a preexilic deuteronomistic redaction. This sweeping redaction under the reign of Josiah did not flinch at reworking previous history, in particular the final judgment regarding the fall of Samaria[27] and, in part, the judgment rendered on

24. Van Seters, "Histories," 169 n. 103: "most curious."

25. Weippert, "Die 'deuteronomistischen' Beurteilungen," 325, 327.

26. Cortese, "Lo schema deuteronomistico"; Van Seters, "Histories and Historians"; Timm, *Die Dynastie Omri*.

27. Cf. M. Cogan, "Israel in Exile: The View of a Josianic Historian," *JBL* 97 (1978) 40–44.

Hezekiah. This process was executed both by the reordering of the previous material and by insertion of new material, a fact that makes the literary criticism of these passages all the more difficult. It will suffice here to underscore the fact that, compared with the religious reforms of Hezekiah, the reforms of Josiah are characterized by the elimination of the worship of the 'hosts of heaven' (*kōl-ṣĕbāʾ haššāmayīm*) that, it is reported, had developed previously, perhaps under Assyrian influence at the time of Manasseh and Amon (cf. 2 Kgs 21:3, 5; 23:4–5). This cultic worship is not mentioned in regard to the prior kings of Judah,[28] and reference to it may serve as a distinguishing criterion of the redaction under Josiah.

(B) The judgments rendered on the kings of Judah and Israel, from the divided kingdom until ca. 850, were probably written toward the end of this period. In fact, in addition to the observations of Weippert regarding the judgment formulas for these kings, we can highlight here two literary and ideological traits that seem characteristic of this redaction.

(B1) For the Northern Kingdom, regarding Baasha (1 Kgs 15:34; cf. 16:2), Zimri (16:19), Omri (16:26), and Ahaziah (22:53), as well as, implicitly, Nadab (cf. 15:26) and Ahab (cf. 22:53), it is said:

> *wayyēlek/lāleket bĕ(kol-)derek yārobʿām (ben-nĕbāṭ) ûbĕḥaṭṭāʾtô ʾăšer heḥĕṭîʾ/ʿāśâ lĕhaḥăṭîʾ ʾet-yiśrāʾel*
> [[and he walked / to walk in (all) the way of Jeroboam (son of Nebat) and in his sin which he made Israel to sin]]

and we should note that the pattern *bĕderek yārobʿām* [['in the way of Jeroboam']] is not to be found elsewhere in the books of Kings; only 1 Kgs 13:33 comes close, mentioning regarding Jeroboam I 'his evil ways' (*lōʾ-šāb yārobʿām middarkô hārāʿâ* [['Jeroboam did not turn from his evil way']]), and confirming in this way that the following series begins with the judgment rendered on the reign of Jeroboam I.

(B2) Concerning the kingdom of Judah, we should note the special role played by the *qādēš* 'male shrine prostitute' at that time. Male shrine prostitutes (*qādēš*) existed in the country under Rehoboam, according to 1 Kgs 14:24; then his son Abijah "walked in all the sins of his father, which he had done before him" (1 Kgs 15:3). In contrast, Asa "expelled (*wayyaʿăber*) the male shrine prostitutes from the land" (1 Kgs 15:12), and this reform was continued and completed by his son Jehoshaphat, who 'walked in all the way of Asa his father' [[229]] (*bĕkol-derek ʾāsāʾ ʾabîw*, 1 Kgs

28. The mention of the cult worship of the "hosts of heaven" in the judgment rendered on Samaria (2 Kgs 17:16) should probably be associated with the redaction under Josiah, for it repeats word for word 2 Kgs 21:3.

22:43),[29] 'and the remnant of the male cult prostitutes who remained in the days of his father Asa, he exterminated from the land' (*wĕyeter haq-qādēš ʾăšer nišʾar bîmê ʾāsāʾ ʾābîw biʿēr min-hāʾāreṣ*, 1 Kgs 22:47). The shrine prostitutes are only mentioned again once,[30] in 2 Kgs 23:7, probably because Josiah is described as taking up and finishing all of the previous religious reforms.

These two characteristics, the use of *bĕderek yārobʿām* ⟦'in the way of Jeroboam'⟧ and the mention of *qādēš* ⟦'male prostitute'⟧, seem to indicate that Weippert's classification needs to be refined and that, in addition to the exilic deuteronomistic redaction, the preexilic deuteronomistic redaction under Josiah, and the protodeuteronomistic redaction under Hezekiah, we must account for an earlier redaction of the books of Kings, toward the middle of the ninth century B.C. It is immediately apparent that the date for this earlier redaction easily explains why the redaction under Hezekiah begins by judging kings who died after 850. In fact, the protodeuteronomistic redaction simply took up and continued an ancient synchronic royal chronicle where it had left off.

It is helpful at this point to stop for a minute and explore further this redaction/edition of the mid–ninth century B.C. in order better to grasp its historical context. We should first observe that, according to a systematic study of the "ways of Jeroboam," this redaction probably originates from the kingdom of Judah, likely from Jerusalem. Further indications regarding the shrine prostitutes seem to be tied to the religious reforms of Jehoshaphat, who continued and finished the reforms of his father, Asa (cf. 1 Kgs 15:11–15). More importantly, this redaction probably dates back to the end of the reign of Jehoshaphat, since it includes a judgment on the reign of Ahaziah of Israel (853–852). A date toward 850 B.C., or between 852 and 846 at any rate, seems very probable, making this redaction contemporaneous with the first years of Joram, king of Israel (852–841). At this time, two historical circumstances come to bear that explain

29. It would be natural to associate the formula *bĕkol-derek ʾāsāʾ ʾābîw* ⟦'in all the way of Asa his father'⟧ and *derek yārobʿām* ⟦'way of Jeroboam'⟧ with the same redactor who took aim at the kings of Israel (see also 1 Kgs 22:53, *bĕderek ʾābîw* ⟦'in the way of his father'⟧). Similar expressions can only be found in 2 Kgs 21:21 (*wayyēlek bĕkol-hadderek ʾăšer hālak ʾābîw* ⟦'He walked in all the way in which his father walked'⟧) and 2 Kgs 22:2 (*wayyēlek bĕkol-derek dāwid ʾābîw* ⟦'and walked in all the way of David his father'⟧). It is possible that these last two formulas used by the redactor under Josiah's reign are more or less conscious borrowing/adaptations of the redaction from the middle of the ninth century.

30. It is interesting to note that in the books of Chronicles the four references to the shrine prostitutes found in Kings have been deleted, probably because this institution had almost disappeared from Judah: cf. P.-E. Dion, "Did Cultic Prostitution Fall into Oblivion during the Postexilic Era? Some Evidence from Chronicles and the Septuagint," *CBQ* 43 (1981) 41–48.

the establishment of a synchronic history of the kings of Judah and Israel after the schism. [[230]]

(1) The two kingdoms were reconciled to each other in the middle of the ninth century. According to 1 Kgs 22:45[44], "Jehoshaphat made peace with the king of Israel," a peace that became an alliance sealed by the marriage[31] of Jehoshaphat's son Joram (who would become king of Judah ca. 848–846–841) to the daughter of the king of Israel, Athaliah, probably "daughter of Ahab" (2 Kgs 8:18 = 2 Chr 21:6) and granddaughter of Omri (see 2 Kgs 8:26 = 2 Chr 22:2). This political and military alliance is illustrated by the joint expedition of Joram of Israel and Jehoshaphat of Judah against Mesha, king of Moab,[32] who had revolted approximately 852 (2 Kgs 3:4ff.). This context of reconciliation and political alliance between Judah and Israel explains the willingness of a Judean redactor to write down in the same book the histories of both kingdoms after their division. In a similar way, under Hezekiah, the desire to welcome Northern Israelites after the fall of Samaria explains the continuation of the same synchronic double history.

(2) The redaction of this double history under the reigns of Hezekiah and Josiah was clearly linked to the religious reforms and, more precisely, cultural reforms of the two kings; the redaction served as an ideological tool that helped implement these reforms. It seems that the same motivation existed at the time of Jehoshaphat who, as we have seen, completed the reforms begun by his father, Asa (1 Kgs 15:11–15), by totally eliminating the male shrine prostitutes (1 Kgs 22:43–47). This religious and cultural reform explains the fact that the books of Chronicles dedicate at least four chapters (2 Chronicles 17–20) to his reign. Furthermore, in spite of the fact that the historical value of many accounts in Chronicles has been debated, we should note that 2 Chr 17:7–9 seems to describe the systematic organization or reorganization of religious teaching in [[231]]

31. This marriage may be dated to approximately 864, since Ahaziah, product of this union, was 22 years old when he ascended to the throne in 841 (cf. 2 Kgs 8:26). This approximate date implies that the reconciliation between Judah and Israel was probably the work of Ahab.

32. Regarding this expedition, see J. R. Bartlett, "The 'United' Campaign against Moab in 2 Kings 3:4–27," in *Midian, Moab and Edom* (ed. J. F. A. Sawyer and D. J. A. Clines; 1983) 135–46, although Bartlett is tempted to reject the mention of Jehoshaphat in the account (especially pp. 143–45) due to an inaccurate chronology. K. H. Bernhardt ("Der Feldzug der drei Könige," in *Schalom: Studien zu Glaube und Geschichte Israels—Festschrift A. Jepsen* ([ed. K. H. Bernhardt; 1971] 11–22) places this campaign toward 800, but this shift seems arbitrary and historically unlikely. Regarding the uniqueness of the mention of Jehoshaphat in the account, see M. Weippert, *Edom* (unpublished dissertation, Tübingen, 1971) 316–18; S. J. DeVries, *Prophet against Prophet* (1978) 88–89; A. R. Green, "Regnal Formulas in the Hebrew and Greek Texts of the Books of Kings," *JNES* 42 (1983) 167–80, especially pp. 175–77.

Judean towns. This teaching was probably administrated by the Levites and linked to a reform in the administration of the royal justice system (2 Chr 19:4–5).[33]

Such a historical context makes the creation of a first redaction of the synchronic history of the kings of Judah and Israel after the divided kingdom seem perfectly reasonable.

In fact, without entering here into the details of the literary criticism of the books of Samuel and the beginning of the first part of 1 Kings, we see that this first redaction of the synchronic history of the two kingdoms must have very naturally followed suit to the previous history of the unified kingdom already existing in the form of two redactions of the story of David (the main theme of 1 Kings 1–2)[34] under Abiathar[35] and Zadok[36] (or possibly Nathan?[37]) and a "wisdom" or "sapiential" redaction on the work of Solomon (the theme of 1 Kings 3–12:19).[38]

Thus, leaving aside sources specific to each of the two kingdoms, sources that themselves may have seen several stages of redaction—such as the account justifying the division of the kingdom at the time of Jeroboam (1 Kgs 11:26–40),[39] the account collating the stories of Elijah and Elisha,[40]

33. Cf. W. F. Albright, "The Judicial Reform of Jehoshaphat (2 Chron 19:5–11)," in *A. Marx Jubilee Volume* (1950) 61–82; R. Knierim, "Exodus 18 und die Neuordnung des mosäischen Gerichtsbarkeit," *ZAW* 73 (1961) 146–71, especially pp. 162–66; G. C. Macholz, "Zur Geschichte des Justizorganisation in Juda," *ZAW* 84 (1972) 314–40, especially pp. 317–33; H. Reviv, "The Traditions concerning the Inception of the Legal System in Israel: Significance and Dating," in *ErIsr* 14 (*H. L. Ginsberg Volume*; 1978) 19–22 and 122ff., especially p. 21; K. W. Whitelam, *The Just King* (JSOTSup 12; Sheffield: JSOT Press, 1979) 185–206 and 268–71; H. D. Hoffmann, *Reform und Reformen* (1980) 95–96; D. Matthias, *ZAW* 96 (1984) 33–34.

34. See the comments of M. Noth, *Könige I* (1968) 9–12.

35. Cf. B. Duhm, *Das Buch Jeremia* (KHC 11; 1901) 3; K. Budde, *Geschichte der althebräischen Literatur* (2d ed.; 1909) 38–41; H. Schulte, *Die Entstehung der Geschichtsschreibung im Alten Israel* (BZAW 128; 1972) 218; F. Langlamet, "Pour ou contre Salomon?" *RB* 83 (1976) 481–528, especially pp. 519–23; A. Caquot, "Hébreu et araméen," *Annuaire du Collège de France* 76 (1976) 451–60; 77 (1977) 523–30, especially p. 523; 78 (1978) 559–70; 79 (1979) 465–77; 80 (1980) 555–65.

36. Caquot, "Hébreu et araméen."

37. Cf. J. Gray, *I and II Kings* (1970) 18–19.

38. Cf. ibid., 46–48, 133–34, 174–75, 208; Cf. also the essays of J. Liver, "The Book of the Acts of Solomon," *Bib* 48 (1967) 75–101; B. Porten, "The Structure and Theme of the Solomon Narrative," *HUCA* 38 (1967) 93–128; Van Seters, "Histories and Historians," 182–83.

39. Cf. especially H. Weippert ("Die Ätiologie des Nordreiches und seines Königshauses [I Reg 11,29–40]," *ZAW* 95 [1983] 344–75), who distinguishes between two predeuteronomistic redactions, one at the end of the reign of Solomon and the other before Baasha's coup d'état.

40. These accounts have been heavily studied: cf. G. Fohrer, *Elia* (2d ed.; 1968); O. H. Steck, *Überlieferung und Zeitgeschichte in den Elia-Erzählungen* (1968); L. Bronner, *The Stories of Elijah and Elisha* (1968); R. Smend, *VT* 25 (1975) 525–43; E. von Nordheim, *Bib* 59 (1978)

[[232]] the justification for Jehu's coup d'état[41] (1 Kings 17–2 Kings 10 + 13[42]), and the account justifying the coup d'état against Athaliah (2 Kings 11[43])—we can outline the creation of the books of Kings through seven successive redaction/editions:

1. The Abiatharite account of David, written around 970, probably at the end of David's reign and ending with the crowning of Solomon.
2. The Zadokite (or Nathanite?) edition of the same account, probably written during the first years of Solomon's reign, perhaps around 960.
3. The redaction of the history of Solomon's reign, ending with the divided kingdom, probably written around 920 during the reign of Rehoboam.
4. The redaction/edition comprising the history of the two kingdoms of Judah and Israel until their reconciliation, written around 850, during the reign of Jehoshaphat.
5. The protodeuteronomistic redaction/edition of the history of both kingdoms until the fall of Samaria and Hezekiah's reform, probably written around 710–705.
6. The deuteronomistic redaction/edition linked with Josiah's reform, written around 620–609.
7. The exilic deuteronomistic redaction/edition written around 560.

153–73; E. Ruprecht, *VT* 28 (1978) 73–82; E. Würthwein, *ZThK* 75 (1978) 375–97; Timm, *Die Dynastie Omri*.

41. G. Garbini ("'Narrativa della successione' o 'Storia dei re'?" *Henoch* 1 [1979] 19–41) sees an important redaction at the beginning of Jehu's reign covering the materials included in Judg 9:1 to 2 Kgs 10:14, but he finds support only in similarities of "literary motifs," a vague enough notion that does not seem to provide sufficient basis for literary criticism. There was in fact a redaction at this time, but it aimed principally at justifying Jehu's coup d'état and followed the classic pattern for royal propaganda used to justify political or military coups. Regarding this genre of literature, see M. Liverani, "L'Histoire de Joas," *VT* 24 (1974) 438–53.

42. Without going into the details of the analysis, it seems to me that we must distinguish between:

- Stories about Elijah that were retold and perhaps written down by Elisha; these stories were then taken up again at the time of Jehu and joined with stories about Elisha, probably by Gehazi, Elisha's servant.
- The account justifying Jehu's coup d'état, written in the early years of his reign.

These two accounts were subsequently collated and completed around 800 B.C. during the reign of Joash of Israel, who called the old Elisha "my father" (2 Kgs 13:14) and who is probably the king who asked Gehazi, the servant of the man of God, "Tell me about all the great things Elisha has done" (2 Kgs 8:4).

43. Cf. Liverani, "L'Histoire de Joas"; cf. also C. Levin's essay, "Der Sturz der Königin Atalia," *SBS* 105 (1982).

[[233]] The two books of Kings therefore appear to be the culmination of literary activity spanning more than four centuries[44]–that is, approximately the same time span as the events recounted in the text. At each of these literary stages these books were revised and updated: not only was recent history appended to the text, but previously recorded history was revised and systematically corrected when necessary.

Therefore, if the present text is indeed the edition that was revised and edited by the last important redactor–that is, the exilic deuteronomistic redactor, as M. Noth argued–the redactor did not create a continuous history of more than four centuries by pulling together material from disparate sources. Rather, the exilic deuteronomistic redaction should be seen as a final revised and corrected edition of a book that had already seen a literary history of about four centuries.

Why was this history written and rewritten and periodically updated both historically and ideologically for more than 400 years? Who wrote it, and for whom? What was its purpose? It is important to comment here, however briefly, on the historical and cultural significance of the long literary history of the books of Kings that we have just elucidated.

First of all, it is clear that each of the redactors and, consequently, each edition of this recorded history aimed at more than simply recording a succession of facts as they occurred. Rather, the text's goal is to inculcate in the reader a certain ideology, both political and religious,[45] corresponding to the reforms in vogue at that time. As a result, the text takes on a *didactic* flavor of varying intensity.[46] The didactic characteristics of the deuteronomistic editions that are often associated [[234]] with a "school"[47] have been well studied recently, and we have just demonstrated the fact that the redaction from the middle of the ninth century seems to have

44. The textual variants in the Greek text suggest that the books of Kings were subsequently transmitted in two different versions. Cf. especially the work of J. Trebolle Barrera: *EstBib* 38 (1979–80) 189–220; *RB* 87 (1980) 87–103; *Salomón y Jeroboán: Historia de la recensión y redacción de I Reyes 11–12, 14* (1980); *Salmanticensis* 28 (1981) 137–52; *Jehú y Joás* (1984).

45. G. von Rad, "Die deuteronomische Geschichtstheologie in den Königsbüchern," in *Gesammelte Studien zum A.T.* (1958) 189–204; H. W. Wolff, "Das Kerygma des deuteronomistischen Geschichtswerks," *ZAW* 73 (1961) 171–86; cf. also E. Zenger, "Die deuteronomistische Interpretation der Rehabilitierung Jojachins," *BZ* 12 (1968) 16–30.

46. Cf. for example M. Noth (*Überlieferungsgeschichtliche Studien*, 100 [[= *Deuteronomistic History*, 134]]): "Dtr hat sein Werk nicht zur Unterhaltung in müßigen Stunden oder nur Befriedigung des Interesses an der nationalen Geschichte verfaßt, sondern zur *Belehrung* [emphasis mine] über den echten Sinn der Geschichte Israels . . ." [['Dtr did not compose his work for entertainment in times of idle leisure or only for the gratification of an interest in national history but, rather, for the *teaching* [. . .] of a true sense of the history of Israel . . .']].

47. Cf. for example J. Fichtner, *Das erste Buch von den Königen* (1964) 18: "eine ganze Schule" [['an entire school']]; J. Delorme and J. Briend, "Les livres des Rois," in *Introduction critique à l'A.T.* (ed. H. Cazelles; 1973) 2.301–27, especially 320: "we should rather think of a

been linked to a reform in teaching enacted in the kingdom of Judah at the time of Jehoshaphat.

Second, it is evident that the various redactor-editors of the books of Kings were scribes at the heart of the royal court[48] and were very likely quite close to the king. They had direct access to the royal archives and made their talents available to the administration's propaganda favoring various religious and political reforms that the king was carrying out.[49] From one end to the other, from David to Jehoiachin, this is a "history of kings," characterized by *royal ideology*. When the Temple, the priests, or the prophets are mentioned in this history, it is because they were in direct relation to the king, either as counselors or in opposition to him.

The royal and didactic character of the various redaction/editions of the books of Kings suggests that they were probably written for and used as a teaching instrument to inculcate in the future civil servants of the kingdom a sense of national consciousness and service to the king–that is, of royal ideology. They were also used as a tool to explain the present political situation of a given administration, based not only on great historical deeds but also on the errors of the past. This signifies that the history of the redaction of the books of Kings is probably best explained as the growth of a historical reference work–we would say today a historical textbook–used in the teaching of the royal school of Jerusalem.[50] [[235]]

---

school whose work started before 587 and continued thereafter"; Radjawane, "Das deuteronomische Geschichtswerk," 212; Porter, "Old Testament Historiography," 134ff.

48. Cf. M. Weinfeld, *Deuteronomy and the Deuteronomic School* (Oxford: Oxford University Press, 1972; repr. Winona Lake, Ind.: Eisenbrauns, 1992) especially pp. 158–71 and 184; Porter, "Old Testament Historiography." 144.

49. On the links between literature and politics, compare A. Weiser, "Die Legitimation des Königs David," *VT* 16 (1966) 325–354; Liverani, "L'Histoire de Joas," 438–53; K. W. Whitelam, "The Defence of David," *JSOT* 29 (1984) 61–87; see, regarding Egypt, G. Posener, *Littérature et politique dans l'Egypte de la XIIème dysnastie* (1956).

50. Cf. A. Lemaire, *Les écoles et la formation de la Bible dans l'ancien Israël* (OBO 39; 1981) especially pp. 67–68 and 78–81.

Chronological Table

David (1010–1003–970)	
Solomon (971–970–931)	
Rehoboam (931–914)	Jeroboam I (931–910)
Abijah/Abijam (914–912)	
Asa (912–871)	Nadab (910–909)
	Baasha (909–886)
	Elah (886–885)
	Zimri (885)
	Omri (885–881–874)
	Tibni (885–881)
Jehoshaphat (871–846)	Ahab (874–853)
	Ahaziah (853–852)
	Joram (852–841)
Joram (848–846–841)	
Ahaziah (841)	
Joash (841–835–802) Athalia (841–835)	Jehu (841–814)
	Jehoahaz (819–814–803)
Amaziah (804–802–776)	Joash (805–803–790)
	Jeroboam II (790–750)
Uzziah/Azariah (790–776–739)	
	Zechariah (750)
	Shallum (750)
	Menahem (750–741)
Jotham (749–739–735/4)	Pekahiah (741–740)
	Pekah (750–740–732)
Ahaz (735/4–719)	Hoshea (731–722)
Hezekiah (727–719–699)	
Manasseh (699–645)	
Amon (645?–640)	
Josiah (640–609)	
Jehoahaz (609)	
Jehoiakim (609–598)	
Jehoiachin (598–597)	
Zedekiah (597–587)	
Exile–Liberation of Jehoiachin (561)	

Ephraimite versus Deuteronomistic History

ALEXANDER ROFÉ

In contrast to the influential hypothesis of Noth for one exilic edition of the Deuteronomistic History, Rofé revives an older hypothesis, which conceives of the material in Deuteronomy through Kings as being composed in blocks by a succession of at least three groups of authors. One such block is the original book of Deuteronomy. The second section, which ranges from Joshua 24 to the end of 1 Samuel 12, is nondeuteronomistic in character. The third block is the rest of Samuel and Kings, which comprises the original work of the Deuteronomists. Noth's theory agrees with distinguishing between the first and third blocks but does not allow the second. In Rofé's view, the second block, Joshua 24 through 1 Samuel 12*, constitutes a predeuteronomistic history. This history can stand on its own and reflects an Ephraimite (Northern Israel) setting and orientation. Only at a later point was this unit incorporated into the larger Deuteronomistic History. Each of the three major units has its own distinctive theological platform. Whereas Deuteronomy guardedly allows for the introduction of kingship and the Deuteronomistic History is positively inclined toward it, the Ephraimite History is anti-kingship in orientation. Rofé's essay, which has not received the scrutiny it deserves, calls attention to the diversity of perspectives embedded within the corpus of Deuteronomy and the Former Prophets.

[[221]] The purpose of this short paper is to cope, at least partly, with Martin Noth's thesis concerning the deuteronomistic (= Dtr) historical work. The somewhat unconventional direction adopted here may be in line with Prof. J. A. Soggin's scholarly contribution on historical and historiographical problems, since he too repeatedly sought new directions and

Reprinted with permission from *Storia e Tradizioni di Israele: Scritti in Onore di J. Alberto Soggin* (ed. D. Garrone and F. Israel; Brescia: Paideia, 1991) 221–35.

alternative solutions, first in his paper on the "Question of the Children,"[1] and recently in his original answer to the query as to where a critical history of Israel should begin.[2]

As well known, nearly fifty years ago, Noth came forth with an innovative hypothesis, most consequential for the research of the Pentateuch and the Former Prophets.[3] According to him, the literary sequence Deuteronomy 1–2 Kings 25 constitutes one single composition, the Dtr historical work. It narrated the history of Israel from Horeb to Babylon, having as a subject the story of the covenant between the LORD and Israel: the LORD enjoined Israel to observe his precepts and installed them in the Land; Israel repeatedly broke the covenant, and the LORD, after recurring warnings, banished them from His presence, exiling them to Assyria and Babylonia. This great opus was composed by one author, who remained in the Land during the Babylonian Exile,[4] on [[222]] the basis of a variety of sources at his disposal. The author's own comments mostly appear in the epitomes by which he either introduced or concluded the tale of each period of his history.

The impact of Noth's theory was enormous, both in Germany and abroad, especially in the English-speaking countries. Though not a few tentatives were made to refine and improve the hypothesis. His followers in Germany singled out a series of Dtr redactors: a historian, a prophetic disciple and one upholding the Torah-piety.[5] In the United States, on the other hand, the various Dtr redactions were differentiated according to the distinct historical settings of their compilers, either before or after the Exile.[6] Nevertheless, Noth's hypothesis has remained a cornerstone for all

1. J. A. Soggin, "Kultätiologische Sagen und Katechese im Hexateuch," *VT* 10 (1960) 341–47.

2. J. A. Soggin, *Storia d'Israele*, Brescia 1984, 53–57.

3. M. Noth, *Überlieferungsgeschichtliche Studien* 1, Halle 1943, 1–110; English Translation: *The Deuteronomistic History* (JSOTSup 15) Sheffield 1981.

4. Aliter J. A. Soggin, "Der Entstehungsort des deuteronomischen Geschichtswerkes," *ThLZ* 100 (1975) 3–8. Having highlighted the elements in the Dtr opus that emphasized the Exile (such as Joshua 23, 2 Kgs 21:10ff.), Soggin concluded that the whole work was directed to the exiles and must have been written in Babylon.

5. R. Smend, "Das Gesetz und die Völker. Ein Beitrag zur deuteronomischen Redaktionsgeschichte," *Probleme biblischer Theologie–Festschrift G. von Rad*, München 1971, 494–509 [[translated in this volume, pp. 95–110]]; W. Dietrich, *Prophetie und Geschichte* (FRLANT 108), Göttingen 1972; T. Veijola, *Das Königtum in der Beurteilung der deuteronomistischen Historiographie* (An. Ac. Scient. Fen. 198), Helsinki 1977.

6. F. M. Cross, "The Themes of the Books of Kings and the Structure of the Deuteronomistic History," in his: *Canaanite Myth and Hebrew Epic*, Cambridge, Mass., 1973, 274–89 [[reprinted in this volume, pp. 79–94]]; R. E. Friedman, *The Exile and Biblical Narrative* (HSM 22), Chico, Calif., 1981; R. D. Nelson, *The Double Redaction of the Deuteronomistic History* (JSOTSup 18), Sheffield 1981.

subsequent scholarship, even if, as usual in our discipline, full agreement has never been achieved.[7]

However, it seems to me that some weighty arguments against Noth have not yet been stated. In the first place, one should note that the unity of the Dtr composition has not been demonstrated, but merely asserted by Noth.[8] This is a remarkable point, in view of the evidence adduced by A. Kuenen—more than fifty years before [[223]] Noth—to the effect that the Dtr redaction of the Former Prophets was not the doing of one author.[9] And what is more: exactly twenty-five years before the publication of Noth's conjecture, C. F. Burney documented, mainly on stylistic grounds, that the redaction of the original Book of Judges—Joshua 24–1 Samuel 12—was not Dtr, but belonged to a different historical school which he named Late-Elohistic.[10] Noth, who dealt with the subject after the mentioned scholars, should have set out by refuting their arguments before expounding his thesis about the unity of the Dtr opus. Surprisingly enough, he did not cope with his predecessors.

In my opinion, Kuenen and Burney had it right. In what follows, I shall adopt Burney's hypothesis, restating it in my own way: the composition which he defined Late-Elohistic will be called here "Ephraimite," a term less committed to the Documentary Hypothesis; the bounds of this composition will be fixed anew while taking into account textual witnesses other than the Masoretic Text; the main emphasis of the discussion will be

7. Cf., e.g., G. Fohrer, *Introduction to the Old Testament*, London 1974, 192–237. All the same, present Biblical scholarship is Dtr-minded indeed; cf. H. Weippert, "Das deuteronomistische Geschichtswerk. Sein Ziel und Ende in der neueren Forschung," *TRu* 50 (1985) 213–49.

8. His only proof, "the chronological framework" (*Deuteronomistic History*, 18–25), does not stand the test. Noth resorted to three devices: he explained away the evidence for three periods (Joshua from the Conquest to his death, the elders who outlived him, Samuel from his victory over the Philistines to his old age), deleted one record (1 Sam 4:18b) and interpreted some spans as being contemporary (from Judg 13:1 to 1 Sam 7:6). All the same he concludes: "This then is another proof . . . that Dtr's history is a planned self-contained unity." (*Deuteronomistic History*, 25)!

9. A. Kuenen, *Historisch-kritische Einleitung in die Bücher des alten Testament* (Deutsche Ausgabe), 1, 2, Leipzig 1890, 6–101; cf. more recently: G. von Rad, *Old Testament Theology* 1, London 1962, 346–47.

10. C. F. Burney, *The Book of Judges, with Introduction and Notes*[2], London 1920, repr. New York 1970, xli–l. To some extent Burney was preceded by Budde, Cornill and Steuernagel; cf. the analysis of 1 Samuel 7–12 in: K. Budde, *Die Bücher Richter und Samuel, ihre Quellen und ihr Aufbau*, Giessen 1890, 169–88; C. H. Cornill, "Noch einmal Sauls Königswahl," *ZAW* 10 (1890) 96–109; C. Steuernagel, *Lehrbuch der Einleitung in das Alten Testament*, Tübingen 1912, 311–15. In recent scholarly discussion a similar position has been upheld by W. Beyerlin; cf. his "Gattung und Herkunft des Rahmens im Richterbuch," *Tradition und Situation* (*Fs. A. Weiser*), Göttingen 1963, 1–29.

shifted from the stylistic to the conceptual analysis, thus highlighting the theological ideas of both schools, the Dtr and the Ephraimite, one against the other.

One cannot tell where the Ephraimite history started or where it ended, as we do not know if any part of it was lost. What is preserved is now extant between Joshua 24 and 1 Samuel 12. This is an ancient version of the Book of Judges which also included the stories about Eli the Priest, who "judged Israel forty years" (1 Sam 4:18), and Samuel who vanquished the Philistines and "judged Israel all the days of his life" (1 Sam 7:3–17). From this work one [[224]] should subtract the stories extraneous to its theme, in the first place Judges 17–21, chapters that do not mention either judge or savior. These chapters were appended to the present Book of Judges, because they tell about the times when "no king was in Israel" (Judg 17:6, etc.). Another subtraction is less obvious, but not less certain; Judg 1:1–3:11. These seventy verses were not extant in the Vorlage of the Septuagint to Joshua 24. After the death of Eleazar (v. 33) and his son Phineas, the Greek relates the Israelites' worship to Astarte and to the gods of the nations around (Judg 2:12–13?), immediately going on to the eighteen years' subjection to King Eglon of Moab. Plausibly, this same text was known to the author of the Covenant of Damascus, as I pointed out in an earlier article.[11] There is enough evidence here of a different edition of Joshua-Judges (or at least Joshua 24 + Judges); this edition, to be sure, did not contain early material about the Conquest (Judg 1:1–2:5), however, neither did it include the late–partially Dtr–introduction to Judges (Judg 2:6–3:6), nor the fictitious story about the Judahite judge Othniel (3:7–11).[12]

Deleting as we do Judg 1:1–3:11, we obtain, between Joshua 24 and 1 Samuel 12, a totally North-Israelite account. Its heroes are Joshua the Ephraimite, Ehud the Benjaminite, Deborah from Mount Ephraim, Barak from Naphtali, Gideon from Manasseh, Jephthah the Gileadite (from Gad or Manasseh), Samson the Danite, Eli the priest from Shilo (Mt. Ephraim), Samuel the Ephraimite. Once Othniel is excluded, there is not even one savior-judge from Judah.

The same applies to the places of worship. Jerusalem is not mentioned, while the following holy localities are prominent, either explicitly

11. A. Rofé, "The End of the Book of Joshua according to the Septuagint," *Henoch* 4 (1982) 17–36. *Aliter* H. N. Rösel, "Die Überleitungen vom Josua–ins Richterbuch," *VT* 30 (1980) 342–50.

12. I cannot subscribe to Malamat's attempt to save the authenticity of the Othniel story; cf. A. Malamat, "Cushan Rishataim," *JNES* 13 (1954) 321–42. As for the Introduction to Judges, the late composition of its main portion (2:11–19) has been pointed out by Beyerlin, *Tradition.*

as sites of worship or implicitly as places where one presents himself "before the LORD": Shechem (Josh 24:1, 25), Ophrah in the Lower Galilee (Judg 6:24), Mizpah of Gilead (Judg 11:11), [[225]] Shilo (1 Sam 1:7, 9, etc.),[13] Mizpah of Benjamin (1 Sam 7:5–9), Ramah (1 Sam 7:17, 9:5–25) and Gilgal (1 Sam 11:15), all places belonging to the Northern tribes.

Thus, this extensive composition preserves historical traditions originating in Northern Israel. Benjamin is included therein, but the most prominent tribe is Ephraim whose heroes Joshua and Samuel open and close the story. On this ground the title "Ephraimite history" appears to be an appropriate name for this writ.

It is obvious that Northern traditions alone do not impeach the Dtr character of any given work. Joshua 1–23 and 1 Kings 11–2 Kings 17 contain no little Northern material, yet no one would contest their being Dtr. Even the book of Deuteronomy contains remnants of Northern literature, such as the precepts connected with Gerizim and Ebal (Deut 11:26–30 + 27:12–13; 27:4–8). The real test for the literary affiliation of a work remains its style and ideas. In the case of extensive compilations in which long excerpts of older sources are embedded, the test will center on those passages which already have been identified as written by the compiler(s)—namely the speeches attributed to the LORD, His prophets or the righteous leaders of Israel and the epitomes made by the writer in his own name. Since an analysis of the style has already been undertaken,[14] I will limit myself to a comparison of some basic ideas inherent to the Ephraimite (= Ephr) and Dtr histories.

A basic tenet of the Dtr school through all its phases is the injunction of the unification of worship. Indeed, the various versions of this law reflect the history of the deuteronomic-deuteronomistic school.[15] The first Deuteronomists assumed the unification to have become positive law only when the conditions of "rest and inheritance" be attained (Deut 12:8–12), i.e., in the days of Solomon (1 Kgs 5:17–19). Later Dtr authors [[226]] conceived of the unification as being enforced immediately upon the Conquest (Deut 11:31–12:7) when the Tent of Meeting was established at Shiloh (Josh 18:1, 6, 8, 10; 19:51; 22:29). These, however, were just unhistorical theories. In practice the deuteronomic law was enforced in the days of Josiah only; therefore the Dtr scribes were confronted with the

13. The description of the Shilo sanctuary as *ʾōhel môʿēd,* in 1 Sam 2:22b MT, is a late addition; cf. the LXX and 4QSam[a] (F. M. Cross Jr., "A New Fragment etc.," *BASOR* 132 [December 1953] 15–26).

14. Cf. Burney, *Judges*.

15. A. Rofé, "The Strata of the Law about the Centralization of Worship and the History of the Deuteronomic Movement," *Congress Volume* (VTSup 22), Uppsala 1971; Leiden 1972, 221–26.

problem, how to describe the cultic realities before Josiah, as these contradicted their legal conceptions.

The writers of the first phase distinguished between the times before the building of Solomon's sanctuary, when the "high-places" were still tolerated (1 Kgs 3:2), and after the consecration of the Temple when the "high-places" were rejected as sinful (1 Kgs 12:31, 14:23, 15:14, etc.). The writers of the next phase, as they dealt with upright leaders, such as Joshua and Eleazar, ignored the very existence of any cultic centers outside of Shiloh. Even the valedictory oration of Joshua (Joshua 23) takes place nowhere! As against those Dtr scribes, the authors of the Ephr history, as we have seen, mention no less than seven cultic sites in Northern Israel. What is more, they are sometimes mentioned even in conjunction with editorial sermons such as Josh 24:1–28; 1 Sam 10:17–27, 11:14–12:25. These writers are not troubled by the legitimacy of those centers: they do not have to assert that a place was legitimate because elected by the LORD, nor do they justify the worship as being performed under duress. In short, the Ephr authors act as if they have never heard of the law of worship unification; alternatively they knew but did not adhere to it.

The election of a place of worship goes hand in hand with the election of a king. This binary, shows in some royal Psalms (Ps 78:67–72, 132:11–13) and prefaces the Dtr "Prayer of Solomon" (1 Kgs 8:15–21, 23–53, 56–61). In this important text, v. 16 has been mutilated by a homoioteleuton, which perhaps accounts for its being neglected by scholars; it must be completed by the parallel 2 Chr 6:5–6: "Since the day that I brought my people out of the land of Egypt, I chose no city in all the tribes of Israel in which to build a house, that my name might be there [and I chose no man as prince over my people Israel; but I have chosen Jerusalem that my name may be there] and I have chosen David to be over my people Israel."[16] [[227]] There is no doubt here as to the basic concept: the single sanctuary and the monarchy join together to inaugurate a new, exalted era in the history of Israel. This era, having dawned with David's anointment and his conquest of Jerusalem, fully materialized with Solomon, who accomplished what had been denied to his father: the building of a house for the name of the LORD (1 Kgs 8:17–20 = 2 Chr 6:7–10). This is how the Dtr school developed, in its own vein, the original concept of the royal chapel of the Davidides. This basic idea concerning the twofold election lends significance to the Dtr passages that quote an oracle to David (not preserved in the book of Samuel), running; "There shall not fail you a man on the throne of Israel" (1 Kgs 2:4, 9:5; cf. 8:25 as well as Jer 33:17).

16. Oddly enough, the LXX to 1 Kgs 8:16 offers a rendering which is a midway between the MT of Kings and Chronicles.

This is a promise of an eternal Davidic dynasty. And it is once more joined to the election of Jerusalem in the passages that assure David of an eternal lamp before the LORD in Jerusalem (1 Kgs 11:36, 15:4; 2 Kgs 8:19). All in all, the Dtr school maintains the eternity of the Davidic line as a consequence of the LORD's election of David to be a prince over Israel. The election of David and that of Jerusalem are both acts of grace the LORD has conferred on Israel.

How different is the attitude to the monarchy of the Ephr school! Its writings not only incorporated older sources which opposed the monarchy on practical issues, such as the Jotham fable (Judg 9:8–15) and the "practice of the king" (1 Sam 8:11–18); in its editorial passages it overtly assaulted the monarchy on theological grounds. It repeatedly asserted that the monarchy is illegitimate (Judg 8:23), that it is a sin, as it implies the rejection of the kingdom of the LORD (1 Sam 8:17; 10:19a; 12:12, 17). The various tentatives suggested so far, to minimize this opposition, relativizing it as time conditioned[17] or as referring to certain functions of the king only,[18] [[228]] are, in my opinion, doomed to failure. What we face here is a fundamental anti-monarchism. It corresponds to Hosea's stand, in that both the prophet and the Ephr historian condemn the people's request of a king (1 Sam 8:6, Hos 13:10) and insist that the LORD is the sole savior of Israel (1 Sam 10:19a, 12:7–11; Hos 13:4, 10). Plausibly, then, the Ephr historian belongs to the same milieu as Hosea.[19] The historical setting is the twilight of the Kingdom of Northern Israel and the ideology reflects the historical experience of that state.

In my opinion, there is no way of harmonizing this attitude to the monarchy with that of the Dtr school, by arguing that the Dtr work opposed the monarchy in general, but condoned the Davidic dynasty.[20] Such an argument finds no support in the texts. To the contrary, the Dtr formula "In those days there was no king in Israel; every man did as he pleased" (Judg 17:6, 21:25; cf. Deut 12:8) is appended to the *chronique*

17. Y. Kaufmann, *The Religion of Israel*, translated and abridged by M. Greenberg, London 1961, 262–66.

18. H. J. Boecker, *Die Beurteilung der Anfänge des Königtums in den deuteronomistischen Abschnitten des I. Samuelbuches* (WMANT 31), Neukirchen-Vluyn 1969. For instance, to say that the issue in the editorial passages of 1 Samuel 7–12 is not opposition to kingship, but to its pretension to save the people (Boecker, *Beurteilung*, 43) begs the question: the very essence of the king in ancient Israel is his function as *môšîʿa* [['deliverer']]. See infra.

19. Pace F. Crüsemann, *Der Widerstand gegen das Königtum* (WMANT 49) Neukirchen-Vluyn 1978, 88–92.

20. Or, as Clements put it, that the Dtr approved only of those kings that were chosen by the LORD, i.e., David and his line; cf. R. E. Clements, "The Deuteronomistic Interpretation of the Founding of the Monarchy in I Sam VIII," *VT* 24 (1974) 398–410.

scandaleuse of the period of the Judges (Judges 17–21) in order to demonstrate the anarchy caused by the absence of monarchy in Israel.[21]

Midway between the Ephr and the Dtr histories stands the law of the king in Deut 17:14–20 (D). Kingship here is considered an imitation of the customs of the nations (v. 14) which makes it reprehensible to D. The king, however, is chosen by the LORD (v. 15), a quality that in D is usually commendable, other divinely chosen objects in D being Israel, the single sanctuary and the Levitical priests. Further on, the law does not specify the king's functions nor his prerogatives, only obligations and limitations. Thus D accepts the monarchy though with reservations. It does not view the monarchy as a revolt against the divine kingship, but neither as an eternal divine grace. Since it is implausible that the Ephr history should antagonize the monarchy after it had been [[229]] authorized by the D law, the sequence of our sources would appear to be the following: first, the Ephr school (eighth century) assailed kingship conceiving of it as a sin; later, the law of D (seventh century) expressed a qualified acceptance of this institution; finally, the Dtr school (seventh–sixth centuries) building on the foundations of the D law, glorified the Davidic throne as an eternal grace bestowed by the LORD upon Israel.

Correlated to D's acceptance and Dtr's glorification of human kingdom is their absolute silence about the kingdom of the LORD. Nowhere in their writings is the LORD referred to as king![22] This is most remarkable since D and Dtr do insist on the LORD's sole dominion of the world: Exod 19:5; Deut 4:34–35, 39; 10:14; Josh 2:11; 2 Sam 7:22; 1 Kgs 8:23, 60. The reasons for this position cannot be explained here. In any case it clearly contradicts Ephr's insistence upon the LORD's kingship over Israel.

How deeply the attitude towards the monarchy is ingrained in the theological views of each school will be realized by considering the correlation of their concepts of king and war. Such a correspondence is only to be expected, since a foremost function of the king was his leading of the people into war (1 Sam 8:20, 2 Sam 5:1–2, etc.). How then do the writings of these two schools describe the Israelite wars?

The Ephr school, conforming with its view concerning the monarchy, keeps to an utterly quietistic outlook. In Joshua 24 five clashes between Israel and the nations are described: with Egypt, the Amorites of Transjordan, Balak king of Moab, the citizens of Jericho and the Amorites of Cisjordan. In all of these encounters Israel was passive. They did not fight; they wandered, led by the LORD, were assailed by other nations, the LORD

21. Cf. Veijola, *Königtum*, 15–29.

22. Deut 33:5 does not belong to the D [[deuteronomic]] document; *basileū tōn theōn* [['king of gods']] in Deut 9:26 LXX is a late liturgical expansion; cf. Tob 11:1S (10:14); Jdt 9:12.

intervened and delivered them. Most eloquent in this respect is the description of the conquest of all Cisjordan in v. 12: "And I sent the hornet ahead of you, it drove them out before you, twelve[23] kings of the Amorite, [[230]] not by your sword nor by your bow." A similar view is reflected in the story of Gideon. Thirty-two thousand Israelites had gathered to do battle against Midian, but the LORD instructed Gideon to send home more than ninety-nine percent of this multitude "lest Israel vaunt themselves against Me, saying my own hand has delivered me (*hôšîʿâ lî*)" (Judg 7:2). Further the LORD says: "By the three hundred 'lappers' I will deliver you" (*ʾôšîaʿ ʾĕtkem*) (Judg 7:7). Indeed, the LORD did it, but the blind people did not understand; they attributed the victory to Gideon and offered him the kingship, because "you have delivered us (*hôšaʿtānû*) from the Midianites" (Judg 8:22).[24] Not much different is the lesson taught by the story of Samuel at Mizpah (1 Sam 7:7–14). The Philistines assaulted the Israelites and frightened them. The Israelites asked Samuel "to cry out to the LORD our God that He will deliver us (*wĕyōšiʿēnû*) from the Philistines" (1 Sam 7:8). Samuel complied, the LORD intervened and confused the Philistines who were defeated before Israel. With some variations the pattern repeats itself: Israel is passive and cries to the LORD; the LORD fights and delivers His people; therefore he must be acknowledged as king. The short historical summary in 1 Sam 12:7–11, by the Ephr editor, follows these lines.

The Dtr theology, however, is completely different; it is activistic. The king, the LORD's chosen, fights aided by divine assistance. Such is the description of Hezekiah by the author of Kings: "And the LORD was always with him; he was successful wherever he turned. He rebelled against the king of Assyria and did not serve him. He overran Philistia," etc. (2 Kgs 18:7–8). Even more characteristic is the account of early times in Deuteronomy 1–3: Joshua 1–11: the norm is that Israel fights and the LORD is on its side. More exactly: every step taken by Israel is preceded by the LORD's instructions. And when Israel's leader acted on his own, uninstructed by the LORD, as in the sending of the spies by Moses (Deut 1:22–23) or in Joshua's first assault on Ai (Josh 7:2–4), the deed ended up in failure and disaster. The LORD's directions are reported in a uniform style, e.g.: "The LORD said to me: You have [[231]] compassed this mountain long enough; turn you northward" (Deut 2:3; cf. 1:6–7:42; 2:9, 17–19, 24, 31; 3:2; Josh

23. Following the LXX *dōdeka* [['twelve']]. The unique notion about the number of the Amorite kings fits in with the singular tradition embedded in Josh 24:1–28:31; hence it must be reckoned as the original reading. Cf. A. Dillmann, *Die Bücher Numeri, Deuteronomium und Josua* (KEHAT²), Leipzig 1886, 586, with reference to Hollenberg.

24. Cf. W. Beyerlin, "Geschichte . . . von Richter VI–VIII," *VT* 13 (1963) 1–25, esp. pp. 21–22; I. L. Seeligmann, "Menschliches Heldentum und göttliche Hilfe," *ThZ* 19 (1963) 385–411, esp. 408–10.

1:2; 6:12; 8:1; 10:8; 11:6). Surprisingly enough the nearest analogy to this recurring formula is found in the Mesha Stone: "And Chemosh said to me: Go, seize Nebo against Israel" (line 14); [And] Chemosh [s]aid to me: Go down, fight against Horonen" (line 32). In this inscription too it is emphasized that the leader exactly complied with the divine instructions.[25] The LORD's participation in the battle is usually mentioned, but it only means an assistance to his fighting people. "So Joshua, with all his fighting men, came upon them suddenly at the Waters of Merom, and pounced upon them. The LORD delivered them into the hands of Israel," etc. (Josh 11:7–8)—this approximately is the style of the battles of the LORD and Israel, allied against the nations of Canaan. This activistic theology befits, as we have said, the pro-monarchic outlook, since the king embodies the human enterprise in political and military life.

A minor point enhances the difference between Dtr activism and Ephr quietism. It refers to the fate of the Canaanites. According to D and Dtr they should be, and were, exterminated by the law of the ban (*ḥērem*) (Deut 7:2, 24; 20:16–18; Josh 11:16–20, etc.) enforced by Israel. As against it, the Ephr narrative speaks of their being expelled (*grš*) by the LORD (Josh 24:12, Judg 6:9) according to the promises given in the ancient predeuteronomic sources (Exod 23:28, 29, 30; 33:2; 34:11).

Coming back to the addresses of the LORD to Moses and Joshua, one notes that they contain both directions and predictions. The leader keeps to the direction and the prediction comes true. Thus we touch upon one more aspect of the Dtr theology: the quality of the LORD's word, that it is always fulfilled. The matter has already been discussed in recent scholarship.[26] In the book of Joshua the [[232]] Dtr view is emphasized in the summary of the conquest: "Not one of the good things which the LORD had promised to the House of Israel went unfulfilled; they all came true" (Josh 21:23).[27] In the book of Kings entire series of prophecies and their fulfillments obtain,[28] thus exemplifying that every true prophecy finds its realization in history. All this is in line with the instruction appended to the

25. The fact that the "Mesha formula of divine instruction" does not show in the Dtr account of righteous Judean kings corroborates the distinction between the Dtr history in Deuteronomy–Joshua on one hand and the Dtr edition of Kings on the other.

26. Beginning with G. von Rad's seminal study: "The Deuteronomistic Theology of History in the Books of Kings," in his: *Studies in Deuteronomy* (SBT 9), London 1953, 74–91.

27. Cf. I. L. Seeligmann, "From Historical Reality to Historiosophy in the Hebrew Bible" [Hebrew], *Pᵉrāqîm* 2 (1971) 273–313, esp. 288.

28. I. L. Seeligmann, in his "Die Auffassung der Prophetie in der deuteronomistischen und chronistischen Geschichtsschreibung," 29, *Congress Volume, Göttingen 1977* (VTSup 29), Leiden 1978, 254–84, esp. 258–64, aptly pointed out the disjointed nature of some of the 'prophecy-fulfillment' occurrences in the book of Kings. In my own work I have tried to differentiate between two distinct series; cf. A. Rofé, *The Prophetical Stories*, Jerusalem 1988, 99–105.

law of the prophet in Deut 18:21–22: "And should you ask yourselves, 'How can we recognize the word not spoken by the LORD?'—if the prophet speaks in the name of the LORD, but the word does not come true, that word was not spoken by the LORD; the prophet spoke it presumptuously; do not dread him."

Here again, the Ephr school takes a different stand. The prophets have a distinct role. They are not predictors;[29] rather they castigate the people on past transgressions (Judg 6:7–10; cf. 1 Sam 10:18–19a and the address of the LORD in Judg 10:11–14) or present them with alternatives, prodding them to choose the right way.[30] This characterizes Joshua's speech to the assembly of Shechem (Josh 24:1–28) and Samuel's valedictory oration at Gilgal (1 Sam 11:14–12:25). Both these personalities appear here as prophets: Joshua starts his speech with "Thus says the LORD" and Samuel calls upon the LORD (a prophetic function) to make a portent. Indeed, prophecy in the Ephr work attains a higher status than in the DH; albeit the authority of Joshua and Samuel is limited, without means of coercion, their moral ascendancy is great. On this basis Joshua makes a covenant in Shechem and both he and Samuel do away with the foreign gods (Josh 24:23, 1 Sam 7:3). This style of [[233]] rebuke and warning is present in additional sources from Northern Israel, such as Deuteronomy 32[31] and Psalm 81. It apparently characterized one of the currents in Israelite prophecy before the fall of Samaria and certainly stood nearer to classical prophecy than the prophets quoted in the Dtr work.

A basic point with the Dtr school is the observance of the Torah, its laws and precepts; indeed, the entire output of this school carries on the tenor of the deuteronomic Torah. Hence, Moses, Joshua and David, before their death, urge the people to observe the Torah (Deut 32:45–47, Josh 23:6, 1 Kgs 2:2–3). Moreover, the theodicies of the Exile count the transgression of the laws of the Torah as one of the foremost sins (2 Kgs 17:13, 16; 21:8). The Torah is made a constant standard by which both the community and the individual are assessed.

This is not the case with the Ephr history. Here the prophets call to fear the LORD, to hearken His voice and serve Him exclusively. They never

29. A single exception being 1 Sam 2:27–36—probably a Dtr expansion; cf., however, Seeligmann (preceding note), 262–63.

30. The same position was upheld again by the late-Dtr editors of Jeremiah's words; cf. Seeligmann, "Auffassung," 279–84.

31. The predeuteronomic prologue to the Song of Moses, Deut 31:16–22, usually attributed to E (cf. A. Kuenen, *The Origin and Composition of the Hexateuch*, London 1886, 155, 256–58), adheres to the same view of prophecy; the Song is written and taught not to predict Israel's destiny, but to castigate the people: their future complaint that the LORD does not save them (*ʾên ʾĕlōhay bᵉqirbî*, v. 17) will be answered by the Song that the LORD is hiding His face from them, because of their evil deeds.

mention the observance of the Torah.[32] In the general context of loquacious hortatory speeches, the absence of any reference to the Torah is conspicuous. This phenomenon finds its explanation in a chapter central to this history, Joshua 24. The assembly of Shechem is concluded as follows (vv. 25–26): "So Joshua made a covenant for the people that day and established for them law and judgment (*ḥōq ûmišpāṭ*) in Shechem. And Joshua wrote these words in the book of the Torah of God (*bᵉsēper tôrat ʾĕlōhîm*)."

Here we see: Joshua makes laws and writes (the laws? the covenant?) in a book of Torah. The identification of the Torah, even in its first, restricted sense–the D document–with the activity of Moses is yet to come. Torah is still a general concept: the [[234]] instruction given to Israel by any religious leader.[33] In the case of authors zealous for the LORD, such as the Ephr and Dtr scribes, there is no greater sign to distinguish between two religious schools.

Actually, besides a general resemblance of parenetic genre and style,[34] the Dtr and the Ephr schools share only one element: the demand for an exclusive worship of the LORD, and its derivative–the condemnation of idolatry. This denominator is too low to allow the entering of all the editorial work of the Former Prophets under one caption. To the contrary, even in the matter of idolatry there is room for the drawing of a distinction: the Ephr work limits itself to the condemnation of the worship of foreign gods, whereas the Dtr school introduces a new issue, the polemics against the use of images in the Worship of the LORD; it demands an aniconic worship. Hence, the condemnation of the calves of Jeroboam in the book of Kings (1 Kings 12ff.). Hence also the description of the construction of the Ark fashioned without cherubim in Deut 10:1–5. Hence, finally, the detailed and well-grounded warning against all images in the cult of the LORD in Deut 4:9–24. And what is more, the punishment of Exile is justified by this very sin (Deut 4:25–31); in another instance the historical fate of Northern Israel is explicitly connected with their iconic worship (2 Kgs 17:16).

32. Cf. Budde, *Richter*, 184: "Wo bleiben ferner in den Reden die 'Satzungen und Rechte und Gebote und Gesetze Jahwe's, die Thora Mose's'?" [['What is left, furthermore, in the speeches of the statutes and prescriptions and laws of Yahweh, the Torah of Moses?']].

33. Remarkable in this context is the fact that in addition to Josh 24:25, also Judg 2:1–2 and 6:8–10 assume that (some of) the laws were given by the LORD to Israel in Canaan; cf. G. Schmitt, *Der Landtag von Sichem* (Arb. z. Theol. 1, 15), Stuttgart 1964, 42–46. All three passages were considered in the past to belong to the E histories.

34. Resemblance, indeed, but not identity: The style has been studied by Burney, *Judges*. As for the genre, the Dtr authors make use of the plain oration (e.g., Joshua 23; 1 Kgs 8:14–53); as against them, the Ephr writers compose entire scenes and express their views through dialogues (Josh 24:1–28; Judg 8:22–23, 10:10–15; 1 Samuel 8, 12); cf. Budde, *Richter*, 184.

We have thus distinguished between two major schools of historians in ancient Israel. What remains is to determine their historical setting. The Dtr school started to develop with the first edition of D, in the second half of the seventh century B.C.E. It flourished during the Exile and the Restoration in the sixth and down to the fifth centuries. As for the Ephr work, the evidence points at a date not much later than the eighth century: it was founded on traditions from the area of the Northern Kingdom [[235]] which perished in 722 B.C.E.; its anti-monarchial position comes near to that of Hosea; it appears to be unaware of the D law of the king. Moreover, the silence of the Ephr authors about the Torah of Moses seems to indicate that such an opus was not known to or not accepted by them. The Ephr school flourished at the end of the Northern Kingdom. It preserves some of the cultural and religious legacy of the lost Ten Tribes.

Redaction, Recension, and Midrash in the Books of Kings

JULIO TREBOLLE BARRERA

The past century has witnessed a series of manuscript discoveries that have clarified the relationship between the Greek and Hebrew texts of Samuel and Kings. Although some scholars have regarded the versions as essentially paraphrases, expositions, and interpretations of the MT, other scholars have cited evidence provided by the Dead Sea Scrolls to offer another explanation. In this essay, Trebolle Barrera pursues some detailed comparisons between the MT, the LXX, and the Old Latin witnesses to the text of Kings to show that the array of variants that exist in the Greek, Hebrew, and Latin witnesses to Kings are not all tendentious corruptions of the Hebrew (MT). Some reflect a type of the Hebrew text of Samuel–Kings used by the Chronicler and evident in the Qumran manuscripts 4QSam^{abc}. By recognizing the existence of distinct textual families among the witnesses to books of Samuel, Kings, and Chronicles, textual critics are considerably aided in their primary tasks of *recensio* (recension), *examinatio* (examination), and *emendatio* (emendation). The implications of Trebolle Barrera's study extend, however, beyond the field of textual criticism. Given that the length, content, and sequence of a passage within one textual tradition can reflect an earlier stage of composition than that of another tradition, textual criticism becomes foundational to literary, historical, tradition, and redaction criticism. In other words, textual criticism and other forms of scholarly criticism are all interrelated.

[[12]] Research on the books of Kings has been dominated in these last decades by the work of M. Noth on the deuteronomistic *redaction.*[1] His

Reprinted with permission from *Bulletin of the International Organization for Septuagint and Cognate Studies* 15 (1982) 12–35.

Author's note: I wish to thank Professor John Strugnell of Harvard for offering corrections in the manuscript and F. Normand Bonneau of Worcester, Massachusetts, for translating the Spanish original into English.

1. M. Noth, *Überlieferungsgeschichtliche Studien* 1: *Die sammelnden und bearbeitenden Geschichtswerke im Alten Testament* (Schriften der Königsberger Gelehrten Gesellschaft, Geisteswissenschaftliche Klasse 18; Halle: Niemeyer, 1943).

masterpiece opened up new paths and proposed new models of research. After every masterpiece, however, research sooner or later becomes "scholasticized" and confines itself tamely to the lines traced by the master. Furthermore, the impact of a masterpiece tends either to marginalize earlier paths of research or to close them off entirely. Thus in the work of Noth and his disciples very little importance has been given to the contributions to be drawn from the versions (esp. the LXX and the VL [[Vetus Latina = 'Old Latin']]) for the *recension* history and text history of the books of the Bible. In the books of Kings these versions offer many important variant readings with respect to the MT. Noth's work in 1943 coincided with a generalized "return to the MT" movement.[2] At that time the Greek version came to be considered mostly as a targum or as a *midrashic* paraphrase of the Hebrew. J. W. Wevers at mid-century and more recently D. W. Gooding and R. P. Gordon developed this line of research by studying the "principles of exegesis" underlying the Greek version of Kings and the midrashic elements it contains.[3]

If the early decades of this century were characterized by both the use and abuse of conjecturally restoring the 'primitive text' (*Urtext*) by choosing among the many variants found in the versions, [[13]] these last decades have seen the analogous abuse of conjecturing, on literary grounds, what was the 'primitive form' (*Urform*), and this on the basis of the Masoretic text alone. Consequently, if on the one hand the history of the tradition and redaction of Kings (10th–5th century B.C.) now appears excessively complicated, on the other hand we are content with a very simple history of the transmission of the text. In the long span stretching from the 5th century B.C. up to the medieval Masoretes, it is currently assumed that there existed but a simple and direct line of textual transmission in Hebrew (Noth);[4] the variants of the versions are considered to be merely tendentious deviations from a uniform Hebrew text.

2. H. S. Nyberg, "Das textkritische Problem des Alten Testaments am Hoseabuche demonstriert," *ZAW* 52 (1934) 241–54. A work of earlier times, as valuable as it is forgotten, is that of H. Hrozný, *Die Abweichungen des Codex Vaticanus vom hebräischen Texte in den Königsbüchern* (Leipzig: Drugulin, 1909).

3. J. W. Wevers, "Exegetical Principles Underlying the Septuagint Text of 1 Kings ii 12–xxi 43," *OTS* 8 (1950) 300–322; "Principles of Interpretation Guiding the Fourth Translator of the Book of the Kingdoms (3 K. 22:1–4 K. 25:30)," *CBQ* 14 (1952) 40–56; D. W. Gooding, "Problems of Text and Midrash in the Third Book of Reigns," *Textus* 7 (1969) 1–29; *Relics of Ancient Exegesis: A Study of the Miscellanies in 3 Reigns 2* (SOTSMS 4; Cambridge: University Press, 1976); R. P. Gordon, "The Second Septuagint Account of Jeroboam: History or Midrash?" *VT* 25 (1975) 368–93.

4. M. Noth, *Die Welt des Alten Testaments: Einführung in die Grenzgebiete der alttestamentlichen Wissenschaft* (2d ed.; Berlin: Töpelmann, 1953) 286.

The study of the biblical manuscripts of Qumran, in particular of 4QSam[a, b, c], has facilitated a new understanding of the parallel history and parallel evolution of the Hebrew and Greek texts of Samuel–Kings. This new knowledge creates the need for an interdisciplinary dialogue between the practitioners of redaction history (Noth and his school) and those of the study of the transmission and recension of the text (e.g., W. F. Albright, F. M. Cross, D. Barthélemy, etc.).[5]

In such a dialogue it will be accepted that many of the variants in the versions do not represent isolated phenomena or occasional acts of negligence on the part of the translators and/or copyists. Rather, they represent complete patterns all their own which correspond to different types of text that once existed in the Hebrew tradition. It will also be accepted that the plurality of textual types can even reflect different stages in the earlier process of the redaction and editing of the text.

Our study begins with the textual and literary analysis of selected passages. From these analyses a working method will be extracted which will prove to be better adapted to the textual and literary characteristics of the books of Kings. As a result, we [[14]] will see the need for a return to textual criticism and frequently to the *Urtext* as found in the text of the versions. Instead of being an arsenal for random corrections to the current Hebrew text, these versions will serve as evidence for the existence of a non-Masoretic Hebrew type of text or a pre-Masoretic recension-form of the text. For its part, textual criticism will be seen to need the literary-critical method to help it isolate merely textual phenomena such as glosses, omissions, and transpositions.

Jeroboam at the Assembly at Shechem: MT 1 Kgs 12:2 // LXX 11:43

1 Kings 12:2 is one of the most important and most discussed passages in the books of Kings. The history of the Assembly at Shechem depends on the correct interpretation of this text. The majority of authors tend to correct the MT *wayyēšeb . . . b*ᵉ [['and he settled in']] to *wayyāšob . . . min* [['and

5. W. F. Albright, "New Light on Early Recensions of the Hebrew Bible," *BASOR* 140 (1955) 27–33; D. Barthélemy, *Les Devanciers d'Aquila* (VTSup 10; Leiden: Brill, 1963); F. M. Cross, "The History of the Biblical Text in the Light of Discoveries in the Judaean Desert," *HTR* 57 (1964) 281–99; "The Evolution of a Theory of Local Texts," *Qumran and the History of the Biblical Text* (ed. F. M. Cross and S. Talmon; Cambridge, MA / London: Harvard University, 1975) 306–20; E. C. Ulrich, *The Qumran Text of Samuel and Josephus* (HSM 19; Missoula: Scholars, 1978); E. Tov, "Determining the Relationship between the Qumran Scrolls and the LXX: Some Methodological Issues," *The Hebrew and Greek Texts of Samuel* (1980 Proceedings IOSCS; Jerusalem: Academon, 1980) 45–67.

he returned from'⟦, in conformity with Alexandrinus (LXX^A) and with the parallel in Chronicles: "Jeroboam returned from Egypt."[6]

The expression *wayyēšeb b^e* appears frequently in contexts speaking of a flight into exile, forming part of a fixed narrative structure: '(. . . when X heard these things,) he sought to kill Y; Y was afraid, and he fled from the presence of X and settled in Z' (. . . *wyšmʿ* . . . *ʾt dbryw wybqš* . . . *lhmyt ʾt* . . . *wyrʾ* . . . *wybrḥ mpny* . . . *wayyēšeb b^e* . . . ⟦'. . . when he heard his words, he sought . . . to kill . . . and he was afraid . . . and he fled from . . . and he settled in . . .'⟧). The flights of Moses, Jephthah, David, Absalom, and Jeremiah are all expressed in this narrative pattern (cf. esp. Exod 2:14–15; Jer 26:21; cf. also Judg 9:21, 11:3; 1 Sam 19:2, 23:14–15, 27:1–4; 2 Sam 4:1–3, 13:37–38). This conventional expression is found in narratives from such diverse epochs as, for example, the story of the flight of Idrimi (14th century B.C.) and the NT flight of Joseph into Egypt.[7] In these notices the fleeing protagonist ends up "residing in" or "settling in" a place of exile.

The text in 12:2 reproduces essential elements ('he fled . . . and settled in . . .' = *wybrḥ* . . . *wyšb b* . . .) of that narrative sequence (above). ⟦15⟧ This proves the value of the reading *wayyēšeb* . . . *b^e* against the generally proposed correction. Furthermore, it renders impossible the proposed separation of the two verbs by consigning one to the parenthetical sentence and one to the main sentence: "When Jeroboam, son of Nebat, learned of this (for he was still in Egypt, whither he had fled from King Solomon), then Jeroboam returned from Egypt." The expression *wayyēšeb b^e* also forms part of the inserted parenthesis. The corresponding passage in the Old Greek, located in 11:43, confirms this conclusion: here the parenthesis includes and closes after the expression 'and Jeroboam settled in Egypt' (*hōs ephygen ek prosōpou Salōmōn kai ekathēto en Aigyptō* ⟦'he fled from the presence of Solomon and settled in Egypt'⟧). Then follows the apodosis of the main sentence: 'he set out and came to his city in the land of Sareira, in the mountains of Ephraim' (*kateuthynei kai erchetai eis tēn polin autou eis tēn gēn Sareira tēn en orei Ephraim*).

The subject of the apodosis must be the same as the subject of the protasis, "Jeroboam." Furthermore, the same verb, *wybʾ*, is attested in all the forms of the manuscript tradition: in the Q *wybʾ* ⟦'and he came'⟧ of 1 Kgs 12:3 and in 17 manuscripts (K *wybʾw* ⟦'and they came'⟧); in LXX 11:43 and in LXX 12:24f.; in the Hexaplaric text of LXX^A 12:3 (including

6. J. A. Montgomery, *The Books of Kings* (ICC; Edinburgh: Clark, 1951) 249; M. Noth, *Könige* (BKAT 9/1; Neukirchen-Vluyn: Neukirchener Verlag, 1968) 265; A. Jepsen, *Die Quellen des Königsbuches* (2d ed.; Halle: Niemeyer, 1956) 2; J. Gray, *I and II Kings: A Commentary* (2d ed.; London: SCM, 1970) 301.

7. Matt 2:3–15; cf. S. Smith, *The Statue of Idri-mi* (London: The British Institute of Archaeology in Ankara, 1949) 14–15.

the Armenian and Syrohexaplar versions); and in 2 Chr 10:3. The nucleus of the original apodosis, then, is contained in the expression: 'When Jeroboam learned of this . . . , *he came to* . . .' (*wyb' yrb'm*).

This main sentence is found outside its proper context in both the MT and the Old Greek. In the MT it interrupts the sequence between verses 1 and 3b (cf. LXX): "[v 1] Rehoboam went to Shechem, where all Israel had come to proclaim him king. [v 3b] They said to Rehoboam. . . ." In the Old Greek it is interpolated by means of the process of *Wiederaufnahme* ⟦'repetitive resumption'⟧, between the concluding formulas of Solomon's reign: "*Solomon rested with his ancestors*; he was buried in the City of David his father (LXX: When Jeroboam, son of Nebat, learned of this. . .). *King Solomon rested* ⟦16–18⟧ *with his ancestors*, and his son Rehoboam succeeded him as king."[8] ⟦see table on pp. 491–92⟧

According to the arrangement of the text in the MT, Jeroboam returns from Egypt when he learns that all Israel and Rehoboam have assembled in Shechem (cf. v. 1); thus, the *šm'* of 12:2 now in the MT refers to the assembly. The Old Greek, on the contrary, alone preserves an original element: Jeroboam returns from Egypt when he learns that Solomon has died; thus, the *šm'* ⟦'he heard'⟧ of 12:2 (= the *ēkousen* ⟦'he heard'⟧ of LXX 11:43) originally referred to the death of Solomon and connected with 11:40, of which it is the direct continuation. Accordingly, "[Jeroboam] remained in Egypt until the death of Solomon . . . ; when Jeroboam learned of [the death of Solomon] . . . , he came. . . ." A similar passage in 1 Kgs 11:21 has a formally similar element: Hadad also returned from Egypt upon hearing of the death of David (*šm'*. . . *ky* [*mṭ*] . . . ⟦'he heard that (he died)'⟧).[9]

A further confirmation is found in the text of a notice preserved in the so-called "supplement" or "midrash" of the Old Greek in 12:24c (d, f). This form of the notice represents or closely approximates the original. It even contains a formal element of the literary genre "flight notice" which is absent in MT / LXX 11:40, that is, the "fear" of the persecuted (*wyr'* = *kai ephobēthē* [both] ⟦'and he was afraid'⟧): "[v 24c] Solomon sought to kill Jeroboam; Jeroboam *was afraid* and fled to Egypt where he found refuge with Shishak, and he settled there until the death of Solomon. [24d] When Jeroboam learned in Egypt that Solomon had died . . . , [24f] he *came to*. . . ."[10] All the essential elements of the "flight notice" are found here assembled in the proper order: (1) the persecution (*wybqš* . . . *lhmyt*

8. D. W. Gooding, "The Septuagint's Rival Versions of Jeroboam's Rise to Power," *VT* 17 (1967) 173–89, cf. 178; R. W. Klein, "Jeroboam's Rise to Power," *JBL* 89 (1970) 217–18.

9. Cf. also 1 Kgs 21:15: *wyhy kšm'*. . . *ky sql nbwt wymt* ⟦'when she heard . . . that Naboth had been stoned and died'⟧.

10. Cf. the text of the MSS boc$_2$e$_2$ in 11:43: (*ēkousen*) . . . *hoti tethnēke Solomōn* . . . ⟦'(he heard) . . . that Solomon died . . .'⟧.

ʾt . . . ⟦'and he sought to kill'⟧); (2) the flight of the persecuted (*wybrḥ* ⟦'and he fled'⟧); (3) the temporary residence in exile of the persecuted person (*wyšb/wyhy b* . . . ⟦'and he settled/and he was in'⟧); (4) the news of the persecutor's death (*wyhy kšmʿ ky mt* ⟦'and when he heard that he died'⟧); and (5) the return (*wybʾ* . . . ⟦'and he came'⟧).

Such an argument of literary criticism, based on the literary genre of the "flight notice" and based on form rather than on content, allows us to resolve here a question of textual criticism: ⟦19⟧ which of the two is the preferred reading, "settled in" or "returned from"? It equally allows us to discover the limits of the present literary unit.

The "flight notice" of the MT/LXX 11:40 (= also LXX 12:24c) continues and ends with the sentence: "When Jeroboam heard . . . , he came to . . ." (MT 12:2; LXX 11:43 and 12:24d, f). The LXX texts 11:43 and 12:24f. both identify this place as Sareira. This "flight notice" is a part of the whole narrative beginning with the abortive revolt of Jeroboam (MT 11:26–28; LXX 12:24b) and following with the account of the Assembly at Shechem (MT 12:3b–21; LXX 12:24nβ, p–x). There can be no doubt, then, that Jeroboam was at the Assembly at Shechem from its very outset.[11] He is not, however, expressly mentioned as being present. In fact, the only people who intervene in the deliberations are those who are authorized, such as the elders of the people and, in opposition to them, the young friends and counselors of Rehoboam's court.

The Accession Formula: Text and Composition

It is not possible to discuss here the text of the so-called "supplement" or "duplicate" in LXX 12:24a–z. Since the time of Meyer (1906)[12] it was quite simply set aside as being late "midrash." Gooding qualified it as pedantic in its chronology and as biased against, and insulting to, Jeroboam. The first verse of this "supplement" (LXX 12:24a) appears to be a "duplicate" of the accession formula of Solomon and Rehoboam.

11. J. Wellhausen, *Israelitische und Jüdische Geschichte* (2d ed.; Berlin: Reimer, 1895) 57; R. Kittel, *Geschichte des Volkes Israel* (7th ed.; Stuttgart: Kohlhammer, 1925) 2.219–20; M. Noth, *Geschichte Israels* (6th ed.; Göttingen: Vandenhoeck & Ruprecht, 1966) 208. For the contrary view, cf. J. A. Montgomery, *Kings* (1951) 248; J. Bright, *A History of Israel* (2d ed.; London: SCM, 1972) 226. For the whole discussion, cf. J. Trebolle, *Salomón y Jeroboán: Historia de la recensión y redacción de 1 Rey. 2–12; 14* (Bibliotheca Salmanticensis, Dissertationes 3; Salamanca/Jerusalén: Universidad Pontificia/Instituto Expañol Bíblico y Arqueológico, 1980) 226–31.

12. Cf. E. Meyer, "Bericht der Septuaginta über Jeroboam," *Die Israeliten und ihre Nachbarstämme* (Alttestamentliche Untersuchungen; Halle: Niemeyer, 1906) 363–70.

The stereotyped phraseology of the accession formula recurs frequently throughout the books of Kings. This therefore allows us another approach to the study of the process of the recension and composition of the books. Despite the rigidity of its formulation, the accession formula nevertheless undergoes numerous variations. As an explanation for this phenomenon Bin-Nun supposes a plurality of formulations in the original source. E. Cortese thinks rather of a redactor's literary variations upon the primitive [[20]] formula. These authors do not take into account the textual variants of the Old Greek and, in the case of Rehoboam, do not pay the least attention to the text of LXX 12:24a.[13]

The accession formula is as follows: 'In the year . . . of X, king of Israel/Judah, there became king Y, son of Z, king of Judah/Israel . . .' (*bšnt . . . l . . .* [*bn . . .*] *mlk yśrʾl/yhwdh mlk . . . bn . . . ʾl yhwdh/ysrʾl*).

In five cases in the MT, the formulation of the phrase presents a common anomaly, repeated by LXX^{B} in the *kaige* [[a revision of the Old Greek]] section. This anomaly consists in inverting the order of the sentence in such a way that the synchronism shifts to the second position: "Y, son of Z, became king over Judah/Israel in the year . . . of X, king of Israel/Judah" (1 Kgs 16:29 Ahab; 22:41 Jehoshaphat; 22:52 Ahaziah of Israel; 2 Kgs 3:1 Jehoram of Israel; 12:1 Joash of Judah).

In these cases, the text of the Old Greek, reflected in the *kaige* section only by the Antiochene text, always preserves intact the original formulation with the synchronism in the initial position: *en tō eniautō* . . . [['in the year']]. The change in the MT is always occasioned by the transposition of the whole formula to a different context from its primitive location. A displacement of the formula in the ensemble of the composition provokes a readjustment in the formulation of the phrase.

The anomaly in the formulation of MT 1 Kgs 16:29 (Ahab), 22:41 (Jehoshaphat), and 22:52 (Ahaziah of Israel) is in each case due to the transposition of the occurrence of the formula in reference to Jehoshaphat. The original position of Jehoshaphat's accession formula was in 1 Kgs 16:28a. This is attested by the Old Greek (LXX^{BL} in a non-*kaige* section), which has here the formula in its regular form. The original position fits the pattern of synchronisms which structures the composition of 1–2 Kings.[14]

13. Sh. R. Bin-Nun, "Formulas from Royal Records of Israel and Judah," *VT* 18 (1968) 414–32; E. Cortese, "Lo schema deuteronomistico per i re di Giuda e d'Israele," *Bib* 56 (1975) 37–52; J. Debus, *Die Sünde Jerobeams: Studien zur Darstellung Jerobeams und der Geschichte des Nordreiches in der deuteronomistischen Geschichtsschreibung* (FRLANT 93; Göttingen: Vandenhoeck & Ruprecht, 1967) 86; J. Trebolle, *Salomón y Jeroboán*, 84–109.

14. Cf. S. R. Driver, *An Introduction to the Literature of the Old Testament* (5th ed.; Edinburgh: Clark, 1894) 179; J. D. Shenkel, *Chronology and Recensional Development in the Greek Text of Kings* (HSM 1; Cambridge, MA: Harvard University, 1968) 58, 73–86.

[[21]] In the same way the anomaly of the MT in the formulation of 2 Kgs 3:1 (Jehoram of Israel) is motivated by the transposition of the formula. Its original position was in 2 Kgs 1:18a. This fact is attested by the Old Greek (LXX^{L} in the *kaige* section and Josephus),[15] which here has the normal formula; it corresponds, furthermore, to a second principle of the composition of the books: that compositional units (notices or historical narratives, prophetic oracles and narratives, etc.) must be integrated within the framework of that reign with which they are synchronized. In the text-form reflected by the Old Greek, the prophetic narratives of chap. 2 are set within the framework of the reign of Joram. On the contrary, in the MT they remain outside the framework of any reign.[16]

The MT of 2 Kgs 12:1 first gives the age of Joash of Judah at the moment of his accession to the throne, followed by the synchronism for his accession. The Old Greek, represented here by LXX^{L}, preserves once more the habitual formulation.

In an earlier passage the MT presents the synchronism in the accession formula for Ahaziah of Judah in 8:25 ("In the 12th year of Joram son of Ahab"), but in 9:29 it adds a different synchronism corresponding to the chronological system of the Old Greek: "in the 11th year of Joram son of Ahab, Ahaziah began to reign over Judah." This phrase and its synchronism belong to the original text of the regnal formula of Ahaziah as preserved in the so-called "addition" of LXX^{L} VL after 10:36. The formula comes immediately before the "conspiracy notice" (*qšr ʿl*) of Jehu, redacted according to the narrative pattern of the "conspiracy" or "*coup d'état*" (*hkh, Putschbericht*):

> . . . καὶ Ὀχοζίας υἱὸς ἦν εἴκοσι καὶ δύο ἐτῶν ἐν τῷ βασιλεύειν αὐτόν, καὶ ἐνιαυτὸν ἕνα ἐβασίλευσεν ἐν Ιερουσαλημ. καὶ ὄνομα τῆς μητρὸς αὐτοῦ Γοθολία θυγάτηρ Αχααβ βασιλέως Ισραηλ. καὶ ἐπορεύθη [[22]] ἐν ὁδῷ οἴκου Αχααβ. . . . Καὶ ἐπορεύθη Ὀχοζίας ἐπὶ Αζαηλ βασιλέα Συρίας εἰς πόλεμον. Τότε συνῆψεν Ιου υἱὸς Ναμεσσει ἐπὶ Ιωραμ υἱὸν Αχααβ βασιλέα Ισραηλ, καὶ ἐπάταξεν αὐτὸν ἐν Ιεζραηλ, καὶ ἀπέθανεν. καὶ ἐτόξευσεν Ιου καὶ τὸν Ὀχοζίαν βασιλέα Ἰούδα ἐπὶ τὸ ἅρμα, καὶ ἀπέθανεν. καὶ ἀνεβίβασαν αὐτὸν οἱ παῖδες αὐτοῦ ἐν Ιερουσαλημ καὶ θάπτουσιν αὐτὸν μετὰ τῶν πατέρων αὐτοῦ ἐν πόλει Δαυειδ. (2 Kgs 10:36+)
>
> [['Ochozias [Ahaziah] was twenty-two years old when he began to reign and he reigned in Jerusalem for one year. The name of his mother was Gotholia [Athaliah], daughter of Achaab [Ahab] king of Israel. And he walked in the way of the house of Achaab. . . . Ochozias went to war

15. Cf. Shenkel, *Chronology*, 69, 73, 82.
16. O. Eissfeldt, *The Old Testament: An Introduction* (Oxford: Blackwell, 1965) 294.

against Azael [Hazael] king of Syria. At that time Jou [Jehu] son of Namessei [Nimshi] conspired against Ioram [Joram] son of Achaab king of Israel and he wounded him in Jezrael [Jezreel] so that he died. And Jou shot (with an arrow) Ochozias king of Judah upon a chariot so that he died. His servants brought him into Jerusalem and buried him with his fathers in the City of David'.]]

The Old Greek (cf. VL) here preserves the text of Jehu's *coup d'état* notice integrally and in its proper place, that is, after the initial formula of Ahaziah and before the beginning of chap. 11. Also in the MT the initial sentence of the notice (8:28a) follows the initial formula of Ahaziah (8:25–27). Nevertheless, the remainder of this notice, taken from the Annals of Judah, now appears in the MT in pieces scattered throughout a prophetic narrative which comes from the Northern Kingdom and recounts the revolt of Jehu (8:28a; 9:14a, 28).[17]

The composition of the books of Kings appears then as a process in three stages: (1) At first there was a synchronic scheme of the reigns of Israel and Judah. (2) Within this scheme were integrated notices from the Annals of both kingdoms (e.g., "conspiracy notices"). Also in the second stage, narratives gathered from prophetic and historical sources were incorporated into the framework of the respective reigns with which they were synchronized. (3) Finally, deuteronomic comments were added at various stages difficult to define precisely for each case.[18]

One thing is clear: in order to reconstruct the history of the *redaction* and composition of the books it is necessary first to reestablish correctly the history of the *recension* of the text. The type of text on which the Old Greek is based occasionally shows knowledge of a text in which not all of the deuteronomic [[23]] additions had yet been made or in which these had been arranged according to a different compositional plan.[19] Thus, for example, the regnal formula of Rehoboam in LXX 1 Kgs 12:24a lacks the Dtr addition found in MT/LXX 14:21–22 and ignores the anomalous formulation found in 14:21a. Again, the narratives of the consultation of Ahijah of Shiloh and of the Assembly at Shechem are presented in LXX 12:24g–z in a pre-Dtr form. Or again, in the LXX the account of the construction of the Jerusalem temple lacks the Dtr addition found in MT 1 Kgs 6:11–14; this addition is demarcated in the MT by means of *Wiederaufnahme* [['repetitive

17. Note the comment of J. A. Montgomery (*Kings* [1951] 434) concerning Lucian's "faculty of putting things in their right place."

18. Cf. A. Jepsen, *Die Quellen.*

19. This is a very promising field of research. For the moment, see J. Trebolle, *Salomón*, 168–85.

resumption']], where the expression "Solomon built the temple and completed it" is repeated (6:9 and 14).

A final example will summarize and confirm the above conclusions. In the MT of 2 Kgs 13:10–13, and consequently in the *kaige* text of LXX^B, the initial and final formulas of Jehoash of Judah follow immediately one upon the other. No space is left, then, for any narrative material which belongs to the reign of Jehoash. The prophetic narrative of 13:14–21 and the notice of the verses 22, (23), 24–25 are found outside the framework of his reign. This is contrary to the principle of integration of literary units which governs the composition of the book. Moreover, a duplication of the concluding formula of Jehoash is reproduced in the MT/LXX^B at 14:15–16. Finally, the notice in MT and *kaige* 13:22, 24–25, taken from the Annals, appears interrupted by the Dtr insertion of v. 23:

OG (LXX^L)		MT/LXX^B
13:3–7, 23	Dtr comments	13:3–7
13:10–11	accession formula	13:10–11
	epilogue formula	13:12–13
13:14–21	prophetic narrative	13:14–21
13:22, 24–25	notice	13:22, (23 Dtr), 24–25
13:25+	epilogue formula	

On the other hand, in the text of the OG (LXX^L) and Josephus the concluding formula of Jehoash, here located after 13:14–25, [[24]] encloses the prophetic narrative and the historical notice corresponding to his reign (vv. 14–25). Furthermore, this same OG text ignores the repetition of the concluding formula as found in the MT of 14:15–16. It also locates 13:23 inside the Dtr commentary composed of vv. 3–7 and 23. The notice of the victory over the Arameans, then, does not undergo the deuteronomic interruption found in the MT (13:23). Moreover, this OG notice preserves an ending (cf. 13:25, now missing in the MT) in which reference is made to a war in Aphek. All these literary units (prophetic narrative, notice, and Dtr comments) are linked among themselves by mutual references: all revolve around the "salvation" in the war at Aphek (*tšwʿh*, *sōtēria*, cf. 13:5, 17, 24–25).

In the above examples we have used an analysis which combines textual ("lower") and literary ("higher") criticism, that is, *recension history* and *redaction history*. We applied this method to the two text-types of 1–2 Kings, the proto-Masoretic and that underlying the Old Greek. This kind of analysis allows us to discover an earlier stage of the composition of the books in which distinct literary units maintain a greater degree of literary unity and integrity, and in which they are not as fragmented and riddled with interruptions as they are in the proto-Masoretic text.

The Construction of Solomon's Palace: MT 1 Kgs 7:1–12 // LXX 7:38–50

J. W. Wevers, D. W. Gooding, and L. Prijs have stressed the midrashic and targumic character of the LXX translation in the books of Kings. It is now necessary to establish the criteria which will allow us to answer the question: "*Vorlage* ⟦'source text'⟧ or *Targum*?" In order to do this we now propose two further examples for discussion.

In the MT and in the OG of 1 Kgs 6:2–7:51 the differences in order of the literary units are as follows [the LXX verse numbers have their counterpart in the MT listed in brackets]: ⟦25⟧

	LXX		MT
Chronological note	6:4–5a[6:37–38a]		
Temple	6:6–34[6:2–36]	6:2–36	Temple
		6:37–38a, b	Chronological note
		7:1–12	Palace
Temple	7:1–37[7:13–51]	7:13–51	Temple
Palace	7:38–50[7:1–12]		

In the MT the description of the construction of the palace is found inserted in the middle of the account of the construction of the temple. The LXX, by contrast, first presents the narrative of the construction and decoration of the temple and only later makes reference to the palace. It appears intentionally to separate the temple from the palace. Gooding sees in this a separation of the religious from the profane and accordingly rejects this "reverent" order. He attributes it to the typical piety and pedantry of the translator in questions of chronology.[20]

Methodologically speaking, however, an argument based on the formal aspects of a given text should take precedence over an argument based on its possible "tendencies." It also comes first in order as one applies the several critical methods. *Tendenzkritik* ⟦'critical analysis of ideological tendencies'⟧ is very much exposed to the fantasies and the biases of each exegete. In the present case the valid formal criteria derive from a principle already demonstrated above: when a textual corruption is related to a transposition in a given text, the corruption is probably caused by, and is a sign of, that same transposition. In this case the transposition could have been made under the influence of the process of ring composition or *Wiederaufnahme*.

20. D. W. Gooding, "Pedantic Timetabling in the 3rd Book of Reigns," *VT* 15 (1965) 153–66, cf. 155–56; contrast Trebolle, *Salomón*, 307–20.

The proto-Masoretic text has transposed the ensemble formed by the two literary units 6:37–38a and 7:1–12a. The evidence for [[26]] these two transpositions is found in the discrepancies which have been left in the present text. The insertion of this block of material in a new context has caused the corruption of the form of the MT in the two verses which constitute the points of insertion and suture: 6:36 and 7:12b (LXX 6:34). The text of these verses is as follows:

LXX^B		MT
6:34[6:36]		6:36
καὶ ᾠκοδόμησεν		ויבן
τὴν αὐλὴν τὴν ἐσωτάτην		את החצר הפנימית
τρεῖς στίχους ἀπελεκήτων		שלשה טורי גזית
καὶ στίχος κατειργασμένης κέδρου		וטור כרתת ארזים
κυκλόθεν (סביב)		
κὰι ᾠκοδόμησε καταπέτασμα		
τῆς αὐλῆς		
τοῦ αἰλὰμ τοῦ οἴκου (לאלם הבית)		
τοῦ κατὰ πρόσωπον τοῦ ναοῦ		
	TRANSPOSITION	7:37–38a, (b) 7:1–11
7:49[7:12a]		7:12a
τῆς αὐλῆς τῆς μεγάλης κύκλοι		וחצר הגדולה סביב
τρεῖς στίχοι ἀπελεκήτων		שלשה טורים גזית
καὶ στίχος κεκολλημένης κέδρου		וטור כרתת ארזים
		7:12b
		וכחצר בית יהוה הפנימית ולאלם הבית

6:34[6:36] [['and he built the inner court of three courses of hewn stones and one course of cedar beams surrounding, and he built the curtain of the court for the portico of the temple which was in front of the shrine']]

7:49[7:12a] [['and the large surrounding court of three courses of hewn stones and one course of cedar beams']]

7:12b [['for the inner court of the temple of Yhwh and for the portico of the temple']]

The two passages (LXX 6:34[6:36] and MT 7:12) use identical expressions to refer to the portico of the temple (*ʾlm hbyt*), the interior court (*ḥṣr hpnymyt*), and the type of construction composing the interior and exterior court walls (*sbyb šlšh ṭwry[m] gzyt wṭwr krtt ʾrzym*; in the LXX the only difference is that 6:34[6:36] *kyklothen* = *sbyb* [['surrounding']] appears at the end of the sentence). This [[27]] textual parallelism is heightened by a parallelism of context. The two verses cited above, MT 7:12b and LXX 6:34[6:36], mark the transition to a similar block of material (MT 7:13–51 // LXX 7:1–37) also referring to the portico of the temple (cf. LXX 7:3[7:15] *to ailam tou oikou*) and to the interior court, in which are found the cult objects mentioned in the sequel (columns, "sea," and bronze basins, etc.). This double parallelism of text and context facilitates the movement from one text to the other and simplifies the insertion of the block MT 7:1–9(10–11) between the two, with 7:12 forming a *Wiederaufnahme* of 6:36.

As it now stands, the insertion of 7:1–11 has provoked a textual corruption in the MT in its forms of the two verses, 7:12b and 6:36, between which the foreign piece has been forcibly interpolated:

(1) The MT 7:12b has little meaning in itself and even less in its present context (7:1–12a). The context makes reference to the construction of the palace and of its large outer court. It makes no sense to refer, as does 12b, to the interior court and the portico (*ʾulam*) of the temple. This reference, however, helps smooth the transition to the following description in MT 7:13–51 of the cult objects found in the *ʾulām* and the interior court of the temple. This shift to a description of the temple is the reason for the "addition" by *Wiederaufnahme* of 7:12b in the MT.

(2) Furthermore, the MT form of 6:36 has lost its ending, which was in part transposed to provide 7:12b in the MT. The reference to the vestibule of the temple (*lʾlm hbyt*) retains its original context in LXX 6:34. After the description of the *dᵉbîr* [['inner shrine']] and the *hêkāl* [['great hall']] with their respective doors (6:18aβ–33[6:19–35]), we pass logically to the description of the third section of the temple: the *ʾulām* or vestibule framed by its bronze pillars (7:13–22). Such is the sequence in the LXX where the link between the references to the vestibule and those to its two pillars is expressed [[28]] by the common allusion to the "vestibule of the temple" in 6:34[om MT] and 7:3[7:15] (*to ailam tou oikou*).

The Translation Equivalent *lkn* = *ouch houtōs* (*lʾ kn*): *Vorlage* or *Targum*?

S. R. Driver qualified as "strange" the occasional LXX translation of the particle *lkn* [['therefore']] by an (interrogative?) *ouch houtōs* [['not so']], as though one were dealing with *lʾ kn* [['not so']]: 1 Kgs 22:19; 2 Kgs 1:4, 6, 16; 19:32; 21:12; 22:20.[21] All these passages are found in the *kaige* section γδ of

21. S. R. Driver, *Notes on the Hebrew Text of the Books of Samuel* (2d ed.; Oxford: Clarendon, 1913) 44; cf. L. Prijs, *Jüdische Tradition in der Septuaginta* (Leiden: Brill, 1948) 59–61.

the Greek text of 1–2 Kings. According to L. Prijs, the "LXX" in this case employs a "targumic" interpretation of the type *ʾal tiqra*, which consists in understanding a word by dividing it into two parts.

This "strange" version, however, is not the original in the OG. It is a clue which betrays a later recension of the text. Wherever it occurs, the Antiochene text, or at least some one of its representatives, such as the *Vetus Latina* ⟦'Old Latin'⟧ or the Armenian version in its intermediate stage,[22] preserves the old version.

Thus, in 2 Kgs 1:16 the Antiochene text (boc_2e_2) has *dia touto* ⟦'on account of this'⟧ where we find the reviser's phrase *ouch houtōs* in the rest of the MSS of the LXX. In two other cases, 2 Kgs 1:4, 6, the LXX^L offers a double reading, the reviser's reading followed by the primitive reading: *ouch houtōs dia touto*. In 2 Kgs 19:32 there is an omission in the LXX^L, but the Armenian version attests *propter hoc* ⟦'on account of this'⟧; the intermediate stage of this version depends upon the proto-Lucianic text and consequently attests *dia touto* in the OG. In two other cases, 2 Kgs 21:12 and 22:20, the LXX^L now presents the reviser's translation, but again the Armenian version here joined by Lucifer (*propter hoc*) reflects the primitive Greek *dia touto*. Finally, in LXX^L at 1 Kgs 22:19 the reviser's form reappears, but significantly enough Theodoret ignores it.

⟦29⟧ In Samuel–Kings the Hebrew particle *lkn* appears only five more times: 1 Sam 2:30, 3:14, 27:6, 28:2; 1 Kgs 14:10. The first four cases correspond to the section α, non-*kaige*, of the Greek text. In 1 Sam 2:30 and 27:6 all the MSS offer *dia touto*, confirming our supposition that this was the original version of the LXX. In 3:14 the reviser's form reappears in the G MSS *oud'/ouch houtōs* ⟦'not so'⟧, but the VL (*Palimpsestus Vindobonensis*) offers *ideo* and the Ethiopic version ($Aeth^a$) has *et propterea*, which attests a Greek *dia touto*. In 1 Sam 28:2 the transmitted version is *houtō* ⟦'thus'⟧, which can equally come from *ouch houtōs* or *dia touto*. The passage in 1 Kgs 14:10 forms part of a larger Hexaplaric addition (vv. 1–20) which was never part of the OG and here is taken from Aquila. Its version, *dia touto*, is in this case the typical Aquilan version.

In order to obtain a more complete view of the translations of the particle *lkn*, we need to take into account also the rendering of the expression *lʾ kn* from which the reviser's version is derived. In the only case of *lʾ kn* in a non-*kaige* section (1 Sam 30:23) the OG translation for *lʾ tʿśw kn* ⟦'you shall not do so'⟧ is *ou poiēsete houtōs* ⟦'you shall not do so'⟧. All the other cases of the reading *ouch houtōs* (= MT *lʾ kn*) are found in the *kaige* sections of the G text. This does not help to make a comparison between the pos-

22. B. Johnson, *Die armenische Bibelübersetzung als hexaplarischer Zeuge im 1. Samuelbuch* (ConBOT Series 2; Lund: Gleerup, 1968) 96.

sible readings of the old version and those of the proto-Theodotionic or *kaige* recension found elsewhere: 2 Sam 20:21, 23:5 (*hoti ouch houtōs* [['that not so']] boc$_2$e$_2$ VL); 2 Kgs 7:9 (*ti houtōs* [['one so' or 'something']] boc$_2$e$_2$); 2 Kgs 17:9 (*adikous* [['unjust']] boc$_2$e$_2$ VL).

However, the case of 2 Sam 18:14 is in itself very eloquent:

MT	*lʾ kn ʾḥylh* [['thus I will not wait']]
LXX^B	*touto egō arksomai ouch houtōs menō* [['I will begin this; I will not remain so']]
LXX^L	*dia touto egō arksomai* [['on account of this, I will begin']]
Arm	*propter hoc quidem praeteribo* [['on account of this, indeed I will pass by']]

The current text of the LXX offers a double reading. The first element preserves the old version, albeit in a truncated form [[30]] without *dia*; the same form is attested by the Antiochene text, reflected in the Armenian version as well, presupposing the *Vorlage lākēn ʾāḥēllāh* [['therefore I will begin']]. The second element corresponds to the reviser's version made according to the proto-MT.[23]

Thus, in the books of Samuel–Kings the translation *lkn* = *ouch houtōs* is not that of the Old Greek. It corresponds instead to the later hebraizing recension represented by the *kaige* revision.

Conclusion: Method in Identifying the Original Text of Kings

The Hebrew, Greek, and Latin variants must be studied and assessed from the perspective of the history of the biblical text. The correct use of the principles of textual and literary criticism in restoring the *Urtext* [['original text']] depends in great measure upon following a correct theory of the history of the biblical text.

The new understanding of the history of the text of (Samuel–)Kings gained in the light of the MSS discovered in Cave 4 at Qumrân grounds the possibility of assigning a high value to the readings and the passages of the OG and (in the *kaige* sections) of the Antiochene text.

The OG translated a type of Hebrew text which had already been used by Chronicles and which has now reappeared in Hebrew, especially in 4QSam^{a,b,c}. Around the turn of the eras the OG was revised according to

23. Barthélemy, *Les Devanciers*, 116.

a Hebrew text of the proto-Masoretic type. This *kaige* revision in the MS tradition replaced the OG text in the sections 1 Kgs 1–2:11 and 1 Kings 22–2 Kings and may have left traces in the non-*kaige* section in some MSS. In those sections then, the only path capable of leading us back to the primitive form of the Greek version is that which retraces the pre-Lucianic substratum of the Antiochene MSS. Consequently, a working method consisting of a three-stage approach is needed for the establishment and exegesis of the Hebrew *Urtext* of Kings:

⟦31⟧ (1) The first stage is that of rediscovering the OG. This consists in re-ascending the path traced by the successive revisions ("proto-Lucianic," proto-Theodotionic or *kaige*, Hexaplaric, and Lucianic).

(2) The second stage is that of approaching as nearly as possible to the Hebrew *Vorlage* of the first translation and its revisions.[24] In the dilemma *Vorlage* or *Targum* (and here we speak only for the text of Samuel–Kings) the balance weighs in favor of a non-Masoretic *Vorlage* which is reproduced with a high degree of literalness by the OG translation. This primary version does not reflect more or less isolated Greek variants from a constant proto-Masoretic text, but rather an independent type of Hebrew text which had a different development.

(3) The third stage consists in moving still farther back toward the Hebrew archetype (*Urtext*). This implies a critical *examinatio* of the two basic types of text: the one represented by the proto-Masoretic text, reflected by the *kaige* and Hexaplaric recensions, and the other represented by the Hebrew text of Chronicles (and by 4QSam^{a,b,c} in Samuel) and reflected by the OG.[25]

This *examinatio* ⟦'examination'⟧ must be carried out before any argumentation based on possible biases in the content of the text, and it must utilize formal criteria such as the fixed structure of literary formulas and genres, the literary procedure of transposition and insertion of one passage into another by, e.g., *Wiederaufnahme*, and the general principles of composition of the books of Kings.

24. On the whole question of the reconstruction of the Hebrew text underlying the LXX, see E. Tov, *The Text-Critical Use of the Septuagint in Biblical Research* (Jerusalem Biblical Studies 3; Jerusalem: Simor, 1981).

25. The question about the "better text" then concerns the earlier period of the editors, rather than that of more or less careless or innovative later copyists. At that earlier stage the limits between higher and lower criticism become rather fluid and both methods must work side by side. Cf. D. Barthélemy, "Notes critiques sur quelques points d'histoire du texte," *Etudes d'histoire du texte de l'Ancien Testament* (Orbis Biblicus et Orientalis 21; Fribourg/Göttingen: Editions Universitaires Fribourg/Vandenhoeck & Ruprecht, 1978) 289–303, esp. 296–97; "La qualité du texte massorétique de Samuel," *The Hebrew and Greek Texts of Samuel*, 1–44.

Editors, translators, and critics of the books of Kings have had frequent recourse to the Lucianic text in the *kaige* sections. It is all the more significant that this preference for the Lucianic text as "the better text" in these cases does not stem from a tendency favorable to it, but rather overcomes a prejudice widespread since the days of Rahlfs against the Lucianic revision and [[32]] against any possible existence of a "lucian before Lucian."[26] Such modern authors, then, must assign a high critical value to the type of text represented by the OG and/or by the pre-Lucianic or Antiochene text. This should not remain a merely occasional recognition, confined to those passages where the MT presents an insuperable corruption or difficulty. The two types of texts must first be studied separately on their own merits. Either or both of the two text-types may sometimes reflect previous secondary redactional activity. Consequently, the analysis of the recensional history of these texts constitutes a necessary step methodologically prior to the literary analysis of the chronologically prior history of the composition and redaction of the critically-identified *Urtext*.

	LXX^{B}		LXX^{B}	MT	
			καὶ τοῦτο τὸ πρᾶγμα	וזה הדבר	11:27a
12:24b	καὶ ἦν ἐπαιρόμενος		ὡς ἐπήρατο χεῖρας	אשר הרים יד	
	ἐπὶ τὴν βασιλείαν		ἐπὶ βασιλέα . . . (vv. 27–39)	(vv. 27–39) . . . במלך	
24c	καὶ ἐζήτει Σαλωμὼν	11:40	καὶ ἐζήτησεν Σαλωμὼν	ויבקש שלמה	11:40
	θανατῶσαι		θανατῶσαι	להמית	
	αὐτόν		τὸν Ἰεροβοάμ	את ירבעם	
	καὶ ἐφοβήθη				
			καὶ ἀνέστη	ויקם ירבעם	
	καὶ ἀπέδρα αὐτὸς		καὶ ἀπέδρα	ויברח	
			εἰς Αἴγυπτον	מצרים	
	πρὸς Σουσακεὶμ		πρὸς Σουσακεὶμ	אל שישק	
	βασιλέα Αἰγύπτου		βασιλέα Αἰγύπτου	מלך מצרים	
	καὶ ἦν μετ᾽ αὐτοῦ		καὶ ἦν ἐν Αἰγύπτῳ	ויהי במצרים	
	ἕως ἀπέθανεν Σαλωμών		ἕως οὗ ἀπέθανεν Σαλωμών	עד מות שלמה	
		11:43	. . . καὶ ἐγενήθη	ויהי	12:2
24d	καὶ ἤκουσεν Ἰεροβοὰμ		ὡς ἤκουσεν Ἰεροβοὰμ	כשמע ירבעם	
			υἱὸς Ναβάτ,	בן נבט	
			καὶ αὐτοῦ ἔτι ὄντος	והוא עודנו	
			ἐν Αἰγύπτῳ	במצרים	
			ὡς ἔφυγεν ἐκ προσώπου	אשר ברח מפני	
				המלך	

[[table continues on next page]]

26. Rahlfs, *Lucians Rezension der Königsbücher* (Septuaginta Studien 3; Göttingen: Vandenhoeck & Ruprecht, 1911) 290–95.

	LXX^{B}		LXX^{B}	MT	
			Σαλωμὼν	שלמה	
			καὶ ἐκάθητο	וישב	
	ἐν Αἰγύπτῳ		ἐν Αἰγύπτῳ,	ירבעם במצרים	
	ὅτι τέθνηκεν Σαλωμών . . .		(ὅτι τέθνηκε Σολομῶν boc$_2$e$_2$)		
24f	καὶ ἐξῆλθεν Ἰεροβοὰμ		κατευθύνει(ν)		
	ἐξ Αἰγύπτου,				
	καὶ ἦλθεν		καὶ ἔρχεται		
			εἰς τὴν πόλιν αὐτοῦ		
	εἰς γῆν Σαρειρὰ		εἰς τὴν γῆν Σαρειρὰ		
	τὴν ἐν ὄρει Ἐφράιμ . . .		τὴν ἐν ὄρει Ἐφράιμ . . .		
				וישלחו	
				ויקראו לו	
				ויבאו ירבעם	
				וכל קהל ישראל	
24p	Καὶ εἶπεν	12:3	Και ἐλάλησεν	וידברו	12:3
	ὁ λαός		ὁ λαὸς		
	πρὸς Ῥοβοὰμ . . .		πρὸς τὸν βασιλέα Ῥοβοὰμ . . .	אל רחבעם . . .	

The Royal Novella in Egypt and Israel

A Contribution to the History of Genre in the Historical Books of the Old Testament

SIEGFRIED HERRMANN

The thesis of the essay is that two Old Testament narratives, 1 Kgs 3:4–15 and 2 Samuel 7, can be understood in the light of the Egyptian royal novella, an established literary form, based on an actual type of ceremony, from the Egyptian Middle Kingdom into the Late period. The aim of the novella in Egypt was to explain events and institutions as having their origin in decisions of the king. The adoption of the form in Israel was deliberate, reflecting the confidence of the young Davidic-Solomonic empire. It shows necessary modifications because of both the recentness of the empire and the Israelite royal ideology. The idea of the king as "son" of God, for example, is conceived in natural terms in Egypt, while in Israel it is a sonship by adoption, a transformation that underlies a variety of Old Testament texts, especially in Psalms and Isaiah.

The premises of the argument include the idea of the patterning of the Davidic administration on Egyptian models and the historical value of the Old Testament narratives in question. Today the former premise stands, while the latter is more controversial. The thesis has a methodological difficulty in its concept of the royal novella as a fixed form, yet manifesting various changes in its adoption by Israel and its inclusion in a larger narrative framework. (For an assessment of the article's reception, see P. K. McCarter, *II Samuel* [AB 9; New York: Doubleday, 1984]

Reprinted and translated with permission from "Die Königsnovelle in Ägypten und in Israel: Ein Beitrag zur Gattungsgeschichte in den Geschichtsbüchern des Alten Testaments," originally published in *Wissenschaftliche Zeitschrift Universität Leipzig* 3 (1953–54) *Gesellschafts- und sprachwissenschaftliche Reihe* 1, 51–62; here based on the version reprinted in S. Herrmann, *Gesammelte Studien zur Geschichte und Theologie des Alten Testaments* (Munich: Chr. Kaiser, 1986) 120–44. Translation by Peter T. Daniels. The RSV has been used in this essay for English scripture quotations.

212–15.) However, it throws light on important points of contact between Egypt and Israel, not only in the concept of the king as "son" of God, but also in their shared ideal of the king as responsible for justice. The close link between the royal ideology and Temple-building provides an illuminating backcloth to the narrative's play on the term "house" in 2 Samuel 7.

–for Albrecht Alt on his 70th birthday
with thanks and honor

[[120]] The term "royal novella" is not at home in Old Testament studies. In Egyptology, though, it has become established, signifying a literary form found in a series of historical documents. It makes immediate sense that, given the prominent position of the Egyptian monarchy, a proper literary genre of its own came into existence, crystallizing around the figure of the king. But the fact that the person of the king stands at its heart is not the sole characteristic of the royal novella, nor should it be thought of in the sense of a biography. The peculiarity of the royal novella instead lies in its etiological character. Its purpose is to trace deeds, events, and institutions back to the king; it seeks to understand him as their creator and initiator by portraying him communicating his latest resolutions in as much detail as possible before the assembled court. The two are most closely connected: the king and the historical decision or institution called into existence by him, which continues to operate into the future. This preoccupation with the objective justifies the name "royal novella" for this literary genre. Its concern is "an outstanding event that will be influential in future ages, and it is always the king, not so much as an individual but as an archetypal figure, who stands at its heart."[1]

The literary peculiarity of the literary form called the "royal novella" has occasionally been pointed out in the course of publishing relevant documents.[2] Alfred Hermann and, recently, Eberhard Otto have treated it in summary fashion and collected the material.[3] This short [[121]] article[4] builds on the essential observation presented in those two works—

1. Alfred Hermann, *Die ägyptische Königsnovelle* (LÄS 10; Glückstadt, 1938). This work won general acceptance for the term "royal novella" in Egyptology.

2. E.g., A. Erman, *Die Sphinxstele* (SPAW; Berlin, 1904) 438.

3. A. Hermann, *Die ägyptische Königsnovelle*; Eberhard Otto, Handbuch der Orientalistik 1/2 (Leiden, 1952) 140ff. No treatment dealing with comparative philological and stylistic details yet exists. The work of A. Hermann has brought out the essential factual points but has not exhausted all the nuances that a deeper philological treatment of the texts would uncover.

4. I have had the opportunity to discuss all the details with my Egyptology teacher, Prof. Dr. S. Morenz, and thank him profusely.

that the royal novella literary genre, which appeared in the Middle Kingdom and survived into the Late Egyptian period,[5] did not remain limited to Egypt but under specific historical conditions also influenced the form of historiography elsewhere, leaving recognizable traces.

The shaping power of the royal novella as it is found in Egyptian texts lies in the strict treatment of a simple literary schema, reporting the course of a court ceremonial in the context of which the king promulgates his resolutions. Its most general form is this: the king "appears," he reports his intention to the assembled officials, they respond with a song of praise for the king and his wise thoughts, and the carrying out of the orders is immediately begun. A series of further elements can be added to this basic schema: The king may become aware of the will of the divinity in a dream, which he then passes on to the officials. The speech to the high governmental dignitaries may be extended by praising Ra, whose son the king is. In this context, the king may describe his election even before his birth and the deeds of his youth before he ascended to the throne. He may thus legitimize both himself and his kingship. Finally, the fulfillment of the royal resolution may prompt the king to sacrifice or to pray. The treatment of all the individual elements of this general schema is loose and nonobligatory, yet such that several elements always occur together, and they schematically determine the course of the external event and thereby give the literary whole the distinct structure that gives rise to the label "royal novella." Thus, both the content that has been included in the schema and the king's resolutions and intentions should be taken seriously by the historian, for they relate to historical facts. And the historical kernel of the royal novella consists in this, that these facts must have originated in direct connection with the king's will. The royal novella is most commonly found in the context of building projects, especially temples and their service.[6] The high temple walls inspired inscriptions praising the king as creator of the lordly precincts and giving the pharaoh opportunity to thank the gods suitably for his position and his divine gifts. Only secondarily does a series of [[122]] temple inscriptions and stelas in the style of a royal novella commemorate other kinds of events brought about by the king's memorable directives in the course of his reign. These include war-related decisions[7] and in a few cases matters of

5. Otto, *Handbuch der Orientalistik*, 1/2.144.

6. The attested material is collected in Hermann, *Die ägyptische Königsnovelle*, 9–10; and Otto, *Handbuch der Orientalistik*, 1/2.140ff.

7. Kamoses's campaign against the Hyksos, the so-called "Carnarvon Tablet," translated in A. Erman, *Die Literatur der Ägypter* (Leipzig, 1923) 82ff. Defeat of the Nubians by Thutmosis II, *Urk.* IV, 137–41. The so-called "War Counsel at Iḥm" from the Annals of Thutmosis III, *Urk.* IV, 649–51, also belongs in this context. See also n. 75 in regard to the assumed predominance of history over the genre in the "War Counsel at Iḥm."

domestic policy.[8] Finally, there is a "prophetic" text cast in the form of the royal novella.[9] In the Late period several other legendary pieces adopted the schema.[10]

The editors of the royal novellas have expressed the opinion that this literary genre can also be found in the Old Testament.[11] In favor of this opinion, at the outset, is the fact that the area of Syria and Palestine belonged to the sphere of Egyptian influence from the time of the Old Kingdom on, albeit with fluctuating intensity. External influence, however, is not enough to cause literary forms like the royal novella to come into existence. Internal conditions, bearing on the influenced party, must exist as well. The Canaanite dynasts of the time of Amenophis III and IV, for example, who are known from the Amarna correspondence, appear to have been too minor for us to think that they consciously remade their kingship [[123]] on a foreign model. A dependent princedom, whose power extended over only limited territory, was no terrain for the royal novella. It required absolute power extending over an impressive domain. At the time of the decline of the New Kingdom, however, the Egyptians gradually had to decommission their positions in Palestine, especially Philistia.[12] The shift of power relations toward the northeast then began, which helped the peoples of Syria–Palestine finally to achieve independence and to maintain it for at least several centuries. In Palestine, these conditions made it possible for a separate Israelite kingdom to establish itself, elicited and reinforced by the confrontation with the Philistines, and to hold its ground and become established in its struggle with neighboring peoples. Already its second ruler, David, quickly succeeded in forming a great

8. Punt expedition, *Urk.* IV, 349–54, translated in J. H. Breasted, *Ancient Records of Egypt* (hereafter cited as *ARE*; Chicago, 1906), vol. 2, §§292–95; inscription of Sethos I in the Temple of Redesije, text in C. E. Sander-Hansen, *Historische Inschriften der 19. Dynastie* (BAeg; Brussels, 1933) 25–26, translated in Breasted, *ARE* (Chicago, 1906), vol. 3, §§282–93; care of workers and craftsmen on the stela of Ramses II from Heliopolis, in *RT* 30 (1908) 213ff., translated in Hermann, *Die ägyptische Königsnovelle*, 53ff.

9. This is the "Prophecy of Nefer-rehu," which is not discussed in this context by Hermann or Otto; translated by Erman, *Literatur der Ägypter*, 151; latest translation by J. A. Wilson in "Egyptian Oracles and Prophecies," in *ANET*, 442ff. The problematic text of the actual prophecy is here included in the linguistically and materially straightforward standard framework of royal novella. It is highly probable that the result of conscious editorial activity is visible in it. [Instead of "Nefer-rehu" we now read "Neferti."]

10. Bentresh stela from the Chons Temple in Karnak, translated in Hermann, *Die ägyptische Königsnovelle*, 56ff. A genuine Egyptian royal novella is rendered in a Greek text known as the "Dream of Nectanebo." Details and bibliography in ibid., 39ff.

11. Ibid., 39 n. 64; Otto, *Handbuch der Orientalistik 1/2.*144, where several figures in the citation of passages are confused by typographical errors. 2 Kgs 3:1–28 should read 1 Kgs 3:1–28 and 2 Kgs 5:1–8, 66 should probably read 1 Kgs 8:1–5, 66.

12. A. Alt, "Ägyptische Tempel in Palästina und die Landnahme der Philister," *Kleine Schriften* (Munich, 1953) 1.216–30; originally published in *ZDPV* 67 (1944–45) 1–20.

power, unique in the history of the people of Israel.[13] Once the power structure of this young state had been established, it became necessary for its founder, David, to create conditions under which the positions he had achieved would be secured for the future. The monarchy in Israel thus had to be placed on a broader and more certain foundation than was at first possible under Saul. The primary question was that of the succession. In place of charismatic leadership, which was still the basis on which David's predecessor was chosen, a hereditary dynasty was now established. Out of the purely military kingship of Saul grew a territorial kingdom symbolized by a royal court, for which David had created the prerequisite political context by conquering Jerusalem. New possibilities then opened up, since the royal household provided the impetus for surrounding the person of the king and his governmental activity with an aura that could be symbolically expressed by the assumption of titles and, closely connected to this, by the construction of royal ceremonies. We already know[14] that in these external forms of its internal character the young Davidic kingdom followed the [[124]] Egyptian model, and the question must be asked how much of its content came over as well.

This young monarchy, finally, gave rise to the last and most significant step on the way to its essential perfecting, in that it became the object of a historiography until that time unparalleled in the world.[15] The founding by power politics of an independent kingdom in Israel, the establishment of a court, and the conceptual formation of the kingdom, together with an interest, developed in the meantime, in the person of the king create the conditions of meaning that appear to make plausible an openness in Israel to texts of the Egyptian kingdom and their literary forms. The undertaking of a historiography dedicated to David's monarchy provides the concrete historical point of contact at which the Egyptian royal novella could become effective as a model. If the royal ritual was already highly indebted to Egypt, then the borrowing of the royal novella represented merely the most sublime expression along the path of the outer and inner renovation that was occasioned by the cessation of

13. On this whole question, see the comprehensive investigations of A. Alt, *Die Staatenbildung der Israeliten in Palästina* (Reformationsprogramm der Universität Leipzig, 1930); idem, "Das Großreich Davids," *TLZ* 75 (1950) 213ff.

14. G. von Rad, "Das judäische Königsritual," *TLZ* 72 (1947) 211ff. Most recently A. Alt, "Jesaja 8,23 bis 9,6 Befreiungsnacht und Krönungstag," in the Bertholet Festschrift (Tübingen, 1950) 29ff.; see esp. 42ff.

15. E. Meyer, *Geschichte des Altertums* (2d ed.; Stuttgart, 1931) 2.285–86; idem, *Die Israeliten und ihre Nachbarstämme* (Halle/Saale, 1906) 478ff. Meyer's purely secular-historical conception, in which the religious element of the Old Testament texts in question has not been adequately acknowledged, is evaluated critically by Alt, *Die Staatenbildung*, 43 n. 5; and G. von Rad, [["The Beginning of Historical Writing in Ancient Israel," *The Problem of the Hexateuch and Other Essays* (Edinburgh: Oliver and Boyd / New York: McGraw Hill, 1966) 166–204.]].

real Egyptian power in Palestine and its replacement there by the formation of new states.

David as founder of his dynasty was at once its beginning and its apex. None of his successors matched, let alone surpassed, him. However, with the state already sufficiently secured externally, his direct successor, Solomon, was able to develop and organize it internally. But it then broke into the two constituent parts from which David had welded it together. The Davidic dynasty remained on the throne in the South at least, where its incumbents and subjects fed to the utmost on the exalted self-awareness conferred on it by David, and they gave permanent expression to this awareness in the idea of the coming "Messiah." But nothing fundamentally new was to ensue after David with regard to the internal development of the concept of kingship or the dynastic idea. Thus, if its essential affinity with Egypt was ever consciously felt, the period of David and Solomon comes first into consideration–but also in quite a unique way.

[[125]] The second significant creative act that the Davidic-Judahite Kingdom produced, the Josianic Reform, had nothing to do with either the institution of the kingdom or with its originality. It stands in a wider historical context, not limited to Israel, but observable also in Egypt and Mesopotamia and most clearly understood as the first example of an explicit "classicism" that, at least in Egypt, encompassed many areas of life.

If, then, we are going to find the royal novella with certainty anywhere in the Old Testament, the only possibility is in the era and tradition of David and Solomon. Only then in the history of the people Israel were the intrinsic prerequisites found that corresponded to the nature and meaning of the royal novella and made possible the taking over of this literary form. It is the time of Solomon, in fact, to which the Old Testament texts belong and to which the Egyptologists have hitherto directed attention, though admittedly without decisive, detailed comparison in the content of the royal novella.[16] But in addition, a text from the time of David, which has also been frequently discussed, though in some respects it has not been explained satisfactorily, must undoubtedly be explained in terms of the Egyptian-influenced royal novella, on the basis of its structure, content, and place in the framework of a larger literary whole.

The first text to be connected with the royal novella is 1 Kgs 3:4–15. Solomon is at the heart of it. He has sacrificed on the "great height" of the sanctuary at Gibeon and at night he has a vision of Yahweh in a dream. Upon awakening, he goes immediately to Jerusalem, where once again he makes a sacrifice and decrees a feast for the people of the court. Already this brief outer framework has points of close contact with that of an

16. Cf. above, n. 11.

Egyptian royal novella, the text of the so-called "sphinx stela."[17] Thutmoses IV, who used to hunt in the region of Memphis, goes for a walk in the shadow of the great sphinx, which was honored by the inhabitants of Memphis and the whole region and was bedecked with sacrifices. At this holy spot, the king is overcome by sleep. The sphinx speaks to him in a dream. He wakes but tells no one what he has heard ("he kept silently in his heart") but immediately orders a swift return to the city and a great sacrifice to the god. The strikingly parallel features of the Israelite and Egyptian reports–dream in or at the sanctuary, king's silence, return to the city, sacrifice–appear the more significant because both texts have made the same election from the available [[126]] fixed topoi of the royal novella. Most noteworthy is the absence of any dialogue between the king and the bureaucracy or other representatives of his region, which in Egypt is missing only in the rarest cases.[18]

It has been recognized for a long time that 1 Kgs 3:4–15 is actually a small, self-contained unit, an originally independent older piece that was inserted into the larger context of the Solomon narratives in 1 Kings 3–11.[19] But its literary character and its actual purpose only [[127]] become

17. Erman, *Die Sphinxstele*, 428ff.; most recent translation by J. A. Wilson, "A Divine Oracle through a Dream," in *ANET*, 449.

18. Note that the parallel report in Chronicles (2 Chr 1:2–13) may reflect knowledge of an address by Solomon to his people before the move to Gibeon, if we actually have old traditions before us in this passage. In 2 Chr 1:2, in addition to the speech to "all Israel, " we find the enumeration of a series of high officials whom Solomon consulted. But without proper transition, there follows directly in v. 3 the move of Solomon "and the entire assembly (*qāhāl*)" to the great height of Gibeon. If in its present context v. 2 might also create the impression that it describes the summoning of all the powerful to a state occasion, we still must ask whether this verse, introduced by וַיֹּאמֶר שְׁלֹמֹה, originally meant this. Its wording and its unsatisfactory continuation suggest seeing it as a fragment of an introduction to a longer speech by Solomon to the audience mentioned.

19. Difficulties faced the exegetes (Kittel, Noth) simply because of the problem of the unity of the passage. Sacrifice and dream (vv. 4–5) are apparently performed in Gibeon, but the king appears in Jerusalem once again to sacrifice in v. 15. This discrepancy can be resolved if we remove the king's vision from the setting surrounding it in 1 Kings 3, into which it was inserted independently as an afterthought and anchored at a specific place, in order to introduce the Solomon stories historically. It is not impossible that the vision was transferred to Gibeon only secondarily. Verse 4 reports the great sacrifice in Gibeon, and v. 5a links with the vision (v. 5bff.), whose beginning, בְּגִבְעוֹן, brackets the preceding with the following and at the same time establishes the unity of place for both traditions. For the purposes of historiography, this question is basically irrelevant. It is interesting only to the extent that Solomon's dream is preceded or followed by a sacrifice. There are Egyptian parallels for both possibilities. Without wanting to overstep the bounds of historiography, I still must ask whether not at least one of the two mentioned sacrifices depends on a stylistic constraint suggested by the royal novella and whether it was only later that the necessity for placing this sacrifice at particular sanctuaries arose. That the vision text was originally independent is also indicated by the sudden change in divine name in vv. 5b and 11, where אֱלֹהִים

clear in its fullest extent through the content of Solomon's vision. Following God's invitation, "Ask what you would like me to give you," Solomon speaks first as in a hymn about the development and nature of his kingdom, which he understands as a continuation of the grace bestowed on his father David. His birth, like his elevation to king כַּיּוֹם הַזֶּה [['this day']] (v. 6), are acts of Yahweh, which weigh all the more heavily on him because the call to kingship had already come to him when he was נַעַר קָטֹן [['but a little child']], one who "did not know how to go out or come in" (v. 7). In v. 8 Solomon remembers the fact that Yahweh has chosen all of Israel, in whose midst he is now permitted to be king, and only in v. 9 does he respond to Yahweh's initial invitation and make his request for an "understanding mind."

This praise of the deity inserted in vv. 6–8, which also represents the self-legitimization of Solomon's kingship, can only be properly explained and understood as a specific stylistic constraint, namely, a feature of the Egyptian royal novella. Several Egyptian texts attest that the king, before he begins to speak about his particular goals, independently of this, praises his kingship and the act of his vocation to it before the assembled nobles, in the style of the hymns. In this vocation to the kingship, his relationship to the divinity is the decisive element. In the so-called leather manuscript[20] (a parade example of the royal novella), in which Sesostris I determines to build a temple in Heliopolis, the king expands at surprising length, in hymnic language, on the origin of his kingdom. Thus: "He (Re) bore me to do what (must) be done for him; . . . he made me protector of this land . . . I am a king of his kind . . . he named me lord of mankind (*rḫj.t*), he created me in the face of mankind (*ḥnmm.t*). . . ." But special attention is paid to the memory of earliest childhood, which the divine election already reached back to. Thus: "I already conquered as a nestling (*ṯꜣ*) and, already great in the egg, I 'lived' as a youth (*inpw*);[21] he (Re) enlarged me to be lord of the Two Lands as a child (*nḫn*) . . . he decreed me to be palace-dweller as an (unborn) child (*wḏḥ*), before I ever emerged from the thighs (of my mother)." That this already involves a canonically stamped manner of speech is shown by the great inscription of Thutmosis III on

appears instead of יְהוָה, and by the surprising note in v. 15, וְהִנֵּה חֲלוֹם, which appears not to presuppose v. 5a in its present form, where already clearly a "dream" was spoken of. Verse 14 is an addition by the Deuteronomist, who has also intervened in v. 15. Cf. M. Noth, *Überlieferungsgeschichtliche Studien* (Halle/Saale, 1943) 1.110.

20. Latest edition of the text by A. de Buck, in *Studia Aegyptiaca* (AnOr 17; Rome, 1938) 1.48ff. Translations in Erman, *Literatur der Ägypter*, 79ff.; and Hermann, *Die ägyptische Königsnovelle*, 49ff.

21. The word *inpw* denotes specifically the royal child, the 'prince'.

the southern outer wall of the temple at Karnak.[22] In it, [[128]] the king, before the assembled nobles, the 'friends of the king' (*śmr.w nśwt*), begins his great speech, describing his coronation and at the end speaking about the erection of temple buildings, in a similar way, with a look back at his youth:[23] "He (Amon) commanded me to be on his throne when I was still one who is in his nest (*ỉmj sš.f*).[24] He begat me in the middle of the heart[25] . . . since I was a youth (*ỉnpw*), when I was still a small child (*wḏḥ*) in his temple and my introduction as prophet[26] had not yet taken place. . . ." Unfortunately, what comes immediately after this has been destroyed; the text continues with the mention of a further priestly office, which the prince must have occupied, and then leads directly to the description of the enthronement. It is clear enough, however, that this text both contextually (at the beginning of the royal reign) and conceptually represents a parallel to the leather manuscript. However, 1 Kgs 3:6–8 belongs in the same immediate context, where v. 7, with the words וְאָנֹכִי נַעַר קָטֹן לֹא אֵדַע צֵאת וָבֹא [['I am but a little child; I do not know how to go out or come in']], especially stands out. Semantically, this passage may be set alongside the Egyptian expressions and concepts, *ṯꜣ*, *ỉnpw*, *nḫn*, *wḏḥ*, *ỉmj sš.f*. It matches exactly the theme of the royal novella,[27] which portrays human powerlessness alongside divine election from the time of the beginnings of physical growth. In Egypt as in Israel, these forms of expression serve to secure the dynastic principle, which here is being traced back to its ultimate roots, to the divine will, in the sense of predestination. This is particularly necessary in Israel, where the dynastic principle was first instituted with Solomon. The [[129]] Egyptian model furnished the form here also, in order to validate this principle among the Davidides.[28]

22. *Urk.* IV, 155ff. Cf. also J. H. Breasted, *A New Chapter in the Life of Thutmose III* (UGAÄ 2; Leipzig, 1900). German translation in K. Sethe, *Urkunden der 18. Dynastie*, vol. 1 (Leipzig, 1914).

23. For further similarities between the leather manuscript and the Thutmosis text, see de Buck, *Studia Aegyptiaca*, 1.54 n. 6.

24. For this expression in similar contexts, see Breasted, *Thutmose III*, 11 n. 2.

25. According to Sethe, an expression for 'sincerity'.

26. Conventional translation of a priestly title.

27. The series of examples in which pharaohs speak about their youth in the framework of royal novellas can be extended. See, for example, Sphinx stela 4–5 in Erman, *Die Sphinxstele*, 430–31. There is also a parallel to the Thutmosis text here in the expression 'but his majesty was a child like Horus the boy in Chemmis' (*ỉśt ḥm.f m ỉnpw mj Ḥr nḫn m ꜣḫ-bj.t*). The Thutmosis text reads: 'I was in appearance and form as an *Inmwtf*-priest, as Horus was young in Chemmis' (*mj nḫn Ḥr mꜣḫ-bj.t*), *Urk.* IV, 157, line 12. The praise of the election and youth of the king, recited not by himself but by the dignitaries, can be read in the Kuban stela, lines 13–19; text edited by P. Tresson, "La stèle de Koubân," *BEt* 9 (Cairo, 1922). Translation in Breasted, *ARE* 3, §§282ff.

28. In view of the comparative Egyptian materials, the following translation of 1 Kgs 3:7 recommends itself: "Now, then, Yahweh, it is you who has made your slave into a king in

The great inscription of Thutmosis III at Karnak may also clarify 1 Kgs 3:4–15 in other ways. Further along in the inscription, the king describes his coronation day, in the process veiling the actual events in mythological dress. In the northern, papyrus-columned hall of the Karnak Temple, Thutmosis experiences an epiphany of Amon. Amon has approached the temple in a procession and goes around the papyrus-columned hall during great sacrificial ceremonies. He seeks the king among the festival throng and finally stops before him.[29] The king prostrates himself before Amon and rises again in order to undergo the actual act of coronation, standing, at the "place of the lord."[30] The gates of heaven are opened, he is permitted to see the secret (*bs*) of god, who himself sets the crown on the head of the ruler and establishes the titulary (*nḫb.t*), the five names of which are described at length. It is not difficult to see a relationship with 1 Kings 3 on the basis of the overall character and individual details of this report, which is the king's personal report before his *śmr.w* [['king's friends']]. On Coronation Day the title and names of his kingship are bestowed on the new king in an encounter with god. The wording כַּיּוֹם הַזֶּה [['this day]] at the end of v. 7 shows that 1 Kings 3 is also such a "ceremonial text," a sort of ἱερὸς λόγος [['foundation legend']], which establishes the names and concepts associated with future royal dignity. This wording should be taken as marking the coronation day and [[130]] shows finally the clusters of terms that will be used elsewhere in the Old Testament again and again in connection with the king. This is especially the case in the so-called "royal psalms"–2, 21, 22, and 89–and the "messianic" passages–Isa 9:5, 6 and 11:1–5.[31] Psalm 21 is virtually a para-

---

place of my father David, *while* I was still a small child, who was unskilled in leadership." The possible wide age-range that נַעַר [['youth']] can represent is deliberately restricted by קָטֹן [['small']]. According to one point of view (which needs to be substantiated in more detail), that this may be the component of a ritual, in v. 7b we would expect no information about Solomon's actual age at the moment of his enthronement. Cf. R. Kittel, *Die Bücher der Könige* (HKAT; Göttingen, 1900) at 1 Kgs 1:11. In connection with the assessment of the division of the Israelite kingdom, see also n. 65 below.

29. This must concern some sort of divine decision in the temple. So H. Kees, *Kulturgeschichte des alten Orients* (Munich: Beck, 1933) 1.175. The divine judgment itself and its record were probably requested because of uncertainty in this case regarding the succession.

30. The significant clause that provides, if not the direct model, at least a parallel for the special place of the Davidic king in the Temple in Jerusalem (cf. 2 Kgs 11:14 + 2 Chr 23:13 and 2 Kgs 23:3 + 2 Chr 34:31) reads: *sʿḥʿ.kwj r ʿḥʿw n (?) nb* 'I was installed on the place of the lord', *Urk.* IV, 159, line 1. A further example has already been adduced by von Rad, "Das judäische Königsritual," 213. Cf. also Breasted, *Thutmose III*, 16–17.

31. The messianic passages in Isaiah, particularly Isa 9:5–6 and 11:1–5, which will also be cited frequently below, are therefore appropriate for comparison because Isaiah is here sketching the conceptual ideal of the Davidides, whom he expects on the throne in the not-too-distant future (see Alt's explanations of Isa 8:23–9:6 in the Bertholet Festschrift, esp.

phrase of the royal requests and divine gifts cited in 1 Kings 3. An allusion to the entire scene may also lie behind Ps 20:5–6. The verb שאל [['to ask']] (1 Kgs 3:5, 10, 11, 13) is especially favored there and, besides the passages mentioned, is also found in Ps 2:8. The phrases חֶסֶד גָּדוֹל [['great and steadfast love']] (1 Kgs 3:6) and especially חַסְדֵי דָוִד [['steadfast love for David']] are recalled in many passages (Ps 21:8; 89:25[24], 29[28], 34[33]). The ideal governmental functions of a ruler on the throne of David are indicated in 1 Kgs 3:4–15 by citing a series of concepts familiar from the royal ritual, which are here densely grouped together in a form easily remembered. The ideal is a "righteous" king, where the word "righteous" is to be understood in its Old Testament sense as corresponding to norms laid down by Yahweh. The norms binding on the king coincide with those established by Israel's covenant with Yahweh and thus also bind the people as a whole. The king alone, thanks to the gifts bestowed on him by Yahweh (cf. Isa 11:2), is uniquely and entirely their executor.[32] His governmental function is described as a שפט [['judge']], which not only refers to royal verdicts but stands representatively for all governmental activity (see Isa 11:3).[33] [[131]] Words like צְדָקָה [['righteousness']],[34] אֱמֶת [['truth']], אֱמוּנָה [['faithfulness']],[35] בִּינָה [['understanding']],[36] and חָכְמָה [['wisdom']][37] contribute to this conceptual ideal of the Davidic ruler, but all stand in close connection to the charismatic gifts bestowed on the king, and it is these gifts that enable him to make his decisions in direct correspondence to divine will.

---

pp. 39ff.). It is clear that this conceptual ideal in the Isaiah prophecies connects with the overall message of the prophet, but Isaiah in his description does not go beyond what the tradition had already formed, which, of course, appears in Isaiah's mouth in elevated speech.

32. Cf. G. von Rad, "'Gerechtigkeit' und 'Leben' in den Psalmen," in the Bertholet Festschrift (Tübingen, 1950) 418ff., esp. the remarks on principles, p. 423.

33. Kittel, *Die Bücher der Könige*, at 1 Kgs 3:9. This concept can be compared with an Egyptian concept as well. The king, who lives on the basis of "truth," sees his highest duty as upholding the "right," which is directly bound up with the notion of peace. See Kees, *Kulturgeschichte des alten Orients*, 1.175–76. The entire breadth of a self-contained fixed order in which truth and legal right are combined is encompassed in the Egyptian concept *mꜣʿ.t*. Characteristic for our context is this idea combined with ideal royal governmental activity, as it is expected in the prophecy of Nefer-rehu of Amenemhet I, which deals in its own words with peace on the eastern borders of Egypt (lines 68–69): "The 'right' (*mꜣʿ.t*) will again achieve its place; the 'unright' (*ỉsf.t*) is driven out." On the breadth and comprehensiveness of the *mꜣʿ.t* concept, see R. Anthes, *Die Maat des Echnaton von Amarna* (JAOS Supplement 14; Baltimore, 1952).

34. With 1 Kgs 3:6, compare Isa 9:6; 11:4, 5; 32:1.

35. With 1 Kgs 3:6, compare Isa 11:5; Ps 89:25, 34.

36. With 1 Kgs 3:9, 11, 12, compare Isa 11:2.

37. With 1 Kgs 3:12, compare the parallel in Chronicles, which has the word חָכְמָה [['wisdom']] (1 Chr 1:10ff.); also Isa 11:2.

The right recognition of earthly realities through divine gifts is described as 'hearing' (שמע), which is not hearing with ears (see Isa 11:3), but 'hearing' with the heart. Thus the king requests a לֵב שֹׁמֵעַ ⟦'heart that hears'⟧, specifically לִשְׁפֹּט אֶת־עַמְּךָ לְהָבִין בֵּין־טוֹב לְרָע 'to govern your people, to discern between good and evil' (1 Kgs 3:9). But still more explicitly, the wish for governmental activity to flow directly from God's will is expressed in the nearly paradoxical sentence 1 Kgs 3:11: "but you have asked לְהָבִין לִשְׁמֹעַ מִשְׁפָּט to possess insight to hear the right," not "to speak the right." Thus, in his heart the king knows about everything human as well as the divine–Yahweh's will. He judges and decides after he has perceived both and has rightly "heard" both.[38] However, the other gifts that Yahweh promises to Solomon also belong squarely among the components of the royal ritual, in particular, long life[39] and triumph over enemies.[40]

38. This passage confirms the theory of S. Morenz about the phenomenon of spiritual hearing as the root of the religion of the book. S. Morenz, "Entstehung und Wesen der Buchreligion," *TLZ* 75 (1950) 709ff.

39. Here Egypt offers such rich comparative material that individual examples can be dispensed with. Let us simply recall the formula *dj ʿnḫ* 'gifted with life', which can be expanded to *dj ʿnḫ ḏ.t* or *dj ʿnḫ r nḥḥ* 'gifted with eternal life'. Independent of the question of grammatical form, it should be understood as a statement of or a wish for a divine gift to the king. In the Old Testament, compare Ps 21:5 with 1 Kgs 3:11, not to mention Phoenician and Syrian inscriptions that ask the divinity for "length of days" for the king. The most beautiful parallel for such royal wishes in Semitic sources has recently been found in the Karatepe inscription, which reads (col. III 2ff.): "And may Bʿl Krntrjš bless Azitawadda with life (חים) and health (שלם) and mighty strength (עז אדר) more than any king, while Bʿl Krntrjš and all the gods of the country grant Azitawadda length of days (ארך ימם) and fullness of years (רב שנת) and good government(?) (רשאת נעמת) and mighty strength (עז אדר) more than any king!" Cf. A. Alt, "Die phönizischen Inschriften von Karatepe," *WO* 4 (1949) 272ff. The first three gifts with which Azitawadda is to be blessed, namely חים, שלם, and עז אדר, recall (at least in the first two terms) Egyptian *ʿnḫ wḏꜣ śnb* as a wish for the king: 'May he live, be hale and healthy'.

40. Triumph over enemies is a widespread wish throughout the Orient. From the rich Egyptian illustrative material let us refer first to a passage from a song to the city of Ramses, in which a familiar form of the royal novella follows the subject of triumph over enemies: ". . . you, victorious king, . . . who in the egg was a king majestic like Horus. He conquered the lands through his victories, he subdued the two lands by his thoughts. The nine peoples lie trodden under his feet; all people are dragged to him with their tribute and all lands are set on the one path to him [that is, to his palace]" (Erman, *Literatur der Ägypter*, 338). In addition to his triumph over the Libyans, Merenptah celebrates his triumph at court. This has been transmitted to us in the form of a royal novella in Merenptah's inscription at Karnak (Breasted, *ARE* 3, §§590–92). Long life and triumph over enemies also play a role in the titulary. So we read of Ramses II in an inscription in the rock temple of Abu Simbel: "The conqueror of the adversary, rich in years, great in victories (*wśr rnpw.t ꜥꜣ nḫwt*)" (C. X. R. Lepsius, *Denkmäler*, 195a [1849; repr. Osnabrück, 1970]; translated in Erman, *Literatur der Ägypter*, 323ff.). A further step is taken in a passage from a hymn to Thutmosis III (ibid., 318ff.), in which Amon says: "The great ones of every foreign land are united in your fist; I myself extend the hands and bind them to you. I tie up the Nubian troglodytes together with myriads and thousands and the northern peoples in hundred thousands, captive." This is a virtual

[[132]] 1 Kgs 3:4–15 thus proves to be a unity in both form and content, conceived according to fixed perspectives–in fact, according to the very same perspectives that also belong to the Egyptian royal novella. What is said about the king is not to be understood biographically but as, in each individual feature, typical. What is described as unique and specific should be understood generally–it aims to bring together in concrete narrative context what is institutionally familiar and effective. It thus appears that the young Israelite monarchy is indebted to the Egyptian model even as far as the literary form of its official texts. In this way, the moment is preserved in which royal ceremonial names and concepts are pronounced by the divinity. At the same time, it is clear that this model was modified in some details, specifically in regard to the particular religious situation in Israel. The ruler ideal of the Davidides has its own characteristics, and the royal novella of 1 Kgs 3:4–15 has incorporated the Judahite royal ritual that has retained its individuality by means of the unconditional binding of the Davidide king to Yahweh. This particular characteristic of the Davidic king finds its most eloquent expression in the request for a "hearing heart," which is by nature Israelite [[133]] and is without parallel. Next to this request, the usual requests–long life, riches, and honor–distinctly take second place.

1 Kgs 3:4–15 stands at the beginning of the stories about Solomon in 1 Kings 3–11, just as the description of Thutmosis III's accession introduces the great inscription at Karnak. There has also been an effort to compare the continuation of the text in 1 Kings with the conception in Egyptian documents.[41] Probably the most tempting passage for comparative purposes is the great Temple construction report that begins with the preparations for construction in 1 Kgs 5:16 and ends with the dedication of the Temple in 1 Kings 8. There are indeed points of contact here that support the comparison.[42] However, as for the Solomon narratives in

---

commentary on what countless Egyptian depictions show: the king grasps the heads of his enemies by their topknots and is in the process of smiting them with a club. The victorious power of the king is expressed in his title *kȝ nḫt* 'strong bull', which is an indispensable component of the titulary from Thutmosis I on (E. Otto, *Beiträge zur Geschichte der Stierkulte in Ägypten* [UGAÄ 13; Leipzig, 1938] 2–3). In the Old Testament, compare 1 Kgs 3:11 with Ps 21:9ff., 89:22–24. See also Ps 18:32ff.

41. Hermann, *Die ägyptische Königsnovelle*, 39 n. 64; Otto, *Handbuch der Orientalistik*, 1/2.144.

42. The sole overseer of Temple construction, as in Egypt, is the king himself; see 1 Kgs 6:2, 7:1, etc. Furthermore, the description of the individual components of the Temple and the enumeration of its equipment has its parallels; see, among others, the great inscription of Thutmosis III at Karnak (*Urk.* IV, 166–75); the building inscription of Amenhotep III in Thebes (Breasted, *ARE* 2, §§878–92); recently also the translation by J. A. Wilson, "From Amen-hotep III's Building Inscription" (*ANET*, 375–76).

their present complete form within the Deuteronomistic History, a decision whether literary models exist for further details must await a thorough examination, which is not possible here.[43] In any case, a distinct context of the sort found in 1 Kgs 3:4–15, directly comparable to the royal novella, is not identifiable elsewhere.[44]

Another closed, fully developed unit in the sense and style of the royal novella is found, however, in another text dedicated to David's kingdom, a text which purports to be the ultimate founding document of the Davidic dynasty, 2 Samuel 7. This text, fraught with literary complications, demands [[134]] a brief review of the facts. A detailed explanation of the problems has been provided by Leonhard Rost.[45] Martin Noth agreed with him, on the whole.[46] Rost recognized a basic core, gathered from older material, in vv. 1–7, 11b, 16, 18–21, 25–29, supplemented by vv. 8–17, all of which lay before the Deuteronomist, who then added vv. 13a, 22–24. In juxtaposition to this division of the chapter into older and newer layers is a simpler arrangement, which is organized according to the actual course of events: after David's conversation with Nathan (vv. 1–3), Nathan has a night vision (vv. 4–16), whose content he reveals to David (v. 17), whereupon David offers a prayer of thanksgiving (vv. 18–29). That this arrangement is not secondary but already existed in the old, basic form of the text is confirmed by the literary-critical finding that Nathan's conversation, his vision, and David's prayer already were components of the oldest layer of the composition. The literary-critical problems have arisen, essentially, from matters of content. The beginning of the chapter is dedicated to the question of whether a permanent edifice should be

43. For instance, the question needs to be asked whether the "Book of the Acts of Solomon," cited in 1 Kgs 11:41 by the Deuteronomist as the principal source of his presentation of the Solomon story (whose content Noth, *Überlieferungsgeschichtliche Studien*, 1.109 seeks to outline), could have been comparable in arrangement to Egyptian texts. But efforts to answer this question will have little success and certainly will be unable to make any claim to certainty, since the Deuteronomist himself schematically divided the material of the Solomonic stories into two parts–Solomon's acts pleasing to God and his fall–in the process separating originally adjacent materials. Cf. Noth, ibid. Furthermore, 1 Kgs 3:16ff. is, in contrast to the preceding, a new unit that in this location gives an example of the wisdom granted to the king and exemplifies it by a case from the realm of law. Noth, ibid.

44. This includes 1 Kgs 9:1ff., where it is clear that the Deuteronomist adapted Solomon's dream, in 1 Kings 3, for his own purposes. It also goes for the verses probably (see n. 11) intended by Otto (Handbuch der Orientalistik 1/2.144), 1 Kgs 8:1–5, 66, which cannot be plucked out of their wider context in this way. Cf. Noth, *Überlieferungsgeschichtliche Studien*, 1.112 [70].

45. L. Rost, *Die Überlieferung von der Thronnachfolge Davids* (BWANT 3/6; Stuttgart, 1926) 47–74.

46. Noth, *Überlieferungsgeschichtliche Studien*, 1.106.

constructed for the Ark of Yahweh. This train of thought reaches a conclusion in v. 7, but in v. 8 goes in a new direction, which has at its heart the person of David alone. A clear-cut expression of this appears in v. 11b with the affirmation: David will not build a house for Yahweh, but Yahweh will build a house for David. Here the word "house" unexpectedly shifts to "house" in the sense of "monarchy" and "dynasty." This word בַּיִת is the pivot on which the movement of thought in the chapter turns. As soon as the talk is of a "house," as a designation for the Davidic kingdom, the Ark is no longer mentioned. This double focus of the material gives the chapter a peculiar mediating position when one tries to place it in a larger literary whole. Thus, the beginning, with the Ark problem, connects directly to the preceding chapter, in which the transportation of the Ark to Jerusalem is recounted. But the further course of 2 Samuel 7, which does not mention the Ark, finds its main significance as a prelude to the narrative of the succession to David's throne, which in its main part comprises 2 Samuel 9–20 and 1 Kings 1–2.

The difficulties that literary criticism has long had with this text give rise to the question whether 2 Samuel 7 as a whole or in its individual parts still should be recognized as an independent conception that was only muddied by later interventions but that can provide a [[135]] starting point for clarification of its present form. Alternatively, should it simply be seen as a melting pot for various traditions? The latter alternative, however, is excluded from the start by the extraordinary meaning of the utterances of 2 Samuel 7, whose weight in themselves could not have been without influence on the adjacent component parts of the text. It therefore needs to be asked whether 2 Samuel 7 as a whole or in its parts exhibits features of a specific genre that might permit its apparently different themes—Ark, Temple construction, monarchy, dynasty—to be unified, that might, in fact, necssitate the unifying of these otherwise disparate topics. Features of just such a genre are indeed present, for Temple construction and royal theology are the principal themes of the Egyptian royal novella. Their juxtaposition is neither surprising nor disconcerting but, given the background of a larger form-critical context, is explicable and understandable.

The similarity of 2 Samuel 7 to the Egyptian royal novella, however, is not limited to the commonality of material but is demonstrated by a whole series of characteristics. The chapter begins with the king sitting in his house.[47] This trivial-looking introduction, which omits any exact historical context, is the essential presupposition for the general meaning of what follows. This form of introduction is a stylistic feature of the royal novella.

47. Verse 1b, "When Yahweh had given him rest from all his enemies round about," is deuteronomistic and similarly to be found in Josh 23:1 and Deut 12:10 and 25:19.

The humdrum is deliberately described first; only later is something unique and special introduced. So reads the beginning of the prophecy of Nefer-rehu:[48] "On one of these days it happened that the bureaucracy of the residence of the palace entered to perform the greeting [of the king] [lit., to inquire after the welfare],[49] and they went back out, so that they [again] greeted, as was their daily custom."[50] Only after the description of this ordinary ceremony does the specific action begin: the custodians of the seal are called back at the command of the king so that a task can be assigned to them. The residence of the king in his palace, especially in the columned hall (*ḏꜣdw*),[51] is the most common motif.[52] The [[136]] seating of the king in his house is therefore virtually a standard introduction.

Then David's conversation with Nathan begins. The Egyptian texts have the dialogue of the king with his officials, either enumerated in long lists[53] or subsumed generally as "friends of the king,"[54] in this position, but Nathan stands as an individual before the king. Yet even this is not without Egyptian parallels. On the memorial of King Amosis from the funerary chapel of his grandmother *Ttj-šr*, which he built in Abydos, we read the introduction of a royal novella, which comes closest to the text in 2 Samuel 7:[55] "But it happened that His Majesty sat in the column hall (*ḏꜣdw*),[56] . . . while the . . . king's wife . . . was before His Majesty; one said to the other. . . ." To be sure, 2 Samuel 7 does not mention the king's wife, but it does contain a private conversation between two people. That Nathan enters alone as a single official must be explained, furthermore, on the basis of the concrete relationships of the emerging Davidic state and court monarchy: a strongly defined bureaucracy, available to the king in a representative way, is not yet to be reckoned with. Rather, the royal government in the newly-won metropolis is supported by a chosen circle of reliable followers. Nathan appears in this case as an influential personality in the young state and in one person represents an entire bureau-

48. See n. 9 above.

49. See A. Erman and H. Grapow, *Wörterbuch* (Berlin: Akademie, 1982) 2.373 on *nḏ-ḫr.t.* What it probably means is a tour of officials of various functions, who daily pay their homage to the king and the highest dignitaries and if necessary give reports.

50. *mj n.t-ʿ.śn n.t rʿ nb.*

51. So, for example, in the leather manuscript; also *Urk.* IV, 26 (Amosis for Ttj-šr) and *Urk.* IV, 349 (Punt expedition).

52. See the prophecy of Nefer-rehu, leather manuscript, inscription of Thutmosis III at Karnak, great Abydos inscription of Ramses II, etc. Latest translation in Breasted, *ARE* 3, §§251–81.

53. For example, the leather manuscript and the great Abydos inscription of Ramses II.

54. *Urk.* IV, 156 (inscription of Thutmosis III at Karnak).

55. *Urk.* IV, 26ff. Translation in Hermann, *Die ägyptische Königsnovelle,* 51ff.

56. The omissions contain titles.

cracy,[57] which is only possible in the court of a long-established state.[58] Here, too, the concrete Israelite situation has modified the foreign model.

[[137]] How much David's conversation with Nathan has borrowed from the style of the royal conversation with the entire bureaucracy in the Egyptian model is shown by the end of v. 3: "And Nathan said to the king, 'Go, do all that is in your heart; for Yahweh is with you.'" Precisely corresponding with this phrase in the schema of the royal novella is the hymn of the officials in which they give assent to the king's wise decision.[59] This approval seems peculiar in 2 Sam 7:3 because it contradicts what happens in the next verse, but because of this reveals itself as an element constrained by foreign style.

The continuation in v. 4 introduces the nocturnal vision in which Yahweh orders Nathan to stop David from building the planned Temple, the element of the dream in the narrative with which 1 Kgs 3:4–15 already dealt. What David considered and what Nathan at first confirmed (vv. 1–3) is negated by Yahweh's speech. By divine command, the king must renounce his intention. This same alteration of original intent is found in the Egyptian royal novella in the form of the king's independently asserting his decision against the opinion of his officials.[60] These passages are

57. The fact that in addition to the representative bureaucracy the Egyptian king also had permanent high officials is indicated by the role of the seal custodians, to which the officials appeal, in the just-mentioned Nefer-rehu prophecy: "Then spoke His Majesty to the seal custodians who were at his side (*ntj r gś.f*)." Finally, the entire prophecy is structured as a conversation between the king and a single person, the priest Nefer-rehu, who reads aloud. The seal custodian at the side of His Majesty is introduced and instructed to call the officials in the same way as above, in the great Abydos inscription of Ramses II; Breasted, *ARE* 3, §264; and the Kuban stela, §287.

58. The fact that the spotlight is on Nathan confirms his preeminent and highly influential position in 1 Kings 1. Nathan belongs to the *homines novi* along with Zadok. We encounter them as ἀγενεαλόγητοι [['persons without genealogy']] in Jerusalem in leading positions, after David won the city. The sources do not distinguish between Nathan's prophetic and his political activities, since his appearance in 2 Samuel 12 and—as will be more clearly shown—here in 2 Samuel 7 is only limited to the framework of older traditions. It is precisely these chapters, however, that offer the only examples of his prophet status. The work of M. Simon, "La Prophétie de Nathan et le Temple," *RHPR* (1952) was not available to me.

59. Characteristic examples appear, for instance, in the leather manuscript and the great Abydos inscription of Ramses II.

60. So in the battle of King Kamose against the Hyksos, the so-called "Carnarvon tablet" (translated in Erman, *Literatur der Ägypter*, 82ff.), and, pushing the boundary of diary style (see n. 7 and the text at the end of this work), in the war counsel of Thutmosis III in Iḥm, ibid. On the latter, see A. Alt, "Pharao Thutmosis III. in Palästina," *PJ* 10 (1914) 53ff., esp. 70ff. On the intrusion of Late Egyptian linguistic forms in this annal text, but especially on the abbreviated diary style of his reports (infinitive predicate forms), in which longer pieces with narrative content are included only sporadically, H. Grapow has recently considered: *Studien zu den Annalen Thutmosis des Dritten und zu ihnen verwandten historischen Berichten des*

actually not directly comparable to the negative message of Yahweh to David, since this message is God's word and not the opinion of officials—not Nathan's personal understanding. Furthermore, David does not think of asserting himself, as does the Egyptian king. But in one point the Egyptian texts go further. The Egyptian texts introduce the contradiction of the officials as a stylistic element of the royal novella, which serves to let the king's decision appear [[138]] all the more his own decision.[61] In 2 Samuel 7 we must at least consider the possibility that a similar purpose is being pursued by the skillful selection of the literary resources. With the initial agreement of Nathan and the subsequent turn of events brought about by Yahweh, it appears as if human planning and the absolute will of God are brought into confrontation. In this sense, David assumes the role of the Egyptian officials, who have to obey the higher authority unconditionally. This is virtually a Copernican Revolution for the royal novella in the Israelite context, where in the end not the king but Yahweh's claim to absolute right rules, before which the king himself must sink to the level of עֶבֶד [['servant']]. These considerations are confirmed when we recall the historically burning question Yahweh's speech is intended to answer. Yahweh's speech answers the question why David had not yet built the Temple: Yahweh himself had willed it so!

The problem of building the Temple is first concluded in v. 7. Nathan's night vision continues, after a new introductory formula, and extends to v. 16. Verses 8–16 are a self-contained unit in terms of content, at the heart of which stands David's kingship.[62] Verse 8 reaches back into David's youth

---

Neuen Reiches (ADAW.PH 2, 1947; Berlin, 1949); on the war counsel in Iḥm and the problem of the diary style, see pp. 40, 43, 44–46, 50. The historical problems of the annals have been discussed by M. Noth: "Die Annalen Thutmosis' III. als Geschichtsquelle," *ZDPV* 66 (1943) 156–74.

61. Alt, "Pharao Thutmosis III," 82.

62. All agree that a break occurs between an earlier introductory passage (vv. 1–7) and a later continuation (vv. 8ff.), where the problem of the Ark and Temple is separated from the discussions of David's kingship. Traces of the reediting of a probably older basic core of the text are noticeable in the entire chapter. So right away, vv. 1–3, where one reads only הַמֶּלֶךְ [['the king']] (without דָּוִד [['David']]), are detached from the rest of the context. Whether the transition is right after the first words of v. 4 cannot be said with certainty. The new introduction in v. 8 is surprising, and the continuation of the text presents a few difficulties that later hands must have caused. Both groups of text, vv. 1–7 and 8–16, should nonetheless not be considered independent but as held together by the features of the royal novella and the concept of בַּיִת [['house']], dominant in both. The question remains open whether the word בַּיִת documents the original unity of the chapter or only later became an accidental connecting link between the Temple-building problem and dynastic considerations. In 2 Samuel 7 it has the character of wordplay, and since Egyptian loves wordplay, it should at least be recalled that Egyptian *pr* 'house' is related to *pr.t* 'descendants' in consonantal makeup, though not by root, and it would fit in the context of Temple-building and dynasty-founding, as it appears in

and lets Yahweh report how he had plucked him from the herd and called him to be a נָגִיד [['prince']] [[139]] over the people of Israel. He has accompanied him this far and will eventually make for him "a great name like the name of the great ones of the earth." The recollection of the choice in youth coincides most closely with 1 Kgs 3:6–7. Just as the נַעַר קָטֹן [['little child']] in v. 7 found points of contact with a series of examples of formulaic speech from Egypt, so in 2 Sam 7:9 the phrase "make a name" has been proved to be an Egyptianism by S. Morenz.[63] In 2 Sam 7:8–9, in addition to formulaic phrases such as destruction of enemies (see 1 Kgs 3:11), there are also concrete statements, especially David's call from being a shepherd to being a נָגִיד [['prince']]. Egyptian texts also allow a more detailed historical treatment of the life of the king before his accession at this point in the framework of the royal novella. For example, it is at this point that Ramses II finds occasion to speak to the question of his co-regency.[64]

In 2 Sam 7:10–11, as in 1 Kgs 3:8, the view widens to take in the people of Israel. But, whereas in 1 Kgs 3:9 Solomon begins to present his request, in 2 Sam 7:11b Yahweh commences with his promises to King David and his entire posterity. These promises are crowned by Yahweh's promise that between him and the Davidic descendants there will be a father-son relationship (v. 14) and that the House of David will be firmly established for eternity (v. 16). The elevation of the king to son of the divinity is doubtless connected to the Egyptian model. The Egyptian kings stress their completely physical sonship of god, which allows them to be gods themselves, far beyond the framework of the royal novella. This principle of divine sonship holds also for the Davidic monarchy, but the Israelite monarchy has given up the mythological character of the principle in favor of the historical. It is not physical sonship that unites the king with the divinity but the historically powerful engagement of Yahweh in the concrete conditions of his chosen people that has called the Davidides to the throne and elevated them to Yahweh's sons κατ' ἐξοχήν [['par excellence']]. In this sense, the Davidides are *adopted* as sons of Yahweh.[65] It is noteworthy that

---

2 Samuel 7. Unfortunately, an example of this wordplay in Egyptian texts eludes me. It is quite questionable, however, whether such wordplay would consciously have been taken over into Hebrew. Nonetheless, it is firmly established that inner closure is inherent in 2 Samuel 7 because of the word בַּיִת, despite many other textual difficulties.

63. S. Morenz, "Ägyptische und davididische Königstitulatur," *ZÄS* 79 (1954) 73–74.

64. See the great Abydos inscription of Ramses II, in Breasted, *ARE* 3, §§267–68.

65. From the point of view of adoption of the Davidic ruler and the ritual elements essential to it that must have played a role in the coronation act, in addition to the cardinal passage Ps 2:7, 1 Kgs 3:4–15 also deserves a deeper examination in regard to a few points. For the whole cluster of ideas connected with נַעַר קָטֹן [['small child']] fits with the concept of this tent as a tent with ritual elements of the coronation day. That is, in Isa 9:5 we have a passage in which a descendant of David is prophesied as coming to power with the words "A

the election of the king is placed immediately adjacent ⟦140⟧ to the historical election of the entire people and receives its confirmation from that fact. The election of the king at the same time has its substance in the fact that it is an election for the people of Yahweh. This is expressed in the verses where, in the royal novella, the focus is directed away from the person of the king to the whole people (1 Kgs 3:8 and 2 Sam 7:10–11). The people of Israel are Yahweh's people on the basis of the בְּרִית ⟦'covenant'⟧ Yahweh made with them; likewise, the relationship of the Davidides to Yahweh must be understood on the level of such a covenant.[66]

Adoption of the king by Yahweh and the promise of the permanence of the dynasty are the essential components of the Davidic royal ritual.[67] 2 Sam 7:8–16 thus proves itself to be parallel to 1 Kgs 3:4–15, because in both, familiar terms from the royal ritual that are announced to the king are placed in Yahweh's mouth. That David does not receive them directly, like Solomon, but through Nathan's mediation, is the view forced on us by 2 Samuel 7. With reference to v. 27, Rost raised the possibility that it was not Nathan but David himself who may have been the direct recipient of Yahweh's speech,[68] in which case here too the formal features would correspond to 1 Kings 3. This possibility should be acknowledged; ⟦141⟧ especially Yahweh's speech in vv. 8ff. could be regarded without difficulty as addressed directly to David.[69]

---

child is born to us, a son is given to us." Isa 9:5 refers not to a physical birth but to the accession of a Davidide to the throne, who according to the Israelite perception can legitimately accept rulership only when he has been adopted as Yahweh's son. This has been discussed by Alt, *Jesaja*, 41–42. The Egyptian parallels to נַעַר קָטֹן concern a physical birth that incorporates election as king, as discussed above. Through Isa 9:5 we become aware of the significant modification of this Egyptian basis for Israel in 1 Kgs 3:7 as well. The idea of the newborn, understood in Egypt physically to include the choice as king, is adopted in Israel, but now in a transferred sense as of the new ruler adopted by Yahweh as his son. Completely excluded by this viewpoint is the possibility that נַעַר קָטֹן in 1 Kgs 3:7 designates a person's age. Nonetheless, it is extremely likely that it is not simple predicates of human inadequacy and weakness that are meant by this designation but, over and above this, the possibility that the phrase is an adaptation for the Davidides, who are raised by it to the level of adoptive sons of Yahweh.

66. This is discussed in detail by von Rad, *Das judäische Königsritual*, 214–15.

67. Father–son relationship in Ps 2:7 and 89:27; permanence of the dynasty in Ps 89:37; see Isa 9:6.

68. Rost, *Die Überlieferung von der Thronnachfolge Davids*, 63–64. He opts to assume that there were two parallel traditions, one of which contained the report of God's speaking to David, the other the same speech to Nathan. Each was spliced into the other so much that the prophecy to David could be replaced by the prophecy to Nathan.

69. Investigation and relationship of older material and possible later reworking are definitely the problem in 2 Samuel 7. The mediating role of the word בַּיִת ⟦'house'⟧ and the internal unity of the chapter has already been discussed in n. 62. The completeness of a thought complex, though with formal deficiences in detail, can best be seen as the result of

Regardless of whether Nathan is to be considered the original mediator or not, in form and content the Egyptian royal novella is evident as a model for 2 Samuel 7,[70] and comparison with 1 Kings 3 shows the specific content that this literary form had taken in Israel. It consists throughout in the elements of the Judaic royal ritual of the Davidides, which are legitimated in the framework of a royal novella.

The commonality between 1 Kgs 3:4–15 and the Egyptian sources is also apparent in the position in which 2 Samuel 7 is placed within the framework of the larger literary whole–namely, at the beginning of the Succession Narrative. Just as 1 Kings 3 introduced the story of Solomon and the coronation of Thutmosis III appeared at the beginning of the great inscription at Karnak, so the programmatic content of 2 Samuel 7 is even more striking than in those texts. 2 Samuel 7 prophesies the eternality of the throne of David from the mouth of Yahweh. The establishment and receiving of this Davidic monarchy through dynastic progeny are the theme and goal of the Succession Narrative. It is not a hero-narrative, but as objectively as possible narrates and seeks to explain the development of the dynastic principle of the House of David and, through its interest in these facts, proves to be genuine historiography. Its program includes 2 Samuel 7, which recounts the investiture of David as king legitimated by Yahweh and tells of a prophecy that reaches beyond the person of David.[71]

[[142]] Rost, finally, attempted to date this important section, 2 Sam 7:8–17, by assigning a specific period to each of the layers he had identified.[72] The oldest layer, to which vv. 11b and 16 are supposed to belong, probably stemmed, he thought, from the time of David. But Rost wishes to assign all the rest, with the exception of the deuteronomistic v. 13, to the time of Isaiah, particularly to the period after the fall of the Northern

---

a stylistic constraint that, for the sake of the larger direction, caused some inconsistencies in detail but even so was successful. The recognition of the fact that this constraint on 2 Samuel 7 emerged from the Egyptian royal novella ought to add a new, fundamental aspect to the evaluation of this chapter.

70. For a prayer at the close of the royal novella, as found here in 2 Sam 7:18–29, see the great Abydos inscription of Ramses II, in Breasted, *ARE* 3, §279. Also the Redesije inscription of Sethos I, ibid., §174.

71. Rost's investigation has shown that the beginning of the Succession Narrative is dovetailed into the end of the Ark narrative, and the Succession Narrative begins already with the Michal scene in 2 Sam 6:20b–23. In deliberate opposition to the observation in 2 Sam 6:23 that Michal remained childless to the end of her life, 2 Samuel 7 relates Nathan's prophecy of eternality for the dynasty. Rost, "Die Überlieferung von der Thronnachfolge Davids," 120. Cf. also von Rad, "Die Anfänge der Geschichtsschreibung," 12–14. This little prologue in 2 Samuel 6 is of secondary importance for the present investigation, but it indicates how much actual weight is attached to the dynastic problem of 2 Samuel 7.

72. Rost, *Die Überlieferung von der Thronnachfolge Davids*, 63ff.

Kingdom. Rost supports this late dating essentially on the basis of vv. 14b–15, where the possibility of the chastening of the Davidides is mentioned. It must now be reexamined, however, because we have shown that 2 Sam 7:8–16, except for vv. 11b and 16, contains a whole series of demonstrably old traditional elements, whose thorough assimilation at an earlier time must be assumed. The terminus a quo for the formation of the royal novella in Israel can be taken as the time when the Davidic royal ritual took on a sufficiently self-contained form. This timepoint should be assigned as closely as possible to the time of David and Solomon themselves, when awareness of the origin of the ritual was still present.[73] The fact that 2 Samuel 7 remained open to minor alterations until the Deuteronomist is shown (besides v. 13) by the additions to the prayer of David (vv. 22–24).[74] All of the insertions, however, have not rendered unrecognizable the characteristics of the old tradition preserved in 2 Samuel 7.

The investigation and researching of literary genres is accompanied by a final, deeper question, the question of the relationship between literary form and actual history. The literary dependence of Israel on Egypt has been demonstrated for one genre above, and it will be good to give the answer to the question posed here on the basis of this concrete case, without generalizing beforehand. Though the schema that the Egyptian royal novella uses is distinctive, it is striking how many possibilities exist for its variation and adaptation to particular events and conditions. For instance, the king need not sit in the palace. He can stroll and hunt; he can even be on a campaign. His speech does not need to be addressed to officials and [[143]] dignitaries. It can be with his wife; it can even give way to a "prophet's" monologue. These variants are only clues to altered historical circumstances, but they indicate the essential flexibility of the genre, which allows it to come closer to the historical and factual. Real history and genuine events are palpable in the royal decisions, without which the framework of the royal novella would also be meaningless. The constructions, temples, and stelas are the stone remnants of the royal will to power. They owe their origin to it and their inscriptions witness to it. One example that stretches the boundary between literary schema and dramatic reality is the war counsel of Thutmosis III at Iḥm. Here every indi-

73. The report of the fall of Athaliah and the installation of Joash in 2 Kings 11 already gives clear indications of fixed traditions of the monarchy (for example, placing the king by the pillars), especially the strong dynastic consciousness that dominated the Judahite country population. Thus, in all probability the above-discussed texts, or at least the assumptions underlying them, had reached maturity by this period.

74. Rost, *Die Überlieferung von der Thronnachfolge Davids*, 53–54.

vidual trait can be a story; here the urgent course of events blasts open the constraint of the genre.[75]

However, the close connection of the royal novella with genuine history is confirmed by the comparison we have made with Israel, where, though adapted to a new environment, it remains unmistakable in its fundamental elements while also adapting to the new context insofar as possible. In the case of the texts of the Old Testament cited above, which as in Egypt concern monarchy and temple construction, we discussed this adaptation to the concrete Israelite situation as it was expressed in external events (dream at Gibeon, journey to Jerusalem, conversation of the king with Nathan, the problem of Ark first, then Temple) and as it was modified internally, in its content (physical god-kingship in Egypt, historical-adoptive kingship in Israel). This adaptation in form and content has, not least, given rise to the literary problematic of the text, especially for 2 Samuel 7. This problematic actually can only be rightly understood when, on the one hand, the broader stream of literary tradition is viewed, in which these Old Testament texts stand and which constitutes the unifying thread even for apparently mutually exclusive details. But, on the other hand, it can only be understood when the concrete historical conditions are also kept in mind, which the royal novella has actually embraced, in the case of the Davidic monarchy, in the Israelite context. When Rost,[76] commenting on 2 Samuel 7, maintains the historicity of a divine revelation, "however controversial the How," this possibility is not to be dismissed out of hand. The single event, however, as the narrative of the dream, conversation, and prayer suggests to us, pales before the historical impact, which the actual content of the narrative has shown and which, even though in form it follows a foreign model, is the property of the people of [[144]] Israel. The royal novella in Israel at core preserves the dynastic notions of the Davidides, as well as the seed of the messianic idea. Its root lies in the court in Jerusalem, and it owes its historical energy to the inner shaping, determined by Yahweh himself, of the Judahite royal ritual, a process in which Egypt and the royal novella played their part. Thus, as a result of its trajectory through Israel, the Egyptian royal novella has been able to influence world history.

75. Even in the field the king did not do without a certain degree of ceremony. Cf. A. Alt, "Höfisches Zeremoniell in Feldlager der Pharaonen," *WO* 1 (1947) 2ff.

76. Rost, *Die Überlieferung von der Thronnachfolge Davids*, 54–55.

The Counsel of the "Elders" to Rehoboam and Its Implications

MOSHE WEINFELD

The pursuit of parallels in ancient Mediterranean literature to biblical idioms and concepts has long been a staple of Weinfeld's research. In this essay, Weinfeld offers some detailed comparisons between the advice Rehoboam receives at the Assembly at Shechem (1 Kgs 12:6–7) and the advice provided to officials in Classical and ancient Near Eastern diplomatic texts. The notion that the king should be a servant of the people is not unusual in ancient Greece, much less in the Hebrew Bible and early Jewish literature. Weinfeld compares the advice to Rehoboam on forced labor with the exemptions given to Mesopotamian officials, temples, and cities from certain taxes, corvée labor, and military service. The revocation of such privileges is cited, at least in some instances, as the occasion for revolt. Comparison with Assyrian writings, especially a document from the reign of Ashurbanipal, suggests that the counsel given to Rehoboam to speak good things (ודברת דברים טובים) to his people indicates that these good things refer to tangible deeds, perhaps even an agreement or grant, rather than to niceties or gestures. The parallels between phraseology in Kings and phraseology found in Mesopotamian texts shed some light, in turn, on the Chronicler's version of this incident (2 Chr 10:7). Weinfeld suggests that this later rewriting, occasioned by the impression that the Kings text presented the monarch as too obsequious to his people, diminishes the force of the original advice.

[[27]] In the biblical account of the "elders'" counsel to Rehoboam we read: "If you will be a servant (עבד) unto this people this day and will serve them (ועבדתם) and respond to them and speak good words unto them, then they will be your servants forever" (1 Kgs 12:7). The Chronicler modified the phraseology out of respect for the Davidic house and read: "If

Reprinted with permission from *MAARAV* 3/1 (1982) 27–53.

Author's note: This is an expanded version of my article in Hebrew in *Lešonénu* 36 (1971) 3–13.

you be kind (לטוב)[1] to this people, and please them (ורציתם), and speak good words to them, they will be your servants forever" (2 Chr 10:7). He considered the formulation in the book of Kings to be obsequious and degrading to a king of Davidic descent; so he softened it, speaking about a king who will be kind and pleasing to his people rather than a servant and thus subservient, as he appears in the book of Kings. By changing the phrase: "You will be a servant unto this people this day and will serve them" into: "if you be kind to this people," the Chronicler removed the basic import of the verse: because the intent of the "elders," as it is expressed in the original version in Kings, is "if you concede and be their servant *today,* they will be your servants for *all the days.*" The same applies–as will be seen later–to the [[28]] change of "if you respond to them" in the verse in Kings into "if you please them" in Chronicles.

I

The notion of the king as *the servant of the people* seemed extraordinary to some commentators;[2] however, this is not the only verse in the Bible which presents such an idea. In 1 Sam 12:2 we hear that the new king, as well as the Judge Samuel who preceded him in the leadership, 'walk about before the people' (התהלך לפני (עם that is, serve them.[3] It is no coincidence that the latter verse appears within the framework of an anti-monarchic polemic.

The idea finds its continuation in Rabbinic literature. Rabban Gamliel turns to those to whom he is offering his leadership and says: "Do you imagine that I offer you rulership? It is servitude that I offer you; as it is said, 'And they spoke to him saying: "If you will be a servant unto this people this day"'" (*b. Hor. 10a–b*), and there (page a) one learns from the verse concerning Uzziah וישב בבית החפשית [['and he resided in the house of freedom']] (2 Kgs 15:5) that only by his becoming a leper was he free (חפשי), previously being a slave to his kingship.[4]

1. The addition of the ל to the predicate (תהיה לטוב instead of תהיה טוב [['if you be kind']]) is characteristic of the Chronicler's style; cf. 1 Kgs 22:22: והייתי רוח שקר [['I will be a lying spirit']] with 2 Chr 18:21 והייתי לרוח שקר [['I will be a lying spirit']] and see A. Kropat, *Syntax des Autors der Chronik* (BZAW 16; Giessen: Töpelmann, 1909) 14.

2. See, e.g., J. Gray, *1–2 Kings* (3d ed.; Old Testament Library; London: SCM, 1970) 305: "The use of *ʿebed* [['servant']] and *ʿābad* [['to serve']] of the king in relation to the people is somewhat strange."

3. For the understanding of the expression and its parallels in Akkadian, see below, pp. 31, 41 [[520, 528]].

4. See the words of Maimonides in *Hilkot Məlakim* 2:6.

> Just as the scripture honored him (the king) and commanded everyone to honor him, so it commanded him to have a meek and humble heart, as it says (Ps 109:22),

[[29]] The text of 1 Kgs 12:7 not only brings up the matter of the service of this king towards the people, but also emphasizes–and this is in fact the real intention of the verse–the benefit to be bestowed upon the king as a result of his service, that is, the loyalty of the people to the king: should the king demonstrate loyalty to his subjects, they likewise will respond with loyalty towards him.

In this vein, indeed, Josephus portrays the negotiations between king Rehoboam and the people in *Antiquities* 8.213–14. According to his account, the people demand an easing of servitude (δουλεία) and if the king would lighten the yoke of the kingdom, they would be loyal (εὐνουστέροι) to him,[5] "and will lovingly accept upon themselves servitude[6] if treated with kindness[7] than if made to fear him." The advice of the elders to Rehoboam (ibid., 215–16) is portrayed accordingly. These elders advise the king to respond graciously to the people, since in this manner he will

---

> "for my heart is pierced within me," and he may not be overly haughty to a fellow Israelite, since it says (Deut 17:20), "Thus he will not act haughtily toward his brothers." And he should be merciful and pitying toward the weak and powerful, and he should come and go in a way that satisfies them and that they find becoming. And he should respect the honor of the least significant among them, and when he speaks to the assembled community in plural language, he should speak tenderly, as it says (1 Chr 28:2), "Hear me my kinsmen and my people," and it also says (1 Kgs 12:7), "If you will be a servant to these people today. . . ." He should always be exceedingly modest, as there was no one greater than Moses our teacher, and he says (Exod 16:8), "What is our part? Your grumbling is not against us." And he shall tolerate their troubles and their burdens and their complaints (Num 11:12) "as a nurse carries an infant." The scriptures called him a shepherd (Ps 78:71), "To the shepherd of his people Jacob."

For a similar conception of Moses as a humble king see Philo *De Vita Mosis* 1.148–62; 2.48–51.

Moses does indeed view the leadership as a burden in Num 11:14, 17; Deut 1:9, similar to βάρος τῆς ἡγεμονίας [['the burden of rule' or 'the heavy weight of governing']] mentioned by Josephus in connection with Vespasian in *Jewish War* 4.616 (see n. 9 below).

5. On εὐνοέω meaning 'to be loyal', see my article "The Loyalty Oath in the Ancient Near East," *UF* 8 (1977) 383–84.

6. καὶ ἀγαπήσειν τὴν δουλείαν. The intention is to willing responsiveness and not by force, as shown by the continuation. On love and joy as expressions of willingness in ancient Hebrew and cuneiform literature, see Y. Muffs, "Joy and Love as Metaphorical Expressions of Willingness and Spontaneity in Cuneiform, Ancient Hebrew and Related Literatures," in *Christianity, Judaism and Other Greco-Roman Cults* (J. Neusner, ed.; Leiden: Brill, 1975) 1–36. Compare also in the Jewish evening prayer: "His kingdom they accepted willingly" (S. Singer, *The Standard Prayer Book* [New York: Bloch, 1943] 135) and see my comments in "The Loyalty Oath" (n. 5 above) 407 n. 254 and in "Pentecost as a Festival of the Giving of the Law," *Immanuel* 8 (1978) 11.

7. ἐπιεικεῖα [['fairness, clemency']] appears frequently in the Hellenistic literature in relation to the ideal quality of the king; see O. Murray, "Aristeas and Ptolemaic Kingship," *JTS* NS 18 (1967) 353, and G. Zuntz, "Aristeas Studies I," *JSS* 4 (1959) 28. In his terminology Josephus is influenced by Hellenistic literature. Compare the Letter of Aristeas, §188.

assure their loyalty, and since it is only natural that subjects cherish generosity and equanimity on the king's part.

[[30]] Students of Hellenistic culture found the concept of the *king as servant of the people* expressed for the first time by king Antigonos Gonatas, the Macedonian philosopher (320–239 B.C.E.) who, in his rebuke to his son concerning the oppression of the citizens, says: "Do you not understand, my son, that our kingdom is held to be a noble servitude?" (εὔδοξος δουλεία).[8] The idea of "a noble servitude" is thereafter reflected in the words of Stoic authors and philosophers,[9] and the Principat of Augustus, Caesar of Rome, was described in the spirit of this notion.[10] Moreover, even the words of the Jewish elders in the Letter of Aristeas in regard to the true function of the kingship and the obligations of the king toward the people have been interpreted against the background of this canon of Stoic philosophy.[11]

The formulation of the most sublime conception of kingship was thus attributed to Antigonos Gonatas, as for example W. W. Tarn in his book on Antigonos Gonatas puts it: "It was he who laid down the highest view of kingship that the ancient world ever saw."[12] For some reason, scholars have failed to notice that the concept of the king as the servant of the people is found fully expressed in the Old Testament, especially in 1 Kgs 12:7. This verse, which describes the king as the servant of the people, appears in the context of rebellion on account of the heavy taxation. It serves to instruct that the king, who is not submissive to the will of the people and who burdens them with taxes, is destined to fail (see below). The Stoic philosophy also determined [[31]] that taxes must be imposed with the agreement of the people, since the property of the people is not

8. Aelian *Varia Historia* 2.20.

9. See, e.g., the words of Seneca on the subject: *tu non experiris istud* [[*imperium*]] *nobilem* (not *nobis*, cf. U. Wilamowitz, "Lesefruechte," *Hermes* 37 [1902] 307) *esse tibi servitutem* [['Are you not aware that this rule is a noble service for you?']] (Seneca *De Clementia* 8.1). Cf. E. Kostermann, "Statio principis," *Philologus* 87 (1932) 436, and compare Suetonius in connection with Tiberius (24), who relates that a rigorous and encumbering servitude is cast upon him (*miseram et onerosam injungi sibi servitutem* [['a wretched and weighty slavery is put upon you']]). Note also the words of Josephus in regard to Vespasian, who takes upon himself 'the burden of rule' [[better: 'the heavy weight of governing']] τὸ βάρος τῆς ἡγεμονίας (*Jewish War* 4.626); see also Dion Chrysostomos, περὶ βασιλείας 3.55.

10. See L. Delatte, *Les Traités de la Royauté d'Ecphante, Diotogène et Sthénidas* (Bibliothèque de la Faculté de philosophie et lettres de l'Université de Liège, fasc. 97; Liège: Faculté de la philosophie, 1942) 123–63.

11. See recently the various references on this matter in the article of D. Mendels, "'Kingship' in the Temple Scroll and the Symposia in the Letter of Aristeas," *Shnaton* 3 (1978) 245–52 (Hebrew).

12. W. W. Tarn, *Antigonos Gonatas* (Oxford: Clarendon, 1913) 253.

the property of the king. On the contrary: the kingdom is the property of the people.[13]

In Mesopotamia we do not hear that the king is considered the servant of the people. However, from a Mesopotamian document from the first millennium B.C.E. we learn that also in Mesopotamia it was endeavored that the king submit to the will of the people. So, for example, we read in the so-called "Advice to a Prince":[14]

> A king who does not heed justice, his people will be thrown into chaos and his land will be devastated, (a king) who does not heed his nobles, his life will be cut short, (a king) who does not heed his adviser, his land will rebel against him.[15] If he heeds a rogue his land will get into a state of confusion. . . .[16] If citizens of Nippur (the holy city) are brought to him for judgment, and he accepts bribes from them and treats them with disrespect, Enlil, lord of the lands, will bring forth a foreign army against him. . . . If he mobilized the whole of Sippar, Nippur and Babylon and imposed forced labor on the people . . . Marduk, the sage of the gods . . . will turn his land over to his enemy. . . .

Similarly, we hear about the Assyrian king Shalmaneser V (726–722 B.C.E.) who failed and lost his kingdom because he imposed a heavy tax on the city of Asshur[17] (see below).

Diodorus Siculus, who describes the practices of the kings of ancient Egypt, drawing upon Hecataeus of Abdera,[18] also extols [[32]] the reciprocal relations between the king and the people in Egypt. After describing the ideal relations between the king and his people (Book 1.70) he relates

13. Such things are said in regards to Antigonos Gonatas, ibid., 255 n. 120.

14. W. G. Lambert, *Babylonian Wisdom Literature* (Oxford: Clarendon, 1960) 112–15.

15. Cf. below, pp. 35–36 [[523–24]].

16. In 1 Kings 12 we find good advisors and bad advisors; the king's failure is due to his heeding the bad advisors. The relation of a king to his good and bad advisors is reflected also in the proverbs related to the king in Prov 16:12–13: "Wickedness is abhorrent to kings, for a throne rests firm on righteousness. Honest speech is the desire of kings, they love a man who speaks the truth," and also Prov 29:12: "A prince who listens to falsehood, all his servants are wicked." On the ideal advisor to the king see also Ps 101:6–7: "My eyes are on the trusty men of the land, to have them at my side . . . he who speaks untruth shall not stand before my eyes." Cf. also the testament of Darius in W. Hinz, *Altiranische Funde und Forschungen* (Berlin: de Gruyter, 1969) 56–57, §8b.

17. See H. W. F. Saggs, "Historical Texts and Fragments of Sargon of Assyria: I. The Assur Charter," *Iraq* 37 (1975) 11.

18. On the reliability of Hecataeus' account see F. Jacoby, *PW* 7.2764; E. Meyer, "Gottesstaat, Militärherrschaft und Standeswesen in Agypten," *Sitzungsberichte der preussischen Akademie der Wissenschaften* (Philosophische-historische Klasse, 1928) 529. On the reliability of the first book of Diodorus, see A. Burton, *Diodorus Siculus I, Commentary* (Études préliminaires aux religions orientales dans l'Empire romain 29; Leiden: Brill, 1972).

that, because the kings followed a righteous course dealing with their subjects, the people demonstrated loyalty (εὔνοια) to them (ibid., 71.4).[19]

The concept of the kingdom as an institution subservient to the people is not, therefore, the innovation of Stoic philosophy. Its roots are in the Near East. In the light of the identity found between 1 Kgs 12:7 and the saying of Antigonos Gonatas concerning the kingship as servitude, the question is, of course, raised if perhaps this notion reached the Stoics from the Orient. It seems to me that we can answer this question in the affirmative. Antigonos Gonatas was the pupil of Zenon, the founder of the Stoic school,[20] who came from a Phoenician settlement in Kition in the isle of Cyprus.[21] It is then not impossible that Zenon imported this canon from the East.

In another place, I endeavor to show that the literary genre of advice for the king, περὶ βασιλείας, which was so popular in the Hellenistic and Roman periods, is rooted in the East.[22] If so, it is surely reasonable that the view of *the king as the servant of the people* also, which stands behind these rules, was not necessarily born in Greece.

II

Up to now we have discussed the general idea of the king as servant of the people expressed in the first part of 1 Kgs 12:7. [[33]] Now we pass to the second part of this verse, which, as will be shown, refers to the practical side of the issue: grants and exemptions established by the king. The phrase ועניתם ודברת אליהם דברים טובים should be rendered 'and you will respond to them and set good conditions'. Let us adduce the evidence for this rendering.

The form ועניתם [['and you will respond to them']] was dropped not only in Chronicles but in the LXX translation of 1 Kgs 12:7 as well[23]–

19. On a parallel to Diodoros' ideal description of the Egyptian king in the Temple Scroll from Qumran, see my article, "The Royal Guard according to the Temple Scroll," *RB* 87 (1980) [[394–96]].

20. On Zenon as the teacher of Antigonos see Tarn, *Antigonus*, 31–36.

21. His father was Mnaseas = Manasses (see U. Wilamowitz, *Staat und Gesellschaft der Griechen und Römer* [Die Kultur der Gegenwart, T. 2, Abt. 4, 1; Berlin: Teubner, 1910] 167), which is Hebrew 'Menasseh' and in Phoenician *mnsy*. On *mnsy* in Phoenician see F. L. Benz, *Personal Names in the Phoenician and Punic Inscriptions* (Studia Pohl 8; Rome: Pontifical Biblical Institute, 1972) s.v.

22. See my article, "Temple Scroll," *Shnaton* 3 (1978) 224–31.

23. It was restored to the Greek version by Origen in the Hexapla, following Aquila and Symmachus: καὶ εἴξεις αὐτοῖς [['and he submitted to them']] (cf. F. Field, *Origenis Hexaplorum quae supersunt* [2 vols.; Oxford: Clarendon, 1875] 1.620; J. Reider, N. Turner, *Index to Aquila* [VTSup 12; Leiden: Brill, 1966] 67) and from there it seems to have entered the Vulgate: *et petitioni eorum cesseris* 'and submit to their request', a translation which is exactly in accord

apparently due to the translator's difficulty in understanding it.[24] Exegetes and linguists rightly felt that this term expresses responsiveness and appeasement,[25] but thus far, no evidence for this usage has been found [[34]] elsewhere in the Bible. The clause ודברת דברים טובים 'and speak good words unto them' has also not been sufficiently clarified. Usually the phrase is translated by some form of 'speaking kindly to them'. But would the king actually appease the people with pleasant words? Do not people rather demand concrete action to relieve their plight? Our discussion will therefore revolve around these expressions and attempt to clarify them with reference to the relationships of a king to his subjects, as expressed in ancient Near Eastern royal documents.

To begin our search for a solution to the problem we will refer to an Assyrian text, which reflects a special situation very reminiscent of 1 Kgs 12:7 and its context. This text is one of a series of documents of exemptions and grants awarded by the Assyrian king to his loyal servants.[26] Part

---

with the Greek εἴκειν. (This verb is not found in LXX to any canonical book; cf. E. Hatch, H. Redpath, *A Concordance to the Septuagint* [2 vols.; Graz: Akademische Druck und Verlagsanstalt, 1954] 1.377.) Even though the rendition in the LXX and Vulgate makes sense in the present context, it does not reflect the Hebrew *Vorlage* because ענה, meaning 'submit', appears with the preposition מן [['from']] (Isa 31:4) or מפני [['from before']] (Exod 10:3) and not with the accusative.

24. E. L. Ehrlich, *Randglossen zur Hebräischer Bibel* 7 (Leipzig: Hinrichs, 1914) 244, emends the passage to ועניח ודברת [['and you will respond and speak']]. But this is a purely arbitrary correction. In addition, it should be pointed out that ענה ודבר [['responded and spoke']], in contrast to ענה ואמר [['responded and said']] is a rare expression in the Bible; and, where it does occur (Josh 22:21; 2 Kgs 1:12), it introduces direct speech.

25. Cf., e.g., W. Gesenius, F. Buhl, *Hebräisches und Aramäisches Handwörterbuch über das AT* (17th ed.; Berlin: Springer, 1949) 603: "auf seine Wünsche eingehen." *BDB* 772: 'be responsive, answer kindly, grant request'. Perhaps somewhat similar is Qoh 10:19 הכסף יענה את הכל [['money meets every need']]; see H. L. Ginsberg, *Qohelet* (Tel-Aviv/Jerusalem: Newman, 1961) 124 (Hebrew), where he interprets the passage: 'as one who complied with a request'. However, his comparison with Hos 2:23–24 (following Ibn-Ezra on Hosea) is not cogent in my opinion. It seems to me that Hosea is speaking of responsiveness with erotic overtones and against the background of fertility imagery, for which compare Sultantepe Tablet 136 in the incipit of an incantation: *kīma šamû u erṣetu ana aššūti innaḫazū* 'as heaven and earth were joined in marriage' (O. R. Gurney, P. Hulin, *The Sultantepe Tablets* 2 [London: British Institute of Archaeology at Ankara, 1964] no. 136). Compare also in connection with marriage between heaven and earth: "Heaven spoke with the earth and the earth spoke with heaven" (V. Dijk, "Le motif cosmique dans la pensée Sumérienne," *AcOr* 28 [1964] 36–37, lines 10–15). On the concept of cohabitation of heaven and earth for fertility purposes (*hieros gamos* [['sacred marriage']]) in Greece see M. P. Nilsson, *Geschichte der Griechischen Religion* 1 (3d ed.; München: Beck, 1967) 120–22.

26. On this matter see J. N. Postgate, *Neo-Assyrian Royal Grants and Decrees* (Studia Pohl, Series Maior 1; Rome: Pontifical Biblical Institute, 1969) 27–38. On grants at Ugarit, see A. F. Rainey, "The System of Landgrants at Ugarit in its Wider Near Eastern Setting," *Fourth World Congress of Jewish Studies* 1 (1967) 187–91; and for the Middle Babylonian period, see F. R.

of it reads as follows:[27]

> I, Ashurbanipal, king of Assyria, . . . who responds in goodness / in kindness ([*ina*] *damqāt*[*ī*]) to courtiers who serve him [lit., stand before him] and returns kindness to the reverent who keeps his royal command . . . PN . . . who served wholeheartedly his master served me [lit., stood before me] with truth, acted perfectly [lit., walked in perfection][28] . . . and kept the guard of my kingdom . . . I ⟦35⟧ took favorable thought for him[29] and I have established his gift.[30] Fields, orchards and people, which he acquired under my protection, . . . I have exempted (from taxes), wrote down and sealed with my royal seal; . . . corn taxes of that land shall not be collected, the levy on their herds and flocks shall not be levied. The (people) of the fields and orchards shall not be called up for corvée labor (*ilku tupšikku*) and for military conscription (*dikût māti*).

The special privileges granted here to servants of the king of Assyria, especially exemption from corvée labor, were in fact also given to entire cities in Mesopotamia, and particularly to temple cities.[31] Cancellation of these privileges was seen as sufficient cause for the breakdown of authority and the overthrow of the royal dynasty. Thus, Sargon, king of Assyria,

---

Kraus, "Ein mittelbabylonischer Reschtsterminus," *Symbolae Martino David Dedicatae* 2 (Leiden: Brill, 1968) 9–40.

27. See texts 9, 10, 11 in Postgate, *Neo-Assyrian Royal Grants*, 27–34. Postgate newly edited the texts published in cuneiform by C. H. J. Johns, *Assyrian Deeds and Documents* 4 (Cambridge: Bell, 1924) 164–70, nos. 646–48; transliteration by L. Köhler, A. Ungnad, *Assyrische Rechtsurkunden* (Leipzig: Pfeiffer, 1913) nos. 15–18. The texts are identical in content and our text citations are from Postgate, *Neo-Assyrian Royal Grants*, no. 9, lines 4–35, 10:4–35, 11:4–32. For clarification of the terms for loyalty and the typological parallels in the OT to those texts, with particular reference to the covenants with Abraham and David, see my article, "The Covenant of Grant in the Old Testament and in the Ancient Near East," *JAOS* 90 (1970) 184–203, and my book, *Deuteronomy and the Deuteronomic School* (London: Oxford Univ., 1972) 75–81 ⟦repr. Winona Lake, Ind.: Eisenbrauns, 1992⟧.

28. On the meaning of this idiom and its biblical parallels see my "Covenant of Grant," 185–86.

29. According to Postgate's new reading (after collation): [*ṭa-a*]*b-ta-šu aḫ-su-us-ma* (*Neo-Assyrian Royal Grants*, pl. 7, line 22) in place of the earlier reading *īnā at-ta-šu aḫsusma* (Köhler and Ungnad, *Assyrische Rechtsurkunden*, no. 16).

30. I suggested the reading *ši-ri-*[*ik*]*-šu* even before the appearance of Postgate's book ("Covenant of Grant," 188 n. 32). Postgate suggests *ši-ri-i*[*k-ta-šu*] (*Neo-Assyrian Royal Grants*) 28, line 22), but also *širku* ⟦'gift'⟧ occurs as a grant in Neo-Assyrian texts; cf. my article "Covenant Terminology in the Ancient Near East and Its Influence on the West," *JAOS* 93 (1973) 195 n. 77.

31. See H. Tadmor, "Temple Cities and Royal Cities in Babylonia and Assyria," in *The City and Community, Collected Lectures Presented at the Twelfth Congress of Historical Study* (1968) 179–205 (Hebrew); cf. also most recently H. Reviv, "Kidinnu, Observations on Privileges of Mesopotamian Cities," *Shnaton* 2 (1977) 205–16 (Hebrew).

recounts[32] that his predecessor (Shalmaneser V, 727–722 B.C.E.), who did not fear the gods, imposed on the city of Asshur *ilku tupšikku* (= corvée)[33] obligations. For this the god Asshur decided to put an end to his reign and replace him with Sargon, who returned to Asshur its *zakūtu* (exemption from royal obligations). Besides the exemption from corvée work, the *zakūtu* included exemption from military conscriptions (*dikût māti*),[34] from the herald's cry [[36]] (*šišīt nāgiri*)[35] and from dues on quay and crossing (*miksi kāri nēbiri*).[36]

In another Mesopotamian document, "Advice to the Prince," quoted above, which consists of a list of warnings to the king who oppresses and suppresses his people, we read:[37] "if he mobilized the whole of Sippar, Nippur and Babylon and imposed forced labor (*tupšikku*) on the people, exacting from them a corvée (*ilku*) at the herald's proclamation, Marduk . . . will turn his land over to his enemy" (lines 23–27). These warnings, especially the threat of the country rising up against the king, are most helpful for illuminating the pericope with which we are dealing in 1 Kgs 12:7. Note that in v. 4, preceding the pericope, Rehoboam, the new king, is called upon to free his people from his father Solomon's heavy yoke (מעלו הכבד) and the hard labor (עבדת אביך הקשה) involved with corvée. The 'heavy yoke' and 'hard labor', which Solomon imposed (נתן) upon the people and from which they wish to be freed, are none other than forced labor: סבל and מס, about which we are told in the preceding chapters (1 Kgs 5:27–29; 9:21; 11:28), and which are of a type now known from the cuneiform sources in the West (Alalaḫ, Mari and El-Amarna[38]). Furthermore, the

32. Cf. Saggs, "Historical Texts," 11.

33. For *ilku tupšikku* [['corvée labor']] and the nature of *ilku* [['corvée']] service, see J. N. Postgate, *Taxation and Conscription in the Assyrian Empire* (Studia Pohl, Series Maior 3; Rome: Pontifical Biblical Institute, 1974) 80–81.

34. Ibid., 218.

35. The phrase *šisīt nāgiri* is equivalent, in my opinion, to *qōl nōgēś* in Job 3:18. The *nōgēś* in the Bible is one who (usually in the name of the authorities) exacts forced labor (cf. the *nōgəśîm* assigned to oversee the סבלות 'burdens' (= corvée) of the Israelites in Exod 5:6, 10, 13, 14) and payment of taxes (2 Kgs 23:35 and cf. Isa 3:5, 12). In the Old Babylonian period this task is carried out by the *mušaddinu* (one who causes one to give) who, like the *nāgiru* also 'calls' (*šasû*) for the payment of a debt (cf. F. R. Kraus, *Ein Edikt des Königs Ammisaduqa von Babylon* [Leiden: Brill, 1958] §4, pp. 28, 50–56).

36. For these, see references in Postgate, *Taxation*, 131–33.

37. See Lambert, *Babylonian Wisdom Literature*, 112–15. The tablet bears a colophon which states that the text was selected for the perusal of the king (cf. I. M. Diakonoff, "A Babylonian Political Pamphlet from about 700 BC," in *Studies in Honor of B. Landsberger on His Seventy-Fifth Birthday* [M. G. Güterbock, Th. Jacobsen, eds.; Assyriological Studies 16; Chicago: Univ. of Chicago, 1965] 349 n. 24), which reminds us of the Law of the King (Deut 17:14–20), which is destined for his reading (vv. 18–19).

38. See P. Artzi, "Sablum = סבל," *BIES* 18 (1954) 66–70 (Hebrew); M. Held, "The Root ZBL/SBL in Akkadian, Ugaritic and Biblical Hebrew," *JAOS* 88 (1968) 90–96; A. F. Rainey, "Compulsory Labour Gangs in Ancient Israel," *IEJ* 20 (1970) 191–202.

idioms used for the imposition of corvée also appear in their Akkadian forms in Mesopotamia in [[37]] connection with the laying on and freeing from a yoke. The 'heavy yoke' (עלו הכבד in 1 Kgs 12:4) is the equivalent of *nīru kabtu* encountered in Akkadian literature in connection with carrying the yoke of domination,[39] i.e., the yoke of tribute and forced labor.[40] The 'hard labor' (עבדת אביך הקשה in 1 Kgs 12:4) is equivalent to *dullu dannu* [['difficult work']].[41] The *ʿōl* 'yoke' and *ʿăbōdâ* 'labor', when objects of the verb נתן, are semantically equivalent to *dulla/nīra emēdu* [['to impose labor/service']].[42]

It seems quite reasonable then that the Israelite assembly (קהל ישראל) and especially the people of Shechem, the capital of Ephraim, demanded exemption of the type granted to important [[38]] and sacred cities in the ancient Near Eastern world and apparently also to Jerusalem and other parts of Judah.[43]

39. Cf., e.g., *nīr bēlūtiya kabta elišunu ukīn* 'I placed the heavy yoke of my overlordship upon them' (*The Annals of the King of Assyria* [L. W. King, E. A. Wallis Budge, eds.; London: Longmans, 1902] 57, col. 3, lines 85–86 [Tiglath-Pileser I]); cf. also R. Borger, *Die Inschriften Asarhaddons Königs von Assyrien* (AfO, Beiheft 9; Graz: Selbstverlag des Herausgebers, 1956) 51, line 55; also S. Langdon, *Neubabylonische Königsinschriften* (Leipzig: Hinrichs, 1912) 68, line 18: *ina nirišu kabti ušazziqu nišīm māti* '(the Assyrian king who) has made the people of the country suffer from the heavy yoke', to which compare Isa 47:6–7: "You showed them no mercy . . . *you made your yoke very heavy* (הכבדת עלך מאד); you thought 'I shall always be the mistress'" (applied here to Babylon).

40. Cf., e.g., in the Ashurbanipal annals: *nīr Aššur ēmissunūti . . . biltu maddattu bēlūtiya . . . ēmissunūti* 'I imposed on them the yoke of Aššur . . . the tribute of my overlordship I imposed on them' (M. Streck, *Assurbanipal* 2 [Leipzig: Hinrichs, 1916] 40, IV, lines 103–4). Compare also *ʿol* 'yoke' in connection with סבל of Assur in Isa 9:3: "the yoke of his load (סבלו = 'basket'), the shackle (read מֹטֹת; cf. Lev 26:13; Ezek 34:27) of his shoulder" (cf. Ps 81:7: "I relieved his shoulder of the load (סבל); his hands were freed from the basket"); also Isa 14:25: "his yoke shall drop off them, and the load (סבל) shall drop from his shoulder." For the idiom "carrying the yoke of the king," cf. El-Amarna 296:38: GIŠ *nīri* (gloss *ḫullu* = *ʿol*) *šarri bēliya ana k*[*iš*]*ādiya u ubbalušu* 'the yoke of the king my lord is upon my n[e]ck and I carry it'; cf. also 257:15 (*Die El-Amarna-Tafeln* [J. A. Knudtzon, ed.; Leipzig: Hinrichs, 1915]).

41. L. Waterman, *Royal Correspondence of the Assyrian Empire* (Ann Arbor: Univ. of Michigan, 1930) 336–37, letter no. 479, reverse, line 2; E. Ebeling, *Neubabylonische Briefe* (Abhandlungen der Bayerischen Akademie der Wissenschaften, Philosophisch-historische Klasse N.F. Heft 30; München: Bayerische Akademie der Wissenschaften, 1949); *passim*; cf. Index in E. Ebeling, *Glossar zu den Neubabylonischen Briefen* (Sitzungsberichte der Bayerischen Akademie der Wissenschaften, Philosophisch-historische Klasse, Jahr 1953, Heft 1; München: Bayerische Akademie der Wissenschaften, 1953).

42. See references in *CAD* E, 142–43 in connection with the idioms *dulla emēdu* [['to impose a task']], *kudurra emēdu* [['to impose forced labor']], *nīra emēdu* [['to impose a yoke']], *tupšikka emēdu* [['to impose corvée service']], and cf. Held, "ZBL/SBL," 94–95.

43. The district of Judah is not mentioned in the list of the twelve districts burdened with provisions for the king (1 Kings 4). For the favoritism shown to Judah by David and its consequences (i.e., the revolt of the North), see most recently F. Crüsemann, *Der Widerstand gegen das Königtum* (Neukirchen-Vluyn: Neukirchener, 1978) part 2.

Exemption of cities from taxes, corvée and military services are known to us in Mesopotamia from the beginning of the second millennium onwards. Thus we hear that Išme-dagan, the king of Isin (1953–1935 B.C.E.), freed Nippur, the holy city, from taxes and that he put down the weapons of the army (UGNIM-BI GIŠ TUKUL-BI-HÉ-GA-AR).[44] In other documents we hear about exemption from military obligation (EREN-BI KASKAL-TA).[45] Lipit-Ištar, king of Isin (1934–1924 B.C.E.), tells us in the prologue to his Code that he summoned brothers of the "paternal house" for only 70 days yearly (see below), whereas from the "house of the young men" he summoned for 10 (days) monthly.[46] Another king of Isin, whose identity is not established, proclaims: "In Isin I established equity . . . the grain taxes, which reached to one fifth, I reduced to one tenth; I imposed on the *muškenum* [['commoner']] 4 days' work monthly. . . ."[47]

Such exemptions were sometimes integrated within a reform applied to the whole country, the so-called *mīšārum* [['redress (as a legislative act']] and *andurārum* [['freedom']].[48] Thus we find in the Edict of Ammiṣaduqa[49] that the [[39]] soldier and the fisherman should be exempted from the *ilku* service, following the proclamation of the *mīšārum*. Similarly, we hear that Samsuiluna (within the framework of a reform) freed the soldier and the fisherman from their debts to the crown.[50] Exemption of major religious cities from tax and corvée, the so-called *kidinnūtu* [['tax']] and *zakūtu* [[read: *zakûtu* 'exemption']], are known to us from the Kassite period[51] onward. In the first millennium B.C.E. *kidinnūtu* marks the special rights of sacred cities in Mesopotamia.[52]

44. D. O. Edzard, *Die Zweite Zwischenzeit Bayloniens* (Wiesbaden: Harrassowitz, 1957) 80, B, line 47.

45. Ibid., 81 (cf. R. J. Stephens, *Votive and Historical Texts from Babylonia and Assyria* [YOS 9; New Haven: Yale Univ., 1937] 25, line 11).

46. Edzard, *Zwischenzeit*, 96.

47. Cf. D. O. Edzard, "'Soziale Reformen' in Zweistromland," *Acta Antiqua* (Academiae Scientarum Hungaricae) 22 (1974) 151.

48. See J. Levy, "The Biblical Institution of *Deror* in the Light of Akkadian Documents," *Eretz Israel* 5 (1958) 27–31; F. R. Kraus, *Edikt*, 224–47; J. Finkelstein, "Ammisaduqa's Edict and the Babylonian 'Law Codes,'" *JCS* 15 (1961) 91–104. On *andurārum* see *CAD* A/2, s.v. That the corvée exemptions were associated with the *andurāru* may be learned from the royal title of Merodach Baladan II: *šākin andurāri, ḫātin ṣābē kidini* = '(he who) establishes freedom, protects the people with the *kidinnu* privileges' (see Reviv, "Kidinnu," 208); for *kidinnu* [['security, protection']] see below.

49. F. R. Kraus, *Edikt*, 39, §17 and J. Finkelstein in *ANESTP*: 526–27, §19. Finkelstein has published two additional paragraphs of the Edict (see "The Edict of Ammisaduqa: A New Text," *RA* 63 [1969] 45–46) and thus the numbers of the paragraphs have changed.

50. Cf. Kraus, *Edikt*, 226.

51. See J. A. Brinkman, "The Monarchy of the Kassite Dynasty," *Le Palais et la Royauté, XIXe Rencontre Assyriologique Internationale* (Paris; Geuthner, 1974) 407 and n. 37.

52. Cf. Reviv, "Kidinnu," 205–16.

Similar exemptions were apparently demanded by the people of northern Israel in Shechem. The corvée imposed by Solomon on the Israelites and especially the corvée of בית יוסף [['Joseph's house']] (cf. 1 Kgs 11:28) may be exemplified by 1 Kgs 5:27–32. Thirty thousand people were subject to מס [['service']] and were sent to work in Lebanon, while another 150 thousand were engaged in סבל [['labor']] and in "quarrying." It seems that מס and סבל are to be identified with the two Mesopotamian terms for compulsory service, *ilku* [['(state) corvée']] and *tupšikku* [['(building) labor']]. The former denotes service for the state in general– military or civilian– and, as may be learned from the etymology of the word *ilku* (← *alāku* [['to walk']]) and from its combination with *ḫarranu* [['campaign']],[53] it originally denoted the service involved in going on a campaign.[54] The latter term, *tupšikku*, however, is limited to work connected with "carrying the basket," i.e., building construction. Similarly, *mas* [['service' or 'corvée']] in Hebrew and *massu* [['service']] in the cuneiform documents from the West[55] imply general service,[56] like *ilku*, usually performed far from home;[57] while סבל, like *tupšikku* is limited to building [[40]] activity[58] and was associated with carrying on the "shoulder."[59]

The demand for release from the heavy yoke of Solomon may be put in perspective by comparing it with the alleviation of the corvée by Lipit-Ištar, referred to above. Lipit-Ištar boasts that he summoned the men of the paternal house for seventy days a year (approximately a fifth of the year) while Solomon's summons were for a third of the year.[60]

53. Cf. *ilkum ḫarranum* [['campaign service']] (*CAD* Ḫ, 112) and *ālik ḫārrani* [['going on a campaign']] (*CAD* A/1, 342). See also in the Advice to the Prince: *ana ḫarrāni ušeṣṣušunūti* '(if) he sends them on a campaign', Lambert, *Wisdom*, 114, line 52.

54. In later Neo-Assyrian times the distinction between *ilku* [['(state) corvée']] and *tupšikku* [['(building) labor']] was blurred, and they became a kind of hendiadys denoting work for the crown in general. Cf. Postgate, *Taxation*, 81.

55. Cf. Rainey, "Labor Gangs," 192–202.

56. *Massu* [['service']] in Alalaḫ was used with the verb *alāku* [['to walk']] (cf. D. J. Wiseman, *The Alalakh Tablets* [London: British School of Archaeology, 1953] *169:18, *259:15–17, and see Rainey, "Labor Gangs," 192–93) which, like *ilku alāku* means to perform corvée work.

57. Compare 1 Kgs 5:27–28: "King Solomon raised *mas* [['service' or 'corvée']] from all Israel and the *mas* was thirty thousand men. He sent them to Lebanon. . . ."

58. Cf. Held, "ZBL/SBL," 90–96. Note that *sablum* at Mari is associated with 'youth' *ṣeḫrum* (cf. Rainey, "Labor Gangs," 195). This may explain the specification of Jeroboam as נער in connection with commissioning him "over all the *sēbel* of the house of Joseph" (1 Kgs 11:28).

59. See n. 40 above.

60. "One month in Lebanon and two at home" (1 Kgs 5:28). Compare a Hittite document concerning feudal obligations: "PN will work four days for the king's land and four days for his house (É-*ti-šu*); see R. K. Riemschneider, "Zum Lehnswesen bei den Hethitern," *ArOr* 33 (1965) 337–38, lines 2–7. For the expression לביתו [['for his house']] (= É-*ti-šu*) in the context discussed here, compare Deut 24:5 "he shall be exempt one year for his house (לביתו)."

In sum: the assembly of Israel demands release of the "heavy yoke," that is, exemption from *mas* and *sēbel* [['labor']] which Solomon had imposed upon them. These terms are equivalent to *ilku* and *tupšikku*, from which important Mesopotamian cities were exempted, not only on behalf of the king, but also on behalf of the gods.[61] This manner of forced labor for the king was considered a religious crime in Israel, as may be learned from Jer 22:13–14. In these verses Jehoiakim, who is known from elsewhere in exacting heavy tribute from the people (2 Kgs 23:35), is accused of constructing his palaces by making his fellow men work without pay.[62] He thus violates "righteousness and justice" (v. 13)[63] which constitute "knowledge of God" (v. 16).

Let us now turn to our comparison of the passage from 1 Kgs 12:7 with Ashurbanipal's exemption document; for, in light of our discussion, we can learn more now about the answer of the *zəqēnîm* [['elders']] to Rehoboam.

[[41]] Of crucial importance is the first sentence of the Assyrian document: "Who answers (constantly = Gtn)[64] in goodness (or kindness)." The word translated as 'answers' is *it-ta-nab/p-ba/pá-lu*. It is generally associated with the verb *abālu* ('to carry'); and, in the present context, it is given the meaning 'treat, behave',[65] even though there is no concrete evidence for this interpretation.[66] I suggest reading the word with the alternate sign values *it-ta-nap-pá-lu* [['responds']],[67] and deriving it from *apālu* ('to answer'). This reading is supported by two passages from Esarhaddon's vassal treaty with the Medes.[68] Although Wiseman reads *tatanabbalšūni*

61. Cf. my forthcoming monograph on *Justice and Righteousness in Israel and the Nations; Equality and Freedom in Israel in Light of Ancient Near Eastern Concepts of Social Justice* [[pub. as *Social Justice in Ancient Israel and in the Ancient Near East* (Jerusalem: Magnes/Minneapolis: Fortress, 1995]].

62. For wages paid to corvée workers compare *idi* LÚ MEŠ *massi* and *igir* LÚ MEŠ *massi* in Alalaḫ (cf. Wiseman, *Alalakh Tablets*, 15–17, 269:18, 268:14, and Rainey, "Labor Gangs," 192–93).

63. For משפט וצדקה and its connection with royal exemptions, see my *Justice and Righteousness*.

64. Compare עניתם [['and you respond']] in 1 Kgs 12:7, which follows an imperfect, (אם) תהיה [['(if) you are']], and expresses a repetitive action; see S. R. Driver, *Hebrew Tenses* (Oxford: Clarendon, 1892) 127, §113 (4a).

65. See, for example, *CAD* A/1, 23 n. 7b: 'who treats (graciously)', and also Postgate's translation of this sentence: 'who behaves (kindly)' (*Taxation*, 36).

66. It is interesting that the meanings assigned to *abālu* in the paragraph under discussion in *CAD* A/1, 23 n. 7b are: 'to direct, manage, organize', while in the translation of our passage the form is read 'treats', thus deviating significantly from the definitions given initially.

67. In the Neo-Assyrian syllabary *ba* has the value *pá*; cf. W. von Soden, W. Röllig, *Das Akkadische Syllabar* (2nd ed.; AnOr 42; Rome: Pontifical Biblical Institute, 1967) 2.

68. D. J. Wiseman, "The Vassal Treaties of Esarhaddon," *Iraq* 20 (1958) 35, line 98; 47, line 236.

therein,[69] R. Borger correctly realized that this form should be read *tatanappalšūni*.[70] Thus we read: "If you do not hold fast perfect truth,[71] if you do not respond to him (*tatanappalšūni*) (with) uprightness and integrity,[72] speak with a [[42]] true heart[73] (lines 96–99; cf. line 236 and Borger's comment to it).

The citation from the grant document of Ashurbanipal appears similar in background to the passage from the Esarhaddon treaty, except that in the former the king "responds with goodness to his servants who proved their loyalty," while in the Esarhaddon treaty the servants (i.e., the vassals) were commanded to respond in truth and honesty to their king. A like double usage of an expression of loyalty may be found in the Bible in such idioms as עמד לפני [['stand before']] or התהלך לפני [['continually walk before']]. The expression הלך//התהלך לפני [['walk before']], like עמד לפני,[74] usually expresses the service or the devotion of a faithful servant to his king,[75] whether human[76] or divine.[77] However, in 1 Sam 12:2 the roles are

69. Cf. also *CAD* A/1, 23 n. 7b.

70. See on these lines R. Borger, "Zu den Asarhaddon-Verträgen aus Nimrud," *ZA* 20 (1961) 177, 182. E. Reiner's objection in *ANESTP* 99 n. 7 (= *ANET*[3] 535) is not substantiated.

71. *Kittu šalmitu la tukallani. CAD* contradicts itself in the translation of this phrase: in K, p. 469 we read: "(if) you do not report the full truth," whereas on p. 515 of that volume the phrase occurs under the meaning 'to grant a boon', which might be reflected in E. Reiner's translation 'to offer complete truth' (*ANESTP* 99 = *ANET*[3] 535). Wiseman's translation is still the best: 'You will hold perfect justice' and a similar rendering may be recognized in *AHW* 503: 'Recht einhalten', which is to be compared to החזיק בצדקה/בתום [['maintain righteousness/integrity']]; cf. Job 2:3, 9; 27:6.

72. *Kīnāte tarṣāti* like *damqāti* (see below) are plural substantives which express the attributes of loyalty and integrity; cf. Hebrew טובות [['good deeds']], צדקות [['righteousness']], ישרים [['integrity']] and especially הלך צדקות ודבר מישרים in Isa 33:15, 'he who walks in righteousness and speaks uprightly'.

73. For the loyalty to the king expressed here by truth, uprightness and integrity of heart, compare the loyalty of David to God: 'because he walked before you in truth, righteousness and integrity of heart' כאשר הלך לפניך באמת ובצדקה ובישרת לבב עמך (1 Kgs 3:6). For צדקה in the sense of loyalty, cf. my article "Covenant of Grant," 186 n. 17.

74. For these terms cf. Weinfeld, "Covenant of Grant," 186 n. 19.

75. In contrast to הלך אחרי and *alăku arki* 'to go after', which expresses passive allegiance of the vassal (see, for instance, W. Moran, "The Ancient Near Eastern Background of the Love of God in Deuteronomy," *CBQ* 25 [1963] 82 n. 35), עמד לפני [['stand before']], הלך לפני and the Akkadian equivalents *alăku/uzzūzu ina pāni* [['to walk/stand in the presence of']], indicate the active service of the loyal servant who goes before his master, paving the way, or who stands before him and serves him.

76. 1 Kgs 1:2; 10:8; Jer 52:12.

77. Thus, the patriarchs before God: Gen 17:1; 24:40; 48:15 (התהלך לפני ה' [['continually walk before the LORD']]); referring to Enoch and Noah: Gen 5:22, 24; 5:16; the priests and Levites: Deut 10:8; 18:7; Judg 20:28; Ezek 44:15 (עמד לפני). Ps 51:4; 56:14c (להתהלך לפני אלהים באור החיים [['to walk before God in the light of life']]) and 116:9 do not express service, but rather existence on earth in the presence of God or by His grace. Cf. the Babylonian prayer, "Marduk, the great lord, give me life and I will be satiated to walk before you in light (*maḫarka*

reversed and we find the king and the prophet walking before the people (see above, p. 28 [[517]]).

In any case, we have learned that the verb 'answer' in Akkadian has the sense 'be responsive', particularly in regard to relationships between a king and his subjects. This, too, appears to be the nuance of ועניתם [['and you respond']] in 1 Kgs 12:7.

III

ודברת אליהם דברים טובים 'And Speak Good Words unto Them'

[[43]] This passage is usually taken to mean: 'say to them kind words which are pleasant to their ear'. However, in Ashurbanipal's exemption document, from which we quoted, the good things (*damqāti*) which the king answers are not mere niceties but rather good deeds which the king performs for his servants. There is no doubt that this is the import in our passage as well; for what the people demand is a relaxation of their burden, not empty gestures of placation.

A thorough examination of all occurrences of the idiom *dibbēr dābār* (cf. דברת . . . דברים in 1 Kgs 12:7) reveals that in general it does not mean simply 'to speak a word', but rather 'to arrive at a decision through bargaining (usually at a gathering)'. So, for example, דברו דבר ולא יקום in Isa 8:10 means 'reach a decision, but it will not be realized'; compare H. L. Ginsberg's translation in the new *JPSV*: 'agree on action–it shall not succeed'.[78] The passage עצו ודברו in Judg 19:30 and its continuation הנה כלכם) בני ישראל) הבו לכם דבר ועצה[79] הלם in 20:7–both ought to be interpreted in the same way: 'agree upon and decide'. The passage במצפה וידבר . . . את כל דבריו לפני ה׳, referring to Jephthah in Judg 11:11, is likewise to be understood as '*set his terms* before the LORD in Mizpah'. This was apparently

namriš atalluka)"; see E. Ebeling, *Die Akkadische Gebetsserie 'Handerhebung'* (Berlin: Akademie, 1953) 64, lines 21–22. See further p. 134, line 84: "In light . . . with living (people) I will come into the market place."

78. See S. D. Luzzatto, ספר ישעיה, מתורגם איטלקית ומפורש עברית (Padova: Bianchi, 1867) on this verse: "עצו עצה–agree in your minds as in זאת העצה היעוצה על כל הארץ [['this is the counsel that is counselled for the whole land']] (Isa 14:26); had the intent been to discuss with the advisors, it would not likely to be said afterwards ותופר [['and it shall be foiled']], because something not yet agreed upon cannot be annulled. Similarly דברו דבר connotes a decree, as in יצא מפי צדקה דבר ולא ישוב [['Righteousness has issued from my mouth; a word that shall not return']] (Isa 45:23), and were it not a decree it would not be followed by ולא יקום [['and it shall not succeed']]." For יצא דבר in the sense of decision, cf. Gen 24:50 and Jer 44:17.

79. The phrase דבר ועצה functions as a hendiadys like *ṭēmu* [['report, action']] *u milku* [['resolution']] in Akkadian. The terms עצה and *milku* do not only mean taking counsel but also refer to the decision reached thereby. Von Soden (*AHW* s.v.) rightly translates *milku* as 'Ratschluss'.

done in the framework of a solemn pact concluded with the people's representatives, the elders.[80] In a like manner דבר דבר in Isa 58:13 should be taken to mean that business transactions or bargaining[81] are not to be carried out on [[44]] the Sabbath. In fact all the three stipulations in this verse–מצא חפץ [['do business']], עשות דרך [['carry out an enterprise']], דבר דבר [['make an agreement']]–are associated with business transactions. Like דבר דבר (see below), מצא חפץ and עשה דרך have their semantic equivalents in Akkadian expressions that are clearly connected with business transactions and business journey, and it even seems that we meet here with Babylonian influence on the rhetoric of the prophet.

Both עשות חפץ and מצא חפץ (cf. also Isa 58:5) are equivalent to Akkadian *epēš ṣibûti* 'doing business' and *kašād ṣibûti* 'completing the enterprise'.[82] On the other hand, עשות דרך finds its [[45]] equivalent in Akkadian

80. Cf. A. Malamat, "The Period of the Judges," in *Judges* (B. Mazar, ed.; *The World History of the Jewish People*, First Series: *Ancient Times*, 3 [Tel-Aviv: Massadah, 1971) 158. For the translation of Judg 11:11 compare the new *JPSV*: 'Jephtah repeated *all these terms* before the Lord at Mizpah'.

81. Cf. the new *JPSV* translation of this verse by H. L. Ginsberg: 'nor look to your affairs, nor strike bargains'. The verse was similarly understood in the Qumran writings: אל [[(18) ישפוכו (= ישפוטו) על הון ובצע אל ידבר בדברי המלאכה והעבודה . . . לעשות את עבודת חפצו השבת 'He is to discuss neither riches nor gain. (19) He is not to speak about matters of work or of the task . . . (20) to carry out the work he wishes (21) on the sabbath']] (CD 10: 18–21) and see L. Ginzberg, *An Unknown Jewish Sect* (New York: Jewish Theological Seminary, 1976) 59, 108–9; cf. further the Rabbinic sources: *m. Šabb.* 23:1–3; *t. Šabb.* 17(18):10; *b. Šabb.* 150a, and cf. also R. Weiss, "Two Notes," *Lešonenu* 37 (1972–1973) 306 (Hebrew). One must add, however, that in Qumran, as well as in Rabbinic sources, the verse was also understood in the sense 'to refrain from uttering mean words'. CD 10:17–18: אל ידבר איש דבר נבל ורק 'let no man speak a lewd or villainous word' (or 'a vain [הבל instead of נבל] or empty word', cf. Ch. Rabin, *The Zadokite Documents* [Oxford: Clarendon, 1958] 52). Compare Tg. Jon. Isa 58:13: למללא מלין דאונים 'to utter words of violence'. Compare further v. 9 there, where דבר און [['speak evil']] is translated by למללא מלין באונים [['to utter words of evil']]. For the Rabbinic sources cf. *y. Šabb.* 15a; compare also *b. Šabb.* 113a–b, and see *Leviticus Rabbah* (*Midrash Leviticus Rabbah* [M. Margulies, ed., 5 vols.; Jerusalem: American Academy for Jewish Research, 1953–1960]) 34, 16 (pp. 814–15) and the references cited there. This tradition has penetrated the Christian sources. Thus we read in the Apostolic Constitutions vii, 36:5: 'That no one may desire to utter a word in anger on the day of Sabbath' ὅπως μηδὲ λόγον τις ἐκ ὀργῇ ἐκ τοῦ στόματος αὐτοῦ προέσθαι θελήσῃ ἐν τῇ ἡμέρα τῶν σαββατῶν (F. X. Funk, *Didascalia et Constitutiones Apostolorum* [Paderbornae: Schoeningh, 1905] 434). For uttering a word in anger (ἐν ὀργῇ) compare 1QS 7:2 דבר בחמה [['speak in wrath']]. In the same section (7:9) we have ידבר בפיהו דבר נבל [['he shall speak with his mouth an empty word']], a phrase virtually identical with the one in CD 10:17–18 quoted above.

82. For חפץ [['business']] in the sense of business and commerce see especially 1 Kgs 5:22–24, 10:13 and cf. M. Eilat, *Economic Relations in the Lands of the Bible* (Jerusalem: Mosad Bialik, 1977) 191 (Hebrew), and for *ṣibûtu* cf. *CAD* E, 218; Ṣ, 169–70. The phrases *epēš ṣibûti* [['do business']] and *kašād ṣibûti* [['complete the enterprise']] occur often in Neo-Babylonian letters and contracts and strengthen our supposition that Babylonian-Aramaic influence may

ḫarrānu epēšu 'to undertake a business journey'.[83] Furthermore, in the Neo-Babylonian sources we find side-by-side the expressions for undertaking a journey and doing business in the same vein as Isa 58:13. Thus, for example: "You went on a journey with me but you were not doing my business"[84] or "this day is favorable for taking a journey . . . and undertaking a business enterprise."[85] The prophet's admonition about refraining from business activities on the Sabbath is to be seen against the background of the Exile and Restoration when there was apparent laxity in this matter. This may be deduced from the admonition in Jer 17:19–22 and the rigorous action of Nehemiah, as described in Neh 13:15–22.

The expression דבר דבר in the sense 'make an agreement' occurs in 1 Sam 20:23: והדבר אשר דברנו אני ואתה הנה ה׳ ביני ובינך עד עולם [['As for the pact that we made, you and I, may Yhwh be witness between you and me forever']]. Here דבר דבר refers undoubtedly to the covenant[86] and oath which were exchanged according to vv. 14–17 of the same chapter. The *NEB* rightly translates this verse: 'the LORD stand witness between us forever to the pledges we have exchanged'. This is also the case of Hos 10:4: "Uttering words (דברו דברים), swearing falsely, making a covenant"; where the דברים, as explained by the context, mean reaching an agreement and making a covenant, similar to דבר דבר in Isa 8:10, which we discussed above.[87] In Akkadian, too, *awātam dabābu* [['speak a word']] connotes reach-

be reflected in Isaiah 58. Aramaic צבו/צבותא equals Hebrew חפץ; cf. G. R. Driver, *Aramaic Documents of the Fifth Century B.C.* (2nd ed.; Oxford: Clarendon, 1965) 31–32; J. C. Greenfield, "Studies in Legal Terminology of the Nabatean Funerary Inscription," in *H. Yalon Memorial Volume* (E. Y. Kutscher, S. Lieberman, M. Z. Kaddari, eds.; Ramat-Gan: Bar-Ilan Univ., 1974) 67. For צבו as business, cf. especially in the Palmyrene inscriptions: *wsyʿ tgryʾ bkl ṣbw* 'and he helped the merchants with everything (= with all the business)' (*Inventaire des inscriptions de Palmyre* fasc. 10 [J. Starcky, ed.; Damascus: La Direction Générale des Antiquités de Syrie, 1949)] 31, no. 44, line 6). A striking parallel to עשׂות חפציך ביום קדשי '(refrain) from pursuing business on my holy day' can be found in the Assyrian hemerologies which specify the days which are not fit for any enterprise (*ana epēš ṣibûtu lā naṭû* [['[the day] is not fit for enterprise']]); cf. *CAD* E, 218.

83. Cf. *CAD* Ḫ, 110–11 and E, 208.

84. *ḫarrāna ittiya tattalak ṣibûtâ ul tēpuš* [['you traveled with me but you were not in my employ']]; see *CAD* E, 218.

85. *ana alāk ḫarrāni . . . u epēš ṣibûtu šalmat* [['for embarking on a trip . . . or any enterprise']]; see *CAD* E, 218.

86. For דבר in the sense of covenant cf. Hag 2:5: הדבר אשר כרתי [['the promise which I ratified']]; Deut 9:5 הקים את הדבר [['confirm the promise']], which is to be compared with הקים את בריתו [['confirm his promise']] in 8:18; Ps 105:8 where דבר parallels ברית. See my article "בְּרִית" in *TWAT*: 1.786 [[Moshe Weinfeld, "בְּרִית: bᵉrîth," *TDOT* 2 (Grand Rapids: Eerdmans, 1975) 253–79]].

87. Cf. H. W. Wolff, *Hosea* (Hermeneia; Philadelphia: Fortress, 1974) 175: "The phrase 'uttering (empty) words' denotes meaningless political agreements also in Is 8:10 (cf. Is 58:13)."

ing an agreement, as in *ištu awātum ša idbubu ibbalakkitu* '(if) he breaks his word which he spoke (namely, the agreement which he made)'.[88]

⟦46⟧ In an Aramaic legal settlement between two persons from the seventh century B.C.E.[89] we read similarly about an *ʾm*, i.e., a 'word' (= 'settlement')[90] that the parties made: *ʾmhm śmw* ⟦'their settlement they made'⟧. As in the Akkadian text quoted immediately above, this Aramaic text contains a warning clause against withdrawal or 'return to suit one against the other': *mn ʿl mn yšb.*[91]

We have spoken thus far only of *dibber dābār*, but the expression which actually appears in 1 Kgs 12:7 is דברים טובים . . . דברת ⟦'speak . . . kind words'⟧. One might rightfully disagree, therefore, with our suggested explanation and claim that, nonetheless, appeasement is spoken of, as it is with the angel speaking in Zechariah: "good words, comforting words" (1:13). However, we shall see immediately that the qualification of דברים ⟦'words' or 'promises'⟧ by טובים ⟦'kind'⟧ does not invalidate our proposed understanding, but, to the contrary, advances it even further. In a detailed treatment of the word טבתא in the Aramaic Sefire treaty, W. L. Moran rightly claimed[92] that this word means 'amity established by treaty'.[93] In the course of his discussion he also touched on the Akkadian evidence. There he found that 'good words' or 'good things' can have a specific connotation of treaty and covenant. So, for instance, a Mari text states:[94] *awātim damqātim birītiya u birītišu nīš ilim u riksātim dannātim nišakkan* 'We will establish "good things," a divine oath and a binding [lit., strong][95]

88. E. A. Speiser, R. H. Pfeiffer, *One Hundred New Selected Nuzi Texts* (AASOR 16; New Haven: J. D. Nies Publication Fund, 1936) 55, line 44.

89. Cf. P. Bordreuil, "Une tablette araméenne inédite de 635 av. J. C.," *Semitica* 23 (1973) 96–102; S. A. Kaufman, "An Assyro-Aramaic *egirtu ša šulmu*," in *Essays on the Ancient Near East in Memory of Jacob Joel Finkelstein* (Maria de Jong Ellis, ed.; Hamden: Connecticut Academy of Arts and Sciences, 1977) 119–27.

90. Aramaic *ʾm* here equals Akkadian *amātu* 'word', although the form is not necessarily cognate; see Kaufman, "*egirtu*," 122.

91. Cf. Kaufman, "*egirtu*," 124, who compares it with Akkadian *mannu ša ina eli mannu ibbalakkatuni.*

92. W. L. Moran, "A Note on the Treaty Terminology of the Sefire Stelas," *JNES* 22 (1963) 173–76 to Sefire I C:4–5, 19–20; II B:2; cf. J. A. Fitzmyer, *The Aramaic Inscriptions of Sefire* (BibOr 19; Rome: Pontifical Biblical Institute, 1967) 73–74.

93. On 'brotherhood' and 'friendship' expressing covenantal relationship in the ancient Near East as well as in the Greco-Roman sphere see my "Covenant Terminology," 190–93.

94. G. Dossin, "Iamhad et Qatanum," *RA* 36 (1939) 57, lines 7–10.

95. Akkadian *danānu* and Hebrew אמן have implications of both strength and validity; but in Akkadian the element of strength supersedes the element of validity, while in Hebrew just the opposite is so. For נאמן as 'strong' see, e.g., היתד התקועה במקום נאמן ⟦'the peg established in a firm place'⟧ (Isa 22:25, cf. v. 23) and מכות (גדלות) נאמנות ⟦'great and strong plagues'⟧ (Deut 28:59) which should be compared with Akkadian *miḫiṣtu dannat* ⟦'persistent

covenant[96] between me and him'. Moran [[47]] believes that the 'good things/words' (*awātim damqātim*) are the friendly relations established by covenant and oath. He finds similar expressions in the Amarna letters, e.g.: "Between kings (there should be) brotherhood, friendship, peace and nice

blow']] (cf. Lambert, *Wisdom*, 44, line 99). For *dannu* in the sense 'stable, valid', cf. *našpāru dannu* (S. Langdon, *Die Neubabylonischen Königsinschriften* [Leipzig: Hinrichs, 1919] 277, lines 17–18) which should be translated 'faithful messenger' or in the language of Proverbs, ציר אמונים [['faithful envoy']] (13:17). Also see on this issue J. J. Rabinowitz, "Neo-Babylonian Legal Documents and Jewish Law," *Journal of Juristic Papyrology* 13 (1961) 148. We therefore suggest changing E. Sollberger's rendition of *našpāru dannu* ("Samsuiluna's Bilingual Inscriptions C and D," *RA* 63 [1969] 33, line 33) from 'strong' to 'reliable' messenger. It is interesting to compare *dannatu* (= contract) with Hebrew אמנה [['faithfulness' or 'firmness']] (see my "Covenant of Grant," n. 58) and Nabatean כתב תקף [['legitimate document']] , תקף [['valid, legitimate']] (see Y. Muffs, *Studies in the Aramaic Legal Papyri from Elephantine* [Leiden: Brill, 1969] 208; J. C. Greenfield, "Legal Terminology," 73–74). In "The Counsel of the Elders to Rehoboam," *Lešonenu* 36 (1971) 9, I have noted that תקף in Esth 9:29 means 'valid document' and this was independently stated by S. E. Loewenstamm, "Esther 9:29–32: The Genesis of a Late Addition," *HUCA* 42 (1971) 119. Following this recognition, many misunderstood legal expressions may be correctly comprehended. Thus, *riksu dannu* is the semantic equivalent of ברית נאמנה [['enduring covenant']] (cf. Ps 89:29) and עדות נאמנות [['enduring decrees']] (cf. Ps 93:5; 19:8; also *adê* [['stipulations']] in Akkadian and עדן [['stipulations']] in Aramaic; see my article "בְּרִית," 785–86 [[Eng. trans: "בְּרִית," *TDOT* 2.257–58]]. These equivalent expressions connote a covenant of lasting validity; cf. Isa 55:3: ברית עולם חסדי. דוד הנאמנים [['an everlasting covenant, the enduring loyalty (shown to) David']]. (For ברית and חסד as a hendiadys cf. my "Covenant Terminology," 191–92). Similarly, *māmītu* (NAM. ÉRIM) *dannu* in the Idrimi inscription, line 50 (E. L. Greenstein and David Marcus, "The Akkadian Inscription of Idrimi," *JANES* 8 [1976] 59–96) is not a 'mighty oath', as translated by S. Smith (*The Statue of Idri-mi* [Occasional Publications of the British Institute of Archaeology in Ankara 1; London: British Institute of Archaeology in Ankara, 1949] line 50), but a 'binding (valid) oath'. By the same token *ṭuppu dannu* (cf. *AHW*, s.v. *dannu* 7, p. 161; *dannatu* 3, p. 160) is certainly not a 'feste Tafel' but a 'reliable, valid document'. Therefore also *dunnunu*, which appears in context with a covenant, is not to be rendered 'to strengthen' but 'to validate' (see, e.g., M. Streck, *Assurbanipal*, II, 4, lines 20–23; Wiseman, *Vassal Treaties*, lines 23, 65). Hittite *dašša*, which appears along with NI-IŠ DINGIR MEŠ (= divine oath) is *Keilschrifturkunden aus Boghazköi* 36 (1955) 106, lines 9′–10′ (transliteration and translation in H. Otten, "Zwei althethitische Belege zu den Hapiru (SA.GAZ)," *ZA* 52 [1957] 217) and also *Keilschrifturkunden aus Boghazköi* 30 (1939) 45, 110:10 (Otten, "Belege," 220) in connection with *lingāiš* ('oath'), also expresses strength and legal validity; cf. E. Forrer, *Forschungen* Band 1, Heft 1 (Berlin: Selbstverlag, 1926) 32. The Aramaic expression that corresponds to Akkadian *riksa dunnunu* [['validate the agreement']] is לתקפה אסר [['to sanction an oath']], which occurs in parallel to לקימה קים [['to confirm a decree']] in Dan 6:8. The term *riksu* [['contract, agreement']], as well as ברית [['covenant']] and קים [['confirm, establish']], basically denote 'obligation' or more precisely, 'obligatory bond'; cf. Weinfeld, "בְּרִית," 784–85. In Ugaritic *ʾsr* and *ṣmt* (*ṣmd* = 'bind') signify covenantal relationship (cf. 2.1[137].37, 64[118].17); see J. C. Greenfield, "Some Aspects of Treaty Terminology in the Bible," *Fourth World Congress of Jewish Studies* 1 (1967) 117.

96. For the word pair *niš ilim, riksātum* ('oath and bond') cf. my "Covenant Terminology," 190–91.

⟦48⟧ words."[97] Likewise: "I and my brother pledged each other friendship[98] and thus declared: 'as our fathers were friends (*ṭābu*) with each other we shall be friends too.'"[99] That 'nice/proper words' (*amātu banātu*) refer to friendly political relations while 'improper words' connote 'rebellious deeds' may be learned from the letter of Tušratta to Amenopis III:[100] "Tuhe did 'improper things' (*amāta la panīta*) against my country and has killed his ruler." 'Bad things' are rightly translated by the *CAD* as 'hostile acts'.[101]

Covenantal relations are expressed not only by 'proper, friendly words' but also by 'upright words'. Thus in another Mari text we read:[102] "Kill a donkey-foal of peace (= conclude a ⟦49⟧ covenant)[103] and speak with *uprightness* (or speak *correctly*, i.e., come to a formal agreement);[104] his encampment[105] is peaceful, and there is neither fraud nor felony." In another

97. *šarrāni aḫḫūtu ṭābūtu šalīmu . . . u amātu* [*banītu*] ⟦'[among] the kings there are brotherhood, amity, peace, and [good] relations'⟧, El-Amarna 11:rev. 22 and see Moran, "Treaty Terminology," 175, n. 20 for the plural of *amātu*.

98. El-Amarna 8:8–9, *anāku u aḫiya itti aḫāmeš ṭabūta nidabbub* ⟦'My brother and I made a mutual declaration of friendship'⟧. Note Moran's comment to the translation: "The two parties did more than discuss (*CAD* III 8) friendship; they spoke, that is, *pledged* to each other. This meaning seems required by context" ("Treaty Terminology," 175, n. 99).

99. El-Amarna 8:8–12, cf. 9:7–9: "Since the time when my ancestors and your ancestors pledged each other friendship, and sent each other gifts (*šulmānu*)." For *šulmānu* in connection with covenant at Ugarit, see Greenfield, "Legal Terminology," 119, n. 74.

100. El-Amarna 17:12–13.

101. *CAD* B, 82, n. 4′, s.v. *banû* ⟦'to build'⟧.

102. *ḫayaram ša salīmim qutulma . . . išariš dub*[*u*]*b, nawûšu šalmat . . . sārtum u gullultum ul ibašše* (G. Dossin, "Les archives epistolaires du Palais de Mari," *Syria* 19 [1938] 109, line 23), and cf. Job 5:23–24: 'for you have a covenant with the stones of the field and the beasts of the field concluded peace with you [cf. Hos 2:20], then you will know that it is well in your tent, you will look around your encampment and find nothing amiss' כי עם אבני השדה בריתך וחית השדה השלמה לך וידעת כי שלום אהלך ופקדת נוך ולא תחטא. Compare also Job 8:6: 'if you are innocent and upright, then indeed will he protect you and will grant well-being in your righteous abode' אם זך וישר אתה כי עתה יעיר עליך ושלם נות צדקך (compare the Ugaritic standard greeting formula: *ilm tǵrk tšlmk* ⟦'may the gods grant you protection and well-being'⟧). For נות צדק ⟦'legitimate abode'⟧ compare Jer 31:23 where נוה צדק is parallel in meaning to קריה נאמנה ⟦'faithful town'⟧, עיר הצדק ⟦'righteous city'⟧ of Isa 1:26. In these contexts צדק means 'loyalty' (see my "Covenant of Grant," 186, n. 17). As in the passage from Mari, so the verses in Job speak therefore about good reward for true covenantal relations.

103. Cf. M. Held, "Philological Notes on the Mari Covenant Rituals," *BASOR* 200 (1970) 33.

104. See *CAD* I–J, 223–24 n. 2′d, s.v. *išariš* ⟦'duly, correctly'⟧; *myšrym* in Dan 11:6 and *yšrym* in v. 17 mean 'treaty'—cf. the LXX translation of these terms by συνθήκη ⟦'covenant'⟧ in both verses (also in Theodotion's translation of v. 6). It has not been recognized that δίκαια ('just things') appears in the Book of the Maccabees in the sense 'treaty'; cf. 1 Macc 7:12; 11:33 (cf. 10:26); 2 Macc 10:12 (τὸ δίκαιον ⟦'the just things'⟧); 11:14; 13:23.

105. For *nawû* ⟦'encampment'⟧ cf. A. Malamat, "Mari and the Bible: Patterns of Tribal Organization," *JAOS* 82 (1962) 146; P. Artzi, *Encyclopedia Miqrait* 5.791–94, s.v. נוה.

text: *anāku u [att]a išariš ni[db]ubbu* 'I and [yo]u have sp[ok]en with uprightness/correctly', with the meaning: 'we have come to a formal agreement'.[106]

In the vassal treaties of Esarhaddon we often find the words *ṭābtu* 'good', *damiqtu* (SIG$_5$-*tu*) 'proper', *tarīṣu* 'right, straight', and *banītu* 'nice' describing the relations with the sovereign. The 'good thing' (*amātu ṭābtu*), which the vassals are asked to keep, is loyalty, whereas disloyalty is expressed by the opposite: 'not good' (*lā ṭābtu*), 'not proper' (*lā damiqtu*), 'not right' (*lā tariṣu*), and 'not nice' (*lā banītu*).[107]

[[50]] The expression *dibbēr ṭōbâ* with the meaning 'establish a covenant relationship' is found explicitly in the Bible. A. Malamat has already observed[108] that ותדבר אל עבדך את הטובה הזאת 'you have spoken this *good thing* to your servant' in 2 Sam 7:28 refers to the covenant which the LORD made with David (cf. 2 Sam 23:5; Ps 89:4, 29, 34, 50) concerning dynasty, and that David here acknowledges it. It should be added that this matter is also referred to when Abigail says to David: והיה כי יעשה ה׳ לאדני בכל אשר דבר הטובה עליך וצוך לנגיד על ישראל 'When the LORD has made to my master all the "good thing" that God has spoken about you and has made you prince over Israel' (1 Sam 25:30).[109]

106. Cf. *CAD* I–J 223, n. 2′c, s.v. *išariš*, and see now *Archive Royale de Mari*, vol. 10; *Correspondance féminine* (G. Dossin, A. Finet, eds.; Paris: Geuthner, 1978) 11, line 20; 177, line 9 (for the latter cf. W. H. Ph. Römer, *Frauenbriefe* [AOAT 12; Neukirchen-Vluyn: Neukirchener, 1971] 42).

107. Cf. Wiseman, "Vassal Treaties," lines 296–97 and in the negative, lines 67–68, 73–74, 108–9, 125. See further M. Weinfeld, "The Loyalty Oath in the Ancient Near East," *UF* 8 (1976) 412 with nn. 289, 290. Cf. also the phrase 'the word which is not good' (*amat lā ṭābti*) meaning 'betrayal' in the fealty oath pledged by the Assyrian officials (to Ashurbanipal): "If any guard . . . or plotter speaks a word that is not good" (L. Waterman, *Royal Correspondence*, no. 1105:12–13). Compare also 'bad deed' (*epšu lemnu*) in the sense of rebellious activity in El-Amarna 287:71; Borger, *Inschriften*, 43, 1:55; 47, 2:50; cf. *CAD* L, 121, n. 2′. The same applies to ועושה רעה בעמו [['to commit evil against one's people']] in the Temple Scroll (Y. Yadin, *The Temple Scroll* [3 vols.; Jerusalem: Israel Exploration Society]: cf. col. 64, line 7. Identical terms in the context of seditious agitation are found in the Hittite treaties (*idaluš memiyaš* = 'bad words') and in the Sefire treaty מלין לחית ('bad words'); see J. C. Greenfield, "Stylistic Aspects of the Sefire Treaty Inscriptions," *AcOr* 29 (1965) 8–9. For 'speaking kindly' (KA.KA DÙG.GA) in the sense of making an agreement, cf. Postgate, *Taxation*, 390, line 4, in connection with allowing the Tyrians to cut wood on Mt. Lebanon; see also B. Oded, "Assyria and the Cities of Phoenicia during the Time of the Assyrian Empire," in *Beer Sheva* 1 (Y. Avishur, S. Abramsky, H. Reviv, eds.; Jerusalem: Kiryat Sepher, 1973) 148, n. 80 (Hebrew).

108. A. Malamat, "Organs of Statecraft in the Israelite Monarchy," in *The Biblical Archaeologist Reader* 3 (E. F. Campbell, D. N. Freedman, eds.; New York: Doubleday, 1970) 195–98.

109. This verse should be interpreted by rearranging the words to read בכל הטובה אשר דבר עליך or את הטובה בכל אשר דבר עליך. See S. R. Driver, *Notes on the Hebrew Text and Topography of the Books of Samuel* (2nd ed.; Oxford: Clarendon, 1912) 202; M. H. Segal, *Siphre Shmuel* (Jerusalem: Kiryat Sepher, 1976) 200 (Hebrew).

To be sure, exegetes[110] were at a loss to explain which "good thing" is referred to, but after the new interpretation of 2 Sam 7:28 there is no doubt that it is the dynastic promise, as expressed in Nathan's prophecy. That the address of Abigail in 1 Sam 25:25–31 contains motifs from the dynastic oracle of Nathan in 2 Samuel 7 may be deduced from 1 Sam 25:28. In this verse Abigail refers to the promise of establishing a בית נאמן [['enduring dynasty']] for David, a promise which occurs again in 2 Sam 7:16 and is alluded to in the oracle of the "man of God" in 1 Sam 2:35.[111]

M. Fox[112] has provided additional evidence for טוב and דבר טוב in the covenantal sense in the Bible; and I have endeavored to show elsewhere[113] that דבר טוב [['good thing']] in the *Emet weYaṣib* liturgy, [[51]] recited after the *Shemaʿ*, refers to the fealty oath to God, the King, which this liturgy actually represents. This corresponds to the "good thing" in the fealty oaths' pledges by the subjects to their sovereign in the ancient Near East.

Alongside 'good word' (הטובה), we find in 2 Sam 7:28 also an allusion to 'words of truth' (ודבריך יהיו אמת). These two expressions, "goodness and truth," appear in their Akkadian form in a letter to the king of Ugarit as a hendiadys (*kittu ṭābūtu*), meaning covenant.[114] One can further compare חסד ואמת, an expression which also serves to indicate covenant relationships.[115]

In the light of all this, the "good words" in 1 Kgs 12:7 have to be understood as a legal arrangement according to which the northern population will be exempted from corvée work and heavy taxes imposed on them. A release proclaimed by a king and expressed by דבר טובה may be found in 2 Kgs 25:28. In connection with the release of Jehoiachin during the accession year of Evil-Merodach we find the sentence וידבר אתו טבות which should also be understood as an official privilege formula.[116] We are told here that Evil-Merodach decreed the release of Jehoiachin at the beginning of his reign (apparently in the framework of an *andurārum* [['freedom']]): "He exalted his throne above those of other kings . . . and he (Jehoiachin) ate 'bread' regularly"[117] in his presence all the days of his

110. See, e.g., H. P. Smith, *The Books of Samuel* (ICC; Edinburgh: Clark) 226.

111. As in other biblical speeches (see my book *Deuteronomy*, 51–58), here too the scribe (apparently from the Davidic house) used Abigail as a means of presenting his own ideology.

112. M. Fox, "Ṭôb as Covenant Terminology," *BASOR* 209 (1973) 41–42.

113. Weinfeld, "Loyalty Oath," 412–13.

114. See Moran, "Treaty Terminology," 174 and nn. 17 and 30.

115. See my "Covenant Terminology," 191–92.

116. This has been raised as a possibility by Malamat, "Organs," 197.

117. The לחם [['bread']] of the king (cf. 1 Sam 20:24, 27, 34; 2 Sam 9:7, 10; 1 Kgs 5:2) is 'the king's meal'; compare Aḥiqar col. 3, line 33 (cf. A. Cowley, *Aramaic Papyri of the Fifth Century B.C.* [Oxford: Clarendon, 1923] 213): [ובוסמסכן ח]ד מן רבי אבי זי לחם אבי [אכל] '[Nabu-šum-

life" (2 Kgs 25:28–29), וארחתו ארחת תמיד נתנה לו מאת המלך דבר יום ביומו כל ימי חיו 'and a regular daily allocation of food was given him by the king as long as he lived' (v. 30).

The act of Evil-Merodach may be paralleled by Sargon's act towards Ullusunu, the king of the Manneans, as told in Sargon's [[52]] account of the eighth campaign:[118] "Before Ullusunu (who expressed his submission to the Assyrian king) I spread a heavy table and made his throne higher than that of Iranzu, the father who begot him.[119] I seated Ullusunu and his men with the people Assyria at a joyous table (*paššur ḫidâti*)."[120]

Eating at the king's table or at his expense was a privilege of high officials and the palace staff.[121] Thus we read in the Aḥiqar story that Nabušumiškun was one of Sennacherib's high officials (חד מן רבי) who "ate his bread."[122] Similarly, we hear about Mephibosheth, the grandson of Saul, who was privileged to eat at the king's table (2 Sam 9:7; 19:29). The sons of Barzilai the Gileadite, whom David wanted to reward for his loyalty towards him (2 Sam 19:32–33), also were given a place at the king's table (1 Kgs 2:7). These royal acts are defined as חסד (עשה) [['act loyally' or 'show mercy']], which, like טובה [['goodness, kindness']], expressed a formal grant (see above).

Those who were privileged to sit at Solomon's table, כל הקרב אל שלחן המלך שלמה [['all who approached the table of King Solomon']][123] (1 Kgs 5:7 [Hebrew]), were apparently high officials of a similar type. In Ugarit we encounter the term *ṯrmm* 'the diners (of the king)' who have their estates in the province.[124] In 2 Kgs 25:30, which continues the privilege formula

---

iškun, on]e of my father's big officials who din[ed] with my father'. The phrase בא אל הלחם [['come to the meal']] in 1 Sam 20:27 is to be compared with *ana napteni erēbu* 'to enter for the meal' (cf. K. F. Müller, *Das assyrische Ritual* [*MVAG* 41/3] 59–60; and see J. Kinnier Wilson, *The Nimrud Wine Lists* [London: British School of Archaeology, 1972] 43). Another expression for the 'king's meal' is שלחן המלך (cf. 2 Sam 9:13), which is the equivalent of *paššur šarri* [['table of the king']]. For the "king's meal" in Assyria cf. recently Wilson, pp. 34–35.

118. F. Thureau Dangin, *Une relation de la Huitième Campagne de Sargon* (Paris: Geuthner, 1912) 12, lines 62–63.

119. *paššur takbitti maḫaršu arkusuma, eli ša* ^{m}*Iranzi abi ālidišu ušaqqi kussâšu.*

120. A nice illustration of participating at a royal "joyous table" is the scene from the Khorsabad reliefs (see now Wilson, pl. 2), where we see Assyrian officers sitting on high chairs before a table with food and holding their rhytons aloft.

121. Cf. Wilson, 78–79.

122. See n. 118 above.

123. Compare in connection with Barzilai in 1 Kgs 2:7: כי כן קרבו אלי בברחי מפני אבשלום. It seems that קרב here expresses the privileged of the king (the ones who are close to him); cf. Assyrian *qurubūte* (for which see Wilson, 48–49). We should then translate the verse 'they became my close (friends) when I was fleeing from Absalom'.

124. See A. Rainey, *The Social Structure of Ugarit* (Jerusalem: Mosad Bialik, 1967) 51–53 (Hebrew); idem, "Institutions: Family, Civil, and Military," *RSP* 2.89.

of v. 28, דבר יום ביומו [['daily allotment']] and תמיד [['regular']], are equal in meaning to *riksu ša ūmi* [['agreement in perpetuity']][125] *gimû* and *sadru* (*sadrūti*) [['standard quality']], found in the Assyrian [[53]] lists of regular daily delivery for palace personnel or for the temple.[126] As in 2 Kgs 25:30 so in Dan 1:5 the daily ration of food and wine for the Jews of royal descent in the Babylonian king's palace is defined as דבר יום ביומו.

The phrase וידבר טבות in 2 Kgs 25:28 is then to be understood as a formal act establishing a grant, and not just "speaking kindly." This demonstrates that ודברת דברים טובים [['speak good words']] in 2 Kgs 12:7 refers to concrete royal acts formulated in written agreements of the *zakūtu* or *andurārum* type known also from the Neo-Assyrian period. Whether this meant exemption from corvée of the whole northern Israelite population or of the city of Shechem only cannot be established because of lack of evidence.

125. For the meaning of this term and its Hebrew equivalent ערך, cf. M. Weinfeld, "Recent Publications: A Survey," *Shnaton* 2 (1977) 249.

126. Cf. J. N. Postgate, *Neo-Assyrian Royal Grants and Decrees*, 92–93 for *sadrūti* and Wilson, *Wine Lists*, 112–13 for *ginû* [[normally translated 'regular']]. Note that Hebrew ערך which equals Akkadian *riksu* [['bond, contract, agreement']] (see n. 126) is translated in *Tg. Onq.* to Exod 40:23 by סדר [['arrangement']].

The State of Israelite History

Baruch Halpern

For the past two centuries, most biblical scholars have been intensely interested in two subjects: the history of ancient Israel and the history of Israel's literature. In pursuing these interests, scholars assumed a close relationship between topics–ancient Israel's literature could be used as a source, perhaps the major source, to write Israel's history. This consensus no longer holds. As Halpern points out, some scholars deem the deuteronomistic work, and all biblical literature for that matter, to be late and unreliable guides to the worlds of ancient Israel and Judah. If histories of ancient Palestine are to be written, according to this view, they must be based on material evidence and not on works of theology and literature. Hence, the debate has shifted from whether one could reconstruct the Ancestral Age as a distinct historical era or whether one could speak of the exodus as an actual historical event to whether one can even speak of a united monarchy and separate states of Israel and Judah in the preexilic period. The author agrees with the emphasis on obtaining as much information as possible from the material remains, but he also thinks that this evidence, supplied by tell archaeology, surface surveys, and epigraphy, points to the existence of Israelite and Judahite states. On the basis of comparisons with Northwest Semitic epigraphy and archaeology, Halpern defends the claim that the Deuteronomist's work qualifies as an example of ancient history writing.

The following is a reflection on a number of recent works. Among their number are: T. L. Thompson, *Early History of the Israelite People*; P. R. Davies, *In Search of Ancient Israel*; J. Van Seters, *Prologue to History*; G. W. Ahlström, *History of Ancient Palestine*. Each of these works in its own way attempts to overturn a consensus of long standing to the effect that there is material of value for the reconstruction of history in the Former Prophets, and that this material does not merely embrace the time in which the texts were written but also that to which they refer. Whether one accepts the so-called "minimalist" revision, the latter issue remains a key point: historical texts, after all, mediate information both about themselves and about a time anterior to themselves. To illustrate this point, the following treatment focuses on Kings, the softest of the potential targets for this purpose. Similar representations can certainly be made regarding large sections of Samuel, and even portions of Judges. However, the concentration of historical material subject to clear correlation with external sources is much heavier in Kings than in these other accounts.

The earliest universally acknowledged external attestation of an Israelite state occurs in the annals of Shalmaneser III, regarding the year 853 B.C.E. In the last years, however, numerous books have appeared, each of which directly or indirectly questions the existence of David and Solomon, 80 to 150 years earlier.[1] These works have been written from literary, archaeological, anthropological, and philosophical perspectives.[2] What they share is a sharply minimalist approach to Israelite history. Indeed, the same scholars deny the existence of a state in Judah, or a kingship in Jerusalem, until *its* attestation in external inscriptions–specifically, the mention of Ahaz in the annals of Tiglath-Pileser III. More recently, a bevy of scholars (mostly the same ones) deny that the reference to a

1. J. Van Seters, *In Search of History: Historiography in the Ancient World and the Origins of Biblical History* (New Haven: Yale University Press, 1983; repr. Winona Lake, Ind.: Eisenbrauns, 1997); idem, *Prologue to History: The Yahwist as Historian in Genesis* (Louisville: Westminster/John Knox, 1992); T. L. Thompson, *Early History of the Israelite People: From the Written and Archaeological Sources* (Studies in the History of the Ancient Near East 4; Leiden: Brill, 1992); P. R. Davies, *In Search of Ancient Israel* (JSOTSup 148; Sheffield: Sheffield Academic Press, 1992); J. W. Flanagan, *David's Social Drama. A Hologram of Israel's Early Iron Age* (Social World of Biblical Antiquity 7; JSOTSup 73; Sheffield: Sheffield Academic Press, 1988); D. W. Jamieson-Drake, *Scribes and Schools in Monarchic Judah: A Socio-archeological Approach* (Social World of Biblical Antiquity 9; JSOTSup, 109; Sheffield: Sheffield Academic Press, 1991). Sociologically, note the recurrent Sheffield imprint. Related work includes G. W. Ahlström, *The History of Ancient Palestine from the Palaeolithic Period to Alexander's Conquest* (JSOTSup 146; Sheffield: JSOT Press, 1993); G. Garbini, *History and Ideology in Ancient Israel* (London: SCM, 1988); N. P. Lemche, "Is It Still Possible to Write a History of Ancient Israel?" *SJOT* 8 (1994) 165–90; J. Van Seters, *Abraham in History and Tradition* (New Haven: Yale University Press, 1975); K. W. Whitelam, *The Invention of Ancient Israel: The Silencing of Palestinian History* (London: Routledge, 1996).

2. Part of the problem is that the creeping critical rejection of biblical accounts has reached its natural limits. First the patriarchs, then the Exodus underwent rejection by historians. Now the Conquest has suffered the same fate, and in some cases and in many respects the period of the Judges. Now scholarly skepticism has butted up against the United Monarchy, a period for which written records must have been available at least from David's formation of a state bureaucracy forward.

"house of David" in the Tel Dan stela has anything to do with a state centered in Jerusalem.[3]

One source of difficulty here is the nature of the field of biblical studies. Typically, professionals in this area are trained either in theological seminaries or in departments of Near Eastern studies or religion. Their exposure to the discipline of history, as it is practiced on other times and places, is very often marginal. In fact, many years ago, my own graduate program in Near Eastern Languages and Civilizations refused my request for a minor field in the philosophy of history: philological method, not historical method, was the centerpiece of the Albrightian tradition–indeed, of all professional biblical scholarship since the Middle Ages. While "historical-critical" method was of the essence, an added minor in historiographic self-consciousness was a waste of everyone's time.

There is much to be said for philological method. And nothing can be more repugnant to any real intellectual than playing the "union card": so-and-so is not a "historian." In fact, the compartmentalization not so much of knowledge as of claims to knowledge, the idea that one must have a doctorate in some field in order knowledgeably to discuss that field–whether history or comparative literature or economics (if economics can be knowledgeably discussed even by its Ph.Ds)–is a chronic affliction of academic discourse and the main obstacle to meaningful interdisciplinary dialogue.[4]

Furthermore, philology is after all the basis of all further work. The exegete, for example, can never be any better than his or her philology in a given text. The history of language, as well, although often pursued to levels of extreme fragility in biblical studies, can when responsibly undertaken, furnish a clear and convincing base line for the relative dating of texts. It is not the object of this discussion to review the hard philological evidence that establishes, for example, the preexilic dating of a great deal of biblical historiography and other literature. However, the "minimalist" case depends on the view that the authors of such texts as Kings–and

3. For full bibliography, including of some forthcoming studies, see the acerbic article of Niels Peter Lemche and Thomas L. Thompson, "Did Biran Kill David? The Bible in the Light of Archaeology," *JSOT* 64 (1994) 3–22; further, P. R. Davies, "*Bytdwd and Swkt Dwyd*: A Comparison," *JSOT* 64 (1994) 23–24; Ehud ben-Zvi, "On the Reading 'Bytdwd' in the Aramaic Stele from Tel Dan," *JSOT* 64 (1994) 25–32. See latterly G. Knoppers, "The Vanishing Solomon: The Disappearance of the United Monarchy from Recent Histories of Ancient Israel," *JBL* 116 (1997) 19–44, with comprehensive coverage of the discussion.

4. Guild officials limit access in two ways: by writing obscurely and by insisting on ticket-punching. The maintaining of guild standards has two effects: discouraging distraction by the incompetent and discouraging competition from competent outsiders. Though sensible, this system is far from perfect, since insiders can be incompetent and outsiders insightful (though less frequently than the reverse).

especially their audiences–had no access to preexilic sources, which alone explains how they could, for example, have invented a United Monarchy and states as early as the 10th and 9th centuries. The hard philological evidence, thus, is crippling to their views.[5]

In that sense, the philological background of recent entrants into the ranks of those who debate the history of ancient Israel is no argument against their positions, though their failure to come to grips with the linguistic evidence itself certainly is. These new voices–Thompson, Van Seters, Davies, Lemche, Cryer, Jamieson-Drake, and, in very different senses, Ahlström, Knauf, and others–call into question various aspects of the biblical paradigm for Israelite history. In fact, they reject it, on the grounds that it is not wholly reliable. Each does so from a unique perspective and with unique argument. Lemche, for example, is centrally concerned with the social structure of the Judahite community. Flanagan, with the firmest grasp of archaeology, worries justifiably whether one can unify data from disparate archaeological sites. Ahlström rewrites the early history but more or less accepts the biblical presentation from the beginnings of the state on down to the Exile.

In some of these cases, however, philological positivism asserts itself against traditional historical method, and history is the loser. The problem is that different logics actuate the two. Philology is the "science of language," as Müller put it already in the 19th century. To put it differently, philology is a sort of elementary algebra: What is the common denominator of X in the following? X, speaking from his home in Plains, promised that on assuming office, he would govern without deceit or cronyism; X's wife, at Kennebunkport prior to the inauguration, promised to make America's children her highest priority; X, speaking from the State House in Little Rock, announced plans to offer universal health care to a population reluctant to aid its neighbors. If your answer was "the President-Elect," you qualify as a philologist. If, however, you believe that any of the actions described was based primarily on some conviction regarding the common good, you fail as a historian: intrinsic merit and political advocacy have little to do with one another.

And that is the difference between history and philology. Historians live in the mental space between action, including expression, and its myriad strategic, tactical, and ingenuous motivations. In the 19th century, when fledgling social scientists believed that life was rationally determined (it was before the quantum theory, and the universe was still Newtonian), philology furnished one of the models for history. If we could

5. Some of the evidence of this ilk, starting with the very important studies of Avi Hurvitz on Aramaic loanwords, will be reviewed in my *History of Israel* (New York: Doubleday, forthcoming).

know all the details, the facts, we could create a grand synthesis: the laws of history, like those of physics, would expose history's grand design. There is a direct line from Darwin to Ranke, Marx, Freud, Toynbee, Spengler. That is the point: philology is deterministic, algebraic, mathematical. It is as certain as any theoretical science can be and, applied to history, it reduces the complexities of human interaction, the complexities of war, politics, society, economics, art, emotion, and thought to schemes of rules, laws, regulations. For a philological historian, things human can never be more than the sum of their parts, and their parts are few indeed.

History, however, as Robin Collingwood observed, concerns itself with human intentions and their results. And in that sense it is an example of what Edward Lorenz would call a chaotic system: identical actions in similar circumstances do not necessarily yield similar results. No one cognizant of the history of the 20th century maintains that history is a stable system, the opposite of the chaotic in Lorenz's typology. Given this, history is not a field in which the application of philological method is appropriate: philology, like theoretical mathematics, is preeminently a science of stable systems.

Sometimes, of course, history is less than a science of human intentions–when we are in doubt concerning the very course of international or domestic politics. But sometimes we can try to understand what was in the minds of the authors of our texts. Many literary theorists deny this latter possibility, and their logic, from a literary perspective, may be impeccable. But from a historical standpoint–and historians ask questions peculiar to their discipline–the attempt to understand our authors' intentions is a moral imperative, because those intentions are the subject of the study. A converse immorality is unsurprising: the discourse of politics trades perpetually in demonization and the imputation of malice. Yet absent self-interest, even politicians' intentions tend to be beneficent. The abdication of any effort to construe intention, its deliberate misconstruction, is the literary extension of human political culture.

Why is the United Monarchy un-"historical"? The professed reason is that there is a *remote* possibility that the whole construct is a lie. In other words, biblical allegations (in the books of Samuel and Kings, for a start, but in other works as well) of a pan-Israelite state centered in Jerusalem in the 10th century are themselves insufficient evidence on which to base a reconstruction of that period. Any reconstruction. For the biblical texts were both invented wholecloth and brought to their final form in the Persian (or even Hellenistic) era. Life is a conspiracy; Persian Judah schemed to create a past for itself. Intentions were bad all around.

This is a quintessentially philological, not historical, argument. Its proponents claim to isolate archaeological from textual data and to rely overwhelmingly on the former.[6] Such strategies are useful as heuristic devices: they answer the question "what is the minimum that we can know from one corpus of data?" But precisely in discarding rather than reserving to the side one variety of evidence, the whole approach evinces a mechanistic, Newtonian approach toward the construction of knowledge. The idea is that archaeological remains in themselves, without knowledge gleaned from other sources, place the interpreter in some superior epistemic location. The reality is that there is no such thing, in historical archaeology, as the interpretation of remains without at least an indirect dialectical relationship to the historical tradition. The more indirect this relationship, the less controlled are the archaeological interpretations—and, the historical ones. This is not even to mention the problem of archaeological interpretation itself, from stratigraphy (which is often problematic) and on to everything that depends on it, such as chronology. In fact, however, the question "what is the minimum we can know?" is a question that impoverishes historical interpretation if it is not followed by the question "what in addition can we reasonably surmise?" Indeed, the *historical* question is "what is the most probable, not the certain, course of events and causation to posit?" Certainty is a stock-in-trade of theoretical sciences, such as philology; history is an applied human science.

The most extreme forms of the new historiography do not even engage the actual archaeology.[7] They appeal to the construct of archaeology and to some archaeologists' history-writing to subvert the validity of the textual presentation. The real logic operating here is the old tradition of historical-critical biblical exegesis. Individual texts in Samuel and Kings can be dated anywhere from the 10th to the 5th centuries B.C.E., depending on an exegete's vision of the development of Israelite and Judahite culture, and some are dated as late as the 3d or 2d century by the most extreme scholars. It is certain, however, that the present books of Kings were completed no earlier than the mid–6th century. In regard to the Pentateuch, though the individual sources are considerably older,[8] the present, combined narrative is no older than the 6th century and is possibly as late as the 5th. Thompson and Davies, in particular, simply equate the

6. Thompson, Flanagan, Jamieson-Drake, Davies—all cited in n. 1. For a constructive example of the method, see J. S. Holladay, "Religion in Israel and Judah under the Monarchy: An Explicitly Archaeological Approach," in *Ancient Israelite Religion: Essays in Honor of Frank Moore Cross* (ed. P. D. Miller, P. D. Hanson, and S. Dean McBride; Philadelphia: Fortress, 1987) 249–99; idem, "The Kingdoms of Israel and Judah: Political and Economic Centralization in the Iron IIA–B (ca. 1000–750 B.C.E.)," in *The Archaeology of Society in the Holy Land* (ed. T. E. Levy; London: Facts on File, 1995) 368–98, 586–90.

7. The most responsible scholars cited by the "minimalists" are, in alphabetical order, Ahlström, Flanagan, and Garbini (for references, see above, n. 1).

8. See R. E. Friedman, *Who Wrote the Bible?* (New York: Summit, 1987).

content with the period of literary completion and deny extensive use of sources. Van Seters is even more vehement, while dating the combination of J and E (his J) in the Pentateuch quite late: no earlier sources were used in any Israelite writing about the past. Welcome to the world of positivist philology: to quote Wolfgang Pauli, this work "isn't *even* wrong";[9] it merely exudes despair at recovering the past from works written in a more recent present. Except, of course, that the proponents of the method pretend to provide access to the past in their own present-day works. Their apology is that our ancient authors were less interested in history than we. Yet it is the "minimalists" whose rhetoric reflects a deep-seated discomfort with the tradition. They seem at least as interested in contemporary politics as in history, and one might polemically maintain that their accusations against the ancient historians represent projections of self-knowledge onto others. After all, like the so-called minimalists, biblical historiography cites sources, starting from Joshua forward, and provides many other indexes of antiquarian interest; indeed, source citations involving Menander of Ephesus (Josephus, *Ag. Ap.* 1.106ff.; 2.18), among others, confirm the reality of earlier sources in biblical historians' work.

Consideration of some positive evidence inverts this litany of negatives. First, there is the character of the books of Kings. Were these wholly or largely a product of the Persian era and written without access to preexilic sources, we should expect multiple errors both about chronology and about the names of major public figures, such as kings. Herodotus, writing at or even before the time when Davies, Thompson, and Van Seters posit the activity of our biblical authors, commits such errors with obstinate regularity, despite the fact that he traveled extensively in the lands on which he reports. He relied, it would seem, primarily on oral sources. Yet Herodotus is still understood, and rightly, to be "the father of history." Ktesias, in the Persian court around 400, seems to be no more reliable, and perhaps even less, than Herodotus.

Yet the books of Kings preserve some very accurate information on international affairs. 2 Kings 15–25 place Israel's and Judah's contact with Babylonia and Egypt in the 7th–6th centuries, and with Assyria and Aramea in the 8th–7th centuries, in precisely the right times, naming accurately the Assyrian, Aramean, Babylonian, and Egyptian monarchs with whom contact was made.

Consider precisely what is involved here, from the 6th century on back. It is not terribly surprising that the books of Kings accurately recollect the names of the last kings of Judah before the Exile, in particular the name Jehoiachin, whose captivity in Babylon is attested in cuneiform

9. See Jeremy Bernstein, "Julian: 1918–1994," *American Scholar* (Spring, 1995) 241.

sources. Nor is it surprising that they recall the campaigns to the west of Nebuchadnezzar, king of Babylon, from 605 onward. The conflict between Pharaoh Necho (II) and Babylon is also accurately reflected, including Necho's abortive attempt to shore up the remnants of the Assyrian kingdom in 612–609. Reflexes of the fall of Nineveh and the subsequent era of the Babylonian Empire remain, too, in the prophetic books of Nahum and Jeremiah—books that on the "minimalist" hypothesis must have been composed in the Persian era as well. A little more surprising, then, is the fact that various courtiers and functionaries named in Jeremiah (and Kings) are now attested in the form of seal stamps from 7th-century Jerusalem.[10] Preserving the memory of these individuals' status was something of a feat for scribes composing freely 150 or more years later.

Inside the 7th century, Kings does not often mention the names of Assyrian kings. (Ezra mentions Esarhaddon and Asshurbanipal.) It does, however, accurately preserve the name of a king of Judah, Manasseh, who appears in the historical records of Esarhaddon and Asshurbanipal. Moreover, in the first quarter of the century, 2 Kgs 19:37 preserves not just the name of the Assyrian king, Sennacherib (705–681), but also the name of one of his sons and assassins.[11] The same account recalls that there was an Assyrian (but not Babylonian or Persian) official with the title Rab-Shaqeh.

In 701 B.C.E., the campaign of Sennacherib to the west is covered in some detail in the Assyrian's annals and reliefs on the one hand and in 2 Kings 18–20 (// Isaiah 36–39) on the other. There has been considerable embellishment in the Kings account, which combines three versions of the events, at least one of them transmitted orally. But there are important points of contact, particularly in the matters of Sennacherib's devastation of the countryside and siege of Lachish and of intervention by an Egyptian field force at the specific site of Elteqeh. (This last point cannot possibly have been recovered by later writers without excellent written

10. Among those attested: Jerahmeel, the king's son; Gemaryah ben-Shaphan; Seraiah ben-Neriah. See for the most pertinent collections N. Avigad, *Hebrew Bullae from the Time of Jeremiah* (Jerusalem: Israel Exploration Society, 1986); Y. Shiloh, "A Hoard of Hebrew Bullae from the City of David," *ErIsr* 18 (1985) 73–87, esp. p. 80.

11. Arad-Mulissi, correctly identified in various manuscript traditions as Sennacherib's son: the Hebrew equivalent would be *ʾrdmlš*, which owing to the similarity of *r* and *d*, and sometimes of *š* and *k*, has been corrupted in the MT into *ʾdrmlk* during transmission. It is important to note, however, that the corruption is graphic and not audial, as one might expect were the source an oral one. The name of the other assassin, Saruzur, is not known from any source outside of Kings. See generally S. Parpola, "The Murder of Sennacherib," in *Death in Mesopotamia* (ed. B. Alster, Mesopotamia 8; Copenhagen: Akademisk, 1980) 171–82. Eckardt Otto remarked in public discussion at the 1998 Oslo IOSOT conference that the appropriation of Assyrian treaty curses in Deuteronomy presupposes both political contact with Mesopotamia at this time and the survival of its deposit in writing thereafter.

sources.) Further, Hezekiah's submission and the sparing of Jerusalem from conquest and the order of magnitude of Hezekiah's tribute are all more or less agreed upon by Assyrian and biblical sources. Indeed, contemporary descriptions of the countryside by Isaiah and Micah match up well with the accounts both of Sennacherib and of Kings. So, too, does the biblical claim that Hezekiah "smote the Philistines unto Gaza," reflecting his alliance with or domination of Gath, Eqron, Ashdod, and Ashkelon.[12] Even more interesting is the biblical tradition of Hezekiah's alliance with Merodach-Baladan of Babylon (2 Kgs 20:12–19). This is certainly not inserted in chronological sequence (biblical historiography is often thematic, rather than chronological, in its organization).[13] But the tradition is reliable in this matter—a recollection of diplomatic contact with a distant rebel against Assyria 200 years before the writing of Kings as alleged by those who date all this literature to the Persian or later eras.

Nor is this all. Isa 20:1 includes a recollection of the Assyrian king, Sargon II (722–705), Sennacherib's predecessor, and of his campaign by proxy against Ashdod. Sargon is the king who deported the last of "the ten tribes" of Israel. 2 Kings 17, however, while not explicit on this point, does contain a recollection that Shalmaneser (727–722), Sargon's predecessor, was the king who first proceeded against the rump kingdom of Israel, based in Samaria. Moreover, 2 Kings 15–17 names several kings mentioned in the annals of Tiglath-Pileser III (745–727): Ahaz of Judah and, starting from the last, Hoshea, Pekah, and Menahem of Israel. These appear in precisely the order in which Tiglath-Pileser came into contact with them. Tiglath-Pileser's annals confirm what we should also otherwise have suspected, namely, that Rezin II of Damascus, who reputedly combined with Pekah of Israel against Ahaz (2 Kgs 16:5–9), was indeed on the throne at the time and was indeed subjected, along with Israel, by Tiglath-Pileser. 2 Kgs 15:29 even reports, again with striking corroboration in the Assyrian annals, that it was Tiglath-Pileser who initiated the deportation of Israelites. Isa 14:29 may even preserve a recollection of Tiglath-Pileser's campaigns against Philistia.[14]

12. On the events of 701, see my "Jerusalem and the Lineages in the 7th Century B.C.E.: Kinship and the Development of Individual Moral Liability," in *Law and Ideology in Monarchic Israel* (ed. B. Halpern and D. W. Hobson; JSOTSup 124; Sheffield: JSOT Press, 1991) 11–107.

13. D. Glatt, *Chronological Displacement in Biblical and Related Literatures* (SBLDS 139; Atlanta: Scholars Press, 1993).

14. So H. Tadmor and M. Cogan, *II Kings* (AB 11; Garden City, N.Y.: Doubleday, 1988). It is conceivable that the reference is to the death, not of Tiglath-Pileser, but of Ahaz himself, who would then be the "staff who smote" Philistia, and that expansion in the direction of Philistia began before Hezekiah but was concealed by tendentious reportage in Kings. If so, the likeliest target is the town of Gath, which is not apparently on the map in Sennacherib's time. Gath plays no significant role in any literature after the 9th century.

It remains a question whether Tiglath-Pileser's annals also mention Uzziah (Azaryah) of Judah.[15] And before Tiglath-Pileser's time, we lack detailed Assyrian records about the west for a considerable time. Yet where there is contact, sometime around 800, the name of Joash, the king of Israel, again appears, this time as a tributary in the Tell al-Rimah stela of Adad-Nirari III, along with Mariʾ ('Lord') of Damascus, presumably Ben-Hadad, son of Hazael,[16] a king whose expansion is attested in the Zakkur inscription. Kings credits Joash of Israel with the recovery of his predecessors' losses to Aram (2 Kgs 13:25; probably 2 Kgs 13:5, with Qimḥi). But it is clear that in the aftermath of Hazael's program of expansion, reported in Kings and reflected in the Assyrian annals, Assyrian resurgence gave Israel the opportunity to recuperate, as Kings claims. Further, both biblical and extrabiblical evidence[17] names Ben- or Bar-Hadad as Hazael's successor.

Here, we are entering the realm of the 9th century, four centuries or more before the time when the revisionist school dates the composition of Kings, and three centuries before the last event it records. Yet accurate representation of regnal sequences and of a general international political situation continues. Hazael, of course, is remembered in Kings as the great Aramean scourge of Israel and Judah: the annals of Shalmaneser III tend in all particulars to corroborate this picture. In 841, Shalmaneser relates that Jehu "son of Omri" (i.e., of "the House of Omri," the dynastic name for the Israelite kingdom) submitted to him. Sometime between 845 and 841, Hazael, a usurper according to Shalmaneser ("the son of a nobody"), succeeded Hadadezer on the throne of Damascus. Kings did get Hadadezer's name wrong—calling him Ben-Hadad instead. But what it does get right is the fact that Hazael succeeded Hadadezer before Jehu came to the throne in Israel (2 Kgs 8:28). The order and, indeed, the

15. See esp. the treatment of M. Weippert, "Israel und Juda," *RLA* 5.205; also Cogan and Tadmor, *II Kings*, 165–66, with the thesis that Azriyau was a Yahwistic filibuster. While I formerly made the same suggestion concerning Iaubiʾdi of Hamath in the late 8th century ("Sectionalism and the Schism," *JBL* 93 [1974] 519–32), the most satisfying explanation may be that of S. Dalley, "Yahweh in Hamath in the 8th Century B.C.: Cuneiform Materials and Historical Deductions," *VT* 40 (1990) 21–32. Dalley suggests that Yhwh was an indigenous deity in central Syria from the Late Bronze Age forward. All the same, although improbable on its face, it is not altogether out of the question that the Azriyau of Tiglath-Pileser's account of the year 739–738 is in fact the king of Judah.

16. Hazael certainly held the title *mrʾ*, as observed by Dalley ("A Stela of Adad-Nirari III and Nergal-Ereš from Tell al Rimah," *Iraq* 30 [1968] 149) and as confirmed by Hazael's booty inscriptions, on which see I. Ephʿal and J. Naveh, "Hazael's Booty Inscriptions," *IEJ* 39 (1989) 192–200; A. Lemaire, "Joas de Samarie, Barhadad de Damas, Zakkur de Hamat. La Syrie-Palestine vers 800 av. J.-C.," *ErIsr* 24 (1993) 148*–157*; F. Bron and A. Lemaire, "Les inscriptions araméennes de Hazaël," *RA* 83 (1989) 35–44.

17. In the instance, the inscription of Zakkur, king of Hamath—*KAI* no. 202.5.

chronology are right for *foreign* rulers. Surely the suggestion is that the authors of Kings, whenever one dates them, relied on historical sources.

A more controversial source of potential confirmation for data in the biblical record is the so-called Tel Dan stela. This fragmentary text, from the Iron Age gate plaza, may originally have been part of a set of orthostats.[18] The text dates from the late 9th century (to my mind the last decade or two of the century). It documents three things of relevance in a 9th-century context: First, Hazael did, as Kings maintains, expand at Israel's expense. Second, there were probably contemporaneous kings of Israel and Judah named "[Jeho]ram son of [Ahab]" and "[Ahaz]yahu son of [Jehoram]." The author of the stela probably claims that he or his father killed these kings, an instance of a conqueror claiming responsibility for a domestic coup.[19] This would confirm both the chronology of 2 Kings 8–9 and arguably the claim that both of these kings were killed in Jehu's coup (an event also presupposed in Mesha's triumphalism about the fall of the Omrides (*KAI* no. 181.7, *wʾrʾ bh wbbth wyśrʾl ʿbd ʿbd ʿwlm* ⟦'But I witnessed his undoing, and that of his dynasty, for Israel has perished, perished forever'⟧). The third point is subtler. By calling Judah "the house of David," but calling Israel "Israel," the stela suggests that the biblical account is correct in placing the establishment of an abiding national-dynastic identification earlier in Jerusalem than in Tirzah and Samaria.[20]

Prior to the submission of Jehu, Shalmaneser III's annals also mention conflict with Ahab of Israel. Ahab is master of a huge chariotry arm in Shalmaneser's account–whether the number (2000) is correct or not, this contingent dwarfs those of Shalmaneser's other opponents. Further, Ahab's chariotry is not accompanied by cavalry, while Damascus and Hamath, the

18. This suggestion was made by E. A. Knauf in conversation in June, 1995.

19. For the Tel Dan stela, B fragment, see A. Biran and J. Naveh, "The Tel Dan Inscription: A New Fragment," *IEJ* 45 (1995) 1–18. For the A stela fragment and its readings, see Biran and Naveh, "An Aramaic Stele Fragment from Tel Dan," *IEJ* 43 (1993) 81–98, as modified either in their more recent publication, or in my "Stela from Dan: Epigraphic and Historical Considerations," *BASOR* 296 (1994) 63–80; idem, "Notes on the Second Fragments of the Stela from Tel Dan," in *The Tel Dan Stela* (ed. F. Cryer; JSOTSup; Sheffield: JSOT Press, forthcoming), the latter with a contemporary (853!) parallel to a conqueror (ambiguously) claiming credit for a domestic coup, and further bibliography. On the *byt*-PN nomenclature, see N. Naʾaman, "Beth-David in the Aramaic Stela from Tel Dan," *BN* 79 (1995) 20–21; Halpern, "Construction of the Davidic State"; further, latterly, Knoppers, "Vanishing Solomon," 36–40.

20. So Z. Kallai, "The King of Israel and the House of David," *IEJ* 43 (1993) 248. Kallai is perhaps on less firm ground in claiming that the location of Moabite stelae at Dibon and Kerak and of the Damascene stela at Dan demonstrates "the centrality" of those sites. Stelae were indeed erected in central locations but also at border sites (the Ashdod stela, for example) and other areas conquered, including mountain peaks (Shalmaneser III in the Amanus, with the stelae of his predecessors, and at Baʿli-Raʾsi, for example).

other major chariotry powers, field equal numbers of cavalry and chariotry. Further, whereas Damascus fields 16.7 foot soldiers per chariot and Hamath either 14.3 or 28.6, Israel fields 5. Later references suggest that this distinction is not arbitrary: Israelite charioteers were incorporated *as a closed military unit* into the Assyrian army, indicating that their tactics were both effective and distinctive. And the numbers of chariots attributed to Ahab indicate that the creation of the Israelite state was not a recent development–not so recent even as twenty years before. Indeed, the probable Egyptian background of the Israelite chariotry tradition suggests that the inspiration for that tactical doctrine was transferred during a period of intimate Israelite-Egyptian cooperation, either during the United Monarchy or just after Shishaq's conquest of the country.[21] In this respect it is surprising that attention has not so far been directed to the fact that the author of the Tel Dan stela also attributes immense quantities of chariotry to his or his father's Omride Israelite (and Davidic Judahite) antagonist. The Omride chariot arm, attested in 853, suggests a period of capital formation, territorial expansion, and long acquisition and training, on the order of 50–100 years.

Shalmaneser's conflict with Ahab occurs in 853. Ahab's two sons are accorded reigns that could at most total 12 years in Kings. Jehu submits to Shalmaneser in 841. While the tightness of this chronology has sometimes occasioned skepticism, the fact that there is a close fit (Ahab dying in 853, after the battle of Qarqar) is rather a confirmation of Kings's version of the political succession. Furthermore, the association of Jehu with "the House of Omri" suggests that Omri was regarded, at least in Assyria, as the founder of the state of Israel. Omri is understood in Kings to be Ahab's father. All this is perfectly consonant with biblical testimony. There is extraneous material, such as the tradition that Ahab died fighting the Arameans (1 Kings 22), which has been accepted by our historians from oral rather than literary sources. Yet contradictory literary traditions, such as that of Ahab's peaceful death (1 Kgs 22:40), are also preserved.[22]

21. See D. D. Luckenbill, *ARAB*, 611. On the Israelite chariotry tradition, see esp. S. Dalley, "Foreign Chariotry in the Armies of Tiglath-Pileser III and Sargon II," *Iraq* 47 (1985) 31–48. On the Egyptian background of the Israelite tradition, note G. Reisner ("Tombs of the Egyptian 25th Dynasty at El Kurruw," *Sudan Notes and Records* 2 [1919] 252–54), who observed that Egyptian horses even in the late 8th century were always attached to chariots, never ridden alone. This comports both with the Kurkh Monolith on Ahab and with Sargon's use of chariotry attached from Israel in the late 8th century (for which, see Dalley). It may be added that the 1998 results of the Megiddo Expedition cast grave doubts on the identification of compounds 1576 and 364 there as stables. Further testing of the hypothesis is, however, in progress.

22. The programmatic work on Ahab's death and the traditions of Omride warfare with Damascus was done by J. M. Miller: "The Elisha Cycle and the Accounts of the Omride

The result is a sort of standoff, admittedly, at the literary level, but external evidence then determines how one reconstructs the transmission of information (here, with the aim of shifting evidence of divine favor onto the Omrides from the Nimshides). The Dan stela, for example, confirms that conflict with Damascus did begin in the Omride period.

Still another point relating to the 9th century confirms that the authors of Kings exploited reliable sources. Jezebel, Ahab's vilified queen, is the daughter of Ethbaal, king of Tyre (1 Kgs 16:31). An Ittobaal (Ethbaal) occurs in the Tyrian king list cited by Josephus (*Ag. Ap.* 1.123) from Menander of Ephesus and belongs precisely to the right era. Further, the dynastic alliances between Israel, Tyre, and Judah that are portrayed in Kings in this era make eminent sense precisely in this era, when coalitions of western states attempted, rather successfully, to hold off the Assyrian onslaught. Oddly, Kings makes no such allegations about other periods, only this one.

Indeed, the form of the Tyrian king list preserved in Josephus again suggests that the authors of Kings relied on such archival materials for their composition. For the kings of Tyre, the king list preserves both length of reign and age at death. The authors of Kings provide this data for kings of Judah in the form of length of reign and age at accession. Other Near Eastern king lists supply lengths of reigns but not length of life or age at accession. Strikingly, the authors of Kings do not provide age at accession or death for kings of Israel. This suggests, again, that the information was *not* present in the sources for the Northern Kingdom but was *indeed* present in the sources concerning Judah. The similarity between the records of Judah and of Tyre is most likely to be traced to 10th-century connections between the two. Because age at accession is first reported, in Kings, for Rehoboam and because this would have been a difficult detail to reconstruct after a lapse of a few decades, the most natural reconstruction is that it was in fact recorded, beginning with the end of the United Monarchy. On the other hand, the absence of age reports for Solomon, Abijah, and Asa might suggest that the age for Rehoboam was somehow recovered later from a source other than a king list (such as a funerary monument); in this case it would have been in the Omride era that Tyrian influence asserted itself in Judah.[23] This seems less likely on

Wars," *JBL* 85 (1966) 441–55; idem, "The Fall of the House of Ahab," *VT* 17 (1967) 307–24; idem, "The Rest of the Acts of Jehoahaz (I Kings 20; 22:1–35)," *ZAW* 80 (1968) 337–42. For further bibliography and discussion, see Halpern and D. S. Vanderhooft, "The Editions of Kings in the 8th–7th Centuries B.C.E.," *HUCA* 62 (1991) 230–35.

23. There is no report on age at accession for Abijah (1 Kgs 15:2) or Asa (15:10). However, the accession formulas for these kings were at least somewhat disturbed, because they are the only two figures to share the same queen-mother (Maacah, daughter of Absalom).

the face of it, because one would expect Tyrian influence to have been exercised via the court at Samaria.

There is one last episode of the mid-9th century that deserves mention. Kings relates that Mesha, king of Moab, revolted against Israel at the time of the death of Ahab or his son—in the period shortly before Hazael's accession in Damascus. This is wholly consonant with the implications of Mesha's own propaganda (*KAI* no. 181) and with developments in Assyro-Aramean relations in the midcentury. What is remarkable, once more, is the biblical recollection of a decidedly marginal foreign monarch and his relations with the Israelite (not Judahite) state. Again, the inference is that the authors of the account are employing reliable sources. In fact, four-hundred-odd years before Davies and his congeners envision the composition of a work essentially not based on written sources, such accuracy is virtually unimaginable. Mesha is not exactly a figure who cast a shadow on later tradition. Nor should it be neglected that 2 Kgs 8:20 dates a revolt by Edom against Judah to the same period: these claims are consonant with a general power shift in Transjordan after Hazael's coup in Damascus (especially 2 Kgs 10:33). A report of a contemporary secession by Libnah (2 Kgs 8:22), recovered by Judah in the 8th century (2 Kgs 19:8), is another index of weakness—the only town secession recorded in Kings.

The most impressive intersections with extrinsic textual sources stem from the 10th century, at a remove of five full centuries from the alleged forgeries of the Persian or Hellenistic era. The earlier of these is the correspondence of David and Solomon with Hiram of Tyre. Hiram's reign is attested, again, in the Tyrian annals examined by Menander of Ephesus. According to any sensible chronology (indeed, almost any chronology that has been suggested to date), the synchronism of Solomon with Hiram goes back to about 970. As noted, the Tyrian annals record not just length of reign but, parallel to the records concerning the kings of Judah, also the lifespan: they do so already for figures in the 10th century. It might be argued that in this respect the Tyrians aped Judah, but it is difficult to imagine why they might do so.

More important, however, is the campaign of Shoshenq I to Judah, Israel, and Philistia. Shoshenq's campaign is recorded in 1 Kgs 14:25 as well as in Egyptian epigraphs.[24] Davies notes that Shoshenq does not mention Israel in the record of his campaign to Judah and Israel. He observes that

---

This may simply mean that Maacah survived her son Asa and retained the office of Queen Mother into Asa's reign; but the very confusion entailed in later times may have led a historian to delete, as implausible, age information that led him perhaps to assume that this woman gave birth to a son, and then to a son of that son at some impossibly later date.

24. See K. A. Kitchen, *The Third Intermediate Period in Egypt* (3d ed.; Warminster: Aris & Phillips, 1986) 432–47.

one cannot conclude from this text that there was a United Monarchy focused in Jerusalem (or anywhere else). Yet 1 Kings 14 specifically places Shoshenq in the right time and place and relates that Rehoboam ransomed the city of Jerusalem from assault, a fact that might explain why it does not appear on Shoshenq's itinerary.[25] The same text furnishes evidence for a reign, not just of Rehoboam, but also of Solomon (1 Kgs 14:26–27). Second, Shoshenq's list enumerates settlements, not kingdoms, and it is arguable that no Egyptian king would enumerate territorial states in the region, because none after the early New Kingdom was willing to concede even their nominal independence.[26] Finally, Shoshenq's list is fragmentary, yet the pharaoh claims to have taken Tirzah, which was shortly after the capital of the Northern Kingdom, according to Kings. What is more, the pharaoh's campaign does not materially exceed the borders of the Israelite United Monarchy in any direction, as these are most sensibly reconstructed (below). There could be little reason for such a coincidence unless it were intentional on his part—the Solomonic state, though sundered by the schism under Jeroboam, was the object of the campaign.

The placement of Shoshenq in the late 10th century by collectors of "fragments" in the Persian era would represent, were it actually the case, one of the most remarkable achievements of any historian of that era. Davies hypothesizes that local archives were available in the land of Israel after the Exile but not transported to Babylon in the Exile.[27] But, reservations about that assumption aside, Shoshenq's campaign *and date* are not something scribes picked up isolated from any other information in an archive, which led them to invent a Rehoboam. In fact, the reference clearly stems from a chronicle or annal of some sort: information from this source was incorporated into the extensive narrative of Kings no later than the 7th century. The same can probably be said of the report that Jeroboam fled, after the failure of his attempted coup against Solomon, to the court of the same Shoshenq, no doubt newly established on the throne of Egypt. In the account of Solomon's reign in 1 Kings, Shoshenq is implicitly but accurately understood to have undone the previous alliance between Egypt and Jerusalem. He is not, thus, identified as the pharaoh whose daughter Solomon wed (1 Kgs 3:1, 9:16), despite the fact that biblical texts otherwise rarely furnish a pharaoh's name, rather than title.[28] And what are the odds that a text reflecting knowledge of Sho-

25. What the criteria were for inclusion in the list is not certain.

26. G. N. Knoppers, in correspondence, 1998.

27. Davies, *In Search of Ancient Israel.*

28. Taharqa, probably mistakenly displaced in time, in 2 Kgs 19:9; Isa 37:9; possibly Osorkon (2 Kgs 17:4). Even where the pharaoh lends his name to a site (Ramses, Merneptah), no recollection of the pharaoh's own name is preserved.

shenq's campaign five years after Solomon's death and of Jeroboam's flight to Shoshenq's court is in error about the question of who built a Temple that still stood in the 6th century? A Temple, moreover, that is mentioned by Isaiah, Micah, Jeremiah, and Ezekiel, let alone Kings and Ezra. In all, even were there no king of the United Monarchy called Solomon, we would have to posit another figure of the same–not name–but variety. Of course, king lists in historical time tend to be reasonably reliable in the ancient Near East, and Kings neglects the fact that Shoshenq campaigned north of Judah. It may even be the case that the Egyptian raid, not Judahite inactivity, secured the independence from Jerusalem of the Northern tribes. But like the accounts of other historians, Samuel-Kings demands that its historian-readers distinguish event and fact, at the level of probability, from omission, embellishment, and surmise.

The last piece of evidence concerning the reliability of Kings is its peculiar insistence that the founder of the royal dynasty in Jerusalem was David. In the ancient Near East, royal propagandists are typically anxious to tie Temple foundation to dynastic foundation and to date it as early as possible. Yet 2 Samuel and Kings perversely insist that, while David founded the dynasty, it was his son, Solomon, who constructed the Temple. The best the authors can do is claim that David expressed an interest in building a temple but was refused permission by Yhwh (2 Samuel 7).

Precisely because it is at variance with Near Eastern convention, this picture is believable in itself. Still, some of the scholars to whom this study responds have questioned the existence or activity of a "David." The discovery of the Tel Dan stela now confirms, not just the existence of a "David," but also the plain fact that in the late 9th century, at least, a kingdom in contact with Damascus and in alliance near midcentury with Israel, was called 'the house of David' (*bytdwd*): that is, Judah was identified in an Aramaic inscription as an entity ruled or formerly ruled by a dynasty that traced its royal lineage to David. The locution "house of RN," meaning "state now or formerly ruled by the dynasty stemming from RN," is attested widely in Assyrian literature and is attested as well in another Aramaic stela (*KAI* no. 202.5) and the Bible (in Amos 1:4).[29] It may also have been applied to Judah (as "house of David") in the Mesha stela.[30]

In assigning Samuel-Kings to the Persian or to the Hellenistic era, in denying any historical content in the parts of them without contact to

29. Amos 1:4 is particularly interesting in that it refers to "the house of Hazael" and "the royal buildings of Ben-Hadad." If the reference, as is probable, is to Hazael's successor, Bar-Hadad, then Hazael's takeover may be linked to a subsequent building program–parallel in a sense to the relationship, as traditionally understood, between David and Solomon.

30. *KAI* no. 181.31, as read by É. Puech, "La stèle araméenne de Dan: Bar Hadad II et la coalition des Omrides et de la maison de David," *RB* 101 (1994) 215–41 (p. 227); A. Lemaire, "'House of David' Restored in Moabite Inscription," *BAR* 20/3 (1994) 30–37.

external sources, the minimalists abdicate the primary responsibility of historians: to understand a source's purposes and then to ascertain what are the received particulars on which its authors base their views and what thinking underlies the reconstructions or embellishments they create on that basis. Furthermore, despite a rhetoric of engagement with it, the minimalists also evade the evidence from the archaeological record.

There is not much doubt that the archaeological record of the 8th–6th centuries comports in almost every particular with the general political picture that we derive from epigraphs and the biblical record, critically regarded. In the 8th–7th centuries, most of Israel was depopulated, and there was a swath of destruction cut throughout Judah in 701, followed by a gradual resurgence. Judahite settlement then plummeted in the 6th century, reflecting Babylonian policy in the region.

In the 8th century, both Israel and Judah reached their height in numbers of settlements and probably in terms of land under exploitation. There is very little evidence, though some had earlier been manufactured from a confusion of strata at Tell Farʿah, for significant social stratification in the average settlement of this period. But there is extensive archaeological testimony to the persistence of kinship groups, as one would expect from traditional texts, in the form of clan-section tombs, expanded-family housing compounds, and the distribution of artifacts (such as cooking and storage facilities and domestic cult items) by housing compound. In addition, sets of fortifications in the Shephelah of Judah and in the Jezreel Valley and southern Beqaʿ of Israel, while not necessarily indicating the presence of a nation-state in each locality, are at least strongly suggestive of it. (Public buildings are increasingly prominent at the entrances to such circumvallations in the 8th century.) Very important in this respect is the character of Stratum IVA at Megiddo, which is, if not entirely devoid of normal domestic quarters, certainly largely given over to huge public developments. This is an administrative center without a population and so bespeaks the existence of a larger state, of which it is one part. Indeed, the center of the site seems to have been kept relatively clear of construction to permit the mustering of troops.

At the beginning of the 8th century and into the 9th, the picture is considerably more murky. What is reasonably plain, however, is that from the mid-10th century into the 9th, neither Megiddo nor Hazor, two key northern fortresses, housed any significant intramural domestic population whatever. It would be strange enough to find one such site without evidence of a central power based elsewhere. But it surpasses imagining that two such centers should occupy prominent strategic positions: were they city-states, after all, they would concentrate population within the fortifications. They are instruments of national control, rather than independent polities. Significantly, on its incorporation into the Assyrian Empire as a city-state, in Stratum III, Megiddo again becomes a population center as well as an administrative outpost: regional security problems cannot even conceivably account for this alteration. The 10th–9th century evidence clearly indicates the presence of an unusual umbrella state in the north.

It is in the 10th century that the coincidence of archaeological remains with critically-regarded textual evidence is most striking, since this evidence concerning the kingdom is at such a remove from the Persian era. First, there is an efflorescence of settlement in the Negev, suggesting either central control of pastoralists or, more likely, a national interest in the southern caravan trade.[31] This latter is the more likely in that Solomon, after the accession of Shoshenq, reportedly outfitted a southern port, in cooperation with Tyre and apparently in competition with Egypt.[32] Concern with the southern trade led to a similar alliance, of Jehoshaphat with Israel (itself an ally of Tyre) in the 9th century, and to military activity aimed at the recovery of Edom under Amaziah. Interest in the area is constant in Kings, which was written during a period when control of the southern trade was contested and when Judahite settlements were again pushed out through the Arava. Indeed, the conflict between Josiah and the pharaoh Necho in 609 may in the end have turned on the question of controlling the spice routes. Necho later dug a canal down the Wadi Tumeilat to bring commodities into the Delta. Not too long afterward, Babylon erected a royal residence in Teima, no doubt to trump the Egyptian project. In almost all periods, indeed, down to the Byzantine era, prosperity in the region of Judah was tied to exploitation of resources in the south. The dating of the burst of settlement in the Negev is at least assured by Shoshenq's campaign list: these single-period settlements were there to be destroyed in the late 10th century; they were shortlived outcroppings of Solomon's trade policy. But the juxtaposition of Shoshenq's accession, during Solomon's reign, to the sea-change in Solomon's trade and fortification policy (in both the Negev and the north–see below) as well as to the raid in Rehoboam's time reflects reliance on sources rather than free composition: this is not the sort of connection made in ancient Near Eastern policy reports.

Second, we have in the 10th century (at latest, the early 9th) the remarkably similar gates of Megiddo, Hazor, and Gezer, all three attributed in 1 Kgs 9:15 to Solomon. David Ussishkin, in particular, has questioned

31. See recently Z. Meshel, "The 'Aharoni Fortresses' near Quseima and the 'Israelite Fortresses' in the Negev," *BASOR* 294 (1994) 39–67, for discussion and bibliography.

32. See my "Sectionalism and the Schism," *JBL* 93 (1974) 519–32.

the attribution of these gates to the 10th century (and thus, to Solomon): he compares to them the later but similar gates of Ashdod and Lachish.[33] The dating at Ashdod and Lachish is probable but not entirely firm—an archaeological period is a grosser dating device than a historical one. Moreover, at Hazor and Gezer, the gates connect to casemate defensive walls; the same is at least probably true at Megiddo, where a casemate system sat on the edge of the tell under a later solid wall. This is not the case with the "later" gates. There is certainly a legitimate question as to whether the Megiddo gate in fact belongs to the 10th-century stratum VA–IVB.[34] Still, on the available evidence, it looks as though Yadin's reconstruction of a gate-type introduced under Solomon (and perhaps serving as a template for later construction) was correct. An 8th-century structure of this sort has latterly been excavated and carbon-dated by Michele Daviau at Tell el-Mudayna in Jordan (Ammonite).

Further excavation may not securely determine the stratigraphic status of the Megiddo gate. If Ussishkin is right, we would still have evidence of the coordination or at least the regional influence of fortification plans in the 9th century—though it is then a question why Judahite and Philistine fortifications conform to Israelite. In the more probable instance that 1 Kgs 9:15 is right (and that the gate of Megiddo VA–IVB originally connected, like those of Hazor and Gezer, to a casemate fortification system), we have stunning confirmation (as we already have at Hazor and Gezer) of the allegations of Kings as to Solomon's building activities, a confirma-

33. See D. Ussishkin, "Was the 'Solomonic' City Gate at Megiddo Built by King Solomon?" *BASOR* 239 (1980) 1–18; idem, "Notes on Megiddo, Gezer, Ashdod, and Tel Batash in the Tenth to Ninth Centuries B.C.," *BASOR* 277–78 (Feb.–May 1990) 71–91; idem, "Megiddo," *ABD* 4.666–79. For the converse view, see Y. Yadin, *Hazor* (Schweich Lectures; London: British Academy, 1972) 150–64; Y. Yadin, Y. Shiloh, and A. Eitan, "Megiddo," *IEJ* 22 (1972) 161–64; Y. Shiloh, "Solomon's Gate at Megiddo as Recorded by Its Excavator, R. Lamon, Chicago," *Levant* 12 (1980) 69–76. For an attempt to down-date Gezer's fortification system, see I. Finkelstein, "Penelope's Shroud Unravelled: Iron II Date of Gezer's Outer Wall Established," *Tel Aviv* 21 (1994) 276–82, against W. G. Dever, "Late Bronze Age and Solomonic Defenses at Gezer: New Evidence," *BASOR* 262 (1986) 9–34.

34. This attribution of VA–IVB to the tenth century is now in dispute: see I. Finkelstein, "The Date of the Settlement of the Philistines in Canaan," *Tel Aviv* 22 (1995) 213–39; idem, "The Archaeology of the United Monarchy: An Alternative View," *Levant* 28 (1996) 177–87, for dating of VIA to the mid–10th century; for a defense of the traditional dating, see A. Mazar, "Iron Age Chronology: A Reply to I. Finkelstein," *Levant* 29 (1997) 157–67. The stratigraphic attribution of the gate and the dating of the stratum in question (VA–IVB) is treated more extensively and with further bibliography in my "Gate of Megiddo and the Debate on the Tenth Century," in *Congress Volume, Oslo, 1998* (ed. A. Lemaire; VTSup; Leiden: Brill, forthcoming). Because removal of the remaining structure seems impractical and may not be warranted by the results, a suggestion concerning possible excavation strategy is made there.

tion that archaeology is rarely able to bring to any short-term development other than destruction. The gate at Gezer is sandwiched between two destructions–presumably those of Shoshenq in the late 10th century, after Solomon, and of Solomon's pharaonic father-in-law, as reported in 1 Kgs 9:16. The fit is close, as in the case of Ahab and Jehu; the odds are that, in regard to gross political developments, Kings is providing the honest guff. At a minimum, we have further evidence of the operation of a state authority above the level of the individual site.[35]

Third, recent research at rural sites in the Lower Galilee makes it probable that a major change occurred in that region in the 10th century. Surveyors, such as Zvi Gal, report a huge increase in the foundation of settlements in this period. More recently, J. P. Dessel has investigated two settlements: Tel Wawiyat in the Beth Netopha Valley (with Tel Hannaton at its mouth) and Tel ʿEin Zippori, some 6 km to the south of Hannaton. His preliminary conclusion is that village sites in the region survived into the 10th century (in the case of Zippori) and were then perhaps supplanted by farmsteads. Whether this represents the operation of the United Monarchy, as Dessel suggests,[36] or Sheshonq's legacy is unclear. What is very likely, again, is that major social transformations mark the 10th century, as Kings suggests.

At the textual level, several further arguments can be advanced. First, 2 Samuel in large measure defends David against charges of murdering opponents from various sections of the country and factions of the body politic, in whom interest would be minimal in the Judah of the 9th century or thereafter.[37] Second, the actual literature about David's conquests in 2 Samuel is not nearly as expansive as the claims regarding Solomon's state in 1 Kings or subsequent sources.[38] Indeed, it is quite modest in restricting itself to the coast at Dor plus inland Cisjordan south of Abel Bet

35. See esp. W. G. Dever, "Monumental Architecture in Ancient Israel in the Period of the United Monarchy" in *Studies in the Period of David and Solomon and Other Essays* (ed. T. Ishida; Winona Lake, Ind.: Eisenbrauns, 1982) 269–306; idem, "Archaeology and the 'Age of Solomon': A Case-Study in Archaeology and Historiography" in *The Age of Solomon: Scholarship at the Turn of the Millennium* (ed. L. Handy; SHANE 11; Leiden: Brill, 1997) 217–51; Holladay, "The Kingdoms of Israel and Judah," in 368–98.

36. Dessel, private communication, 28 April 1996. For the Lower Galilee survey, see Z. Gal, *Lower Galilee during the Iron Age* (ASOR Dissertation Series 8; Winona Lake, Ind.: Eisenbrauns, 1992).

37. See my "Text and Artifact: Two Monologues?" in *The Archaeology of Israel: Constructing the Past, Interpreting the Present* (ed. N. A. Silberman and D. Small; JSOTSup 237; Sheffield: JSOT Press, 1997) 311–41.

38. See my "Construction of the Davidic Empire: An Exercise in Historiography," in *The Origins of the Ancient Israelite States* (ed. V. Fritz and P. R. Davies; JSOTSup 228; Sheffield: JSOT Press, 1997) 44–75.

Maacah, Edom, parts of Moab and Ammon, and the southern reaches of Damascus. Finally, the reportage regarding David and Solomon fits closely with the absence of great-power projection into Canaan during its period. Is this an accident precipitated by speculation from the 5th–2d centuries, or is it the result of consultation with historical sources? Obviously, the former explanation is to be eschewed, the more so in that sources from those eras uniformly presuppose a Davidic empire reaching the Euphrates.

None of this is altogether surprising to historians working with Kings. What is perhaps a little more shocking is the fact that the population of the territory of Israel exploded in the period preceding the monarchy, which is to say, in the 13th–11th centuries. While predictions of such an explosion came in advance of the surveys that confirmed it,[39] the facts in the ground clearly indicate that the biblical tradition of a premonarchic period of settlement and expansion is perfectly reasonable. Moreover, the excavation of Izbet Sartah (II) indicates either that social stratification preceded the onset of the Monarchy (so the excavators) or immediately followed it. In either case, the fit remains a tight one. Just before the explosion of the Iron I comes the reference to Israel in Merneptah's stele as well. The earliest reference to Israel thus derives from the late 13th century B.C.E., in conformity with the archaeological evidence that piles up during the next century for its presence in Canaan. Incidentally, in the handful of sites where paleozoological collection permits analysis, pig is notable for its almost complete absence from what we would normally identify as Israelite levels.[40] What is also of greatest interest is that the housing stock and its exploitation in Israelite areas clearly bespeaks a form of economic organization derived from a prestate background, one without significant centralized redistribution organized around household-based agrarian capitalism; at the same time, the evolution of sheep/goat ratios over time in the same settlements indicates the operation of complex exchange arrangements (focused on sheep) that demand the economic security offered only by state control.[41]

39. As in my *Emergence of Israel in Canaan* (SBLMS 29; Atlanta: Scholars Press, 1983).

40. This conclusion is heavily based on the work of B. Hesse and P. Wapnish. For bibliography, see my "Settlement of Canaan," *ABD* 5.1120–43.

41. On the housing stock, Holladay, "Kingdoms of Israel and Judah"; on the sheep/goat ratios, R. Redding, "Subsistence Security as a Selective Pressure Favoring Increasing Cultural Complexity" *Bulletin on Sumerian Agriculture* 7 (1993) 77–98; P. Wapnish and B. Hesse, "Mammal Remains from the Early Bronze Sacred Copmound," in *Megiddo III: The 1992–1996 Seasons* (ed. I. Finkelstein, D. Ussishkin, and B. Halpern; 2 vols.; Monograph Series 18; Tel Aviv: Tel Aviv University Institute of Archaeology, 2000) 2.429–62.

Contention about this early period is unending. Israelite material culture is virtually identical with that of settlements in Transjordan that would later be incorporated into Ammon and Moab. Some participants in the discussion have therefore argued that Israel was an indigenous, not allochthonous people, as the biblical account claims. It is probably an error to concern oneself with origins. It is a Heideggerian concern, a romantic concern, of the sort that led the Nazis to identify with some very elusive ancient Aryans. But the identity of Israelite and Ammonite or Moabite material culture in the Iron I is hardly evidence of anything other than that the same influences were at work on each, as distinct from the coasts and lowlands. In fact, much later biblical testimony claims that these cultures were of the same vintage, and indeed the same ancestry, as Israel's. The idea of "Hebrews," embracing everyone surviving in the region other than the Canaanites, Phoenicians, and Philistines, is very much an Israelite idea.[42]

Thus archaeology, epigraphy, and the critical assessment of biblical texts all land us in the same place. This leaves the question, why are the *fin-de-siècle* revisionists so insistent? Back as late as the 1970s, the standard histories of ancient Israel (with the exception of the "critical" textbook of Martin Noth for the early history) were nothing more than asymptotes of the biblical record. What Kings said was the history. What Exodus said was the history. Sometimes, what Genesis said was the history. Figures such as W. F. Albright, John Bright, G. E. Mendenhall, and E. A. Speiser were still holding the line on the existence of a "patriarchal age."

No one with a whiff of independent intellectual integrity on the subject accepted this on an a priori basis as likely. First of all, the evidence for the patriarchal age was at its best evidence of the antiquity of some practices possibly reflected in the narratives. That such practices might have survived after their early attestation was never taken into account (this was the essence of Van Seters's critique) and, as Thompson argued, they may have been mismatched to the narratives. Kenneth Kitchen argues the reverse, and there is a great deal to be said for his point of view. The fact remains, however, that the "Albrightian" defense of the patriarchs as "historical" led the way to serious fissures in the sociology of the field.

The similar accounts of the Exodus in JEPD and the Psalms and Prophets have long occasioned problems. Starting at least in the 1850s, critical scholars attempted to make sense of them, without according them unquestioned fidelity. Even more egregious was the account of Joshua's conquest. Archaeology, to which Albright and others, such as

42. Deut 2:5, 9–12, 19–25; 3:1–17, with the JP folk genealogy in Gen 10:25–30, 11:14–22. See further my "Settlement of Canaan."

Yadin, long appealed to sustain the Bible's claims, in the end completely infirmed them.

The inevitable revolt against the tyranny of orthodoxy was led by some of the scholars now regarded as representatives of extreme positions–Van Seters, Thompson, Ahlström–and also by other figures–for example, Donald Redford. These scholars were in large measure merely following the lead of continental scholars such as Noth and Engnell, themselves heirs to scholars of the 19th century, who had already indicted the testimony of the book of Joshua on the basis of materials in Judges. The modern representatives of this movement, such as Lemche and Cryer, have naturally gone much further than the preceding generation ever meant to go.

In sum, the reaction against tradition is emotional, not intellectual. Or to put it differently, it is difficult to separate the issues of emotion from issues of the intellect. This is the origin of the field of biblical studies recapitulated: the Deists, such as Jefferson and Payne, scoffed at inconsistencies and contradictions; the defenders of the faith, such as Richard Simon and Jean Astruc, discovered source-criticism and claimed Moses or some subsequent figure had divergent sources on which to rely. The higher criticism was in fact invented as a defense against attacks on the Church.

The original Deist critique of the reliability of biblical narrative was almost exclusively focused on the Pentateuch, where it is ringingly appropriate–it was applied to myths and legends whose character was not materially different from the character of Greek tales about the generations before the Trojan War and often used information in the Former Prophets as a standard against which to find Pentateuchal claims wanting (it was, in this sense, truly historical-critical). Nowhere is this Pentateuchal orientation clearer today than in the work of Davies, Thompson, and Van Seters who, finding no formal distinction between Kings and Genesis or Exodus, declare that both are cut from the same epistemic cloth. Earlier readers were not so insensitive to genre. Only a late-20th-century philologist would expect to see a formal distinction between legend presented as though it were historical and history presented as such. Only a philologist would expect history to be devoid of untruth.

The difference between history, which is one type of fiction, and romance, which is an altogether different type of fiction, is that the historian tries to avoid communicating what was not so. To this end, particularly in antiquity, the historian might use vehicles of presentation–speeches, for example, explicitly in Thucydides, but also psychologizing, assignment of abstract causation (for example, economics, geopolitics, providence, luck) –that are literally false but communicate a view of what the issues were at the time.

This is a condition that modern history has not altogether escaped: the work of scholars such as Simon Schama or C. V. Wedgewood or E. H. Carr continues to be imbued with elements of presentation that are false at the literal level but that communicate aspects of their reconstruction. Thus, understanding history requires that the reader be able to distinguish literal statements from the intent with which they are made. This is certainly never a subject of philological training and is rarely a concern and often dismissed altogether in the contemporary training of literary critics. Yet even outdated works of history, even works that were dead wrong, remain works of history after their reconstructions are discredited. Accuracy is not a measure of historiographic haecceity. In history, conscious intention is everything. Thompson's work is history, even if I thoroughly disagree with it. Amazing then that he does not accord the same courtesy to his ancient colleagues, in light of clear evidence that they were trying their best, in 2 Samuel and Kings, to get things right.

And this looks as though it were again a projection from contemporary, scholarly, politics. A recent article by Lemche and Thompson[43] invokes a series of methodological issues (falsifiability, among other bugbears) to accuse opponents of "the worst abuses of the biblical archaeological movement of the 1930s–1960s," of "fundamentalist reading of the Bible," and other iniquities. But there is a difference, it seems to me as a reader of history, between taking Kings seriously, as Lemche's and Thompson's opponents do, and relying on Genesis or Arthurian legend. Lemche and Thompson and other "minimalists" equate, at least in their rhetoric, any reliance on Kings, however critical (for example, the view that a United Monarchy did exist), with the wholesale historical acceptance of the Garden of Eden story.[44] But in this failure to distinguish the categories represented in myth and folklore from categories reflected by the synchronistic chronologies and multiple historiographic and archaeological correlations in Kings, the "minimalists" reveal that they are readers unsympathetic to the *intention*, to the meaning rather than the exact words, of the texts they are interpreting. They are, in a word, the ultimate positivists, for their logic dictates that any error at all in a source, any inaccuracy, shows that the source is not at all historical in character but a mere composite of fantasies. A reading that relies on the source, then, is "fundamentalist," motivated by blind ideological commitment.

What is fundamentalism in fact? It is the unwillingness to distinguish between the parts of the text (or the parts of an ideology) according to their genre and according to the question being asked of them. It is the

43. Lemche and Thompson, "Did Biran Kill David?" 3–22.

44. Ibid., 17–18.

insistence on a homogeneous and universal applicability—to the past, to the present, to the future—of the text or of the ideology. One can fight fundamentalism with fundamentalism of another sort—another refusal to distinguish genres. But this is ultimately sterile. Nor is the response to fundamentalism of much use. To know, after all, that David existed is to know very little indeed. To reason that he founded a dynastic state from biblical, archaeological, and, now, epigraphic evidence says next to nothing about his methods or achievements. The best evidence for these remains the biblical record; and yet, that record is precisely the propaganda of his dynasty and is extremely unreliable in its particulars.[45] Reasoned deconstruction of what are often exaggerated claims, typical of Near Eastern royal texts, is the only method by which some sort of historical reality can be approximated. Jettisoning the texts altogether, even for the purpose of keeping archaeologists honest, will not generate positive results. Nor is it the case that the material evidence entitles one to bypass the necessary critical engagement with historiography, literature, political commentary, divination, cosmological speculation, epigraphs, statues, reliefs, paintings, glyptics, and the like. These, too, demand careful reflection before any attempt at correlation with the archaeological record can be made. There are no short-cuts to any sophisticated grasp of ancient reality. No fundamentalism—no doctrine either of inerrancy or of complete errancy—is a substitute for working out the historical processes that generated the evidence, of all sorts, as we have it. One can never rely on a historical work. And one cannot simply dismiss historiography with accurate information, out of hand.

As the minister responsible for Britain's rearmament, Sir Winston Leonard Spencer Churchill once replied to the question "Where will it all end?" "The gentleman reminds me," he said, "of the man who received a telegram from Brazil informing him that his mother-in-law had died, and asking for instructions. He answered, 'Embalm, cremate, bury at sea. Take no chances!'" At the base of the extremism of contemporary "minimalism" lies a hysteria no less profound than that one. One may question the motives of the hysteria. They differ in different scholars. One can probably do no better than to quote that eminent American authority, Salder Bupp:

> Of Roman history,
> Great Niebuhr's shown,

45. In "Text and Artifact," as noted, I argue that 2 Samuel's main purpose is to acquit David of charges of serial murder, of which he was very likely guilty, and that the implication is that it stems from David's reign or the early part of Solomon's. Contemporary records tend to put a heavy spin on events (see my "Construction of the Davidic State"), while later ones tend to embellish them more shamelessly.

'Tis nine-tenths lying.
Faith, I wish 'twere known,
Ere we accept Great Niebuhr as a guide,
Wherein he blundered, and how much he lied.[46]

It is neither my brief nor my instinct to defend the detailed allegations of Kings and Samuel. All the same, the general picture these texts present of international relations in Iron II is fully consonant with external sources, with archaeological evidence, and with common sense. In addition, all manner of linguistic evidence–not susceptible to quick presentation here–coincides with this verdict.[47] Did Niebuhr lie? The answer is, he didn't really understand the evidence as we do today. Did Thompson and Lemche kill Biran? The answer is, they are laying down lines for the future, as Niebuhr did. But the most effective means of charting the future would be to take into account all of the data–properly philological, historiographic, archaeological–and account for it in detail. This is the stage to which the discussion must now turn and, if either the "fundamentalists" or the "minimalists" are to keep up with those between, they too must join in precisely such a dialogue.

46. Cited in Salder Bupp, "History," *The Devil's Dictionary* (New York: Oxford University Press, 1999).

47. I have shared some of the linguistic evidence with Ron Hendel, whose own argument to related conclusions appears in "Finding Historical Memories in the Patriarchal Narratives," *BARev* (July–August 1993) 52–57, 72. In addition to the materials forthcoming in my *History of Israel*, note that Rezin (*rn) is represented *rzn* in 1 Kings but *rṣn* in 2 Kings and Isaiah. This change is remarkable in several respects, but the early (and unrepresentative) reflection of the phoneme is clear evidence that there was a difference between the reception of Aramaic phonology in the 10th century and in the 8th. The two dental plosive emphatics of proto-Semitic were the least stable elements in West Semitic philology, and their phonemic representations remained polyphonous into the 7th century in many dialects. The regularization of their realization at the phonemic and phonetic levels by the late 6th century provides a chronological lever for dating material to periods before the Persian era, including parts of JE, Samuel, and Kings.

New Directions in the Study of Biblical Hebrew Narrative

DAVID M. GUNN

The premise of this essay is that the older disciplines of historical criticism and the history and religion of Israel have failed and that the shift to a new "literary" paradigm in the study of the Hebrew Bible is well established (already in 1987). This is so much the case that the term *literary criticism* can no longer be used, without qualification, for the analysis of texts into the underlying units from which they were deemed to have been composed. And Gunn declares independence, on behalf of the newer literary approaches, from historical critical enquiry. This puts the present essay in quite a different category from most of the other methodological essays included here. It finds an echo in the present volume in D. Jobling's article on 1 Samuel (pp. 601–14).

Gunn does not enter the debates concerning the number of redactions in the DH and their respective meanings and intentions. Rather, he is interested centrally in the relationship between text, reader, and meaning. This requires thinking afresh about literary boundaries, and in this connection he shows that the concept of "books," as well as of accepted literary blocks such as the DH and the Pentateuch, are not immune to reevaluation. In advocating such reevaluation, his main interest is not historical criticism but what he sees as the error of some newer literary approaches, typified by M. Sternberg (*The Poetics of Biblical Narrative* [Bloomington: Indiana University Press, 1985]), which assume that the reader can discover the voice of the "reliable narrator." The important issue facing readers of the Hebrew Bible is not the relative merits of synchronic and diachronic analyses but the concept of a "normative meaning." Such a concept, for him, is complicated by questions of limits, that is, canonical questions, as well as by intrinsic problems of understanding texts, particularly whether statements made by the narrator might be

Reprinted with permission from *Journal for the Study of the Old Testament* 39 (1987).

Author's note: [[This was originally]] a paper delivered to the Rhetorical Criticism Section: "Directions in Biblical Literature," SBL Annual Meeting, November 23, 1986.

ironical. Gunn brings into the open, therefore, the interrelatedness of literary and canonical questions, or put differently, hermeneutical and theological ones, which are often not articulated in historical and traditional literary-critical studies. Whether, as he proposes, the traditional historical and the newer literary types of study can simply proceed independently of each other must remain an open question.

⟦65⟧ Plainly things have changed. The study of narrative in the Hebrew Bible has altered dramatically in the past ten years, at least as far as professional biblical studies is concerned. That is now a truism. Nor has there been any lack of commentators charting that change. This brief paper, therefore, risks offering more of the obvious by presenting some further thoughts about directions that have been taken and directions that might be taken in our field of study.

So striking is the change, it has led me on more than one occasion to suggest that "literary criticism" was becoming, has become perhaps, the new orthodoxy in biblical studies. But perhaps I enjoy overstating the position and, in any case, the varieties of "literary approach," present and foreseeable, look like having the potential to fracture any too neat party line that might emerge to choke the reading of the Hebrew Bible.

Nevertheless, I believe it is true to say that criticism of biblical texts using the reading methods of contemporary critics of other bodies of literature has, in a relatively short time, become entrenched among the disciplines of the professional guild of biblical critics and will not go away in a hurry. Inexorably the label "literary criticism" is being displaced as the label for "source criticism" or "source analysis," a symbolic displacement.

If the historical critics still dominate, the domination is fast eroding. Already the textbooks are beginning to appear that signal the shift–Norman Gottwald's *The Hebrew Bible* ⟦1985⟧ pays attention to ⟦66⟧ the new literary approaches, though in my view this material hovers still on the fringes of his work, while James Crenshaw's *Story and Faith* ⟦1986⟧ goes further, basing his book (like Brevard Childs's pioneering *Introduction* ⟦1979⟧) on the shape of the Hebrew canon rather than an historical scheme and taking seriously questions of aesthetic criticism. There are many of us who look forward to the introductory textbook which radically reverses the present priority and consistently (and logically) places literary questions–which might include, in the case of narrative texts, attention to structure, plot, informational gaps, redundancy, allusion, metaphor, modes of speech, point of view, irony–ahead of questions of history and development.

The life-force of modern historical criticism was a determination to deal with the biblical text in the same way as secular texts were treated, even if that should lead to the shaking of some dearly held verities. And that assumption, ironically, is at the heart of the current challenge which historical criticism faces–a challenge to both its notion of history and its notion of a text.

For two hundred years Western biblical criticism has been concerned with the question of historicity (the history of Israel) and with the history of biblical literature. The two ran hand in glove, for without the one the other could not be written. Despite some spectacular successes, the major failure of both programs is now becoming obvious.

What compositional units have been securely established and dated (beyond, that is, the mere convenience of consensus)? Even those cornerstones of historical critical endeavor, the Pentateuch and (to a lesser extent) the book of Isaiah are currently the subject of rethinking, some of it radical, in this regard (see, e.g., Rendtorff [[1977, 1986]], Van Seters [[1975]], Merendino [[1981]], Schmitt [[1979]], Vincent [[1977]]). It is no exaggeration to say that the truly assured results of historical critical scholarship concerning authorship, date and provenance would fill but a pamphlet.

As for the history of Israel, the problems confronting this enterprise are daunting. Of particular concern for our present subject are those that are intimately bound up with the historian's understanding of the nature of biblical texts, especially the major narrative texts. Miller and Hayes in their major new volume (*A History of Ancient Israel and Judah* [[1986]]) are unwilling to discuss the history of Israel before the "eve of the establishment of the monarchy" (in practice Solomon is their starting point), and thereafter are constantly admitting to the fact that what follows is largely [[67]] intelligent guesswork. Yet, as Burke Long has remarked in a review of their work [[1987]], despite the

> reordering and evaluating, occasional discarding and rewriting of the Biblical tradition, the fact remains that, without much of either corroborative or disconfirming information from outside the Bible, Miller and Hayes have swallowed the biggest pill of all: they follow the large outline [of Kings], the as-found built-in selectivity, the perspectives and implicit evaluations implied by an ancient writer's choices, and the causal coherence (supposedly separated out from divine agency) at the heart of the version of history they chose to depend on. In short, because they cannot write from sources, they must write from historiography, and from a single one at that.

In other words, he suggests, this "history" is still essentially a paraphrase of the books of Kings. If there is to emerge something *other* than a paraphrase it will come, it seems to me, through the efforts of the social-world critics, using models drawn from sociology and anthropology, recognizing patterns of material organization (the domain of actions) in mute remains, and seeking in the texts the embedded data which encodes some of the cultural or ideational concerns (the domain of notions) of the society (see Flanagan). The result will be nothing like a what-happened-next history, its periodization will be broad, and it will depend upon literary criticism (including structuralist criticism) for its appropriation of texts.

The move away from historical critical study gained impetus from a variety of sources, including the rise of canon criticism and its concern for the final form of the text (Childs ⟦1979⟧). Dissatisfaction has also stemmed from a renewed appreciation of what critics in other disciplines are doing with, and saying about, texts and criticism. Earlier in the 1970s this showed up in two ways (amongst others), one, the importing of structuralist modes of analysis into the study of biblical narrative (and it was mostly on narrative), especially in France and through the pages of *Semeia* in the United States, and the other, the growth of close reading loosely related to what has become known as the "New Criticism." With this latter movement belonged essentially James Muilenburg's "rhetorical criticism" which influenced the work of a number of key pupils (I think, for example, of James Ackerman ⟦1974, 1982⟧ at Indiana University, himself a figure of significant influence), and new critical concerns were much in evidence in the work of others both within the United States and elsewhere (as, for example, in Europe, Luis Alonso Schökel, to whom David Clines and ⟦68⟧ I in England early looked for support). If structuralism was more theoretically sophisticated and had, as I believe, a powerful effect in promoting the legitimacy of synchronic study of the text, it could also be somewhat arcane and remote from the non-afficionado. (The work of David Jobling ⟦1986⟧ has served a notable mediating function.) It has been, above all, the "new critical" interest in the surface composition of the text that has continued to generate and reform critical practice among the readers of biblical narrative; and although much of this work has appeared in the form of short essays, lengthier treatments of more extensive texts are beginning to appear (see recently, e.g., Eslinger ⟦1985⟧ and Miscall ⟦1983, 1986⟧).

Robert Alter's timely book on the "art" of biblical narrative ⟦1981⟧ capped this movement of the seventies and gave it a huge fillip. Adele Berlin's book on the poetics of biblical narrative ⟦1983⟧ also stands in this tradition–concerned with the mechanics, the how, of narrative composition and the discipline involved in moving from mechanics to meaning. Meir Sternberg's recent book on poetics ⟦1985⟧ moves such a narratology into a whole new dimension of discrimination and sophistication and will be fundamental to the emerging generation of narrative critics (reading Sternberg will be the new graduate hurdle, equivalent to reading Martin Noth in German!). So let me dwell on this book for a moment.

Brilliant as Sternberg's poetics is, I would risk suggesting that his *hermeneutic* is less satisfying. At base he seems to be saying that the narrative offers a determinable meaning, determinable through the practice of sophisticated reading habits. Despite the ambiguities of the text, despite the gaps (about which he has excellent things to say), there is security to be found in the reliable narrator who is aligned with God, and offers the voice of divine authority. (God, it almost seems, is author, narrator and main character.) Ambiguities, tensions, gaps, multivalence–these should not deflect the reader from perceiving in the text its ideological truth. The ideological concerns the reader brings can and must be filtered out, allowing an essentially objective deployment of reading technique which will enable the sifting of right and wrong readings and the delineation of that authoritative voice. It is rather like the classical distinction between exegesis and interpretation–the distinction between discovering the root meaning and applying or relating it to oneself or one's social context. Exegesis is the discovery of the truth in the text. To listen to Sternberg (always an immensely stimulating thing to do) is to get the impression of having finally found the path to truth-in-the-text. [[69]] "Interpretation" is not his concern. In other words, such a poetics seems to be still moored, theoretically speaking, to something like the new critical position of the text-in-itself as the locus of meaning. Perhaps this is to misunderstand him or misstate his position. But I gnaw at the matter because it touches a fundamental question of direction.

It has become my conviction, if not always affecting my critical practice, that the major challenge to biblical criticism mounted by literary criticism cannot be expressed in terms simply of a shift from "diachronic" to "synchronic" analysis but rather involves the question of normative reading. This is especially so for those many among biblical scholars who are interested in theology and, in whatever tradition, the authority of the Bible. For it seems clear to me that those theorists who recognize the reader's inextricable role in the production of meaning in texts have the future on their side (see Culler [[1982]], Detweiler [[1985]], Eagleton [[1983]], Suleiman and Crosman [[1980]]; cf. Barton [[1984]], Keegan [[1985]]). That is not to say that Sternberg is not interested in the reader. On the contrary, he would claim, rightly, to be extremely concerned to chart the ways in which manipulations of text manipulate readers. But others would say, more radically, that meaning is also and always the manipulation of the text by the reader. "Readers make sense," as Edgar McKnight nicely puts it (1985: 12). There is no poetics, however discriminating, that will settle the question of meaning (for a provocatively indeterminate reading of Samuel, see Miscall [[1986]]). There is no objective, ideologically sterile reader to appropriate an ideological prescription embedded in the text.

Reader-oriented theory legitimizes the relativity of different readings and thus threatens to unnerve conventional understandings of biblical authority. This has already happened at the level of critical practice through the challenge of feminist criticism (cf. Fewell [[1987]])–which, even when deployed in a seemingly new-critical mode, as for example by Phyllis Trible [[1978, 1984]], operatives out of convictions about reading that align closely with reader-oriented theory. The step from Trible's kind of reading (especially in *Texts of Terror* [[1984]]) to "deconstructionist" criticism is but a short and natural one: deconstruction appears to offer powerful opportunities to feminist and other critics, whose reading is overt in its ideological (or theological) commitment. Many religiously conservative/orthodox critics are finding in literary criticism (especially of "historical" narrative) a refuge from the hobgoblin of historicity. Yet my prediction is that [[70]] troubling times lie ahead as the reader theory of the secular critics begins to corrode the edges of normative exegesis and doctrines of biblical authority which insist on viewing the Bible as divine prescription. The problem of the gap between "original setting and intention" and "contemporary interpretation" will merely have given place to the gap between reader and reader.

In one sense, therefore, we might say that there has not really been a change at all: the more it changes the more it is the same–there will be no end of readings and reflections and papers and books and the endless round of exegetical and theological disputation. Yet in the midst of all that there are great possibilities for a resurgence of participation in the joy of critical reading–by scholarly, student and lay readers alike. Biblical narrative read critically through an orientation to the reader's experience and commitment has great power to enliven that experience, especially in the context of a particular community of readers and the sharing of readings. I see the beginnings of this both in writing and in changing methods of studying biblical narrative (and in this regard readers in the Western "first world" countries have something important to learn from the reading practices of the "base communities" of Central America).

We have moved from the poetics of biblical narrative to more general talk of hermeneutics. Let me come back to poetics and raise an issue that relates closely, I think, to the question of (in)determinacy and the relativizing of readings. Sternberg is but giving clear voice to general practice when he emphasizes as he does the reliability of the biblical narrator. In the spirit of deconstruction, let me cast doubt on this conventional and convenient reading assumption.

One has only to take the story of David, a favorite among the newer critics, to make the point that the narrator seems to have gone to some lengths to subvert this notion of reliability. The story has hardly started before we are faced with what most of us here would recognize as two factually irreconcilable accounts of the young David's arrival at court. Sternberg (as Alter previously) may speak of the provision of depth and perspective to the portrait, yet that does not really address the issue of reliability. And, of course, the classic disrupter is yet to come (2 Sam 21:19)—who *did* kill Goliath? When the books of Samuel are read in their final form (which Sternberg does not do) this question cannot be dismissed lightly (unless the reader wishes to pull historical-critical rabbits out of the hat). I would suggest that the so-called supplement at the end of 2 Samuel can be read as having a complex role of subversion to play, [[71]] reinforcing rival views of David that have already come into focus and forcibly pulling our attention back to this very issue of the narrator's reliability that faced us at the onset. That is all part of an engineered collapse of reader confidence as the story of the great king fragments to an end.

When Samuel–Kings is read alongside Chronicles, where is the reliable narrator? Where for that matter is the reliable narrator of the four Gospels? Or, to put it another way: Who among the four narrators is reliable? What *did* Jesus say? We can only maintain an unsullied notion of a reliable narrator by maintaining the compositional segmentation of the Bible—and postulating whole hosts of narrators who have nothing to do with each other. So it is no small irony that Sternberg's poetics turns out to be still locked into historical criticism through the controls of source analysis, the old "literary criticism." I suppose my point is really a canonical one—reading biblical narrative in terms of its final form really is a more radical proposition than perhaps is realized by those who most enthusiastically have embraced the program (and mocked its historical-critical predecessor). Are the books of Samuel a book or not? Is this work a narrative? What about Deuteronomy to 2 Kings? Or the whole Hebrew canon? In each case, is the question whether we have "a" narrator, let alone a reliable one, real? In short, what counts as the poetics of biblical narrative depends on what the theorist means by biblical narrative. And it is time the theorists of poetics took seriously what Brevard Childs has been wrestling with for a decade and more.

Bearing also on the issue of the reliable narrator is a feature of literary works that has long fascinated me and is now gaining consistent attention from critics—namely, irony. When appealing to irony as an interpretive strategy I have been constantly rebuffed by those who counter that this is but a tactic of last resort. What I have come to realize is that such rebuttal is itself but a disguised declaration of the rebutter's critical ideology—very likely a by-produce of a commitment to a particular understanding of revelation and the authority of scripture. But as we attune ourselves to listening more openly for irony in biblical texts, we need to be thoroughgoing about it. It is one thing for characters to be presented trading ironic speech or action with each other—where the narrator lays out the elements of the irony in such a way as both to share its savor and yet to stay detached. What, however, if the irony be embedded in the very language that is being used by the narrator? It is inviting to read ⟦72⟧ thus the evaluations of David and Solomon in Kings, where the little word 'except' or 'only' (*raq*) harbors tremendous subversive possibilities (see 1 Kgs 3:3 [cf. 3:11!], 15:4 [cf. 9:4, 14:8]; and compare 2 Kgs 14:1–4 and 15:1–4, of Amaziah and Azariah). Another well-known passage well served by an ironic reading is Josh 11:23 ("So Joshua took the whole land, according to all that Yahweh had spoken to Moses"). Or, more radically, what if it is the *narrator* (rather than an explicit character within the discourse) who is the object of the irony (e.g., through the espousal of naive judgments, as in an alternative reading of those evaluations of David and Solomon)? If irony is at all pervasive in biblical narrative, as is increasingly being recognized, what makes us shy away from locating irony also in the treatment of the narrator by the (implied) author? The kind of formalist reading that Robert Polzin ⟦1980⟧ has offered of Deuteronomy to Judges suggests just this very possibility—the narrator is but one voice of several, and none is immune from undermining (and irony is a classic mode of undermining). Richard Nelson's treatment ⟦1988⟧ of Uspensky ⟦1973⟧ and the Deuteronomistic History leads in the same direction.

The issue of reliability is bound up with discriminations concerning point of view. This is a matter of crucial importance which will increasingly shape the direction of radical criticism of biblical narrative.

I close with a few further prognostications. First, I expect to see soon appearing some major new readings of extensive segments of narrative, with the book of Judges a favorite subject, Kings following hard in its wake, and soon the whole Deuteronomistic History. Yet as fast as that happens we shall see the demise of the Deuteronomistic History and the adoption of Genesis to 2 Kings as a standard unit (so already, from very different standpoints, both Miller and Hayes ⟦1986⟧ and Miscall 1986). (And readings of this unit which include the book of Ruth should gain some attention, at least from those concerned with the Christian canon.) We should also see growing interest in the poetics of the books of Chronicles, Ezra and Nehemiah, and, likewise, other monologue-oriented narrative such as we find in the Pentateuch and Joshua—it is here that we may see the growth of the kind of rhetorical analysis that has become a feature of New Testament studies, grounded in an understanding of the rhetorical manuals of the Greco-Roman world. And I come back to a subject briefly mentioned above: the impact of feminist criticism of biblical narrative is still only beginning to be felt—it will force some major [[73]] shifts in its own right. (A major new impetus may well come from Mieke Bal's work [[1985]], soon to appear in English [[1987]].)

One last thought, to end where I began (a good rhetorical principle)—with historical criticism. The cry is for a rapprochement between the old and the new. A few scholars have been able to accommodate this—I think of David Clines for one (both in *The Theme of the Pentateuch* [[1978]] and in his new book on Esther [[1984]]), of Lee Humphreys [[1985]] for another, and of that inimitable master of intersecting disciplines, Walter Brueggemann [[1985]]. But I think this will continue to be rare. I see separate roads for a long way ahead. My view is that, practically speaking in the doing of major varieties of literary criticism, historical critical inquiry does not make much contribution. It is not necessarily that it is wrong. It is just that it is going somewhere else.

Bibliography

Ackerman, James S.

1974 "The Literary Context of the Moses Birth Story," in Kenneth R. R. Gros Louis, ed., with James S. Ackerman and Thayer S. Warshaw, *Literary Interpretations of Biblical Narratives: Vol. I* (Nashville: Abingdon) 74–119.

1982 "Joseph, Judah, and Jacob," in Kenneth R. R. Gros Louis, ed., with James S. Ackerman, *Literary Interpretations of Biblical Narratives: Vol. II* (Nashville: Abingdon) 85–113.

Alter, Robert

1981 *The Art of Biblical Narrative* (New York: Basic Books).

Bal, Mieke

1985 *Femmes Imaginaires: L'Ancien Testament au risque d'une narratologie critique* (Montreal: Editions Hurtubise HMH; Utrecht: HES Uitgevers). [[English translation: *Lethal Love: Feminist Literary Readings of Biblical Love Stories* (Bloomington: Indiana University Press, 1987).]]

Barton, John

1984 *Reading the Bible: Method in Biblical Study* (London: SPCK and Philadelphia: Westminster).

Berlin, Adele

1983 *Poetics and Interpretation of Biblical Narrative* (Bible and Literature Series 9; Sheffield: Almond). [[Reprinted, Winona Lake, Indiana: Eisenbrauns, 1994.]] [[74]]

Brueggemann, Walter

1985 *David's Truth in Israel's Imagination and Memory* (Philadelphia: Fortress).

Childs, Brevard, S.

1979 *Introduction to the Old Testament as Scripture* (London: SCM and Philadelphia: Westminster).

Clines, David J. A.
1978 *The Theme of the Pentateuch* (JSOT Supplement Series 10; Sheffield: JSOT).
1984 *The Esther Scroll: The Story of the Story* (JSOT Supplement Series 30; Sheffield: JSOT).
Collins, Adela Yarbro (ed.)
1985 *Feminist Perspectives on Biblical Scholarship* (Chico, California: Scholars).
Crenshaw, James L.
1986 *Story and Faith: A Guide to the Old Testament* (New York: Macmillan).
Culler, Jonathan
1982 *On Deconstruction: Theory and Criticism after Structuralism* (Ithaca, New York: Cornell University).
Detweiler, Robert
1985 *Reader Response Approaches to Biblical and Secular Texts* (= *Semeia* 31; Decatur, Georgia: Scholars).
Eagleton, Terry
1983 *Literary Theory: An Introduction* (Minneapolis: University of Minnesota).
Eslinger, Lyle
1985 *Kingship of God in Crisis: A Close Reading of 1 Samuel 1–12* (Bible and Literature Series 10; Sheffield: Almond).
Fewell, Danna Nolan
1987 "Feminist Reading of the Hebrew Bible: Affirmation, Resistance and Transformation," *Journal for the Study of the Old Testament* 39: 77–87.
[[Flanagan, J. W.
1985 "History as Hologram: Integrating Literary, Archaeological, and Comparative Sociological Evidence," *SBL Seminar Papers, 1985* (ed. K. H. Richards; Atlanta: Scholars Press) 291–314.]]
Gottwald, Norman K.
1985 *The Hebrew Bible: A Socio-Literary Introduction* (Philadelphia: Fortress).
Gunn, David M.
1980 *The Fate of King Saul: An Interpretation of a Biblical Story* (JSOT Supplement Series 14; Sheffield: JSOT).
[[1989]] "In Security: The David of Biblical Narrative," *Semeia* [forthcoming]. [[This has now appeared in *Signs and Wonders: Biblical Texts in Literary Focus* (ed. J. C. Exum; Semeia Studies; Atlanta: Scholars Press) 133–51.]]
Humphreys, W. Lee
1985 *The Tragic Vision and the Hebrew Tradition* (Overtures to Biblical Theology; Philadelphia: Fortress).
Jobling, David
1986 *The Sense of Biblical Narrative: Structural Analyses in the Hebrew Bible*. Vols. 1 and 2 (JSOT Supplements 7 and 39; Sheffield: JSOT). [The first edn. of vol. 1 appeared in 1978.]
Keegan, Terence J.
1985 *Interpreting the Bible: A Popular Introduction to Biblical Hermeneutics* (Mahwah: Paulist).

Long, Burke O.
1987 "On Finding the Hidden Premises," *Journal for the Study of the Old Testament* 39: 10–14. [[75]]
McKnight, Edgar V.
1985 *The Bible and the Reader: An Introduction to Literary Criticism* (Philadelphia: Fortress).
Merendino, R. P.
1981 *Der Erste und der Letzte* (Vetus Testamentum Supplements 31; Leiden: Brill).
Miller, J. Maxwell, and John H. Hayes
1986 *A History of Ancient Israel and Judah* (Philadelphia: Westminster).
Miscall, Peter D.
1983 *The Workings of Old Testament Narrative* (Semeia Studies; Philadelphia: Fortress and Chico, California: Scholars).
1986 *1 Samuel: A Literary Reading* (Indiana Studies in Biblical Literature; Bloomington, Indiana: Indiana University).
Nelson, Richard D.
1988 "The Anatomy of the Book of Kings," *Journal for the Study of the Old Testament* [[40: 39–48]].
Polzin, Robert M.
1980 *Moses and the Deuteronomist: A Literary Study of the Deuteronomic History, Part One: Deuteronomy, Joshua, Judges* (New York: Seabury).
Rendtorff, Rolf
1977 "The 'Yahwist' as Theologian? The Dilemma of Pentateuchal Criticism," *Journal for the Study of the Old Testament* 3: 2–10 (and see the further discussion, pp. 11–60).
1986 *The Old Testament: An Introduction* (translated from the German by John Bowden; Philadelphia: Fortress) 157–64.
Russell, Letty M. (ed.)
1985 *Feminist Interpretation of the Bible* (Philadelphia: Westminster).
Schmitt, H.-C.
1979 "Prophetie und Schultheologie im Deuterojesajabuch," *Zeitschrift für die Alttestamentliche Wissenschaft* 91: 43–61.
Sternberg, Meir
1985 *The Poetics of Biblical Narrative: Ideological Literature and the Drama of Reading* (Indiana Studies in Biblical Literature; Bloomington, Indiana: Indiana University).
Suleiman, Susan, and Inge Crosman (eds.)
1980 *The Reader in the Text: Essays on Audience and Interpretation* (Princeton: Princeton University).
Trible, Phyllis
1978 *God and the Rhetoric of Sexuality* (Overtures to Biblical Theology; Philadelphia: Fortress).

1984 *Texts of Terror: Literary-Feminist Readings of Biblical Narratives* (Overtures to Biblical Theology; Philadelphia: Fortress).

Uspensky, Boris

1973 *A Poetics of Composition: The Structure of the Artistic Text and Typology of a Compositional Form* (translated from the Russian by Valentina Zavarin and Susan Wittig; Berkeley, Los Angeles/London: University of California).

Van Seters, John

1975 *Abraham in History and Tradition* (New Haven and London: Yale University).

Vincent, J. M.

1977 *Studien zur literarischen Eigenart und zur geistigen Heimat von Jesaja, Kap. 40–55* (Beiträge zur biblischen Exegese und Theologie 5; Frankfurt and Bern: Peter Lang).

The Centre Cannot Hold

Thematic and Textual Instabilities in Judges

J. Cheryl Exum

The essay represents one type of the newer literary study of the Old Testament narratives. It is a "final form" reading of Judges, in which Exum quite consciously puts her study into direct dialogue with the conventional critical theory of "deuteronomistic" authorship. In this respect hers is like all interpretations that imply that the narratives are subtler than the conventional interpretations have realized. Her use of the concept of irony, for example, has echoes in the work of Lillian Klein (*The Triumph of Irony in the Book of Judges* [JSOTSup 68; Sheffield: JSOT Press, 1988]) and Barry Webb (*The Book of the Judges* [JSOTSup 46; Sheffield: JSOT Press, 1987]). Yet she goes further. The heart of her argument is that the structural pattern, as postulated by the deuteronomistic theory, breaks down, and this is a sign of dissolution consistent with the theme of the book. The disturbance of such patterns, moreover, is part of an aim to disturb conventional ways of thinking about God and Israel. Her reading, which has something in common with that of Robert Polzin (*Moses and the Deuteronomist* [New York: Seabury, 1980]), may therefore be called "deconstructionist." She hints that such a reading, if extended to the historical books more widely, would necessitate some rethinking of the deuteronomistic theory.

[[410]] The book of Judges exhibits an enigmatic complexity; so much transpires on different levels that multiple interpretations are inevitable, as the plurality of views in current scholarship illustrates. Judges is frequently dissected into a series of unrelated deliverer stories plus other traditional material (e.g., the "minor judges"), held together by a deuteronomistic

Reprinted with permission from *Catholic Biblical Quarterly* 52 (1990) 410–31.

framework illustrating the retributive cycle of disobedience/oppression/appeal for help/deliverance (a pattern that does not actually hold true). The apparent lack of clear lines of diachronic development in Judges poses a challenge for a holistic literary reading, a challenge recent literary studies have only begun to address.[1] The present study suggests a coherent literary interpretation of [[411]] the book by focusing on (1) the increasingly problematic character of its human protagonists,[2] and (2) what to my knowledge has been a generally neglected area, the increasingly ambiguous role of the deity.[3] Most commentators deal with Judges in terms of Israel's sin,

1. Yairah Amit, "The Art of Composition in the Book of Judges" (Ph.D. dissertation: Tel Aviv University, 1984 [Hebrew]); David M. Gunn, "Joshua and Judges," *The Literary Guide to the Bible* (ed. R. Alter and F. Kermode; Cambridge, MA: Harvard University, 1987); Barry G. Webb, *The Book of the Judges: An Integrated Reading* (JSOTSup 46; Sheffield: JSOT, 1987); Lillian R. Klein, *The Triumph of Irony in the Book of Judges* (JSOTSup 68; Bible and Literature Series 14; Decatur, GA: Almond, 1988). Most influential on my analysis have been Robert Polzin, *Moses and the Deuteronomist: A Literary Study of the Deuteronomic History*, Part 1 (New York: Seabury, 1980) and D. W. Gooding, "The Composition of the Book of Judges," *ErIsr* 16 (1982) 70–79. The parallels are more extensive than Gooding's brief analysis is able to show. If Samson balances Othniel because of the theme of intermarriage with nationals versus marriage within one's own group, the Samson story also balances the Song of Deborah, with Delilah and Jael taking on similar roles (Gooding matches Jael with Abimelech's killer). As Gooding observes, Jephthah is like Ehud in that both do battle at the fords of the Jordan, but he is more like Gideon, who disputes with Ephraim. Webb notes many instances of cross-referencing, as does Robert G. Boling, *Judges* (AB 6A; Garden City, NY: Doubleday, 1975). In addition to the sources mentioned below, see also M. Buber, "Books of Judges and Book of Judges," *Kingship of God* (3d ed.; Harper Torchbooks; New York: Harper & Row, 1967) 66–84; J. P. U. Lilley, "A Literary Appreciation of the Book of Judges," *TynBul* 18 (1967) 94–102; and Dennis J. McCarthy, "The Wrath of Yahweh and the Structural Unity of the Deuteronomistic History," *Essays in Old Testament Ethics (J. Philip Hyatt, In Memoriam)* (ed. J. L. Crenshaw and J. T. Willis; New York: Ktav, 1974) 97–110. W. J. Dumbrell ("'In Those Days There Was No King in Israel; Every Man Did What Was Right in His Own Eyes': The Purpose of the Book of Judges Reconsidered," *JSOT* 25 [1983] 23–33) examines Judges as an editorial unity; Boling (*Judges*, 29–38), as a redactional unity. For insightful analyses of the framework, see E. Theodore Mullen, Jr., "The 'Minor Judges': Some Literary and Historical Considerations," *CBQ* 44 (1982) 185–201; and Frederick E. Greenspahn, "The Theology of the Framework of Judges," *VT* 36 (1986) 385–96. On the editing of Judges, see Baruch Halpern, *The First Historians: The Hebrew Bible and History* (San Francisco: Harper & Row, 1988) 121–40.

2. Polzin (*Moses and the Deuteronomist*), Gooding ("Composition"), Webb (*Judges*), Klein, (*Triumph of Irony*), and K. R. R. Gros Louis ("The Book of Judges," *Literary Interpretations of Biblical Narratives* [ed. K. R. R. Gros Louis with J. S. Ackerman and T. S. Warshaw; Nashville: Abingdon, 1974] 141–62) recognize in the so-called deuteronomistic framework (esp. 2:11–23 and passim) the theological clue to the present arrangement of Judges and point to a decline in the character of the judges as illustrative of the chaos of the time.

3. God is, after all, a character in the narrative, to be examined in the same way as the other characters. A crucial difference is that God alone acts, paradoxically, both to further and to thwart the fortunes of Israel, or, to put it in structuralist terms, who fills the roles of both sender and opponent.

its disobedience and lack of trust in Yhwh, its turning to other gods. In doing so, they are often at pains to exonerate God, to demonstrate that Israel alone bears responsibility for its suffering. In proposing here a reading that acknowledges God's complicity in the dissolution that takes place in Judges, I shall focus on a particular dimension of the text that resists easy solutions. This dimension reflects the uncertain, sometimes ambivalent, nature of reality, about which the Bible is disarmingly honest. Occasionally auspicious and reassuring moments relieve the vision of moral and social deterioration in Judges, but on the whole, increasing corruption and an atmosphere of hopelessness characterize the book. A corresponding dissolution of coherence occurs at the book's structural level.

The deuteronomistic framework presented in 2:11–23, and immediately illustrated by the judge Othniel in 3:7–11, provides the theoretical and theological context and a preview of the stories that follow. It is not, as often observed, a pattern of apostasy/punishment/repentance/deliverance but [[412]] rather one of apostasy/punishment/cry for help/deliverance (or as Robert Polzin puts it, punishment/mercy).[4] Although we are led to expect a consistent and regular pattern, what happens is that the framework itself breaks down.[5] Rather than attributing the lack of consistency in the framework pattern to careless redaction, I take it as a sign of further dissolution. The political and moral instability depicted in Judges is reflected in the textual instability. The framework deconstructs itself, so to speak, and the cycle of apostasy and deliverance becomes increasingly murky.

Within the framework occur the stories of the "major judges" or "charismatic deliverers," to use two common descriptions.[6] All are unlikely heroes in some sense: Ehud is left-handed or "bound in his right hand" (perhaps ambidextrous [LXX, Vg]); Shamgar is an obscure figure suspiciously related to a Canaanite goddess; Deborah has a reluctant general, and the victory over Sisera is neither hers nor his (many commentators consider her an unlikely choice for judge because she is a woman, though the text does not make gender an issue); Gideon is the least of the least of the tribes; Jephthah, an outcast, the son of "another woman"; and Samson, a Nazirite who does not live up to his promise. But more than being unlikely deliverers, some of these leaders exhibit highly question-

4. *Moses and the Deuteronomist*, 155.

5. See Greenspahn, "Framework of Judges."

6. For purposes of this analysis, I am not concerned with drawing distinctions between "judges" and "deliverers." Othniel, Ehud, Shamgar, Gideon, Tola, and Samson fall into the category of deliverer; Othniel, Deborah, Tola, Jair, Jephthah, Ibzan, Elon, Abdon, and Samson, into that of judge. But there are problems; see the discussions of Alan J. Hauser, "The 'Minor Judges'—A Re-evaluation," *JBL* 94 (1975) 190–200; and Mullen, "The 'Minor Judges.'"

able behavior. Although no neatly progressive pattern emerges, a turning-point occurs with Gideon.[7] Gideon and the important figures after him reveal disturbing weaknesses, if not serious faults. By the end of the story of Samson, the cyclical pattern of punishment/deliverance has exhausted itself. The temporal aspect remains, but time is now characterized negatively, by absence, the absence of a king, and the protagonists who appear next are reprehensible and wholly unsympathetic.

What, we might ask, is the deity's role in all this? Is there a connection between success or failure, the character of the judge (or protagonist in chaps. 17–21), and the role of the deity, and if so, what is it? Just as the human protagonists of Judges are not arranged on a scale from good to bad, so also God's role is not easily categorized. Some of the protagonists receive ambiguous and ambivalent treatment in the narrative, and so too, at times, does God. God plays an active part in the affairs of Deborah and Gideon, [[413]] bears direct responsibility for Abimelech's downfall, is implicated in Jephthah's tragic vow, and assumes a controlling, though behind-the-scene, role in the volatile exploits of Samson. Curiously aloof from the action in chaps. 17–19, God has a major role in the internecine war of chaps. 20–21. Consideration of each of the major divisions of Judges reveals a crisis of leadership on human and divine levels.[8]

Judges begins with a double introduction, balanced by a double conclusion often misleadingly called "appendixes" or "additions." Though Canaanites are (surprisingly) still in the land after Joshua's death, events begin propitiously, with Yhwh promising victory to Judah ("I have given the land into its hand") and then fulfilling the promise ("Yhwh gave the Canaanites and the Perizzites into their hand" [1:4]). This phraseology will echo importantly in the succeeding stories. Initial successes, however, are

7. Gooding ("Composition") sees a relative progression except for the minor judges; see also David Jobling, *The Sense of Biblical Narrative: Structural Analyses in the Hebrew Bible* 2 (JSOTSup 39; Sheffield: JSOT, 1986) 55–56, 60; Webb, *Judges*, 157–58.

8. As part of the picture of dissolution we can trace a corresponding deterioration in the position and the treatment of women. This subject merits careful study in its own right; see, e.g., Mieke Bal, *Death and Dissymmetry: The Politics of Coherence in Judges* (Chicago: University of Chicago, 1988). From the opening story of Achsah's forceful claim to property, we move to Deborah's leadership and Jael's heroism. But thereafter comes the sacrifice of Jephthah's daughter, followed by the murder of Samson's wife (but note his mother's significant role; see J. Cheryl Exum, "Promise and Fulfillment: Narrative Art in Judges 13," *JBL* 99 [1980] 43–59), and finally, the brutal rape and murder of the Levite's nameless wife and the repetition of this crime on a mass scale in the abuse of the women of Benjamin, Jabesh-gilead, and Shiloh. On Judges 11 and 19–21, see Phyllis Trible, *Texts of Terror: Literary-Feminist Readings of Biblical Narratives* (Philadelphia: Fortress, 1984) 65–116; Esther Fuchs, "Marginalization, Ambiguity, Silencing: The Story of Jephthah's Daughter," *Journal of Feminist Studies in Religion* 5 (1989) 35–45; J. Cheryl Exum, "Murder They Wrote: Ideology and the Manipulation of Female Presence in Biblical Narrative," *USQR* 43 (1989) 19–39.

followed by serious setbacks, as various tribes are unable to wrest all of the land from the Canaanites. Success and failure intermingle, but the overall impression is increasingly negative, a pattern mirrored in the Book of Judges as a whole. Whereas the first part of the introduction (chap. 1) deals with Israel's military problem, the second (chap. 2) raises a religious problem, providing an "ideological account" in contrast to the more "objective account devoid of excuses or moralistic explanations."[9] A messenger of Yhwh accuses Israel of disobedience: in spite of Yhwh's past actions on their behalf, the Israelites have made covenants with the inhabitants of Canaan. Consequently Yhwh will not drive out the Canaanites before them (2:3). The charges leveled against Israel in this speech will be repeated at crucial junctures in the narrative. Understandably the people weep.

Against the backdrop of Israel's military problem and its theological explanation, a pattern emerges that provides a framing device for the book (2:11–23). [[414]] Its essential features are: the people of Israel do what is evil in the eyes of Yhwh (understood as worship of other gods); they provoke Yhwh to anger so that Yhwh gives them over to plunderers (the statement about provocation is sometimes missing); as a result of their groaning, Yhwh is moved to pity and raises up judges who deliver them. Israel is doomed at the outset to repeat this pattern:

> Whenever Yhwh raised up judges for them, Yhwh was with the judge, and saved them from the hand of their enemies all the days of the judge; . . . but whenever the judge died, they turned back and behaved worse than their ancestors. . . . (2:18–19)

Already the implicit question becomes, how will Israel break out of this cycle? The answer, as we shall see, is not through a dramatic change (as, e.g., the adoption of monarchy, which Samuel and Yhwh later see as a rejection of God's role) but rather through the cycle's inability to sustain itself (thus *opening* the way for the new pattern of leadership the monarchy will offer).

Othniel (3:7–11) conforms so completely to the pattern that many scholars view him as an editorial fabrication, created to provide a judge from the South. He illustrates precisely what we have been led to expect: the Israelites do evil in the eyes of Yhwh; Yhwh's anger is provoked and Yhwh sells them into the hand of Cushan-rishathaim, whom they serve for eight years. The Israelites cry to Yhwh and Yhwh raises up a deliverer, Othniel. Beyond what we know of Othniel from 1:12–15, we learn only that the spirit of Yhwh came upon him as it will later animate Gideon,

9. Polzin, *Moses and the Deuteronomist*, 146.

Jephthah, and Samson, and that he "judged Israel," a phrase later applied to Deborah, Tola, Jair, Jephthah, Ibzan, Elon, Abdon, and Samson. Othniel is victorious and the land has rest for forty years.

After Othniel's death (3:11), the cycle resumes: the Israelites continue to do evil in the eyes of Yhwh; Yhwh strengthens Moab, whom Israel serves for eighteen years; the Israelites cry to Yhwh and Yhwh raises up a deliverer, Ehud. The framework leads directly into the story, producing a connection that invites us to see Ehud as the instrument of Yhwh in spite of the fact that, as events unfold, Yhwh is not particularly involved. The only references to Yhwh's participation occur on Ehud's lips. He masks his plan for the assassination of Eglon as "a message from God for you" (3:20), and later he urges on his followers with the promise that, as noted above, will become a familiar one in Judges, "Yhwh has given your enemies the Moabites into your hand" (3:28). At this point in the book, particularly in view of the relation of the deuteronomistic framework to the Ehud story, we are disposed to accept [[415]] Ehud's leadership as Yhwh's curious form of deliverance.[10] Only in retrospect will we note the irony produced by the conjunction of several elements that reappear at the end of the book: a left-handed deceiver from the tribe of Benjamin; a location in the hill country of Ephraim; and the double reference to the *psylym* [['sculptured images']] which seem incidental here until seen in the light of the *psl* [['image']] and other cultic objects in chaps. 17 and 18.

For Shamgar, who comes next, no deuteronomistic framework appears; this and the fragmentary nature of 3:31 have led commentators to question his place in the book. His killing of six hundred Philistines with an oxgoad foreshadows Samson's slaughter of a thousand Philistines with another unlikely instrument, the jawbone of an ass. We are told that Shamgar too delivered Israel, but this deliverance, like Samson's, is not complete, as the Philistines remain a formidable enemy until the time of David.

Not only is there no deuteronomistic framework for the information about Shamgar (easy enough for a redactor to supply), but in addition, Shamgar is not acknowledged as part of the cyclical pattern. The appearance of the phrase "after Ehud died" in the Deborah story (4:1) calls attention to the "interruption" of the cycle with Shamgar. Some LXX manuscripts place the Shamgar notice after 16:31. In any event, we shall see that despite its regularity, the pattern is not firmly established at the beginning of the book. Other accounts will later have a tenuous connection with the cyclical pattern; in particular the Abimelech story, loosely

10. See Yairah Amit, "The Story of Ehud (Judges 3:12–30): the Form and the Message," *Signs and Wonders: Biblical Texts in Literary Focus* (ed. J. C. Exum; Decator, GA: Scholars, 1989) 97–123.

associated with the Gideon story, appears at the point where the framework noticeably breaks down.

Deborah provides the only unsullied her of the book. Her story is not connected to the framework in the same way as Othniel's and Ehud's. The Israelites continue to do evil in the eyes of Yhwh; Yhwh sells them into the hand of Jabin, king of Canaan, who oppresses them for twenty years; the Israelites cry to Yhwh. We expect to hear that Yhwh raised up a deliverer, but instead we meet Deborah as already judging Israel. Moreover Deborah is a prophet, who speaks authoritatively in Yhwh's name: "Does not Yhwh the God of Israel command you. . . . I will draw out Sisera . . . and I will give him into your hand . . . for into the hand of a woman Yhwh will sell Sisera" (4:6–9). "This is the day that Yhwh has given Sisera into your hand. Does not Yhwh go out before you?" (4:14). As in chap. 1, Yhwh's proclamation (here through his prophet) finds immediate fulfillment: "Yhwh routed Sisera and all his chariots and all his army before the sword before Barak" (4:23). Once [[416]] again Yhwh fights for Israel, as in the days of Joshua. In fact, a harmony prevails between God and Israel's leader not witnessed since Joshua and not to be seen again until another judge/prophet, Samuel, appears. This harmony is celebrated in a triumphant song that attributes victory to Yhwh, praises Deborah as a "mother in Israel," and extols Jael as Sisera's assassin. The song is unique in Judges; it might be argued that only Deborah provides the occasion for such celebration. The honors accorded women in Judges 4 and 5 will be radically transformed by the final stories of Judges.[11]

A few elements cast a shadow: Barak hesitates (a fault magnified in Gideon), and therefore the glory will not be his (similarly Yhwh reduces Gideon's troops lest Israel under Gideon claim the victory). Jael gives Sisera refuge and then kills him, reflecting and outdoing Ehud's grotesque murder of Eglon. Some tribes fail to join the battle and consequently are reproved. Nonetheless, Judges 4 and 5 suggest that conditions in Israel have improved. True, we know from 2:6–3:6 that Israel will fall back into sin, but we have also seen that the periods of rest are longer than the years of oppression, and thus we have reason to hope that Israel under the judges/deliverers might fare well. But the forty-year period of rest after

11. D. F. Murray ("Narrative Structure and Technique in the Deborah-Barak Story [Judges IV 4–22]," *Studies in the Historical Books of the Old Testament* [VTSup 30; ed. J. A. Emerton; Leiden: Brill, 1979] 155–89) sees both the prose and poem as affirming the leadership of women, contra Barnabas Lindars, "Deborah's Song: Women in the Old Testament," *BJRL* 65 (1982–83) 158–75. Mieke Bal (*Murder and Difference: Gender, Genre, and Scholarship on Sisera's Death* [Bloomington: Indiana University, 1988]) reads Judges 4 and 5 as "masculine" and "feminine" accounts respectively.

Deborah is shorter by half than the period of rest after Ehud, and we move back into the cycle, not at all prepared for Gideon.

No character in the book receives more divine assurance than Gideon and no one displays more doubt. Gideon is, significantly, the only judge to whom God speaks directly, though this privilege does not allay his faint-heartedness. The story begins typically: the Israelites do evil in the eyes of Yhwh; Yhwh gives them into the hand of Midian for seven years; the Israelites cry to Yhwh (6:1–6). In response, God sends a prophet. Thus far it appears as if the pattern of the Deborah story might be repeated. Instead, the anonymous prophet accuses Israel of unfaithfulness and disappears abruptly, without even delivering the customary lecture on the consequences of disobedience.

> Thus says Yhwh, the God of Israel: "I brought you up from Egypt and I led you out of the house of bondage, and I delivered you from the hand of Egypt and from the hand of all who oppressed you, and I drove them out before you, and [[417]] I gave you their land. I said to you, 'I am Yhwh your God; you shall not serve the gods of the Amorites in whose land you are dwelling.' But you did not obey my voice." (6:8–10; 6:7–10 are lacking in 4QJudges)

Since we have heard this charge twice before, we know its consequences: God will not drive out the indigenous population of the land, and their gods will become a snare (*mwqš*) for Israel (2:1–5; cf. 2:20–23). The omission of the threat here will find ironic compensation at the end of the story.

The story of Gideon takes longer to get under way than the previous accounts. On the one hand, God does not raise up a deliverer at the beginning, as in the cases of Othniel and Ehud; on the other hand, our expectations that we might have another prophet-judge like Deborah are not fulfilled. After a lengthy introduction, a more dramatic form of divine involvement occurs; a divine messenger appears to Gideon–surely a portent of his future greatness! (We will have a similar buildup and letdown in the Samson story.) Whereas the stories of Othniel and Ehud merely reported that Yhwh raised up a deliverer (*wyqm Yhwh mwšyʿ*), here we find God commissioning the deliverer (*hwšyʿ* [['he delivered']] is a key word in this story). But the divine intent meets with resistance. Gideon, in a conventional scene with affinities to the call of Moses,[12] cannot believe that God will deliver Israel by his hand (6:36, 37). When we meet Gideon, he is beating out wheat in the wine press, hiding from Midianite view, and he

12. Webb (*Judges*, 148–53) explores the parallels interestingly. I disagree, however, that Gideon "is a model of Mosaic piety" (151).

reveals his fearful, hesitant nature in his skeptical response to the messenger, "If Yhwh is with us, why has all this come upon us and where are all his wonders . . . ?" (6:13). It is a very good question. It takes a theophany to convince Gideon that God is with him, but even so, he remains apprehensive. He follows Yhwh's command to tear down the Baal altar, but does it at night out of fear (6:27). He tests God twice with the fleece (6:36–40); and he again reveals his fear when, at Yhwh's suggestion, he goes to the Midianite camp and overhears the dream (7:9–15). Ironically, only after Gideon ceases to be afraid does Yhwh stop giving him instructions.

Besides receiving direct communication from God, Gideon is also possessed by the spirit of Yhwh (6:34). Othniel, our paradigm judge, was possessed by the spirit and was victorious in battle. Gideon's possession may be viewed similarly; but in light of what happens later, when the spirit comes upon Jephthah and Samson, we might question the spirit's awesome nature. Yhwh's spirit comes upon Gideon and afterward he wants assurance ("If [*ʾm*] you are delivering Israel by my hand . . ." [6:36]). After the spirit comes upon Jephthah, he seeks to guarantee success ("If [*ʾm*] you will indeed give the Ammonites into my hand . . ." [11:30]). To be sure, Gideon's test and Jephthah's vow are different matters and serve different functions. What they have in common is their position in the narrative, following upon possession ⟦418⟧ by Yhwh's spirit. What is the connection, if any, between animation by the spirit and the subsequent revelation of the judge's weakness of character?

The story contains repeated references to Yhwh's giving Midian into Gideon's and Israel's hand: Yhwh promises it (7:7, 9), though in such a way that Israel cannot claim success by its own hand (7:2); Gideon finally accepts the idea (7:15); a Midianite even dreams about it (7:13–14); and later Gideon will appease the Ephraimites with the argument that God has given Oreb and Zeeb into their hand (8:3). As in the story of Deborah and Barak (4:15, 23), Yhwh fights for Israel: "Yhwh set every man's sword against his fellow and against all the army" (7:22). Yet Gideon lacks Deborah's confidence and the harmony between God and judge is undercut. It has taken a good deal of narrative time to get past Gideon's timorousness to this victory, and the glory is short-lived. In contrast to the confident ending of the Deborah story, we encounter a series of disappointing events. D. W. Gooding observes a chiastic pattern in the Gideon story: (a) Gideon counters idolatry by breaking down the Baal altar (6:1–32); (b) he fights Israel's enemies (6:33–7:25); (b′) he fights his own nationals (8:1–21); (a′) Gideon himself lapses into idolatry (8:22–32). As Gooding demonstrates, Gideon presents an ambiguous turning point in the book.[13]

13. "Composition," 74; for a different view, see Webb, *Judges*, 146–53.

Interestingly, God does not participate in the events of b′ and a′, and thus we might well reconsider God's role, an issue Gideon had already drawn to our attention in his initial speech (6:13).

The crucial shift occurs in chap. 8, with Gideon's dispute with Ephraim. Gideon applies shrewd diplomacy to a situation Jephthah later handles catastrophically. His self-deprecatory rejoinder, "What have I done now in comparison with you? Is not the gleaning of the grapes of Ephraim better than the vintage of Abiezer?" (8:2), is totally in character, yet paradoxically the speech bears witness to Gideon's ability to handle matters himself. We recall that earlier, when a similar contentious question was raised (cf. *mh hdbr hzh ʿśyt lnw* [['what have you done to us?']] [8:1] with *my ʿśh hdbr hzh* [['who did this thing?']] [6:29]), Gideon's father stepped in to defend his son. Having successfully used God's name to defuse a potential internal threat (8:3), Gideon proceeds to deal ruthlessly with Succoth and Penuel. He confidently speaks of a time when "Yhwh will have given Zebah and Zalmunna into my hand" (8:7), though when he captures them there is no reference to divine involvement. When his son Jether, who seems to have inherited his father's timorousness, is afraid to slay Zebah and Zalmunna, Gideon must kill them himself. "As the man is, so is his strength" (8:21). Once fearful and hesitant, Gideon has developed a new self-assertive destructiveness. Simultaneously God has disappeared from the action. Is God still with Gideon, as God had assured him in his commission (6:12, 16)?

[[419]] At one point we learn something about divine motivation. Resorting like Gideon to a test, Yhwh reduces the number of Israelite troops "lest Israel vaunt themselves against me, saying, 'My own hand has delivered me'" (7:2–7). Victory is to be Yhwh's, not Israel's or Gideon's, though Gideon's name appears beside Yhwh's in the battle cry, "For Yhwh and for Gideon" (7:18, 20). It is interesting to note, then, that Gideon is offered the kingship because, according to the Israelites, *he* delivered them (8:22). Gideon's refusal of hereditary kingship might appear laudatory, but it will shortly be overturned by his son, who bears the suggestive name Abimelech, and it is followed by his apostasy. If his rejection of kingship is sincere, Gideon has no such hesitation about appropriating priestly authority.[14] Out of the spoil of battle, he made an ephod, which he placed in Ophrah, where he had earlier built an altar to Yhwh (6:24). "All Israel played the harlot after it there, and it became a snare (*mwqš*) to Gideon and to his house" (8:27). What was suppressed at the beginning of the story—that idolatry will become a snare to Israel—occurs at the end, as a

14. Baruch Halpern, "The Rise of Abimelek Ben-Jerubbaal," *Hebrew Annual Review* 2 (1978) 84–85.

result of Gideon's leadership (recall that Gideon also bears a Baal-name, 6:32; 7:1; 8:35). Hereafter the deliverers will complicate Israel's problems rather than relieve them. According to 8:28, Midian is subdued and the land has rest forty years in the days of Gideon–apparently in spite of Gideon's idolatry.

With Gideon's death (8:33), focus shifts to his house and to the fate of his son Abimelech, who is neither judge nor deliverer. Abimelech's story forms a disastrous interlude in the cycle of deliverer stories–a sequel to the Gideon narrative that, like the brief account of Shamgar, stands outside the deuteronomistic framework. The introduction resembles the framework, though the wording is more like that of 2:17: "After Gideon died, the Israelites turned and played the harlot after the Baals" (8:33). (Are we to regard this as a progression over playing the harlot after Gideon's ephod [8:27]?) They make Baal-berith their god, do not remember Yhwh, and do not show loyalty to Gideon's family. These conditions do not, as we might expect, lead God to hand Israel over to plunderers, though perhaps Abimelech is the wrath of God. Although Gideon had refused a hereditary monarchy, proclaiming, "I will not rule over you and my son will not rule over you," suspicion is cast on his resolve, for it appears from Abimelech's speech to the Shechemites that all seventy sons of Gideon-Jerubbaal are ruling (9:2).[15]

⟦420⟧ The Abimelech story offers a case study in retribution, as T. A. Boogaart's plot analysis illustrates.[16] The principle is stated unambiguously both early in the narrative and as a didactic conclusion.

> Thus God repaid Abimelech for the evil he committed against his father in killing his seventy brothers; and God also made all the evil of the men of Shechem fall back upon their heads, and upon them came the curse of Jotham the son of Jerubbaal. (9:56–57; cf. vv. 23–24)

Some details remain problematic, however. God allows Abimelech to rule for three years before intervening; then God sends an evil spirit between Abimelech and the men of Shechem. If Abimelech's usurpation of power is equivalent to God's giving Israel over to plunderers in the deuteronomistic schema, then sending the evil spirit corresponds to raising up a deliverer. On the other hand, it may be simply a delaying tactic, since after Abimelech a deliverer arises.

15. G. Henton Davies ("Judges VIII 22–23," *VT* 13 [1963] 151–57) argues that v. 23 is an acceptance of kingship "couched in the form of a pious refusal with the motive of expressing piety and of gaining favour with his would-be subjects" (p. 154); but cf. Halpern, "Abimelek Ben-Jerubbaal," 84–85 and n. 12.

16. "Stone for Stone: Retribution in the Story of Abimelech and Shechem," *JSOT* 32 (1985) 45–56.

According to Boogaart, "the evil spirit is none other than the evil of Abimelech and the men of Shechem, which continued to exist after their evil acts had been committed and which God, belatedly, directed back upon them."[17] This interpretation tries to explain God's behavior rather than confronting it as problematic. That Yhwh sends an evil spirit to undermine a king of whom he does not approve (and perhaps regards as a usurper of divine authority) will happen again with Saul, though Saul's case will be more disturbing, since Saul is a more sympathetic character than Abimelech. The three-year hiatus between crime and punishment raises questions about divine procedure, which Boogaart rightly acknowledges.[18] We may note, however, that three years is less than the periods of time Israel suffers under oppressors in the deuteronomistic schema. In retrospect, we will perceive an ironic contrast between the Abimelech debacle, where God returns evil for evil, and chaps. 19–21, where, rather than operating according to the principle of retribution, God allows the crimes of Benjamin to be repeated on a larger scale.

Abimelech's murder by a woman wipes out Gideon's house, except for Jotham, the only one left of his seventy brothers. The next major judge, Jephthah, brings an end to his own house when he sacrifices his daughter, and Samson, who kills himself along with his enemies, has no progeny. Even [[421]] the judges themselves cannot escape calamity, and by the end of the book, the Israelites will decimate the houses of Benjamin and of Jabesh-gilead.

The Jephthah story is framed by the list of "minor judges" (10:1–5; 12:8–14). The list has been described as an annalistic source split up by the insertion of the story of Jephthah, who belongs to both the major and the minor judges.[19] Recent criticism views the distinction between "major" and "minor" judges as a literary one, not necessarily reflecting a difference in role or function.[20] Two things stand out about the nature and arrangement of material in the list: the progressive breakdown of the deuteronomistic cyclical pattern, and the heightening of Jephthah's tragedy through contrast with other judges noted for their many offspring.[21] The

17. Ibid., 56 n. 12.

18. Ibid., 56 n. 11.

19. Martin Noth, "Das Amt des 'Richters Israels'," *Festschrift Alfred Bertholet* (ed. W. Baumgartner; Tübingen: Mohr, 1950) 404–17; Wolfgang Richter, "Zu den 'Richtern Israels'," *ZAW* 77 (1965) 40–72.

20. Hauser, "The 'Minor Judges'"; Mullen, "The 'Minor Judges'."

21. The numerous offspring of the minor judges and their holdings of land and livestock also indicate their status; see Keith W. Whitelam, *The Just King: Monarchical Judicial Authority in Ancient Israel* (JSOTSup 12; Sheffield: JSOT, 1979) 59–60; cf. Boling, *Judges*, 216; Jobling, *The Sense of Biblical Narrative*, 77–78. For a different view, see Matitiahu Tsevat, "Two Old Testament Stories and Their Hittite Analogues," *JAOS* 103 (1983) 323–26.

list sets up a series that disrupts the deuteronomistic cyclical pattern, while the Jephthah story in turn disrupts the list with an unexpected development in the deuteronomistic pattern. The pattern changes considerably after Gideon, the last judge for whom the rest formula occurs. After Abimelech, Tola "arise to deliver Israel," a departure from the usual expression, "Yhwh raised up a deliverer." Moreover, the other minor judges in the series merely "judged Israel." The list betrays no recognition of divine intervention. It appears here as if Israel can manage on its own, though how well it can manage, with or without Yhwh's involvement, is open to question in the Jephthah story.[22]

The first sign of something seriously amiss occurs in the introduction (10:6–16). We seem to be back within the familiar pattern: the Israelites continue to do evil in the eyes of Yhwh; Yhwh's anger is kindled and he sells them into the hand of the Philistines and the Ammonites; the Israelites cry to Yhwh. For the first time, a dialogue between Israel and Yhwh occurs within the framework, and for the first time in the Book of Judges, Israel repents. It is therefore surprising that Yhwh refuses to intervene (10:13). The repetitive fate predicted for Israel in 2:11–23 approaches its end, not in the [[422]] form of deliverance from the vicious cycle but rather in the threat of divine abandonment. Though often read as a sign that Yhwh is moved to intervention by Israel's suffering, Judg 10:16 states only that Yhwh became impatient with Israel's hardship, leaving the issue of his response on their behalf perplexingly open.[23]

Though Jephthah delivers Israel from Ammonite oppression, he is not "raised up" by Yhwh. The elders of Gilead appoint Jephthah their leader, and only later does Yhwh's spirit come upon him, confirming, as it were, the elders' selection. A mysterious and terrible force, the spirit often plays a role in Israel's victories over its foes (3:10; 6:34; 13:25; 14:6, 19; 1 Sam 10:10; 11:6; 16:13). Since the spirit comes upon Jephthah just before he vows a sacrifice to Yhwh in return for victory, it might be argued that he utters his ill-fated vow while under its influence. The narrative sequence prevents us from deciding whether victory comes as the result of Yhwh's spirit upon Jephthah or as the result of his vow, or both.

It is not the making of the vow that is so disturbing but rather its content. Whether Jephthah intended to offer God a person or an animal is a moot question, since *hywṣʾ* [['the one coming forth']] could be, and we know it will be, a human sacrifice. Jephthah, however, seems blind to the

22. Boling (*Judges*, 189, 215) and Webb (*Judges*, 176) see the list of minor judges as representing periods of peace. Boling (p. 214) deems Jephthah an exemplary judge, "the best since Othniel." Whatever happened to Deborah? In my view, Jephthah is the worst of the lot, though not merely through a fault of his own.

23. See Polzin, *Moses and the Deuteronomist*, 177; Webb, *Judges*, 46–48.

implications of his vow; his response makes clear that he had not expected "the one coming forth" to meet him to be his only child. Significantly, Jephthah does not seek an alternative to fulfilling the vow. Even his daughter accepts her fate without protest.[24]

If Jephthah appears negatively in the narrative, what can be said of Yhwh? Apart from animating Jephthah by the spirit, Yhwh's only other direct involvement is to give the Ammonites into Jephthah's hand. If not a tacit acceptance of the vow, this act nevertheless implicates the deity in the terrible events that follow. Moreover, Yhwh does not intervene to prevent Jephthah from offering to him a human sacrifice. Jephthah's tragedy lies not simply in his own guilt but also in the divine silence.[25] From the initial refusal to deliver Israel (10:13), God remains strangely aloof from the affairs of Jephthah and Israel, although the other characters–Jephthah, the elders, and Jephthah's daughter–consistently invoke his name.

Jephthah's victory over Ammon occurs against the backdrop of failed negotiations and comes at great personal cost. The text does not report God's reaction to the sacrifice or its effect upon Jephthah, though it hints at the low ⟦423⟧ point Jephthah has reached when it recounts his failure to avert conflict with Ephraim (12:1–6). Unlike Gideon before him, and in marked contrast to his own lengthy attempt at negotiation with the Ammonites (11:12–28),[26] Jephthah does nothing to prevent fighting among the Israelites themselves. The Gileadites repeat Jephthah's sin on a tribal scale, the slaughter of their own flesh and blood. Human sacrifice to Yhwh and needless fighting between Israelite tribes hardly yield an impressive record for a judge. Disorder reigns in spite of Jephthah's military victories.

With Samson, the deuteronomistic framework breaks down altogether. The narrative begins typically, with the Israelites continuing to do evil in the eyes of Yhwh and Yhwh giving them into Philistine hands for forty years (13:1), but it ends without deliverance having been effected. If in the Jephthah story the people repent but Yhwh rebuffs their appeal for help (10:10–16), in the Samson story a curious kind of reversal occurs. For the first time in the Judges cycle, the Israelites do not cry out, yet God intervenes spectacularly. Othniel and Ehud were "raised up"; Deborah is introduced as a prophet who already judges Israel; Gideon's commission was

24. On the daughter's complicity, see Exum, "Murder They Wrote."

25. For detailed discussion, see J. Cheryl Exum, "The Tragic Vision and Biblical Narrative: The Case of Jephthah," *Signs and Wonders: Biblical Texts in Literary Focus* (ed. J. C. Exum; Decatur, GA: Scholars, 1989) 59–83.

26. Both Jobling (*The Sense of Biblical Narrative*, 128–31) and Webb (*Judges*, 54–57) analyze insightfully the ambivalent and uneasy nature of Jephthah's suit, Jobling suggesting that "Jephthah is dissatisfied with his case" (p. 129), and Webb noting that "these are not the words of a man who is desperate for peace" (p. 55).

elaborately related; Abimelech usurped power; and Jephthah was selected by the Gileadite elders. Now, in the most dramatic form of intervention since Gideon, Samson is chosen by God before birth and set apart as a Nazirite "to begin" or "to be the first" to deliver Israel from the Philistines. Like the messenger's appearance to Gideon, the angel's appearance to Samson's mother promises great things, especially if we recall other biblical birth announcements. But our expectations are not fulfilled.[27] Although commentators frequently blame Samson for failure to live up to his calling, the story contains no explicit censure of Samson and, what is more, attributes his unconventional behavior to Yhwh (14:4, 19; 15:14–15).

In contrast to Gideon, Abimelech, and Jephthah, with their unfavorable qualities, Samson is genuinely amoral. In many respects he resembles the well-known trickster figure, a marginal character with abnormal strength and an enormous libido, witty, uncontrollable, destructive, and beneficial, finally destroying himself.

> [Trickster] is positively identified with creative powers [in Samson's case as an instrument of Yhwh] . . . and yet he constantly behaves in the most antisocial manner we can imagine. Although we laugh at him for his troubles and his [[424]] foolishness and are embarrassed by his promiscuity, his creative cleverness amazes us and keeps alive the possibility of transcending the social restrictions we regularly encounter.[28]

Is Samson's amorality reflected in the deity? Yhwh achieves victory over the Philistines through Samson (16:23–30). Although the Philistines credit Dagon (16:23, 24), actually Yhwh delivers Samson into their power (16:20). Whereas Yhwh triumphs when Samson destroys the Philistine temple, killing thousands, the deliverer dies also, and the Philistine threat remains. Yhwh's "behind-the-scene" activity produces double-edged results. Is God perhaps the divine trickster? If one appreciates the creative and destructive sides of Samson, should one not be prepared to accept the creative and destructive sides of the God he represents?

Three prayers appear in the Samson story, and all are answered, though on divine rather than human terms.[29] But no dialogue ever takes place between Yhwh and Samson, and even in the theophany to Manoah and his wife, God remains evasive and secretive. To appreciate just how

27. See Edward L. Greenstein, "The Riddle of Samson," *Prooftexts* 1 (1981) 237–60.

28. Barbara Babcock-Abrahams, "'A Tolerated Margin of Mess': The Trickster and His Tales Reconsidered," *Journal of the Folklore Institute* 11 (1975) 147. On the comic dimension of Samson's character, see J. Cheryl Exum and J. William Whedbee, "Isaac, Samson, and Saul: Reflections on the Comic and Tragic Visions," *Semeia* 32 (1984) 28–33.

29. J. Cheryl Exum, "The Theological Dimension of the Samson Saga," *VT* 33 (1983) 30–45.

secretive one has only to recall the patient and extensive exchanges between God and Gideon.

Throughout Judges 13–16, the participants remain ignorant of God's will and God's intentions. Samson's mother and father—and, as events indicate, Samson as well—do not know that Samson's desire for a Philistine wife (or perhaps the woman herself; note the pronoun *hy*ʾ [['she']]) was "from Yhwh, for he was seeking an occasion against the Philistines" (14:4). Though Yhwh's chosen deliverer, Samson displays no understanding of his mission. He is merely an instrument of Yhwh (13:25; 14:4). Like Othniel, Gideon, and Jephthah before him, he is animated by Yhwh's spirit. I suggested above that Jephthah might have uttered his vow under the spirit's influence. Certainly the spirit drives Samson to perform bizarre and violent deeds: killing a lion with his bare hands; killing thirty Philistines for their garments; killing a thousand Philistines with the jawbone of an ass.

Everything is determined by God without the knowledge (or consent?) of those involved.[30] Samson is passive with regard to the most important events of his life, making and breaking the Nazirite vow. Nazirite injunctions are placed upon him before his birth, and his hair is cut while he sleeps. After [[425]] he has been shaved, he does not know that Yhwh has left him (16:20), a reversal of the book's introductory rubric, "Yhwh was with the judge" (2:18). Nevertheless, Yhwh does not abandon Samson, any more (or less) than Yhwh has abandoned Israel in the cycles of judges. Like the Israelites who cried out to Yhwh in their distress, Samson calls upon Yhwh in his hour of need, but—again like Israel, with the exception of 10:10–16—he does not repent. The absence of Israel's cry at the beginning of the Samson story perhaps finds compensation in Samson's prayer to Yhwh in 16:28–30. The prayer for vindication is granted, but the petitioner dies. In the other two prayers of the saga, we are told that Yhwh (or Elohim) responded. Here direct reference to the deity is lacking. God has withdrawn, as at the end of the Jephthah story, and as will happen in the stories to follow.

Only in death does Samson fulfill his destiny to begin Israel's deliverance from the Philistines. What purpose has his life served? He accomplishes no lasting deliverance. He never leads Israelite troops into battle but remains a marginal figure, who lives an isolated existence and dies without offspring. He is betrayed by his wife and by Delilah, whom he loved, as well as by the Judahites, who hand him over to the Philistines (15:11–13). Yhwh, too, hands Samson over to the Philistines, who blind and enslave him, and make him an object of amusement. In all this, is he

30. Francis Landy, "Are We in the Place of Averroes?," *Semeia* 32 (1984) 140–42.

also betrayed by God? Yhwh's most dramatic involvement is, in a sense, a spectacular failure. There is no rest formula, as there has not been since Gideon. We are back where we started, but not quite. It is not that the repetitive way of life indicated by the cyclical pattern of Judges does not continue after Samson, but that it cannot continue.

Judges 17–21 forms a double conclusion to the Book of Judges, balancing its double introduction. Cyclical time now exhausted, we move into time characterized preeminently by absence: "in those days there was no king in Israel" (17:6; 18:1; 19:1; 21:25). The concluding stories illustrate the depravity and anarchy of the times, a time when there is no king but Yhwh (8:23), whose beneficial guidance, it seems, cannot be assumed. Neither judges nor deliverers, the protagonists in these stories include a motley selection of individuals, a couple of unscrupulous Levites, a clan acting independently, and a highly organized tribal assembly. Israel's enemy is no longer external but internal.

Judges 17 begins much like the Samson story: "Now there was a man from the hill country of Ephraim and his name was Mikayehu" (cf. "Now there was a certain man from Zorah from the clan of the Danites and his name was Manoah" [13:2]). Momentarily we might wonder if God will again intervene miraculously. But immediately we hear of a theft and the making of a molten image. A man who steals eleven hundred pieces of silver from his mother (the amount each Philistine lord brought to Delilah) engages in disturbingly syncretistic religious practices which belie his name, "Who is like Yhwh?" ⟦426⟧ If we recall the dangers of syncretism in chaps. 2, 6, and 10, the consequences of Gideon's ephod, and the scandal of Jephthah's human sacrifice, we rightly anticipate problems. Whereas Gideon made an ephod that became a snare to the people, Micah has a *psl* ⟦'sculptured image'⟧, a *mskh* ⟦'molten image'⟧, an *ʾpwd* ⟦'ephod'⟧, and *trpym* ⟦'teraphim'⟧. The building up of terms is surely ironically emphatic; note simply the repetition with interesting variations in 17:3, 4, 5; 18:14, 17, 18, 20, 24, 27, 30, 31.[31]

The Danites do not come off much better, since they steal these dubious objects for their cultic center (18:30–31). Their appearance, seeking an inheritance, looks back to their predicament at the beginning of the book (1:34), when Israel was not given all the land because of its apostasy. Ironically the Danites' actions here suggest that same sin. We recall, too, that the Danite Samson failed as a deliverer, in spite of the victory won at his death. The Danites reveal themselves as a ruthless lot, threatening Micah with violence when he protests their theft of his god, and wiping

31. *Psl wmskh* ⟦'sculptured image and molten image'⟧ is probably hendiadys; see Boling, *Judges*, 256.

out the unsuspecting population of Laish in a campaign that sounds like holy war with its imposition of the *ḥerem* ⟦'utter destruction'⟧, but otherwise lacks its religious trappings. The Levite, too, appears in a negative light as an opportunist happy to abet the Danites' theft of Micah's cultic objects and to accompany them as their priest. One even wonders about Micah's mother, who consecrates stolen silver to Yhwh to make an image and apparently keeps the larger portion.

Yhwh does not participate in the events of this story. The divine absence is especially noteworthy after an account where Yhwh had controlled everything from offstage. It is as if, with the failure of the judges to bring any real resolution, Yhwh abandons Israel to its own devices.

The characters in the story, however, are quite content to view their affairs as under the auspices of the deity. In Yhwh's name, Micah's mother blesses the restorer of her silver, who is also the thief, and she consecrates the silver to Yhwh for an image made by human hands. Micah, having set up his shrine and installed the Levite, is sure Yhwh will prosper him because he has a Levite as a priest (17:13). But Yhwh does not prosper him; his "gods which I made" (18:24) and his priest, who is both father (17:11) and son (17:12) to him, are stolen by the Danites. It is no small irony that the image they steal and set up for themselves in their newly conquered homeland was made of stolen money. The Danite spies inquire of God through the Levite (18:5) and, having received an oracle they consider favorable, come upon Laish. They tell their compatriots that "God has given it into your hands" (18:10), a display of confidence in providential disposition similar to Micah's. They fare better than Micah, for they succeed in defeating Laish and establishing an inheritance for themselves. But nowhere, except in their own words, is ⟦427⟧ God said to have played a part in granting them success. Indeed, the oracle the Levite gives them is, as Polzin points out, delphic in its ambiguity: "Before [or "opposite"] Yhwh is your way" (*drkkm* [18:6]),[32] an answer befitting a tribe which inquires about the success of its way (*drknw* [18:5]) from an opportunistic Levite seeking his way (*lʿśwt drkw* [17:8]). Yhwh's equivocal involvement in the Danites' venture recalls the ambiguity surrounding Yhwh's role in Jephthah's vow. The divine purpose, which in the Samson story was revealed to us though hidden from the participants, is here hidden from us.

The next story also takes place when "there was no king in Israel" (19:1). An important connective, this description concluded the account of Micah's graven image and introduced the Levite who would become his priest (17:6). Next it concluded the account of the Levite's installation and introduced the Danites (18:1). Here it concludes the account of "Micah's

32. Polzin, *Moses and the Deuteronomist*, 198.

image which he made" (18:31) and introduces another Levite, who will turn out to be not simply worse than the first Levite, but possibly the most disreputable character in the book. Like the other Levite, he appears in the hill country of Ephraim (17:8; 19:1). The other Levite, from Bethlehem in Judah, journeyed from Bethlehem to Ephraim, and later to Dan. This Levite's wife of secondary rank comes from Bethlehem in Judah, and he journeys from Ephraim to Bethlehem and back home, on the way spending a fateful night in Gibeah of Benjamin. Finally he appears at the assembly at Mizpah, before vanishing from the picture. One Levite ends his journey with a joyful heart (18:20); the other has a joyful heart when he feasts and drinks with his hosts (19:6, 9, 22), but in Gibeah his merriment is suddenly interrupted by wanton and violent men (19:22).

The Levite's weakness of character is hinted at as the story begins, when he allows his father-in-law repeatedly to persuade him to remain in Bethlehem. First he is too irresolute to leave on his journey at a reasonable hour, and then too stubborn to remain yet another night. Had he left early in the morning as intended, the outrage at Gibeah might have been avoided.

The first suggestion of decay within Benjamin comes through contrast with the Jebusites, "foreigners who do not belong to the people of Israel" (19:12). Though hospitality would be expected from fellow Israelites in Gibeah, no one takes the travellers in for the night, until an old man from Ephraim, a resident alien in Gibeah, comes upon them in the square. The depravity of the Benjaminites of Gibeah comes to light when ruffians demand that the Levite be brought outside so that they might sexually assault him. [[428]] The baseness not just of the men of Gibeah but also of the Levite and his host is revealed in the treatment of the Levite's wife. Either the Levite or his host–the ambiguity shields the true culprit and paradoxically exposes the guilt of both men–throws the woman out to the mob. The men rape and abuse her all night.[33] (Although the host also offered his virgin daughter, somehow she is spared.) When the Levite opens the door in the morning "to go on his way"–not to see what has happened to his wife–and finds her lying on the threshold, his crass response is shocking: "Get up, so we can go" (19:28). More shocking yet are his actions: he puts her on his ass, travels home, and–in a morbid parody of Saul's muster of the tribes in 1 Samuel 11–chops her body into twelve pieces which he sends throughout the territory of Israel. It is not at all

33. The verb *ʿnh* [['ravish, force, rape']], which appears in 19:24 and 20:5, is used of Samson's treatment [['tie up']] by Delilah and the Philistines, 16:5, 6, 19. See also Gen 34:2, 2 Sam 13:12, 14.

clear that the woman was dead when he dismembered her![34] The Israelites are scandalized, apparently by the dismemberment, since they have not yet heard the Levite's version of events (20:4–6). We certainly have reason to include the Levite's deed in the "evil" (20:3) which elicits their dramatic response.[35]

The Levite's report to the Israelite assembly confirms his baseness. He stresses the threat to himself ("me they sought to kill" [20:5]) and neglects to mention that he remained in the safety of the house while "my wife they ravished." His final word, *wtmt* ⟦'and she died'⟧, preserves the ambiguity whether the woman was dead or alive when he dismembered her.

In Genesis 22, God intervenes at the climactic moment to save Abraham's "only son Isaac whom [he] love[s]"; no such last-minute intervention averts the sacrifice of Jephthah's daughter. Similarly, in Genesis 19, God intervenes to save Lot's guests, but in the gruesome counterpart in Judges 19, Yhwh does not appear.[36] Moreover, and in contrast to chaps. 17–18, Yhwh is not mentioned, apart from the Levite's statement in 19:18 that he is going to the house of Yhwh (where LXX reads *kai eis ton oikon mou* ⟦'and into my house'⟧. The situation reverses in the sequel, chaps. 20–21, which relates the Israelites' response ⟦429⟧ to the crime. Yhwh's intervention here recalls the introductory chapters of Judges, but in a way that accentuates a qualitative difference. The cyclical pattern of the deliverer stories and the more linear, kingless time have brought us full circle, revealing the futility of Israel's situation under the judges, and also, it appears, under Yhwh. Israel, once again acting as a theocratic unity (20:1 and 2), assembles at Mizpah (recall Jephthah's association with a place of the same name). The assembly, composed of Israelites from Dan (with its syncretic images stolen from Micah) to Beersheba, including Gilead, take counsel and proceed against Benjamin, without consulting Yhwh. (The Gileadites have acted without divine counsel before, when they chose Jephthah to lead them against the Ammonites. In the wake of that victory came human sacrifice and internecine fighting.)

34. LXX cannot rest with the ambiguity. It adds in v. 28, "for she was dead."

35. Stuart Lasine ("Guest and Host in Judges 19: Lot's Hospitality in an Inverted World," *JSOT* 29 [1984] 41–42) points out the bizarre and problematic significance of the Levite's action by comparing it to Saul's dismemberment of the oxen in 1 Samuel 11: "The 'message' sent by the Levite by means of the severed body is made more bizarre because he is not quoted as declaring the exact significance of the message, unlike Saul, who makes it clear that the dismembered oxen represent what will happen to the oxen of those who do not rally to his call" (42). The differences in LXX do not resolve the problems posed by v. 30.

36. See the comparison by Lasine, "Guest and Host," 38–41; see also Susan Niditch, "The 'Sodomite' Theme in Judges 19–20: Family, Community, and Social Disintegration," *CBQ* 44 (1982) 365–78.

Only after the Benjaminites refuse to hand over the criminals[37] and the battle lines are drawn, do the Israelites go to Bethel and inquire of God, "Who of us shall go up first to fight against the Benjaminites?" (20:18). God responds, "Judah first." When almost the identical question appeared in Judges 1 ("Who of us shall go up first against the Canaanites to fight against them?"), the divine answer was, "Judah shall go up; I have given the land into its hand" (1:1–2). Here Yhwh does not promise victory and, indeed, Benjamin defeats Israel (recall the Levite's inquiry of God on Dan's behalf and the ambiguous answer [18:6]). Just as in Judges 2, the Israelites wept before Yhwh when confronted with the reason for their failure to defeat the Canaanites, so here they weep in the face of their failure to rout Benjamin. Again they inquire of Yhwh, this time asking not who should lead the attack but whether they should attack at all. Their words draw attention to their relationship to Benjamin (*bny bnymn ʾḥy* [['our kinfolk the Benjaminites']] [20:23]). Yhwh responds "Go up against them," and once more the Israelites suffer defeat. Again they weep and make offerings to Yhwh. A third time they inquire of Yhwh, whose presence among them is symbolized by the ark of the covenant, which we now learn resides at Bethel. They repeat their question about attacking the Benjaminites, their own people (*bny bnymn ʾḥy* [20:28]), and add, as if to state the question as ambiguously as possible, "or shall we cease?" (20:28). Doubtlessly it is perplexing, as well as embarrassing, that Yhwh keeps sending them to defeat. For the first time, Yhwh promises victory, "Go up, for tomorrow I will give them into your hand."

Disturbing questions attend the divine response. Why has this promise of victory been so long in coming? Why does Yhwh allow the Israelites to fail twice, if he intends to give Benjamin to them? What purpose does the excessive slaughter serve? Apparently not only the protracted fighting but also [[430]] the destruction of one Israelite tribe by the others has divine support. Is Israel, like Samson, abandoned to its own folly and being brought to ruin by Yhwh?[38]

On the third day, the Israelites set an ambush for the Benjaminites who "did not know that evil was close upon them" (20:34). The description recalls Samson, for whom the Philistines and Delilah set an ambush (16:2, 9, 12) and who "did not know that Yhwh had left him" (16:20). The

37. Cf. Judah's willingness to turn over Samson to the Philistines.

38. Webb (*Judges*, 194 and passim) sees the fighting and Israel's defeat as chastisement of Israel by Yhwh; similarly, Klein, *Triumph of Irony*, 178–85. This is, in fact, the typical explanation: if Israel suffers, it is because it is being deservedly punished; if Israel does not suffer harm, it is because God is merciful. In such a schema, God's behavior is never called into question. On the framework as reflecting Israel's suffering as punishment and its salvation as the result of God's mercy, see Greenspahn, "Framework of Judges," 394–96.

whole story resembles the Abimelech interlude, where God sends an evil spirit to create discord between Abimelech and the Shechemites. Abimelech, too, fights his own kin, and achieves victory through an ambush (9:32, 34, 43). There is also a variation on a motif of the Gideon story: the size of the Israelite army is reduced twice—to give glory to God!

According to Judg 20:35, "Yhwh routed Benjamin before Israel." The earlier stories of Deborah and Gideon assigned Yhwh direct responsibility for overcoming Israel's enemies (4:15, 23; 7:22). In the Jephthah story, Yhwh also defeated Israel's enemies (11:32), but Jephthah's victory was pyrrhic, requiring him to fulfill his vow. Yhwh's intervention here is similarly double-edged, with the fighting among the tribes taking place on a larger scale than in Judges 12. In what amounts to a "holy war" (20:48), the victorious Israelites destroy the cities of Benjamin. Then they come to Bethel and again weep bitterly before God, ironically, now, not because they could not defeat Benjamin, but precisely because they have. They pose an urgent question that is never answered: "Why, Yhwh God of Israel, has this happened in Israel . . . ?" (21:3).

Bound by an oath, whose consequences they now regret, the Israelites find themselves in a predicament not unlike Jephthah's. In contrast to Jephthah, they seek a way out of the dilemma, but ironically, like Jephthah, they end up killing their own flesh and blood. Responsibility for their situation is placed upon Yhwh, who "had made a breach in the tribes of Israel" (21:15), whereas the Israelites are said to have compassion on Benjamin (21:6, 15). On their own initiative, the Israelites reach a solution to Benjamin's plight; they carry out the ban (21:11) against Jabesh-gilead, sparing only four hundred virgins to provide wives for the surviving Benjaminite men. To punish the violence done to one woman (and threatened against one man), the Israelites kill many innocent women, women from Benjamin and women from Jabesh-gilead [[431]] who are not virgins. They take by force four hundred virgins from Jabesh and instruct the Benjaminite men to capture others from Shiloh. They thus repeat on a mass scale the crimes they found so abhorrent in the men of Gibeah.

At the end of Judges, Israel is without direction. Individuals behave as they please; "the best lack all conviction, while the worst are full of passionate intensity."[39] Let us consider the final statement of the book in the light of two others.

> The Israelites continued to do evil in the eyes of Yhwh. . . .
>
> "I will not rule over you, and my son will not rule over you; Yhwh will rule over you."

39. William Butler Yeats, "The Second Coming."

> In those days there was no king in Israel, and every man did what was right in his own eyes.

Throughout the Book of Judges, Israel has repeatedly done what was right in its eyes and evil in the eyes of Yhwh. Even the judges were not able to remedy this condition, and we have reason, especially with Gideon and the judges after him, to question Yhwh's role in this state of affairs. The last judge, Samson, for example, stubbornly pursues "the right one in my eyes" (14:3), never realizing that "it/she was from Yhwh" (14:4). Judg 21:25 suggests that this anarchy results from the lack of a king. But Israel has a king; Yhwh rules over Israel. In Judges 17–21, Yhwh's rule is ineffectual, either because Yhwh does not intervene in events or because Yhwh intervenes in ways that result in destruction rather than benefit. Yhwh thus shares with Israel responsibility for the disorder with which Judges ends.

The foregoing reading of Judges exposes problems in the presentation of God that disrupt the stable meanings some interpreters seek in the text. I have focused on the negative side of that presentation, since most commentators, whether intentionally or not, pursue the positive. To be sure, Judges portrays God more complexly than it has been possible to sketch here, and analyses are called for that treat the individual tales in greater detail. Investigation of the entire Deuteronomistic History along these lines should open further interpretive possibilities. As it turns out, Israel does not fare much better under human kings. If the end of Judges looks toward the establishment of the monarchy, leaving open the question whether or not human kingship can solve Israel's problems, the answer of Samuel and Kings is that kingship, too, is a flawed institution.

What, If Anything, Is 1 Samuel?

DAVID JOBLING

Jobling's essay exemplifies general issues raised by Gunn's essay in the present volume (pp. 566–77). Specifically, Jobling draws attention to the canonical book-divisions as interpretative acts of the ancient canonizers but claims that this often passes unnoticed in modern scholarship, where they are often treated in practice as raw data. The adoption of certain points in the larger narrative (the historical books broadly speaking) as *beginnings* makes a bid, which he calls "political," for the parts of the narrative to be read in particular ways. His thesis is that it matters for interpretation whether events and information from *earlier* in the narrative are allowed to affect the reader's understanding of the text as s/he reads it. The effect of surrounding material on interpretation is also illustrated by the various canonical decisions respecting the placement of the book of Ruth.

The essay aims to demonstrate how the adoption of a beginning point affects the Song of Hannah–whether 1 Samuel, according to the traditional canonical division, or Judges 2, in line with a large body of modern scholarship. The two beginnings result in "forward" and "backward" readings respectively and thus give quite different results in terms of the Song's alignment or nonalignment with the royal theology of the books of Samuel. While Jobling is mainly concerned to show that the identification of "beginnings" is a part of interpretation itself, he is specially critical of certain literary treatments, like L. Eslinger's of 1 Samuel 1–12, that adopt the beginning of a book in an exclusive way. If the traditional book-divisions are not taken as absolute, it may be asked whether the canonical beginning- and ending-points need preclude either "forward" or "backward" readings. Jobling, therefore (like Gunn), poses the question of the relationship between literary and theological criteria in reading.

Reprinted with permission from *Scandinavian Journal of the Old Testament* 7/1 (1993) 17–31.

Drawing the Lines

[[17]] At the beginning of his treatment of "1 and 2 Samuel" in *The Literary Guide to the Bible,* Joel Rosenberg speaks of "the Masoretic parceling of books," whereby a long narrative work was divided into the "books" of the canon.[1] He hints that other divisions would have been possible and perhaps as good.[2] Robert Polzin similarly recognizes "that the division of the text into books is itself artificial and must have taken place much later than the composition of the [Deuteronomic] History."[3] Yet both scholars draw back from any implication of arbitrariness. Rosenberg's sentence goes on: ". . . the Masoretic parceling of books gives Samuel a beginning and end *that most fully accord* with the shape of [the] larger argument" (my italics). And Polzin continues, "Nevertheless, by whatever process this division took place, . . . this process, by and large, has recognized and remained faithful to the structural plan of the History that I assume existed in the original composition." In particular, Polzin claims, the opening chapter of each book of the Deuteronomic History "is a carefully organized introduction to the 'book' that follows."

There is something odd, on the face of it, about these statements. Rosenberg is apparently saying that a certain "argument," merely implicit in the previously unbroken narrative, was marvelously *exposed* by the Masoretic creation of the book of Samuel. Polzin, likewise, is suggesting that certain sections of the "original composition," not composed as introductions (since they weren't the beginning of anything) have become "carefully organized introductions" as a result of the process of book-division. It only adds to the oddness of their claims that Rosenberg and Polzin are talking about two *different* divisions into [[18]] books! Rosenberg is referring to the *single* Masoretic book of Samuel, while Polzin works within the LXX-Christian canonical tradition of *two* books of Samuel.[4]

The sheer "givenness" of the biblical "books," it seems, makes even critical readers tend to accept statements which, like the above, do not bear much examination. Being a book of the Bible makes "1 Samuel" an

1. *The Literary Guide to the Bible* (ed. Robert Alter and Frank Kermode; Cambridge, MA, 1987) 122–45 (quote from p. 123).

2. 1 Samuel 1–7 put with Judges, or 1 Kings 1–2 put with Samuel (ibid., 122, 138).

3. Robert Polzin, *Samuel and the Deuteronomist. A Literary Study of the Deuteronomic History: Part Two: 1 Samuel* (San Francisco, 1989) 230. For convenience, I shall, like Polzin, retain the term "Deuteronomic History."

4. This statement requires some nuancing in both cases. *The Literary Guide* compromises between Jewish and Christian traditions, giving the books (in the chapter titles) their Christian names, but treating them in the Jewish order; Rosenberg in fact pays no attention to the division between 1 and 2 Samuel. Polzin sometimes bases his argument on the single book of Samuel (for an example, cf. below, on the song of Hannah), but the scope of his book is 1 Samuel, and he claims that 1 Samuel 1 serves to introduce 1 Samuel.

"authorized" literary object,[5] so that we talk about it in ways that occlude the question of whether it is an appropriate or meaningful literary object. We write a lot of books whose topic, even whose title, is "1 Samuel"; and in doing so we assert, at some level, the *rightness* of beginning to read at 1 Samuel 1 and stopping at 1 Samuel 31. Many of these books, of course, are constrained by being part of a series on the books of the Bible. But other authors, *not* so constrained, still take 1 Samuel as their scope—for example, Polzin, or Peter Miscall.[6] There are, to be sure, works which take as their topic some literary object not coterminous with 1 Samuel—Lyle Eslinger on 1 Samuel 1–12, or J. P. Fokkelman on 1 Samuel 13–2 Samuel 1[7]—and these call in question our natural tendency to let the canonical tradition decide into what bits we divide the Bible for the purpose of study. But I surmise that authors who let the canon define the scope of their books get more contracts, and sell more copies, than those who don't.

What, if anything, is 1 Samuel? For those in the Christian canonical tradition, it is a potent thing. But in the Masoretic canon, 1 Samuel isn't any "thing." It is a matter of where you draw the lines. My title is borrowed from Stephen Jay Gould's "What, if Anything, Is a Zebra?"[8] which, in an altogether different context—evolutionary [[19]] biology—has to do with where you draw the lines. This essay will concentrate on the drawing of just one line—the line which makes the beginning of Samuel (or 1 Samuel) *into* a beginning. It is a line common to both canons. But even this statement needs qualification. In the Masoretic canon, the line is drawn between Samuel and Judges, but in the Christian canons Ruth intervenes at this point. A scholar like Polzin, taking 1 Samuel as the scope of his book, still tacitly assumes that what precedes 1 Samuel is Judges. While this is natural for one who is working within the framework of the hypothesis of the Deuteronomic History, it is an error; for the only canons which make 1 Samuel a "book" place the book of Ruth between it and Judges![9]

5. Many anglophones still refer to "The Authorised Version" of the Christian Bible—that is, the King James Version.

6. Polzin, *Samuel and the Deuteronomist*; Miscall, *1 Samuel: A Literary Reading* (Bloomington, 1986).

7. Eslinger, *Kingship of God in Crisis: A Close Reading of 1 Samuel 1–12* (*Bible and Literature* 10; Sheffield, 1985); Fokkelman, *Narrative Art and Poetry in the Books of Samuel: A Full Interpretation Based on Stylistic and Structural Analyses. Volume II: The Crossing Fates (I Sam. 13–31 & II Sam. 1)* (Assen/Maastricht, 1986).

8. *Hen's Teeth and Horse's Toes: Further Reflections in Natural History* (New York and London, 1984) 355–65.

9. Technically, of course, the Christian canons are preceded in this by the LXX (where "1 Samuel" is "1 Kingdoms"). In this essay, I shall treat Ruth very little; I have extended my analysis in that direction in "Ruth Finds a Home: Canon, Politics, Method," forthcoming in *The New Literary Criticism and the Hebrew Bible* (ed. David J. A. Clines and J. Cheryl Exum; Sheffield, 1993).

Both Rosenberg and Polzin see the beginning of (1) Samuel as determined secondarily to the creation of the larger narrative. Both see this division as *effecting* something, and both claim that what is effected is somehow *right*, "true" to the larger narrative. But neither takes a critical view of the division, or seriously considers any alternative. In this essay, I want to demonstrate that where one draws the lines makes a difference to meaning, to reading. This requires that we seriously consider *alternative* divisions. Where shall we go for a canon in which the present beginning of Samuel is *not* a beginning? There is, of course, no such canon in the usual meaning of the term. We could invent one, proposing our own subdivision of the Deuteronomic History on some grounds or other. But I prefer to try out the division proposed by Martin Noth, and refined by Dennis McCarthy,[10] based on passages of "deuteronomic" theological reflection which occur from time to time in the History. Though these scholars do not do so, one might perfectly well call their divisions "books." One of these "books," which I shall call "the extended Book of Judges," runs from Judg 2:11 through 1 Samuel 12, the next from 1 Samuel 13 through 2 Samuel 7, and so on. We have no ancient attestation for any such division; but the conviction it has carried with scholars of modern times, greater than that of any other proposal, represents another sort of canonicity.

⟦20⟧ On the basis of several examples, I shall show how our reading of what we now know as the early chapters of 1 Samuel depends on the division of the Deuteronomic History–Masoretic, LXX-Christian, or Noth-McCarthy–which we are assuming. I shall turn around Polzin's mystifying claim about the beginning of 1 Samuel; those who established it, far from revealing a "natural" introduction to what follows, wielded considerable *power* over subsequent reading precisely by *making 1 Samuel 1 into* an introduction.[11]

But it is not the purpose of this essay simply to compare different readings on their literary merits (whatever that may mean). My context is a highly politicized literary criticism, much under the impact of feminist, Marxist, and psychoanalytic criticism, as this has been related to the Bible through feminist and liberation theologies.[12] When I speak of "the difference it makes," I mean the political difference. When I speak of the canonizers' "power" over reading, I mean political power.

10. Martin Noth, *The Deuteronomistic History* (Sheffield, 1981 [1957]) 4–11 and passim; Dennis J. McCarthy, S.J., "II Samuel 7 and the Structure of the Deuteronomic History," *JBL* 84 (1965) 131–38.

11. Miscall, *1 Samuel*, 8, problematizes "the space between Judg 21:25 and 1 Sam 1:1" in a very useful way (though still without reference to Ruth!).

12. For a discussion, see David Jobling, "Writing the Wrongs of the World: The Deconstruction of the Biblical Text in the Context of Liberation Theologies," *Semeia* 51 (1990) 81–118.

But what constitutes a political reading? At a very basic level it means taking seriously the fact that our biblical texts are already the object of feminist and liberation exegesis.[13] This is a fact to which recent literary treatments have paid little or no attention. But an adequately political reading seems to me to be much more than an *including* of liberation readings among a variety of readings. The methods one adopts, the questions one asks, are also political issues within the current interpretive scene. The literary division between Judges and Samuel will prove to be implicated in the politics of the text's production and interpretation; even the attitude of suspicion towards so "natural" a fact as the book division is a consequence of adopting political methods of reading. A political reading, then, is not one which takes "neutral" results and assesses them in a political framework. It is one which is political at every step.

There seem to me to be two main trends in recent literary work on 1 Samuel. Both are responses to a common perception of this text–[[21]] that it is a particularly *complex* text, one which seems often to be in trouble over what it means to say, to teeter on the edge of, or to fall into, self-contradiction on major issues. One response is to try to exert control, to solve the text's problems by showing that the diversity expresses a single, though complex, ideological perspective. This approach shows great concern, even anxiety, over the perspective of the *narrator*, as if appropriate reading must necessarily demonstrate the narrator's *control* over the narrative. The other is to accept the problems, or even rejoice in them as creating the interest or fun of the text; to delineate the problems, but not to solve them.[14] Is it fanciful to see in this dichotomy a playing out at the level of interpretation of the final verse of Judges, which in some sense sets the program for 1 Samuel? Interpreters like Miscall, and in a broader sense the radical reader-response critics, see positive value in each interpreter "doing what is right in his/her own eyes." Others, like Polzin, want somebody to be in control, a "king in Israel," whether it be the narrator or the modern commentator (which amounts, in fact, to the same thing). Is not a certain stance being adopted, in these very methodological choices, to the political matter of the text? If so, what are the likely consequences for reading?

13. For representative readings, in addition to the feminist ones discussed in this essay, cf. George V. Pixley, *God's Kingdom: A Guide for Biblical Study* (Maryknoll, NY, 1981) 20–24; Bruce C. Birch, *Let Justice Roll Down: The Old Testament, Ethics, and Christian Life* (Louisville, KY, 1991) 204–12; Alice L. Laffey, *An Introduction to the Old Testament: A Feminist Perspective* (Philadelphia, 1988) 93–96, 105–7.

14. To the first line belongs Eslinger, *Kingship of God in Crisis*, and Polzin, *Samuel and the Deuteronomist*; to the second, Miscall, *1 Samuel*, and, to a lesser extent, James S. Ackerman, "Who Can Stand before YHWH, This Holy God? A Reading of 1 Samuel 1–15," *Prooftexts* 11 (1991) 1–24.

It is perhaps to avoid the implications of such a question that virtually all the literary approaches distance themselves from the political matter of the text. I do not mean that they fail to *describe* it. Polzin, for example, certainly sees a struggle going on in 1 Samuel between the ideologies of judgeship and kingship, and deals at length with the ideological commitments of the characters, the narrator, and even the reader; but this "reader," like Polzin's own authorial voice, has no particular location, and feminist or liberation criticism goes unheard.[15] My reading will reveal, I hope, my political framework, and let the political aspects of text and interpretation stand out, while continuing to be a *literary* reading informed by the great richness of recent literary readings of 1 Samuel.

Examples of Reading

[[22]] My first example is a quite small one from the work of Eslinger. But it proves to be the tip of an iceberg, and leads into my second example, the assessment of judgeship and kingship. My final example is a feminist reading, centered on Hannah and especially her song. I preface my examples with a general comment. To take the beginning of 1 Samuel as a literary "beginning" creates a tremendous tendency to read its opening chapters *forward* rather than *back*. Eslinger makes this into a point of method; he tells us that he has decided to read "from the context of 1 Samuel 1–12," a decision "no more or less arbitrary than any other."[16] Polzin's reading of the story of Hannah and Elkanah as a "parable" of the later rise of kingship, brilliant as it may be, is eminently a reading forward, and *tends to exclude* any equally significant reading backward. The tendency to read forward is insidious; even Miscall, whose careful problematizing of 1 Samuel 1 as a beginning I have commended, reads the Song of Hannah entirely forwards.

Defeat by the Philistines

The portion of the Deuteronomic History that Eslinger reads has a canonical starting-point (at 1 Samuel 1) and a Noth-McCarthy end-point (at 1 Samuel 12)! It is his starting-point that concerns me here, and it is rendered particularly important by Eslinger's theory of reading. His reader is entirely under the control of the narrator, who gives instructions in the narrative about how to read it. What makes this interesting rather than boring is that the instructions are not always easy to spot, so that the reader

15. E.g., *Samuel and the Deuteronomist*, 96; but such free-floating "ideological" discussion occurs throughout the book.

16. *Kingship of God in Crisis*, 136.

is required to participate in an active way, but only in order to discover for himself that the instructions are, in fact, complete and unambiguous.

I am not sympathetic to this theory, which minimizes the participation of the reader in the creation of meaning; but let us for present purposes play the game Eslinger's way. What is vital to know is the *framework* within which the instructions for reading are given. Eslinger's reader is one who began to read at 1 Samuel 1.[17] The exegetical difference this makes is exemplified in the issue of whose the fault is that leads to Israel's defeat by the Philistines and the capture of the ark (1 Samuel 4). Eslinger is tremendously insistent that it is the fault of Hophni and Phinehas (more ambiguously, of Eli), and *not* any fault of the people as a whole. Consequently, the reader must speculate about whether the [[23]] punishment fits the crime, and worry theologically about a god who punishes the many for the sins of the few.[18] Now it is true that such a reader–one who began to receive his reading instructions at 1 Samuel 1–*will* be theologically perplexed over this matter, and will be further baffled by the ceremony of national repentance in which Samuel leads the people in chap. 7. Of *what* are they repenting?[19] But the reader of "the extended Book of Judges," who began to read at Judges 2, finds herself laboring under a quite different set of instructions. Has the narrator ever released this reader from the instructions given in Judges 2, to see the narrative time as divided into *judge-cycles*, and to be clear about where the story is, at any given point, in relation to these cycles? I cannot see where or how she has been released. Admittedly, it has become very difficult, by the time she reaches 1 Samuel, to interpret these earlier instructions. But if she tries to do so, there are things she will process otherwise than Eslinger's reader. When the *Philistines* appear, she will recall that they were not dealt with in Judges according to established convention–the formulae for foreigners' subjugation to Israel (see Judg 3:30, 4:23, etc.) were missing at the end of the Samson account–so that their (re)appearance can and should still have something to do with the national apostasy which led to Samson's appointment. This is all puzzling, but our reader will surely let out a cry of recognition when she comes to 1 Samuel 7, which returns fully to the logic of the judge-cycles, including a subjugation formula: "So the Philistines were subdued" (7:13). And she will conclude, in contrast to Eslinger's reader, that the defeat in chap. 4 was still related to national sin, though the matter is certainly complicated by the sin of the priests.

17. "So far the narrator has given the reader no real clues as to any historical cause or situation that might have prompted [Yahweh's response]" (ibid., 88; my italics). "So far" clearly means "so far in 1 Samuel."

18. E.g., ibid., 134–35.

19. Eslinger's own embarrassment with this passage is obvious; ibid., 234–35.

Judgeship versus Kingship

The first example is, as I said, the tip of an iceberg, for the question of the relationship between the sin of the people and the sin of the leadership brings us straight into the problematic of judgeship versus kingship in the Deuteronomic History. Let me briefly sketch (since much of the following is implicit in my earlier work)[20] how this problematic looks according to the Noth-McCarthy and the canonical schemes.

The "books" implied by the Noth-McCarthy scheme conclude each with a covenant-like passage: 1 Samuel 12, 2 Samuel 7 (1 Kings 8, etc.)[21] 1 Samuel 12 [[24]] brings kingship under the selfsame covenant that ruled the time of the judges (vv. 14–15, etc.). So what *links* kingship to judgeship seems suddenly to outweigh what *separates* them, to the extent that one wonders how *real* this kingship is. This impression that Saul's kingship achieves nothing new seems to me to be confirmed in various ways. For example, by the literary form of 1 Samuel 12 as a *false valedictory*. The reader is set up to read the chapter as "the last words of Samuel," which, as last words, mark the moment of transition to something new–just like the last words of Joshua or of Moses. But Samuel does not then die! He goes on to live almost as long as Saul, and we know that as long as he lives, despite the *supposed* monarchy, judgeship is still in place, for "Samuel judged Israel all the days of his life" (1 Sam 7:15). Again, whereas 1 Samuel 12 precisely *fails* to solve the problem of unworthy leaders (cf. the Eslinger example)–it will be "like people, like king," giving Israel no greater guarantee under the king than it had under the judges–the ending of the next Noth-McCarthy "book," 2 Samuel 7, *does* solve this problem, excluding the kings from the conditionality of the covenant. At 2 Samuel 7, we finally have a kingship which has separated itself *theologically* from judgeship.

The Noth-McCarthy system of "books" precisely foregrounds this problematic of a kingship which isn't one. What, by contrast, is the effect of the Masoretic canon? It "backgrounds" the theological problematic of the relationship of kingship to covenant. What it foregrounds is the present ending of Judges–"no king in Israel" as a negative state of affairs–so that we begin to read "Samuel" not only expecting a monarchy, but expecting monarchy to improve things. Samuel loses his rooting among the judges, and becomes a "John the Baptist" of monarchy. To illustrate this

20. *The Sense of Biblical Narrative: Structural Analyses in the Hebrew Bible II* (JSOTSS 39; Sheffield, 1986) 44–87.

21. Perhaps also Joshua 24. Noth and McCarthy include among their epochal passages both Joshua 23 and Judg 2:11–23. I prefer to regard the whole of Joshua 23–24 as marking the end of a "book," and to see the beginning of Judges as an interlude set off by resumptive repetition (Josh 24:28–31 is repeated in Judg 2:6–9). See my "Ruth Finds a Home."

readerly process, consider Polzin's "parabolic" reading of 1 Samuel 1. In Elkanah's resentment that Hannah desires something other than himself ("Am I not more to you than ten sons?" [1:8]), Polzin finds a prefiguration of Yahweh's resentment that Israel desires something other than himself (". . . they have rejected me from being king over them" [8:7]). Polzin provides what he sees as a powerful metaphoric link between 1 Samuel 1 and what follows: Hannah demanding a child *is* Israel demanding a king, "the story of Samuel's birth is the story of Saul's birth as king of Israel." This reading is certainly brilliant, but I would ask whether anyone would propose it who was [[25]] not a priori thinking of this chapter as a beginning.[22]

The LXX-Christian canon seems to carry further this tendency of the Masoretic canon. In Judges, Ruth, 1 Samuel, it produces a sequence of "books" which *end* (a) with the *need* for monarchy (Judges), (b) with the announcement of the coming of David, founder of the "true" monarchy (Ruth), and (c) with the resolution (through Saul's death) of the complication of an *alternative* monarchy to the true one (1 Samuel).

But more needs to be said about 1 Samuel.[23] In terms of the ideological tendency which I am suggesting in the canonical process, the legitimation and "deproblematization" of Davidic kingship, this book– and this is my most direct answer to the question in my title–strikes me as a very successful literary production. Defined by its contents, 1 Samuel is surely "The Book of Samuel and Saul." It exactly covers the lifetime of both characters, beginning with the birth of the older and ending with the death of the younger. It has many dramatic scenes of interaction between them, including the first appearance of Saul and the last, posthumous appearance of Samuel. It even presents their names as somehow related, and confusable. Why would this "double biography" seem the appropriate scope for a canonical book? Because, I suggest, it exploits the intertwining of these two lives to foreground their relation *to each other*, and hence to *background* both the identification of Samuel with the judges and the identification of Saul with the kings. This diverts attention from two central questions. Detaching Samuel from the judges diverts attention from the question of whether the transition from judgeship to monarchy was theologically justified; we focus on the present ending of Judges, with its suggestion that judgeship was a failure, and forget its apparent rehabilitation in the figure of Samuel (1 Samuel 7). Detaching Saul from the kings diverts attention from a second question: How, if monarchy is hereditary, could Saul's monarchy *legitimately* give place to David's? Having devoted

22. *Samuel and the Deuteronomist,* 22–26 (quote from p. 26). I shall also go on to suggest that this strong metaphoric link between Hannah and kingship may be a compensation for the fact that the metonymic link is not nearly so strong as Polzin would wish!

23. For more on the book of Ruth in this connection, see my "Ruth Finds a Home."

an essay to each of these questions, and to the extraordinarily hard textual work going on in the deuteronomic narrative to give a plausible response to them—work which, impressive as it is, leaves the persistent or resistant r.eader baffled with ambiguities and loose ends—I am struck with admiration of the canonbuilders who hid the hard [[26]] questions from view by quarantining within their own book the characters who most raised them, so that the last judge and the first king somehow cancelled each other out.[24]

Hannah Backwards and Forwards

My final example puts the discussion into the context of feminist reading of the Bible, and draws upon some recent feminist discussions bearing on the reading of Judges and Samuel. 1 Samuel begins with a memorable woman's story, that of Hannah, and I begin with a few superficial observations about it. Hannah is defined by her *family* situation, as a favored but barren wife in her husband's house—the story seems to belong to Genesis. Not only her trouble, but also her eventual reward, are defined in these terms—we last hear of her as the mother of six (2:21). But, *within* the family, she acts with a striking independence, above all in her assumption of complete control over he firstborn son. At no point is any question raised as to her right to make her own vow to Yahweh regarding this child, and to carry it out.

And Hannah sings a song (2:1–10). For a feminist and liberationist reading, it is an odd song. Most of it celebrates Yahweh's liberation of the oppressed, including women, in terms compatible with a theology of revolution. But its final half-verse assumes, and celebrates, kingship, in terms which remind us of the so-called Royal Psalms ("The Lord . . . will give strength to his king, and exalt the power of his anointed").

Does Hannah's story invite us to read forward or back? Obviously the reader who knows anything about the Bible will be expecting something special concerning the longed-for child. But Hannah's story does not intrinsically suggest that a new *era* is being inaugurated. Her song does not announce a coming kingship, but assumes an existing one, so that its closing verse seems anachronistic, as well as ideologically at odds with the rest of the song. To find in this verse a *narrative anticipation* of kingship seems to me entirely the consequence of reading the beginning of "Samuel" *as* a beginning.

24. For the first question, see above, n. 20; for the second, *The Sense of Biblical Narrative: Structural Analyses in the Hebrew Bible I* (JSOTSS 7; 2nd ed.; Sheffield, 1986) 12–30. Polzin (*Samuel and the Deuteronomist*, 26–30) seems to identify essentially these same questions as the most critical in 1 Samuel.

There is, in the literature, an enormous tendency to read Hannah's song forward. Most of what Polzin, on whom I want to concentrate, says about the song is based on a parallel he alleges between it and David's song in 2 Samuel 22. Polzin is here very consciously reading within the framework of the single Masoretic book of Samuel; the [[27]] two supposedly parallel songs mark its beginning and end (and his discussion takes in also the song in 2 Samuel 1).[25] But Polzin's parallel is to me entirely unpersuasive, and this is related directly to the political context in which I read. First, he pays no attention to the issue of *gender*; a feminist reading would not, without comment, parallel a woman's and a man's (David's) song.[26] Second, his detailed comparisons of Hannah's and David's songs are based on a literary sensibility quite at odds with that of liberation readings, so that I simply cannot imagine a South American reader (say) finding these two songs similar, or being persuaded by Polzin that they are. He pays no attention to what seems obvious to me, that Hannah's song speaks of *general social* upheaval, whereas David's speaks of an upheaval (in any case highly mythicized) through which *the king alone* is rescued from his enemies. His parallels, in other respects interesting and even impressive, carefully avoid the socioeconomic.[27]

To what extent is Polzin's reading of Hannah's song determined by the "Samuel" context in which he reads it? That the songs to which he relates it are songs of David *tends* to focus his reading on the monarchical; this is appropriate for the final verse of Hannah's song, but tends to miss the point of the non-monarchical (perhaps even antimonarchical) rest of the song. For contrast, let us read Hannah's song as one of the songs in "the extended Book of Judges." We will *then* relate it to the song of another woman, Deborah, in Judges 5, with its sweeping away of the vaunted power of kings by the waters of Kishon; and perhaps also to the antimonarchical fable of Jotham–a man's song, but one which finds its fulfillment in a woman's assassination of a king (Judg 9:8–15:53–54)!

25. *Samuel and the Deuteronomist*, 31–35.

26. Gender is never, for Polzin, a category of narrative analysis. Elsewhere (ibid., 23–24), when he compares Hannah's vow with Jephthah's, he does not ask about the difference between a father dedicating a daughter and a mother dedicating a son–or about the striking difference in the fate of the dedicatees. Again, when he tells us that Elkanah and Hannah are a parable of Yahweh and Israel, he fails to pursue the obvious gender implications (which would lead to Hosea 1–3, and elsewhere).

27. Ibid., 33–34. For the verse in Hannah's song richest in such terms (v. 5) Polzin finds no parallel. "Poor" in v. 7 has no parallel, and in v. 8 it is paralleled with "my enemies" (2 Sam 22:43, by implication). The nearest to a socioeconomic parallel is the one between 1 Sam 2:7 ("he brings low, he also exalts") and 2 Sam 22:28 ("Your eyes are upon the exalted to bring them down").

I do not argue the *superiority* of reading in this context, merely that doing so will make us *see* different things in Hannah's song that Polzin sees. Our focus will be on the social revolution that *gets rid* of kings, and the reference to the king in the final verse will seem all the odder. But [[28]] what I am suggesting has extensive methodological implications. For Polzin is encouraged in his reading by canonical decisions made long ago; reading according to canonical units tends to make him read the way he does. It is but a small step to suggest that the canonical decisions were an integral part precisely of a process whereby readers were led to read Hannah's song the way Polzin reads it! My alternative derives not only from the different eyes with which I read one particular text (Hannah's song), but also from my suspicion of the canonical divisions. Already within the text, I perceive in the final half-verse a monarchical cooption of a song which otherwise is not in the least monarchical. Making the song part of the monarchical book of Samuel extends the cooption, as does Polzin's paralleling it with a Royal Psalm.

I wish to underline this suggestion by reference to recent feminist work bearing upon the role of women in the transition from judgeship to monarchy. Some of the work sees this transition primarily in literary terms–more or less, the transition from Judges to Samuel–while some of it suggests the historical framework of an actual transition to monarchy in Israel. It is characteristic of feminist scholarship, I think, that no one wants to make a hard and fast distinction between the two sides. But for present purposes, I shall confine myself to the primarily literary.[28]

Mieke Bal's thesis, in *Death and Dissymmetry*, is that the Book of Judges is the literary product of a struggle over the transition from one pattern of kinship/marriage to another–from "patrilocal" (the husband moves to the wife's father's house) to "virilocal" (the wife moves to the husband's house; Bal adjusts the customary anthropological terms "matrilocal" and "patrilocal" to ones based on the wife's perspective).[29] She suggests that patrilocal marriage provides women with *relatively* wider options than virilocal; not that it is beneficial for women, but that, among the various forms of "patriarchy," there are relative differences which it is meaningful and necessary to analyze.

Regina Schwartz has recently discussed the role of stories featuring women and sexuality in the accounts of the incipient monarchy, arguing

28. For a review of this work, see my "Feminism and 'Mode of Production' in Ancient Israel: Search for a Method" in *The Bible and the Politics of Exegesis: Essays in Honor of Norman K. Gottwald on His Sixty-Fifth Birthday* (ed. D. Jobling et al.; Cleveland, 1991) 239–51. I there take up the work of Carol Meyers and Naomi Steinberg, as well as that of Bal and Schwartz.

29. *Death and Dissymmetry: The Politics of Coherence in the Book of Judges* (Chicago, 1988). See esp. 85–86.

that power over women functions as both a metaphor and a metonym [[29]] for political power.[30] She concentrates on three stories of David's women (Abigail, Michal, Bathsheba), noting in each case how it is a man (Nabal, Paltiel, Uriah) who appears as the "victim," the woman being only a pawn in the male power-struggle.

Hannah is the female character who appears most precisely at the point of transition indicated by Bal and Schwartz, and it is fascinating to read her in relation to the alternatives they offer. She seems fully integrated into the *virilocal* household, so that one might see her as the forerunner of Schwartz's women, mere pawns in patriarchal/monarchical games. This would make her cooption for monarchical ends–by biblical authors and canonizers, and by modern commentators like Polzin–understandable. Yet her assumption of control over her son–much more compatible with patri- than with virilocality–invites us to read her story as another episode in the struggle Bal perceives in Judges. In this connection, of course, we will not miss the link between Hannah's story and that of "The Levite's Concubine," so central to Bal's case. Both stories–a mere three chapters apart–begin with "a certain man/Levite of the hill country of Ephraim" (Judg 19:1, 1 Sam 1:1).

The foregoing discussion has considered the Noth-McCarthy and Masoretic divisions of the Deuteronomic History. The LXX-Christian canon again raises the issue of the book of Ruth. I deal with its impact on a feminist-canonical reading in my other essay,[31] and merely summarize here. The character Ruth, like Hannah, appears at the point of transition from Balian to Schwartzian woman. But she seems to me to help to *achieve* that transition (I side with those feminist readers who see Ruth and her book as subserving male agenda). The book tells how she is successfully incorporated into the virilocal system (in striking contrast to her sister Orpah, who represents the alternative option, but who disappears from the story). Her relationship to Naomi, celebrated by some feminists as an example of female bonding unique in the Bible, in fact valorizes a relationship–mother-in-law to daughter-in-law–on the success of which the peace of the virilocal household depends. And the result of her incorporation is that she becomes the ancestor of kings.

In summary, a feminist reading of the figure of Hannah provides an exemplary view of the effect of the various framings of the deuteronomic narrative. To read her in "the extended book of Judges" maximizes her relative strength and independence. To read her in "Samuel" [[30]] downplays these aspects in favor of seeing her as involved in the transition to

30. "Adultery in the House of David: The Metanarrative of Biblical Scholarship and the Narratives of the Bible," *Semeia* 54 (1991) 35–55.

31. Cf. above, n. 9.

monarchy, and as herself exemplifying the status of women in monarchical Israel. To read her in "1 Samuel" is to confirm this separation between the world of Samuel and that of Judges, inasmuch as Ruth acts as a buffer between these worlds, and further valorizes monarchy.

Conclusion

What, if anything, is 1 Samuel? Like any other literary object, it is a piece of literary production within an ideological field of forces. Like any other literary object, it asserts its "somethingness" *ex nihilo,* out of the arbitrariness of language and hence the unfoundedness of linguistic discourse; this self-assertion constitutes ideological work within language and discourse. What is peculiar about 1 Samuel is merely the *means* of production–it is not a new and separate literary object, but a bit of an old one. The ideological work, put very simplistically, is the presentation of the transition from rule by judges to rule by Davidic kings as "the will of God." In the current interpretive scene, it is out of contexts where people seek liberation from the imposition of *modern* versions of "royal" power that the impulse comes to examine such ideological work in the biblical text and its interpretation.[32] Where scholars simply accept "1 Samuel" as a given, they are absenting themselves from such ideological discussion for reasons which are themselves ideologically analyzable. And where scholars assert, in full awareness of the issues, the *rightness* of the textual division which results in "1 Samuel," for mysterious reasons which seem to amount to some sort of literary or divine inspiration (are these really so different?), they make themselves complicit in the ideological work going on in the text.

32. See again my "Writing the Wrongs of the World" (above, n. 12).

Index of Authors

Index of Scripture

Scripture is indexed according to Hebrew chapter and verse divisions; where the English versification differs, English chapter and verse are supplied in brackets.

Hebrew Bible

New Testament

Deuterocanonical Works